EDITORS' FOR...

This book is designed [...] who enjoy driving. Despite [...] includes common everyday [...] minivan to complement the u[...] introduction, we chose more than 130 models that possess the ability to accelerate, stop and turn more capably and confidently than most of the vehicles for sale on the new car market today.

Each listing includes at least one representative photo of the covered model. Below each photo is an analysis of the vehicle, which may include information about the vehicle's features, historical background, editors' opinions or comparisons to competing models. To make your decision making a tad easier, we also supply performance and safety data on each of the models including crash test grades for both driver (D) and passenger (P), when available.

Our editors and contributors drove just over half of the vehicles included in this guide, and were inspired to write a bit about the experiences. Evaluations and impressions are provided for those models, and we hope they inform as well as entertain you.

As is Edmund's practice, we provide you, the smart consumer, with detailed information on dealer invoice prices and Manufacturer's Suggested Retail Prices (MSRP). On the printed page, each vehicle's base invoice price and MSRP are listed right after the editorial text, followed by listings of standard equipment, and then optional accessories with their associated costs.

Throughout the book, a series of short articles are provided which allow you to find out how well a particular model did in government crash tests, where a particular model was assembled, and what kind of profit the dealer is *really* making, among others. Please see the table of contents to locate these articles. Use these articles and the included costing form worksheets to apply the pricing information toward making your best deal on the vehicle of your choice.

Finally, in keeping with the performance theme of this issue, the indices at the back of the book lists all the models in order of overall performance (based on a composite score) and in alphabetical order with each vehicle's particular performance data and the page number where you can find that vehicle. Additionally, three listings provide you with the top 25 vehicles in each of the following categories: acceleration time from zero to 60 mph; braking distance from 60 mph to zero; and the vehicle's ability to go around a corner, which is measured as a percentage of one g of force.

Good luck in hunting for a new, fun-to-drive car, pickup, sport utility or minivan, and in utilizing the information printed within to *your* advantage.

Most people have three things in common when they buy a car.

They pay too much.

They waste time.

They hate the experience.

Which is exactly why you should call the Car Club. We offer the quickest and most convenient way to save time and money when you buy a new car or truck. Simple as that. No haggling. No hassles. No games. Just tell us the vehicle and options you want (and make or model - foreign or domestic) and we'll get you a lower price than you can get on your own. Guaranteed in writing. For more information, call us today, **1-800-CAR-CLUB** (1-800-227-2582).

The Smart New Way to Buy Your Car™

Edmund's Perfect Partners

USED CARS: PRICES & RATINGS

For 30 years, Edmund's has guided smart consumers through the complex used car marketplace. By providing you with the latest wholesale and retail pricing, you are able to determine fair market value before negotiations begin.

Whether buying, selling, or trading, Edmund's *Used Cars: Prices & Ratings* gives all the information you need to get your very best deal.

√ Prices All American and Imported Used Cars, Pickup Trucks, Vans, and Sport Utilities

√ Shows Summary Ratings Graphs for Most Used Vehicles

√ Listings Cover Models Over Last 10 Years

√ Price any Vehicle Quickly and Accurately

√ Adjust Value for Optional Equipment and Mileage

Edmund's *Used Cars: Prices & Ratings* takes on a completely new organization and format, patterned after the familiar dictionary model and designed for your ease of use...

$5.99
CANADA
$6.99

For information on all Edmund's Automotive Books, call 914-962-6297

"Car dealers take advantage of their knowledge and the customer's lack of knowledge... Edmund's New Car Prices... provides standard costs for cars and optional items."
—Steve Ross
Successful Car Buying
(Harrisburg, PA: Stackpole Books, 1990)

"How much should you pay for a new car?... Your goal is to buy the car for the lowest price at which the dealer will sell it... To be accurate about profit margins, you should use the most recent edition of Edmund's Car Prices."
—Dr. Leslie R. Sachs
How to Buy Your Next Car For a Rock Bottom Price
(New York: Signet, 1986)

"Edmund's publishes a variety of useful guides... Edmund's is a great source of information. You might find it useful to buy the guide that deals specifically with the type of car you need.

Wouldn't it be nice if you could know beforehand the dealer's cost for the new vehicle you just fell in love with? Wouldn't it be even nicer if you knew how much to offer him over his costs, a price he would just barely be able to accept?

Well you are in luck. You can find out exactly what the car cost the dealership... Look up the information yourself in... Edmund's specialty auto books."
—Burke Leon
The Insider's Guide to Buying A New or Used Car
(Cincinnati, OH: Betterway Books, 1993)

Get MORE For Your Used Car.

Before trading or selling your used car, make sure you know its TRUE value on today's market.

Our automated line gives you current wholesale and retail prices, *including* adjustments for mileage and equipment on any used car, 1985-1994.

CALL NOW.

1-900-9-EDMUND

(1-900-933-6863)

$1.95 per minute (Average call is 3 to 5 minutes.)

Must be 18 or older to use this service.

Edmund Publications Corporation, El Segundo, CA

1995

Edmund's

NEW HIGH-PERFORMANCE AUTOMOBILES BUYER'S GUIDE

"THE ORIGINAL CONSUMER PRICE AUTHORITY"

Publisher: Peter Steinlauf

NEW HIGH-PERFORMANCE AUTOMOBILES
1995 Buyer's Guide
VOL. H2901

TABLE OF CONTENTS

Published by:
Edmund Publications Corp.
300 N. Sepulveda Bl., #2050
El Segundo, CA 90245

ISBN: 0-87759-463-5
ISSN: 1079-1485

Editor-in-Chief
Michael G. Samet, Ph. D.

Automotive Editors:
Christian Wardlaw
William Badnow

Special Contributor:
James M. Flammang

Creative Design:
Debra Katzir

Cover Design:
Jozsef Nagy

Information Specialist:
Victor Friedman

Advertising Manager:
Brenda Davis

© 1995 by Edmund Publications Corporation. All rights Reserved. No reproduction in whole or in part may be made without explicit written permission from the publisher.

Printed in the United States

Cover photo: 1995 Pontiac Firebird Formula Convertible

Introduction 10
Where Are the Cars Built? 12
Focus on Safety 16
Understanding the Language
  of Auto Buying 18
Abbreviations 20
How to Buy Your Next
  New Automobile 22
Step-by-Step
  Costing Form 23
Dealer Holdbacks 24
Warranties &
  Roadside Assistance 26
Automobile Listings 28
Step-by-Step
  Costing Form 348
Specifications 349
How Fuel Economy
  Estimates Are Obtained . 373
Crash Test Data 374
Customer Assistance
  Numbers 378
Leasing Tips 380
**Automobile Dealer
  Directory 388**
Index to Performance 390

ACURA
Integra 28
Legend 32
NSX 35

ALFA ROMEO
164 37

AUDI
90 39
S6 42

BMW
3-Series 45
5-Series 49
8-Series 53

BUICK
Park Avenue Ultra 56
Riviera 59

CADILLAC
Eldorado Touring Coupe 62
Seville STS 65

CHEVROLET
C1500 Pickup 68
Camaro Z28 72
Caprice Classic 76
Corvette 79
Impala SS 84
Lumina LS 87
Monte Carlo Z34 90
S10 SS Pickup 93

CHRYSLER
Concorde 96
LHS 99

DODGE
Intrepid ES 102
Neon 105
Ram Sport Pickup 110
Stealth 114
Viper 117

EAGLE
Summit ESi Coupe 119
Talon TSi 121
Vision TSi 124

FORD
Contour SE 128
Escort GT 131
F150 Pickup 134
Mustang GT 136
Probe GT 140
Ranger Splash Pickup 143
Taurus SHO 146
Thunderbird 149

Look for Edmund's CD-ROM offer on page 384 and Edmund's NEW Used Car Price Hotline offer on page 6

SPECIAL OFFER from 1-800-CAR-CLUB
details on page 3

GMC
Sierra Pickup 154
Sonoma SLS Pickup 157

HONDA
Accord EX 160
Civic EX Coupe 162
Civic del Sol VTEC 164
Prelude Si 166

INFINITI
G20t 169
J30 170
Q45t 172

JAGUAR
XJ-Series 174
XJS 177

JEEP
Grand Cherokee 180

LEXUS
ES 300 185
GS 300 187
LS 400 189
SC Coupes 191

LINCOLN
Mark VIII 196

MAZDA
626 ES 200
Millenia S 202
MX-5 Miata 204
MX-6 LS 207
Protege ES 209
RX-7 211

MERCEDES-BENZ
C-Class 213
E-Class 216
S600 220
SL-Class 222

MERCURY
Cougar XR7 227
Mystique LS 231

MITSUBISHI
3000 GT 234
Eclipse 238
Mirage LS Coupe 242

NISSAN
240SX 244
300ZX 247
Altima 250
Maxima 253
Sentra SE-R 257

OLDSMOBILE
Aurora 259
Cutlass Supreme Conv. 262
Eighty-Eight LSS 264
Silhouette 267

PLYMOUTH
Neon 270

PONTIAC
Bonneville 275
Firebird 281
Grand Prix 286

PORSCHE
911 Carrera 291
928 GTS 299
968 304

SAAB
900 SE 309
9000 Aero 312

SATURN
SC2 315
SL2 318
SW2 321

SUBARU
SVX 324

TOYOTA
Camry 327
Celica GT 330
MR2 333
Supra 336

VOLKSWAGEN
GTI 339
Jetta III GLX 341
Passat GLX 343

VOLVO
850 Turbo 345

NOTE: All information and prices published herein are gathered from sources which, in the editor's opinion, are considered reliable, but under no circumstances is the reader to assume that this information is official or final. All prices are represented as approximations only, and are rounded to the highest whole dollar amount over 50 cents. Unless otherwise noted, all prices are effective as of 11/15/94, but are subject to change without notice. The publisher does not assume responsibility for errors of omission or interpretation.
• The consumer information services advertised herein are not operated by nor are they the responsibility of the publisher. • The publisher assumes no responsibility for claims made by advertisers regarding their products or services.

EDMUND'S 1995 HIGH-PERFORMANCE AUTOMOBILES

INTRODUCTION

Those of you familiar with Edmund's Buyer's Guides will notice a big change of format in this first issue of *New High Performance Automobiles*. We've focused on a specific niche of autos for this guide, and have included reviews, specifications, and, of course, pricing information for each vehicle listed. More than half include driving impressions written by Christian Wardlaw, Edmund's' automotive editor, or James Flammang, freelance auto writer and editor of *Tirekicking Today*. All in all, this guide is quite a contrast with our more comprehensive but less informative new car and truck buyer's specialized price guides.

Those of you unfamiliar with Edmund's Buyer's Guides will be happy to know that this book was designed with you in mind. We wanted to reach a segment of consumers who wanted more than just information on MSRP and dealer prices. We wanted to provide insightful, educated reviews and reports on the hottest performing cars and trucks for sale in the United States this year. Additionally, safety data and performance statistics provide smart consumers like yourselves with crash test data (when available), acceleration times and fuel economy numbers, among other important factors. Vehicle specifications and price information that includes both dealer invoice cost and manufacturer's suggested retail price (MSRP) are the frosting on a decidedly rich cake.

Looking at the table of contents, you might find our claim that we've included only high performance cars a stretch of our imagination. Chevy Lumina LS? C'mon. Here's how we chose the list of vehicles. We wanted at least 100 cars and trucks to make the cut, or the book wouldn't have been worth doing. Using published performance data from a variety of reliable sources, we decided that each car to be included had to accelerate to 60 mph within 8.75 seconds, stop from 60 mph within 140 feet, and go around a flat, smooth corner pulling better than .77 g's of force. The parameters for trucks were relaxed a bit, with 9.5 seconds the time limit to arrive at 60 mph, 155 feet allowed to stop from 60 mph, and an adhesion limit of .75 g's of force in turns.

INTRODUCTION

Most performance purists would likely scoff at the high tolerances we have used to include vehicles in this guide. However, this book has been conceived with the notion that its audience will be largely comprised of consumers looking for a **fun-to-drive** mode of transportation to get to the office, the supermarket, and soccer practice; not performance nuts looking for their next SCCA race car. In short, for the intended reader, the performance parameters outlined above are more than adequate.

The sharpie's among you will note that some vehicles are missing from the contents page, for instance, the all-new BMW 7-Series and the Ford Mustang Cobra. The reason for these omissions is a distinct lack of press material and prices as we reached our deadline. But we look at it this way: if one of these cars is what you're dying to drive, what we have to say about either of them would probably not sway your decision. Others, like the Pontiac Sunfire GT and Dodge Avenger ES simply didn't make the performance cut. In the case of these two cars, published acceleration times over nine seconds were their downfall.

Finally, in this buyer's guide we've tried to provide you with all the information you need to make an educated decision about the new high-performance fun-to-drive automobiles and to enable you to get one at a reasonable price. We'd love to hear your comments and suggestions about this book. Please write to us at:

Edmund Publications Corporation
300 N. Sepulveda Blvd., Suite 2050
El Segundo, CA 90245
Attn: Automotive Editor

or send us an e-mail message to *Edmund@enews.com*.

With that, dive in and enjoy your search for that fun-to-drive new car, sport utility, minivan or pickup!

WHERE ARE THE CARS BUILT?   1

A new law went into effect for the 1995 model year. It requires all manufacturers to paste a sticker on each car it sells in the United States that provides consumers with important data regarding the percentage of imported and domestic content of the vehicle in question.

Not surprisingly, automakers are calling foul, especially those from across the Pacific, who seem to be getting the short end of the stick. The people who designed this law and the rules governing it have saddled automakers with tons of extra administrative and research costs, which are ultimately transferred to consumers, and have created loopholes for domestic automakers who sell rebadged versions of popular imports without suffering the import stigma. One example of the loophole at work is the difference between a Geo Prizm, which is sold through General Motors' Chevy dealerships, and a Toyota Corolla. They are both assembled on the same line out of the same parts by the same people who work in the same Fremont, California plant. Yet, the Prizm somehow comes out with more domestic content. Magic? No. Incompetence and ignorance, yes.

To build a strong economy, Americans need jobs. Those jobs are provided increasingly by companies headquartered in other countries, as they move design and production to the United States and buy components from U.S. suppliers. Our economy is built on the premise that competition is healthy. It has been exactly this sort of competition that has forced American automakers to rethink the way they have been designing and producing automobiles, giving consumers some of the best cars and trucks available anywhere for any price.

The new law is misleading consumers. If keeping Americans working is one of your goals when buying a new car, take the information on the label with a grain of salt, and use the following list of build locations to supplement that information.

Model	Assembly Location(s)
Acura Integra	Suzuka, Japan
Acura Legend	Sayama, Japan
Acura NSX	Tochigi, Japan
Alfa Romeo 164	Milan, Italy
Audi 90	Ingolstadt, Germany
Audi S6	Neckarsulm, Germany
BMW 3-Series	Regensburg, Germany; Munich, Germany; Spartanburg, South Carolina
BMW 5-Series	Dingolfing, Germany
BMW 8-Series	Dingolfing, Germany
Buick Riviera	Orion Township, Michigan
Buick Park Avenue	Flint, Michigan
Cadillac Eldorado	Hamtramck, Michigan
Cadillac Seville	Hamtramck, Michigan

WHERE ARE THE CARS BUILT? 2

Chevrolet C1500	Ft. Wayne, Indiana; Moraine, Ohio; Pontiac, Michigan; Oshawa, Ontario, Canada
Chevrolet Camaro	Ste. Therese, Quebec, Canada
Chevrolet Caprice	Arlington, Texas
Chevrolet Corvette	Bowling Green, Kentucky
Chevrolet Impala SS	Arlington, Texas
Chevrolet Lumina	Oshawa, Ontario, Canada
Chevrolet Monte Carlo	Oshawa, Ontario, Canada
Chevrolet S-10	Shreveport, Louisiana; Linden, New Jersey
Chrysler Concorde	Bramalea, Ontario, Canada; Newark, Delaware
Chrysler LHS	Bramalea, Ontario, Canada
Dodge Intrepid	Bramalea, Ontario, Canada; Newark, Delaware
Dodge Neon	Belvidere, Illinois
Dodge Ram	Warren, Michigan
Dodge Stealth	Nagoya, Japan
Dodge Viper	Detroit, Michigan
Eagle Summit	Mizushima, Japan
Eagle Talon	Normal, Illinois
Eagle Vision	Bramalea, Ontario, Canada
Ford Contour	Kansas City, Missouri
Ford Escort GT	Wayne, Michigan
Ford F-150	Kansas City, MO; Twin Cities, MN; Wayne, MI; Norfolk, VA; Louisville, KY
Ford Mustang	Dearborn, Michigan
Ford Probe	Flat Rock, Michigan
Ford Ranger	Louisville, Kentucky; Twin Cities, Minnesota; Edison, New Jersey
Ford Taurus	Atlanta, Georgia; Chicago, Illinois
Ford Thunderbird	Lorain, Ohio
GMC Sierra	Ft. Wayne, Indiana; Pontiac, Michigan; Oshawa, Ontario, Canada
GMC Sonoma	Pontiac, Michigan; Shreveport, Louisiana; Linden, New Jersey
Honda Accord	Marysville, Ohio; Sayama, Japan
Honda Civic	E. Liberty, Ohio; Alliston, Ontario, Canada; Suzuka, Japan
Honda Civic del Sol	Suzuka, Japan
Honda Prelude	Sayama, Japan
Infiniti G20	Oppama, Japan
Infiniti J30	Tochigi, Japan
Infiniti Q45	Tochigi, Japan
Jaguar XJ-Series	Coventry, England
Jaguar XJS	Coventry, England
Jeep Grand Cherokee	Detroit, Michigan
Lexus ES300	Tsusumi, Japan
Lexus GS300	Tahara, Japan
Lexus LS400	Tahara, Japan

EDMUND'S 1995 HIGH-PERFORMANCE AUTOMOBILES

WHERE ARE THE CARS BUILT? 3

Lexus SC300/SC400	Motomachi, Japan
Lincoln Mark VIII	Wixom, Michigan
Mazda 626	Flat Rock, Michigan
Mazda Milllenia	Hofu, Japan
Mazda MX-5 Miata	Hofu, Japan
Mazda MX-6	Flat Rock, Michigan
Mazda Protege	Hiroshima, Japan
Mazda RX-7	Hiroshima, Japan
Mercedes C-Class	Bremen, Germany
Mercedes E-Class	Sindelfingen, Germany; Rastatt, Germany
Mercedes S-Class	Sindelfingen, Germany
Mercedes SL-Class	Bremen, Germany
Mercury Cougar	Lorain, Ohio
Mercury Mystique	Kansas City, Missouri
Mitsubishi 3000GT	Oye, Japan
Mitsubishi Eclipse	Normal, Illinois
Mitsubishi Mirage	Kurashiki, Japan
Nissan 240SX	Kyushu, Japan
Nissan 300ZX	Shatai, Japan
Nissan Altima	Smyrna, Tennessee
Nissan Maxima	Oppama, Japan
Nissan Sentra SE-R	Smryna, Tennessee
Oldsmobile Aurora	Orion Township, Michigan
Oldsmobile Cutlass	Fairfax, Kansas
Oldsmobile LSS	Orion Township, Michigan; Flint, Michigan
Oldsmobile Silhouette	Tarrytown, New York
Plymouth Neon	Belvidere, Illinois
Pontiac Bonneville	Orion Township, Michigan
Pontiac Firebird	Ste. Therese, Quebec, Canada
Pontiac Grand Prix	Fairfax, Kansas
Porsche 911	Zuffenhausen, Germany
Porsche 928	Zuffenhausen, Germany
Porsche 968	Zuffenhausen, Germany
Saab 900	Trollhattan, Sweden
Saab 9000	Trollhattan, Sweden
Saturn SC2	Spring Hill, Tennessee
Saturn SL2	Spring Hill, Tennessee
Saturn SW2	Spring Hill, Tennessee
Subaru SVX	Gunma, Japan
Toyota Camry	Georgetown, Kentucky; Tsutsumi, Japan
Toyota Celica	Tahara, Japan
Toyota MR2	Tokyo, Japan
Toyota Supra	Tahara, Japan
Volkswagen GTI	Puebla, Mexico
Volkswagen Jetta	Puebla, Mexico
Volkswagen Passat	Emden, Germany
Volvo 850	Ghent, Belgium; Goteborg, Sweden

Out In The Cold When You Go To Buy a Car?

Nothing Warms Up Negotiations Like Knowing The Facts <u>Before</u> You Sit Down To Buy.

You can obtain a quote on the car or truck of your choice.

•

You may choose your options and know exactly what each one costs.

•

You can use your itemized options quote as a reference or as a bargaining tool for the future.

We can supply a vehicle at the quoted price if you are unable to make a deal.

•

Your purchase will be made from the comfort of your home.

•

Our huge inventory provides immediate availability on many models.

Pay as little as $50 over dealer invoice.

•

Your vehicle has a full factory warranty and financing is available.

•

Your vehicle will be shipped to the destination of your choice.

We have over 28 years of experience to put to work for you.

NATIONWIDE Auto Brokers, Inc.
17517 West Ten Mile Road Southfield, MI 48075 • 810-559-6661 • FAX 810 559-4782
FIRST QUOTE $11.95, EACH ADDITIONAL QUOTE $9.95. ADD $6.95 FOR FAXES

※ Some vehicles will be higher. Some specialty imports and limited production models and vehicles may not be available for delivery to your area or through our pricing service. A message on your printout will advise you of this. You will still be able to use the printout in negotiating the best deal with the dealer of your choice. New car pricing and purchasing services are not available where prohibited by law.

Call Nationwide Auto Quotation Line 1-800-521-7257

FOCUS ON SAFETY

Traction Control: Do you need it? Yes!

We just spent several hundred miles behind the wheel of a Ford Thunderbird LX, equipped with Ford's magnificent 4.6-liter V-8 engine and traction control. The V-8 T-Bird is powerful, fast, and is driven by the rear wheels. This combination is fine for dry, fair weather climates and for conducting adolescent experiments that focus on the effects of heat and friction on rubber, but in the rain and snow a drivetrain such as the one in our Thunderbird makes for nightmarish driving conditions.

Not so in the Thunderbird with traction control. The system cuts power to the rear wheels as they slip, and gives the hefty T-Bird good grip in a variety of conditions. Fortunately, a button that shuts the system off resides in the center console for those times when wheelspin is a good thing, like rocking yourself out of the snowdrift the plow left at the foot of your driveway or terrorizing the neighbors with smoky 4,000 rpm burnouts at the stop sign...not that we condone that sort of thing.

Traction control is becoming as important a safety feature on modern cars as anti-lock brake systems (ABS) have, but like ABS, they require a shift in traditional driving styles to take advantage of their benefits. If you buy a car equipped with traction control, find a deserted and safe place to test out some of the characteristics of the particular system you have. Often, manufacturers will provide detailed instructions inside the owner's manual, which is that silly little book you got for free when you bought the car. It usually sits in the glovebox. Read it.

There are three types of traction control, and we'll briefly outline each system.

1) Limited-slip differential. This system transfers engine torque to the wheel that has the best traction in any given situation. It is not an electronic system, and generally doesn't perform as well as newer types of traction control. Modern limited-slip differentials are able to transfer power to the good wheel before slippage occurs, however, if both wheels are on a slippery surface, this system will leave you just as stuck as a car wihout it.

FOCUS ON SAFETY

2) Brake System Traction Control. Working just like ABS in reverse, this type of system uses the same sensors and hardware that ABS does to apply the brakes and keep a wheel from spinning. Each wheel is individually controlled, making this setup a perfect match for a variety of slippery surfaces. Generally inexpensive and highly effective, this system is designed for low speed slippage. Because the braking components are used, higher speed slip control would generate too much friction and heat, damaging the braking components.

3) Drivetrain Traction Control. Our Thunderbird was equipped with this system, which retards power delivery to the slipping wheel or wheels at any speed. Using the same ABS-type sensors as the brake system traction control setup, this one employs a processor that will do one of four things: (a) close the throttle, which is how the cheapest of these systems works; (b) cut the fuel supply; (c) retard spark timing; or (d) shut down cylinders. The most advanced drivetrain traction control systems will do all of these things, plus push the accelerator against your foot to tell you it's working. Because this system cuts power in all slippery situations, a button is almost always provided to turn the system off for situations where slippage is desired.

Our experience with traction control has convinced us that it is one more in a series of important automotive safety breakthroughs. We highly recommend it, especially for people who commonly drive in adverse weather conditions.

Understanding the Language of Auto Buying

Many consumers are justifiably confused by the language and terms used by automobile manufacturers and dealers. To assist you, here are some basic definitions:

MSRP — Manufacturer's Suggested Retail Price The Manufacturer's recommended selling price for a vehicle and each of its optional accessories.

Dealer Invoice The amount that dealers are invoiced or billed by the manufacturer for a vehicle and each of its optional accessories.

Dealer Holdback Many maufacturers provide dealers with a *holdback allowance* (usually between 2 and 3% of MSRP) which is eventually credited to the dealer's account. That way, the dealer can end up paying the manufacturer less than the invoiced amount — meaning that they could sell you the vehicle at cost and still make a small profit. Holdback is also known as a 'pack.'

Destination Charge The fee charged for shipping, freight, or delivery of the vehicle to the dealer from the manufacturer or Port of Entry. This charge is passed on to the buyer without any mark-up.

Preparation Charges These are dealer-imposed charges for getting the new car ready to drive away including a full tank of gas, checking and filling the fluid levels, making sure the interior and exterior is immaculate, etc.

Dealer Charges These are highly profitable extras that dealers try to sell in addition to the vehicle itself. Items such as rustproofing, undercoating and extended warranties fall into this category. Most consumer experts do not recommend the purchase of these extras.

Advertising Fee The amount you are charged to cover the cost of national and local advertising. This fee should be no more than 1-1½% of the MSRP.

Manufacturer's Rebate/Dealer Incentives Programs offered by the manufacturers to increase the sales of slow-selling models or to reduce excess inventories. While manufacturer's rebates are passed directly on to the buyer, dealer incentives are passed on only to the dealer — who may or may not elect to pass the savings on to the customer.

Trade-in Value The amount that the dealership will give you for the vehicle you trade in. Generally, this amount will be about 5% below wholesale value of the vehicle. The trade-in value will be deducted from the price of the new vehicle.

Upside-down When you owe more on your car loan than your trade-in is worth, you are *upside-down* on your trade. When this happens, the dealer will add the difference between the trade-in value and what you owe to the price of the new vehicle.

Note: Occasionally there will appear in the "Dealer Invoice" and "MSRP" columns, prices enclosed in parenthesis, example: (90), which indicate a credit or refunded amount is involved.

ABBREVIATIONS

16V	16 Valve Engine	CAP	Capacity	FS	Flareside
2WD	Two Wheel Drive	CASS	Cassette	F/S	Fleetside
3A/4A	3-Speed/4-Speed Automatic	CD	Compact Disc	FWD	Front Wheel Drive
		CFC	Chloroflorocarbon	GAL	Gallon
4M/5M/6M	4-Speed/5-Speed/6-Speed Manual	CNTRY	Country	GRP	Group
		COL	Column	GVW	Gross Vehicle Weight
4SP	4 Speed Transmission	CONV	Convertible	GVWR	Gross Vehicle Weight Rating
4SPD	4 Speed Transmission	CPE	Coupe		
4WD	Four Wheel Drive	CRS	Cruise	HBK	Hatchback
4WS	Four Wheel Steering	CTRL	Control	HD	Heavy Duty
5SP	5 Speed Transmission	CUST	Custom	HO	High Output
5SPD	5 Speed Transmission	CU IN	Cubic Inches	HP	Horsepower
5SPD/AT	5 Speed, Automatic Transmission	CVRS	Covers	HUD	Heads Up Display
		CYL	Cylinder	HVAC	Heating/Ventilation/Air Conditioning
6SP	6 Speed Transmission	DFRS	Dual Facing Rear Seats		
6SPD	6 Speed Transmission	DLX	Deluxe	HVY	Heavy
ABS	Anti-Lock Braking System	DOHC	Dual Overhead Camshaft	HT	Hardtop
				ILLUM	Illuminated, Illumination
AC	Air Conditioning	DR	Door		
ADJ	Adjustable, Aduster	DRW	Dual Rear Wheels	INCLS	Includes
AIR COND	Air Conditioning	EFI	Electronic Fuel Injection	INCLD	Included
ALT	Alternator	ELEC	Electronic, Electronically	INJ	Injection
ALUM	Aluminum			INT	Interior
AMP	Amperes	ENG	Engine	L	Liter
ANT	Antenna	EQUIP	Equipment	LB	Longbed
AT	Automatic Transmission	ETR	Electronically Tuned Radio	LBK	Liftback
AUTO	Automatic			LBS	Pounds
AUX	Auxiliary	EXT	Extended, Exterior	LD	Light Duty
AVAIL	Available	F&R	Front & Rear	LH	Left Hand
AWD	All Wheel Drive	FBK	Fastback	LKS	Locks
BLK	Black	FI	Fuel Injection	LR	Left Rear
BSW, BW	Black Sidewall (tires)	FRT	Front	LTD	Limited

ABBREVIATIONS

LTHR	Leather	PERF	Performance	SPT	Sport
LUGRK	Luggage Rack	PGM FI	Programmed Fuel Injection	SRS	Supplemental Restraint System (Airbag)
LUX	Luxury	PKG	Package		
LWB	Long Wheelbase	PKUP	Pickup Truck	SRW	Single Rear Wheels
LWR	Lower	PNT	Paint	ST	Seat(s)
MAN	Manual	PREM	Premium	STD	Standard
MAX	Maximum	PS	Power Steering	STS	Seats
MED	Medium	PW	Power Windows	SU	Sport Utility
MIN	Minimum	PWR	Power	SW	Station Wagon
MLDGS	Moldings	QTR	Quarter	SWB	Short Wheelbase
MPI, MPFI	Multi-Port Fuel Injection	RDSTR	Roadster	SYNC	Synchromesh, Synchronized
MPG	Miles Per Gallon	REQ	Requires		
MPH	Miles Per Hour	RH	Right Hand	SYS	System
MT	Manual Transmission	R, RR	Rear	TACH	Tachometer
NA, N/A	Not Available, Not Applicable	RPM	Revolutions Per Minute	TBI	Throttle Body Injection
		RWD	Rear Wheel Drive	TEMP	Temperature
NBK	Notchback	RWL (Tires)	Raised White Letters	TP	Tape
NC	No Charge	SB	Shortbed	TPI	Tuned Port Injection
OD	Overdrive	SBR (Tires)	Steel Belted Radial	TRANS	Transmission
OHC	Overhead Camshaft	SDN	Sedan	TRBO	Turbo
OHV	Overhead Valves	SEFI, SFI	Sequential Fuel Injection	TURB	Turbo
OPT	Optional			VOL	Volume
OS	Outside	SFTTP	Soft Top	W/	With
OZ	Ounce	SNRF, S/R	Sunroof	W/O	Without
P/U	Pickup Truck	SOHC	Single Overhead Camshaft	W/T	Work Truck
PASS	Passenger			WB	Wheelbase
PDL	Power Door Locks	SP, SPD	Speed	WGN	Wagon
PEG	Preferred Equipment Group	SPFI	Sequential Port Fuel Injection	WHL(S)	Wheel(s)
				WS	Wideside
PEP	Preferred Equipment Package	SPKRS	Speakers	WSW, WW	White Sidewall (tires)

EDMUND'S 1995 HIGH-PERFORMANCE AUTOMOBILES

How to Buy Your Next New Automobile

Every new automobile buyer has but one thought in mind - to save money by getting a good deal. Your goal should be to pay 2-5% over the dealer invoice, not the 8-10% the dealer wants you to pay. To select a dealer who will appreciate your Edmund's-supplied knowledge of dealer costs, check the Automobile Dealer Directory at the back of this book. Use the following guide to help you plan your new vehicle purchase:

Step 1 Study alternatives carefully and choose the make, model and accessories you want.

Step 2 Visit a local dealership to test drive the model you intend to buy. Pay special attention to safety features, performance factors, design and comfort, visibility, handling, acceleration and braking, ride quality, etc.

Step 3 Once you've decided on a particular model, check with your insurance company to make sure the cost of insuring the vehicle falls within your budget.

Step 4 Contact your bank or credit union to obtain loan-rate information. Later on, you can compare their arrangement with the dealer's financing plan.

Step 5 Use the information in this book to determine the dealer's actual cost. Then...

a) Total the dealer invoice column for the model and equipment you want using the costing form on the opposite page.

b) To this total, add destination and preparation charges, dealer extras and the advertising fee.

c) Add to the dealer's cost what you think is a reasonable dealer profit (on most vehicles, a reasonable amount is 3% over invoice — this excludes hot selling models which will command a higher dealer profit). *Remember the dealer also makes an additional profit because of the dealer holdback.*.

Step 6 Bargain for the best price — visit several dealerships. The dealer who comes closest to your "target price" should get your business. Be sure that the dealer's price quote will be your final cost. Beware of extra dealer charges! Don't buy items such as rustproofing, undercoating, extended warranties, etc., unless you really want them.

Step 7 Deduct any manufacturer's rebates or dealer incentives from your final cost.

Step 8 If your present vehicle will be used as a trade-in, negotiate the highest possible value for it. Try to accept an amount that is not less than 3% below the trade-in vehicle's wholesale value. (Consult Edmund's *Used Car Prices* book). If you trade-in your old vehicle, deduct its agreed-upon value from the cost of the new vehicle. If you owe more on your trade-in than the dealer will give you for it, you are *upside-down* on your trade and must add your *trade-in deficit* at this point.

Step 9 Add applicable state and/or local taxes and registration fees.

Step 10 Enjoy your new vehicle, knowing that you did everything to get the best possible deal.

Alternatively, if you want to save lots of time and effort, call 1-800-CAR-CLUB (1-800-227-2582). Their expert buyers will find the exact vehicle you want at a dealer near you, and they will negotiate the best and final price, which could be less than 2% over the total invoice amount. They will even arrange competitive financing or an attractive lease for you in many markets.

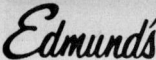

STEP-BY-STEP COSTING FORM

MAKE: EXTERIOR COLOR:

MODEL: INTERIOR COLOR:

BODY STYLE: ENGINE SIZE/TYPE:

ITEMS	MSRP	INVOICE	BEST DEAL
Basic Model Price Only			
Optional Equipment/Accessories			
1.			
2.			
3.			
4.			
5.			
6.			
7.			
8.			
9.			
10.			
11.			
12.			
13.			
14.			
TOTAL			
ADD Destination Charge			
ADD Preparation Charge			
ADD Dealer Charges ("Extras")			
ADD Advertising Fee			
ADD Dealer Profit			
SUBTRACT Rebate Amount			
SUBTRACT "Trade-In" Amount or ADD "Trade-In" Deficit			
FINAL PRICE			
ADD Sales Taxes and Fees			
TOTAL COST			

EDMUND'S 1995 HIGH-PERFORMANCE AUTOMOBILES

DEALER HOLDBACKS

Look in last Sunday's newspaper, and you will likely find a car dealer advertising inventory at one dollar below dealer invoice. Many people discount proclamations such as these, thinking that there's gotta be a catch. Yes, there is. The dealer is most likely receiving some factory incentives to move the merchandise, and will be keeping any rebates currently available on the car. Additionally, the dealer probably has profit built into every vehicle they sell. That built in profit is called a holdback, or *pack*.

You should take dealer holdback into consideration when bargaining the price of a new car or truck. Since dealer holdbacks are usually about 3% of the MSRP amount, you ought negotiate the price of the car down to about 2% above the dealer invoice amounts listed in this guide. Then subtract dealer incentives and rebates from that figure. You get a sweet deal, and the dealer makes about a 5% profit on the car.

For example, take a Ford Probe GT with package 263A, anti-lock brakes and leather seats. Retail price of such a vehicle would be $20,450 including destination charges. Dealer invoice would be $18,537, which includes a holdback of 3% of the MSRP, amounting to $613 of built-in profit to the dealer. The price you should shoot for in negotiations is $18,908 (2% above dealer invoice of $18,537), which would still give the dealer a profit of $984 or about 5% of his actual cost.

Now assume that this particular Probe qualifies for a $500 rebate. Deduct the $500 from your target price of $18,908. Ask if the dealer qualifies for any factory incentives, and deduct that amount from the target price as well. To get the latest information on rebates and incentives, go to your local library and consult the lastest issue of *Automotive News,* or, call the dealer anonymously and inquire about them. Good luck!

DEALER HOLDBACKS

Make	Holdback
Acura	No holdbacks
Alfa Romeo	Unknown
Audi	No holdbacks
BMW	2% of the MSRP
Buick	3% of the MSRP
Cadillac	3% of the MSRP
Chevrolet	3% of the MSRP
Chrysler	3% of the MSRP
Dodge	3% of the MSRP
Eagle	3% of the MSRP
Ford	3% of the MSRP
GMC	3% of the MSRP
Honda	Unknown
Infiniti	No holdbacks
Jaguar	2% of the MSRP
Jeep	3% of the MSRP
Lexus	No holdbacks
Mazda	No holdbacks
Mercedes-Benz	No holdbacks
Mercury	3% of the MSRP
Mitsubishi	2% of dealer invoice
Nissan	3% of MSRP
Oldsmobile	3% of MSRP
Plymouth	3% of the MSRP
Pontiac	3% of the MSRP
Porsche	No holdbacks
Saab	3% of the MSRP
Saturn	Unknown
Subaru	3% of the MSRP
Toyota	2% of MSRP in Alabama, Georgia, Florida, South Carolina & North Carolina only
Volkswagen	2% of the MSRP
Volvo	$700 on the 850; $900 on the 940 & 960

WARRANTIES & ROADSIDE ASSISTANCE

All new vehicles sold in America come with at least two warranties and many include roadside assistance. Described below are the major types of warranties and assistance provided to consumers.

Basic. Your basic warranty covers everything except items subject to wear and tear, such as oil filters, wiper blades, and the like. Tires and batteries often have their own warranty coverages, which will be outlined in your owner's manual. Emission equipment is required to be covered for five years or 50,000 miles by the federal government.

Drivetrain. Drivetrain coverage takes care of most of the parts that make the car move, like the engine, transmission, drive axles and driveshaft. Like the basic warranty, parts subject to wear and tear like hoses and belts are not covered. However, most of the internal parts of the engine, such as the pistons and bearings, which are subject to wear and tear are covered by the drivetrain warranty. See your owner's manual or local dealer for specific coverages.

Rust. This warranty protects you from rust-through problems with the sheetmetal. Surface rust doesn't count. The rust must make a hole to be covered by the warranty. Keep your car washed and waxed, and rust shouldn't be a problem.

Roadside Assistance. Most manufacturers provide a service that will rescue you if your car leaves you stranded, even if it's your fault. Lock yourself out of the car? Somebody will come and open it up. Run out of gas? Somebody will deliver some fuel. Flat tire? Somebody will change it for you. See your owner's manual for details, or ask the dealer about the specifics, and don't pay for extended coverage if your insurance company already provides this type of assistance.

WARRANTIES & ROADSIDE ASSISTANCE

Make	Basic (yrs/mi)	Drivetrain (yrs/mi)	Rust (yrs/mi)	Roadside Assistance (yrs/mi)
Acura	4/50,000	4/50,000	4/Unlimited	4/50,000
Alfa Romeo	3/36,000	3/36,000	6/60,000	3/36,000
Audi	3/50,000	3/50,000	10/Unlimited	3/Unlimited
BMW	4/50,000	4/50,000	6/Unlimited	4/50,000
Buick	3/36,000	3/36,000	6/100,000	3/36,000
Cadillac	4/50,000	4/50,000	6/100,000	4/50,000
Chevrolet	3/36,000	3/36,000	6/100,000	3/36,000
Chrysler	3/36,000	3/36,000	7/100,000	3/36,000
Dodge	3/36,000	3/36,000	7/100,000	3/36,000
Eagle	3/36,000	3/36,000	7/100,000	3/36,000
Ford	3/36,000	3/36,000	6/100,000	3/36,000
GMC	3/36,000	3/36,000	6/100,000	3/36,000
Honda	3/36,000	3/36,000	3/Unlimited	N/A
Infiniti	4/60,000	5/70,000	7/Unlimited	4/60,000
Jaguar	4/50,000	4/50,000	6/Unlimited	4/50,000
Jeep	3/36,000	3/36,000	7/100,000	3/36,000
Lexus	4/50,000	6/70,000	6/Unlimited	4/Unlimited
Lincoln	4/50,000	4/50,000	6/100,000	4/50,000
Mazda	3/50,000	3/50,000	5/Unlimited	3/50,000 (929,Millenia,RX-7only)
Mercedes	4/50,000	4/50,000	4/50,000	Unlimited
Mercury	3/36,000	3/36,000	6/100,000	3/36,000 (Towing only)
Mitsubishi	3/36,000	5/60,000	5/Unlimited	5/60,000
Nissan	3/36,000	5/60,000	5/Unlimited	None Available
Oldsmobile	3/36,000	3/36,000	6/100,000	3/36,000
Plymouth	3/36,000	3/36,000	7/100,000	3/36,000
Pontiac	3/36,000	3/36,000	6/100,000	3/36,000
Porsche	2/Unlimited	2/Unlimited	10/Unlimited	2/Unlimited
Saab	4/50,000	N/A	6/Unlimited	4/50,000
Saturn	3/36,000	3/36,000	6/100,000	3/36,000
Subaru	3/36,000	5/60,000	5/Unlimited	3/36,000 (SVX only)
Toyota	3/36,000	5/60,000	5/Unlimited	None Available
Volkswagen	2/24,000	10/100,000	6/Unlimited	2/24,000
Volvo	4/50,000	4/50,000	8/Unlimited	4/Unlimited

EDMUND'S 1995 HIGH-PERFORMANCE AUTOMOBILES

ACURA INTEGRA

| CODE | DESCRIPTION | INVOICE | MSRP |

1995 Acura Integra GS-R Sedan

INTEGRA

Acura redesigned its excellent Integra for the 1994 model year, so the '95s have few changes. Mid-level LS models receive a standard power sunroof, and leather is now optional on GS-R models. New Special Edition Integras come in both hatchback and sedan flavors, and are sumptuously equipped with luxury and performance goodies. Dual airbags are standard on all Integras, while anti-lock brakes are optional.

These sport coupes and sedans are quick and comfortable, with excellent build quality. Since 1994, they've sported swoopy, modern styling, featuring quad, circular headlamps. Unfortunately, the front fascia design is marred by a thick, black rubber molding between the edge of the hood and the fascia, and this cutline is painfully obvious on lighter-colored cars.

With Acura's legendary reliability, we recommend the Integra, particularly for those on a budget or in need of a sporty sedan. Starting at about $16,000, the Integra offers cheap thrills and low repair bills.

Performance and Safety

Integra RS/LS

Acceleration (0-60 mph) .... 7.6 sec.	ABS .... Optional (Standard LS)
Braking (60-0 mph) .... 127 ft.	Driver Airbag .... Standard
Cornering .... .82 g's	Passenger Airbag .... Standard
Fuel Capacity .... 13.2 gal.	Traction Control .... N/A
Fuel Economy .... City: 24 mpg	Crash Test Grade .... D: N/A P: N/A
Hwy: 31 mpg	Insurance Cost .... High (Sedan: Average)

INTEGRA ACURA

Integra GS-R

Acceleration (0-60 mph)	7.3 sec.	ABS	Standard
Braking (60-0 mph)	130 ft.	Driver Airbag	Standard
Cornering	.84 g's	Passenger Airbag	Standard
Fuel Capacity	13.2 gal.	Traction Control	N/A
Fuel Economy	City: 25 mpg	Crash Test Grade	D: N/A P: N/A
	Hwy: 31 mpg	Insurance Cost	High (Sedan: Average)

Edmund's Driving Impression

Led by its retro-stylish round headlamps, the sleek body of Acura's front-drive stands out from the mini-sport pack. Better yet, this subcompact drives like a champ—or at least, a contender. Top performance choice is the assertive GS-R, sold as a coupe or sedan, packing a 170-horsepower VTEC engine and close-ratio five-speed gearbox (no automatic offered).

Although acceleration is brisk at takeoff, it won't bring any hearts to a standstill. You can't always tell which gear you're in, either, though the notchy shift lever moves between ranges with minimal effort, via short throws. Clutch behavior is top-notch, with a slightly heavy pedal but delightfully gradual grab. Despite the freely-revving GS-R engine, its 9500-rpm tachometer (with 8000-rpm redline) and 150-mph speedometer are a trifle optimistic.

Most skilled in the handling department, an Integra is sure-footed and stable on the road, without losing too much ride comfort. Those who fear that a GS-R might be a little too jarring might prefer an LS or RS, but don't expect a dramatic difference. Even the GS-R runs quietly, with no exhaust rumble.

Seatbacks are firm and supportive, in a comfortable driving position—provided you favor a low cowl. Cramped visibility (especially to the rear) is worsened by the GS-R's rear wing spoiler and wiper. Anyone who carries more than one passenger should look at the sedan, as the coupe's back seat won't satisfy anyone of voting age.

Even if performance isn't exactly perfect, the Integra's relatively modest price is a welcome surprise, for a car that feels so well-built and tightly constructed. If you cannot bear shifting yourself, or don't need the GS-R's extra zest, look at an LS or RS, which can have Acura's Grade Logic Control automatic transmission.

See Edmund's
Automobile Dealer Directory *(page 388)*
and the back cover of this book to enter our
$10,000 Wheel N'Deal
Give-Away.

EDMUND'S 1995 HIGH-PERFORMANCE AUTOMOBILES

ACURA INTEGRA

CODE	DESCRIPTION	INVOICE	MSRP
INTEGRA			
DC434S	RS 3-Dr Sport Coupe (5-spd)	13272	15460
DC444S	RS 3-Dr Sport Coupe (auto)	13916	16210
DB754S	RS 4-Dr Sedan (5-spd)	13925	16220
DB764S	RS 4-Dr Sedan (auto)	14569	16970
DC435S	LS 3-Dr Sport Coupe (5-spd)	15573	18140
DC445S	LS 3-Dr Sport Coupe (auto)	16217	18890
DB755S	LS 4-Dr Sedan (5-spd)	16260	18940
DB765S	LS 4-Dr Sedan (auto)	16904	19690
DC238S	GS-R 3-Dr Sport Coupe w/Cloth Interior (5-spd)	17470	20350
DC239S	GS-R 3-Dr Sport Coupe w/Leather Interior (5-spd)	18157	21150
DB858S	GS-R 4-Dr Sedan w/Cloth Interior (5-spd)	17754	20680
DB859S	GS-R 4-Dr Sedan w/Leather Interior (5-spd)	18441	21480
DC436S	Special Edition 3-Dr Sport Coupe (5-spd)	17076	19890
DC446S	Special Edition 3-Dr Sport Coupe (auto)	17719	20640
DB756S	Special Edition 4-Dr Sedan (5-spd)	17548	20440
DB766S	Special Edition 4-Dr Sedan (auto)	18192	21190
	Destination Charge:	390	390

Standard Equipment

INTEGRA COUPE - RS: 1.8 liter 16-valve DOHC inline 4 cylinder engine, programmed fuel injection (PGM-FI), 5-speed manual transmission, 4-wheel independent double-wishbone suspension, front and rear stabilizer bars, variable power assisted rotary valve rack and pinion steering, 4-wheel disc brakes with ventilated front discs, P195/60R14 85H M+S tires, driver and front passenger air bag SRS, side-impact door beams, side-intrusion hip pads, 3-point outboard seat belts, front and rear 5-mph bumpers, front and rear crumple zones, projector beam headlights, body color front/rear bumpers, dual power operated door mirrors, protective bodyside moldings, rear window defroster with timer, rear window wiper/washer, body color door handles, galvanized body panels, 3-coat 3-bake paint, driver's seat lumbar adjustment, passenger side walk-in seat, center console with armrest, 50/50 fold-down rear seatback, rear seat divider, rear seat headrests, tilt steering wheel, power windows, AM/FM stereo/cassette with 4 speakers, power antenna, intermittent front wipers with mist, remote trunk/fuel filler door releases.

LS (in addition to or instead of RS equipment): Michelin XGT-H4 P195/60R14 85H M+S tires, anti-lock braking system (ABS), air conditioning, cruise control, power door locks, power moonroof, map lights.

SPECIAL EDITION (in addition to or instead of LS equipment): Cast aluminum alloy wheels, Michelin XGT-V4 P195/55R15 84V M+S tires, Special Edition emblem, leather seating and trim, rear spoiler. GS-R (in addition to or instead of LS equipment): 1.8 liter 16-valve DOHC inline 4 cylinder engine with VTEC, 5-speed manual transmission with close ratios, cast aluminum alloy wheels, Michelin XGT-V4 P195/55R15 84V M+S tires, rear spoiler with integral brake light, AM/FM stereo cassette with 6 speakers.

INTEGRA SEDAN - RS: 1.8 liter 16-valve DOHC inline 4 cylinder engine, programmed fuel injection (PGM-FI), 5-speed manual transmission, 4-wheel independent double-wishbone suspension, front and rear stabilizer bars, variable power assisted rotary-valve rack and pinion steering, 4-wheel disc brakes with ventilated front discs, P195/60R14 85H M+S tires, driver and front passenger air bag

INTEGRA ACURA

| CODE | DESCRIPTION | INVOICE | MSRP |

SRS, side-impact door beams, side-intrusion hip pads, side intrusion shoulder pads, 3-point outboard seat belts, front and rear 5-mph bumpers, front and rear crumple zones, child-proof rear door locks, projector beam headlights, body color front and rear bumpers, dual power-operated door mirrors, protective bodyside moldings, rear window defroster with timer, body color door handles, sashless door glass, galvanized body panels, 3-coat 3-bake paint, driver seat lumbar adjustment, center console with armrest, one-piece fold-down rear seatback, rear seat headrests, seat belt height adjustment, tilt steering wheel, power windows, power door locks, AM/FM stereo/cassette with 4 speakers, power antenna, intermittent front wipers with mist, remote trunk/fuel filler door releases. LS (in addition to or instead of RS equipment): Michelin XGT-H4 P195/60R14 85H M+S tires, anti-lock braking system (ABS), air conditioning, cruise control, power moonroof, map lights.

SPECIAL EDITION (in addition to or instead of LS equipment): Cast aluminum alloy wheels, Michelin XGT-V4 P195/55R15 84V M+S tires, Special Edition emblem, leather seating and trim, simulated wood console.

GS-R (in addition to or instead of LS equipment): 1.8 liter 16-valve DOHC inline 4 cylinder engine with VTEC, 5-speed manual transmission with close ratios, cast aluminum alloy wheels, Michelin XGT-V4 P195/55R15 84V M+S tires, AM/FM stereo/cassette with 6 speakers.

Accessories

Acura accessories are dealer installed. Contact an Acura dealer for accessory availability and pricing.

1995 Acura Integra GS-R Coupe

EDMUND'S 1995 HIGH-PERFORMANCE AUTOMOBILES

ACURA   LEGEND

1995 Acura Legend LS Coupe

LEGEND COUPE / GS SEDAN

New paint colors are the extent of the changes to Acura's flagship for 1995 as a replacement is readied for the 1996 model year. The Legend sedan started the whole Japanese luxury car trend in 1986, and the coupe has epitomized elegance and performance since it first appeared in 1987. While other luxury manufacturers have introduced larger, V-8 powered sedans and lower, smaller and more sporting coupes, Acura sticks with a recipe that calls more for luxury than go-fast capability.

The Legend is no slouch when it comes to acceleration and handling, though. Performance is on par with models from Lexus, and the Acura coupe has a larger interior than the rival Lexus SC coupe. Other amenities include dual airbags, anti-lock brakes, and standard traction control, as long as you opt for the high-line GS sedan or LS coupe. These Acuras come out of the box loaded with equipment, so the dealer-installed options list is short.

While no less expensive than the Lexus SC300, the Legend coupe is the more versatile of the two. The Legend GS sedan is priced competitively with the Lexus GS300, and performs a bit better. The next generation of the Legend is expected to move further upscale in content and size, although a V-8 engine is still not planned. For now though, the 1995 Legend fills its luxury sport shoes perfectly.

Performance and Safety

Acceleration (0-60 mph) .... 7.5 sec.	ABS .... Standard
Braking (60-0 mph) .... 134 ft.	Driver Airbag .... Standard
Cornering .... .85 g's	Passenger Airbag .... Standard
Fuel Capacity .... 18 gal.	Traction Control .... Optional (Standard on LS)
Fuel Economy .... City: 18 mpg	Crash Test Grade .... D: Average P: Good
Hwy: 23 mpg	Insurance Cost .... Average

EDMUND'S 1995 HIGH-PERFORMANCE AUTOMOBILES

LEGEND   ACURA

| CODE | DESCRIPTION | INVOICE | MSRP |

1995 Acura Legend Coupe

LEGEND COUPE

KA816S L 2-Dr Coupe (6-spd)	33029	39400
KA826S L 2-Dr Coupe (auto)	33029	39400
KA17S LS 2-Dr Coupe (6-spd)	36215	43200
KA27S LS 2-Dr Coupe (auto)	36215	43200
Destination Charge:	420	420

Standard Equipment

LEGEND COUPE - L: 3.2 liter 24-valve SOHC 90-degree V6 longitudinally-mounted engine, programmed fuel injection (PGM-FI) with variable induction system, 6-speed manual transmission, 4-wheel independent double-wishbone suspension, variable power assisted rack and pinion steering, anti-lock braking system (ABS), driver and front passenger SRS, front seat belts with automatic tensioners, variable diameter door beams, 3-point outboard seat belts, front and rear 5-mph bumpers, front and rear impact-absorption zones, flush-mounted high efficiency dual lens halogen headlights, tinted glass, dual power-operated body color door mirrors, protective bodyside body color moldings, rear window defroster with timer, heated door mirrors, anti-soiling bottom door guards, galvanized body panels, 4-coat 4-bake paint, leather-trimmed interior and steering wheel, simulated wood trimmed console and power window controls, driver's 8-way power seat with adjustable lumbar support and memory, fold-down rear center armrest, height and tilt adjustable front headrests, rear headrests, air conditioning, Acura/Bose Music System, steering wheel mounted remote control audio system, pre-wiring for CD changer, power-operated moonroof with sliding shade, power windows with key-off feature, power door locks with driver's side dual unlocking feature, theft-deterrent system, electronic tilt and telescopic steering column with automatic tilt-up, seat and steering wheel memory system, center console with armrest/covered storage compartment/beverage holder.

LS (in addition to or instead of L equipment): Traction control system (TCS), burled walnut-trimmed console and power window controls, front passenger 4-way power seat, heated front seats, automatic climate control, Acura/Bose Premium Music System with 8 speakers (incls AM/FM stereo/cassette, Dolby, Dynamic Noise Reduction [DNR], FM diversity antenna system, anti-theft feature), illuminated entry system.

EDMUND'S 1995 HIGH-PERFORMANCE AUTOMOBILES

ACURA
LEGEND

CODE	DESCRIPTION	INVOICE	MSRP

LEGEND GS SEDAN
— 4-Dr Sedan (6-spd) 36049 42000
— 4-Dr Sedan (auto) 36049 42000
Destination Charge: 420   420

Standard Equipment

LEGEND GS SEDAN: 3.2 liter 24-valve SOHC V6 engine, programmed fuel injection with variable induction system, 6-speed manual transmission, 4-wheel independent double wishbone suspension, variable power assisted rack and pinion steering, power assisted 4-wheel disc brakes with anti-lock braking system, driver and front passenger air bags, traction control system, front and rear 5-mph bumpers, halogen headlights, tinted glass, body color dual power operated door mirrors (heated), body color bodyside moldings, rear window defroster with timer, leather-trimmed interior and steering wheel, burled walnut-trimmed console and power window controls, driver's 8-way power seat with adjustable lumbar support and memory, fold-down rear center armrest, front passenger's 4-way power seat, heated front seats, height and tilt adjustable headrests (front and rear), air conditioning, automatic climate control, Acura/Bose Premium Music System (incls AM/FM stereo/cassette, 8 speakers, Dolby Dynamic Noise Reduction, FM diversity antenna system, anti-theft feature), steering wheel mounted remote control audio system, pre-wired for CD changer, power operated moonroof with sliding shade, power windows with key-off feature, power door locks with driver's side dual unlocking feature, theft-deterrent system, electronic tilt and telescopic steering column with automatic tilt-up, seat and steering wheel memory system, illuminated entry system, center console with armrest, Michelin XGT-V4 all-season 215/55R16 91V tires.

Accessories

NOTE: Acura accessories are dealer installed. Contact an Acura dealer for accessory availability.

1995 Acura Legend GS Sedan

1994 Acura NSX

NSX

Since its 1991 introduction, the Acura NSX has been heralded by much of the motoring press as the best sports car ever produced. Certainly, with its 24-valve, 3.0-liter V-6, aluminum body, mid-engine layout and traditionally Honda-correct ergonomics, the NSX is a heckuva car. But the best sports car ever made? We don't doubt it.

For 1995, the slow-selling NSX is slated to get a targa roof, among other changes that Acura has not yet discussed with the media. Acura is hoping the targa option will increase sales of the NSX, which could happen, but few Americans seem to be in the market for $70,000 Japanese two-seaters, especially since the LT1 Corvette offers nearly as good performance for half the asking price and Dodge's Viper offers nostalgic styling, a throaty V-10, and is a guaranteed babe magnet. The 1995 model has been delayed until mid-winter, but dealers should be able to obtain a 1994 edition if you just can't wait.

Still, the exotic looks and excellent engineering of the NSX should prove to be even more attractive with the promise of open-roofed motoring. If the more financially able enthusiasts of America don't agree, we may see the NSX go the way of the Corvette ZR1.

Performance and Safety

Acceleration (0-60 mph)	5.3 sec.	ABS	Standard
Braking (60-0 mph)	118 ft.	Driver Airbag	Standard
Cornering	.95 g's	Passenger Airbag	Standard
Fuel Capacity	18.5 gal.	Traction Control	Standard
Fuel Economy	City: 18 mpg	Crash Test Grade	D: N/A P: N/A
	Hwy: 23 mpg	Insurance Cost	Average

ACURA
NSX

CODE	DESCRIPTION	INVOICE	MSRP
NSX (1994)			
NA115R	2-Dr Coupe (5-spd)	62872	75000
NA126R	2-Dr Coupe (auto)	66227	79000
Destination Charge:		725	725

Standard Equipment

NSX: Cruise control, full instrumentation, rear spoiler, leather upholstery, tinted glass, digital clock, variable intermittent wipers, driver and front passenger air bags, color-keyed front and rear bumpers, dual power mirrors, theft-deterrent system, limited slip differential, dual exhaust system, power windows, power steering (auto trans only), automatic air conditioning, remote decklid release, high performance tires (front - 215/45ZR16, rear - 245/40ZR17), power diversity antenna, power door locks, dual 4-way power seats, power anti-lock 4-wheel disc brakes, aluminum alloy wheels, retractable projector-beam headlights, AM/FM ETR Bose radio with cassette and compact disc pre-wiring, full carpeting including cargo area, traction control system, full center console, front and rear stabilizer bars, electric rear window defroster, tilt/telescopic steering column, 3.0L V6 EFI VTEC 24-valve engine, remote fuel filler door release.

Accessories

NOTE: Acura accessories are dealer installed. Contact an Acura dealer for accessory availability.

1994 Acura NSX

ALFA ROMEO

1995 Alfa Romeo 164 Quadrifoglio

164

Rolled out in 1990 as a replacement for the ill-fated Milano, the Alfa Romeo 164 sports front-wheel drive and a platform shared with other European sedans, such as the Saab 9000. The 164 has never sold well in America, and for 1995 is the sole offering by Alfa Romeo as it contemplates its future on U.S. soil.

This year, the 164 becomes a much safer car, with the addition of standard dual airbags. This sporty Italian sedan is also equipped with anti-lock brakes, but traction control is unavailable. A new steering wheel design and fresh color choices round out the 1995 164.

Reliability on Alfas has improved considerably in the past few years, but is far from the standards set by Pacific Rim builders.. However, it's a European sport sedan by a company with a long racing history, and not many are sold in the States. If you value exclusivity and eccentricity, it's a safe bet that you'll drive many smiling miles without seeing a 164 headed towards you on the other side of the double yellow.

Performance and Safety

Acceleration (0-60 mph) .... 7.2 sec.	ABS .... Standard
Braking (60-0 mph) .... 126 ft.	Driver Airbag .... Standard
Cornering .... .81 g's	Passenger Airbag .... Standard
Fuel Capacity .... 17.2 gal.	Traction Control .... N/A
Fuel Economy .... City: 15 mpg	Crash Test Grade .... D: N/A P: N/A
Hwy: 22 mpg	Insurance Cost .... Average

EDMUND'S 1995 HIGH-PERFORMANCE AUTOMOBILES

ALFA ROMEO 164

CODE	DESCRIPTION	INVOICE	MSRP

164
—	LS 4-Dr Sedan (5-spd)	29635	36140
—	Quadrifoglio 4-Dr Sedan (5-spd)	31930	38940
Destination Charge:		460	460

Standard Equipment

164 - LS: 3.0 liter MPI 24-valve V6 DOHC engine, 5-speed manual transmission with overdrive, power 4-wheel disc brakes with anti-lock braking system, air conditioning with auto climate control, front wheel drive, cruise control, power sunroof, power windows, front and rear fog lights, power assist rack and pinion steering, power door locks, 15" cast alloy wheels, P195/65ZR15 SBR BSW tires, rear window defroster, AM/FM stereo radio with cassette, power antenna, power outside heated folding mirrors, dual air bag supplemental restraint system, rear window sunshades, heated 8-way power leather sport seats, tachometer, automatic dimming interior mirror, illuminated passenger visor vanity mirror, power fuel filler door release, power trunk release, anti-theft security system, headlight washers, intermittent windshield wipers, front suspension (MacPherson struts with lower wishbones, coil springs, anti-roll bar), rear suspension (struts, double transverse links and single trailing link per side, coil springs, anti-roll bar), digital clock, center front and rear armrests, center console, 3.35:1 axle ratio, rear seat reading lamps, ski boot, leather-wrapped telescoping steering wheel.

QUADRIFOGLIO (in addition to or instead of LS equipment): Front air dam, rear decklid spoiler, ground effects package, aerodynamic rocker panel moldings, unique bodyside cladding, electronic sport suspension, 3.41:1 axle ratio, sport alloy wheels.

Accessories

—	Automatic Transmission — 4-speed - LS	740	900
	incls 4.20:1 axle ratio		
—	Metallic Paint — LS	345	420
—	California Emissions	48	48
—	Compact Disc Player — LS	520	625

For expert advice in selecting/buying/leasing a new car, call

1-900-AUTOPRO

($2.00 per minute)

AUDI

1995 Audi 90 CS

90

This will be the final year for the Audi 90, which is due to be replaced in 1996 by an all-new compact called the A4. In the meantime, however, the 90 benefits from a new Sport package that includes a retuned suspension, body color moldings, alloy wheels and sport seats. Also, the Quattro all-wheel drive system has been separated from expensive option packages and is now available across the line for approximately $1,500.

As with the rest of the Audi lineup, the 90 has suffered sales woes since its introduction in 1988. Staid styling aside, the 90 is a competent compact in the German driver's car tradition. The current iteration features a 2.8-liter V-6, the same engine that can be found under the hood of the speedy 100 Series sedans. With much less weight to haul around, the V-6 works quite well in the 90, and we predict that Audi buyers will gravitate toward the new Sport edition.

The 90 isn't the least expensive nor the most refined player in this class, but for driving pleasure, all-weather capability, and a measure of exclusivity, it's hard to beat this Audi.

Performance and Safety

Acceleration (0-60 mph)	8.2 sec.
Braking (60-0 mph)	129 ft.
Cornering	.80 g's
Fuel Capacity	17.4 gal. (16.9 Quattro)
Fuel Economy	City: 18 mpg
	Hwy: 26 mpg

ABS	Standard
Driver Airbag	Standard
Passenger Airbag	Standard
Traction Control	N/A
Crash Test Grade	D: N/A P: N/A
Insurance Cost	Low

EDMUND'S 1995 HIGH-PERFORMANCE AUTOMOBILES

AUDI 90

| CODE | DESCRIPTION | INVOICE | MSRP |

1995 Audi 90 CS Quattro Sport

90
8C24U4	Base 4-Dr Sedan (5-spd)	22578	25670
8C26U4	Sport 4-Dr Sedan (5-spd)	22926	26070
Destination Charge:		445	445

Standard Equipment

90/SPORT 90: 2.8 liter 172 HP V6 engine (incls variable intake path geometry and fully electronic engine control system, knock sensors, electronic idle control, hydraulic valve lifters), hydraulic engine mounts, engine/automatic transmission oil coolers, front-wheel drive, 5-speed manual transmission, long-life exhaust system, power rack and pinion steering, front coil spring/shock absorbers (gas charged) struts with wishbone lower control arm, rear torsion beam linked trailing arms, lowered sport suspension with sport springs and shock absorbers (Sport 90), front and rear stabilizer bars, 7J x 15 10-spoke alloy wheels (90), 7J x 15 5-spoke alloy wheels (Sport 90), 195/65HR15 all-weather tires, power assisted 4-wheel disc brakes (vented front with load-sensitive pressure proportioning), anti-lock braking system (ABS), asbestos-free brake and clutch linings, 4-door sedan body style, unit body using fully galvanized sheet steel (all panels, both sides), multi-step factory rust protection, body color front and rear bumper aprons, body color outside mirrors and door handles, protective bodyside moldings, flush-mounted glass/door handles, aerodynamic halogen headlights, front fog lights integrated in lower bumper apron, rear fog lights integrated in left rear light cluster, high pressure headlight washer system, full-width rear reflective light panel, fuel cap hanger feature, foldable windshield wipers, 5-mph bumpers, right outside convex mirror, flared fenders, clearcoat metallic paint (90), sport uni-color paint: white, red, black (Sport 90); comfort seats with Chenille velour seat upholstery (90), sport seats with Jacquard sport cloth seat upholstery (Sport 90), burled walnut wood inlays (incls instrument panel, center console, door panels), reclining front seats with seat height adjustment, folding front center armrest with height adjustment (90), fold-down rear center armrest, full center console with storage bin (90), beverage holders, front and rear "open" head restraints (foldable rear), driver and front passenger air bags with knee bar (SRS), front 3-point safety belts with height adjustment and automatic tensioners, rear outboard 3-point safety belts, leather-wrapped steering wheel, leather shift knob and boot (Sport 90 manual trans), folding overhead assist handles, individual passenger reading lamps, front seatback storage pockets (90), red backlit instrumentation (incls tachometer, 160-mph electric speedometer, coolant temperature gauge, fuel gauge, digital clock, trip odometer), sports gauge package in lower center console (incls voltmeter, engine oil pressure gauge, oil temperature gauge) (Sport 90), outside temperature gauge (manual trans), driver and passenger illuminated vanity mirrors, illuminated glove box/trunk/lighter/ashtrays, lockable glove box, retained accessory power for windows and optional sunroof, interior lighting with courtesy delay feature, ignition key with integrated light, front and rear color-coordinated carpet floor mats, full-width trunk lid liner, anti-theft vehicle alarm system (incls horn and lights), CFC-free air conditioning, heat and AC vents to rear footwell, tinted glass, windshield with tint band, rear window defogger with automatic timed shut-off feature, electronic cruise control with resume and speed-up features, power windows with child safety lock, driver's window with one-touch down feature, dual power outside mirrors with defog feature, power central locking system (incls trunk and fuel filler door), child safety rear door locks, electronically tuned AM/FM stereo cassette radio with anti-theft coding, 6-speaker sound system with dual diversity antenna system, 2-speed intermittent wipers, gas strut supports for hood and trunk lid, 60/40 split folding rear seatback.

Accessories

CODE	DESCRIPTION	INVOICE	MSRP
OLM	**California Emissions**	NC	NC
OLS	**Massachusetts Emissions**	NC	NC
QTR	**Quattro AWD Pkg**	1500	1500
	NA w/automatic transmission		
—	**Automatic Transmission — 4-speed**	850	900
	incls transmission oil cooler		
3FD	**Power Sunroof**	835	960
—	**Leather Seat Trim**	1079	1240
	Sport 90 req's Quattro AWD Pkg and comfort & convenience pkg		
—	**Pearlescent Metallic Paint**	461	530
PAX	**All-Weather Pkg #1**	296	340
	incls heated front seats and windshield washer nozzles; req's comfort & convenience pkg; req's Quattro AWD Pkg on Sport 90		
PAW	**All-Weather Pkg #2**	383	440
	incls heated front seats, heated door locks and heated windshield washer nozzles		
PCC	**Comfort & Convenience Pkg**	1549	1780
	incls automatic air conditioning, power sunroof, keyless remote locking system, 8-way power driver's seat		

For a guaranteed low price on a new vehicle in your area, call

1-800-CAR-CLUB

AUDI S6

1995 Audi S6

S6

Audi's flagship sedan, the S6, receives new styling and a new name for 1995. The grille, hood, front bumper fascia, air dam and taillights have all been revised for 1995. Also, the front fenders receive subtle flares and the side window trim has been redone. The result is a taut, aggressive look. Otherwise, the car is carried over from 1994's S4 model, which was based on the old Audi 100, which has been renamed the A6 for 1995. Follow?

What has been carried over includes the S4's excellent interior layout, proven Quattro transaxle, and the potent turbocharged five-cylinder engine good for 227 horsepower. This car is a wonder, and you certainly pay a premium for all the high-tech hardware. Priced at just over $50,000, the S6 comes loaded, standard. Still, the exclusivity, Germanic character and outstanding driveability of the S6 makes it a worthy and interesting alternative to such mainstream offerings as the Cadillac Seville STS or the Lexus LS400.

Performance and Safety

Acceleration (0-60 mph) .... 6.5 sec.	ABS .... Standard	
Braking (60-0 mph) .... 115 ft.	Driver Airbag .... Standard	
Cornering .... .87 g's	Passenger Airbag .... Standard	
Fuel Capacity .... 21.1 gal.	Traction Control .... N/A	
Fuel Economy .... City: 18 mpg	Crash Test Grade .... D: N/A	P: N/A
Hwy: 23 mpg	Insurance Cost .... Low	

S6   AUDI

| CODE | DESCRIPTION | INVOICE | MSRP |

Edmund's Driving Impression

Is "character" enough to induce a reasonable person to part with 50 big ones? For a mere automobile? In the case of Audi's performance machine, the answer is a resounding yes.

Once you pass the $30,000 mark, the elements that make a car edge ahead of the pack grow subtle. Simply put, this newly-renamed premium tourer has the credentials that affluent enthusiasts demand—without the need for geegaws to announce its superlative nature.

Handling from the well-proven all-wheel-drive chassis can only be branded superior. An S6 is secure, sure-footed, stable and capable, hugging the road smartly. Super-wide tires help, but even they do not detract from the pleasing ride. Sure, you feel the bumps, but this road tamer takes potholes very much in stride, delivering a smoother trek than expected to its fortunate occupants.

One word of warning: Acceleration can be great, but *only* if you exercise the right combination of gearing, clutch action, and revs. If not, this otherwise-swift Audi can feel as sluggish as a puny subcompact. Hit it right, and you get a nicely satisfying pull and a highly pleasing, macho whine from the 227-horsepower turbocharged engine. Flunk the control test, and you'll get no satisfaction at all.

The gearshift is on the notchy side, likely to emit an occasional "clunk" if the clutch isn't fully depressed, or you try musclecar-style speed-shifting. Manipulating the shift lever actually demands some arm strength, and doesn't zip as easily between ratios as some. Don't try to bypass the exam by requesting an automatic transmission. The S6 comes only with a five-speed.

Boisterous the S6 is not. You get quiet running and a civilized experience. Seats are satisfyingly comfortable and highly supportive. Lesser Audis are decorated with a little wood, but the hot one turns to carbon fiber interior trim—one more touch of that "character" that makes it more than a costly bauble.

S6

4A2555	Turbo AWD 4-Dr Sedan (5-spd)	39630	45270
Destination Charge:		445	445

Standard Equipment

S6: 2.2 liter 227 HP 5 cylinder turbocharged 20-valve engine (incls electronic engine management system with dual knock sensors, turbocharger with separate water cooling system, boost air intercooler), hydraulic engine mounts, engine oil cooler, Quattro-Permanently engaged all-wheel drive with TORSEN center differential and automatic disengage of rear differential lock, 5-speed manual transmission, self-adjusting hydraulic clutch, long-life exhaust system, vehicle speed-sensitive rack and pinion power steering, front coil spring/shock absorber (gas charged) struts with lower control arms, fully independent rear suspension with trapezoidal lower control arms and upper links, front stabilizer bar, 8J x 16 forged 5-spoke alloy wheels, 225/50ZR16 SBR high performance tires, power assisted 4-wheel disc brakes (vented front and rear with load-sensitive pressure proportioning), anti-lock braking system (ABS), asbestos-free brake and clutch linings, 4-door sedan body style, unit body using fully galvanized sheet steel (all panels, both sides), multi-step factory rust protection, integrated body color front/rear bumpers, body color outside mirrors and door handles, body color protective bodyside moldings, flush-mounted glass and door handles, aerodynamic halogen triple headlights (halogen high beam, elliptical projector low beam, and fog lights in one unit), integrated rear fog lights, high pressure headlight washers, heated windshield washer nozzles, full-width rear reflective/light panel, fuel cap hanger feature, foldable windshield wipers, 5-mph bumpers, right outside convex mirror, flared front fenders, clearcoat metallic paint, Seiden Nappa leather seat upholstery, wraparound dash/door panel design, burled walnut wood inlays (incls instrument panel, center console, door panels), color-coordinated lower dashboard trim, reclining front sport seats with

AUDI S6

lumbar and thigh adjustments, 8-way power front seats, driver's 4-position memory seat function and outside mirror adjustments, heatable front/rear outboard seats with individual temperature controls, folding height adjustable front center armrests, hands-free operation cellular telephone with voice recognition feature (stored in front center armrest), fold-down rear center armrest with expandable ski/storage sack, full center console with storage bins and beverage holders, front/rear "Full Cushion" head restraints, driver and front passenger air bags with knee bar (supplemental restraint system), front 3-point safety belts with height adjustment and automatic tensioners, rear outboard 3-point safety belts with comfort adjustment, ratcheting mechanism for securing a child seat, leather-wrapped sport steering wheel, leather shift knob and boot, folding overhead assist handles, individual passenger reading lamps, front seatback storage pockets, red backlit instrumentation with light gray instrument faces, tachometer, 160-mph electric speedometer, coolant temperature gauge, analog clock, voltmeter, fuel/oil temperature/oil pressure gauges, trip odometer, outside temperature gauge, Active Auto Check System, low fuel warning light, driver and passenger illuminated vanity mirrors, illuminated glove box/trunk/lighter/ashtrays, lockable glove box, interior lighting with courtesy delay feature, retained accessory power for windows and sunroof, ignition key with infrared transmitter, front/rear color-coordinated carpet floor mats, fully carpeted trunk, tilt and telescopic adjustable steering column, anti-theft vehicle alarm system (incls horn and lights), CFC-free air conditioner, automatic climate control system, rear seat heat/AC vents, tinted glass, windshield with tint band, electric rear window defogger with automatic timed shut-off feature, electronic cruise control with resume and speed-up features, power windows with driver's one-touch down feature, dual power outside mirrors with defog feature, right outside mirror with reverse tilt, power central locking system (incls trunk and fuel filler door), infrared remote locking system (incls automatic driver's seat/mirror adjustments, alarm arm and disarm, interior illumination), child safety rear door locks/rear window lock-outs, 2-way tilt/slide power glass moonroof with convenience close feature (incls automatic pre-select function and sun shade), Audi/Bose music system with 4 acoustically tuned amplified speaker modules, 2 tweeters, 2 bass modules and dual diversity antenna system; electronically tuned AM/FM stereo cassette radio with anti-theft coding, 2-speed intermittent wipers, electric remote trunk lid release, gas strut supports for hood and trunk, compact disc changer prep.

Accessories

Code	Description	Invoice	MSRP
—	Pearlescent Metallic Paint	461	530
CD2	Compact Disc Changer	687	790
H4R	Sport Alloy Wheels — 6-spoke	NC	NC

incls P215/60VR15 all-season BW tires

USE A MULTIMEDIA CD-ROM TO RESEARCH YOUR NEXT AUTOMOBILE PURCHASE

see ad on page 384 for details

3-SERIES

1995 BMW M3

3-SERIES

BMW has added an M3 model to the 3-Series lineup for 1995, and it's been winning rave reviews from the press and public. The M3 has a 240-hp inline six purring away under the hood, suspension modifications designed specifically for the war-torn roads of America, huge brakes, and supple leather seats—all for less than $40,000.

Also due on our shores within the year, a BMW hatchback based on the 3-Series. To be called the 316i Compact, it should be priced just above the Volkswagen GTI, though performance levels will likely fall a bit short of those of the vaunted VW.

The rest of the 3-Series line carries over for 1995, which is no bad thing. This BMW has won the favor of driving enthusiasts everywhere for its capable handling, first-class ergonomics, and classic styling. Prices start right around the $25,000 mark, just $6,000 above the average price of a new car in this country. The 325i and 325is, two of the three performers in the lineup, do have base prices that are a bit higher.

Bottom rung 3-Series' are powered by a 1.8-liter four-cylinder, while mid-range cars have a 189-hp six doing the motivational work. All 3-Series models have dual airbags and anti-lock brakes, and six-cylinder cars get optional traction control.

For the money, BMW's 3-Series is tough to beat for sophistication, safety and performance, particularly in M3 guise.

BMW   3-SERIES

Performance and Safety

325i/325is

Acceleration (0-60 mph) .... 7.4 sec.	ABS .... Standard
Braking (60-0 mph) .... 126 ft.	Driver Airbag .... Standard
Cornering .... .85 g's	Passenger Airbag .... Standard
Fuel Capacity .... 17.2 gal.	Traction Control .... Optional
Fuel Economy .... City: 20 mpg	Crash Test Grade .... D: Good P: Average
Hwy. 28 mpg	Insurance Cost .... High

M3

Acceleration (0-60 mph) .... 5.6 sec.	ABS .... Standard
Braking (60-0 mph) .... 111 ft.	Driver Airbag .... Standard
Cornering .... .86 g's	Passenger Airbag .... Standard
Fuel Capacity .... 17.2 gal.	Traction Control .... N/A
Fuel Economy .... City: 19 mpg	Crash Test Grade .... D: Good P: Average
Hwy: 28 mpg	Insurance Cost .... N/A

Edmund's Driving Impression

Long known for superlative assembly quality, the starting-level BMWs mix near-perfect fit/finish with precision handling. Tight, solid construction is evident every time a door shuts, with a firm and reassuring grasp.

The 325i's 2.5-liter inline six-cylinder engine is smooth and crisply responsive, though acceleration doesn't exactly rank as dramatic. More than adequate, of course, for most drivers; but for sheer blast-off potential, the new 240-horse M3 coupe is worth a look.

Anyone who likes to shift is in for a treat, because the BMW's five-speed manual gearbox is about as precise as they come. A sheer, silken joy to manipulate, the short gearshift lever virtually cascades from one ratio into the next, never missing a beat. Clutch action is equally pleasing—a perfect match for the gearbox.

BMW's foremost talent, however, lies at suspension level. Taking advantage of traditional rear-drive German precision, a 3-Series coupe or sedan hugs the pavement tenaciously, steering crisply and quickly. Remarkably agile and easy to maneuver, it delivers excellent steering feedback, and the body leans little in corners. Even better, the suspension absorbs lumps and bumps beautifully, for a well-controlled ride both on the highway and around town.

Except for a mildly throaty exhaust, near-silence is the rule. Driving position is excellent, on highly supportive seats with snug side-bolstering. We couldn't ask for much more in a sports sedan, solidly built by true craftspeople.

For a lot fewer dollars, a 318i delivers most of the expected BMW virtues, including near-peerless handling and that unbeatable manual gearshift. In fact, its free-revving, high-winding four-cylinder engine rivals the more powerful 325i for sporty fun on the highway.

3-SERIES BMW

| CODE | DESCRIPTION | INVOICE | MSRP |

1995 BMW 325is Coupe

325i/325iS

—	325i 4-Dr Sedan (5-spd)	26455	31450
—	325iC 2-Dr Convertible (5-spd)	33310	39600
—	325is 2-Dr Coupe (5-spd)	27635	32850
Destination Charge:		470	470

Standard Equipment

325i SEDAN: 2.5 liter DOHC 24-valve inline 6 cylinder engine with variable valve timing, 5-speed manual transmission, Digital Motor Electronics engine management system, direct ignition system with knock control, strut type front suspension, central link rear suspension, front and rear anti-roll stabilizer bars, twin-tube gas-pressure shock absorbers, engine speed-sensitive variable assist power steering, power 4-wheel disc brakes with anti-lock braking system, 15 x 7J cast alloy wheels, 205/65R15 91H all-season radial tires, body color bumpers (damage control to 9 mph), halogen free-form fog lights, 2-speed intermittent windshield wipers, dual power OS mirrors, illuminated master key, courtesy lights with fade-in/out feature, rear reading lights, map reading lights, take-out flashlight in glove box, cruise control, 8-way power front seats, split folding rear seats, storage nets on front seatbacks, electronic analog speedometer and tachometer, LCD main and trip odometers, service interval indicator, analog fuel economy indicator, leatherette upholstery, full center armrest, power windows with one-touch feature, 2-stage rear window defroster, air conditioning, microfiltered ventilation, power 2-way sunroof, radio (anti-theft AM/FM stereo radio/cassette audio system with 10 x 20-watt amplification, 10 speakers), diversity antenna system, pre-wiring for CD changer, drop-down tool kit in trunk, full-size spare wheel and tire, central locking system, drive-away protection, pre-wired for BMW remote keyless entry security system, dual air bag SRS, automatic front seatbelt tensioners.

325is COUPE (in addition to or instead of 325i SEDAN equipment): Seatback easy-entry feature, leather seating, leather manual shift knob, leather steering wheel, leather hand brake grip and boot.

325i CONVERTIBLE (in addition to or instead of 325i COUPE equipment): Rear reading lights deleted, height adjustable steering wheel, rear center armrest, positive side-window sealing system, blower type rear window defogger, power sunroof deleted, fully lined power convertible top, mast antenna.

EDMUND'S 1995 HIGH-PERFORMANCE AUTOMOBILES

BMW 3-SERIES

CODE	DESCRIPTION	INVOICE	MSRP

Accessories

—	Leather Seat Trim — 325i Sedan	1070	1300
—	Automatic Transmission — 4-speed	740	900
—	On-Board Computer	355	430
—	Metallic Paint	390	475
—	Heated Front Seats	370	450
	incls dual power heated mirrors		
—	Rear Fold-Down Seat	225	275
—	Rollover Protection System — 325iC Convertible	1140	1390
—	Premium Pkg — 325i Sedan	1560	1895
	325iC Convertible	570	695
	325is Coupe	570	695
	incls on-board computer, wood interior trim, leather seat trim (325i Sedan), tilt steering column (325i Sedan)		
—	Sport Pkg — 325i Sedan	1145	1395
	325iC Convertible	1065	1295
	325is Coupe	1145	1395
	incls on-board computer, 16" alloy wheels, P225/60ZR16 tires, sport seats, tilt steering column (325i Sedan), sport suspension (325i Sedan, 325is Coupe)		
—	Limited Slip Differential	430	530

M3

M3 2 Dr Coupe (5-spd)		30955	36800
Destination Charge:		450	450

Standard Equipment

M3: 3.0L DOHC 24-valve 6 cylinder engine with variable valve timing, electronic fuel injection, electronic breakerless direct ignition system, Digital Motor Electronics engine-management system with knock control and self-diagnosis capability, variable rpm limiting, 5-speed manual transmission with direct-drive 5th gear, 25% limited slip differential, exhaust system with stainless steel components, 4-wheel independent suspension (front - strut type; rear - central link), twin-tube gas pressure shock absorbers, engine-speed-sensitive variable assist/variable ratio power rack and pinion steering, front and rear anti-roll bars, vacuum-assisted 4-wheel ventilated disc brakes, anti-lock braking system (ABS), 17x7.5J cast alloy wheels (BMW M 10-spoke design), 235/40ZR17 SBR high-performance tires, undercoating and cavity seal, special BMW M paint colors, BMW M aerodynamic features (special front and lower rear spoiler, rocker panels), hydraulic impact bumpers with compressible mounting elements (damage control to 9 mph), halogen free form low-beam headlights, halogen free form fog lights, 2-speed windshield wipers with single-wipe control (car-speed-controlled intermittent operation), dual power/heated outside mirrors, heated driver's door lock and windshield washer jets, illuminating master key, central locking system with double-lock anti-theft feature (incls trunk and fuel filler door), Driveaway Protection (disables engine when double-lock feature is engaged), pre-wiring for BMW remote keyless entry security system, leather-covered height adjustable M-Technic steering wheel, front sports seats with adjustable thigh support and shoulder support/head-restraint height (driver's seat height adjustable), automatic front seat forward movement for access to rear seats, automatic front seatbelt tensioners, dual-airbag supplementary restraint system, Nappa leather seating with special M design, leather shift knob/handbrake grip/boot, velour carpeting, time-delay courtesy lights, impact sensor (unlocks doors, switches on interior lights and 4-way hazard flashers in case of accident), tinted glass with dark upper windshield band, power front windows with key-off operation (1-touch lowering

3-SERIES / 5-SERIES — BMW

CODE	DESCRIPTION	INVOICE	MSRP

and raising, automatic positioning of windows for positive sealing), openable rear side windows, electronic analog speedometer and tachometer, LCD main and trip odometers, Service Interval Indicator (recommends maintenance on basis of actual car use), multi-information display with alphanumeric LCD readout (incls outside temperature display and freeze warning, multi-function digital clock, check control vehicle monitor system), air conditioning and heating with separate electronic temperature control for left and right sides (CFC-free refrigerant), microfiltered ventilation, rear window defroster, anti-theft AM/FM stereo radio/cassette CD-ready audio system (10x25 watt amplification, 10 speakers, diversity antenna system), pre-wiring for BMW CD changer, illuminated locking glove box with rechargable flashlight, split fold-down rear seats, drop-down toolkit in trunklid, full-use spare wheel and tire.

Accessories

—	Heated Front Seats	305	370
—	Power Sunroof	920	1120
	incls cruise control		
—	Cruise Control	375	455
—	On-Board Computer	355	430

1995 BMW 530i

5-SERIES

The vaunted 5-Series is nearing the end of its run in its current form. A redesigned model is due within two years, but that doesn't consign the 1995 model to the dustbin, not by a long shot. Freshened styling and body-colored trim update the 5-Series' look this year, while the 540i gets a six-speed manual transmission and sport-tuned suspension.

Inside, a new steering wheel accentuates the cabin. The artful dashboard houses dual airbags, and anti-lock brakes assure smooth stops. BMW's traditionally firm seats make driving a pleasure, with a great driving position and long-haul comfort.

BMW 5-SERIES

Wrapped in classy, distinctive sheetmetal, with creamy V-8 engines under the hood, the 530i and 540i are among the top ranks of the luxury car class.

Performance and Safety

530i

Acceleration (0-60 mph)	7.0 sec.	ABS	Standard	
Braking (60-0 mph)	132 ft.	Driver Airbag	Standard	
Cornering	.80 g's	Passenger Airbag	Standard	
Fuel Capacity	21.1 gal.	Traction Control	Optional	
Fuel Economy	City: 16 mpg	Crash Test Grade	D: N/A	P: N/A
	Hwy: 24 mpg	Insurance Cost	Average	

540i

Acceleration (0-60 mph)	6.9 sec.	ABS	Standard	
Braking (60-0 mph)	118 ft.	Driver Airbag	Standard	
Cornering	.84 g's	Passenger Airbag	Standard	
Fuel Capacity	21.1 gal.	Traction Control	Optional	
Fuel Economy	City: 17 mpg	Crash Test Grade	D: N/A	P: N/A
	Hwy: 25 mpg	Insurance Cost	Average	

Edmund's Driving Impression

Words like solid, comfortable, capable, confident, and supple describe the 5-Series driving experience. This is the ultimate driving machine. True, the blue and white BMW emblem on the tip of the hood imparts a certain degree of class, sophistication and status—characteristics that in other automobiles may alter the driver's image of himself. However, the 5-Series is one of those rare cars that makes you forget about the message the vehicle is sending to your peer groups. Once behind the wheel, the magic of the BMW name is supplanted by the magic of the BMW itself, and you don't care what moniker is stenciled across the decklid any more than you care why Tonya did it.

The 5-Series may not be as perfectly engineered as a Lexus, or as pedigreed as a Mercedes, but it sure is a blast to drive. Everything fits. This BMW becomes an extension of the driver, communicating the right information from the road and damping the wrong things, like chuckholes and railroad tracks. The interior is an ergonomic delight, with seats that feel as fresh after hours as they do after minutes. The one interior gripe is the Happy Halloween orange-lit gauges at night. While this particular shade does cut down on distractions to the driver, it is somewhat sickly after awhile.

The powertrain is flawless. Power delivery is smooth, with seamless shifts. The 540i is quite quick, and with the new six-speed transmission and revised suspension settings, should prove very satisfying. With prices for the 530i starting at about $45,000, the 5-Series could even save you enough over comparable Lexus and Infiniti models to buy a used Miata for the weekends.

5-SERIES — BMW

CODE	DESCRIPTION	INVOICE	MSRP

530i

—	530i 4-Dr Sedan (5-spd)	34825	41750
	Destination Charge:	470	470
	Gas Guzzler Tax: 530i w/5-spd	1000	1000

Standard Equipment

530i SEDAN: 3.0 liter DOHC 4-cam 32-valve V8 engine, 5-speed manual transmission, Digital Motor Electronics engine management system, direct ignition system with knock control, double-pivot strut-type front suspension, Track Link rear suspension, front and rear anti-roll stabilizer bars, twin-tube gas-pressure shock absorbers, engine-speed-sensitive variable assist power steering, 4-wheel disc brakes (ventilated front discs, vacuum-assisted), anti-lock braking system (ABS), 15" x 7"J cast alloy wheels (cross-spoke design), 225/60R15 96H all-season radial tires, body color bumpers with hydraulic energy absorbers and front compressible elements (damage control to 9 mph), halogen ellipsoid low-beam headlights, halogen fog lights, 2-speed intermittent windshield wipers (incls car-speed controlled wiping speed and interval, single wipe control, windshield washer system with heated washer jets), metallic paint (at no additional charge), dual power/heated outside mirrors, pre-wiring for automatic dimming inside rearview mirror, heated driver's door lock, illuminating master key, time delay courtesy lights with actuation from driver's exterior door handle (automatic switch-on when engine is turned off), map reading lights, take-out flashlight in glove box, telescopically adjustable steering wheel, 10-way power front seats with power head restraints (incls driver's seat power lumbar support, folding front center armrests), electronic analog speedometer and tachometer, LCD main and trip odometers, Service Interval Indicator, fuel-economy indicator, check control vehicle monitor system, onboard computer, leather and wood interior trim (gathered-leather seating surfaces and door trim, leather covered steering wheel/handbrake boot and grip/door armrests/door pulls/manual-transmission shift boot), rear center armrest with storage compartment, seatback storage pockets, velour carpeting, power windows with key-off and operation (incls one-touch lowering of all windows, one-touch lowering and raising of driver's window), 2-stage rear window defroster, air conditioning and heating with separate left/right temperature controls (CFC-free refrigerant, microfiltered ventilation), automatic ventilation system (can be programmed to operate interior ventilation when car is standing), power 2-way sunroof with key-off and one-touch operation, anti-theft AM/FM stereo radio/cassette audio system (incls 10 x 20 watt amplification, 10 speakers), diversity antenna system, pre-wiring for BMW cellular phone (incls hands-free operation, remote functions and audio muting), pre-wiring for BMW CD changer, fully finished trunk with luggage straps and drop-down tool kit, full-use spare wheel and tire (alloy wheel), central locking system with friction anti-theft feature (window and sunroof closing possible from both front door locks), drive-away protection, pre-wiring for BMW remote keyless entry security system, dual air bag SRS with differentiated deployment system, automatic height adjustment for front seatbelts, automatic front seatbelt tensioners, impact sensor (unlocks doors, switches on interior lights and hazard flashers after serious impact).

Accessories

—	All-Season Traction	1110	1350
—	Automatic Transmission — 5-spd w/overdrive	900	1100
—	Heated Front Seats	305	370

EDMUND'S 1995 HIGH-PERFORMANCE AUTOMOBILES

BMW 5-SERIES

CODE	DESCRIPTION	INVOICE	MSRP

540i

—	540i 4-Dr Sedan (6-spd)	40730	48600
—	540iA 4-Dr Sedan (auto)	40185	47950
Destination Charge:		470	470
Gas Guzzler Tax:		1300	1300

Standard Equipment

540i SEDAN: 4.0 liter DOHC 4-cam 32-valve V8 engine, 5-speed electronically controlled automatic transmission, Digital Motor Electronics engine management system, direct ignition system with knock control, double-pivot strut-type front suspension, track link rear suspension, front and rear anti-roll stabilizer bars, twin-tube gas-pressure shock absorbers, engine-speed-sensitive variable assist power steering, 4-wheel disc brakes (ventilated front discs, vacuum assisted; ventilated front and rear discs), anti-lock braking system (ABS), 15" x 7"J cast alloy wheels (honeycomb design), 225/60R15 96H all-season radial tires, body color bumpers with hydraulic energy absorbers and front compressible elements (damage control to 9 mph), halogen ellipsoid low-beam headlights, halogen fog lights, 2-speed intermittent windshield wipers (incls car speed controlled wiping speed and interval, single-wipe control, windshield washer system with heated washer jets), metallic paint (no additional charge), dual power/heated outside mirrors, automatic tilt-down of right outside mirror (for visibility of curb when backing up), pre-wiring for automatic dimming inside rearview mirror, heated driver's door lock, time delay courtesy lights with actuation from driver's exterior door handle (automatic switch-on when engine is turned off), map reading lights, take-out flashlight in glove box, telescopically adjustable power steering wheel, 10-way power front seats with power head restraints (incls driver's seat power lumbar support, folding front center armrests), memory system for driver's seat and seatbelt height/steering wheel/outside mirrors (3 settings), electronic analog speedometer and tachometer, LCD main and trip odometers, service interval indicator, fuel economy indicator, check control vehicle monitor system, onboard computer, leather and wood interior trim (gathered leather seating surfaces and door trim, leather-covered steering wheel/handbrake boot and grip), rear center armrest with storage compartment, seatback storage pockets, velour carpeting, power windows with key-off and operation (incls one-touch lowering of all windows, one-touch lowering and raising of driver's window), 2-stage rear window defroster, air conditioning and heating with separate left/right temperature controls (CFC-free refrigerant, microfiltered ventilation), automatic ventilation system (can be programmed to operate interior ventilation when car is standing), power 2-way sunroof with key-off and one-touch operation, anti-theft AM/FM stereo radio/cassette audio system (incls 10 x 20 watt amplification, 10 speakers), diversity antenna system, pre-wiring for BMW cellular phone (incls hands-free operation, remote functions, audio muting), pre-wiring for BMW CD changer, fully finished trunk with luggage straps and drop-down tool kit, full-use spare wheel and tire (alloy wheel), central locking system with friction anti-theft feature (window and sunroof closing possible from both front door locks), drive-away protection, remote keyless entry security system (keyhead remote), dual air bag SRS with differentiated deployment system, automatic height adjustment for front seatbelts, automatic front seatbelt tensioners, impact sensor (unlocks doors, switches on interior lights and hazard flashers after serious impact).

Accessories

—	All-Season Traction	1110	1350
—	Heated Front Seats	305	370

EDMUND'S 1995 HIGH-PERFORMANCE AUTOMOBILES

8-SERIES

1995 BMW 840Ci

8-SERIES

BMW's megabucks super coupe hasn't sold well since it was introduced in 1991, primarily because of price. It carries over basically unchanged for 1995, and is due to be replaced by a less expensive model based on an upcoming replacement for the 5-Series sedan. So, if the 8-Series is on your shopping list, take advantage of its availability now.

A new V-12 engine bows in the 850Ci for 1995, which gives it increased power and performance. The $70,000 "entry-level" 840Ci continues to offer V-8 power and a pared-down equipment list. The top-rung 850CSi is a fabulous piece of machinery, but costs as much as a three-bedroom house with a pool and a view.

But if you've got the money, and the place you live suffers a cloud-to-sun ratio far in favor of the clouds, the traction-control-equipped 8-Series is a rare alternative to the Mercedes SL convertible.

Performance and Safety

840Ci

Acceleration (0-60 mph) .... 7.4 sec.	ABS .... Standard	
Braking (60-0 mph) .... 113 ft.	Driver Airbag .... Standard	
Cornering .... .83 g's	Passenger Airbag .... Standard	
Fuel Capacity .... 23.8 gal.	Traction Control .... Standard	
Fuel Economy .... City: 16 mpg	Crash Test Grade .... D: N/A	P: N/A
	Hwy: 24 mpg	Insurance Cost .... N/A

BMW 8-SERIES

CODE	DESCRIPTION	INVOICE	MSRP

850CSi

Acceleration (0-60 mph) .... 5.8 sec.	ABS .... Standard		
Braking (60-0 mph) .... 116 ft.	Driver Airbag .... Standard		
Cornering .... .87 g's	Passenger Airbag .... Standard		
Fuel Capacity .... 23.8 gal.	Traction Control .... Standard		
Fuel Economy .... City: 12 mpg	Crash Test Grade .... D: N/A	P: N/A	
	Hwy: 20 mpg	Insurance Cost .... N/A	

840Ci/850CSi

		Invoice	MSRP
—	840Ci 2-Dr Coupe (auto)	58580	69900
—	850CSi 2-Dr Coupe (6-spd)	NA	NA
Destination Charge:	....	470	470
Gas Guzzler Tax:			
	840Ci	1300	1300
	850CSi	NA	NA

Standard Equipment

840Ci: 4.0 liter DOHC (4-cam) 32-valve V8 engine, Digital Motor Electronics engine management system, 5-speed electronically controlled automatic transmission, double-pivot strut type front suspension, 5-link integral rear suspension, front and rear anti-roll stabilizer bars, twin-tube gas-pressure shocks, engine speed-sensitive variable assist power steering, power 4-wheel disc brakes with anti-lock braking system, all-season traction, 16 x 7.5J cross-spoke design cast alloy wheels, 235/50ZR16 tires, body color bumpers (damage control to 9 mph), retractable halogen headlights, flasher beams/auxiliary high beams in bumper, halogen free-form fog lights, 2-speed intermittent windshield wipers with heated washer jets, metallic paint (no additional charge), dual power heated OS mirrors, automatic-dimming inside rearview mirror, heated driver's door lock, illuminated master key, time-delay courtesy lights, map reading lights, locking glove box with beverage holder, rechargeable take-out flashlight, power tilt/telescopic steering wheel with automatic tilt-away for entry and exit, power seats (driver - 10-way w/head restraints/seatbelt height as function of cushion height, power lumbar support; passenger - 8-way w/head restraint/seatbelt height as function of cushion height, power lumbar support), memory system for seat and head restraint/seatbelt height, steering wheel and OS mirrors; split fold-down rear seats, electronic analog speedometer and tachometer, LCD main and trip odometers, leather seats, leather steering wheel, leather lower instrument panel, leather door inserts, leather center console sides, leather sun visors, heated front seats, fixed rear center armrest, velour carpeting, power windows with one-touch feature, 2-state rear window defroster, automatic climate control, microfiltered ventilation, automatic ventilation system, power 2-way sunroof with one-touch operation, radio (anti-theft AM/FM stereo radio/cassette audio system with 10 x 20-watt amplification, 12 speakers, weather band, diversity antenna system, pre-wiring for BMW cellular phone including remote operation and audio muting, pre-wiring for CD changer), velour lined trunk with drop-down tool kit, trunk-to-interior pass-through and ski bag, full-use spare wheel and tire, central locking system, drive-away protection, remote keyless entry security system with keyhead remote, dual air bag SRS.

8-SERIES — BMW

CODE DESCRIPTION INVOICE MSRP

850CSi (in addition to or instead of 840Ci equipment): 5.6 liter SOHC V12 engine, variable RPM limiting, variable throttle linkage, 6-speed manual transmission, dual Digital Motor Electronics engine-management system, one-touch starting, electronic throttles, vehicle speed-sensitive variable assist power steering, limited slip differential, 17 x 8J 5-spoke design forged alloy wheels (front), 17 x 9J 5-spoke design forged alloy wheels (rear), 235/45ZR17 front tires, 235/40ZR17 rear tires, special front and lower rear spoilers, Yew hardwood trim, BMW cellular phone, 6-disc CD changer.

Accessories

— Forged Alloy Wheels — 840Ci 880   1100

1995 BMW 850CSi

FOR A SPECIAL RATE ON AN AUTO LOAN, CALL

1-800-AT-CHASE

CHASE AUTOMOTIVE FINANCE

SIMPLE ◆ FAST ◆ CONVENIENT

BUICK
PARK AVENUE ULTRA

1995 Buick Park Avenue Ultra

PARK AVENUE ULTRA SEDAN

Sporting flowing, Jaguaresque lines, a long list of standard amenities, and all the luxury most buyers require, the Park Avenue Ultra offers value, style and performance in one reasonably priced package.

Look at the facts. This is a big sedan, able to accommodate six people and a good portion of their belongings. Fuel economy, a negligible issue what with all the cheap gas in the States, averages 23 mpg. The Park Avenue blends European savvy and traditional Detroit luxoyacht feel into one very attractive package. Almost every imaginable feature is standard on this car, and base prices start at $33,000. Its supercharged V-6 gets it to 60 mph over a second quicker than a Chrysler LHS, while braking and handling are on a par with the much ballyhooed $45,000 Cadillac STS. This thing is a bargain.

For 1995, the Ultra gets minor revisions, including less confusing climate controls, rear cupholders, and an available heated passenger-side seat. Modifications to the exterior trim and fascias tidy up the already attractive design.

So what if the Park Avenue Ultra doesn't give enthusiasts heart palpitations. It offers an outstanding blend of functionality, power and luxury that many performance-oriented cars lack.

Performance and Safety

Acceleration (0-60 mph)	7.3 sec.
Braking (60-0 mph)	137 ft.
Cornering	.78 g's
Fuel Capacity	18 gal.
Fuel Economy	City: 17 mpg
	Hwy: 27 mpg

ABS	Standard
Driver Airbag	Standard
Passenger Airbag	Standard
Traction Control	Optional
Crash Test Grade	D: N/A P: N/A
Insurance Cost	Very Low

PARK AVENUE ULTRA — BUICK

Edmund's Driving Impression

Confidence is the key word when describing the supercharged Ultra. Whether the subject is acceleration, comfort, handling, dependability, or overall demeanor, the top Park Avenue performs like a bodyguard: a car waiting to respond to your command, to react to your wishes with haste and dispatch.

Because the interior is practically silent, with only the tiniest engine noise audible, passengers tend to feel insulated from the outside world. But that doesn't mean an unnatural feeling (as in a Roadmaster, for instance).

Confidence and assurance begin with the hearty zoom from the engine as it leaps to life, and its reaction when pushed hard. But they extend throughout the driving experience. Soft, cushiony leather seats manage to blend a pillow-like feel with fine support. A linear dashboard layout, with warning lights spread across the top, imparts a spacious feeling. Small but complete gauges deliver all the needed information. The column gearshift is easy to use.

Tromp hard on the gas and the blown V-6 responds faithfully, strongly, almost instantly. The supercharger stands ready to react immediately to what your foot seeks, even though there's little evidence of its presence (no boost gauge, for instance). Throughout, the Ultra produces an impressive but subtle, sophisticated experience.

Steering is light, with just enough resistance to make driving life interesting. The big sedan takes corners reasonably well and handles nicely on snow/ice—more so with traction control operating. No matter what happens, it's almost saying: "There's no problem, sir. We'll take care of this for you."

Bumps are absorbed capably. A tiny wallowiness emerges while traversing certain road obstacles, but then the car responds almost instantly, resuming its usual confident stride.

Now that the base Park Avenue's V-6 engine has been upped to 205 horsepower, does anyone really need the Ultra's 225? Perhaps not, but that extra burst of power comes as a welcome surprise now and then.

PARK AVENUE ULTRA SEDAN 6 CYL

CODE	DESCRIPTION	INVOICE	MSRP
U69	4-Dr Sedan	28618	33084
	Destination Charge:	635	635

Standard Equipment

PARK AVENUE ULTRA SEDAN: 3800 supercharged V6 engine, electronically-controlled 4-speed automatic transmission with overdrive, variable effort power rack and pinion steering, anti-lock power front disc/rear drum brakes, power windows with driver's express-down and passenger lockout feature, automatic programmable door locks, P215/70R15 SBR all-season BW tires, specific 15" aluminum wheels, AM/FM ETR stereo radio with seek/scan/cassette/clock; dual automatic ComforTemp climate control air conditioning, rear seat ComforTemp air conditioning, driver and front passenger side air bag SRS, front seat storage armrest with dual cup holders, passenger assist handles, push-to-set and release parking brake, front bumper guards, front and rear carpet savers, overhead console includes: front seat reading lights/garage door opener storage; electronic cruise control, electric rear window defogger, front/side window outlet defoggers, front wheel drive, electronic warning tone for: seatbelt/ignition key/headlamps/parking brake on; stainless steel exhaust system, electric remote fuel filler door release, Solar-Ray solar control glass, wrap-around composite tungsten-halogen headlamps, adjustable front-seat head restraint, inside release hood lock, center high-mounted stop lamp, lights include: front ashtray/trunk/engine compartment/glove box/instrument panel courtesy, front and rear door courtesy/warning lights, front and rear seat reading/courtesy lights, lighted passenger visor vanity mirror, deluxe body color outside electric rearview mirrors (left/right remote), moldings include: wheel opening/belt reveal/bodyside; basecoat/clearcoat paint with anti-chip lower protection, front seat lap/shoulder seatbelts with shoulder belt comfort adjuster, rear seat lap/shoulder seatbelts with child comfort guide, rear door child security locks, tilt-wheel adjustable

 **PARK AVENUE ULTRA**

CODE	DESCRIPTION	INVOICE	MSRP

steering column, accent stripes, supplemental/extendable sunshades, automatic level control suspension, DynaRide suspension, front and rear independent suspension, remote electric trunk lock release with security switch, full trunk trim, 2-speed wipers with low-speed delay, automatic power antenna, rear seat storage armrest (included with leather seats), heavy duty Delco Freedom II Plus battery, body color door edge guards, twilight sentinel headlamp control, rear seat head restraints, 4-note horn, analog instrumentation gauge cluster includes: tachometer/coolant temperature/ oil pressure/voltage/low fuel indicator/oil level indicator/oil life monitor/trip odometer, front and rear lamp monitors, cornering lamps, automatic dimming inside rearview mirror, driver's lighted visor vanity mirror, rear seat passenger's lighted vanity mirror, moldings include: wheel opening/belt reveal/ wide bodyside/lower panel/door edge guard, specific lower accent moldings, driver and passenger electric seatback recliners, reminder package includes: low washer fluid indicator/low coolant level/ door ajar and trunk ajar indicators; remote keyless entry, retained accessory power includes illuminated door locks and light control, driver and passenger 6-way power reclining seats, 55/45 leather/vinyl seats with front seat storage armrest, Concert Sound II speakers, leather-wrapped steering wheel, theft-deterrent system with starter interrupt, trunk convenience net, electric trunk pull-down.

Accessories

Code	Description	Invoice	MSRP
SC	**Base Pkg**	NC	NC
	incls vehicle plus standard equipment		
SD	**Luxury Pkg**	628	730
	incls radio (power-loading cassette and ETR AM/FM stereo with seek/scan, automatic tone control, clock, steering wheel radio controls), automatic ride control, traction control system		
SE	**Prestige Pkg**	1191	1385
	incls SD Luxury Pkg plus automatic day/night rearview mirror with compass, electric heated left and right remote mirrors (day/night, body color), electric heated driver and passenger seats, two-position memory 6-way power driver's seat and memory mirrors, P215/70R15 whitewall self-sealing tires, trunk mat		
YF5	**California Emissions**	NC	NC
NG1	**Massachusetts Emissions**	NC	NC
CF5	**Astroroof** — electric sliding - w/SD or SE	690	802
D83	**Ultra Solid Exterior Color**	NC	NC
KA1	**Seat** — electric heated driver and passenger - w/SD	103	120
P42	**Tires** — w/SC or SD	129	150
	incls self-sealing steel belted radial-ply whitewall all-season P215/70R15		
QPK	**Tires** — w/SC or SD	(69)	(80)
	w/SE	(198)	(230)
	incls steel belted radial-ply blackwall all-season P215/70R15		
UL0	**Radio** — w/SC	129	150
	incls power-loading cassette and ETR AM/FM stereo with seek/scan, automatic tone control, clock, steering wheel radio controls		
UN0	**Radio** — w/SC	215	250
	w/SD or SE	86	100
	incls power-loading CD player with next/last CD track selector and ETR AM/FM stereo with seek/scan, automatic tone control, clock, steering wheel radio controls		
UP0	**Radio** — w/SC	301	350
	w/SD or SE	172	200
	incls power-loading CD and cassette player with next/last CD track selector and ETR AM/ FM stereo with seek/scan, automatic tone control, clock, steering wheel radio controls		

PARK AVENUE ULTRA / RIVIERA — BUICK

CODE	DESCRIPTION	INVOICE	MSRP
V92	**Trailer Towing Pkg** — w/SD or SE, w/o Y56	(175)	(203)
	w/SD or SE, w/Y56	(198)	(230)
Y56	**Gran Touring Pkg** — w/SD or SE	(253)	(294)
	incls gran touring suspension, 16" aluminum wheels and P215/60R16 touring blackwall tires		

1995 Buick Riviera

RIVIERA (Supercharged V6)

After decades of mediocre personal luxury coupes from Buick, 1995 brings a stunning Riviera that returns the car to its performance roots. Photos do not convey the elegance and beauty of this design. It looks best in dark shades, and from just about every angle, the new Riviera's sheetmetal is intriguing. The stark interior is thankfully devoid of digital wizardry, sporting simple round gauges and a slightly retro look.

Motivating the base front-wheel drive Riviera is GM's tried-and-true 3.8-liter V-6, which puts 205 horsepower to the ground through the front axle. A supercharged version of that motor, which comes standard with bigger wheels and tires, stretches the Riviera's performance envelope a bit. Anti-lock brakes and dual airbags are standard, and traction control is one of the few options available.

Prices start under $30,000 for the supercharged Riviera. While this big Buick won't woo buyers who favor cars like the BMW 3-Series, the Riviera is a fine American luxury coupe with more than a hint of Euro flavor.

BUICK   RIVIERA

| CODE | DESCRIPTION | INVOICE | MSRP |

Performance and Safety

Acceleration (0-60 mph) .... 7.8 sec.
Braking (60-0 mph) .... 139 ft.
Cornering .... .78 g's
Fuel Capacity .... 20 gal.
Fuel Economy .... City: 17 mpg
                                 Hwy: 27 mpg

ABS .... Standard
Driver Airbag .... Standard
Passenger Airbag .... Standard
Traction Control .... Optional
Crash Test Grade .... D: N/A   P: N/A
Insurance Cost .... N/A

Edmund's Driving Impression

Not many cars on the road today can be spotted easily from a distance. Riviera is one of those precious few—and its passionate performance matches the nothing-like-it design.

An utterly magnificent road machine, the all-new Riv is easy to drive, handles with true competence, and delivers a splendid feel of the road. The optional supercharged engine is almost worth the stout extra charge.

From a standstill, acceleration is stunning. A blown Riviera almost pushes occupants back in their seats. Passing from highway speed brings a brief delay for downshifts to second gear, but then a refined thrust forward. Shifts are crisp, yet only mildly perceptible.

New magnetic variable-assist power steering accepts a light touch in the city, but supplies exquisite response on the highway and in turns—exactly as promised by Buick's engineers. Maneuvering smartly for a large car, a Riv stays almost flat on moderate curves.

Sport rather than luxury marks the ride quality, which is bouncier than some buyers might relish. Instead of gliding past imperfections, the body tends to rise and fall as the car passes over holes, cracks, and tar strips. Even so, the suspension is nicely controlled most of the time.

The engine is nearly silent until you push hard on the gas, when a gentlemanly roar and blower whine take charge. Moderate road noise emerges on some pavements.

The distinctive, visored instrument panel looks modern, yet curiously old-fashioned. A large 120-mph speedometer and 7000-rpm tachometer are easy to read, but their full graduations are a touch distracting. Some may prefer a snugger fit from the seats, but bottoms offer good support.

Thick windshield and rear-window pillars block the view a bit, and it's not easy to tell exactly where the front end and long tail are, when parking. Beyond minor quibbles, it's hard to find much wrong with this beautiful, solidly-built Buick.

Riviera Supercharged V6
G07   2-Dr Coupe 24454   27632
Destination Charge: 625   625

Standard Equipment

RIVIERA: Acoustical package, driver and passenger air bags, automatic dual comfortemp climate control air conditioning with rear seat comfortemp, automatic power antenna, front seat armrest with storage and dual cupholders, two rear rail-mounted assist handles, heavy duty Delco Freedom II Plus battery, anti-lock 4-wheel power disc brakes, front and rear carpet savers, heavy duty engine and transmission cooling, electronic cruise control, front and side defogger outlets, electric rear window defogger, automatic power door locks, front wheel drive, electronic warning tone (seat belt,

RIVIERA — BUICK

CODE	DESCRIPTION	INVOICE	MSRP

ignition key, headlamps on, turn signal and parking brake), 3800 "Series II" V6 engine, dual stainless steel exhaust, flash to pass signal, electric remote release fuel filler door, fuel cap holder, solar ray glass, tungsten-halogen headlamps, inside hood lock release, dual horns, instrumentation (speedometer, tachometer, coolant temperature, trip odometer, low fuel indicator, low oil, low washer fluid), electric remote keyless entry, light group, deluxe body color OS electric rearview mirrors (left and right remote), inside rearview day/night mirror, lighted visor vanity passenger mirror, moldings (protective bodyside, belt reveal, wheel opening and rocker panel), clearcoat paint with anti-chip protection, radio (ETR AM/FM stereo with seek/scan, cassette with auto reverse, search/repeat), front auxiliary power receptacle, retained accessory power, 55/45 split bench seat with driver and passenger six-way power seats and power recliners, 6-speaker Concert Sound II speakers, magnetic speed variable assist steering, tilt wheel adjustable steering column, leather-wrapped steering wheel, supplemental/extendable sun shades, 4-wheel independent suspension, automatic level control, Pass Key II theft deterrent system, electronically controlled automatic transmission with overdrive, electric remote control trunk release with security switch, full trunk trim, trunk convenience net, 16" aluminum wheels, power windows with express-down driver's side, 2-speed wipers with low speed delay, P225/60R16 SBR all-season BW tires.

Accessories

Code	Description	Invoice	MSRP
SD	**Luxury Pkg**	406	472
	incls convenience pkg (consists of twilight sentinel and driver lighted vanity mirror), security pkg (consists of programmable auto door locks, theft deterrent system and cornering lamps), accent paint stripe		
SE	**Prestige Pkg**	853	992
	incls SD Luxury Pkg plus traction control, automatic mirrors (incls electrochromatic inside driver and outside rearview), steering wheel remote radio controls, driver's seat lumbar support		
L67	**Supercharged 3800 V6 Engine**	946	1100
	incls 16" aluminum wheels and P225/60R16 Eagle GA touring tires		
AM6	**Leather Split Bench Seats**	516	600
AS7	**Leather Bucket Seats w/Console**	559	650
A43	**Memory/Heated Driver Seat w/Memory Mirrors**	267	310
U1R	**CD Player w/Cassette** — req's bucket seats	373	434
UM3	**CD Player** — replaces cassette	210	244
CF5	**Astroroof w/Power Sunshade**	856	995
YM5	**Paint Stripe Delete**	NC	NC
K05	**Engine Block Heater**	15	18
YF5	**California Emissions**	NC	NC
NG1	**New York Emissions**	NC	NC

GET MORE MONEY FOR YOUR USED CAR BY KNOWING ITS TRUE VALUE

See our ads on pages 4 and 6

EDMUND'S 1995 HIGH-PERFORMANCE AUTOMOBILES

CADILLAC — ELDORADO TOURING COUPE

1995 Cadillac Eldorado Touring Coupe

ELDORADO TOURING COUPE

One of the models that lured Cadillac back from the brink of becoming a laughingstock was this Eldorado Touring Coupe. Introduced in 1992 to critical acclaim, and then substantially improved with the introduction of the Northstar V-8 in 1993, this Eldorado, and its sister car, the Seville, redefined Cadillac for the world.

However, the Eldorado hasn't been selling well. Seems the market for high-priced, traditional luxury coupes has dried up a bit during the past few years, and rumors are circulating about the death of this luxury coupe before the end of the decade.

That would be too bad, because what's here is good. The Northstar V-8 has been called the best production engine on the planet, and for 1995 Cadillac has softened up the Eldorado's creased-and-folded look with redesigned fascias and a new grille. The interior, seemingly inspired by Mercedes-Benz, is rich with leather and wood. It all works beautifully, but buyers evidently balk at spending more than 40 grand for an Eldorado.

While Lincoln's Mark VIII is a tad less expensive with only a slight performance penalty, its retro-futuristic styling themes inside and out do not appeal to us as much as the Eldo's sharp edges, richly-appointed interior, and excellent powerplant.

Performance and Safety

Acceleration (0-60 mph) .... 6.7 sec.	ABS .... Standard
Braking (60-0 mph) .... 138 ft.	Driver Airbag .... Standard
Cornering .... .79 g's	Passenger Airbag .... Standard
Fuel Capacity .... 18 gal.	Traction Control .... Standard
Fuel Economy .... City: 16 mpg	Crash Test Grade .... D: N/A P: N/A
Hwy: 25 mpg	Insurance Cost .... Low

ELDORADO TOURING COUPE — CADILLAC

| CODE | DESCRIPTION | INVOICE | MSRP |

Edmund's Driving Impression

Strong on the road, propelled by the remarkable Northstar engine, loaded with practical comfort/convenience gadgetry, the hottest Caddy coupe fails to perform fully up to expectations.

Don't get us wrong. This is one remarkably competent vehicle, whether in off-the-line takeoffs or around-the-turn prowess. Lots of people love their Eldos, for quiet, suave, highly-poised confidence. They're not wrong at all, yet Cadillac's superlative engineering and advanced technology don't seem to come accompanied by an overly-abundant share of thrills.

Because the 295-horsepower Northstar V-8 is so smooth, so refined, the coupe actually doesn't feel quite as swift as its performance numbers reveal. Tap the pedal, though, and the heavy coupe practically vaults ahead. Accelerating from lower speed, it almost hunkers down—then whips forth like a bullet.

Shifts are barely perceptible. Downshifts come firmly, almost instantly, and the electronically-controlled transmission always seems to be in the correct gear.

Ride comfort is less cushy than expected. Reactions come quickly, yet the road-sensing suspension does not brush aside all bumps. In fact, an Eldo can get shaky when traversing certain spoiled pavements. On the highway, it's a dream—secure and stable, never soft or slushy.

Driving position is excellent for a big car. Don't expect a full load of gauges, though. The 150-mph speedometer and 7000-rpm tach are easy to see, but a fuel gauge is the only other instrument. Slipping into the back seat demands some squirming. Extracting oneself is harder yet.

Clinging neatly to curves, the Touring Coupe delivers keen steering feel and nicely-controlled handling, if not quite as sporting as some might wish. Even when hitting the gas hard, and banging around country roads, an Eldo is hushed and gentlemanly.

Maybe that's the problem. Maybe an Eldo is a little too genteel, too richly fitted, to meld with the potential of its Northstar powertrain.

ELDORADO TOURING COUPE V8

6ET57	Eldorado Touring Coupe	35928	41535
Destination Charge:		635	635

Standard Equipment

ELDORADO TOURING COUPE: 4.6 liter V8 Northstar (300 HP) DOHC engine, automatic transmission, power steering, power four-wheel disc brakes, electrically power windows, electrically powered automatic door locks, all-season mud and snow SBR BW tires, cast aluminum wheels, AM/FM ETR stereo radio with signal seeking/scanner/digital display/cassette player; driver and front passenger air bags, power antenna, anti-lock braking system, ignition anti-lockout feature, center front/rear seat armrests, audible reminders, body-frame integral construction, brake/transmission shift interlock, center high-mounted stop lamp, electronic climate control, digital display clock, on-board computer diagnostics, controlled-cycle wiper system, cornering lights, cruise control, electric rear window defogger, front side window defoggers, driver information center, electronic level control, engine oil life indicator, dual exhaust outlets, stainless steel exhaust, flash-to-pass, front/rear carpeted floor mats, fog lamps, front wheel drive, fuel data center, remote release fuel filler door, 3-channel programmable garage door opener, Gold Key delivery system, tungsten halogen headlamps, wiper-activated headlamps, illuminated entry, leather seating, low fuel warning indicator, low windshield washer fluid level indicator, carpeted luggage compartment, electrochromatic automatic day/night inside rearview mirror, driver side electrochromatic automatic day/night outside mirror, driver and passenger illuminated visor vanity mirrors, electrically powered and heated right/left outside rearview mirrors, multi-function turn signal lever, continuous outside temperature digital display, clearcoat

CADILLAC
ELDORADO TOURING COUPE

paint, automatic parking brake release, Pass Key II anti-theft system, platinum-tipped spark plugs, driver/front passenger power reclining seats, remote keyless entry system, retained accessory power, real-time road-sensing suspension, 6-way power driver/front passenger seat adjusters, front bucket seats, short/long arm rear suspension, Solar-Ray tinted glass, compact spare tire, speed-sensitive steering, tilt steering wheel, leather-trimmed steering wheel rim, rear seat storage armrest, independent four-wheel suspension, theft-deterrent system, full-range traction control, trip odometer, trunk convenience net, power trunk lid pull-down, power trunk lid release, trunk mat, trunk sill plate, twilight sentinel, driver window with express-down feature.

Accessories

CODE	DESCRIPTION	INVOICE	MSRP
CF5	Astroroof	1318	1550
DD7	Electronic Compass	85	100
FE9	Federal Emissions	NC	NC
YF5	California Emissions	NC	NC
NG1	Massachusetts Emissions	NC	NC
UG1	Garage Door Opener	91	107
KA1	Heated Front Seats	102	120
C50	Heated Windshield System	263	309
VK3	License Plate Front Mount Provisions	NC	NC
V1F	Paint — white diamond	425	500
YL3	Paint — pearl red	425	500
—	Radios		
	all radios (including base) are AM stereo/FM stereo, electronically tuned, digital display with signal seeking and scanner, and cassette tape player, Delco Bose Sound System		
U1G	w/compact disc and cassette	826	972
QC8	Chrome Wheels	523	1195

1995 Cadillac Eldorado Touring Coupe

EDMUND'S 1995 HIGH-PERFORMANCE AUTOMOBILES

SEVILLE STS — CADILLAC

1995 Cadillac Seville Touring Sedan

SEVILLE STS SEDAN

When Cadillac introduced the 1992 Seville STS to the motoring press, they reacted with such overwhelming approval you would have thought they had just heard an announcement that People had forever banished the Royal Family from appearing on its cover. They 'ooohed' and 'aahhed' and proclaimed the Seville the best American luxosport sedan ever produced.

Well, they were half right. It was another year before the Seville STS was worthy of that honor with the introduction of the stellar Northstar V-8 engine. The STS became a civilized hot-rod, and while this Cadillac is far from cheap, it is a worthy alternative to pricey luxury sedans from Europe and Asia.

For 1995, the STS is carried over with new alloy wheels and paint colors. Mechanically, the STS is endowed with a new Integrated Chassis Control System, designed to give drivers even more control over braking and turning.

The Seville Touring Sedan has enjoyed several years in the spotlight as America's premier luxury-sport sedan. Lincoln has a new Continental bowing in January, and it promises quite a scuffle for the title between the two.

Performance and Safety

Acceleration (0-60 mph) .... 6.5 sec.	ABS .... Standard
Braking (60-0 mph) .... 133 ft.	Driver Airbag .... Standard
Cornering .... .78 g's	Passenger Airbag .... Standard
Fuel Capacity .... 20 gal.	Traction Control .... Standard
Fuel Economy .... City: 16 mpg	Crash Test Grade .... D: Good P: N/A
Hwy: 25 mpg	Insurance Cost .... Very Low

EDMUND'S 1995 HIGH-PERFORMANCE AUTOMOBILES

CADILLAC

SEVILLE STS

| CODE | DESCRIPTION | INVOICE | MSRP |

Edmund's Driving Impression

Insert the same magnificent engine into a two-door car, and also into its similarly-constructed four-door mate, and you get the exact same driving experience, right?

Wrong! In our view, at least, the extraordinary 300-horsepower Northstar V-8 seems better suited to the Seville Sport Touring Sedan than to the enticing but slightly prosaic Eldorado Touring Coupe (see above).

We can't complain about anything in the Seville's handling, as proffered by Cadillac's road-sensing suspension. It's simply superior, whipping sure-footedly around curves and corners.

Acceleration, too, is outstanding. Tromp the gas at 40-60 mph, and the transmission downshifts quickly to 3rd. If your foot presses hard enough, it hesitates just a moment, drops to 2nd—then *leaps* forward. That's right: the back end drops down, the front raises up, like a dragster—quite a shock when piloting a car of this caliber.

Oh, there's more road and tire noise than you might expect in a Cadillac. When accelerating, the engine isn't exactly silent, either. But this isn't a traditional, sedate Caddy. This is the chest-pounding beast of Cadillacs, targeting 40ish professionals who crave an occasional adrenalin-boosting surge of power.

You don't pay much penalty in riding comfort, either. Certainly, you'll feel the urban bumps and cracks, as well as highway potholes and separators. An STS intends to be firm and vigorous, not slushy and soft. And it succeeds.

Seats are extremely comfortable yet nicely supportive, just right for full-size people. Space is plentiful up front and head room is nice in back, though there's no surplus of leg room. Naturally, all the extras a reasonable person could crave are included. Except for a relatively small 150-mph speedometer and 7000-rpm tach, the only other instrument is a fuel gauge. Mirrors are a tad small, but visibility excellent.

Likely to draw envious glances, Seville presents a distinctive aura. In short, it's "special."

SEVILLE STS SEDAN V8

6KY69	Seville STS Sedan	39734	45935
Destination Charge:		635	635

Standard Equipment

SEVILLE STS: 4.6 liter V8 Northstar (300 HP) DOHC engine, automatic transmission, power steering, power four-wheel disc brakes, electrically powered windows, electrically powered automatic door locks, all-season mud and snow SBR BW tires, cast aluminum wheels, AM/FM ETR stereo radio with signal seeking/scanner/digital display/cassette player; driver and front passenger air bags, power antenna, anti-lock braking system, ignition anti-lockout feature, center front/rear seat armrests, audible reminders, body-frame integral construction, brake/transmission shift interlock, center high-mounted stop lamp, electronic climate control, digital display clock, on-board computer diagnostics, controlled-cycle wiper system, cornering lights, cruise control, electric rear window defogger, front side window defoggers, rear door child safety security locks, driver information center, electronic level control, engine oil life indicator, dual exhaust outlets, stainless steel exhaust, flash-to-pass, carpeted front and rear floor mats, fog lamps, front wheel drive, fuel data center, remote fuel filler door release, 3-channel programmable garage door opener, Gold Key delivery system, tungsten halogen headlamps, wiper-activated headlamps, illuminated entry, leather seating, low fuel warning indicator, low windshield washer fluid level indicator, carpeted luggage compartment, electrochromatic automatic day/night inside rearview mirror, electrochromatic automatic day/night driver side outside mirror, driver and passenger illuminated visor vanity mirrors, electrically powered and heated right/left outside rearview mirrors, multi-function turn signal lever, continuous outside temperature digital display, clearcoat paint, automatic parking brake release, Pass Key II anti-theft system, platinum-tipped

SEVILLE STS
CADILLAC

spark plugs, driver and front passenger power reclining seats, remote keyless entry system, retained accessory power, real-time road-sensing suspension, 6-way power driver/front passenger seat adjusters, front bucket seats, short/long arm rear suspension, Solar-Ray tinted glass, compact spare tire, speed-sensitive steering, tilt steering wheel, leather-trimmed steering wheel rim, rear seat storage armrest, independent four-wheel suspension, theft-deterrent system, full-range traction control, trip odometer, trunk convenience net, power trunk lid pull-down, power trunk lid release, trunk mat, trunk sill plate, twilight sentinel, driver's window express-down feature.

Accessories

Code	Description	Invoice	MSRP
CF5	Astroroof	1318	1550
DD7	Electronic Compass	85	100
FE9	Federal Emissions	NC	NC
YF5	California Emissions	NC	NC
NG1	Massachusetts Emissions	NC	NC
UG1	Garage Door Opener	91	107
KA1	Heated Front Seats	102	120
C50	Heated Windshield System	263	309
VK3	License Plate Front Mount Provisions	NC	NC
V1F	Paint — white diamond	425	500
YL3	Paint — pearl red	425	500
—	Radios		
	all radios (including base) are AM stereo/FM stereo, electronically tuned, digital display with signal seeking and scanner, and cassette tape player, Delco Bose Sound System		
U1H	w/compact disc - L	337	396
U1G	w/compact disc and cassette	826	972
QC8	Chrome Wheels	523	1195

1995 Cadillac Seville Touring Sedan

CHEVROLET
C1500 PICKUP

1995 Chevrolet C1500 Pickup 2WD

C1500 REGULAR CAB PICKUP (5.7L V8)

Pickups have been among the best-selling vehicles in this country for years, but are increasingly purchased for personal rather than business use. In fact, three of the top five selling nameplates in 1993 were affixed to the tailgates of millions of pickups. It's only natural that this phenomenon would spawn performance variants for buyers who want some hot with their haul.

For several years, Chevy marketed a souped-up version of its big C/K Series truck. It was called the 454 SS, and came in black. That truck has been discontinued, but performance has not, because the 5.7-liter V-8 version of the Chevy and GMC 1500 trucks will make tracks rapidly when combined with optional handling packages.

The current big GM pickup has been around since the fall of 1987 with very few changes. This year, a driver's airbag has been added, and the formerly angular dashboard has been totally redesigned. Otherwise, this vehicle soldiers on, doing battle with the aging Ford F-Series and the new Dodge Ram in the full-size truck segment.

The 454 SS is missed, especially since its demise left General Motors without a serious contender to Ford's F-Series-based Lightning. The 5.7-liter Chevy and GMC, though, offer plenty of useable performance in a pickup.

Performance and Safety

Acceleration (0-60 mph)	9.5 sec.	ABS	Standard	
Braking (60-0 mph)	143 ft.	Driver Airbag	Standard	
Cornering	.77 g's	Passenger Airbag	N/A	
Fuel Capacity	25 gal (34 Longbed)	Traction Control	N/A	
Fuel Economy	City: 14 mpg	Crash Test Grade	D: N/A	P: N/A
	Hwy: 18 mpg	Insurance Cost	Average	

C1500 PICKUP — CHEVROLET

CODE	DESCRIPTION	INVOICE	MSRP

C1500 5.7L REGULAR CAB PICKUP V8
C10703/E62	Sportside (117.5" WB)	14403	16475
C10703/E63	Fleetside (117.5" WB)	13691	15662
C10903/E63	Fleetside (131.5" WB)	13936	15942
Destination Charge:		610	610

Standard Equipment

C1500 5.7L REGULAR CAB: 5.7 liter V8 EFI engine, 5-speed manual transmission, driver's air bag, dual in-dash cup holders, side-impact door guard beams, 7-wire trailering wire harness, power front disc/rear drum brakes with anti-lock system, power steering, chrome bumpers and painted argent grille, black break-away outside rearview mirrors, full gauges and instrumentation, tinted Solar Ray glass (all windows), color-keyed headliner, deluxe heater with windshield and side window defoggers, heavy duty radiator, AM/FM ETR radio with seek/scan and digital clock, Scotchgarded carpeting and cloth trim, 3-passenger all-vinyl front bench seat with folding backrest.

Accessories

Code	Description	INVOICE	MSRP
—	**Preferred Equipment Groups** — prices include pkg discounts		
1SAX	**Cheyenne Preferred Equipment Group 1SAX**		
	w/R9A and R9B	(602)	(700)
	w/R9B w/o R9A	(172)	(200)
	w/R9A w/o R9B	(430)	(500)
1SBX	**Silverado Preferred Equipment Group**	1603	1864
	incls air conditioning, power door locks, power windows, AM/FM ETR stereo radio with cassette, dual power mirrors, cruise control, tilt steering column, bright wheel opening moldings (Fleetside), dual horns, chrome bumpers, halogen headlights, front rubber floor mats, black bodyside molding, door map pockets, leather-wrapped steering wheel, additional sound insulation, color-keyed cloth and carpet door trim, behind seat storage		
—	**Marketing Pkgs**		
R9A	**Convenience Pkg**	1148	1335
	incls air conditioning, tilt steering wheel, cruise control, AM/FM ETR stereo radio with cassette		
R9B	**Bright Appearance Pkg** — Sportside	501	582
	Fleetside	527	613
	incls rally wheels, bodyside moldings, deluxe chrome bumpers, chrome grille		
BYP	**Sport Pkg** — Sportside 117.5" WB	179	208
	incls aluminum wheels, painted rear step bumper		
C60	**Air Conditioning** — w/PEG 1SBX or w/R9A	NC	NC
	w/PEG 1SAX	692	805
V22	**Appearance Pkg**	164	191
	incls halogen headlights, chrome grille, dual horns, deluxe front chrome bumper		
—	**Axle, Rear**		
GU4	3.08 ratio	NC	NC
GU6	3.42 ratio	NC	NC
GT4	3.73 ratio	NC	NC
G80	locking differential	217	252
TP2	**Auxiliary Battery**	115	134

EDMUND'S 1995 HIGH-PERFORMANCE AUTOMOBILES

CHEVROLET — C1500 PICKUP

CODE	DESCRIPTION	INVOICE	MSRP
BZY	**Bedliner** — Fleetside	194	225
—	**Bumper Equipment**		
VB3	chromed rear step w/rub strip - w/PEG 1SBX or R9B	NC	NC
	w/o PEG 1SBX or R9B	197	229
	req's Silverado decor or deluxe chrome front bumper		
VG3	chromed deluxe front w/rub strip - w/PEG 1SBX or R9B	NC	NC
V43	painted rear step - w/BYP	NC	NC
	w/o BYP	112	130
EF1	**Rear Bumper Delete**	(172)	(200)
V10	**Cold Climate Pkg**	28	33
	incls engine block heater		
ZQ3	**Convenience Group** — w/PEG 1SBX or R9A	NC	NC
	w/PEG 1SAX	329	383
	incls tilt wheel and speed control		
—	**Cooling Systems**		
KC4	engine oil	116	135
KNP	heavy duty transmission cooling	NC	NC
YF5	**California Emissions**	86	100
BG9	**Floor Covering** — full rubber	(30)	(35)
	replaces carpeting on models w/Silverado decor		
AU0	**Remote Keyless Entry**	108	125
AU3	**Power Door Locks**	134	156
DF2	**Exterior Mirrors** — camper type stainless steel		
	w/PEG 1SBX	(39)	(45)
	w/o PEG 1SBX	46	53
B85	**Moldings** — bodyside bright - w/PEG 1SBX or R9B	NC	NC
	Sportside and PEG 1SAX w/o R9B	65	76
	Fleetside and PEG 1SAX w/o R9B	92	107
—	**Exterior Paints**		
ZY1	solid	NC	NC
ZY2	conventional two-tone	114	132
	req's Silverado decor		
ZY4	deluxe two-tone - Fleetside	209	243
	req's Silverado decor		
—	**Seat Type**		
A52	bench seat - w/vinyl or cloth trim	NC	NC
	w/custom cloth trim	224	261
AE7	reclining 60/40 split bench seat		
	w/custom cloth trim	352	409
	w/vinyl trim	150	174
A95	reclining high back bucket seats	568	661
—	**Shock Absorbers**		
FG5	front and rear, gas, 46mm Bilstein	194	225
F51	heavy duty, front and rear	34	40
V76	**Tow Hooks**	33	38
—	**Tires** — P235/75R15 white lettered		
XFN	front	43	50

C1500 PICKUP — CHEVROLET

CODE	DESCRIPTION	INVOICE	MSRP
YFN	rear	43	50
ZFN	spare	22	25
Z82	**Special Trailering** — w/auto trans	374	435
	w/manual trans	292	339
M30	**Transmission**	800	930
	incls 4-speed automatic w/overdrive		
P06	**Wheel Trim** — rally - w/PEG 1SBX or w/R9B	NC	NC
	w/o PEG 1SBX or w/o R9B	52	60
—	**Wheels**		
N90	aluminum - w/BYP	NC	NC
	w/PEG 1SBX or w/R9B	215	250
	w/o PEG 1SBX or w/o R9B	267	310
A28	**Windows** — sliding rear	97	113
—	**Radio Equipment**		
UM7	radio	NC	NC
	incls electronically tuned AM/FM stereo radio with seek/scan and digital clock		
UM6	radio - w/PEG 1SBX or R9A	NC	NC
	w/o PEG 1SBX or R9A	126	147
	incls electronically tuned AM/FM stereo radio with seek/scan, stereo cassette tape and digital clock		
UL0	radio - w/PEG 1SBX	77	90
	w/R9A	47	55
	w/o PEG 1SBX or R9A	174	202
	incls electronically tuned AM stereo/FM stereo radio with seek/scan, automatic tone control, digital clock, cassette tape, theft lock and speed compensated volume		
UN0	radio - w/PEG 1SBX	163	190
	w/R9A	133	155
	w/o PEG 1SBX or R9A	260	302
	incls electronically tuned AM stereo/FM stereo radio with seek/scan, automatic tone control, compact disc player, digital clock, theft lock and speed compensated volume		
UP0	radio - w/PEG 1SBX	249	290
	w/R9A	219	255
	w/o PEG 1SBX or R9A	346	402
	incls electronically tuned AM stereo/FM stereo radio with seek/scan, automatic tone control, compact disc layer, digital clock, cassette tape, theft lock and speed compensated volume		
UL5	radio delete	(247)	(287)

See the Automobile Dealer Directory on page 388 for a Dealer near you!

EDMUND'S 1995 HIGH-PERFORMANCE AUTOMOBILES

CHEVROLET *CAMARO Z28*

| CODE | DESCRIPTION | INVOICE | MSRP |

1995 Chevrolet Camaro Z28 Convertible

CAMARO Z28

"From the country that invented rock n' roll" claim the advertisements for this Quebec, Canada-built sport coupe. A small technicality, we suppose, but there are no technicalities when it comes to the Z28's performance abilities. This car is blazingly quick, holds the road tenaciously, costs less than the average price of a new car in this country, and gets decent gas mileage when it's not being hammered along a twisty two-lane road.

For 1995, Camaro buyers will note few changes to their favorite pony car. The side mirrors are now body color, and you can have the roof painted the same color as the rest of the car if you like. The Bose stereo is enhanced, and chrome wheels, just the thing for rust-belt buyers, are available.

From a bang-for-the-buck standpoint, the Z28 is unbeatable. A Corvette-derived 5.7-liter V-8 puts 275 horsepower to the pavement through the rear wheels. The interior is functional, if not slightly garish. The Camaro holds a respectable amount of gear in the cargo hold as well. Airbags and anti-lock brakes are standard, and more mature drivers can order traction control, but that option defeats some of the fun of the Z28: smoky, adolescent burnouts that leave the drivers behind choking on charred Goodyears.

Performance and Safety

Acceleration (0-60 mph)	5.7 sec.	ABS	Standard
Braking (60-0 mph)	112 ft.	Driver Airbag	Standard
Cornering	.88 g's	Passenger Airbag	Standard
Fuel Capacity	15.5 gal.	Traction Control	Optional
Fuel Economy	City: 17 mpg	Crash Test Grade	D: Excellent P: Excellent
	Hwy: 25 mpg	Insurance Cost	Very High

EDMUND'S 1995 HIGH-PERFORMANCE AUTOMOBILES

CAMARO Z28 — CHEVROLET

Edmund's Driving Impression

They're loved, and they're hated—just like their long-lived predecessors. While some critics claim that the current Camaro is no better than the former (1982-92) generation, others—including ourselves—brand it better than ever. A lot better.

For many drivers (but not all), a Z28's seat feels virtually custom-made: firm and highly supportive, but promising welcome comfort on a long trip. Coupes are surprisingly easy to slip into, too, even if they look forbidding as the door eases open.

Stomp the gas and the Z's 5.7-liter V-8 delivers an exhilarating leap forward, matched by vigorous response at highway speeds. The Corvette-based powerplant delivers 325 pound-feet of torque—enough wallop to induce wheelspins and wreak hearty havoc, for those so inclined. Despite that vitality, it's an easy car to handle on short shopping excursions.

Accelerating on the highway, the four-speed automatic downshifts quickly. Or, there's the option of six-speed manual shift.

Does anyone outside a race course really need half a dozen ratios? Probably not; but when the gearshift is this easy and fun to manipulate, an extra ratio can't hurt. Like Corvette's, it operates with a forced first-to-fourth-gear shift under light throttle, for fuel economy's sake. Full yellow-on-black gauges include a 150-mph speedometer and 7000-rpm tach (redline near 5700).

Handling, as expected, is firm, taut, sure-footed, stable. Some insist a Z28 rides roughly, but we've felt little pain. Oh sure, it's firm. You feel every bump and dent in the asphalt. Still, it seems exactly right.

Camaros grow frightfully skittish on slippery pavement, unless you order the new traction control, which affects both engine speed and braking. In the snowbelt, you might skip the "Z" and pick the less-potent V-6 engine instead.

To its credit, Camaro hasn't lost its youthful vigor—honed over nearly three decades. Today, the coupe and convertible add mid-1990s refinement and build quality to its performance pedigree.

CAMARO Z28 V8

Code	Description	Invoice	MSRP
1FP87/Z28	Z28 2-Dr Coupe	16392	17915
1FP67/Z28	Z28 2-Dr Convertible	21132	23095
	Destination Charge:	500	500

Standard Equipment

CAMARO Z28 COUPE: 5.7 liter SFI V8 engine, 6-speed manual transmission, power rack and pinion steering, power front/rear disc brakes, P235/55R16 BW tires, 16" aluminum silver wheels, electronically tuned AM/FM stereo radio with seek-scan, digital clock, stereo cassette tape, search, repeat and extended range speakers; limited slip rear axle, single serpentine accessory drive belt, 4-wheel anti-lock brake system, transmission shift interlock (auto trans only), 5-mph energy-absorbing front/rear bumpers with body color fascias, side window defoggers, stainless steel exhaust system, Solar-Ray tinted glass, miniquad halogen headlamps, dual sport body color mirrors (LH remote/RH manual), 2-component clear coat paint, special black roof treatment, gas charged monotube front/rear shocks, platinum tip spark plugs, integral rear spoiler, performance firm ride and handling suspension, 4-wheel coil spring suspension system with computer selected springs, short-long arm de Carbon front suspension, Pass Key II theft deterrent system, high pressure compact spare tire, intermittent wipers, driver and passenger air bags, full carpeting (includes cargo area), center console with cup holder and lighted storage compartment, Scotchgard fabric protector (includes seats/door trim/floor mats/floor carpeting), carpeted front floor mats, gauge package with tachometer, low oil

CHEVROLET — CAMARO Z28

| CODE | DESCRIPTION | INVOICE | MSRP |

level indicator system, dome lamp, day/night rearview mirror with dual reading/courtesy lamps, closeout panel for cargo compartment area, headlamps on reminder, 4-way manual driver's seat adjuster, full folding back rear seat, cloth reclining front bucket seats with integral head restraints, 115-mph speedometer, tilt-wheel steering wheel, door storage compartments, covered LH/RH visor mirrors, check gauges warning light.

Z28 CONVERTIBLE (in addition to or instead of Z28 COUPE equipment): Rear window defogger, glass rear window, 3-piece hard boot with storage bag, body color mirrors, folding power top, full headliner, rear seat courtesy lamp, trunk lamp, Premium speaker system.

Accessories

Code	Description	Invoice	MSRP
1SH	**Z28 Coupe Base Equipment Group**	NC	NC
	incl'd w/model		
1SJ	**Z28 Coupe Preferred Equipment Group 1 — w/MN6**	1191	1385
	w/MX0	1097	1275
UU8	w/UU8 radio, add	301	350
U1T	w/U1T radio, add	521	606

incls air conditioning, electronic speed control w/resume feature, remote hatch release, engine oil cooler (w/MN6 only), fog lamps

Code	Description	Invoice	MSRP
1SK	**Z28 Coupe Preferred Equipment Group 2 — w/MN6**	1876	2181
	w/MX0	1781	2071
UU8	w/UU8 radio, add	301	350
U1T	w/U1T radio, add	521	606

incls air conditioning, electronic speed control with resume speed, remote hatch release, engine oil cooler (w/MN6 only), fog lamps, 4-way manual driver seat adjuster, power windows with driver side express-down, power door lock system, sport twin remote electric mirrors, remote keyless entry with illluminated interior feature, leather-wrapped steering wheel, transmission shifter and parking brake handle

Code	Description	Invoice	MSRP
1SL	**Z28 Convertible Base Equipment Group**	NC	NC
U1C	w/U1C radio, add	194	226
1SM	**Z28 Convertible Preferred Equipment Group 1 — w/MN6**	1161	1350
	w/MX0	1066	1240
U1C	w/U1C radio, add	194	226

incls air conditioning, electronic speed control with resume speed, remote trunk lid release, engine oil cooler (w/MN6 trans only), fog lamps

Code	Description	Invoice	MSRP
1SN	**Z28 Convertible Preferred Equipment Group 2 — w/MN6**	1846	2146
	w/MX0	1751	2036
U1C	w/U1C radio, add	194	226

incls air conditioning, electronic speed control with resume speed, remote trunk release, engine oil cooler (w/MN6 trans only), fog lamps, power windows with driver side express down, power door lock system, sport twin remote electric mirrors, remote keyless entry system with illuminated interior feature, leather-wrapped steering, transmission shifter and parking brake handle

Code	Description		
—	**Radio Equipment** — see pkgs		
U1C	Music system - Convertible		

incls electronically tuned AM/FM stereo radio with seek-scan, digital clock, compact disc player, extended range speakers and Delco Loc II

CAMARO Z28 — CHEVROLET

CODE	DESCRIPTION	INVOICE	MSRP
UU8	Music system - Coupe *incls electronically tuned AM/FM stereo radio with seek-scan, stereo cassette tape and digital clock*		
U1T	Delco/Bose music system - Coupe *incls electronically tuned AM/FM stereo radio with seek-scan, compact disc player, digital clock and Delco LOC II*		
—	**Interior Trim**		
C2	cloth bucket seats	NC	NC
—	Exterior Color — paint, solid	NC	NC
—	**Engines**		
LT1	5.7 liter SFI V8	STD	STD
B35	Floor Covering, Rear	13	15
B34	Bodyside Molding	52	60
D82	Monochromatic Roof — Coupe	NC	NC
DE4	Sunshades — removable roof panel	22	25
GU5	Axle, Optional	215	250
	incls engine oil cooler; reqs MXO trans and QLC or QFZ tires		
VK3	Bracket, Front License Plate	NC	NC
C49	Defogger — rear window, electric	146	170
R9W	Defogger — rear window, delete	NC	NC
AU3	Door Lock System, Power — electric	189	220
YF5	California Emission Requirements	86	100
FE9	Federal Emission Requirements	NC	NC
NG1	Massachusetts Emission Requirements	86	100
1LE	Performance Package — Z28 Coupe	267	310
	incls engine oil cooler and special handling suspension system		
CC1	Roof Panels — removable glass - incls locks - Coupe	834	970
AG1	Seat, Power — driver side only	232	270
AR9	Cloth Bucket Seats	NC	NC
AR9	Leather Bucket Seats — w/o 1SH	429	499
	w/1SH	460	534
—	**Tires**		
QMT	P235/55R16 SBR ply BW	STD	STD
QLC	P245/50ZR16 SBR ply BW - Z28 Coupe	194	225
QFZ	P245/50ZR16 BW all performance	194	225
—	**Transmissions**		
MN6	6-speed manual	NC	NC
MXO	4-speed automatic w/overdrive	645	750
N96	Wheels — aluminum cast 16"	STD	STD
	incls wheel locks		

EDMUND'S 1995 HIGH-PERFORMANCE AUTOMOBILES

CHEVROLET *CAPRICE CLASSIC*

1995 Chevrolet Caprice Classic

CAPRICE CLASSIC (5.7L V8)

Yes, we were surprised too, but published performance figures reveal that Chevy's behemoth Caprice is indeed a competent performer, which explains some of its popularity in police and taxi fleets. Essentially, the Caprice's optional 5.7-liter V-8 is the same engine that propels the Impala SS sport sedan, although in slightly different tune, and combined with the optional sport suspension, the Caprice moves with amazing alacrity.

The Caprice has never been very successful with the buying public, mostly due to its heavy-handed styling. Modifications since the current car's 1991 debut include revised rear wheel wells, restyled tail lamps, and for 1995, it adopts the dog-leg rear quarter window treatment from the sportier Impala SS. Overall, the styling improvements haven't improved the Caprice, which we kind of liked as a pseudo-Hudson.

Inside, the Caprice looks like a taxi. An expansive dash and wide, flat bench greet and seat six passengers in comfort. With the optional V-8, sport suspension and wide tires mounted on alloy wheels, the Caprice offers good performance value for the money.

We prefer the understated, muscular look of the Impala SS, but for buyers who need interior acreage, lots of chrome and miss the good old horsepower-infused days of the '60s and '70s, the Caprice Classic ought to fit the bill.

CAPRICE CLASSIC
CHEVROLET

CODE	DESCRIPTION	INVOICE	MSRP

Performance and Safety

Acceleration (0-60 mph) .... 8.5 sec.	ABS .... Standard		
Braking (60-0 mph) .... 133 ft.	Driver Airbag .... Standard		
Cornering .... .82 g's	Passenger Airbag .... Standard		
Fuel Capacity .... 23 gal.	Traction Control .... N/A		
Fuel Economy .... City: 17 mpg	Crash Test Grade .... D: Good	P: Poor	
	Hwy: 25 mpg	Insurance Cost .... Low	

CAPRICE CLASSIC 5.7L V8
1BL19	4-Dr Sedan...	18245	20860
Destination Charge:		585	585

Standard Equipment

CAPRICE CLASSIC 5.7L SFI V8 ENGINE SEDAN: 4-speed electronic automatic transmission, power steering, 4-wheel anti-lock brake system, power door locks, P235/70R15 BW tires, full wheel covers, electronically tuned AM/FM stereo radio with seek-scan, digital clock and dual front/rear speakers; air conditioning, stainless steel exhaust system, tinted glass, manual outside mirrors (LH remote/RH manual), wide bodyside moldings, base coat/clear coat paint, intermittent windshield wipers, driver and front passenger air bags, cup holders, brake/transmission shift interlock, rear child security door locks, color-keyed front/rear carpeted floor mats, voltmeter/oil pressure gauges, front door courtesy lamps, RH covered visor mirror, oil change monitor, trip odometer, Pass Key theft deterrent system, door map pockets, standard custom cloth 55/45 seats with center front and rear armrests, adjustable head restraints, driver and passenger seat recliners, seat back pockets, Scotchgard fabric protector (seats/door trim/floor covering), tilt-wheel adjustable steering column, low fluid warning light.

Accessories

1SA	**Caprice Classic Sedan Base Equipment Group**	NC	NC
UM6	w/UM6 radio, add	172	200
UL0	w/UL0 radio, add	219	255
UN0	w/UN0 radio, add	305	355
	incls standard equipment		
1SB	**Caprice Classic Sedan Preferred Equipment Group 1**	605	703
UM6	w/UM6 radio, add	172	200
UL0	w/UL0 radio, add	219	255
UN0	w/UN0 radio, add	305	355
	incls electronic speed control with resume speed, power windows with driver's express-down, electric twin remote mirrors		
1SC	**Caprice Classic Sedan Preferred Equipment Group 2**	1189	1382
UL0	w/UL0 radio, add	47	55
UN0	w/UN0 radio, add	133	155
	incls power windows with driver's express down, electronic speed control with resume speed, power trunk opener, electric twin remote mirrors, radio (electronically tuned AM/FM		

CHEVROLET — CAPRICE CLASSIC

CODE	DESCRIPTION	INVOICE	MSRP

stereo radio with seek and scan stereo cassette tape with auto reverse, digital clock and coaxial front and extended-range rear speakers), driver's side 6-way power seat, power antenna, dual reading lamps in rearview mirror, rear compartment reading lamps, illuminated RH covered visor mirror

Code	Description	Invoice	MSRP
1SQ	**Caprice Classic Sedan Preferred Equipment Group 3**	1734	2016
UL0	w/UL0 radio, add	47	55
UN0	w/UN0 radio, add	133	155

incls electric twin remote mirrors, power windows with driver's express-down, electronic speed control with resume speed, power trunk opener, radio (electronically tuned AM/FM stereo radio with auto reverse, digital clock and coaxial front and extended-range rear speakers), driver's side 6-way power seat, power antenna, rear compartment lamps, rear courtesy lamps, cornering lamps, illuminated RH covered visor mirror, automatic day/night rearview mirror (incls dual reading lamps), remote keyless entry, passenger power seat, twilight sentinel headlamp system

Code	Description	Invoice	MSRP
—	**Radio Equipment** — see pkgs for specific radio pricing		
UM6	radio - see pkgs		

incls electronically tuned AM/FM stereo radio with seek/scan, stereo cassette tape with auto reverse, digital clock and coaxial front and extended-range rear speakers

Code	Description	Invoice	MSRP
UL0	radio - see pkgs		

incls electronically tuned AM/FM stereo radio with seek/scan, digital clock with automatic tone control, cassette tape, theft lock and speed compensated volume (incls premium front and rear coaxial speakers)

Code	Description	Invoice	MSRP
UN0	radio - see pkgs		

incls electronically tuned AM/FM stereo radio with automatic tone control, compact disc player, digital clock, theft lock and speed compensated volume (incls premium front and rear coaxial speakers)

Code	Description	Invoice	MSRP
G80	**Axle, Rear Limited Slip Differential**	215	250
VK3	**Bracket, Front License Plate**	NC	NC
AP9	**Cargo Convenience Net**	26	30
C49	**Defogger, Rear Window** — electric		
	w/heated outside mirrors	176	205
	w/o heated outside mirrors	146	170
FE9	**Federal Emission Requirements**	NC	NC
NG1	**Massachusetts Emission Requirements**	86	100
YF5	**California Emission Requirements**	86	100
—	**Engines**		
LT1	5.7 liter SFI V8	STD	STD
K05	**Engine Block Heater**	17	20
B18	**Interior Package, Custom**	112	130

incls cargo net, front courtesy lamps, LH covered visor mirror and custom trim door panels

Code	Description	Invoice	MSRP
D84	**Custom Two-Tone Paint**	121	141
D90	**Pinstriping, Bodyside & Rear**	52	61
F41	**Ride/Handling Suspension**	42	49
AG1	**Seat, Power Driver's Side** — 6-way adjuster	262	305

incld w/PEGS 1SC & 1SQ; NA w/PEG 1SA

CAPRICE CLASSIC / CORVETTE — CHEVROLET

CODE	DESCRIPTION	INVOICE	MSRP
—	**Seat Type**		
AM6	55/45 custom cloth	NC	NC
AM6	55/45 custom leather	555	645
	req's PEG 1SQ		
K34	**Speed Control, Electronic** — w/resume speed	194	225
—	**Suspension**		
B4U	sport	437	508
V92	**Trailering Package**	18	21
	incls heavy duty cooling		
UV8	**Telephone, Cellular Provisions**	39	45
—	**Tires** — all-season steel belted radial-ply		
QMU	P235/70R15 blackwall (incld w/B4U)	NC	NC
QMV	P235/70R15 white stripe	77	90
N81	**Full Size Spare** — steel wheel		
	w/QMU tires	52	60
	w/QMV tires	56	65
—	**Wheels**		
PD4	aluminum - w/locks	215	250
PB1	deluxe wheel covers	60	70
N91	wire wheel covers - w/locks	185	215

1995 Chevrolet Corvette Convertible

CORVETTE

Really, this car needs no introduction. It has been around in current form since late 1983, but has been continually improved each year, enough so that it currently ranks as one of the best sports cars you can buy anywhere at any time. And, compared to most of its upscale competitors, the Corvette offers style, performance, and image at a bargain price.

CHEVROLET — CORVETTE

This year, the Corvette receives new gill panels in the front fenders, de Carbon shock absorbers and standard heavy-duty brakes, among other changes. Also, the ZR1 disappears after 1995. ZR1's have specific alloy wheels, and a thrilling twin-cam aluminum V-8 good for 405 horsepower. Certainly, the '95 ZR1 is destined to become a collectible version of America's sports car.

The Corvette's styling still seems fresh, even after 12 years in production. Still, it's been more than a decade since a thorough redesign, and the Corvette is beginning to show its age. For 1997, Chevrolet is planning to roll out a new Corvette, and it will likely showcase cutting-edge technology and represent a vast improvement over the current model.

Were it not for the excellent Camaro Z28, we'd recommend the Corvette, but the extra 20 grand it costs over the Z car would be better spent on a Jeep Wrangler for weekend treks to the north country and a few coolers full of Killian's Red.

Performance and Safety

Corvette LT1

Acceleration (0-60 mph)	5.6 sec.	ABS	Standard
Braking (60-0 mph)	115 ft.	Driver Airbag	Standard
Cornering	.92 g's	Passenger Airbag	Standard
Fuel Capacity	20 gal.	Traction Control	Standard
Fuel Economy	City: 17 mpg	Crash Test Grade	D: N/A P: N/A
	Hwy: 25 mpg	Insurance Cost	Average

Corvette ZR1

Acceleration (0-60 mph)	5.2 sec.	ABS	Standard
Braking (60-0 mph)	117 ft.	Driver Airbag	Standard
Cornering	.92 g's	Passenger Airbag	Standard
Fuel Capacity	20 gal.	Traction Control	Standard
Fuel Economy	City: 17 mpg	Crash Test Grade	D: N/A P: N/A
	Hwy: 27 mpg	Insurance Cost	N/A

Edmund's Driving Impression

Even the most ardent Corvette fanatics admit that their favorite cars of a decade ago were hard-riding, uncomfortable beasts. Instead of unadulterated joy, a day behind the wheel could turn into an exhausting painful experience.

Today's version of American's preeminent sports car is far superior in ride quality and creature comforts. But fear not: the beloved two-seater hasn't lost a bit of its brazen personality, its boisterous road behavior, or its ability to capture the hearts of millions. Anyone who observed the cavalcade of Corvettes—more than 4,000 strong—headed to Kentucky for the grand opening of the National Corvette Museum last Labor Day cannot doubt the car's lasting appeal.

Starting with the basics, Corvettes are fast. Mighty fast. Whether we're talking about the "ordinary" 300-horsepower LT1 or the ZR1 brute, packing an unbelievable 405 ponies, a 'vette will never disappoint when one's foot pounds the floorboard.

CORVETTE
CHEVROLET

| CODE | DESCRIPTION | INVOICE | MSRP |

The real fun begins as soon as the straightaway ends and you encounter the twisty bits. With traditional rear-drive authority, the legendary sports car conquers the sharpest curves and switchbacks, at velocities that would send lesser vehicles over the edge. Then, as soon as the road turns linear again, a tap of the foot sends this partially-tamed barbarian hurtling up to cruising pace.

Back in civilized surroundings, either model is surprisingly docile, perfectly willing to haul groceries from the market—provided that purchase is limited to a couple of bags. Grandmas and grandpas drive Corvettes, after all, wielding the six-speed gearbox just as enthusiastically as their offspring. Nothing wrong with an automatic-transmission Corvette, but the magnificent six-speed turns gearshifting into a virtually artistic experience.

All this exuberance is accomplished while the car's two occupants sit in sublime comfort, right? Not a chance! Depending on the pavement surface, the 'vette is likely to buck and snort, leap and bounce—and you'll love every second.

Unless you're one of the anti-Corvette crowd, that is. Those folks won't even deign to enter one of these detested machines, and nothing we say here could change that opinion.

Because a ZR1 costs twice as much—a bonus paid mainly for its marvelous twin-cam engine—there's little need to scour the countryside for one of the 448 final examples. Driving a "Z" is admittedly a near-mystical experience, but an LT1 is plenty of car for any rational person.

1995 Chevrolet Corvette ZR1

CORVETTE V8

1YY07	2-Dr Coupe	31451	36785
1YY67	2-Dr Convertible	37334	43665
1YY07	ZR1 2-Dr Coupe (incls ZR1 Perf. Pkg)	57708	68043
1YY67	ZR1 2-Dr Convertible (incls ZR1 Perf. Pkg)	63591	74923
Destination Charge:		560	560

CHEVROLET — CORVETTE

| CODE | DESCRIPTION | INVOICE | MSRP |

Standard Equipment

CORVETTE: 5.7 liter SFI V8 engine (includes aluminum heads, composite valve rocker covers, sequential-port fuel injection, aluminum intake manifold, roller valve lifters), 6-speed manual transmission or 4-speed automatic transmission, power rack and pinion steering, heavy duty 4-wheel anti-lock rear disc brakes, power windows with driver side express-down feature, power door locks, P255/45ZR17 front tires, P285/40ZR17 rear tires, 17" x 8.5" aluminum front wheels, 17" x 9.5" aluminum rear wheels, electronically tuned AM/FM stereo radio with seek-scan, digital clock, stereo cassette tape, power antenna and extended range speakers; manual control air conditioning, acceleration slip regulation, Pass Key II anti-theft system, uniframe-design body structure with corrosion-resistant coating, brake/transmission shift interlock (with auto trans only), 2.5-mph bumpers, rear window defogger, side window defoggers, front cornering/underhood courtesy lamps, passive keyless entry with remote hatch release (Coupe only), clamshell-opening front end for easy engine access, Solar-Ray glass, full-glass rear hatch with two interior remote releases/roller-shade cargo cover (Coupe only), power-operated retractable halogen headlamps, distributorless opti-spark ignition system, outside air induction system, acoustic insulation package, halogen fog lamps, front cornering/underhood courtesy lamps, outside dual electrically heated adjustable rearview mirrors, base coat/clear coat paint, 1-piece removable fiberglass roof panel (Coupe only), full folding roof (Coupe only), de Carbon shock absorbers, independent front/rear suspension with transverse fiberglass leaf springs and forged aluminum A-arms, intermittent wipers, driver and passenger air bags, locking center console includes: coin tray/cassette/CD storage/integral armrest/lighted storage compartment, Scotchgard fabric protector (floor covering), low oil level indicator, electronic liquid-crystal instrumentation with white analog and digital display/switchable English or Metric readouts; day/night rearview mirror with reading, ashtray, and courtesy lights; lighted LH/RH covered visor mirrors, headlamps on reminder, leather seating surface bucket seats with lateral support and back angle adjustment, electronic speed control with resume speed, leather-wrapped tilt-wheel sport steering wheel, integral storage compartment with door armrest.

ZR1 (in addition to or instead of CORVETTE equipment): 5.7 liter DOHC V8 engine, P275/40ZR17 front performance tires, P315/35ZR17 rear performance tires, 17" x 9.5" aluminum front wheels, 17" x 11" aluminum rear wheels, electronic control air conditioning, electronic selective ride and handling suspension package, adjustable power sport bucket seats with leather seating surfaces, low tire pressure warning, Delco/Bose music system w/CD and cassette player.

Accessories

Code	Description	Invoice	MSRP
1SA	**Corvette Coupe Base Equipment Group**	NC	NC
	incls standard equipment		
1SB	**Corvette Coupe Preferred Equipment Group 1**	1120	1333
U1F	w/U1F radio, add	333	396
	incls electronic air conditioning, Delco/Bose music system (incls electronically tuned AM/FM stereo radio with seek/scan, digital clock and stereo cassette tape), driver's side power seat		
1SC	**Corvette Convertible Base Equipment Group**	NC	NC
	incls standard equipment		
1SD	**Corvette Convertible Preferred Equipment Group 1**	1120	1333
U1F	w/U1F radio, add	333	396
	incls electronic air conditioning, Delco/Bose music system (incls electronically tuned AM/FM stereo radio with seek/scan, digital clock and stereo cassette tape), driver's power seat		
U1F	**Radio** — see pkgs for specific radio pricing		
	incls Delco/Bose music system (incls electronically tuned AM/FM stereo radio with seek/scan, digital clock, stereo cassette tape and compact disc player)		

CORVETTE — CHEVROLET

CODE	DESCRIPTION	INVOICE	MSRP
G92	**Axle, Performance Ratio** —reqs auto trans	42	50
FE9	**Federal Emission Requirements**	NC	NC
NG1	**Massachusetts Emission Requirements**	84	100
YF5	**California Emission Requirements**	84	100
LT1	**Engine** — 5.7 liter SFI V8	STD	STD
CC2	**Removable Hard Top** —convertible	1676	1995
	incls rear window defogger		
Z07	**Performance Handling Package** —LT1 coupe	1718	2045
	incls FX3 Selective Ride & Handling, Bilstein adjustable ride control system stiffer springs, stabilizer bars and bushings, 17" x 9.5" wheels and P275/40ZR17/N BL tires		
C2L	**Roof Package** —coupe	798	950
	incls standard solid panel and transparent panel		
—	**Roof Panel**		
24S	transparent, removable, blue tint —coupe	546	650
64S	transparent, removable, bronze tint —coupe	546	650
—	**Seats**		
AG1	6-way power, driver side —incl w/ZR1	256	305
AG2	6-way power, passenger side —incl w/ZR1	256	305
AR9	leather seating surface bucket —incl w/ZR1	NC	NC
AQ9	adjustable sport leather seating surface bucket —incl w/ZR1	525	625
FX3	**Selective Ride & Handling, Electronic** —incl w/ZR1	1424	1695
ZR1	**Special Performance Package** —incl w/ZR1	NC	NC
	incls 5.7 liter SFI DOHC 32-valve V8 engine, P275/40ZR17 front tires and P315/35ZR17 rear tires, 17" x 9.5" front and 17" x 11" rear styled aluminum wheels, electronic air conditioning, selective ride and handling, leather adjustable sport seats, 6-way passenger and driver power seats, low tire pressure warning, Delco/Bose music system with CD and cassette player		
WY5	**Tires** — extended mobility	59	70
	incls P255/45ZR17 blackwall front, P285/40ZR17 blackwall rear		
UJ6	**Low Tire Pressure Warning Indicator** —incl w/ZR1	273	325
N84	**Spare Tire Delete**	(84)	(100)
—	**Transmissions**		
MX0	4-speed automatic —NA w/ZR1	NC	NC
MN6	6-speed manual	NC	NC

GET MORE MONEY FOR YOUR USED CAR BY KNOWING ITS TRUE VALUE

See our ads on pages 4 and 6

CHEVROLET

IMPALA SS

CODE	DESCRIPTION	INVOICE	MSRP

1995 Chevrolet Impala SS

IMPALA SS SEDAN

George Thorogood had the Impala SS in mind when he penned "Bad to the Bone." This car is menacing, with its all-black paint job, wide tires and fat alloys. The 5.7-liter V-8 throbs under the hood, and the exhaust note reads 'Don't mess with me.' Chevy's retro Impala SS delivers the goods, all right, and does so without coming off as a bad joke.

Based on the Caprice police package, the Impala SS carries over unchanged this year, save for the addition of two more paint choices: Black Cherry and Green Gray (no, not the punks currently taking over MTV, that's Green Day). The interior is strictly Caprice-issue, which is the SS's only shortcoming. Leather-trimmed seats offer a bit more support than the Caprice bench, but you won't confuse them with Recaros.

What this car needs is a revised interior, with a center console housing a U-shaped shifter, to really give buyers the warm Genuine Chevrolet fuzzies. The rest is in place: surprisingly good looks, great performance, and a price that doesn't induce heart failure.

Performance and Safety

Acceleration (0-60 mph) ..... 7.1 sec.	ABS .... Standard	
Braking (60-0 mph) .... 120 ft.	Driver Airbag .... Standard	
Cornering .... .83 g's	Passenger Airbag .... Standard	
Fuel Capacity .... 23 gal.	Traction Control .... N/A	
Fuel Economy .... City: 17 mpg	Crash Test Grade .... D: Good	P: Poor
Hwy: 25 mpg	Insurance Cost .... N/A	

EDMUND'S 1995 HIGH-PERFORMANCE AUTOMOBILES

IMPALA SS — CHEVROLET

| CODE | DESCRIPTION | INVOICE | MSRP |

Edmund's Driving Impression

Like its fabled ancestor from the 1960s muscle-car era, the burly Impala SS is both civilized and surly: a mean machine beneath its businesslike exterior. This Impala for the mid-Nineties delivers on its promise in three areas: powertrain, police-adapted suspension, and styling.

Tromp the gas pedal, and the merits of the Corvette-derived 5.7-liter V-8 become evident in an instant. Unleashing the full wallop of its 260 horsepower and 330 pound-feet of torque transforms the sedate two-ton cruiser into a charging beast—but one that does its duty in near-silence, with barely a trace of rowdiness. Acceleration to highway speed is fantastic, and the swollen sedan practically clamors for more. Performance when passing or merging isn't quite as dramatic, but more than adequate, and the four-speed automatic transmission never falters.

Through tight curves and sharp corners, the Impala stays flat and grabs hard, helped by special quick-ratio steering. Even so, it handles more like a Caprice than a full-fledged sport sedan. Unlike the woozy-riding Caprice, though, an SS absorbs bumps with blissful nonchalance, imparting little harshness to its occupants.

Wearing a minimum of decoration, the Impala conceals its Caprice-derived identity well. Passersby tend to toss out wild guesses on its origin. Jaguar? Big BMW? Though large, its identifying badges are so subtly molded to the bodysides as to be nearly invisible. Unique interior touches enhance its separate identity, but we can't understand why Chevrolet doesn't install a tachometer to accompany the otherwise-full set of gauges.

There are two schools of thought on the revived Impala. Advocates exclaim, "Great idea!" and wonder, "Where can I get one?" Skeptics dismiss the SS as a mere curiosity and ask, "What's the point?" Chevrolet isn't worried, since the 6,000-plus examples issued late in the 1994 model year were snapped up in a hurry.

IMPALA SS V8
1BL19/WX3 4-Dr Sedan 20963 22910
Destination Charge: 585   585

Standard Equipment

IMPALA SS: 5.7 liter SFI V8 engine, 4-speed electronic automatic transmission with overdrive, power rack and pinion steering, 4-wheel disc brakes with ABS, power driver's side window with express-down feature, power door locks, P255/50ZR17 BW tires, 17" aluminum wheels, electronically tuned AM/FM stereo radio with seek-scan, digital clock, stereo cassette tape with auto reverse and coaxial front/extended range rear speakers; air conditioning, 3.08 limited slip differential (rear axle), black key lock cylinder, black tail lamp moldings, black satin finish, black base antenna, body color front and rear fascias, body color wheel opening moldings/door handles/rocker moldings, bodyside and rear decklid emblems, stainless steel exhaust system, extra capacity cooling, full size spare tire, tinted glass, cornering lamps, twin electric remote mirrors, narrow bodyside moldings, base coat/clear coat paint, rear quarter window molding, rear spoiler, de Carbon shocks, special ride and handling suspension, transmission oil cooler, intermittent windshield wipers, driver and front passenger air bags, brake/transmission shift interlock, luggage area cargo net, rear child security door locks, voltmeter/oil pressure gauges, front door courtesy lamps, color-keyed front/rear carpeted floor mats, LH/RH covered visor mirrors, oil change monitor, trip odometer, power trunk opener, Pass Key theft deterrent system, door map pockets, dual reading lamps (rearview mirror/rear compartment), door trim and floor covering Scotchgard fabric protector, driver side power seat, 45/45 leather seats, full floor console with cup holders, adjustable head restraints, driver and passenger seat recliners, seat back pockets, electronic speed control, tilt wheel adjustable steering column, low oil level warning light, low fluid warning lights.

EDMUND'S 1995 HIGH-PERFORMANCE AUTOMOBILES

CHEVROLET — IMPALA SS

CODE	DESCRIPTION	INVOICE	MSRP

Accessories

Code	Description	Invoice	MSRP
1SJ	**Impala SS Sedan Base Equipment Group**	NC	NC
UL0	w/UL0 radio, add	47	55
UN0	w/UN0 radio, add	133	155
	incls model with standard equipment		
1SK	**Impala SS Sedan Preferred Equipment Group 1**	765	890
UL0	w/UL0 radio, add	47	55
UN0	w/UN0 radio, add	133	155
	incls automatic day/night rearview mirror, rear window defogger with heated outside rearview mirrors, power antenna, passenger side power seat with 6-way adjuster, remote keyless entry with trunk release, twilight sentinel headlamp system		
VK3	**Front License Plate Bracket**	NC	NC
C49	**Electric Rear Window Defogger**	176	205
	incls heated OS mirrors		
NG1	**Massachusetts Emission Requirement**	86	100
YF5	**California Emission Requirement**	86	100
FE9	**Federal Emission Requirements**	NC	NC
K05	**Engine Block Heater**	17	20
—	**Radio Equipment** — see pkgs for specific radio pricing		
UL0	radio - see pkgs		
	incls electronically tuned AM/FM stereo radio with seek/scan, automatic tone control, digital clock, cassette tape, theft lock and speed compensated volume		
UN0	radio - see pkgs		
	incls electronically tuned AM/FM stereo radio with seek/scan, automatic tone control, compact disc player, digital clock, theft lock and speed compensated volume		

EDMUND'S NEW AUDIO TAPE!

How to Get Your Way at the Auto Dealer

You'll learn how to buy right,
negotiate smart, save money, and
enjoy yourself all at the same time.

see our ad on page 376 for details

LUMINA LS   CHEVROLET

1995 Chevrolet Lumina LS

LUMINA LS SEDAN (3.4L V6)

While in college, one of our younger staffers attended the 1989 North American International Auto Show in Detroit, Michigan. The 1990 Chevrolet Lumina was displayed at the show in coupe and sedan form, and this young man thought the vehicle was some kind of ill-conceived concept car. When it hit the streets for the 1990 model year, he couldn't help but laugh every time one passed him on the street. Amazingly, the Lumina went on to become a best-seller.

These days, a new Lumina prowls Chevy showrooms. It is vastly improved over the old model, offering dual airbags housed in a modern, straight-forward dashboard. The exterior shape is also more modern and attractive. Even more amazing, the new Lumina performs well, although the feel of the car really doesn't transmit any inkling of performance capability.

Still, the numbers are there, when equipped with the optional 3.4-liter V-6, and the Lumina is quicker than rivals from Chrysler and Ford. Braking and cornering abilities are not extraordinary for the class, but the Lumina nonetheless keeps itself planted to terra firma with little fanfare. Good news on the performance front from Chevy boss Jim Perkins; he announced that he wants a Super Sport Lumina on the racks for 1996, equipped with many of the Monte Carlo Z34's go-fast goodies.

Chevy engineers claim the new Lumina is the result of intensive consumer clinics, and the car was designed in accordance with the research findings. Styling was not a strong issue among sedan buyers, a point well proven by the popularity of the previous-generation Lumina. Fortunately, Chevy saw fit to give the Lumina a tidy, attractive look that is marred only by a somewhat characterless and protruding proboscis.

With a competent car and a pricing structure that undercuts Ford and Chrysler, Chevy dealers ought to find that the new Lumina is even more popular than the old one.

EDMUND'S 1995 HIGH-PERFORMANCE AUTOMOBILES

CHEVROLET — LUMINA LS

Performance and Safety

Acceleration (0-60 mph) .... 8.0 sec.
Braking (60-0 mph) .... 132 ft.
Cornering .... .78 g's
Fuel Capacity .... 17.1 gal.
Fuel Economy .... City: 17 mpg
                                 Hwy: 26 mpg

ABS .... Standard
Driver Airbag .... Standard
Passenger Airbag .... Standard
Traction Control .... N/A
Crash Test Grade .... D: N/A   P: N/A
Insurance Cost .... N/A

1995 Chevrolet Lumina LS

LUMINA 3.4L LS 6 CYL

		Invoice	MSRP
1WN69/Z7E	LS 4-Dr Sedan	16212	17930
	Destination Charge:	525	525

Standard Equipment

LUMINA 3.4L LS SEDAN: 3.4 liter SFI DOHC V6 engine, power 4-wheel disc brakes with anti-lock brake system, "anti-whistle" radio antenna, 5-mph impact-absorbing bumpers, stainless steel exhaust system, bodyside molding, power rack and pinion steering, four-wheel independent "soft ride" suspension, Pass-Key II theft deterrent system, P205/70R15 BW tires, 4-speed electronic automatic transmission, 15" x 6.0" steel wheels, side window defoggers, power door locks, child-security rear door locks, Scotchgard fabric protector on all interior fabrics, front and rear color-keyed carpeted floor mats, highly readable analog gauges with trip odometer, rear seat heat ducts, horn pad (operates front anywhere on the steering wheel hub), courtesy lighting with theatre dimming, map lights, dual air bags and 3-point safety belts, rear seat child comfort guide safety belts, 4-way manual driver's seat adjuster, tilt-wheel adjustable steering column, storage includes extra large glove box/front door map pockets/seat-back storage pockets, variable intermittent windshield wipers, air conditioning with CFC-free refrigerant, dual body color sport mirrors (LH remote), power trunk opener, tachometer, illuminated driver and passenger visor vanity mirrors, custom cloth 60/40 split bench seats with storage armrest (includes cup holder), AM/FM stereo/cassette tape player, power windows with driver's express-down feature and power window lockout, deluxe wheel covers.

LUMINA LS — CHEVROLET

Accessories

CODE	DESCRIPTION	INVOICE	MSRP
1SC	**Lumina LS Sedan Base Equipment Group**	NC	NC
UL0	w/UL0 radio, add	64	72
	incld with model		
1SD	**Lumina LS Sedan Preferred Equipment Group 1**	445	500
UL0	w/UL0 radio, add	64	72
	incls luggage area cargo retaining net, electric twin remote mirrors, power trunk opener, remote keyless entry, electronic speed control with resume speed		
—	**Interior Trim**		
AM6	cloth 60/40 seat	NC	NC
AR9	custom cloth bucket w/console	43	48
—	**Exterior Color** — paint, solid	NC	NC
—	**Engines**		
LQ1	**3.4 liter SFI DOHC**	NC	NC
VK3	**Bracket, Front License Plate**	NC	NC
C49	**Defogger, Rear Window** — electric	146	164
D83	**Accent Delete**	(33)	(37)
K05	**Engine Block Heater**	17	19
FE9	**Federal Emission Requirements**	NC	NC
NG1	**Massachusetts Emission Requirements**	89	100
YF5	**California Emission Requirements**	89	100
WG1	**Seats** — power driver side	231	260
K34	**Speed Control** — electronic w/resume speed	193	217
UV8	**Telephone** — cellular provision	38	43
—	**Tires** — all-season steel belted radial ply		
QVG	P225/60R16 blackwall	134	150
MX0	**Transmission** — 4-speed automatic electronic	NC	NC
NW0	**Wheels** — 16" aluminum	223	251
—	**Radio Equipment** — see pkgs for specific radio pricing		
UL0	radio - see pkgs		
	incls electronically tuned AM/FM stereo radio with seek/scan, automatic tone control, digital clock, cassette tape, theft lock and speed compensated volume, premium front and rear coaxial speakers		

For a guaranteed low price on a new vehicle in your area, call

1-800-CAR-CLUB

CHEVROLET
MONTE CARLO Z34

1995 Chevrolet Monte Carlo Z34 Coupe

MONTE CARLO Z34 COUPE

Essentially a Lumina Coupe, the new Monte Carlo is one more marketing trick from the folks who brought us the 'Genuine Chevrolet' ad campaign, resurrected the Impala SS, and are considering future products with innovative names like Malibu and Bel Air. All fine and dandy, if the new product is able to live up to the legend, like the Impala SS has been able to. Our staff differs on this point when considering the new Monte Carlo Z34 (see driving impression).

Sure, the twin-cam, 3.4-liter V-6 under the hood is sweet. Yes, this Monte Carlo handles better than its Lumina Z34 predecessor. But it's still a Lumina coupe, and Chevy stylists did not even try to disguise that fact. It looks nothing like flared-fendered Monte Carlos of yore, which can be either a good or bad thing, but **styling** is what sold so many Montes in the '70s and '80s. This one, while negligibly attractive, has no distinct personality of its own.

We'll bet it works well on the track, though. Ford has been whuppin' the Chevy boys in NASCAR with the slick Thunderbird for years, but this new Lumin...er, Monte Carlo, will surely bring some glory during the 1995 racing season.

The Monte Carlo is better than any Monte before it, but is saddled with vanilla styling that renders it nearly invisible on the road. The Thunderbird is into its seventh model year in current guise, but its classy looks and excellent interior design keep it in the hunt. However, check into a Dodge Avenger ES before buying anything in the personal coupe class, despite its less inspiring straight-line acceleration.

MONTE CARLO Z34   CHEVROLET

| CODE | DESCRIPTION | INVOICE | MSRP |

Performance and Safety

Acceleration (0-60 mph)	7.8 sec.	ABS	Standard
Braking (60-0 mph)	139 ft.	Driver Airbag	Standard
Cornering	.82 g's	Passenger Airbag	Standard
Fuel Capacity	17.1 gal.	Traction Control	N/A
Fuel Economy	City: 17 mpg	Crash Test Grade	D: N/A P: N/A
	Hwy: 26 mpg	Insurance Cost	N/A

Edmund's Driving Impression

Naming its performance-oriented rendition of the Lumina after a well-known model from the past is part of Chevrolet's marketing strategy. In this case, the move makes sense. Both the LS and Z34 Monte Carlos display a persona quite different from the family-focused Lumina sedan.

Some claim the Monte should have been more modern, more refined, closer to European/Asian sport coupes. Maybe so, but we rate the Z34 magnificent (for its class) as it stands, and its LS companion more than competent.

Again cranking out 210 horsepower, the dual-cam 3.4-liter V-6 feels just as delicious as it did in the old Z34. You can expect spirited pickup and frisky response, both around town and on the road. A five-speed manual gearbox would be welcome, as in the first generation; but nearly all likely customers probably would choose the smooth-shifting automatic transmission anyway. Its electronic controls perform admirably, slipping the coupe into the proper gear for every demand.

Steering is lighter than expected, suspension slightly softer than hoped-for, yet the Z34 eases through curves with confidence. The Z's 16-inch tires and aggressive suspension tuning make a difference. Despite its ample dimensions, the Monte maneuvers crisply—more like a compact than a mid-size. Sheer joy on the highway, the coupe rides a bit harshly across urban pavement, but not enough to cause anguish. All-disc brakes are gone, but we noted no lack of stopping power.

Slip inside, and you'll probably feel at home in an instant. There's plenty of space for five, and the optional graphite-colored leather seats are both lovely and highly supportive.

Both models are definitely worth a test-drive, but we'd just as soon pay that extra couple of thou' and drive home a Z34 rather than the Lumina-like LS coupe.

MONTE CARLO Z34 COUPE V6

1WX27/Z7G Z34 2-Dr Coupe	17168	18970
Destination Charge:	525	525

Standard Equipment

MONTE CARLO Z34 COUPE: 3.4 liter DOHC SFI V6 engine, P225/60R16 BW Goodyear Eagle RS-A performance tires, aluminum wheels, 40/40 cloth bucket seats, remote keyless entry system, power trunk opener, luggage-area cargo net, speed control, ETR AM/FM stereo radio w/seek-scan, digital clock, stereo cassette tape, extended range speakers, 4-speed electronic automatic transmission, driver and right front passenger side air bags, 4-wheel anti-lock brakes, air conditioning with CFC-free refrigerant, power front disc/rear drum brakes, courtesy interior lights with theatre dimming, power windows with driver's express-down feature, power window lockout, Scotchgard protection on cloth seats/door trim/floor carpeting/floor mats, tilt-wheel adjustable steering column, stainless steel exhaust system, side window defoggers, power door locks, variable intermittent windshield wipers, low oil level light, Pass-Key II theft deterrent system, front and rear color-keyed floor mats.

EDMUND'S 1995 HIGH-PERFORMANCE AUTOMOBILES

CHEVROLET — MONTE CARLO Z34

CODE	DESCRIPTION	INVOICE	MSRP
	Accessories		
1SG	Monte Carlo Z34 Coupe Base Equipment Group	NC	NC
UL0	w/UL0 radio, add	64	72
	incld with model		
—	**Interior Trim**		
AM6	custom cloth 60/40 seat	(43)	(48)
AR9	custom cloth bucket w/console	NC	NC
AR9	leather bucket w/console	491	552
—	**Exterior Color** — paint, solid	NC	NC
LQ1	**Engine** - 3.4 liter SFI V6 DOHC	NC	NC
K05	**Engine Block Heater**	17	19
VK3	**Bracket, Front License Plate**	NC	NC
C49	**Defogger, Rear Window** — electric	146	164
FE9	**Federal Emission Requirements**	NC	NC
YF5	**California Emission Requirements**	89	100
NG1	**Massachusetts Emission Requirements**	89	100
WG1	**Seats** — power driver side	231	260
UV8	**Telephone** — cellular provision	38	43
—	**Tires** — all-season steel belted radial ply		
QVG	P225/60R16 blackwall	STD	STD
MX0	**Transmission** - 4-speed automatic electronic	STD	STD
—	**Wheels**		
PY0	16" aluminum	STD	STD
16P	16" white aluminum	NC	NC
	req's color 16UX white paint		
—	**Radio Equipment** — see pkg for specific radio pricing		
UL0	radio - see pkg		

incls electronically tuned AM/FM stereo radio with seek/scan, automatic tone control, digital clock, cassette tape, theft lock and speed compensated volume, premium front and rear coaxial speakers

---

See Edmund's
Automobile Dealer Directory (page 388)
and the back cover of this book to enter our
$10,000 Wheel N'Deal Give-Away.

S10 SS PICKUP

1995 Chevrolet S-10 SS Pickup

S10 SS PICKUP

With the surging popularity of compact pickups these days, it's not surprising to find performance variants from each of the Big Three manufacturers. Chevrolet's S-10 SS accelerates, stops, and handles better than many of the vehicles in this guide, and has the capacity to haul just about anything you need to.

Based on the recently redesigned S-10 pickup, the SS gets alloy wheels, suspension modifications, monochromatic paint, four-wheel anti-lock brakes, and a high-output V-6 good for 195 horsepower. The exterior styling is an attractive combination of '90s swoop and '50s style, its optional rear bumper recalling the fabled Cameo pickup from the James Dean years. Inside, the S-10 is comfortable, but the dashboard is really ugly, with a high cowl, obnoxiously bulbous air vents along the top edge, and three different shades of gray plastic for panels and knobs.

For 1995, the SS gets a driver-side airbag and is available in the ever-popular extended-cab body style. No other changes are planned for this hot pickup, but we anticipate the addition of a passenger-side airbag within a couple of years. For now though, the S-10 SS is just about as good as it gets. Speedy, stylish, capable, and affordable, the SS makes a good argument against purchasing a model from the 'hot hatch' class.

Performance and Safety

Acceleration (0-60 mph) .... 7.9 sec.	ABS .... Standard
Braking (60-0 mph) .... 140 ft.	Driver Airbag .... Standard
Cornering .... .79 g's	Passenger Airbag .... N/A
Fuel Capacity .... 20 gal.	Traction Control .... N/A
Fuel Economy .... City: 17 mpg	Crash Test Grade .... D: N/A P: Average
Hwy: 25 mpg	Insurance Cost .... Average

CHEVROLET — S10 SS PICKUP

| CODE | DESCRIPTION | INVOICE | MSRP |

1995 Chevrolet S-10 SS Pickup

S10 SS 4.3L PICKUP V6

	S10 2WD SS Fleetside (6 ft.)	12078	13448
	Destination Charge:	480	480

Standard Equipment

S10 SS 4.3L PICKUP: 4.3 liter 191 hp CPI V6 engine, electronic 4-speed automatic transmission, sport suspension package, LS trim, locking differential, fog lamps, cast aluminum wheels with special bright hub caps, body color grille, SS badging, leather-wrapped steering wheel, P215/65R15 tires, color-keyed bumpers, ETR AM/FM stereo radio with digital clock, color-keyed padded sunshades with slider extensions, halogen headlamps, door trim panels with LH and RH molded pockets, full-floor color-keyed carpeting, day/night mirror with dual reading lamps, Scotchgarding, driver's air bag, 100 amp alternator, air dam, 525 amp battery, power front disc/rear drum brakes and 4-wheel ABS, power steering, tinted glass, full-size spare tire, deluxe heater with windshield and side window defoggers.

Accessories

Code	Description	Invoice	MSRP
C60	Air Conditioning	692	805
UA1	Battery — heavy duty - w/o V10 cold climate	48	56
	w/V10 cold climate	NC	NC
VF6	Bumper Equipment — rear step	47	55
V10	Cold Climate Pkg	77	89
—	Convenience Groups		
ZQ6	power door locks, windows and exterior electric remote mirrors	409	475
ZQ3	tilt steering and speed control	329	383
FE9	Federal Emission Requirements	NC	NC
NG1	Massachusetts Emission Requirements	NC	NC
YF5	California Emission Requirements	NC	NC
B32	Floor Covering — auxiliary front floor mats	17	20

S10 SS PICKUP — CHEVROLET

CODE	DESCRIPTION	INVOICE	MSRP
AU0	**Locks, Keyless Remote**	116	135
—	**Seat Type**		
A52	bench seat	NC	NC
AM6	60/40 reclining split bench seat	NC	NC
AV5	reclining high back bucket seats	164	191
U16	**Tachometer**	51	59
A28	**Window** — sliding rear	97	113
—	**Radio Equipment**		
UM6	radio	105	122
	incls electronically tuned AM/FM stereo radio with seek/scan, stereo cassette tape and digital clock		
UX1	radio	138	160
	incls electronically tuned AM stereo/FM stereo radio with seek/scan, stereo cassette tape with search and repeat, digital clock and graphic equalizer		
U1C	radio	244	284
	incls electronically tuned AM/FM stereo radio with seek/scan, compact disc player and digital clock		

FOR A SPECIAL RATE ON AN AUTO LOAN, CALL

1-800-AT-CHASE

CHASE AUTOMOTIVE FINANCE
SIMPLE ♦ FAST ♦ CONVENIENT

See the Automobile Dealer Directory on page 388 for a Dealer near you!

EDMUND'S 1995 HIGH-PERFORMANCE AUTOMOBILES

CHRYSLER
CONCORDE

1995 Chrysler Concorde

CONCORDE (3.5L V6)

Chrysler's Concorde, along with its corporate twins the Dodge Intrepid and Eagle Vision, heralded a new beginning for the Chrysler Corporation when they were introduced in 1993. Since that time, the company has consistently wowed the world with innovative products at great prices. Unfortunately, one of Chrysler's recent growing pains has been questionable quality control, but for 1995, steps have been taken to eliminate most of those concerns.

Concorde touts 'cab-forward' technology, which is a marketing gimmick that means the wheelbase and greenhouse were stretched in every direction to provide more room inside, and swoopy sheetmetal outside. For 1995, the Concorde's four-speed automatic has been refined, but no other changes are in store.

With prices starting just over $21,000 for the 3.5-liter Concorde, this well-equipped sedan is in the ballpark with the Honda Accord EX and Ford Taurus LX, but offers more room and power than either. However, the Honda performs better, gets more miles per gallon and has a proven reliability and resale value record, so the choice really depends on your individual priorities.

Performance and Safety

Acceleration (0-60 mph) .... 8.7 sec.	ABS .... Standard
Braking (60-0 mph) .... 136 ft.	Driver Airbag .... Standard
Cornering .... .80 g's	Passenger Airbag .... Standard
Fuel Capacity .... 18 gal.	Traction Control .... Optional
Fuel Economy .... City: 18 mpg	Crash Test Grade .... D: Average P: Good
Hwy: 26 mpg	Insurance Cost .... Average

CONCORDE CHRYSLER

Edmund's Driving Impression

Chrysler Corporation has the roles all figured out: Vision is the LH car for the sporty-minded. Intrepid is for families (but with more than a hint of sportiness thrown in). Concorde, then, befitting its Chrysler badge, is the choice of those who want plush comfort along with their impressive performance.

But wait: Don't all three have the same top engine—a strong 3.5-liter V-6, stirring up a capable 214 horsepower? And, isn't the suspension setup pretty much the same?

True enough. The bigger engine is simply an option in the Chrysler camp, rather than supplied in a particular model (as in the Eagle Vision TSi). Also, all Concordes carry the same touring suspension. "Touring" tires are optional, however, to replace the regular "ride-biased" rubber. Speed-proportional power steering comes as part of that tire step-up package.

On the whole, a Concorde rides smoother than the Eagle Vision, with no serious loss of stability or handling skills. The V-6 doesn't feel quite as responsive when propelling a Concorde as it is in an Intrepid or Vision, even if Chrysler's version actually weighs less than Eagle's. The exhaust note also tends to be quieter in a Concorde, revealing its luxury orientation, though other sounds might be heard. Instruments are top-notch, but not a complete gauge setup.

So, does it achieve stellar performance and agile maneuvering? Provided that the sedan is measured against similar vehicles, almost—though "stellar" may be overstating capability by a tad. Keep expectations realistic, and you're likely to be pleased by this spacious four-door, which combines a potent powertrain with zesty modern styling, comfortable seating, and interior elegance. You also get loads of convenience extras.

Accepting the smaller 161-horsepower base engine might be tempting, to save some money, but the 3.5-liter's extra passing power is a bonus.

CONCORDE 3.5L 6 Cyl
LP41	4-Dr Sedan	19130	21275
Destination Charge:		535	535

Standard Equipment

CONCORDE 3.5L: 3.5 liter 24-valve OHC V6 engine, 4-speed automatic transmission, power-assisted rack and pinion steering, P205/70R15 A/ST BSW tires, power-assisted 4-wheel disc brakes with ABS, power windows with driver override and one-touch open feature, power door locks, touring suspension, AM/FM ETR stereo cassette radio with 6 speakers, manual air conditioning with non-CFC refrigerant, floor console with cup holders/rear heat/AC ducts, covered storage, power decklid release, child protection rear door locks, stainless steel exhaust system with aluminized coating, two-tone fascias with bright insert, front and rear floor mats, three folding grab handles, bright grille, woodgrain instrument panel accents with unique graphics, interior lamps include: two front reading/courtesy, two rear reading/courtesy, four door with automatic dimming and time out; luggage compartment cargo net, warning lamps for: door ajar/trunk ajar/low washer fluid/traction control (when equipped)/ABS; dual illuminated visor mirrors, heated/foldaway/outside dual power mirrors, full bodyside cladding with bright insert, electric rear window defroster, front bucket seats with manual driver lumbar support and seatback map pockets, rear contoured seat with center armrest, premium cloth seat trim, speed control with cancel feature, tilt steering column, dual sun visors with sliding extension and secondary visor, compact spare tire, four "Prototec" wheel covers, speed-sensitive intermittent windshield wipers and washers with fluidic high-volume washer nozzles.

CHRYSLER — CONCORDE

CODE	DESCRIPTION	INVOICE	MSRP

Accessories

Code	Description	Invoice	MSRP
C	**Quick Order Pkg C**	551	630
	incls air conditioning with auto temp control, 8-way power driver's seat, remote/illuminated entry group		
D	**Quick Order Pkg D**	1536	1755
	incls quick order pkg C contents plus interior rearview mirror with automatic day/night feature, Chrysler Infinity spatial imaging cassette sound system, security alarm, speed sensitive variable assist power steering		
EGE	**Engine — 3.5 liter 24-valve OHC V6**	STD	STD
CFK	**Child Seat — integrated**	88	100
CUN	**Full Overhead Console — w/pkg C**	331	378
	incls compass/temp/trip computer, garage door opener and sunglass storage compartment, interior rearview mirror with automatic day/night feature, illuminated dual visor vanity mirrors		
NAE	**California Emissions**	89	102
NBY	**Massachusetts Emissions**	89	102
NHK	**Engine Block Heater**	18	20
GWA	**Power Moonroof — w/pkg C**	957	1094
	w/pkg D	627	716
	incls mini overhead console		
ARA	**Radio — w/pkg C**	620	708
	incls Chrysler Infinity spatial imaging cassette sound system (incls AM/FM electronically tuned stereo radio with seek/scan, cassette player with fast forward, auto reverse and DNR 5-band graphic equalizer, 120-watt 8-channel amplifier, 11 Infinity speakers, instructional tape, rear mounted power antenna)		
ARB	**Radio — w/pkg C**	767	877
	w/pkg D	148	169
	incls Chrysler Infinity spatial imaging compact disc sound system (incls AM/FM electronically tuned stereo radio with seek/scan, integral compact disc player, 5-band graphic equalizer, 120-watt 8-channel amplifier, 11 Infinity speakers, instructional CD, rear mounted power antenna)		
AJF	**Remote/Illuminated Entry Group**	193	221
	incld in pkg C and D		
JPV	**Seat — driver side 8-way power**	330	377
	incld in pkg C and D		
JPR	**Seats — w/o pkg C or D**	660	754
	w/pkg C or D	330	377
	incls driver and passenger 8-way power seats		
LSA	**Security Alarm — w/pkg C**	130	149
	incld in pkg D		
TBB	**Conventional Spare Tire**	83	95
BNM	**Traction Control — w/pkg C or D**	153	175
AGC	**16" Wheel & Handling Group — w/Base model or pkg C**	550	628
	w/pkg D	459	524
	incls P225/60R16 all-season touring BSW SBR tires, 16" aluminum "spiralcast" design wheels, variable assist speed sensitive steering		

EDMUND'S 1995 HIGH-PERFORMANCE AUTOMOBILES

CONCORDE / LHS
CHRYSLER

CODE	DESCRIPTION	INVOICE	MSRP
—	**Seats**	935	1069
	incls driver and passenger 8-way power seats (leather faced front buckets, rear bench), leather steering wheel and shift knob; NA w/pkg B or CFK		
—	**Paint** — extra cost		
—	char gold	85	97
—	orchid	85	97
—	metallic red	85	97
—	spruce	85	97
—	bright platinum metallic	175	200

1995 Chrysler LHS

LHS

Based on the highly successful LH-series sedans (Chrysler Concorde, Dodge Intrepid and Eagle Vision), the LHS offers unique and classy styling that extends its length nearly five inches beyond the Chrysler Concorde, is powered by the same 3.5-liter V-6 found in the LH cars, and is tuned for luxury-sport duty rather than family-hauler chores. However, despite its slightly higher curb weight and luxury aspirations, it doesn't handle much different from your garden-variety Dodge Intrepid.

No matter; it's good enough. The LHS is actually quite a car. First, it looks great. The roofline is classic, with curvaceous rear pillars and a convex backlight. No pseudo-BMW dogleg C-pillar for this car, folks. Second, it offers commendable performance and a long list of standard luxury amenities, for about $16,000 less than a Cadillac Seville STS. Sure, you're missing out on the fabulous Northstar V-8 that powers the Cadillac by opting for the Chrysler, but sixteen thousand can buy a truckload of performance goodies, you know? Besides, the only performance parameter in which the Cadillac bests the LHS is straight-line acceleration. At $30,000, the LHS is a fantastic buy.

Not convinced? Drive one. Then spend your savings on a lavish three-week vacation in Hawaii. Or send your kid to college for a year or two. Or park a speedy Ford Ranger Splash in your driveway for weekend duty.

EDMUND'S 1995 HIGH-PERFORMANCE AUTOMOBILES

CHRYSLER — LHS

Performance and Safety

Acceleration (0-60 mph) .... 8.7 sec.	ABS .... Standard
Braking (60-0 mph) .... 126 ft.	Driver Airbag .... Standard
Cornering .... .79 g's	Passenger Airbag .... Standard
Fuel Capacity .... 18 gal.	Traction Control .... Standard
Fuel Economy .... City: 18 mpg	Crash Test Grade .... D: Good P: Good
	Hwy: 26 mpg	Insurance Cost .... Low

Edmund's Driving Impression

At a glance, an LHS doesn't bring high performance to mind. Stylish lines in abundance, yes. Plush creature comforts, of course. Nevertheless, isn't it little more than a lengthened, roomier edition of the capable-but-commonplace LH trio?

Well, yes and no. In Chrysler's parlance, the "S" in LHS is supposed to stand for sport: that is, for handling and performance. (Customers who crave sheer luxury are invited inside the lower-priced, but poshly-equipped, New Yorker sedan.)

Handling is unquestionably impressive—tight and secure. At least that's true when measured against other sizable family sedans, rather than all-out performance machines. Because an LHS also has to please drivers who demand luxury, however, its road-behavior virtues are somewhat disguised, much of the time. In short, it's promising—and delivering—more than is apparent.

Despite riding a stiffer touring suspension than the New Yorker's, an LHS rides with finesse: blissfully smooth, in fact, yet without a hint of slushiness.

An LHS is definitely quick, courtesy of the 214-hp V-6. Don't look forward to slammed-into-the-seat takeoffs, though. After all, it's the exact same engine that powers the top-end versions of the Concorde, Intrepid, and Vision, each of which weighs a couple of hundred pounds less.

Actual dimensions aren't immense, but the car looks huge—inside and out. Rear passengers get plenty of space, because their seat sits farther rearward than in other LH models. The driver faces clear, white-on-black instruments. To no one's surprise for a vehicle this size, entry and exit are a snap. Visibility and driving position might not suit everyone, and it's not easy to tell where the front and rear ends are for parking.

So long as you don't expect boisterous behavior, on the order of Chevrolet's Impala SS, an LHS is a sensible choice.

LHS V6

CP41	4-Dr Sedan	26646	29595
Destination Charge:		595	595

Standard Equipment

LHS: 3.5 liter SMPI V6 engine, 4-speed automatic transmission, variable-assist power rack and pinion steering, power-assisted 4-wheel disc brakes with ABS, power windows with driver override and one-touch down, power door locks, P225/60R16 A/ST Goodyear Eagle GA tires, four aluminum "Spiralcast" wheels, Chrysler/Infinity Spatial Imaging Cassette Sound System with AM/FM stereo radio, air conditioning with automatic temperature control and non-CFC refrigerant, electronic digital clock, floor console includes: two cup holders/rear heat/AC ducts/covered storage/armrest; mini overhead console includes: compass/thermometer/trip computer/two courtesy/reading lamps; child

LHS CHRYSLER

protection rear door locks, door trim with leather bolsters and map pockets, stainless steel exhaust system with dual chrome outlets and aluminized coating, body color fascias (or two-tone with bright insert), front and rear floor mats, "Projector" style fog lights, solar control glass for windshield/side windows/rear window, three folding grab handles, body color grille, automatic on/off/delay headlights, illuminated entry system, interior lamps include: two front/reading courtesy, two rear reading/courtesy, four door with automatic dimming and time out; remote keyless entry, leather steering wheel and shift knob, luggage compartment cargo net, warning lamps include: door ajar/trunk ajar/low washer fluid/traction control/ABS; dual illuminated visor mirrors, dual power foldaway heated mirrors, automatic day/night rear view mirror, moldings include: bodyside cladding and body color with bright insert, black window opening/belt/windshield moldings, body color rear window molding, body color hood and fender leading edge, power moonroof, power antenna, electric rear window defroster, bucket seats with manual driver lumbar support, contoured rear seat with center armrest, leather seat trim, front seatback map pockets, 8-way power passenger and driver seats with power recliner, premium sound insulation, speed control, tilt steering column, dual sun visors with sliding extension and secondary visor, full trunk dress up, conventional spare tire, low speed traction control, power pull-down trunk lid release, vehicle theft security alarm, speed-sensitive intermittent windshield wipers and washers with high-volume washers, woodgrain accents on instrument panel/doors/center stack.

Accessories

CODE	DESCRIPTION	INVOICE	MSRP
NAE	California Emissions	89	102
NBY	Massachusetts Emissions	89	102
NHK	Engine Block Heater	18	20
GWA	Power Moonroof	693	792
ARB	Radio	148	169
	incls Chrysler Infinity spacial imaging compact disc sound (incls AM/FM electronically tuned stereo radio with seek/scan, integral compact disc player, 5-band graphic equalizer, 120-watt 8- channel amplifier, 11 Infinity speakers, clock, instructional CD, rear mounted power antenna)		
—	**Paint** — extra cost		
—	char-gold	85	97
—	metallic red	85	97
—	spruce	85	97
—	bright platinum metallic	175	200

For expert advice in selecting/buying/leasing a new car, call
1-900-AUTOPRO
($2.00 per minute)

DODGE
INTREPID ES

CODE	DESCRIPTION	INVOICE	MSRP

1995 Dodge Intrepid ES

INTREPID ES (3.5L V6)

Until the Intrepid was introduced in 1992, no domestic manufacturer had posed a threat to the best-selling Ford Taurus in the mid-size family sedan category. While the Taurus remains a strong seller, the Intrepid, with its good looks and commodious cabin, has definitely carved a niche for itself on this crowded and scarred battleground.

The top-of-the-line ES is the Intrepid we're concerned with here. It goes, stops and turns as well as some lighter and seemingly more nimble cars. Inside, the ES has seating for five, a floor-mounted shifter, and sporty black-on-white gauges. Underhood, an optional 214-horsepower 3.5-liter V-6 powers the front wheels with alacrity. Unfortunately, a loaded ES tips the scales at $26,000, but for that kind of money you get leather seats, a CD player, a sunroof and a host of other luxury conveniences.

If interior space is your number-one priority in a sedan, the Intrepid is hard to beat. This segment of the market is saturated with good cars, though, so do some comparision shopping before settling on this big Dodge.

Performance and Safety

Acceleration (0-60 mph) .... 8.1 sec.	ABS .... Optional
Braking (60-0 mph) .... 125 ft.	Driver Airbag .... Standard
Cornering .... .81 g's	Passenger Airbag .... Standard
Fuel Capacity .... 18 gal.	Traction Control .... Optional
Fuel Economy .... City: 18 mpg	Crash Test Grade .... D: Good P: Good
	Hwy: 26 mpg	Insurance Cost .... Average

INTREPID ES — DODGE

| CODE | DESCRIPTION | INVOICE | MSRP |

Edmund's Driving Impression

Entering an Intrepid, the first thing that catches the eye is its dashboard. Black-on-white gauges look odd at first, but help impart a sporty demeanor. At night, they inexplicably turn a colorful green, on a black background—two distinct personalities.

For that matter, the car itself has twin personalities, depending on whether it contains the basic 161-horsepower engine or its robust 24-valve, 214-horsepower big brother. That motor springs to life with an exuberance that belies the Intrepid's family-sedan credentials.

Out on the highway, its vitality becomes even more evident. The step-up engine exhibits plenty of muscle, delivering a marvelous pull, whether from a stoplight or when merging onto the freeway. Intrepid feels clearly quicker than a Concorde, with just a hint of engine noise. With the 3.5-liter engine, an Intrepid becomes a super road car—but one that can also grow at least a little acrobatic when such antics are called for.

An ES exhibits an extremely solid, heavy feel (in the best sense of the word). The ride seems more secure, yet less harsh, than in other LH sedans. Even after hitting a hard bump, it recovers immediately.

Steering is on the light side, but the wheel receives welcome feedback from the road, and has a lovely grip. Turning the wheel also demands a bit of effort, in the sporting sense. Expect some body lean on tight curves, but sizable tires maintain their grip.

Spacious the interior is, but lower-than-normal seatbacks don't feel quite right for some drivers and passengers. Seats are quite firm, with short bottoms, for less-than-perfect support on long drives.

Except for "touring" tires, the ES suspension isn't much different from that of base-model Intrepids. Enthusiasts can select a performance suspension option for the ES, with even-heavier rubber. Try it, but watch for added roughness in the ride—a common penalty when upgrading chassis components for tighter handling.

INTREPID ES 3.5L V6

Code	Description	Invoice	MSRP
DP41	ES 4-Dr Sedan	19373	21569
	Destination Charge:	535	535

Standard Equipment

INTREPID ES: Power-assisted 4-wheel disc brakes w/ABS, 3.5 liter 24-valve OHC V6 engine, 16" x 7" JJ steel polycast wheels, P225/60R16 A/ST BSW tires, speed-proportional power steering, power door locks, touring tires, "Extender" aluminum wheels, unique two-tone or body color fascias, fog lights, front and rear floor mats, four door courtesy lamps, luggage compartment cargo net, message center warning lamps include: door ajar/trunk ajar/low washer fluid/traction control (when equipped)/ABS (when equipped), ground effect bodyside cladding, premium style and fabric front seats with manual lumbar adjustment and upgraded door trim, rear contoured bench seat with center armrest, speed control with cancel feature, power trunk lid release, 4-speed automatic transmission, power windows with driver override and one-touch open feature, touring suspension, AM/FM ETR stereo radio with seek, cassette player and 6 speakers; manual air conditioning with non-CFC refrigerant, electronic digital clock (included with radio), floor console includes cup holders, rear seat heater/AC ducts, covered storage and armrest, child protection rear door locks, stainless steel exhaust system with aluminized coating, tinted side windows, windshield/rear window solar control glass, two front reading/courtesy lamps, two rear courtesy lamps with automatic dimming and time out, dual exterior heated power mirrors, dual covered visor mirrors, functional bodyside protection moldings, electric rear window defroster, tilt steering column, compact spare tire, speed-sensitive intermittent windshield wipers and washers with high-volume fluidic washer nozzles.

DODGE
INTREPID ES

CODE	DESCRIPTION	INVOICE	MSRP

Accessories

K	**Pkg K**	NC	NC

incls model with standard equipment

L	**Pkg L**	606	693

incls 8-way power driver's seat, illuminated dual visor vanity mirrors, passenger assist handles (3), remote/illuminated entry group, leather-wrapped steering wheel

M	**Pkg M**	1824	2085

incls 8-way power driver's seat, remote/illuminated entry group, leather-wrapped steering wheel, air conditioning with auto temp control, full overhead console, radio (Chrysler Infinity spatial imaging cassette sound system), security alarm, conventional spare tire, traction control

HAB	**Air Conditioning w/Auto Temp Control** — w/pkg L	133	152
CUN	**Full Overhead Console** — w/pkg L	331	378

incls compass/temp/traveler display, interior rearview mirror with automatic day/night feature, front and rear reading lamps, garage door opener and sunglass storage compartment, dual illuminated visor vanity mirrors with secondary visors and sliding extensions, passenger assist handles (3), rear coat hooks

CFK	**Child Seat** — integrated	88	100
NAE	**California Emissions**	89	102
NBY	**Massachusetts Emissions**	89	102
NHK	**Engine Block Heater**	18	20
GWA	**Power Moonroof** — w/pkg L	957	1094
	w/pkg M	627	716

incls mini overhead console (incls compass/temp/traveler displays, interior rearview mirror with automatic day/night feature, front and rear reading lamps, dual illuminated visor vanity mirrors with secondary visors and sliding extensions, passenger assist handles, rear coat hooks)

TBB	**Conventional Spare Tire**	83	95
JPR	**Seat** — driver and passenger 8-way power - w/pkg L or M	330	377
BNM	**Traction Control** — w/pkg K or L	153	175
LSA	**Security Alarm** — w/pkg L	130	149
AWT	**Performance Handling Group** — w/pkg L or M	190	217

incls P225/60R16 all-season performance BSW SBR tires, performance suspension

ARA	**Radio** — w/pkg L	620	708

incls Chrysler Infinity spatial imaging cassette sound system (incls electronically tuned stereo radio with seek/scan, cassette player with fast forward/rewind and auto reverse, 5-band graphic equalizer, 120-watt 8-channel amplifier, 11 Infinity speakers, clock, instructional tape, rear mounted power antenna)

ARB	**Radio** — w/pkg L	767	877
	w/pkg M	148	169

incls Chrysler Infinity spatial imaging compact disc sound system (incls AM/FM electronically tuned stereo radio with seek/scan, integral compact disc player, 5 band graphic equalizer, 120-watt 8-channel amplifier, 11 Infinity speakers, clock, instructional CD, rear mounted power antenna)

EGE	**Engine** — 3.5 liter 24-valve OHC V6	STD	STD

INTREPID ES / NEON — DODGE

CODE	DESCRIPTION	INVOICE	MSRP
—	**Seats**	STD	STD
	incls cloth front buckets, rear bench w/center armrest		
—	**Seats**	883	1009
	incls leather faced front buckets, rear bench w/center armrest (incls driver and passenger 8-way power seats and leather shifter knob); req's pkg L or M		
—	**Paint** — special color or metallic		
	char gold	85	97
	orchid	85	97
	metallic red	85	97
	spruce	85	97
	bright platinum metallic	175	200

1995 Dodge Neon Highline

NEON

Unless you live in an igloo in the northernmost reaches of Alaska, you've heard about or seen the Neon. Hi, say the ads. Hi, say the jaunty ovoid headlights as they approach in the rearview mirror. Bye, says the raspy exhaust note as the 132-hp sedanlet blows the doors off your jalopy in the stoplight drag race.

The Neon has the compact carmakers trembling. The Escort LX is flat outdated next to this Dodge. The new Tercel is forty horsepower and a personality off the mark. Nissan's new Sentra is expected to be much pricier and not nearly as attractive when it hits showrooms in January. This car's closest competitor in performance, price and features is the stodgy-looking Mercury Tracer LTS, a car sold in such small quantities that you probably don't even know what it is.

The Neon is a solid little sedan, and is joined by a coupe variant for 1995. Also new this year is an optional twin-cam four-cylinder motor good for 150 horsepower, which promises to make other compacts even less competitive. When the new motor comes on line, there really won't be any point in shopping around. Just drop in to any Dodge dealer and drive off in one of the best cars in the small car class.

DODGE   NEON

Performance and Safety

Acceleration (0-60 mph) .... 8.4 sec.	ABS .... Optional
Braking (60-0 mph) .... 135 ft.	Driver Airbag .... Standard
Cornering .... .82 g's	Passenger Airbag .... Standard
Fuel Capacity .... 11.2 gal.	Traction Control .... N/A
Fuel Economy .... City: 27 mpg	Crash Test Grade .... D: Average P: Average
Hwy: 33 mpg	Insurance Cost .... N/A

Edmund's Driving Impression

Maybe the hype gave us some lofty expectations. Maybe the media has been brainwashed. We weren't thrilled with Chrysler's latest star. On paper, the Neon looks unbeatable. In reality, it feels cheap, like it will break if pushed too hard, and that doesn't do much for instilling pride of ownership. True, the powertrain does a marvelous job of getting the Neon down the road in a hurry and the steering is communicative, sharp and direct, but the execution of the rest of the car underwhelms. Chrysler needs to tear down a Toyota Corolla and learn about *feel*.

Moreover, the back seat is very hard to squeeze into. Despite cab-forward styling, the swoopy roofline and rear wheelwell are far too intrusive. Once in, the back seat is relatively comfortable, but head, leg, and foot room are rather tight.

Up front, the seats are mushy, and covered in a low-rent fabric. And what's with the jutting dash? It's huge, putting a lot of acreage between the driver and the base of the windshield. It also encroaches on passenger space, and is constructed of hard, grained plastic. I guess Chrysler figures that with dual airbags, a soft dash isn't necessary. It sure would look nice, though.

Perhaps our largest gripe was with throttle response. It's abrupt and makes smooth clutch modulation difficult. Evidently, Chrysler feels that a touchy accelerator imparts the illusion that the car is more powerful than it actually is. Hey, the Neon is powerful. No need to fake it.

Still, very few manufacturers can touch the Neon in the affordability, performance, or styling departments. Japanese competitors are combating the negative effects of an appreciating yen, and most domestic models are far underpowered compared to the sprightly Neon. There are two models which compete with the Neon dollar-for-dollar and boast smoother, more zingy drivetrains: the Mercury Tracer LTS and the Ford Escort GT. While their styling may not be quite as daring, and the performance may not be quite as strong, they both come across as more refined, substantial and therefore fun-to-drive cars than the Neon.

NEON 4 Cyl

PL42	Base 4-Dr Sedan		8815	9500
PH22	Highline 2-Dr Coupe		10416	11240
PH42	Highline 4-Dr Sedan		10416	11240
PS22	Sport 2-Dr Coupe		12285	13567
PS42	Sport 4-Dr Sedan		12015	13267
Destination Charge:			500	500

NEON — DODGE

Standard Equipment

NEON - BASE: 85 amp alternator, 450 amp maintenance-free battery, 13" power front disc/rear drum brakes, 5-mph front and rear bumpers, child protection rear door locks, warning chimes (for key in ignition, headlights on, seat belts), console, 2.0 liter SOHC 16V SMPI 4 cylinder engine, stainless steel exhaust system, single halogen aero-style headlights, cloth covered headliner, mirrors (left exterior manual remote, black), rearview mirror with day/night feature, passenger side visor vanity mirror, driver and front passenger air bags, seats (cloth with vinyl trim, front high back buckets, rear fixed bench), manual steering, sun visors with driver side sunshade extension panel, ride tuned suspension, P165/80R13 all-season BSW SBR tires, T115/70D14 compact spare tire, 5-speed manual transaxle, carpet floor mat trunk dress-up, 13" steel painted bright silver wheels with black center cap, 2-speed windshield wipers.

HIGHLINE (in addition to or instead of BASE equipment): Front and rear body color fascias, tinted glass, mirrors (dual exterior manual remote, black), dual visor vanity mirrors (driver side covered), body color bodyside moldings, AM/FM stereo radio with clock and 4 speakers, seats (cloth with vinyl trim, front low back buckets, rear 60/40 split folding bench), premium sound insulation, 18:1 ratio power assisted steering, touring tuned suspension, P185/70R13 all-season BSW SBR tires, trunk dress-up (incls molded carpet for wheel houses, spare tire well, carpet covered spare), 13" steel wheels painted black with bright silver wheel covers, 2-speed windshield wipers with variable intermittent feature.

SPORT (in addition to or instead of HIGHLINE equipment): 14" power 4-wheel disc brakes with anti-lock, remote decklid release, rear window defroster, power door locks, 2.0 liter DOHC 16V SMPI 4 cylinder engine (Coupe), front and rear body color fascias with accent color rub strip, fog lights, "power bulge" hood design (Coupe), mirrors (dual exterior power remote, black), accent color bodyside moldings, passenger assist handles, rear decklid spoiler (Coupe), 16:1 ratio power assisted steering (Coupe), tilt steering column, performance tuned suspension (Coupe), P185/65R14 all-season touring BSW SBR tires (Sedan), P185/65R14 all-season performance BSW SBR tires (Coupe), T115/70R14 compact spare tire, 14" cast aluminum painted sparkle silver wheels (painted white with white exterior).

Accessories

	Quick Order Pkgs — prices include pkg discounts	INVOICE	MSRP
A	**Pkg A** — Base Sedan	NC	NC
	incls model with standard equipment		
B	**Pkg B** — Base Sedan	1712	1861
	incls air conditioning, rear window defroster, manual remote dual exterior mirrors, bodyside moldings, radio (AM/FM stereo with clock and 4 speakers), power steering, tinted glass, touring tuned suspension, intermittent windshield wipers		
C	**Pkg C** — Highline	NC	NC
	incls model with standard equipment		
D	**Pkg D** — Highline Coupe/Sedan	626	703
	incls air conditioning, floor-mounted console with armrest and storage bin, remote decklid release, rear window defroster		
F	**Pkg F** — Highline Coupe	1184	1330
	Highline Sedan	1220	1371
	incls pkg D contents plus 14" front disc/rear drum brakes, power door locks, front and rear floor mats, light group, power remote dual exterior mirrors, tilt steering wheel, tachometer and low fuel light, P185/65R14 all-season touring BSW SBR tires, 14" wheel covers		

EDMUND'S 1995 HIGH-PERFORMANCE AUTOMOBILES

DODGE — NEON

CODE	DESCRIPTION	INVOICE	MSRP
J	**Pkg J** — Sport	NC	NC
	incls model with standard equipment		
K	**Pkg K** — Sport Coupe/Sedan	557	626
	incls air conditioning, front and rear floor mats, light group, radio (AM/FM stereo with cassette, clock and 6 speakers)		
23C	**Pkg 23C "Competition"** — Highline Coupe	911	990
	incls 14" power assisted 4-wheel disc brakes, unlimited speed engine controller, front and rear body color fascias with metallic accent, bodyside moldings, heavy duty radiator, radio delete, 16:1 ratio power steering, competition suspension, tachometer with low fuel light, P185/60HR14 all-season touring BSW SBR tires, 14" bright silver cast aluminum wheels (white when ordered with white exterior)		
23D	**Pkg 23D** — Highline Coupe	1536	1693
	incls pkg 23C "Competition" contents plus air conditioning, floor-mounted console with armrest and storage bin, rear window defroster, remote decklid release		
25A	**Pkg 25A "Competition"** — Base Sedan	1449	1575
	incls 14" power assisted 4-wheel disc brakes, unlimited speed engine controller, front and rear body color fascias with metallic accent, painted body color grille bar, tinted glass, dual exterior manual remote mirrors, heavy duty radiator, 16:1 ratio power steering, competition suspension, tachometer with low fuel light, T115/70R14 compact spare tire, P175/65HR14 all-season performance BSW SBR tires, 14" bright silver cast aluminum wheels (white when ordered with white exterior)		
25B	**Pkg 25B** — Base Sedan	2687	2981
	incls pkg 25A "Competition" contents plus air conditioning, rear window defroster, dual exterior manual remote mirrors, intermittent wipers		
ECB	**Engine** — 2.0 liter SOHC 16V SMPI		
	Base Sedan	STD	STD
	Highline	STD	STD
	Sport Coupe	STD	STD
	Sport Sedan	(89)	(100)
ECC	**Engine** — 2.0 liter DOHC 16V SMPI		
	Sport Sedan	STD	STD
	Highline Coupe w/pkg 23C or 23D	138	150
DD4/DD5	**Transmission** — 5-speed manual	STD	STD
DGA	**Transmission** — 3-speed automatic	496	557
4XA	**Air Conditioning Bypass** — Base w/pkg A or 25A	NC	NC
BRH	**Anti-Lock Brakes** — 13" - Base w/pkg A or B	503	565
	Highline w/pkg C or D	503	565
	NA w/AY7 on Highline models		
BRJ	**Anti-Lock Brakes** — 14" - Highline w/pkg D or F	503	565
	req's AY7		
CFK	**Child Seat** — integrated	89	100
AJP	**Power Convenience Group** — Highline Coupe w/pkg D	228	256
	Highline Sedan w/pkg D	264	297
	incls dual exterior power remote mirrors, power door locks; incld in pkg F		

NEON

CODE	DESCRIPTION	INVOICE	MSRP
GFA	**Rear Window Defroster** — req'd in New York State		
	Base Sedan w/pkg A or 25A	154	173
	incld in pkg B or 25B		
	Highline w/pkg C or 23C	154	173
	incld in pkg D, F or 23D		
NAE	**California Emissions**	91	102
NBY	**Massachusetts Emissions**	91	102
CLE	**Floor Mats** — front and rear - Base Sedan, Highline, Sport	41	46
	incld in pkg F and K		
MWG	**Luggage Rack** — roof-mounted	89	100
GTE	**Mirrors** — dual exterior, manual remote — Base Sedan w/pkg A	62	70
	incld in pkg B and 25B		
K37	**Bodyside Moldings** — Base Sedan w/pkg A	27	30
	incld in pkg B		
RAL	**Radio** — AM/FM stereo w/clock and 4 speakers - Base Sedan	297	334
	incld in pkg B		
RAS	**Radio** — AM/FM stereo w/cassette, clock and 6 premium speakers -		
	Base Sedan w/pkg B	223	250
	Highline	223	250
	Sport w/pkg J	223	250
	incld in pkg K		
RBG	**Radio** — AM/FM stereo w/CD player, clock and 6 premium speakers -		
	Base Sedan w/pkg B	434	488
	Highline	434	488
	Sport w/pkg J	434	488
	Sport w/pkg K	212	238
SUA	**Tilt Steering Column** — Base Sedan w/pkg B	132	148
	Sport w/pkg C or D	132	148
	incld in pkg F		
NHM	**Speed Control** — Highline w/pkg D or F	199	224
	Sport w/pkg K	199	224
JHA	**Intermittent Windshield Wipers** — Base Sedan w/pkg A	59	66
	incld in pkg B and 25B		
JFH	**Tachometer & Low Fuel Warning Light** — Highline w/pkg D	83	93
	incld in pkg F		
AY7	**14" Wheel Dress-Up** — Highline w/pkg D	71	80
	incls 14" front disc/rear drum brakes, P185/65R14 all-season touring BSW SBR tires, 14" black wheels, 14" silver wheel covers (white w/quartz center when ordered w/white exterior); incld in pkg F		
—	**Paint** — extra cost	86	97

EDMUND'S 1995 HIGH-PERFORMANCE AUTOMOBILES

DODGE RAM PICKUP

*1995 Dodge Ram Pickup ***

RAM SPORT PICKUP (5.9L V8)

Sport trucks are hot these days, there's no doubt. Dodge joined the fray of performance pickups last year with the Ram Sport, a monochromatic rendition of the successful new Ram. Actually, the Sport is an optional appearance package that can be added to any black or red Ram pickup with the 5.2-liter or 5.9-liter V-8 engine. The package includes chrome wheels mounted on wider, lower profile tires, fog lights, a tachometer, and the aforementioned monochrome trim.

Like many Chrysler products of late, the Ram has become the best of its kind, the yardstick by which all others in its class are measured. Naturally, the Sport variant piques our curiosity, especially since it posts some pretty impressive performance figures.

However, all is not roses. The Ram Sport is actually more bark than bite. Compared to comparably equipped Ford and Chevy trucks, the Ram is smaller, weighs more, gets worse fuel economy and takes longer to get stopped from 60 mph. Where the Ram shines is with its big-rig styling and unsurpassed driving environment. As the most recently designed full-size pickup on the market, the Dodge sweats details that Chevy overlooked in the mid-1980s and Ford flat didn't realize in the late '70s.

Basically, there is much to like in the Ram Sport, but nothing, aside from the unconventional styling, really sets it apart from the Ford or the Chevy enough to recommend it over either of its competitors. What it comes down to is personal taste, and we like the Ram Sport.

* photo of Ram Sport not available at press time.

RAM PICKUP

Performance and Safety

Acceleration (0-60 mph) .... 8.5 sec.	ABS .... Standard
Braking (60-0 mph) .... 149 ft.	Driver Airbag .... Standard
Cornering .... N/A	Passenger Airbag .... N/A
Fuel Capacity .... 26 gal.	Traction Control .... N/A
Fuel Economy .... City: 12 mpg	Crash Test Grade .... D: Excellent P: N/A
Hwy: 16 mpg	Insurance Cost .... Average

Edmund's Driving Impression

Pickup trucks don't ordinarily turn heads. In the case of the current Ram, that's been its blessing—or its curse—since Day One. This is one tough-looking cargo hauler, whether decked out in color-keyed Sport trim or wearing standard-issue chrome plating on its chest-pounding grille.

Not that Rams lack substance to match their macho style. Far from it, but their roadgoing personality depends on what's under the hood. Rams come with a choice of five engines, ranging from a 3.9-liter V-6 to an 8-liter V-10 that blasts out a locomotive-like 450 pounds-feet of torque.

For most buyers (and anyone who desires the Sport package) the 5.2- and 5.9-liter V-8s promise the best mix of economy and performance—even if a Ram doesn't exactly best the competition in either area. Automatic-transmission shifts are firm, but not really harsh. Downshifts arrive promptly for passing and merging—better than in a lot of sedans, with only modest hesitation. The column-mounted gearshift operates easily.

Surprisingly agile for such a large and bulky vehicle, the Ram is also reasonably sure-footed, so long as you don't push too hard. Think twice before making any quick maneuvers.

Tromping the gas from a dead stop produces a lot of roar, but it's the reverberation of vitality. Otherwise, the truck runs reasonably quietly. Ride and handling are so competent that it's possible to forget you're in a full-size pickup, though occupants can expect to perceive plenty of bumps. Visibility is great, the cab spacious, controls excellent.

One problem at the dealership: the choices are bewildering. First, the five engines; then, a selection of regular or club (extended) cab style, of Sport or other trim package, of cargo bed length, of two- or four-wheel drive. Finally, there's the long option list to contend with. Fortunately, the end result is worth the effort.

RAM SPORT 5.9L 2WD PICKUP V8

—	2WD Ram Sport 5.9L (auto)	14223	16197
	(req's ST pkg or Laramie SLT pkg at additional cost)		
Destination Charge:		600	600

Standard Equipment

RAM SPORT 5.9L: 5.9 liter MFI V8 engine, 4-speed automatic transmission, sport package (incls color-keyed grille, color-keyed front bumper, color-keyed taillight bezels, tachometer, sport decal [bodyside rear quarter box], color-keyed dual front bumper sight shields, fog lights, chrome wheels, P225/75R16XL SBR all-season BW tires [incld on models w/ST pkg], P245/75R16 all-season BW tires [incld on models w/Laramie SLT pkg]), electronic ignition system, 600-amp maintenance-free battery, 75-amp alternator, 6.5' pickup box (incls dual wall construction, one-piece high strength steel floor, 2-tier loading capability, bulkhead dividing provision, tie-down loops), heavy duty front/rear gas charged shock absorbers, front stabilizer bar, conventional spare tire with underslung winch spare

DODGE
RAM PICKUP

| CODE | DESCRIPTION | INVOICE | MSRP |

tire carrier, 16" x 7" wheels, power steering, driver side air bag, power front disc/rear drum brakes with rear wheel anti-lock, 26 gallon fuel tank, stainless steel exhaust system, bottle-type axle jack, halogen headlamps, dual 6" x 9" exterior mirrors, tinted glass, vented quarter windows, deluxe 2-speed intermittent windshield wipers, gauges (voltmeter, trip odometer, oil pressure/engine temp), inside hood release, AM/FM ETR stereo radio with two front door speakers, digital clock, day/night rearview mirror, dual color-keyed sun visors, side-guard door beams, single note horn.

Accessories

Code	Description	Invoice	MSRP
21C	**ST Pkg**	428	504
	incls dome and cargo lights, bright front/rear bumper, wheel dress-up with bright trim rings and hub centers, tailgate top protection molding, deluxe cloth upholstery, floor carpeting, 40/20/40 split bench seat storage (behind seat)		
—	**Laramie SLT Pkg**	2078	2445
	incls storage (behind seat), power convenience group (power windows/door locks), tachometer, AM/FM ETR stereo radio with cassette and 4 speakers, air conditioning, light group, premium cloth upholstery, leather-wrapped steering wheel, deluxe convenience group, 40/20/40 split bench seat, bright front/rear bumpers, chrome wheels, bodyside moldings, tailgate top protection molding, bodyside accent stripe, dual front bumper sight shields, floor carpeting, (5) P245/75R16 SBR all-season BW tires, premium decor group (incls door map pockets, 40/20/40 split bench seat, covered right visor vanity mirror, bright front bumper with step pad, black sport leather-wrapped steering wheel, front floor mats, black bodyside moldings, underhood insulation, full floor carpeting, premium cloth upholstery, dual horns, black tailgate, panel applique, bodyside tape stripes, door trim panels with cloth inserts and lower carpeting)		
BGK	**Anti-Lock Brakes**	425	500
NAE	**California Emissions**	87	102
—	**Radio Equipment**		
RAS	radio - w/ST pkg	179	210
	incls AM/FM ETR stereo with cassette, 4 speakers and digital clock		
RAY	radio - w/Laramie SLT pkg	281	331
	incls AM/FM ETR stereo with cassette, graphic equalizer, 6 Infinity speakers and digital clock		
RBC	radio - w/Laramie SLT pkg	434	510
	incls AM/FM ETR stereo with compact disc, graphic equalizer, 6 Infinity speakers and digital clock		
RA8	radio - AM/FM delete	(104)	(122)
	NA w/Laramie SLT pkg		
RCD	radio - 4-speaker system	43	50
RCE	radio - 6-speaker system - w/Laramie SLT pkg	172	202
	incls 6 Infinity speakers		
NHK	**Engine Block Heater**	29	34
HAA	**Air Conditioning** — w/ST pkg	677	797
K17	**Lower Bodyside Moldings** — w/ST pkg	87	102
DSA	**Sure Grip Axle**	218	257
DM	**Rear Axle** — optional ratio	33	39

RAM PICKUP — DODGE

CODE	DESCRIPTION	INVOICE	MSRP
AJK	**Deluxe Convenience Group**	332	390
	incls tilt steering column and cruise control		
AHC	**Trailer Towing Prep Group**	206	242
	incls heavy duty flashers, wiring harness with covered pin connector mounted on hitch, class IV platform hitch receiver; req's ADJ heavy duty service group and rear bumper		
ADJ	**Heavy Duty Service Group**	290	341
	incls heavy duty 750 amp battery, heavy duty 120 amp alternator, maximum engine cooling; auxiliary transmission oil cooler (incld on models w/DGB 4-speed auto trans)		
AWK	**Travel Convenience Group**	196	231
	incls full deluxe headliner, overhead console with compass, automatic dimming day/night rearview mirror, outside temperature display, reading lights, dual bright power mirrors; req's Laramie SLT pkg		
GFD	**Sliding Rear Window**	114	134
JPS	**Seat — 6-way power driver - w/Laramie SLT pkg**	252	296
T9	**Seats —** deluxe cloth 40/20/40 split bench - w/ST pkg	NC	NC
LNC	**Cab Clearance Lights**	44	52
—	**Paint**		
6D	two-tone lower break	112	132
	incls lower bodyside moldings		
6C	two-tone center band - w/ST pkg	207	243
	w/Laramie SLT pkg	155	182
	incls upper bodyside and rear tape stripes, lower bodyside moldings, secondary mid-section color, main upper and lower body color		
P	monotone, extra cost	65	77
—	**Tires**		
TYF	P245/75R16C SBR all-season BW (5) - w/ST pkg	111	130
TYG	P245/75R16C SBR all-season OWL (5) - w/Laramie SLT pkg	107	126
CKQ	Floor Carpeting Delete — w/ST or Laramie SLT pkg	NC	NC
—	**Mirrors**		
GPP	dual bright power 6" x 9"	84	99
GPC	dual bright manual 7" x 10"	41	48

USE A MULTIMEDIA CD-ROM TO RESEARCH YOUR NEXT AUTOMOBILE PURCHASE

see ad on page 384 for details

DODGE STEALTH

1995 Dodge Stealth R/T Turbo

STEALTH RT/RT TURBO

Before the Viper, there was the Stealth. Commissioned from Mitsubishi in 1991, the Stealth was the first hint of what kinds of products Chrysler Corporation would be producing in the near future. When it was introduced, the public went ga-ga over the extravagant styling, scooped and sculpted interior, and the top-of-the-line turbocharged, all-wheel drive powertrain. Now, well, folks ain't quite as impressed.

Pricing was a problem with the Stealth. Sports car buyers weren't ready to spend more for a Dodge-badged Japanese sports car than they would for a Chevrolet Corvette or Nissan 300ZX. Base models of the Stealth weren't perceived to be worth their $20,000 price tag either, not with turbocharged, all-wheel drive Diamond Star coupes coming in at that price.

Then the Viper appeared, totally eclipsing the Stealth from public view. The result is a relatively exclusive and competent rocket. Stealths still turn heads, and they handle inclement climes better than just about any other sports car on the market. Changes for 1995 are minimal, including a switch to 18-inch tires and optional chrome wheels.

We recommend the Stealth for buyers in the snow belt states, even though the advent of traction control has made cars like the Corvette much easier to handle in the flakes. The Stealth is a good car, delivering performance, racy looks and a wide range of standard and optional equipment. It competes in a narrow and highly competitive niche, however, and the competition is darn good.

STEALTH — DODGE

Performance and Safety

Stealth R/T

Acceleration (0-60 mph) .... 8.5 sec.	ABS .... Optional
Braking (60-0 mph) .... 117 ft.	Driver Airbag .... Standard
Cornering .... .89 g's	Passenger Airbag .... Standard
Fuel Capacity .... 19.8 gal.	Traction Control .... N/A
Fuel Economy .... City: 18 mpg	Crash Test Grade .... D: Excellent P: N/A
Hwy: 23 mpg	Insurance Cost .... High

Stealth R/T Turbo

Acceleration (0-60 mph) .... 5.7 sec.	ABS .... Standard
Braking (60-0 mph) .... 120 ft.	Driver Airbag .... Standard
Cornering .... .90 g's	Passenger Airbag .... Standard
Fuel Capacity .... 19.8 gal.	Traction Control .... N/A
Fuel Economy .... City: 18 mpg	Crash Test Grade .... D: Excellent P: N/A
Hwy: 24 mpg	Insurance Cost .... High

STEALTH RT/RT TURBO V6

Code	Description	Invoice	MSRP
DS24	R/T 2-Dr Hatchback	24195	26795
DX24	R/T Turbo AWD 2-Dr Hatchback	33971	37905
	Destination Charge:	430	430

Standard Equipment

STEALTH - RT: 3.0 liter DOHC SMPI V6 engine, 5-speed manual transmission, variable power-assisted rack and pinion steering, power-assisted 4-wheel disc brakes, ultimate sound AM/FM stereo cassette radio with 6 speakers, 6 AM/FM presets, seek/scan, auto reverse, 7-band graphic equalizer and CD jack; 5-mph bumpers, center high mounted stop light (LED - mounted in spoiler), electronic digital clock (included with radio), electric rear defroster, stainless steel exhaust system, body color roof, rear body color spoiler, remote fuel door release, two stage opening glove compartment with lock, aero-style projector halogen headlights with automatic off, two assist handles, retractable cargo cover, storage box with cup holder and padded armrest, cloth door trim inserts, molded pillar garnish moldings, lamps include: dome with delay timer, map, door courtesy, cargo area lamp, foot well, glove box, underhood, ignition key and cigar lighter; remote liftgate release, exterior dual folding power mirrors, visor mirrors, front low back bucket seats with recliners, manual driver's lumbar and height adjustment, split back folding rear seats, full cloth front seat trim, cloth and vinyl rear seat trim, tilt steering column, leather-wrapped steering wheel, 2-speed intermittent windshield wipers and washers, 16" x 8" JJ polycast wheels, P225/55VR15 BSW tires, four aluminum "Sport" wheels with center cap, dual tailpipes with chrome tips, bodyside cladding, R/T style body color front and rear fascias, R/T style black front air dam, body color moldings (A-pillar, roof drip, C-pillar [flying]), projector fog lights, floor mats, electronic speed control with steering wheel mounted switches, "top-sided" taillights with small applique, rear wipers and washers.

DODGE

STEALTH

CODE	DESCRIPTION	INVOICE	MSRP

RT TURBO (in addition to or instead of RT equipment): 3.0 liter DOHC SMPI turbo V6 engine, 6-speed manual transmission with AWD, 17" x 8.5" JJ cast aluminum wheels, P245/45ZR17 BSW tires, power windows with illuminated driver's switches, power door locks with illuminated driver's switches, four aluminum "ultimate" wheels with center cap, manual control air conditioning, gloss black roof, additional electrical accessory outlet, remote keyless entry system (radio-wave type), exterior dual folding power heated mirrors, illuminated visor mirrors, visual and audible security alarm system (door/hatch/hood sensors).

Accessories

CODE	DESCRIPTION	INVOICE	MSRP
G	**Pkg G — R/T**	NC	NC
	incls model with standard equipment		
H	**Pkg H — R/T**	457	531
	incls power door locks, keyless entry, power windows		
M	**Pkg M — R/T**	2059	2394
	incls pkg H contents plus trunk mounted compact disc changer, radio (AM/FM stereo w/cassette, graphic equalizer, clock and 8 Infinity speakers), security group (incls anti-lock brakes and security alarm)		
V	**Pkg V — R/T Turbo AWD**	NC	NC
	incls model with standard equipment		
W	**Pkg W — R/T Turbo AWD**	1501	1746
	incls radio (AM/FM stereo w/cassette, graphic equalizer, clock and 8 Infinity speakers), trunk mounted compact disc changer, leather-faced seating surfaces with vinyl trim		
Y	**Pkg Y — R/T Turbo AWD**	2596	3019
	incls pkg W contents plus sunroof, 18" wheel group (incls 245/40ZR18 BSW SBR tires, 18" chrome cast aluminum wheels, chrome plated lug nuts		
DGB	**Transmission — 4-speed automatic**	759	883
	NA on R/T Turbo AWD		
BRG	**Anti-Lock Brakes — R/T w/pkg G or H**	687	799
REM	**Compact Disc Changer — R/T w/pkg G or H**	466	542
	R/T Turbo AWD w/pkg V or W	466	542
NAE	**California Emissions**	NC	NC
NBY	**Massachusetts Emissions**	NC	NC
GWB	**Sunroof — R/T w/pkg H or M**	310	361
	R/T Turbo AWD w/pkg V or W	310	361
AEC	**18" Wheel Group — R/T Turbo AWD w/pkg V or W**	784	912
	incls 245/40ZR18 BSW SBR tires, 18" chromed cast aluminum wheels, chrome plated lug nuts		
—	**Seats — R/T**	725	843
	R/T Turbo AWD	725	843
	incls leather front buckets, rear split folding bench		
—	**Paint — special color or metallic**	176	205

VIPER   **DODGE**
CODE   DESCRIPTION   INVOICE   MSRP

1995 Dodge Viper RT/10

VIPER R/T 10

The Viper has been the biggest automotive news since the original Mustang, and while its sales totals have been nowhere near those of the legendary ponycar, it has just as many devotees drooling over full-color pictures of its cartoonish structure like winos at a peepshow.

Designed to be the modern incarnation of the Cobra 427, Viper debuted at the North American International Auto Show in Detroit in January of 1989 as a show car. Enough people wrote to Chrysler requesting street versions that plans for production of the rakish roadster were set into motion soon after. Viper was introduced for public sale in 1992, and became the darling of the automotive press, not to mention high-profile stars like Jay Leno. It even got a TV show; a dismal one that lasted one season.

A preview of things to come from Chrysler, the success of the Viper revitalized a company that many thought wouldn't last through the middle of this decade. Originally, the car was available only in red, but since 1992 black, green and yellow have been added as color choices. Also in the Viper pipeline: a radical coupe version, to be called GTS, and due in 1996.

Performance and Safety

Acceleration (0-60 mph) .... 4.5 sec.	ABS .... N/A
Braking (60-0 mph) .... 129 ft.	Driver Airbag .... N/A
Cornering .... .97 g's	Passenger Airbag .... N/A
Fuel Capacity .... 22 gal.	Traction Control .... N/A
Fuel Economy .... City: 12 mpg	Crash Test Grade .... D: N/A P: N/A
Hwy: 21 mpg	Insurance Cost .... Average

EDMUND'S 1995 HIGH-PERFORMANCE AUTOMOBILES

DODGE VIPER

CODE	DESCRIPTION	INVOICE	MSRP
VIPER 10 CYL			
DS27	2-Dr 2-Seat Open Sports Car	48725	56000
Destination Charge:		700	700
Gas Guzzler Tax:		2100	2100

Standard Equipment

VIPER: 8.0 liter SMPI V10 engine, 6-speed manual transmission, power-assisted 4-wheel disc brakes, front tires (P275/40 ZR17), rear tires (P335/35 ZR17), power-assisted rack and pinion steering, AM/FM stereo ETR Chrysler/Alpine radio includes: seek and scan/130 watt dual power amplifiers and digital time/frequency/function display/six speakers (compact disc compatible); soft fascia bumpers with high density foam energy 5-mph absorbers, Euro-look short pile carpeting, chimes for door/key/seat belt/headlamps, center horizontal color-keyed console includes: shifter/park brake lever/ash tray/fog lamp switch, 10-year anti-corrosion protection, limited slip differential (clutch-type), fog lights with covers, manual fuel filler door, tinted windshield glass, aero-polyellipsoid headlights (low beam), halogen headlights (high beam), dual latch hood release with single release located in grille opening, dual horn, instrument cluster includes: analog speedometer/tachometer/gauges for oil pressure/voltage/coolant temperature/fuel level/air outlets/glove box, map/reading lamps (in rearview mirror), inside day/night mirror, outside manual mirrors (L/R breakaway), full width roof support, premium sport style high back bucket seats (includes leather seating surfaces with leather-grain vinyl facings/adjustable lumbar supports/continuously adjustable recliner for precise back adjustment), remote control security alarm system, tilt steering column, leather-wrapped steering wheel, snap-in Tonneau cover, removable folding soft top with side curtains, removable rear window.

Accessories

HAA	Air Conditioning	1020	1200
NAE	California Emissions	NC	NC
NBY	Massachusetts Emissions	NC	NC

1995 Dodge Viper RT/10

EAGLE

SUMMIT ESi COUPE

| CODE | DESCRIPTION | INVOICE | MSRP |

1995 Eagle Summit ESi

SUMMIT ESi COUPE

Eagle dealerships are the only places to find Mitsubishi-built, Chrysler-badged compacts in 1995. The Dodge and Plymouth Colt have, as if it weren't obvious from Day One, been replaced by the Neon. Eagle, which doesn't get a version of the Neon, makes do with the Summit.

The ESi coupe is a sprightly performer. Its rounded bodywork is clean and contemporary, and in ESi trim is filled out by attractive alloy wheels and a spoiler. A 1.8-liter four cylinder pumps 113 horsepower to the front wheels, which may not sound like much, but in a 2200 pound car, it's plenty.

The addition of a passenger-side airbag makes the Summit more competitive in the 1995 marketplace. The Summit ESi Coupe is good-looking, solidly reliable, and offers great performance. The fact that you can't option one out above $13,000 means the Summit is a fine alternative to the Neon Coupe and is a much better deal than the new Toyota Tercel DX.

Performance and Safety

Acceleration (0-60 mph) .... 8.2 sec.	ABS .... Optional
Braking (60-0 mph) .... 115 ft.	Driver Airbag .... Standard
Cornering .... .82 g's	Passenger Airbag .... Standard
Fuel Capacity .... 13.2 gal.	Traction Control .... N/A
Fuel Economy .... City: 26 mpg	Crash Test Grade .... D: N/A P: N/A
Hwy: 33 mpg	Insurance Cost .... Very High

EDMUND'S 1995 HIGH-PERFORMANCE AUTOMOBILES

EAGLE
SUMMIT ESi COUPE

CODE	DESCRIPTION	INVOICE	MSRP
SUMMIT ESi COUPE 4 CYL			
B9XL21	ESi 2-Dr Coupe	10320	10859
	Destination Charge:	430	430

Standard Equipment

SUMMIT ESi COUPE: 1.5 liter 4 cylinder MPI engine, front wheel drive, 5-speed manual transmission, manual steering, power front disc/rear drum brakes, driver and front passenger air bags, passenger door assist grips, maintenance-free battery, passenger and cargo carpeting, cigar lighter, coat hooks, two cup holders, vinyl door trim with cloth insert and dual map pockets, stainless steel exhaust system, front and rear body color fascias, driver side footrest, gauges (engine temp and fuel), aerostyle halogen headlights, single note horn, scissor type jack, dome and ashtray lights, black manual remote dual outside mirrors, day/night rearview mirror, passenger side visor vanity mirror, color-keyed bodyside moldings, cloth faced low back reclining front bucket seats, rear low back bench seat, decklid spoiler, 4-spoke "Sport" design steering wheel, front strut suspension, rear independent multi-link suspension, trip meter, P155/80R13 all-season BSW SBR tires, compact high pressure spare tire, warning lights, 13" styled steel wheels with full wheel covers, 2-speed windshield wipers.

Accessories

EJA	**Engine** — 1.8 liter 4 cylinder MPI	NC	NC
	req's pkg K		
DGB	**Automatic Transmission** — 4-speed	562	654
	req's 1.8 liter engine and pkg K		
K	**Pkg K**	1692	1968
	incls 1.8 liter engine, air conditioning, black dual exterior power remote mirrors, dual note horn, variable speed intermittent wipers, remote fuel filler door release, remote trunk release, split-folding rear seat, tilt steering column, trunk trim dress-up, trunk light, rear window defroster, ESi Group (incls front vented disc brakes, dual tip exhaust, touring tuned suspension, tachometer [manual trans only], P185/65R14 tires, 14" cast aluminum wheels), tinted glass, AM/FM radio with cassette/clock/4 speakers, power steering		
GFA	**Rear Window Defroster**	57	66
	req'd in New York State; incl in pkg K		
NAE	**California Emissions**	NC	NC
NBY	**Massachusetts Emissions**	NC	NC
—	**Paint** — special color or metallic	NC	NC

GET MORE MONEY FOR YOUR USED CAR BY KNOWING ITS TRUE VALUE

See our ads on pages 4 and 6

TALON TSi — EAGLE

1995 Eagle Talon TSi

TALON TSi

The first-generation Diamond-Star coupes won countless awards during their four-and-a-half year run, which began in 1990. They could be had as sporty econocars, turbocharged street racers, and all-wheel-drive all-weather sport coupes. A joint development between Mitsubishi and Chrysler, the coupes were built in Illinois and sold under Eagle, Mitsubishi and Plymouth banners.

This year brings a new generation of Diamond-Stars, and rather than arriving as triplets, they come as Eagle and Mitsubishi twins. The shape is low, wide and provocative. The interior features a sweeping center console and excellent ergonomics. As before, the Talon is equipped with a hatchback and folding seats that increase utility. The engine lineup has been revised, with a Chrysler 2.0-liter four cylinder powering the base models and a tweaked turbo engine motivating the TSi and TSi AWD.

Nice car, this Eagle. It's quick, handles well, and the top-rung model offers the security and stability of all-wheel drive for drivers who regularly pilot rain-slicked or snow-covered roads. However, the rear-end styling treatment needs to be rethought. Not only is the bright-orange reflector surrounding the license plate obnoxious, the billboard-sized lettering spelling T-A-L-O-N across the top of it like a pickup tailgate renders the tail of the car garish and crass. This glaring effect alone makes the Talon's identical twin, the Mitsubishi Eclipse, our recommendation.

Performance and Safety

Acceleration (0-60 mph) .... 6.4 sec.	ABS .... Optional
Braking (60-0 mph) .... 123 ft.	Driver Airbag .... Standard
Cornering .... .87 g's	Passenger Airbag .... Standard
Fuel Capacity .... 15.8 gal.	Traction Control .... N/A
Fuel Economy .... City: 20 mpg	Crash Test Grade .... D: N/A P: N/A
Hwy: 27 mpg	Insurance Cost .... N/A

EDMUND'S 1995 HIGH-PERFORMANCE AUTOMOBILES

EAGLE

TALON TSi

Edmund's Driving Impression

True, not everyone falls for the second-generation Eagle's rear end. Nevertheless, exceptional performance can overcome the occasional stylistic blemish, especially when a car looks sharp overall. Based upon those merits, this Talon—particularly in TSi trim—warrants a heap of praise. It's tight, controlled, substantial, capable, mannerly, well-behaved. Easy maneuverability is helped by quickened steering.

The TSi AWD with a five-speed is tops for acceleration. The 210-hp marvel delivers instant response off the line, as the turbo kicks in almost immediately. Slight clutch harshness can develop when pushing the gas hard, though it's smooth when operated moderately. Despite little lateral movement, the shift lever zips crisply between each ratio.

All told, the AWD edition is surprisingly docile for ordinary driving—until you call for its muscle. A TSi can crawl in second gear through traffic, then accelerate vigorously when the crowd clears.

Performance was disappointing initially from an automatic TSi AWD. The hopefully-hot coupe stood at stoplights like a slug, reluctant to take off, until the turbo finally caught hold. Then, we discovered that it accelerated better by "feathering" the gas pedal. But later in our trial, the car began to take off almost like a shot, with only a moderate degree of turbo lag. On the plus side, the automatic shifts smoothly and surely.

All-wheel-drive grips the pavement like a panther; hangs tight through curves; corners impressively; and sends good road feel to the steering wheel. A TSi emits an invigorating whine when accelerating (a mix of turbo and exhaust gurgle). Otherwise, it's very quiet running except for modest tire noise.

Pleasant riding overall, an Eagle is well-controlled on the highway, elbowing aside all but the harshest bumps. In the city, it hits some bumps and holes quite hard, but doesn't lose its grip. Supplementary gauges are tiny in the performance model, but the 170-mph speedometer and 9000-rpm tach are easy to read.

1995 Eagle Talon TSi

TALON TSi 4 Cyl

CODE	DESCRIPTION	INVOICE	MSRP
XH24	ESi 2-Dr Hatchback	13346	14362
XP24	TSi FWD 2-Dr Hatchback	15989	17266
FS24	TSi AWD 2-Dr Hatchback	17973	19448
Destination Charge:		430	430

TALON TSi — EAGLE

Standard Equipment

TALON TSi: Turbocharged 2.0 liter DOHC 16-valve SMPI 4 cylinder engine, 5-speed manual transmission, power assisted rack and pinion steering, power 4-wheel disc brakes, driver and passenger air bags, 5-mph impact protection bumpers, console-mounted cigar lighter, digital clock, two-stage door checks, blackout treatment includes: roof, pillars, mirrors, window opening moldings; front and rear body color fascias, black liftgate-mounted spoiler with integral center stop light, tinted glass on all windows with windshield sunshade, windshield pillar right assist handle, color-keyed molded cargo area trim, color-keyed cut-pile floor carpet needle punch cargo area, two coat hooks, floor console with armrest/cup holders, covered storage, driver's left foot rest, color-keyed knit headliner, lamps include: ash tray/cargo area/cigar lighter/glove box/ignition key with time delay/dual map/dome with time delay; locking glove compartment, remote fuel filler door and liftgate release, 6-way manual cushion seats, adjustable head restraint, low back bucket passenger seat with recliner, "walk-in" track and adjustable head restraint, tilt steering column, mini spare tire and wheel, warning chime for key in ignition/headlights on/fasten seat belts, 2-speed windshield wipers and washers with variable intermittent wipe, single speed rear window wiper with intermittent wipe, P205/55VR16 A/SP BSW tires, four cast aluminum wheels (white or silver), AM/FM ETR stereo radio with cassette and 6 speakers, electric rear window defroster, dual outlet exhaust system with chrome tips, body color door handles, body color side air dams, front fog lights, cargo net, padded color-keyed door trim panels with cloth insert and map pockets, color-keyed removable shelf panel, leather-wrapped shift knob (manual transaxle only), leather-wrapped steering wheel, cloth sun visors with illuminated mirrors, footwell lamps with time delay, dual power mirrors, "Pulsar" and "Serein" cloth seat fabric, driver seat lumbar and back wing adjustments, 2-passenger rear bench seat with split folding back.

TSi AWD (in addition to or instead of TSi equipment): P215/55VR16 A/SP BSW tires, power windows with driver's one-touch down feature, central door locks, electronic speed control.

Accessories

CODE	DESCRIPTION	INVOICE	MSRP
P	**Pkg P** — TSi FWD	1338	1574
	incls air conditioning, power door locks, front floor mats, speed control, power windows		
S	**Pkg S** — TSi AWD	748	880
	incls air conditioning, front floor mats		
H	**Pkg H** — TSi AWD	2536	2983
	incls Pkg S contents plus radio (AM/FM stereo with cassette, equalizer, clock and 8 speakers), power driver seat, power sunroof, security alarm (incls remote keyless entry)		
EBG	**Engine** — 2.0 liter DOHC 16V I4 turbo - TSi FWD, TSi AWD	STD	STD
DD4	**Transmission** — 5-speed manual	STD	STD
DGL	**Transmission** — 4-speed automatic - TSi FWD	751	883
	TSi AWD	724	852
4XA	**Air Conditioning Bypass**	NC	NC
BRF	**Anti-Lock Brakes**	552	649
DSA	**Limited Slip Differential** — TSi AWD	226	266
JPS	**Power Driver's Seat** — TSi AWD w/Pkg S	282	332
NAE	**California Emissions**	NC	NC
NBY	**Massachusetts Emissions**	NC	NC
RAZ	**Radio** — TSi FWD w/Pkg P, TSi AWD w/Pkg S or H	539	634
	incls AM/FM stereo with CD player, cassette, clock and 6 speakers		
RAY	**Radio** — TSi FWD w/Pkg P, TSi AWD w/Pkg S	603	709
	incls AM/FM stereo with cassette, equalizer, clock and 8 speakers		

EDMUND'S 1995 HIGH-PERFORMANCE AUTOMOBILES

EAGLE

TALON TSi / VISION TSi

CODE	DESCRIPTION	INVOICE	MSRP
JPS	**Power Driver's Seat** — TSi FWD w/Pkg P	282	332
GXR	**Security Alarm** — TSi FWD w/Pkg P	282	332
	TSi AWD w/Pkg S	282	332
	incls remote keyless entry		
GWA	**Power Sunroof** — TSi FWD w/Pkg P	621	730
	TSi AWD w/Pkg S	621	730
—	**Paint** — regular production colors or metallic	NC	NC
ALAH	**Seats** — TSi FWD	388	457
	TSi AWD	388	457
	incls leather and vinyl front lowback buckets, rear split folding bench seat (req's JPS power driver's seat)		

1995 Eagle Vision TSi

VISION TSi

Chrysler's LH-series of sedans has redefined the traditional American luxury car. The Chrysler Concorde emphasizes the luxury portion of the equation, while the Dodge Intrepid has mid-America squarely within its gunsight grille. Eagle's Vision is designed to appeal to those of us who want a dash of flair and sophistication in our family haulers. It is the most sporting and European of the trio, with a distinctive look all its own. However, if Chrysler's sales charts are any evidence, there are few takers for this recipe in the marketplace.

It's too bad the Vision doesn't sell, because it's a great car. Perhaps the jutting grille puts potential customers off. Maybe the Eagle division, formed in 1988, hasn't developed the brand image necessary to move the merchandise. Could be that people don't think 'car' when told to drop by their local Jeep-Eagle dealership for a test drive. No matter. Eagle is heavily advertising the Vision to get the car noticed.

VISION TSi — EAGLE

| CODE | DESCRIPTION | INVOICE | MSRP |

There is much to take notice of; rakish styling, a long list of standard features, and more interior room than all of its competition. The TSi handles very much like its LH bretheren, which is to say, extraordinarily well for a big sedan. We think the Vision TSi is a logical choice for sedan buyers who want a little pizzazz in their daily commute, and sales types are likely to wheel and deal more aggressively than the boys at the Dodge or Chrysler dealer to get the slow-selling Vision onto highways and into driveways.

Performance and Safety

Acceleration (0-60 mph)	8.1 sec.	ABS	Optional
Braking (60-0 mph)	125 ft.	Driver Airbag	Standard
Cornering	.81 g's	Passenger Airbag	Standard
Fuel Capacity	18 gal.	Traction Control	Optional
Fuel Economy	City: 18 mpg	Crash Test Grade	D: Average P: Good
	Hwy: 26 mpg	Insurance Cost	Average

Edmund's Driving Impression

Ever since the LH sedan's inception as a trio of 1993 models, TSi has been the sportier of two Visions, carrying a stiffer suspension as well as a 3.5-liter V-6 (versus 3.3-liter for the similar-looking ESi). Switchable traction control, too, is a TSi-only option.

Although gratifyingly swift from a standstill, TSi acceleration is somewhat disappointing at mid-range velocities. Attempting to pick up the pace from 55 mph can produce a delay that feels nearly endless—then a blast of sound, but a dearth of fast-forward movement.

The sporty Vision hits some bumps surprisingly hard, but almost floats over others. That latter phenomenon can impart a disconcerting, nearly woozy feeling of disconnection from the pavement. On the highway, and in treks across smoother surfaces, the touring suspension and performance-oriented tires deliver on their promise of tight, superior handling, as the Vision clings doggedly to the pavement. Steering is good—quite precise for a large car, in fact—except for that floaty feeling on occasion.

Front seats are comfortable, with plenty of room and many power adjustments. The driver faces a large speedometer and tachometer, plus only fuel and temperature gauges.

Virtues in a Vision TSi are many, but despite impressive performance data, it doesn't produce quite as much feeling of sportiness as might be demanded. Overall, it seems more like a very good—not quite great—family car than an unabashed touring sedan.

Compared to the like-engined Concorde or Intrepid, on the other hand, Vision is the one to try—provided you can cope with its harsher ride. Then too, even the weakest of the LH sedans is a quantum leap ahead of the typical full-size American-built automobile in performance. Traction control is a wise checkoff on the option list, for snowbelt dwellers, as you can really feel its assistance when accelerating on ice.

VISION TSi 6 CYL

XS41	TSi 4-Dr Sedan	20562	22871
Destination Charge:		535	535

EDMUND'S 1995 HIGH-PERFORMANCE AUTOMOBILES

EAGLE / VISION TSi

Standard Equipment

VISION TSi: 3.5 liter SMPI V6 engine, 4-speed automatic transmission, variable-assist power rack and pinion steering, power-assisted 4-wheel disc brakes w/ABS, power windows with driver override and one-touch down feature, power door locks, touring tires and touring suspension, AM/FM ETR stereo radio with seek, Dolby and 6 speakers; electronic digital clock (included with radio), floor console with cup holders, rear seat heat/AC ducts, armrest and covered storage; child protection rear door locks, stainless steel exhaust system with aluminized coating, two-tone fascias, front and rear floor mats, solar control windshield and rear window glass, tinted side windows, three folding grab handles, two front reading/courtesy interior lamps, two rear reading/courtesy lamps with automatic dimming and time out, four door courtesy lamps, message center includes: door ajar/trunk ajar/low washer fluid/two traction control (when equipped)/ABS; dual foldaway heated power mirrors, functional bodyside protection moldings, full bodyside cladding, electric rear window defroster, front bucket seats with manual lumbar adjustment (premium style/fabric/upgraded door trim), contoured rear bench seat with center armrest, speed control with cancel feature, tilt steering column, compact spare tire, power trunk lid release, speed sensitive intermittent windshield wipers and washers with high volume fluidic washers, P225/60R16 A/ST BSW tires, touring tires, touring suspension, four "Caisson" aluminum wheels, air conditioning with automatic temperature control, full overhead console with compass, thermometer, trip computer, storage and two courtesy/reading lamps; fog lights, illuminated entry, remote keyless entry, leather steering wheel and shift knob, luggage compartment cargo net, dual illuminated visor mirrors, 8-way power driver's seat, dual sun visors with sliding extensions and secondary visors.

Accessories

CODE	DESCRIPTION	INVOICE	MSRP
K	**Pkg K**	NC	NC
	incls model with standard equipment		
L	**Pkg L**	986	1127
	incls interior rearview mirror with auto day/night feature, Chrysler Infinity spatial imaging cassette sound system, 8-way power driver and passenger seats, traction control		
M	**Pkg M**	1621	1853
	incls Pkg L contents plus leather faced front buckets, rear bench, security alarm, conventional spare tire		
CFK	**Child Seat — integrated**	88	100
NAE	**California Emissions**	89	102
NBY	**Massachusetts Emissions**	89	102
NHK	**Engine Block Heater**	18	20
GWA	**Power Moonroof — w/pkg L or M**	627	716
AWT	**Performance Handling Group — w/pkg L or M**	190	217
	incls P225/60VR16 all-season performance BSW SBR tires, performance suspension; req's conventional spare tire		
ARA	**Radio — w/pkg K**	620	708
	incls Chrysler Infinity spatial imaging cassette sound system (incls AM/FM electronically tuned stereo radio with seek/scan, cassette player with fast forward, rewind and auto reverse and DNR 5-band graphic equalizer, 120 watt 8 channel amplifier, 11 Infinity speakers, clock, instructional tape, rear mounted power antenna)		
ARB	**Radio — w/pkg L or M**	148	169
	incls Chrysler Infinity spatial imaging compact disc sound system (incls AM/FM electronically tuned stereo with seek/scan, integral compact disc player, 5-band graphic equalizer, 120 watt 8 channel amplifier, 11 Infinity speakers, clock, instructional CD, rear mounted power antenna)		

VISION TSi   EAGLE

CODE	DESCRIPTION	INVOICE	MSRP
JPR	**Seat** — w/pkg K	330	377
	incls driver and passenger 8-way power seats; incld in pkg L and M		
LSA	**Security Alarm** — w/pkg L	130	149
	incld in pkg M		
TBB	**Conventional Spare Tire** — w/pkg K or L	83	95
	incld in pkg M		
—	**Seats**	543	620
	incls leather faced front buckets, rear bench; NA w/pkg K or CFK		
—	**Paint** — extra cost		
—	char gold	85	97
—	orchid	85	97
—	metallic red	85	97
—	spruce	85	97
—	bright platinum metallic	175	200

EDMUND'S NEW AUDIO TAPE!

How to Get Your Way at the Auto Dealer

You'll learn how to buy right, negotiate smart, save money, and enjoy yourself all at the same time.

see our ad on page 376 for details

See the Automobile Dealer Directory on page 388 for a Dealer near you!

FORD
CONTOUR SE

1995 Ford Contour SE

CONTOUR SE

Ford spent $6 billion developing a new "world car" designed to be the best in the compact class in every market in which it was sold. Parts were to be common, regardless of the country of origin, with unique interior and exterior styling tweaks for each model. The program tested Ford's ability to utilize all of its resources to create a car that would allow production to become more streamlined, slicing overhead and building bigger profits.

Who cares? The result is the Ford Contour, and for about the average amount of a typical car purchase in the United States today, you can get one loaded up with equipment, with performance and a feel you never would have expected from a sedan made in America. Actually, the road manners of the new Contour are no mystery, given that Ford of Europe did the development work on this car.

Contour replaces the Tempo, which in 1984 represented cutting-edge styling but was as stale as flat Diet Coke by 1994. The SE variant of the Contour comes with a 24-valve, twin-cam, 170-hp, 2.5-liter V6 engine that doesn't require a tuneup until the 100,000 mile mark, sport suspension, big tires mounted on alloy wheels, and more sporting front seats. Load on air conditioning, power windows and locks, moonroof, cruise, traction control, anti-lock brakes and a CD player with premium sound and the sticker stays under $19,500, with room for negotiation.

The Contour looks good and handles like higher-priced German sedans. The body structure is stiff, and the ergonomically-correct instrument panel features legible dials and well-placed controls. However, Chrysler is introducing the Chrysler Cirrus and Dodge Stratus, two more contenders in this arena, and they look quite promising, offering more room than the Contour but less performance for about the same price.

CONTOUR SE — FORD

| CODE | DESCRIPTION | INVOICE | MSRP |

Performance and Safety

Acceleration (0-60 mph)	7.4 sec.	ABS	Optional
Braking (60-0 mph)	122 ft.	Driver Airbag	Standard
Cornering	.79 g's	Passenger Airbag	Standard
Fuel Capacity	14.5 gal.	Traction Control	Optional
Fuel Economy	City: 21 mpg	Crash Test Grade	D: N/A P: N/A
	Hwy: 30 mpg	Insurance Cost	N/A

CONTOUR SE 6 Cyl

P67	SE 4-Dr Sedan	14134	15695
	Destination Charge:	495	495

Standard Equipment

CONTOUR SE: 2.5 liter DOHC Duratec 24-valve V6 engine, power 4-wheel disc brakes, P205/60R15 BSW tires, 15" cast aluminum wheels, 5-speed manual transaxle with overdrive, power rack and pinion steering, child-proof rear door locks, fixed rear quarter panel mounted antenna, body color "B" pillars, front and rear color-coordinated bumpers with bright insert, flush color-keyed door handles and bezels, dripless roof construction doors with water management system, semi-flush glass with solar tint, grey grille with "floating" oval, flush headlamps with replaceable halogen bulb, wraparound side marker lights, color-keyed bodyside moldings, driver and right front passenger dual front supplemental restraint system air bags, color-keyed manual lap/shoulder safety belts for front and rear outboard seating positions, color-keyed lap belt (rear center seating position), height adjustable front outboard seating position shoulder belt, electronic digital clock, dual rear coat hooks, molded cloth insert door trim panels include armrest/door pull handle/front and rear speakers/front stowage bins; driver's left footrest, lockable illuminated glove box (includes integrated utility hook), grab handles, color-keyed cloth covered molded fiberglass headliner, tilt/height adjustable front headrests, rear passenger compartment heat duct, soft-feel driver oriented instrument panel with side window demisters/knee bolsters/4-positive shut-off registers, backlighted cluster includes: 130-mph speedometer/analog gauges/trip odometer/fuel gauge/high beam warning light/coolant temperature gauge; lights include: low oil pressure/RH-LH direction indicator/hand brake on/catalyst malfunction/seat belt reminder warning lamps; illuminated switches and heater control lights, illuminated rotary master light switch, glove box light, illuminated ashtray/cigarette lighter, front header-mounted interior light with door courtesy switches, courtesy light delay, side wall trim luggage compartment with floor carpet/spare wheel cover, interior cabin pollen filter Micronair filtration system, day/night rearview mirror, driver and passenger visor mirrors, cloth-covered sunvisors, 130 amp alternator, seat belt reminder chime, "driver door open" lights-on chime, remote decklid release, EEC-IV electronic engine controls, sequential multiple port electronic fuel injection, remote fuel filler door release, 14.5 gallon fuel tank with tethered cap, 4-speed blower heater/defroster, dual note horn, tilt steering column, independent MacPherson front suspension with front stabilizer bar, independent quadralink rear suspension, mini spare tire, variable intermittent windshield wipers with fluidic washers, electronic AM/FM stereo radio with cassette player, fog lamps, heated dual power mirrors with body color finish, color-keyed 16 oz. carpet, full length floor-mounted console with armrest/cassette-CD stowage/pop-up cup holders/rear ashtray, tachometer, illuminated driver/passenger mirrors, manual 4-way seat adjust, 60/40 fold-down rear seat with armrest, rear seat back carpet, valance panel stowage, color-keyed spoiler, sport style front seat, LH/RH manual lumbar adjust seat, leather-wrapped steering wheel with center horn control, sport suspension.

FORD
CONTOUR SE

CODE	DESCRIPTION	INVOICE	MSRP

Accessories

Code	Description	Invoice	MSRP
—	**Preferred Equipment Pkgs** — prices include pkg discounts		
239A	**Pkg 239A**	1202	1350
	incls group 2 (incls air conditioning, rear window defroster, power windows), group 3 (incls light group, power door locks)		
—	**Groups**		
—	**Group 2**	846	950
	incls air conditioning, rear window defroster, power mirrors		
—	**Group 3**	307	345
	incls light group, power door locks		
422	**California/Massachusetts Emissions**	85	95
428	**High Altitude Emissions**	NC	NC
—	**Transmissions**		
445	**5-spd manual w/overdrive**	STD	STD
44T	**4-spd automatic w/overdrive**	725	815
99L	**Engine** — 2.5 liter 24-valve V6	STD	STD
572	**Air Conditioning**	694	780
13B	**Power Moonroof**	530	595
552	**Anti-Lock Brakes**	503	565
525	**Speed Control**	191	215
57Q	**Rear Window Defroster**	143	160
	incls dual heated mirrors; req'd in New York State		
553	**Traction Control** — incls anti-lock brakes	712	800
12Y	**Floor Mats** — front and rear, carpeted	40	45
143	**Keyless Remote Entry System**	143	160
41H	**Engine Block Heater**	18	20
—	**Seats**		
Y	cloth, reclining sport bucket	NC	NC
Z	leather, reclining bucket	530	595
	incls leather-wrapped steering wheel		
21A	**Seat Adjuster** — power, driver's side	258	290
—	**Audio**		
913	premium AM/FM stereo with cassette	116	130
585	premium AM/FM stereo with compact disc player	240	270
T35	**Tires** — P205/60R15 BSW	STD	STD

USE A MULTIMEDIA CD-ROM TO RESEARCH YOUR NEXT AUTOMOBILE PURCHASE

see ad on page 384 for details

ESCORT GT   FORD

1995 Ford Escort GT

ESCORT GT

Ford doesn't sell many Escort GTs, and it's a mystery why these hot sport hatches don't fly off dealer lots. Dual airbags, a zingy 127-hp engine, available anti-lock brakes and a host of standard features make this car a performance bargain.

The Escort GT is equipped with a new dashboard for 1995, and loses its leather-wrapped steering wheel and seat cushion tilt function in exchange for a new passenger-side airbag. Popular options include a premium sound system with CD player, anti-lock brakes and power windows and door locks. The GT can also be ordered with a slick power moonroof, cruise control and a tilt wheel.

Gas mileage with the manual transmission is average for the class. The GT gets to 60 mph in a scant 8.5 seconds, with Mazda's torquey twin-cam, 1.8-liter four banger wound out to its 7,000 rpm redline in second gear. This nimble Escort handles well, and the same 15-inch Eagle GT+4 tires that help the GT grip the road haul it down to a stop from 60 mph in short order.

The GT accounts for a tiny 6% of all Escort sales, and could be hard to find optioned the way you want. However, the search will be worth it when the payment book arrives in the mail. If you want one of the current versions of the car, you'll need to hurry. The Escort is due for a total makeover in 1996, to be based once again on Mazda mechanicals and sharing more than a few styling cues with the new Contour.

Performance and Safety

Acceleration (0-60 mph) .... 8.4 sec.	ABS .... Optional	
Braking (60-0 mph) .... 138 ft.	Driver Airbag .... Standard	
Cornering .... .82 g's	Passenger Airbag .... Standard	
Fuel Capacity .... 13.2 gal.	Traction Control .... N/A	
Fuel Economy .... City: 26 mpg	Crash Test Grade .... D: Good	P: N/A
	Hwy. 31 mpg	Insurance Cost .... High

FORD

ESCORT GT

CODE	DESCRIPTION	INVOICE	MSRP

Edmund's Driving Impression

Ford's Escort GT is fun, fast and comfortable. The seats are covered in a durable, grippy fabric, and side bolsters keep you firmly in place when carving up mountain passes. The Mazda four cylinder is weak on the low end, but speed picks up rapidly once the tach needle swings beyond 2,800 rpm, and this engine loves to be revved hard. A pleasant exhaust note, reminiscent of that of the Saab 900 Turbo, accompanies rapid acceleration.

On uneven pavement at full throttle, the GT can be a handful as torque steer threatens to plant the sharp seven-spoke rims into the curb. Clutch takeup is smooth, and the four-wheel disc brakes work with authority. The Goodyear tires, designed for all-season use, do not inspire hard charges around freeway off-ramps, despite the Escort's inherent cornering abilities.

The new dashboard is more bulky than that found in previous GTs, but it is still attractive and functional, and now has a passenger-side airbag. Ford needs to do something about all the tiny buttons on the stereo and the motorized seat belts, but otherwise, ergonomics are sound.

This hatchback carries four full-sized adults with ease, and with a split-fold rear seat, it can accommodate parcels sized up to six feet long, or partially disassembled mountain bikes, or several kegs of beer. However, the rear liftover is unacceptably high, and getting heavy items inside the Escort's hatchback requires two or three well-muscled people.

While the Escort GT's exterior design is somewhat dated, it offers low prices, good performance and a higher level of functionality than normally found in sport coupes in this class.

ESCORT 4 CYL

		INVOICE	MSRP
P12	GT 3-Dr	11687	12700
Destination Charge:		375	375

Standard Equipment

ESCORT GT: 1.8 liter DOHC 16 valve EFI I4 engine, power rack and pinion steering, power 4-wheel disc brakes, 5-speed manual overdrive transaxle, flush windshield and backlight glass, semi-flush side glass, flip-out quarter window aerodynamic single rectangular halogen headlamps, black-out door frame moldings, narrow black beltline moldings, driver/passenger side air bag SRS, motorized front shoulder belt systems with manual lap belts, manual lap/shoulder outside rear safety belts with center lap belt, removable hard-type cargo area cover, cigarette lighter, non-locking glove box, illuminated ignition key bezel, two-tone wraparound soft instrument panel with knee bolsters, 4-spoke soft black steering wheel, heavy duty alternator, 58 amp/hour maintenance-free battery, self-adjusting linkage clutch, side window demisters, electronic ignition, engine malfunction indicator light, engine low coolant warning light, front wheel drive, tinted glass, rear seat heat ducts, 4-speed blower heater/defroster/flow-through ventilation, inside hood release, front/rear stabilizer bar, 4-wheel independent suspension, temperature gauge, mini-spare tire, trip odometer, electronic voltage regulator, 2-speed windshield wipers with variable interval feature, unique body color bumpers, body color door handles, body color bodyside protection moldings, rear reflex applique, cloth door trim with unique armrest, integral map pocket/speaker grille and lower carpeting; 60/40 split fold rear seat with dual release handles, P185/60RX15 84H BSW performance all-season tires, 15" x 5.5" styled aluminum wheels, electronic AM/FM stereo radio with cassette and digital clock (radio credit option available), body color asymmetrical grille with Ford oval, fog lamps/unique front fascia, black dual electronic remote control breakaway mirrors, rocker panel cladding, rear spoiler, deluxe passenger compartment carpeting, center console with bin and removable tray with cup holders, light group includes: dual map lights/cargo area light/engine compartment light/headlamps on warning chime/RH-LH non-illuminated visor mirrors; sport performance cloth reclining bucket seats with unique trim, integral rear seat head restraints, electronic engine controls, 13.2 gallon fuel tank, dual note horn, sport handling suspension, tachometer.

ESCORT GT — FORD

CODE	DESCRIPTION	INVOICE	MSRP

Accessories

CODE	DESCRIPTION	INVOICE	MSRP
330A	**GT Pkg 330A** — GT 3-Dr	335	375
	incls rear window defroster, manual air conditioning		
998	**Engine** — 1.8 liter DOHC	STD	STD
445	**Transmission** — 5-speed manual	STD	STD
44T	**Transmission** — 4-speed overdrive automatic	703	790
422	**California Emissions System**	62	70
428	**High Altitude Principal Use Emissions System**	NC	NC
T39	**Tires** — P185/60R15 BSW performance	STD	STD
—	**Seats**		
X	cloth sport performance buckets	STD	STD
216	child seat, integrated	120	135
572	**Air conditioning** — manual	646	725
552	**Anti-Lock Braking System**	503	565
57Q	**Defroster** — rear window	143	160
41H	**Engine Block Immersion Heater**	18	20
153	**License Plate Bracket** — front	NC	NC
415	**Ultra Violet Decor Group**	356	400
	incls ultra violet clearcoat paint, color-keyed wheels, opal grey cloth sport performance buckets, front floor mats with GT embroidered in violet, leather wrapped steering wheel		
50A	**Luxury Convenience Group**	410	460
	incls tilt steering column, speed control, remote decklid release, leather-wrapped steering wheel		
53A	**Power Equipment Group**	410	460
	incls power locks/windows		
13B	**Moonroof, Power**	468	525
—	**Clearcoat Paint**	76	85
585	**Radio**	143	160
	incls electronic AM/FM stereo/clock/CD player		
913	**Premium Sound System**	54	60
58Y	**Radio Credit Option**	(414)	(465)

For a guaranteed low price on a new vehicle in your area, call

1-800-CAR-CLUB

EDMUND'S 1995 HIGH-PERFORMANCE AUTOMOBILES

FORD
F150 PICKUP

1995 Ford F150 XLT Flareside Pickup

F150 XLT REGULAR CAB (5.8L V8) / LIGHTNING

Ford's F-Series pickup has been the best-selling vehicle in the world for more than a decade. The reasons are obvious: truckish styling, car-like interior comfort, good value for the dollar, and a wide range of model availability. Add performance to the list as well, as long as you're talking about the F-150 with the 5.8-liter V-8 under the hood and the optional handling package stiffening up the suspension. Add blinding performance to the list with the Lightning, the meanest sport truck available in showrooms today.

This year, the F-150 is available in Eddie Bauer trim, which includes such niceties as two-tone paint, aluminum wheels, privacy glass and tie-down hooks. The Lightning carries over unchanged. The F-Series is due to be replaced next year by a slightly smaller, more aerodynamic version that features a steeply-sloping nose and aggressive front styling similar to that of the new 1995 Explorer. Sources haven't said whether or not the stellar Lightning will continue to be available when the new truck goes on sale.

With that in mind, 1995 might be the last year to obtain a Lightning (newly available with white paint, in addition to dark red and black), of which a scant 2500 will be produced, and it will surely be the final year for the current truck's rugged good looks. As far as performance is concerned, most folks will want to opt for the F-150 in XLT or Eddie Bauer trim. It's the more useable truck, and offers enough oomph to make driving interesting. Die-hard performance fans will want the Lightning, which rides rough, looks tough, and drives like a Mustang GT with an XXL trunk.

F150 PICKUP — FORD

| CODE | DESCRIPTION | INVOICE | MSRP |

Performance and Safety

F-150 5.8-liter

Acceleration (0-60 mph) .... 8.9 sec.	ABS .... Standard (rear wheels)
Braking (60-0 mph) .... 144 ft.	Driver Airbag .... Standard
Cornering .... N/A	Passenger Airbag .... N/A
Fuel Capacity .... 34.7 gal. (37.2 Longbed)	Traction Control .... N/A
Fuel Economy .... City: 13 mpg	Crash Test Grade .... D: Excellent P: Excellent
Hwy: 18 mpg	Insurance Cost .... Low

Lightning

Acceleration (0-60 mph) .... 7.2 sec.	ABS .... Standard (rear wheels)
Braking (60-0 mph) .... 143 ft.	Driver Airbag .... Standard
Cornering .... .84 g's	Passenger Airbag .... N/A
Fuel Capacity .... 34.7 gal.	Traction Control .... N/A
Fuel Economy .... City: 12 mpg	Crash Test Grade .... D: Excellent P: Excellent
Hwy: 16 mpg	Insurance Cost .... N/A

F150 XLT 5.8L REGULAR CAB V8 (prices for Lightning N/A)

—	2WD XLT 5.8L Regular Cab Flareside (117" WB)	16176	18766
—	2WD XLT 5.8L Regular Cab Styleside (117" WB)	15636	18130
—	2WD XLT 5.8L Regular Cab Styleside (133" WB)	15826	18354
Destination Charge:		600	600

Standard Equipment

F150 XLT 5.8L REGULAR CAB: 5.8 liter V8 EFI engine, 4-speed automatic transmission, upgraded optional axle ratio, power front disc/rear drum brakes with anti-lock, chrome front bumper with front bumper rub strip, cab steps (Flareside), power steering, tinted glass, digital clock, dual fuel tanks, intermittent windshield wipers, dual horns, vent windows, driver's air bag, halogen headlamps, air conditioning, power door locks, power windows, AM/FM ETR stereo radio with cassette and 4 speakers, tilt steering column, cruise control, interior enhancement/light group (incls under hood light, dual beam dome/map light, headlights on audible alert, map pocket, RH visor vanity mirror, mini console, insulation pkg), P235/75R15XL SBR all-season BW tires, steel spare wheel, chrome styled wheels with bright hub caps, color-keyed cloth headliner, leather-wrapped steering wheel, door courtesy lights, bright wheel opening moldings (Styleside), color-keyed carpeting, chrome grille, dual bright manual mirrors, color-keyed bodyside protection (Styleside), cloth flight bench seat with power lumbar, door trim panels with vinyl inserts and storage bins.

Accessories

952	**Deluxe Two-Tone Paint — Styleside**		234	276
	incls wheel opening moldings			
954	**Lower Two-Tone Paint**		155	183
55S	**Keyless Remote Entry System**		216	254
	incls alarm system			

FORD
F150 PICKUP / MUSTANG GT

CODE	DESCRIPTION	INVOICE	MSRP
422	California/Massachusetts Emissions	85	100
41H	Engine Block Heater	28	33
624	Super Engine Cooling	86	101
924	Rear Privacy Glass	84	99
	req's sliding rear window		
433	Sliding Rear Window	96	113
152	Tachometer	50	59
186	Cab Steps — color-keyed - Styleside	298	350
166	Floor Mats	(16)	(18)
	credit when floor mat replaces carpeting		
582	Radio	254	299
	incls premium AM/FM ETR stereo with CD player and 4 speakers		
543	Mirrors — dual bright power	84	99
632	Heavy Duty Battery	48	56
61A	Light & Convenience Group A	172	202
	incls dual illuminated visor vanity mirrors and automatic day/night mirror		
—	Seats		
B	knitted vinyl bench	(83)	(98)
J	premium cloth 40/20/40 split bench	445	523

1995 Ford Mustang GT

MUSTANG GT

Since Ford introduced a redesigned Mustang for the 1994 model year, sales of the popular pony coupe have surpassed the expectations of even the most optimistic bean counters in Dearborn. The Mustang is selling almost as many copies as the Chevy Camaro and Pontiac Firebird, despite its weaker engine choices and more upright styling, and dealers are clamoring for more of them.

For 1995, Mustang receives few changes. The Cobra models that were introduced in mid-1994 continue, as do the base and GT versions of the coupe and convertible. The standard power driver's

EDMUND'S 1995 HIGH-PERFORMANCE AUTOMOBILES

MUSTANG GT — FORD

seat has been dropped to the options list, and a new CD player option has been added. Still unavailable is an engine that can put the Camaro Z28 and Pontiac Firebird Formula on the bench, but plans for the future include a brutish, 300-horsepower 4.6-liter motor under the Mustang Cobra's snout for 1996.

As it stands for 1995, the Mustang offers good performance value for the dollar, as long as you keep your hands out of the options toy box. True performance junkies will probably want to wait one more year or head over to the nearest Chevy or Pontiac dealer.

Performance and Safety

Acceleration (0-60 mph)	6.7 sec.
Braking (60-0 mph)	125 ft.
Cornering	.86 g's
Fuel Capacity	15.4 gal.
Fuel Economy	City: 17 mpg
	Hwy: 24 mpg

ABS	Optional
Driver Airbag	Standard
Passenger Airbag	Standard
Traction Control	N/A
Crash Test Grade	D: Good P: Good
Insurance Cost	Very High

Edmund's Driving Impression

Not for the modest, the current Mustang coupe and convertible earn high marks for both style and performance. Whether in base or GT form, few cars draw as many covetous leers.

When driving Ford's four-speed automatic transmission, the GT's 215-horsepower V-8 runs quietly, except for a mildly invigorating exhaust note when stomping the gas energetically. Highway acceleration is fine. The V-8 inspires confidence when passing or merging, but doesn't exactly blast forward like a rocket—partly because of a mild delay in downshifting. The car actually feels like it's "digging in" for a moment.

From a standing-start, too, an automatic-equipped GT hangs back for an instant before moving out. The automatic-transmission selector is annoyingly inexact, sometimes appearing to be between ranges. For all-out performance, try a manual-shift GT instead. Or, to attain full-scale Ford "go," there's always the Cobra, with 25 extra horses to unleash.

Though nicely stable on the road, hanging flat through curves and corners, a GT isn't quite as athletic as some rivals. Still, it handles beautifully, hugging the highway tenaciously. The steering wheel feels light at its center point, but demands fairly high effort otherwise.

Ride gets moderately rough on optional 17-inch tires, but instead of the expected stiffness, we noticed a jiggly, even rubbery, reaction. Even if illusory, it can make a person yearn for the base Mustang's smoother ride and acceptable road behavior.

Brakes don't produce as strong a feeling of confidence as we'd like to see, to match the GT's precise handling. The V-8 delivers a satisfying roar when accelerating hard; otherwise all is relatively quiet, except for whine from the oversize tires.

Partly due to their upright stance, Mustangs are surprisingly easy to get into and out of. Passenger space is cozy up front, skimpy in back.

Unless you insist on unsurpassed, totally robust straight-line lustiness, a GT Ford pony makes a fine choice. But, save that Canary Yellow convertible for us.

FORD
MUSTANG GT

CODE	DESCRIPTION	INVOICE	MSRP

MUSTANG GT 8 CYL
P42	GT 2-Dr Coupe	16140	17905
P45	GT 2-Dr Convertible	20315	22595
	Destination Charge:	475	475

Standard Equipment

MUSTANG GT: 5.0 liter SEFI HO (High Output) V8 engine, power side windows, power door locks, P225/55ZR16 BSW all-season tires, 16" x 7.5" 5-spoke cast aluminum wheels with locking lug nuts, front and rear body color fascias with Mustang GT nomenclature (lower rear black), Mustang GT fender badge, fog lamps, single wing rear spoiler, check engine/low fluid warning lights (coolant/oil), 150-mph speedometer, GT bucket seats with cloth trim, cloth 4-way head restraints, adjustable cushion/lateral support and power lumbar support; leather-wrapped steering wheel, traction-lok axle, power decklid release, EEC-IV electronic engine control, stainless steel dual exhaust, power lock group, GT suspension package includes: variable-rate coil springs, Quadra-Shock rear suspension with strut tower brace; 5-speed manual overdrive transmission, power rack and pinion steering, power 4-wheel disc brakes, electronic AM/FM stereo 24 watt radio with seek and 4 speakers, front license plate bracket (molded into front bumper), power retractable convertible top with semi-hard boot, aerodynamic halogen headlamps, wrap-around taillamps, dual electric remote control mirrors (RH convex), color-keyed rocker moldings, driver and right front passenger supplemental restraint system air bags, front ashtray, 3-point active restraint system safety belts, 16 oz. carpet, cigarette lighter, digital quartz clock, console with armrest, integral storage bin, cup holder and CD/cassette storage; driver's footrest, glove box, instrumentation includes: tachometer/trip odometer/voltmeter/temperature/fuel/oil pressure gauges/check engine/overdrive off indicator; dome lamps with front door courtesy switches (integrated in mirror on Convertible), light group includes: engine compartment/glove box/ashtray/cargo compartment/headlamps on alert chime; dual covered visor mirrors (illuminated), split/fold-down rear seatbacks (Coupe), leather-wrapped shift knob (with auto trans), stalk-mounted controls include: turn signals/wipers/washer/high beam headlamps/flash-to-pass; tilt steering wheel with center horn blow, full wrap-over soft flow-through door trim panels with full length armrests and cloth or vinyl inserts, color-keyed cloth headliner, color-keyed cloth sunvisors, heavy duty 130 amp alternator, 58 amp maintenance-free heavy duty battery, power decklid release, side window demisters, 15.4 gallon fuel tank with tethered cap, tinted glass, "power vent" heater/defroster/ventilation with 4 instrument panel registers with positive shut-off, dual note horn, power lock group, tunnel-mounted parking brake, modified MacPherson front strut suspension with stabilizer bars, coil spring 4-bar link rear suspension, aluminum mini spare tire, interval windshield wipers.

Accessories

249A	**GT Pkg 249A — GT**	1372	1540
	incls manual air conditioning, group 2 (consists of dual illuminated visor mirrors, speed control, electronic AM/FM stereo radio with cassette/premium sound), power driver's seat, anti-lock braking system		
99T	**Engine — 5.0 liter SEFI HO**	STD	STD
445	**Transmission — 5-speed manual**	STD	STD
44P	**Transmission — 4-speed automatic overdrive**	703	790
422	**California Emissions System**	85	95
428	**High Altitude Principal Use Emissions System**	NC	NC
—	**Tires/Wheels**		
T27	P225/55ZR16 BSW all-season	STD	STD
64H	wheels, unique 17" aluminum / 245/45ZR17 BSW	338	380

EDMUND'S 1995 HIGH-PERFORMANCE AUTOMOBILES

MUSTANG GT — FORD

CODE	DESCRIPTION	INVOICE	MSRP
—	**Seats**		
2	cloth sport buckets	STD	STD
4	leather seating surfaces sport buckets	445	500
217	**Seat** — power driver's	156	175
	incld in PEP & 249A		
61A	**Group 1**	449	505
	incls power side windows, power door locks, power decklid release		
63A	**Group 2**	454	510
	incls speed control, electronic AM/FM stereo/cassette/premium sound radio		
60K	**Group 3**	276	310
	incls remote keyless/illuminated entry, cargo net		
572	**Air Conditioning** — manual	694	780
552	**Anti-Lock Braking System**	503	565
45C	**Axle** — optional ratio	40	45
57Q	**Defroster** — rear window	143	160
12H	**Floor Mats** — front	27	30
961	**Moldings** — bodyside	45	50
917	**Compact Disc Player**	334	375
58F	**Radio**	STD	STD
	incls electronic AM/FM stereo		
58M	**Radio**	147	165
	incls electronic AM/FM stereo/cassette		
586	**Radio** — w/group 2	334	375
	w/o group 2	596	670
	incls Mach 460 electronic AM/FM stereo/cassette		
41H	**Engine Block Immersion Heater**	18	20

FOR A SPECIAL RATE ON AN AUTO LOAN, CALL

1-800-AT-CHASE

CHASE AUTOMOTIVE FINANCE
SIMPLE ◆ FAST ◆ CONVENIENT

EDMUND'S 1995 HIGH-PERFORMANCE AUTOMOBILES

FORD
PROBE GT

1995 Ford Probe GT

PROBE GT

Probe sales have been off since Ford introduced a revamped Mustang in December of 1994, but that doesn't mean the Probe is a lesser car. It has earned high praise since bowing on the sport coupe scene in 1989, and its current iteration is quick, comfortable and good looking.

For 1995, Probe GT gets a revised front fascia, new alloy wheels, and a revised taillight treatment that moves the license plate from between the lenses to a location in the center of the bumper. The interior has been updated too, with the addition of a second cupholder and revised door panels. The seats can now be clad in Saddle leather, if you wish, but not in Ruby Red or Royal Blue cloth. They were cancelled. Five new colors are available this year, replacing five that are no longer offered. The GT's excellent Mazda-engineered V6 remains unchanged.

Rumors claim that the Probe willl be cancelled after the 1996 model year to make more showroom space for the hot-selling Mustang. That would be a shame. While both cars compete in the sport coupe arena, the Probe and the Mustang are vastly different automobiles that appeal to different types of buyers. The rumor mill indicates that the next Mercury Cougar will be based on Mazda's 626/MX-6 platform, the same one that currently supplies the Probe's running gear. Perhaps the Probe, which has needed a new name since its inception, will adopt the Cougar nameplate and move to Mercury for 1997.

Performance and Safety

Acceleration (0-60 mph) .... 7.5 sec.	ABS .... Optional
Braking (60-0 mph) .... 117 ft.	Driver Airbag .... Standard
Cornering .... .87 g's	Passenger Airbag .... Standard
Fuel Capacity .... 15.5 gal.	Traction Control .... N/A
Fuel Economy .... City: 20 mpg	Crash Test Grade .... D: Excellent P: Good
Hwy: 26 mpg	Insurance Cost .... High

140   **EDMUND'S 1995 HIGH-PERFORMANCE AUTOMOBILES**

PROBE GT — FORD

Edmund's Driving Impression

Our first experience with a GT, soon after its introduction as a '93 model, was so exhilarating, so totally satisfying, that we managed to overlook comfort. A sprint in this year's edition quickly revived the recollection that this is one rough-riding machine.

In comparison, the Mustang GT—Probe's rear-drive counterpart in the Ford stable—feels almost cushiony. A Probe can begin to bounce when traversing even *mildly* uneven pavement. And, there's no suspension adjustment to produce a softer setting.

That being said, Ford's sleek front-drive coupe, in GT trim at least, is a performance/handling dream. The 164-horsepower, 2.5-liter twin-cam V-6 runs smoothly and quietly. With automatic shift, there may be a slight delay when tromping the gas from a standing start, but the suavely-shaped coupe then takes off. Not exactly like a dart, but with reasonable swiftness. Upshifts are crisp and neat.

Early Probes tended to downshift for passing with an unpleasant jolt, but the current edition acts more controlled. Anyone wishing to eliminate all risk of awkward shifts has an easy course: accept the standard manual gearbox, even if it's not the slickest five-speed of them all.

Road behavior, not full-bore acceleration, is the Probe GT's top selling point. Start with a snug-but-beautiful driving position that allows for sportscar-like, "arms-out" control. Full gauges include an 8000-rpm tachometer and 140-mph speedometer, but the ungraduated instruments look a little plain.

Firm, secure seats hold front occupants snugly, in a swoopy interior that includes door cutaways for extra (and welcome) elbow room. Rear occupants drop into cavities—provided that they can find a way to crawl inside.

Add superior visibility in all directions, through scads of glass. Toss in a strong helping of tautness in the GT suspension, and you get a coupe that clings to the pavement like glue: Stable as can be on curves, rock-solid overall, with neatly precise steering. More than most harsh riders, it's almost worth enduring some roughness to get this brand of road reactions.

PROBE GT 6 CYL

CODE	DESCRIPTION	INVOICE	MSRP
T22	GT 3-Dr	14930	16545
	Destination Charge:	360	360

Standard Equipment

PROBE GT: 2.5 liter DOHC V6 engine, 5-speed manual transaxle, driver and right front passenger air bags, power rack and pinion steering, power 4-wheel disc brakes with anti-lock brake system, front and rear stabilizer bars, sport suspension, P225/50VR16 BSW performance tires, fixed rear quarter antenna, lower bodyside cladding, GT exterior treatment (incls unique front and rear fascia with rectangular fog lamps and unique side badging, concealed headlamps, sail mounted manual RH and LH remote mirrors, clear front combination lamp lens, 16" 5-spoke aluminum wheels, cargo net, 12 oz. color-keyed carpeting, electronic digital clock, full center console with folding armrest and cup holder, side window demisters, footrest, locking glove box, performance instrument cluster (incls 140-mph speedometer, trip odometer, tachometer, fuel gauge, water temperature gauge, oil pressure gauge and volt meter), day/night inside rearview mirror, electronic AM/FM stereo with 4 speakers, driver and passenger seatback recline with memory, front bucket seats with dual recliners and cloth integral head restraints, 50/50 fold down rear seat, driver side power lumbar support and seatback side bolsters, floor-mounted shift, leather shift knob (with manual trans only), leather-wrapped steering wheel, cloth covered sun visor with covered RH vanity mirror, warning light system, dome/cargo lights, fog lamps, inside hood release, 2-speed windshield wipers.

FORD — PROBE GT

CODE	DESCRIPTION	INVOICE	MSRP

Accessories

Preferred Equipment Pkgs — prices include pkg discounts

261A — GT Pkg 261A .... 1595 / 1790
incls manual air conditioning, electronic AM/FM stereo/clock/cassette/premium sound, group 1 (incls rear window defroster, dual electric remote control mirrors), group 2 (incls console and storage armrest with cup holder, interval windshield wipers, tilt steering column, remote fuel door/liftgate release, speed control), color-keyed bodyside moldings, front color-keyed floor mats

263A — GT Pkg 263A .... 3113 / 3495
incls GT Pkg 261A contents plus group 4 (incls illuminated entry system, dual illuminated visor vanity mirrors, fade-to-off dome lamp with map lights, remote keyless entry, convenience lights), color-keyed bodyside moldings, front color-keyed floor mats, rear wiper/washer, power driver's seat, rear decklid spoiler, anti-lock braking system

Code	Description	Invoice	MSRP
99B	Engine — 2.5 liter DOHC V6	STD	STD
445	Transmission — 5-speed manual	STD	STD
44T	Transmission — 4-speed automatic w/overdrive	703	790
422	California Emissions System	85	95
428	High Altitude Emissions System	NC	NC
T26	Tires — P225/50VR16 BSW performance and 16" wheels	STD	STD
64X	Tires — P225/50VR16 BSW performance and 16" wheels	347	390
—	**Seats**		
8	GT cloth buckets w/console	STD	STD
7	leather seating surfaces (front buckets only)	445	500
21A	power driver's seat	258	290
—	**Groups**		
65B	Group 1	255	285

incls rear defroster, dual electric remote mirrors

67A	Group 2	454	510

incls console, speed control, interval wipers, tilt steering wheel, remote fuel and liftgate release

43R	Group 3	432	485

incls power side windows, power door locks

97A	Group 4	432	485

incls illuminated entry system, dual illuminated visor vanity mirrors, fade-to-off dome lamp with map lights, remote keyless entry, convenience lights, battery saver, headlamp warning chime

Code	Description	Invoice	MSRP
572	Manual Air Conditioning	797	895

incls tinted glass

Code	Description	Invoice	MSRP
552	Anti-Lock Braking System	503	565
12H	Floor Mats — front color-keyed	27	30
18A	Anti-Theft System	169	190
961	Moldings — color-keyed bodyside	45	50
173	Rear Wiper/Washer	116	130
13B	Power Sliding Roof	547	615
13K	Rear Decklid Spoiler	209	235

PROBE GT / RANGER SPLASH — FORD

CODE	DESCRIPTION	INVOICE	MSRP
—	**Audio**		
589	radio	147	165
	incls electronic AM/FM stereo/clock/cassette		
588	radio	361	405
	incls electronic AM/FM stereo/clock/cassette/premium sound, power antenna		
582	radio	240	270
	incls electronic AM/FM stereo/clock/compact disc player/premium sound		

1995 Ford Ranger Splash

RANGER SPLASH (4.0L V6)

With the compact pickup wars heating up over the past few years, Ford decided to go after a segment of the sport truck market that hadn't yet been tapped. The company wanted to attract younger buyers who wanted a truck for image rather than utility, and didn't want their truck to look like everybody else's. Building upon the restyled 1993 Ranger shortbed, Ford designers created the Splash.

The Splash has a fiberglass flareside bed, lowered suspension, chrome wheels, monochrome trim, and a unique grille treatment to distinguish it from run-of-the-mill Rangers and slab-sided pickups from other manufacturers. The Splash is the first production compact truck to offer a flareside bed. And the one on the Splash offers convenient tie-down cleats in the bottom to secure such things as mountain bikes, camping equipment, or the moldy couch that is going with you to the Delta Chi house in the fall.

You can get your Splash in one of five colors for 1995, and any of the Ranger's drivetrain combinations is available. The 4.0-liter V-6 offers the best horsepower and torque for towing, hauling, or smoking Sunfire GTs on Main Street, and the penalty in fuel economy is a slight one over the 3.0-liter V-6.

EDMUND'S 1995 HIGH-PERFORMANCE AUTOMOBILES

FORD
RANGER SPLASH

| CODE | DESCRIPTION | INVOICE | MSRP |

Inside, the Splash gets a suave new dashboard with a driver-side airbag for 1995. Four-wheel anti-lock brakes are now standard on V-6 editions of the Ranger, and minor styling tweaks on the outside freshen the truck's already good looks.

As sport trucks go, the Splash is among the best. The Chevy S-10 SS beats the Splash in sheer acceleration, but the Ford brakes much better, grips the road more tenaciously and has a more friendly and comfortable cab. In this class of compact trucks, style is among the most important attributes, and the Splash wins that contest hands down.

Performance and Safety

Acceleration (0-60 mph) .... 8.3 sec.	ABS .... Standard		
Braking (60-0 mph) .... 144 ft.	Driver Airbag .... Standard		
Cornering .... .84 g's	Passenger Airbag .... N/A		
Fuel Capacity .... 16.3 gal.	Traction Control .... N/A		
Fuel Economy .... City: 16 mpg	Crash Test Grade .... D: N/A	P: N/A	
	Hwy: 21 mpg	Insurance Cost .... Average	

Edmund's Driving Impression

Our bright-red Splash was quick, turned heads, garnered compliments everywhere we went, and drank premium unleaded like a 1962 Buick. That part was probably our fault, but the truck is only rated at 18 mpg city, with the five-speed manual transmission. Still, this thing is so much fun to drive, and sounds so good when opened up a bit, you can't help but get on the gas.

The cab is comfortable, but doesn't offer much room to spread out in. Drivers over six feet tall will likely want to investigate the Super Cab version of the Splash. Interior materials are first-rate, with logically laid out controls and an excellent stereo system whose teensie buttons require too much effort and concentration to operate. The A-pillars are a tad thick, blocking outward visibility more than we'd like, and the five-speed shifter is bulky and, well, truck-like, but otherwise, the Ranger is a joy to drive.

The Splash is not stealthy, especially in red, or newly-available yellow. With chrome wheels reflecting the sunlight and the look-at-me paint, this truck is a ticket magnet. Fortunately, it's available in blue, white and black.

Speeding is easy to do in the 4.0-liter-equipped Ford. Power is strong, with lots of low-end grunt from the torquey V-6. Handling, on smooth pavement, bests most passenger cars let alone other sport trucks. Rough stuff makes the rear end twitchy, but easily controllable. Wet-weather capability is lousy, the Firestones scrabbling for traction on slick roads. The taut suspension makes for quite a backache on broken pavement, and is bone-jarring over speed bumps.

The Ranger Splash is an excellent combination of style, performance and utility. We recommend it over the Chevy S-10 SS, especially with the improved interior and four-wheel anti-lock brakes for 1995. Just stay away from red or yellow, or your driver's license may be revoked before you've made your first payment.

RANGER SPLASH 4.0L V6 *(1994)*

R10	Splash 4.0L 2WD Regular Cab 108" WB	11829	13339
R14	Splash 4.0L 2WD Supercab 125" WB	13122	14808
Destination Charge:	....	470	470

RANGER SPLASH — FORD

| CODE | DESCRIPTION | INVOICE | MSRP |

Standard Equipment

RANGER SPLASH: 4.0 liter EFI V6 engine, 5-speed manual transmission with overdrive, power steering, power front disc/rear drum brakes with rear anti-lock, front and rear stabilizer bars, digital clock, tinted glass, tachometer (Supercab), P235/60R15 SBR all-season BW tires, passenger assist grip, light group, full-face chrome wheels, front seat center armrest with storage, floor consolette, 60/40 split bench seats with cloth upholstery, door map pockets, color-keyed carpeting, AM/FM ETR stereo radio with 4 speakers, intermittent windshield wipers, color-keyed grille, dual color-keyed power mirrors, RH visor vanity mirror, color-keyed bumpers, heavy duty battery (Supercab), Splash striping, black steering wheel.

Accessories

Code	Description	Invoice	MSRP
44T	**Automatic Transmission w/Overdrive**	842	990
	incls auxiliary transmission oil cooler		
572	**Air Conditioning**	685	806
632	**HD Battery** — Regular Cab	46	54
624	**Super Engine Cooling**	47	55
XAB	**Limited Slip Axle** — performance	215	252
433	**Sliding Rear Window**	96	113
43H	**Pivoting Quarter Windows** — Supercab	41	49
152	**Tachometer** — Regular Cab	47	55
851	**Tape Stripe Delete**	(55)	(65)
52N	**Cruise Control/Tilt Steering Wheel**	336	395
41H	**Engine Block Heater**	26	30
587	**Radio Delete**	(117)	(138)
	deletes AM/FM ETR stereo radio		
588	**Radio** — w/preferred equipment pkg	63	74
	w/o preferred equipment pkg	180	212
	incls premium AM/FM ETR stereo radio with cassette, 4 speakers		
582	**Radio** — w/preferred equipment pkg	314	370
	w/o preferred equipment pkg	431	507
	incls premium AM/FM ETR stereo with compact disc player, 4 speakers		
422	**California/New York Emissions**	85	100
903	**Power Window/Lock Group**	322	379
G	**Seats**	307	361
	incls cloth sport bucket seats and floor console		
873	**Rear Vinyl Jump Seat** — Supercab	192	226
—	**Preferred Equipment Pkgs** — Regular Cab		
866A	**Pkg 866A** — Regular Cab	NC	NC
	incls sliding rear window, AM/FM ETR stereo radio with cassette, 4 speakers; NA in Southwest		
866E	**Pkg 866E** — Regular Cab w/manual trans	558	656
	incls sliding rear window, AM/FM ETR stereo radio with cassette, 4 speakers, air conditioning; avail only in Southwest		
	Regular Cab w/automatic trans	NC	NC
	incls sliding rear window, AM/FM ETR stereo radio with cassette, 4 speakers		
—	**Preferred Equipment Pkgs** — Supercab		

EDMUND'S 1995 HIGH-PERFORMANCE AUTOMOBILES

FORD

RANGER SPLASH / TAURUS SHO

CODE	DESCRIPTION	INVOICE	MSRP
855A	**Pkg 855A** — Supercab .... incls sliding rear window, AM/FM ETR stereo radio with cassette and 4 speakers, rear jump seat	NC	NC
866E	**Pkg 866E** — Supercab w/manual trans .... incls sliding rear window, AM/FM ETR stereo radio with cassette and 4 speakers, air conditioning, rear jump seat; avail only in Southwest	557	656
	Supercab w/auto trans .... incls sliding rear window, AM/FM ETR stereo radio with cassette and 4 speakers; avail only in Southwest	NC	NC

1995 Ford Taurus SHO

TAURUS SHO

More Tauruses are sold in the United States than any other car line. You see them everywhere, and there is good reason for its success. Mainstream styling, good reliability, and room for a family of four means that the Taurus fits the bill for most folks. But what about buyers looking for some performance?

The SHO (Super High Output) variant of the Taurus covers that base. It offers thrill-seekers plenty to keep them entertained, while hauling Junior to soccer practice with equal aplomb. For years, the SHO has been the sport sedan to beat, both in performance and price.

The SHO isn't receiving any changes for 1995. Dual airbags continue as standard equipment, as do anti-lock brakes. Your choice of manual or automatic transmissions is available, and the SHO comes with most comfort and convenience items standard.

In 1996, a new Taurus debuts, with a radical new front styling treatment that incorporates oval headlights like the Neon. The SHO will continue, and a wagon version of this hot sedan is expected. The fate of the excellent Yamaha engine under the hood of the current car remains unknown.

TAURUS SHO — FORD

CODE	DESCRIPTION	INVOICE	MSRP

Because the SHO doesn't differ much from regular Tauri, it's somewhat invisible to traffic cops. But Nissan's outstanding new Maxima offers the same anonymity, with better performance, more solid engineering, lower prices and better resale values.

Performance and Safety

Acceleration (0-60 mph)	7.6 sec.	ABS	Standard	
Braking (60-0 mph)	137 ft.	Driver Airbag	Standard	
Cornering	.80 g's	Passenger Airbag	Standard	
Fuel Capacity	18.4 gal.	Traction Control	N/A	
Fuel Economy	City: 18 mpg	Crash Test Grade	D: Good	P: Good
	Hwy: 26 mpg	Insurance Cost	Very low	

Edmund's Driving Impression

"When you've got it," advised the late film comedian Zero Mostel in *The Producers*, "flaunt it!" That's precisely what Ford avoids doing with the Taurus SHO, a civilized road machine that reveals its identity only by way of subtle lettering molded into the back bumper.

The invigorating whine emitted by the Yamaha-built twin-cam 3.0-liter V-6 is one of this sedan's strongest attractions. Oh, what a magnificent melody it trills, whenever the car slips into fast-forward.

Acceleration is deceptive, however. You don't get the impression of phenomenal pickup, in keeping with performance data. Engine growl—even under moderate acceleration—is a trifle annoying, in contrast with that blissfully captivating whine.

Ford drew praise a couple of years back when it made an automatic transmission available. But let's face facts: manual shifting is what makes this a special machine. Without that five-speed, it's just one more strong-engined sedan.

Unfortunately, the floor shift can get temperamental at times, reluctant to slip into the next gear quite as eagerly as the driver commands. You get used to its slightly-stiff disposition soon enough, but a smoother-operating gearbox would be a better match. The dash holds fuel and temperature gauges only, along with a 140-mph speedometer and 8000-rpm tach (7000-rpm redline).

SHO is more than an engine alone. For one, its suspension is noticeably tighter than a regular Taurus's. While ordinary sedans are fine handlers, the SHO adamantly grasps the pavement on curves, tires firmly planted. The taut stance also helps you feel "in charge," despite the SHO's lack of interior distinction from everyday Taurus sedans.

At the same time, an SHO manages to ride almost as comfortably as an ordinary Taurus. Braking skills don't quite seem to match the car's performance credentials, despite an all-disc anti-lock configuration.

You pay a sizable premium to purchase an SHO, but get a big load of comfort/convenience along with that sweet Yamaha motor.

TAURUS SHO 6 CYL

P54	SHO 4-Dr Sedan	22569	25140
	Destination Charge:	535	535

EDMUND'S 1995 HIGH-PERFORMANCE AUTOMOBILES

FORD

TAURUS SHO

Standard Equipment

TAURUS SHO: 3.0 liter DOHC SEFI 24-valve engine (with manual 5-speed overdrive transmission), 3.2 liter DOHC SEFI 24-valve engine (with 4-speed automatic overdrive transmission), power 4-wheel disc brakes, anti-lock braking system, P215/60ZR16 94V BSW high performance tires (Touring tires with automatic), sparkle unidirectional spoke cast aluminum wheels, high level audio system with dual access remote controls on instrument panel, electronic temperature control air conditioning, front/rear unique color-keyed body color A-gloss painted bumpers, black-out sport surround "B" pillars and door frames, decklid spoiler with LED stop lamp, black-out sport treatment, cornering lamps, valance panel with fog lamps, spoiler brake lamp, 18 oz. color-keyed carpeting with integral sound absorber, full vinyl door trim panels, floor mats, cloth and leather sport bucket seats with dual recliners/armrests/4-way adjustable front head restraints/front seatback map pockets, leather bolster seat trim, leather-wrapped steering wheel, 130 amp alternator (with 3.0 liter engine), 120 amp alternator (with 3.2 liter engine), dual exhaust system, extended range fuel tank, manual parking brake release, power radio antenna, speed control, handling suspension, single aerodynamic halogen headlamps with turn signal lamps (integral to headlamp), wrap-around taillamps with integral back-up lamps and side markers, high-mount brake lamp, sail-mounted dual electric remote control mirrors with tinted glass, color-keyed rocker panel moldings, clearcoat paint, driver and right front passenger dual front supplemental restraint system air bags, front/center/dual armrests (single with bucket/console), center folding rear armrest, front illuminated ashtray, rear door ashtrays, manual front/rear seat lap/shoulder belts (outboard seating positions), lap belts (front/rear center seating positions), 14 oz. color-keyed carpet with integral sound absorber, cigarette lighter, electronic digital clock with dimming feature, cup holder/coin holder, color-keyed door handles, illuminated lockable bin-type glove box, illuminated headlamp switch, positive shut-off climate control registers, courtesy dome light switches (all doors), lights include: glove box/ashtray/luggage compartment/front door curb, delayed dome lamp, carpeted luggage compartment with mini spare tire storage, luggage compartment light, day/night rearview mirrors, tilt steering column, cloth-covered sunvisors with retention clips, safety belt reminder chime, rear window defroster, side window demisters, child-proof rear door locks, concealed drip moldings, EEC-IV electronic engine controls, electronic ignition, tinted glass, windshield/rear solar tinted glass, heater/defroster/ventilation with positive shut-off air registers and rear seat heat ducts, low fuel indicator light, luggage compartment light, manual parking brake release, five-passenger seating capacity (with bucket seats), independent MacPherson front suspension with nitrogen gas-pressurized hydraulic struts and front stabilizer bar, independent MacPherson rear suspension with nitrogen gas-pressurized hydraulic struts and rear stabilizer bar, interval windshield wipers, full vinyl door trim panels, leather bolster seat trim, power rack and pinion variable assist speed-sensitive steering, power side windows with express-down driver's feature (includes lock-out switch), power door locks, color-keyed protective cladding, color-keyed bodyside protection moldings, cargo tie down net, console/floor shift (includes flip-open padded "clamshell" armrest, storage bin and depression for beverage container), front and rear grab handles, light group, dual illuminated visor mirrors, driver/passenger secondary visors for front/side coverage, remote fuel door and decklid/liftgate release, automatic on/off/delay headlamps, illuminated entry, instrumentation includes: tachometer/door ajar light/low brake fluid light/low washer fluid light/low oil level light/lamp out indicator lights.

Accessories

Code	Description	Invoice	MSRP
—	**Engines**		
99Y	3.0 liter DOHC — w/5-speed manual trans	STD	STD
99P	3.2 liter DOHC — w/auto trans	STD	STD
44L	**Transmission** — automatic overdrive	703	790
	incls 3.2 liter engine		
445	**Transmission** — 5-speed manual	STD	STD
422	**California Emissions System**	82	85
428	**High Altitude Principal Use Emissions System**	NC	NC

TAURUS SHO / THUNDERBIRD — FORD

CODE	DESCRIPTION	INVOICE	MSRP
—	**Tires/Wheels**		
T22	wheels, sparkle unidirectional cast aluminum / P215/60ZR16 BSW performance	STD	STD
T25	wheels, sparkle unidirectional cast aluminum / P215/60R16 94V BSW touring	STD	STD
—	**Seats**		
9	cloth and leather sport buckets	STD	STD
H	leather seating surfaces buckets	441	495
53L	**Luxury Convenience Group**	1384	1555
	incls Ford JBL Audio System, driver and passenger power seats, power moonroof, remote control entry		
144	**Remote Keyless Entry System**	191	215
916	**Radio**	445	500
	incls Ford JBL audio system		
917	**Compact Disc Player**	334	375

1995 Ford Thunderbird Super Coupe

THUNDERBIRD LX (4.6L V8) / SC

In 1989, the umpteenth generation of the Thunderbird was introduced sporting BMW 6-Series styling, a supercharged V-6 engine for the SC, and an interior whose switchgear resembled the control panel of a 1976 Whirlpool dishwasher. It was too heavy, and early models suffered reliability problems. For the first time in the Thunderbird's history, a V-8 was not available. How the times change.

This year, the T-Bird still sports those classic BMW lines, but everything else about the car has been revised, restyled and revamped since the car bowed in 1989. The supercharged engine is still available too, but in modest quantities and only in the SC model. Inside, the Thunderbird is a work of art, with a flowing dash that sweeps gracefully between the front seats and houses dual airbags. Excessive weight has been overcome by the addition to the options list of Ford's excellent modular

FORD   THUNDERBIRD

4.6-liter V-8. The front styling, new in 1994, is questionable, but grows on you after awhile. While the front bumper scoops are overwrought, giving the car the look of a grinning idiot, the rest is an improvement over the original. Flared rocker panels and wider wheels on the SC give the Thunderbird an aggressive yet understated look.

Ford's entry into the personal coupe class has evolved into quite a substantial car. Despite sheetmetal that is nearing its expiration date, the car has character and class, and is a worthy alternative to Chevy's new Monte Carlo. New contenders from Chrysler, the Dodge Avenger and Chrysler Sebring, are sure to stir things up, and Japanese coupes, while pricey, offer better fuel economy and perceived value, but the Thunderbird is holding its own in an increasingly crowded personal coupe marketplace.

Performance and Safety

Thunderbird LX V-8

Acceleration (0-60 mph)	8.5 sec.	ABS	Optional
Braking (60-0 mph)	139 ft.	Driver Airbag	Standard
Cornering	.78 g's	Passenger Airbag	Standard
Fuel Capacity	18 gal.	Traction Control	Optional
Fuel Economy	City: 17 mpg	Crash Test Grade	D: Excellent P: Excellent
	Hwy: 25 mpg	Insurance Cost	Average

Thunderbird SC

Acceleration (0-60 mph)	6.8 sec.	ABS	Standard
Braking (60-0 mph)	124 ft.	Driver Airbag	Standard
Cornering	.81 g's	Passenger Airbag	Standard
Fuel Capacity	18 gal.	Traction Control	Optional
Fuel Economy	City: 18 mpg	Crash Test Grade	D: Excellent P: Excellent
	Hwy: 26 mpg	Insurance Cost	Average

Edmund's Driving Impression

T-Birds come in three distinct flavors: mild-mannered V-6, burlier V-8, and coolly sophisticated SC (supercharged). Whatever its underhood contents, this traditional rear-drive sport coupe continues to exercise considerable appeal.

Ford's thoughtfully-engineered 4.6-liter V-8 gives the 'bird a level of performance that was lacking with the old 5.0-liter engine. Acceleration rated merely adequate with that motor—not so much stronger than that supplied by the V-6. The latest overhead-cam V-8 is a far more competent piece of machinery, producing swift off-the-line takeoffs as well as worry-free passing. Mid-range pickup isn't quite as satisfying.

With either engine, an LX aims at riding comfort, even at the expense of handling proficiency. That combination is exactly reversed in the SC, which is capable of scampering to highway speed (and far beyond) in astonishingly quick time. Tap the pedal at a standstill, and an SC hurtles forward, never slowing for a backward glance.

Supercharging is what supplies the SC with its brilliant acceleration aptitude, but its talents are no less intense on rolling rural two-lanes. Wheel-twisting exercises also are this coupe's forte, as the heavy machine endures all that its driver is willing to dish out. Broad-based rubber clings stubbornly to the road surface

THUNDERBIRD — FORD

through exacting calisthenics, as the supercharger transmits extra bursts of authority at the moment they're called for.

Such capabilities don't come cheap, either in dollars or comfort. A word of advice: In an SC, don't dash off in "Firm" mode on a full stomach. Unlike some adjustable suspensions, where you can barely discern one mode from another, the top T-Bird transforms its personality at the touch of that console switch. Brutal is the only way to describe the ride produced in Firm. Tapping the button returns the system to automatic, but eases the ride tension only partially.

T-Birds aren't the worst rear-drive handlers on snow or ice, but we wouldn't want to tackle slippery pavement without traction control. An SC can be ordered with manual shift, but in contrast to some performance machines, automatic doesn't detract from its character.

1995 Ford Thunderbird LX

THUNDERBIRD

Code	Description	Invoice	MSRP
P62	LX 2-Dr Coupe w/4.6L V8	16522	18355
P64	Super Coupe 2-Dr	20419	22735
	Destination Charge:	495	495

Standard Equipment

THUNDERBIRD - LX V8: 4.6 liter EFI V8 engine, 4-speed electronic controlled automatic overdrive transmission with overdrive lock-out, speed sensitive power steering, power front disc/rear drum brakes, power side windows, power lock group, P205/70R15 BSW all-season tires, Bolfon Design styled road wheel covers, electronic AM/FM stereo cassette radio, manual air conditioning with rotary controls, soft color-keyed front and rear 5-mph bumpers, solar tinted windshield/door/quarter window glass, aerodynamic halogen headlamps/parking lamps, color-keyed dual electric remote control mirrors, black windshield/door/quarter moldings, window/backlight moldings, body color double spear-shaped bodyside protection moldings, driver and front passenger dual supplemental restraint system, 3-point active restraint system (front/rear outboard), lap belt (rear center/five seating position), safety belt reminder chimes, foot-operated parking brake, 24 oz. cut-pile carpeting, full-length console with floor-mounted shift/storage, dual console-mounted cup holders, luxury level door trim with courtesy lights and illuminated door switches, driver side footwell lights, illuminated entry system, leather shift knob, lights include: map/dome/luggage compartment/front ashtray/glove box; low liftover design

FORD

THUNDERBIRD

carpeted luggage compartment, dual visor mirrors, luxury cloth bucket seats, driver's 6-way power seat, rear seat center armrest, side window defoggers, speed control, luxury leather-wrapped steering wheel, tilt steering wheel, 130 amp alternator, 72 amp maintenance-free battery, digital clock, EEC-IV electronic engine controls, 18 gallon fuel tank, tethered gas cap, dual note horn, performance analog instrument cluster with trip odometer, fuel gauge/temperature gauge, oil pressure gauge and voltmeter; front long spindle SLA suspension with stabilizer bar, variable rate springs, lower control arm and tension strut; rear independent suspension with stabilizer bar/variable rate springs, mini spare tire, interval windshield wipers.

SUPER COUPE (in addition to or instead of LX V8 equipment): 3.8liter V6 EFI engine with multi-port sequential (supercharged/intercooled with dual exhaust), 5-speed manual overdrive transmission, anti-lock braking system (ABS) with 4-wheel power disc brakes, power lock group deleted, P225/60ZR16 BSW performance tires, 16" x 7" directional cast aluminum wheels with locking lug nuts, electronic semi-automatic temperature control air conditioning, unique rear bumper treatment, lower bodyside cladding, front fascia integral fog lamps, hand-operated parking brake (mounted on console/leather-wrapped handle), driver's footrest, integrated warning lamp module, light group (RH instrument panel courtesy light and engine light), articulated bucket seats in cloth/leather/vinyl trim with power adjustable lumbar support and power adjustable seatback side bolsters, rear seat headrests, speed control deleted, 110 amp alternator, traction-lok axle, 58 amp battery, 72 amp maintenance-free battery (w/auto trans), automatic ride control adjustable suspension.

Accessories

CODE	DESCRIPTION	INVOICE	MSRP
—	**Engines**		
99R	3.8 liter EFI super charged V6 - Super Coupe	STD	STD
99W	4.6 liter EFI V8 - LX (price of engine included in model listing)		
	incls speed sensitive power steering, heavy duty battery		
445	**Transmission** — manual - Super Coupe	STD	STD
44L	**Transmission** — automatic - LX	STD	STD
	Super Coupe (incls heavy duty battery)	703	790
422	**California Emissions System**	85	95
428	**High Altitude Principal Use Emissions System**	NC	NC
—	**Tires**		
T33	P205/70R15 BSW - LX	STD	STD
T37	P215/70R15 BSW - w/aluminum wheels only - LX		
T24	P225/60ZR16 BSW performance - Super Coupe	STD	STD
T29	P225/60ZR16 BSW all-season performance - Super Coupe	62	70
—	**Seats**		
X	luxury cloth buckets - LX	STD	STD
Y	leather seating surfaces buckets - LX	436	490
Z	cloth/leather/vinyl articulated buckets - Super Coupe	STD	STD
1	leather seating surfaces articulated buckets - Super Coupe	547	615
411	**Group 1** — Super Coupe (std on LX)	712	800
	incls power lock group, speed control, 6-way power driver's seat		
432	**Group 2** — LX	280	315
	Super Coupe	143	160
	incls rear window defroster, electronic semi-automatic temperature control (LX)		
463	**Group 3** — LX	187	210
	incls cast aluminum wheels, P215/70R15 BSW		

EDMUND'S 1995 HIGH-PERFORMANCE AUTOMOBILES

THUNDERBIRD — FORD

CODE	DESCRIPTION	INVOICE	MSRP
552	**Anti-Lock Braking System**	503	565
45A	**Axle, Traction Lok** — LX	85	95
153	**License Plate Bracket** — front	NC	NC
12H	**Floor Mats** — front	27	30
144	**Remote Keyless Entry** — LX; Super Coupe w/luxury/lighting group	191	215
	Super Coupe w/o luxury/lighting group	263	295
	req's group 1, 2 and 3		
545	**Luxury/Lighting Group** — LX	313	350
	Super Coupe	290	325
	req's 1, 2 and 3; incls autolamp, power antenna, dual illuminated visor mirrors, light group (LX), ILM (LX), illuminated entry (SC)		
13B	**Moonroof** — power	658	740
	req's groups 1, 2 and 3 and luxury/lighting group		
21J	**Seat** — 6-way power passenger	258	290
	req's group 1		
516	**Cellular Telephone** — "hands-free"	472	530
553	**Traction Assist** — LX	187	210
—	**Tri-Coat Paint**	201	225
58H	**Radio**	STD	STD
	incls electronic AM/FM stereo/cassette		
586	**Radio**	258	290
	incls AM/FM stereo/cassette/premium sound		
585	**Radio**	383	430
	incls electronic AM/FM stereo/CD player/premium sound		
631	**Battery** — heavy duty, 72 amp	23	25
	incld w/LX 4.6 liter engine and Super Coupe auto trans		
41H	**Engine Block Heater**	18	20

1995 Ford Thunderbird LX

GMC SIERRA PICKUP

*1995 GMC Sierra Club Coupe Pickup ***

SIERRA C1500 REGULAR CAB PICKUP (5.7L V8)

Pickups have been among the best-selling vehicles in this country for years, but are increasingly purchased for personal rather than business use. In fact, three of the top five selling nameplates in 1993 were affixed to the tailgates of millions of pickups. It's only natural that this phenomenon would spawn performance variants for buyers who want some hot with their haul.

For several years, Chevy marketed a souped-up version of it's big C/K Series truck. It was called the 454 SS, and came in black. That truck has been discontinued, but performance has not, because the 5.7-liter V-8 version of the Chevy and GMC 1500 trucks will make tracks rapidly when combined with optional handling packages.

The current big GM pickup has been around since the fall of 1987 with very few changes. This year, a driver's airbag has been added, and the formerly angular dashboard has been totally redesigned. Otherwise, this vehicle soldiers on, doing battle with the aging Ford F-Series and the new Dodge Ram in the full-size truck segment.

The 454 SS is missed, especially since its demise left General Motors without a serious contender to Ford's F-Series-based Lightning. The 5.7-liter Chevy and GMC, though, offer plenty of useable performance in a pickup.

Performance and Safety

Acceleration (0-60 mph) .... 9.5 sec.	ABS .... Standard	
Braking (60-0 mph) .... 143 ft.	Driver Airbag .... Standard	
Cornering .... .77 g's	Passenger Airbag .... N/A	
Fuel Capacity .... 25 gal (34 Longbed)	Traction Control .... N/A	
Fuel Economy .... City: 14 mpg	Crash Test Grade .... D: N/A	P: N/A
	Hwy: 18 mpg	Insurance Cost .... Average

* photo of regular cab Sierra not available at press time

SIERRA PICKUP

CODE	DESCRIPTION	INVOICE	MSRP
SIERRA C1500 5.7L REGULAR CAB PICKUP V8			
TC10703	SL Sportside (117.5" WB)	15264	17475
TC10703	SL Wideside (117.5" WB)	14553	16662
TC10903	SL Wideside (131.5" WB)	14798	16942
	Destination Charge:	610	610

Standard Equipment

SIERRA C1500 5.7L SL REGULAR CAB: 5.7 liter V8 EFI engine, 4-speed automatic transmission, driver's air bag, dual in-dash cup holders, side-impact door guard beams, 7-wire trailering harness, power front disc/rear drum brakes with 4-wheel anti-lock system, power steering, full gauges and instrumentation, tinted Solar Ray glass (all windows), color-keyed headliner, deluxe heater with windshield and side window defoggers, heavy duty radiator, AM/FM ETR radio with seek/scan and digital clock, Scotchgarded carpeting and cloth trim, bumpers with black rub strip and bright trim, deluxe front appearance grille, dual composite halogen headlamps, rear quarter swing-out windows, color-keyed floor carpeting, 3-passenger front seat with choice of vinyl or custom cloth front bench with headrest and folding backrest, sport steering wheel.

Accessories

CODE	DESCRIPTION	INVOICE	MSRP
YE9	**SLE Decor**	2463	2864
	incls air conditioning, power windows, power door locks, dual power mirrors, AM/FM stereo radio with cassette, convenience pkg, chrome bumpers, deluxe front appearance pkg, bright wheel trim rings, floor mats, carpeting, leather-wrapped steering wheel, bodyside moldings, wheel lip moldings, halogen headlamps, dual horns		
—	**Marketing Pkgs** — incls pkg discounts		
1SB	**Pkg 2**	718	835
	incls air conditioning, cruise control, tilt steering column, AM/FM ETR stereo radio with cassette		
1SC	**Pkg 3**	1603	1864
	incls SLE decor and wideside or sportside body		
—	**Air Conditioning**	692	805
KC4	**Engine Oil Cooler**	116	135
KNP	**HD Auxiliary Transmission Cooling**	83	96
TB2	**Auxiliary Battery**	115	135
AU3	**Power Door Locks**	134	156
AU0	**Remote Keyless Entry System**		
	req's SLE decor		
BZY	**Bedliner** — Wideside	194	225
ZY2	**Conventional Two-Tone Paint**	114	132
	req's SLE decor		
ZY4	**Deluxe Two-Tone Paint** — Wideside	209	243
A28	**Sliding Rear Window**	97	113
—	**Rear Axle** — optional ratio	NC	NC
G80	**Rear Locking Differential Axle**	217	252
YF5	**California Emissions**	86	100
NG1	**Massachusetts Emissions**	NC	NC

GMC   SIERRA PICKUP

CODE	DESCRIPTION	INVOICE	MSRP
B85	**Bright Exterior Moldings** — Sportside	65	76
	Wideside	92	107
	incls bodyside moldings; wheel opening moldings included on Wideside		
VG3	**Chrome Front Bumper**	22	26
	incls rub strip		
VB3	**Chrome Rear Step Bumper**	196	229
	incls rub strip		
V43	**Painted Rear Step Bumper** — Wideside	112	130
EF1	**Rear Bumper Delete** — models w/SLE decor	(172)	(200)
	credit for chrome rear bumper deletion		
BG9	**Rubber Floor Mat** — models w/SLE decor	(30)	(35)
	credit for replacing carpeting and floor mats		
DF2	**Camper Type Mirrors** — models w/SLE decor	(39)	(45)
	models w/o SLE decor	46	53
V76	**Front Tow Hooks**	33	38
—	**Tires** — P235/75R15 SBR all-season WL		
XFN	front	43	50
YFN	rear	43	50
ZFN	spare	22	25
P06	**Bright Wheel Trim Rings**	52	60
N90	**Cast Aluminum Wheels** — models w/SLE decor or appearance group	215	250
	models w/o SLE decor or appearance group	267	310
N83	**Chrome Wheels** — models w/SLE decor or appearance group	215	250
	models w/o SLE decor or appearance group	267	310
F51	**Shock Absorbers**	34	40
	incls HD front and rear		
FG5	**Shock Absorbers**	194	225
	incls Bilstein gas front and rear		
R9Q	**Appearance Group** — Sportside	501	582
	Wideside	527	613
	incls deluxe front appearance pkg, front and rear chrome bumpers, wheel trim rings and hub caps, bright exterior moldings		
V22	**Deluxe Front Appearance Pkg**	164	191
	incls halogen headlights, dual horns, color-keyed grille		
ZQ3	**Convenience Pkg**	329	383
	incls cruise control, tilt steering column		
V10	**Cold Climate Pkg**	28	33
	incls engine block heater and special insulation		
Z82	**HD Trailering Pkg**	175	204
	req's engine oil cooler; 131" WB models req painted rear step bumper or chrome rear step bumper		
A52	**Seats** — models w/o SLE decor	NC	NC
	incls cloth front bench		
A52	**Seats** — models w/SLE decor	225	261
	incls custom cloth front bench, behind seat storage, center fold-down armrest, dual recliners with power lumbar		

SIERRA PICKUP / SONOMA SLS PICKUP — GMC

CODE	DESCRIPTION	INVOICE	MSRP
AE7	**Seats** — models w/SLE decor	352	409
	incls custom cloth front 60/40 reclining split bench seat, behind seat storage, center fold-down armrest, power lumbar		
A95	**Seats** — models w/SLE decor	568	661
	incls custom cloth front reclining highback bucket seats, behind seat storage, console, inboard armrests, power lumbar		
UM6	**Radio**	126	147
	incls AM/FM ETR stereo with cassette, digital clock, 4 speakers		
UL0	**Radio** — models w/SLE decor	77	90
	incls AM/FM ETR stereo with cassette, digital clock, enhanced performance 6 speakers		
UN0	**Radio** — models w/SLE decor	163	190
	incls AM/FM ETR stereo with CD player, digital clock, enhanced performance 6 speakers		
UP0	**Radio** — models w/SLE decor	249	290
	incls AM/FM ETR stereo with cassette and CD player		
UL5	**Radio Delete**	(247)	(287)
	credit for AM/FM ETR radio deletion		

1995 GMC Sonoma SLS

SONOMA SLS (4.3L 195-hp V6)

Compact trucks are among the hottest selling vehicles in the United States today, and it's easy to understand their popularity. First, their utility is unmatched, except by their full-size pickup brethren. Second, pickups have evolved to the point that many of them offer more car-like comfort and convenience than some cars. Third, they don't all drive like trucks have been traditionally known to. Fourth, some trucks, like the GMC Sonoma SLS equipped with GM's high-output 4.3-liter V-6, perform as well as high-priced sports cars did a decade ago. Now that's progress.

The Sonoma was entirely redesigned for 1994, so few changes accompany it into its second model year. A driver-side airbag has been added for 1995, and daytime running lights (headlights and

GMC
SONOMA SLS PICKUP

taillights that operate at 90% intensity whenever the truck is driven, whether you want 'em on or not) will be added during the course of the year. Otherwise, the fresh design is carried over.

Option the Sonoma SLS properly, and you've got GMC's version of the Chevy S-10 SS in your driveway. The look is bit less aggressive than the Chevy, which may be a good or a bad thing, depending on how much you value subtlety. Inside, the GMC is identical to the S-10, with a comfortable cab but discombobulated dashboard that looks as though it were lifted from some defunct Oldsmobile project.

The 195-hp 4.3-liter V-6 motivates the Sonoma with authority, besting the Ford Ranger Splash to 60 mph, and handling is commendable for a truck. The Sonoma is worth looking at if a powerful performance pickup is what you're looking for.

Performance and Safety

Acceleration (0-60 mph)	7.7 sec.	ABS	Standard
Braking (60-0 mph)	146 ft.	Driver Airbag	Standard
Cornering	.77 g's	Passenger Airbag	N/A
Fuel Capacity	20 gal.	Traction Control	N/A
Fuel Economy	City: 17 mpg	Crash Test Grade	D: N/A P: Average
	Hwy: 24 mpg	Insurance Cost	Average

SONOMA SLS 4.3L V6

CODE	DESCRIPTION	INVOICE	MSRP
TS10603/YC3	SLS 2WD Regular Cab 108" WB	11862	13177
TS10653/YC3	SLS 2WD Club Coupe 123" WB	12835	14252
	Destination Charge:	480	480

Standard Equipment

SONOMA SLS: 4.3 liter CPI V6 engine, engine oil cooler, transmission oil cooler, power front disc/rear drum brakes with anti-lock, 5-speed manual transmission with overdrive, speed sensitive power steering, tinted glass, floor console, digital clock, 20 gallon fuel tank, intermittent windshield wipers, dual horns, full-length headliner, front stabilizer bar, color-keyed grille, reading lights, rally wheels with black center inserts and trim rings, P205/75R15 SBR all-season BW tires, spare tire carrier, driver side air bag, illuminated entry system, complete carpeting, lower body stripe, dual black OS mirrors, dual illuminated visor vanity mirrors, AM/FM ETR stereo radio with 4 speakers, double-wall cargo box, reclining front bucket seats, rear jump seat (Club Coupe), cloth upholstery, map pockets, color-keyed bumpers, halogen headlamps, color-keyed padded sunshades with slider extensions, tachometer.

Accessories

C60	**Air Conditioning**	692	805
AU0	**Remote Keyless Entry System**	116	135
	req's ZQ6 convenience pkg		
G80	**Rear Axle Locking Differential**	217	252
—	**Optional Rear Axle Ratio**	NC	NC
UA1	**HD Battery**	48	56

SONOMA SLS PICKUP — GMC

CODE	DESCRIPTION	INVOICE	MSRP
YF5	**California Emissions**	86	100
	NC w/automatic transmission		
NG1	**Massachusetts Emissions**	86	100
	NC w/automatic transmission		
ZY3	**Special Two-Tone Paint**	255	297
A28	**Sliding Rear Window**	97	113
ANL	**Air Deflector**	99	115
	incls fog lights		
NP5	**Leather-Wrapped Steering Wheel**	46	54
M30	**Automatic Transmission — 4-speed**	851	990
V10	**Cold Climate Pkg**	77	89
	incls engine block heater and heavy duty battery		
N60	**Aluminum Wheels**	213	248
—	**Convenience Pkgs**		
ZQ3	tilt steering wheel and cruise control	329	383
ZQ6	power door locks, power mirrors, power windows	409	475
QCA	**Tires — P205/75R15 SBR all-season OWL**	104	121
ZQ8	**Sport Suspension Pkg — SLS Regular Cab**	272	316
	incls HD shocks, HD springs, P215/65R15 highway SBR WL low-profile sport tires		
YC5	**SLE Decor — SLS Regular Cab**	413	480
	incls aluminum wheels, conventional two-tone paint, 60/40 reclining split bench seat, gray bumpers, gray grille, gray bodyside moldings		
UM6	**Radio**	105	122
	incls AM/FM ETR radio with cassette, 4 speakers, digital clock		
UX1	**Radio**	243	282
	incls AM/FM ETR radio with cassette, graphic equalizer, 4 speakers, digital clock		
U1C	**Radio**	349	406
	incls AM/FM ETR radio with compact disc, 6 speakers, digital clock		
AM6	**Seats — SLS Regular Cab**	(164)	(191)
	SLS Club Coupe	(143)	(166)
	incls cloth 60/40 front reclining split bench seats		

See Edmund's
Automobile Dealer Directory (page 388)
and the back cover of this book to enter our
$10,000 Wheel N'Deal Give-Away.

EDMUND'S 1995 HIGH-PERFORMANCE AUTOMOBILES

HONDA ACCORD EX

1995 Honda Accord EX Coupe

ACCORD EX COUPE/SEDAN

The benchmark. The best-selling car in America. The highest resale value in its class. It needs a V-6. These are all statements that are made with regularity concerning the Accord. It is undoubtedly the most popular car in this country, despite what Ford (who includes fleet sales to such entities as rental car and government agencies in its sales totals for the Taurus) has claimed every year since 1992. The Accord won a loyal base of customers by offering sprightly performance, room for four, frugal fuel economy and a virtual guarantee that, if cared for properly, the Accord would not break.

Those qualities have made it the benchmark. It is consistently the best-selling car to regular retail customers like you. What about resale? The current issue of Edmund's Used Car Prices says that a 1990 Accord EX is worth approximately 60% of its original value. Sure, the Accord is pretty pricey new, but the overall cost of ownership, when repairs, maintenance, and resale value are put into the equation, make it a bargain.

This year, the Accord finally gets a V-6. But, it doesn't perform as well as the four cylinder car. Why? Added weight, different tires, and an automatic transmission collaborate to make the Accord V-6 slower and less nimble than a four cylinder five-speed Accord EX. Hmmm...

The Accord EX is quick, frugal, and loaded with equipment. As an added bonus, it's fun to drive, for a sedan anyway. And knowing that in the end, the Accord will actually cost just half what the sticker reads makes the choice a no-brainer. The Accord is the definitive family sedan.

ACCORD EX

Performance and Safety

Acceleration (0-60 mph) .... 8.1 sec.	ABS .... Optional
Braking (60-0 mph) .... 125 ft.	Driver Airbag .... Standard
Cornering .... .79 g's	Passenger Airbag .... Standard
Fuel Capacity .... 17 gal.	Traction Control .... N/A
Fuel Economy .... City: 23 mpg	Crash Test Grade .... D: Good P: Average
Hwy: 29 mpg	Insurance Cost .... Low

1995 Honda Accord EX Sedan

ACCORD EX COUPE/SEDAN

CD715S	EX 2-Dr Coupe w/o Leather (5-spd)	17770	20110
CD716S	EX 2-Dr Coupe w/Leather (5-spd)	18697	21160
CD725S	EX 2-Dr Coupe w/o Leather (auto)	18432	20860
CD726S	EX 2-Dr Coupe w/Leather (auto)	19360	21910
CD555S	EX 4-Dr Sedan w/o Leather (5-spd)	17946	20310
CD556S	EX 4-Dr Sedan w/Leather (5-spd)	18874	21360
CD565S	EX 4-Dr Sedan w/o Leather (auto)	18609	21060
CD566S	EX 4-Dr Sedan w/Leather (auto)	19537	22110
Destination Charge:		380	380

Standard Equipment

ACCORD EX COUPE: 2.2 liter 145 HP 16-valve VTEC engine with second-order balance system, aluminum alloy cylinder head and block with cast iron liners, electronic ignition, multi-point programmed fuel injection, dual air bags (SRS), effort-sensitive power rack and pinion steering, 5-speed manual transmission, integrated rear window antenna, body color dual power mirrors, multi-reflector halogen headlights, impact-absorbing body color bumpers, air conditioning, power windows, power door locks, cruise control, center console armrest with storage compartment, front 3-point seatbelts, rear 3-point seatbelts with center lap belt, adjustable steering column, fold-down rear seatback with lock,

HONDA

ACCORD EX / CIVIC EX COUPE

quartz digital clock, beverage holder, dual illuminated vanity mirrors, trunk-open warning light, remote fuel filler door release, remote trunk release with lock, rear window defroster with timer, 2-speed intermittent windshield wipers, rear seat heater ducts, low-fuel warning light, maintenance interval indicator, anti-lock brakes (ABS), power assisted 4-wheel disc brakes, 15" alloy wheels, power moonroof, body color bodyside molding, driver's seat with power height adjustment and adjustable lumbar support, AM/FM high-power stereo cassette with 6 speakers (4 x 20-watt).

ACCORD EX SEDAN: 2.2 liter 145 HP 16-valve VTEC engine with second-order balance system, aluminum alloy cylinder head and block with cast iron liners, electronic ignition, multi-point programmed fuel injection, dual air bags (SRS), effort-sensitive power rack and pinion steering, 5-speed manual transmission, multi-reflector halogen headlights, impact-absorbing body color bumpers, center console armrest with storage compartment, front 3-point seatbelts with adjustable shoulder anchors, rear 3-point seatbelts with center lap belt, adjustable steering column, quartz digital clock, passenger vanity mirror, trunk-open warning light, remote fuel filler door release, remote trunk release with lock, rear window defroster with timer, 2-speed intermittent windshield wipers, rear seat heater ducts, low fuel warning light, maintenance interval indicator, rear fender-mounted power antenna, body color dual power mirrors, air conditioning, power windows, power door locks, cruise control, fold-down rear seat center armrest, beverage holder, illuminated dual vanity mirrors, anti-lock brakes (ABS), power assisted 4-wheel disc brakes, 15" alloy wheels, power moonroof, body color bodyside molding, driver's seat with power height adjustment and adjustable lumbar support, AM/FM high-power stereo cassette with 6 speakers and anti-theft feature (4 x 20-watt).

Accessories

Honda accessories are dealer installed. Contact a Honda dealer for accessory availability.

1995 Honda Civic EX Coupe

CIVIC EX COUPE

Never before in the subcompact field has there existed a car that exuded so much quality and class that you would be willing to spend nearly double the asking price for just a few minor drivetrain and trim changes. The Civic EX Coupe looks and behaves like a $26,000 BMW 318is. If equipped with an engine that provided more low-end grunt, alloy wheels and a leather interior, the Civic EX could give the Bimmer some serious competition.

CIVIC DEL SOL VTEC — HONDA

A 1988 redesign brought the CRX star status. The car appealed to all demographic groups by being fun, inexpensive, and good looking. No other manufacturers offered anything like it, and Honda had a choke-hold on the niche, selling every CRX it could import from Japan.

For 1993, Honda redefined the niche, much to the chagrin of the CRX faithful. The company produced the del Sol, a slightly pudgier, less attractive vehicle than the CRX. It was called del Sol (Spanish for 'of the sun') because it was a pseudo-convertible; it had a removable targa roof and a rear window that slid down into the mid-section of the car. The trunk was reasonably sized, and performance with the Si version equalled the defunct CRX, but the car didn't feel as good. To top it off, it was much more expensive than the lovable CRX.

Last year, a 160-horsepower VTEC motor was installed under the hood of the del Sol. The car's personality was instantly transformed, becoming an aggressive open-air sport coupe. Critics quieted down a bit, but still grumbled about the del Sol's wind-up-toy looks, rattly and leaky targa top, and excessive weight. Because the del Sol had convertible aspirations, it was always compared to the stellar Mazda Miata, often unfairly.

We miss the CRX. It was a great car; as instantly familiar as an old friend. The del Sol doesn't have nearly as much personality, coming off as an expensive Barbiemobile with wannabe performance aspirations. However, we do think it would be easier to live with as a daily driver than the Miata. Honda should have dropped the top on the sophisticated Civic coupe and left the CRX true to its roots.

Performance and Safety

Acceleration (0-60 mph)	7.4 sec.	ABS	Standard
Braking (60-0 mph)	126 ft.	Driver Airbag	Standard
Cornering	.87 g's	Passenger Airbag	Standard
Fuel Capacity	11.9 gal.	Traction Control	N/A
Fuel Economy	City: 26 mpg	Crash Test Grade	D: N/A P: N/A
	Hwy: 30 mpg	Insurance Cost	High

CIVIC DEL SOL VTEC

EG217S VTEC 2-Dr Coupe (5-spd)	17226	19200
Destination Charge:	380	380

Standard Equipment

DEL SOL - VTEC: Electronic ignition, 5-speed manual transmission, dual air bags (SRS), impact-absorbing body color bumpers, removable roof panel, quartz halogen headlights, center armrest with storage compartment and beverage holder, centrally locking rear storage compartments, driver's footrest, fully carpeted floor/trunk, sun visors with vanity mirror on passenger side, remote fuel filler door release, remote trunk release with lock, power side windows, power rear window, 3-point seat belts, reclining seatbacks, trunk-open warning light, cigarette lighter and front ashtray, rear speakers, rear window defroster with timer, 2-speed intermittent windshield wipers with washer, adjustable steering column, tachometer, automatic transmission mode indicator, quartz digital clock, interior

HONDA CIVIC DEL SOL VTEC / PRELUDE Si

light, cargo area light, power assisted rack and pinion steering, power assisted 4-wheel disc brakes, alloy wheels, body color dual power mirrors, 4 x 20-watt AM/FM high-power stereo cassette, power door locks, cruise control, 1.6 liter 160 HP 16-valve DOHC VTEC engine, anti-lock braking system (ABS), automatic transmission mode indicator deleted.

Accessories

Honda accessories are dealer installed. Contact a Honda dealer for accessory availability.

1994 Honda Prelude Si

PRELUDE Si / Si VTEC

Usually, when a carmaker introduces a model with unusual styling, we assume that the styling will grow on us, becoming attractive as the rest of the carmakers introduce models with similar styling themes. Since we first laid eyes on the Prelude in the fall of 1991, only two cars have dared tread where Honda designers did when creating the current-generation Prelude. The new Supra's roofline and greenhouse share the Prelude's proportions, and the Lincoln Mark VIII sports an interior as radical as that found in the Prelude. Needless to say, we still haven't grown accustomed to, or very fond of, this Honda's looks, inside or out.

Underneath the questionably attractive sheetmetal is where the Prelude shines, at least in Si and Si VTEC form. The Si gets a 160-horsepower 2.3-liter twin-cam engine; the Si VTEC a 2.2-liter twin-cammer good for 190-horsepower. The VTEC motor is sweet, with a high redline and rev-me-red personality, but it costs an extra $3,000 and reduces the Prelude's acceleration times by a scant half a second over the Si. We don't think it's worth it.

A deeply slotted dashboard greets the front passengers, running the length of the cowl and housing a combination of digital and analog gauges. At either end is a speaker housing and chintzy-looking speaker grille. The design provides an ample amount of interior room for the front passengers, but compared to Honda's previously-brilliant interior layouts, this one is cheesy and ineffective.

PRELUDE Si — HONDA

The frontal styling is downright ugly, and the alloy wheels look as though they were heisted from a Saturn SL2. The Prelude is a fun car, with reliability that is nearly matchless. However, we think Honda blew it with this version. The 1988-1991 Prelude was nicer to look at, more user-friendly, and less expensive. No wonder they hold their value so well.

Performance and Safety

Prelude Si

Acceleration (0-60 mph)	7.8 sec.	ABS	Standard
Braking (60-0 mph)	133 ft.	Driver Airbag	Standard
Cornering	.89 g's	Passenger Airbag	Standard
Fuel Capacity	15.9 gal.	Traction Control	N/A
Fuel Economy	City: 22 mpg	Crash Test Grade	D: Good P: Excellent
	Hwy: 27 mpg	Insurance Cost	Very High

Prelude Si VTEC

Acceleration (0-60 mph)	7.2 sec.	ABS	Standard
Braking (60-0 mph)	131 ft.	Driver Airbag	Standard
Cornering	.89 g's	Passenger Airbag	Standard
Fuel Capacity	15.9 gal.	Traction Control	N/A
Fuel Economy	City: 22 mpg	Crash Test Grade	D: Good P: Excellent
	Hwy: 27 mpg	Insurance Cost	Very High

PRELUDE (1994)

CODE	DESCRIPTION	INVOICE	MSRP
BB215R	Si 2-Dr Coupe (5-spd)	18944	21850
BB225R	Si 2-Dr Coupe (auto)	19594	22600
BB216R	Si 4WS 2-Dr Coupe (5-spd)	21372	24650
BB226R	Si 4WS 2-Dr Coupe (auto)	22022	25400
BB117R	VTEC 2-Dr Coupe (5-spd)	21675	25000
Destination Charge:		350	350

Standard Equipment

PRELUDE Si: 2.3 liter 160 HP 16-valve DOHC engine with second-order balance system, aluminum-alloy cylinder head and block with fiber-reinforced metal cylinder walls, electronic ignition with knock sensor, dual stage induction system, driver and front passenger airbag (SRS), variable-assist power rack-and-pinion steering, 5-speed manual transmission, power-assisted 4-wheel disc brakes with anti-lock, power sunroof with tilt feature, rear fender-mounted power antenna, body-colored dual power mirrors, multi-reflector halogen headlights, body-colored impact-absorbing bumpers, dual-outlet exhaust, center console armrest with storage compartment, power windows, cruise control, digital clock, tachometer, adjustable steering column, 2-speed intermittent windshield wipers, 3-point front and rear seat belts, reclining front seatbacks, right-side fold-down rear seatback with lock, remote trunk and fuel filler door releases, rear window defroster with timer, cargo area light, child safety-seat anchors, driver and passenger vanity mirrors, beverage holder, alloy wheels, anti-lock

HONDA
PRELUDE Si

braking system (ABS), chin spoiler, driver's seat adjustable lumbar support, air conditioning, ignition switch light, power door locks, AM/FM high-power 4x20 watt stereo cassette with 6 speakers.

4WS (in addition to or instead of Si equipment): Electronic 4-wheel steering, rear spoiler w/integral LED stoplight, leather-trimmed seats and door panel inserts, map lights.

VTEC (in addition to or instead of 4WS equipment): 2.2L 190HP 16-valve DOHC VTEC engine w/second-order balance system, electronic 4-wheel steering deleted, AM/FM high-power 5x20 watt stereo cassette w/7 speakers.

Accessories

Honda accessories are dealer installed. Contact a Honda dealer for accessory availability.

1994 Honda Prelude VTEC

For expert advice in selecting/buying/leasing a new car, call
1-900-AUTOPRO
($2.00 per minute)

G20t — INFINITI

1995 Infiniti G20t

G20t

On one hand, we can't understand why Infiniti has such a hard time selling the G20. It's very attractive, offers decent all-around performance, and gets good fuel economy. Priced within a few thousand dollars of top-rung models from Honda and Toyota, the G20 has the added prestige and dealer service of the Infiniti brand name.

On the other hand, Nissan's Maxima makes the G20 pretty much redundant. It has more room, more power, better performance, and more modern engineering. Priced at the same levels as the G20, the Maxima simply makes more sense.

If you do opt for the G20, which is often advertised at unbeatable lease rates, you get a 140-horsepower twin-cam 2.0-liter four under the hood. A V-6 is not available. The G20 is front-wheel drive, and has anti-lock brakes and dual airbags standard. The G20 is based on Nissan's home-market Primera sedan, which is about to be redesigned. Chances are good that the G20 will be all-new for '96 or '97, or will be replaced entirely by the soon-to-be-introduced I30, which will be based on the Maxima.

Really, the G20 is a good car. It's speedy, good looking, and competitively priced, especially for an Infiniti-badged sedan. However, there are other offerings in this class that provide the same amount of style, with a bit more substance.

Performance and Safety

Acceleration (0-60 mph) .... 8.4 sec.	ABS .... Standard
Braking (60-0 mph) .... 125 ft.	Driver Airbag .... Standard
Cornering .... .82 g's	Passenger Airbag .... Standard
Fuel Capacity .... 15.9 gal.	Traction Control .... N/A
Fuel Economy .... City: 22 mpg	Crash Test Grade .... D: N/A P: N/A
Hwy: 28 mpg	Insurance Cost .... Average

EDMUND'S 1995 HIGH-PERFORMANCE AUTOMOBILES

INFINITI
G20t / J30

CODE	DESCRIPTION	INVOICE	MSRP
G20t			
92755	4-Dr Sedan (5-spd)	21819	25975
92715	4-Dr Sedan (auto)	22659	26975
	Note: Model prices include cost of Touring Pkg ($2604 dealer invoice; $3100 MSRP).		
Destination Charge:		450	450

Standard Equipment

G20t: 2.0 liter 16-valve 4 cylinder EFI engine, power heated outside mirrors, tinted glass, 3-coat/3-bake paint with clearcoat, halogen headlights, body color bumpers/moldings, bright grille and door handle accents, contoured front bucket seats, driver's seat lumbar support and seat height adjustment, leather-wrapped steering wheel and shift knob, carpeted floor mats, non-CFC R134a air conditioning, cruise control, tilt steering column, driver's and passenger's windows with one-touch down, power door locks, power trunk release, power fuel filler door release, rear window defroster with timer, driver and passenger front seatback pockets, illuminated driver and passenger vanity mirrors, fade-out interior lamp, cargo net in trunk, driver and passenger side air bags, driver and passenger side seatbelt pre-tensioners, height adjustable rear seat head restraints, child safety rear door locks, energy-absorbing front/rear bumpers, protective side door guard beams, anti-theft system, 6-speaker premium audio system with 2 A-pillar mounted tweeters, 160-watt amplifier, in-dash CD player, automatic power antenna and diversity antenna system, electronic speedometer, analog tachometer, coolant temperature and fuel gauges, trip odometer, digital quartz clock, 5-speed manual transmission, power 4-wheel disc brakes with anti-lock braking system, power steering, leather-appointed power front sport seats with adjustable lumbar support and lateral bolsters, split fold-down rear seat, fog lights, power sunroof, rear decklid spoiler, wide all-season tires on alloy wheels, limited slip differential, remote keyless entry system, padded leather center console armrest.

1995 Infiniti J30

J30

When the Infiniti J30 was introduced, its designers said it represented a departure from the "tyranny of the wedge." True, the J30 has unusually rounded flanks front and rear that conspire to produce a different, though bland, shape in the near-luxury class. The look was unique on introduction day, and inspired people to either love it or hate it, with little middle ground to stand on.

J30 — INFINITI

Then Nissan released the Altima sedan; $20,000 less expensive than the J30 and borrowing heavily from the Infiniti's basic shape, the Altima was a much better looking car. New J30 owners felt cheated and cheapened, but others didn't much care about the family resemblance. J30 sales have been steadily increasing since then, though crosstown rival Lexus is selling quite a few more ES300s.

No doubt, the J30 is a solid, substantial luxury automobile that can hold its own in the stoplight drag race, not that you'd ever see one of these things smoking away from the corner of 3rd and Main. We didn't much care for the J30's look when it came out, finding the front styling too aggressive and the rear a bit dumpy looking. We've always maintained that the wheel design of a car influences the visual impression of the entire vehicle, and with the J30t's lace-spoke wheels, the J30 looks pretty good.

Inside, you get coddled in sumptuous leather seats. The interior of the J30 is small, but in a cozy way. Just don't try to stuff more than four adults inside its subcompact dimensions. Ergonomics are nearly flawless, with beautiful gauges and a dashboard clock that would more accurately be described as a fine timepiece.

We're lukewarm about the styling, but the rest of the J30 is sure to please the most discerning drivers.

Performance and Safety

Acceleration (0-60 mph)	8.3 sec.	ABS	Standard
Braking (60-0 mph)	129 ft.	Driver Airbag	Standard
Cornering	.79 g's	Passenger Airbag	Standard
Fuel Capacity	19 gal.	Traction Control	N/A
Fuel Economy	City: 18 mpg	Crash Test Grade	D: Good P: Good
	Hwy: 23 mpg	Insurance Cost	Average

J30

Code	Description	Invoice	MSRP
97015	4-Dr Sedan	31997	38550
	Destination Charge:	450	450

Standard Equipment

J30: 3.0 liter EFI V6 engine, 4-speed ECT automatic transmission, power 4-wheel disc brakes with anti-lock braking system, speed-sensitive power steering, dual air bags, leather seating, power windows, tinted glass, power sunroof, cruise control, clock, front and rear stabilizer bars, anti-theft alarm system, limited slip differential, tachometer, automatic air conditioning, trip odometer, cast aluminum alloy wheels, radio (AM/FM ETR stereo with Dolby, cassette, compact disc, 6 Bose speakers), rear seat center armrest, dual 8-way power front bucket seats (heated), center console, keyless remote entry, dual power OS mirrors, automatic dimming day/night rearview mirror, tilt steering column, power trunk/fuel filler door releases, power door locks, cargo convenience net, leather-wrapped steering wheel, P215/60HR15 SBR all-season tires, floor mats.

Accessories

R01	**Touring Pkg**	1660	2000

incls rear spoiler, performance alloy wheels, revised stabilizer bar diameters, recalibrated sprins

INFINITI
Q45t

CODE   DESCRIPTION   INVOICE   MSRP

1995 Infiniti Q45t

Q45t

European automakers scoffed when, in 1989, Nissan announced a new luxury division called Infiniti. They assumed Americans wouldn't want a Japanese luxury car because it would lack prestige and pedigree. They were wrong, and now find themselves playing ball by much different rules.

The Q45 is Infiniti's luxo-barge entry, though we use the term barge loosely. Powered by a silky V-8 and possessed with road manners nearly as confident as the most powerful sports cars available today, the Q45 is undoubtedly one of the most sporting luxury cars you can buy. True, its competition from Toyota, the Lexus LS400, outsells the Q45 by a margin of about 2 to 1, but that just means the Q45 is a more exclusive car to drive.

For 1995, base Q45s get alloy wheels. No other changes are being made to the Q as Infiniti gears up for the introduction of the 1996 I30, which will slot in between the G20 and the J30.

Lexus has a completely revamped LS400 for sale for 1995, but don't discount the more attractive Q45. Just imagine how much more exclusive the Infiniti will be when everybody starts snatching up the new Lexus.

Performance and Safety

Acceleration (0-60 mph)	7.2 sec.	ABS	Standard
Braking (60-0 mph)	121 ft.	Driver Airbag	Standard
Cornering	.85 g's	Passenger Airbag	Standard
Fuel Capacity	22.5 gal.	Traction Control	Optional
Fuel Economy	City: 15 mpg	Crash Test Grade	D: N/A P: N/A
	Hwy: 22 mpg	Insurance Cost	Average

Edmund's Driving Impression

On an Infiniti, the "t" stands for touring. And if that's your goal, you can't ask for much more luxury—or for much greater handling prowess and performance in a full-size, rear-drive sedan.

Q45t
INFINITI

| CODE | DESCRIPTION | INVOICE | MSRP |

Though fleet-footed from a standstill, acceleration is less impressive on the open road. The Q45's masterful engine responds well enough, and the transmission downshifts readily; yet, the car doesn't take off quite as hurriedly as anticipated. Shifts arrive neatly enough but a bit abruptly—in the sporting sense, just like a touring sedan should.

Handling is a joy, expedited by a sporting "feel" to the steering, though a "Q" can produce a slightly odd feeling on curves, as if it's oversteering. Presumably, that's the four-wheel steering coming into play, but it's not very noticeable—or helpful—otherwise.

Stability on the road is outstanding, producing a welcome sense of sure-footedness. On the other hand, the full-grown sedan hits bumps rather hard for a luxury model. If you relish softer rolling, consider the non-touring model, or the Q45a with its Full-Active suspension.

All controls are easy to reach, though not necessarily in positions where you'd expect to find them. Round gauges include a 160-mph speedometer and 8000-rpm tach. Visibility is okay, but the rear view is marred by thick C-pillars, and small back windows don't help much.

Quiet? You bet! Sound isolation is superb. With the engine running, you barely hear more than the air conditioner, and feel apart from the world.

Seats are a touch firm, but highly supportive. Everything seems tight and thoughtfully put together. Doors need no slamming at all, shutting with little more pressure than a breeze might provide.

Switchable traction control and a limited-slip differential can be a blessing in slippery weather. This is a rear-wheel-drive sedan, after all, with plenty of horses trying to grab a toehold.

Q45t

—	4-Dr Sedan (auto)	46543	55850

Note: Model prices include cost of Touring Pkg ($2863 dealer invoice; $3450 MSRP).

Destination Charge:		450	450

Standard Equipment

Q45t: 4.5 liter 4-cam 32-valve V8 engine with SMPFI, speed sensitive power assisted rack & pinion steering, power 4-wheel disc brakes with anti-lock, P215/65VR15 performance tires with performance alloy wheels, CD autochanger, heated front seats, rear stabilizer bar, rear decklid spoiler, "t" badging, limited slip differential, power sunroof, power heated outside mirrors, tinted glass, 3-coat/3-bake paint with clearcoat, halogen headlights, 10-way driver/8-way passenger power seats, driver's entry/exit system with 2-position memory, leather seating surfaces/head restraints, leather-wrapped steering wheel & shift knob, front center console with storage compartment, rear center armrest, illuminated trunk, carpeted floor mats, wood appointments, automatic temperature control air conditioning with non-CFC R134a refrigerant, cruise control, tilt & telescoping steering column, power windows with one-touch down driver's window, power door locks, power trunk release, power fuel filler door release, rear window defroster with timer, illuminated entry/exit system with time delay fade-out, automatic anti-glare rearview mirror, cargo net in trunk, driver/passenger side air bags, 3-point front seat belts with pre-tensioners, 3-point rear outboard seatbelts with 2-point center belt (A/ELR elts for outboard passengers), front/rear head restraints, child safety rear door locks, energy-absorbing body color front/rear bumpers, protective side door guard beams, anti-theft system, pick-resistant door lock cylinders, 12-cut key design, keyless remote entry system (electronic), 5-mph energy absorbing front/rear bumpers, 6-speaker Bose audio system with 4 amplifiers and 2 A-pillar tweeters, AM/FM stereo tuner with auto reverse & full-logic cassette deck, automatic power antenna, diversity antenna system, pre-wiring for Infiniti cellular phone, in-glass cellular phone antenna, analog speedometer and tachometer, dual trip odometers, fuel level/coolant/temperature gauges, analog quartz clock, 10-point diagnostic information display system.

Accessories

| B02 | Traction Control Pkg | 1517 | 1850 |

JAGUAR

XJ-SERIES

1995 Jaguar XJ12

XJ-SERIES

Finally, a Jaguar to be proud of. It's not going to break and leave you stranded in eveningwear on the Dan Ryan at two a.m. No more rides home sitting on cold vinyl seats in the secretary's rusted Toyota with Big Mac boxes strewn about your feet. No more Lexus owners pointing and laughing as steam boils from the chrome grille at the country club. Well, Jaguar hopes so, at least. A big plus: it looks better than the previously quintessential Jaguar design, the Series III sedan from the early Eighties.

Yes, Ford Motor Company, who bought Jaguar in 1989, has much to do with the metamorphosis of the XJ from a traditionally unreliable British stodgemobile into a sleek, sexy, and reliable (so Ford and Jaguar claim) luxury sedan. Despite the involvement of the boys from the Blue Oval, the Jaguar...uh...mystique remains intact. Dual airbags have been installed to protect you from a tree's worth of wood on the dash in the event of a crash, but otherwise the Jag's interior ergonomics are much as they were before—muddled. However, the switchgear is improved, and sumptous leather is still the order of the day. And, the Jag is still built in England, not Michigan, albeit on a new, more modern assembly line, and a Lincoln-badged version isn't available. Thus, the XJ heritage remains pretty much intact, despite Ford's influence.

Three models will be available: the XJ6, powered by a new 4.0-liter six cylinder engine; the XJ12, with a 6.0-liter V-12 beating under the hood; and the XJR, a to-die-for supercharged terror that does away with much of the XJ's chrome in favor of a more aggressive, purposeful look. And what a look it is—the new XJ is deja vu to Series III fans, but with a Nineties twist. In our opinion, it is one of the finest looking cars on the road today, expressing individuality without screaming "LOOK AT ME!" Beautiful.

Jaguar's pricing structure is a bit above competitors from Germany, Japan and the United States, but how often do you lay your eyes on a car and find that no matter how hard you try not to, you keep looking?

EDMUND'S 1995 HIGH-PERFORMANCE AUTOMOBILES

XJ-SERIES JAGUAR

Performance and Safety

XJ6
Acceleration (0-60 mph) .... 8.7 sec.	ABS .... Standard
Braking (60-0 mph) .... 132 ft.	Driver Airbag .... Standard
Cornering .... N/A	Passenger Airbag .... Standard
Fuel Capacity .... 23.1 gal.	Traction Control .... Optional
Fuel Economy .... City: 17 mpg	Crash Test Grade .... D: N/A P: N/A
Hwy: 23 mpg	Insurance Cost .... N/A

XJ12
Acceleration (0-60 mph) .... 8.3 sec. (est.)	ABS .... Standard
Braking (60-0 mph) .... 134 ft. (est.)	Driver Airbag .... Standard
Cornering .... N/A	Passenger Airbag .... Standard
Fuel Capacity .... 23.1 gal.	Traction Control .... Standard
Fuel Economy .... City: 12 mpg	Crash Test Grade .... D: N/A P: N/A
Hwy: 16 mpg	Insurance Cost .... N/A

XJR
Acceleration (0-60 mph) .... 6.8 sec. (est.)	ABS .... Standard
Braking (60-0 mph) .... 121 ft. (est.)	Driver Airbag .... Standard
Cornering .... .80 g's	Passenger Airbag .... Standard
Fuel Capacity .... 23.1 gal.	Traction Control .... Standard
Fuel Economy .... City: 15 mpg	Crash Test Grade .... D: N/A P: N/A
Hwy: 21 mpg	Insurance Cost .... N/A

1995 Jaguar XJR

JAGUAR — *XJ-SERIES*

CODE	DESCRIPTION	INVOICE	MSRP

XJ-SERIES

—	XJ6 4.0L 4-Dr Sedan (auto)	43615	53450
—	Vanden Plas 4.0L 4-Dr Sedan (auto)	50755	62200
—	XJR 4.0L 4-Dr Sedan (auto)	53040	65000
—	XJ12 6.0L 4-Dr Sedan (auto)	63036	77250
Destination Charge:		580	580

Standard Equipment

XJ6 4.0L SEDAN: 4-speed automatic transmission, 4-wheel disc brakes with anti-lock braking system (ABS), power assisted steering, speed-sensitive steering, tilt and telescopic manually adjustable steering wheel, body color bumpers, body color door mirrors, protective body color side molding, Connolly leather-trimmed interior, walnut trim, dual illuminated sun visors and map lights, driver and passenger air bags, height adjustable upper anchorage for front seat belts, front fog lamps, rearguard fog lamps, vehicle security system with remote entry and courtesy headlamp delay, driver-only unlock/drive-away locking feature, overhead console with sunglasses storage compartment, cellular phone pre-wire, central locking doors/trunk/fuel filler door, 2-speed intermittent windshield wipers with single wipe and heated jets, heated rear window, electrochromic rearview mirror, curb illumination door lamps, multi-adjustable power front seats with power lumbar support, power adjustable heated door mirrors, power windows, one-touch down driver's window, outside temperature indicator, trip computer, automatic climate control with CFC-free air conditioning, cruise control, premium audio system, remote trunk release, retractable cup holders, child seat safety belt locking.

Vanden Plas 4.0L SEDAN (in addition to or instead of XJ6 4.0L SEDAN equipment): Electrical tilt and telescopic steering wheel with auto tilt-away feature, body color door mirrors deleted, chrome bodyside moldings, premium leather interior with walnut picnic trays, inlaid burl walnut trim, wood/leather steering wheel, lambswool passenger footwell rugs, his/her remote memory activation feature, integrated 4-channel garage door/entry gate opener, 3-position driver-seat/steering/door mirror memory, electrical tilt and sliding sunroof.

XJR 4.0L SEDAN (in addition to or instead of VDP 4.0L SEDAN equipment): Limited slip differential, traction control, XJR Sport Pkg (incls 17" wheels, high performance tires, sport-tuned steering and suspension), body color door mirrors, chrome bodyside moldings deleted, premium leather interior with walnut picnic trays deleted, walnut trim deleted, stained Birds Eye Maple trim and gear shift knob, inlaid burl walnut trim deleted, lambswool passenger footwell rugs deleted, All-Weather Pkg (incls traction control and heated front seats), compact disc autochanger (6-disc capacity), Harman Kardon audiophile sound system with compact disc autochanger.

XJ12 6.0L SEDAN: 4-speed automatic transmission, traction control, 4-wheel disc brakes with anti-lock braking system (ABS), power assisted steering, speed-sensitive steering, electrical tilt and telescopic steering wheel with auto tilt-away feature, body color bumpers, protective body color side moldings, chrome bodyside moldings, Connolly leather-trimmed interior, premium interior with walnut picnic trays, autolux leather/ruched seating/walnut gearshift knob/gold hood badge, walnut trim, inlaid burl walnut trim, wood/leather steering wheel, lambswool passenger footwell rugs, dual illuminated sun visors and map lights, driver and passenger air bags, height adjustable upper anchorage for front seat belts, front fog lamps, rearguard fog lamps, vehicle security system with remote entry and courtesy headlamp delay, his/her remote memory activation feature, driver-only unlock/drive-away locking feature, overhead console with sunglasses storage compartment, integrated 4-channel garage door/entry gate opener, cellular phone pre-wire, central locking doors/trunk/fuel filler door, 2-speed intermittent wipers with single wipe and heated jets, All-Weather Pkg (incls traction control and heated front seats), heated rear window, electrochromic rearview mirror, curb illumination door lamps, multi-adjustable power front seats with power lumbar support, power adjustable heated door mirrors, 3-position driver seat/steering/door mirror memory, power windows, one-touch down driver window, outside temperature indicator, trip computer, automatic climate control with CFC-free air conditioning,

XJ-SERIES / XJS   JAGUAR

CODE	DESCRIPTION	INVOICE	MSRP

cruise control, premium audio system, compact disc autochanger (6-disc capacity), Harman Kardon audiophile sound system with compact disc autochanger, remote trunk release, electrical tilt and slide sunroof, retractable cup holders, child seat safety belt locking.

Accessories

—	**California Emissions Equipment**	25	30
—	**Chrome Wheels** — XJ6, Vanden Plas, XJ12	1200	1500
—	**Chrome Hood Ornament**	160	200
—	**Compact Disc Player** — XJ6, Vanden Plas	640	800
—	**Engine Block Heater**	80	100
—	**Full Size Spare Tire**	80	100
—	**All-Weather Pkg** — XJ6, Vanden Plas	1600	2000

incls traction control and heated front seats

—	**Paint** — non-standard color	1600	2000
—	**Premium Sound System** — XJ6, Vanden Plas	1440	1800

incls CD player

—	**Luxury Pkg** — XJ6	2320	2900

incls 3-position driver seat, steering and door mirror memory with his/her remote activation feature, electrical tilt and telescopic steering wheel with auto tilt-away feature, electrical tilt and slide sunroof, and integrated 4-channel garage door/entry gate opener

1995 Jaguar XJS Convertible

XJS

   Jaguar's aging personal coupe and convertible benefit from increased horsepower and torque this year as they adopt the new six and twelve cylinder engines from the fresh XJ6, but otherwise soldier on unchanged. This car just doesn't make sense—it guzzles gas, holds two people (and maybe their prize-winning poodles), rides on an outdated chassis, feels and smells like a luxury car but performs like a sports car, and costs an outrageous amount of money.

JAGUAR   XJS

True, it's the only alternative to the Mercedes SL or ragtop E320 in this stratospheric price range, but the Benzes are so much better that there really is no comparision. Even the slightly less-expensive (and less-prestigious) Mitsubishi Spyder makes more sense, and it provides better reliability, drivability and performance than the Jaguar.

Probably doesn't matter to Jag fans. The XJS isn't meant to be practical. Owners don't care about engineering excellence. They want to be coddled, go fast, and maybe even put the top down. They want people to know that they can toss eighty grand away on a toy, so cost is not an object. In this regard, the XJS gets a five star rating. However, rational folks with money to spend will likely be more satisfied with the luxury and performance of a Mercedes, or the sheer speed and all-wheel drive capability of Mitsubishi's rolling tanning booth.

Performance and Safety

XJS 4.0-liter

Acceleration (0-60 mph) .... 7.8 sec.	ABS .... Standard
Braking (60-0 mph) .... 125 ft.	Driver Airbag .... Standard
Cornering .... .80 g's	Passenger Airbag .... Standard
Fuel Capacity .... 24 gal.	Traction Control .... N/A
Fuel Economy .... City: 17 mpg	Crash Test Grade .... D: N/A P: N/A
Hwy: 24 mpg	Insurance Cost .... Average

1995 Jaguar XJS Coupe

XJS

—	4.0L 2-Dr Coupe (auto)	43575	53400
—	6.0L 2-Dr Coupe (auto)	59038	72350
—	4.0L 2-Dr Convertible (auto)	50225	61550
—	6.0L 2-Dr Convertible (auto)	67361	82550
Destination Charge:		580	580

XJS   JAGUAR

CODE	DESCRIPTION	INVOICE	MSRP

Standard Equipment

XJS 4.0L COUPE: 4-speed automatic transmission, limited slip differential, 4-wheel disc brakes with anti-lock braking system (ABS), power assisted steering, manually adjustable tilt steering wheel, body color bumpers, Connolly leather-trimmed interior, walnut trim, dual illuminated sun visors and map lights, driver and passenger air bags, height adjustable upper anchorage for front seat belts, rearguard fog lamps, vehicle security system with remote entry and courtesy headlamp delay, cellular phone pre-wire, central locking doors/trunk/fuel filler door, 2-speed intermittent windshield wipers with single wipe and heated jets, heated rear window, curb illumination door lamps, multi-adjustable power front seats with power lumbar support, power adjustable heated door mirrors, 2-position memory door mirrors and driver seat, power windows, automatic climate control with CFC-free air conditioning, cruise control, premium audio system, full-size spare tire.

6.0L COUPE (in addition to or instead of 4.0L COUPE equipment): Body color door mirrors, rear decklid spoiler, autolux leather/ruched seating/walnut gearshift knob/gold hood badge, inlaid burl walnut trim, All-Weather Pkg (incls headlamp power wash, engine block heater, heated seats), trip computer, compact disc autochanger (6-disc capacity), full-size spare tire deleted.

4.0L CONVERTIBLE: 4-speed automatic transmission, limited slip differential, 4-wheel disc brakes with anti-lock braking system (ABS), power assisted steering, manually adjustable tilt steering wheel, body color bumpers, power operated lined convertible top with glass rear window, Connolly leather-trimmed interior, walnut trim, dual illuminated sun visors and map lights, driver and passenger air bags, rearguard fog lamps, vehicle security system with remote entry and courtesy headlamp delay, cellular phone pre-wire, central locking doors and trunk, 2-speed intermittent windshield wipers with single wipe and heated jets, heated rear window, curb illumination door lamps, multi-adjustable power front seats with power lumbar support, power adjustable heated door mirrors, 2-position memory door mirrors and driver seat, power windows, automatic climate control with CFC-free air conditioning, cruise control, premium audio system, full-size spare tire.

6.0L CONVERTIBLE (in addition to or instead of 4.0L CONVERTIBLE equipment): Body color door mirrors, rear decklid spoiler, autolux leather/ruched seating/walnut gearshift knob/gold hood badge, inlaid burl walnut trim, All-Weather Pkg (incls headlamp power wash, engine block heater, heated seats), trip computer, compact disc autochanger (6-disc capacity), full-size spare tire deleted.

Accessories

—	California Emissions Equipment	25	30
—	Chrome Wheels	1200	1500
—	All-Weather Pkg — 4.0L	240	300
	incls heated front seats, power headlight washers and engine block heater		
—	Compact Disc Player — 4.0L	640	800
—	Paint — non-standard color	1600	2000
—	Sport Suspension — 4.0L	400	500

See the Automobile Dealer Directory on page 388 for a Dealer near you!

EDMUND'S 1995 HIGH-PERFORMANCE AUTOMOBILES

JEEP GRAND CHEROKEE

1995 Jeep Grand Cherokee Limited

GRAND CHEROKEE (5.2L V8)

For years, the Ford Explorer has been the best-selling sport utility vehicle in this country, but in 1993 a new challenger called Grand Cherokee arrived to try to wrest the sales crown away from the champ. It was not successful. However, it did outsell every other sport utility on the market, and became the Explorer's biggest threat.

Currently, the Jeep is still number two, but behind Chevrolet's all-new Blazer. While Ford has sold more Explorers than either Jeep or Chevy have of Grand Cherokees or Blazers for all of 1994, October sales put the Chevy in the lead for that month. Worse news for Jeep—a revamped Explorer should be in showrooms about the first of the year. Does all this mean that Jeep doesn't have a shot at the title in the near future? Probably, but only because the factory can't make enough to meet demand, not because of any inherent flaws with the Grand Cherokee itself.

Indeed, this is the most car-like of sport utilities. It has a driver-side airbag, four-wheel anti-lock disc brakes, lots of equipment choices and trim lines, and can be optioned with one of three four-wheel drive systems, if you want it at all. New for 1995 is an integrated child seat option, available sunroof, optional flip-open rear glass, and a new model sponsored by the Orvis outdoor outfitter folks. As you can see, Jeep isn't resting on its laurels waiting for the competition to leave the Grand Cherokee in the dust.

The exterior is all hard edges and angles, but is instantly recognizable as a Jeep product and looks pretty good. Inside, the angular theme continues, with a slightly outdated dash design and big, flat seats. Another retro touch we could do without—the location of the spare tire. Now, the Grand Cherokee doesn't have tiny tires, and the cargo area is among the smallest in the class to begin with, so why is the tire in the cargo area? It should be under the cargo floor or mounted under the truck. Otherwise, we have few quibbles with this sport ute.

GRAND CHEROKEE — JEEP

Performance and Safety

Acceleration (0-60 mph) .... 8.0 sec.
Braking (60-0 mph) .... 126 ft.
Cornering .... .75 g's
Fuel Capacity .... 23 gal.
Fuel Economy .... City: 15 mpg
                                 Hwy: 20 mpg

ABS .... Standard
Driver Airbag .... Standard
Passenger Airbag .... N/A
Traction Control .... N/A
Crash Test Grade .... D: Good   P: Average
Insurance Cost .... Average

Edmund's Driving Impression

Until we drove a V-8 Grand Cherokee Limited, we were underwhelmed by the new sport ute. It seemed overstyled, underdeveloped and its unibody construction made us question its durability off the road. Most of our fears have been assuaged, and we now recommend the Grand Cherokee.

The V-8 provides astounding acceleration for a sport utility, and while it still feels somewhat tippy and bouncy, this truck doesn't ride like one. It goes, stops, and turns better than Uncle Morty's Accord LX, and the interior is not as small as the exterior design would indicate.

The seats are flat and wide, but offer good support with an excellent driving position that provides a panoramic view in all directions. Headroom is more than sufficient, and the tall side windows impart a feeling of spaciousness. The interior, while robbed of vital space by the spare tire, managed to carry five and their luggage in comfort for several hours of Interstate travel. Coddled by leather and entertained by an excellent stereo system, the five travelers uttered nary a complaint about the duration of the trip. However, the fake wood on the dash is just too much, and the overall design of the dashboard is less than pleasing.

While the Grand Cherokee is competent and easy to drive, nothing about it makes us want to own one. It's somewhat bland, and some of its styling cues are overwrought. The body cladding is cheesy and easily collects grime, and the grille could be toned down somewhat. Also, few of our staff members spend much time off-road or in inclement weather, so most of the Grand Cherokee's virtues are lost on us. As an alternative to an all-wheel drive van, the Cherokee fails. For those who need serious off-road capability with space for five, or just want the latest in a suburban status vehicle, the Grand Cherokee can't be beat.

GRAND CHEROKEE 5.2L V8

Description	Invoice	MSRP
SE 4WD 5.2L V8 4-Dr Wagon	23315	25757
Limited 4WD 5.2L V8 4-Dr Wagon (models ordered w/pkg G)	28313	31420
Limited 4WD 5.2L V8 4-Dr Wagon (models ordered w/pkg L at additional cost)	28214	31303
Destination Charge:	495	495

EDMUND'S 1995 HIGH-PERFORMANCE AUTOMOBILES

JEEP GRAND CHEROKEE

CODE	DESCRIPTION	INVOICE	MSRP

Standard Equipment

GRAND CHEROKEE SE: 5.2 liter MFI V8 engine, power steering, power 4-wheel disc brakes with anti-lock, 4-speed automatic transmission, 2-speed Command Trac transfer case, driver side air bag, power door locks, tachometer, electric rear window defroster, digital clock, power windows, air conditioning, tinted glass, cruise control, extra-quiet insulation package, intermittent windshield wipers, rear window wiper/washer, dual horns, floor console with storage, tilt steering column, black bodyside moldings, black bumper guards, argent and black bumpers, cloth headliner, leather-wrapped steering wheel, dual black OS mirrors, illuminated keyless remote entry system, front stabilizer bar, silver full-face steel wheels, color-keyed carpeting, courtesy lights, roof-mounted luggage rack, front reclining high back bucket seats, 60/40 split fold-down rear seat, cloth and vinyl trim, compact spare tire, P215/75R15 SBR all-season BW tires, AM/FM ETR stereo radio with cassette and 4 speakers, remote fuel filler door release, silver grille, trailer tow prep group.

LIMITED (in addition to or instead of SE equipment): Luxury group (incls night vision safety rearview day/night mirror, automatic headlamp system, 6-way power front seats, vehicle information center), air conditioning with auto temp control, alarm system, fog lights, protection group (incls cargo cover, convenience area net, floor mats), full-time Quadra-Trac transfer case, color-keyed grille, color-keyed bumpers with gold insert, sunscreen glass, gold paint stripes, power antenna, AM/FM ETR stereo with cassette, graphic equalizer, and Infinity Gold sound system, dual color keyed heated power OS mirrors, automatic dimming rearview mirror, dual illuminated visor vanity mirrors, map pockets, dual power reclining low back wingback front bucket seats, crosswire aluminum wheels, overhead console, bodyside cladding, leather/vinyl upholstery, P225/70R15 OWL tires.

Accessories

B	**Pkg B** — SE	NC	NC
	incls model with SE decor group		
E	**Pkg E "Laredo"** — SE	536	631
	incls Laredo decor group, dual electric mirrors, protection group, 15" x 7" sport wheels (4)		
F	**Pkg F "Laredo"** — SE	2412	2838
	incls pkg E contents plus overhead console, deep tinted sunscreen glass, luxury group, radio (incls AM/FM radio with cassette, 6 speakers and graphic equalizer), security alarm, "select trac" transfer case		
G	**Pkg G** — Limited	NC	NC
	incls model with Limited equipment (incls air conditioning with auto temp control, 4-wheel disc brakes with anti-lock, floor console, rear window defroster, deep tinted sunscreen glass, luxury group, dual electric heated mirrors, protection group, radio (AM/FM cassette with 6 speakers and graphic equalizer), roof rack, security alarm, P225/70R15 OWL all-terrain tires (4), "quadra-trac" transfer case, 15" x 7" luxury aluminum wheels (4)		
L	**Pkg L "Orvis"** — Limited	564	663
	incls trailer tow prep group, "Up Country" suspension, Orvis edition decor group (incls moss green fascias and cladding with roan red insert and maize stripes, body color grille and maize "Jeep" and "V8" nameplates, maize "Grand Cherokee" decal on front doors, "Orvis" decal on front cladding, door trim panels with dark green upper bolsters, "Orvis" medallion added to woodgrain applique, leather/vinyl seating with champagne/dark green inserts, black storage nets on seat backs, unique champagne/dark green with roan red accent spare tire cover with zippered storage, 3 storage pockets with velcro flaps, black storage net and "Orvis" name and logo, unique color-keyed console, "Orvis" name added to front floors [16 oz.])		
DSA	**Axle** — rear trac-lok differential	242	285

GRAND CHEROKEE

CODE	DESCRIPTION	INVOICE	MSRP
CUN	**Overhead Console** — SE w/pkg E	197	232
	incls compass, trip computer, keyless entry receiver, 4 lamps, sunglass and garage door opener storage compartments		
NHK	**Engine Block Heater**	26	31
AWL	**Fog Lamp/Skid Plate Group** — SE w/pkg B, E or F	216	254
	w/AWE (SE w/pkg B, E or F)	94	110
	Limited w/pkg G	122	144
GEP	**Glass** — flipper liftgate	77	90
GEG	**Glass** — deep tinted sunscreen - SE w/pkg B or E	192	226
AFF	**Luxury Group** — SE w/pkg E	567	667
	incls night vision safety rearview mirror (day/night), automatic headlamp system, 6-way power front seats, vehicle information center		
GTK	**Mirrors** — dual electric - SE w/pkg B	81	95
GTM	**Mirrors** — dual electric, heated - SE w/pkg B	119	140
	SE w/pkg E or F	38	45
ADB	**Protection Group** — SE w/pkg B	100	118
	incls floor mats (4), retractable rear cargo cover, convenience area net		
RAY	**Radio** — SE w/pkg B or E	524	617
	incls 5-band equalizer, 8 premium sound Infinity speakers, 120 watt power amplifier, power antenna, clock		
RBC	**Radio** — SE w/pkg B or E	669	787
	SE w/pkg F	145	170
	Limited w/pkg G or L	145	170
CFK	**Seat** — integrated child - SE w/pkg B, E or F	128	150
	Limited w/pkg G	128	150
LSA	**Security Alarm** — SE w/pkg B or E	127	149
GWA	**Sunroof** — power - SE	912	1073
	Limited	645	759
	avail w/all pkgs; overhead console incld on Limited		
AWE	**Up Country Suspension Group** - SE w/pkg B	675	794
	SE w/pkg E or F	491	578
	Limited	360	423
	incls skid plate group, tow hooks, P245/70R15 OWL all-terrain tires, front and rear high pressure gas shocks, unique front and rear springs (1" higher ride height), conventional spare tire, matching 5th wheel		
TRT	**Tires** — SE w/pkg B	209	246
	incls P225/75R15 OWL all-season (4)		
TRN	**Tires** — SE w/pkg B	266	313
	SE w/pkg E or F	57	67
	Limited w/pkg G	NC	NC
	incls P225/75R15 OWL all-terrain (4)		
TBB	**Tires** — SE w/pkg B	111	130
	SE w/pkg E or F	136	160
	Limited w/pkg G	136	160
	incls conventional spare and steel wheel WJD		

EDMUND'S 1995 HIGH-PERFORMANCE AUTOMOBILES

JEEP — GRAND CHEROKEE

CODE	DESCRIPTION	INVOICE	MSRP
AHT	**Trailer Tow Group III**	305	359
	incls 5000 lbs. maximum trailer weight, 750 lbs. maximum tongue weight, 25' maximum travel trailer length, frame mounted equalizer hitch receptacle, 7-wire harness, auxiliary automatic transmission oil cooler, 3.73 axle ratio		
AHX	**Trailer Tow Group IV** — SE w/pkg B, E or F	206	242
	Limited w/pkg G or L	206	242
	incls 6500 lbs. maximum trailer weight, 750 lbs. maximum tongue weight, 25' maximum travel trailer length, frame mounted equalizer hitch receptacle, 7-wire harness, 3.73 axle ratio		
NAE	**California Emissions**	105	124
NBY	**Massachusetts Emissions**	105	124
—	**Seats** — SE w/pkg B	NC	NC
	incls Jasper cloth and vinyl high back bucket seats		
—	**Seats** — SE w/pkg E or F	NC	NC
	incls cloth and vinyl high back bucket seats		
—	**Seats** — SE w/pkg E or F	490	576
	Limited w/pkg G	NC	NC
	Limited w/pkg L	NC	NC
	req's AFF on SE; incls leather and vinyl low back bucket seats		
—	**Seats** — Limited w/pkg G	255	300
	incls luxury leather and vinyl low back bucket seats		

1995 Jeep Grand Cherokee Orvis Edition

EDMUND'S 1995 HIGH-PERFORMANCE AUTOMOBILES

ES 300

1995 Lexus ES 300

ES 300

Based on the hugely successful Toyota Camry, the ES 300 is the 'entry-level' Lexus. Priced at about the same level as larger, more plush premium American sedans, the smaller ES 300 is more nimble, solid and refined, and is as reliable as a sunrise.

The only options available on this car are leather trim, a sunroof, heated front seats and a CD player. Everything else is standard. A 3.0-liter twin-cam V-6 powers the front wheels, providing swift acceleration. Four-wheel anti-lock brakes haul the ES down from 60 mph in short order, and your choice of Goodyear, Dunlop or Firestone V-rated tires keep the ES 300 glued to the road.

The cabin is well insulated from the buzz of the outside world, and a premium Nakamichi sound system does a fair impression of the Boston Pops performing at the Hollywood Bowl. The optional leather seats are well bolstered and provide an excellent seating position. Ergonomics, in the Lexus tradition, are unbeatable.

For 1995, the ES has undergone a slight revision of the front and rear fascias, and chrome wheels are optional. The ES 300 is a remarkable car, but we have a difficult time justifying buying one. The Toyota Camry XLE V-6, outfitted with leather and all the trimmings, is powered by the same drivetrain and rides on many of the same underpinnings for thousands less. If a Lexus badge really means that much to you, the ES 300 is a great car, but we'll opt for the less prestigious Camry and use the savings to go white water rafting or something.

LEXUS — ES 300

Performance and Safety

Acceleration (0-60 mph) .... 8.2 sec.	ABS .... Standard
Braking (60-0 mph) .... 134 ft.	Driver Airbag .... Standard
Cornering .... .81 g's	Passenger Airbag .... Standard
Fuel Capacity .... 18.5 gal.	Traction Control .... N/A
Fuel Economy .... City: 20 mpg	Crash Test Grade .... D: N/A P: N/A
Hwy: 28 mpg	Insurance Cost .... Average

ES 300

Code	Description	Invoice	MSRP
9000	4-Dr Sport Sedan (auto)	26145	31500
	Destination Charge:	480	480

Standard Equipment

ES 300: 3.0L 188HP 4-cam 24 valve V6 engine, 4-speed electronically controlled automatic transmission with intelligence (ECT-i), vehicle-speed-sensing progressive power rack and pinion steering, front-wheel drive, 4-wheel independent MacPherson strut-type suspension, MacPherson struts, front and rear stabilizer bars, 4-wheel power-assisted ventilated disc brakes, 4-wheel anti-lock braking system (ABS), 15" aluminum alloy wheels, 205/65R15 V-rated tires, halogen double projector low-beam headlamps, halogen double projector high-beam headlamps, dual power remote-controlled and color coordinated outside mirrors with defoggers, variable intermittent full-area windshield wipers with mist control, color keyed lower bodyside cladding, remote entry system, electronic analog instrumentation, driver and front passenger airbag supplemental restraint system (SRS), 3-point safety belts (front and outboard rear), rear center lap belt, automatic locking retractor (ALR)/emergency locking retractor (ELR) safety belts for all outboard positions except driver, manual tilt steering wheel with driver side airbag, driver and front passenger power seat adjustments (seat fore/aft movement, recline, front and rear vertical height, manual headrest fore/aft, driver's seat manual lumbar support), power window with driver's side "auto-down" feature, retained accessory power for windows and optional moonroof, power door locks with driver's door two-turn unlock feature, R-134a CFC-free air conditioning system, walnut wood trim, automatic climate control, automatic on/off headlamps, rear window defogger with timer, vehicle theft-deterrent system, dual illuminated visor vanity mirrors, center sun visor, remote electronic trunk lid and fuel-filler door releases, outside temperature indicator, Lexus/Pioneer AM/FM ETR with auto-reverse cassette and 8 speakers, automatic AM/FM power mast antenna with FM diversity antenna on rear window glass, pre-wired for optional Lexus cellular telephone, tool kit, first aid kit.

Accessories

Code	Description	Invoice	MSRP
HH	**Heated Front Seats**	320	400
	req's leather pkg		
DC	**Remote CD Changer**	750	1000
LA	**Leather Pkg**	1040	1300
CW	**Chrome Wheels**	880	1100
WL	**Wheel Locks**	30	50
FT	**All-Season Tires** — models w/chrome wheels	NC	NC
SR	**Power Moonroof**	720	900
LM	**Trunk Mat**	38	63
CF	**Floor Mats** — carpeted	66	110

GS 300

1995 Lexus GS 300

GS 300

Some readers may think we're goofy, but when the GS 300 first appeared we kept confusing it with the Ford Mustang when one of them approached us on the road. Understandable perhaps, since the Mustang was released at about the same time. We don't know if this similarity in front styling is a good or a bad thing. It could be good that the Lexus sport sedan resembles the quintessential American sport coupe, lending the GS a decidedly rakish look. It could be bad if status-seeking buyers interested in a premium sport sedan find that the car looks like a brash boy-racer hot rod. Whatever the verdict, we were quite embarassed when discovering that the approaching Mustang GT was in fact the new Lexus, but the way cars are styled these days, it's often difficult to tell what brand, let alone what model, a vehicle is from a distance of ten feet or more.

From the side, this Lexus is easily identifiable. The unique roofline gives it away instantly. The GS 300 is a very attractive car, aside from an odd taillight design and rather hefty-looking rear quarters. Inside, the GS is pure Lexus, with electro-luminescent gauges, near perfect control placement, and luxury touches everywhere you look.

The GS 300 is powered by a 220-horsepower 3.0-liter inline six cylinder, which provides slightly sluggish acceleration for a sport-minded sedan. For 1995, this Lexus receives no changes.

Slotted between the ES 300 and the LS 400, the GS doesn't come cheap. It is a solid, competent car, but lacks a distinct personality. Sometimes the relentless pursuit of perfection can lead to some rather dull consequences.

LEXUS GS 300

Performance and Safety

Acceleration (0-60 mph) .... 8.7 sec.	ABS .... Standard
Braking (60-0 mph) .... 124 ft.	Driver Airbag .... Standard
Cornering .... .82 g's	Passenger Airbag .... Standard
Fuel Capacity .... 21.1 gal.	Traction Control .... Optional
Fuel Economy .... City: 18 mpg	Crash Test Grade .... D: Average P: Average
Hwy: 23 mpg	Insurance Cost .... Average

GS 300

Code	Description	Invoice	MSRP
9300	4-Dr Sedan (auto)	35441	42700
	Destination Charge:	480	480

Standard Equipment

GS 300: 3.0L 220HP twin-cam 24-valve in-line 6 cylinder engine, 4-speed electronically controlled automatic transmission with intelligence (ECT-i), vehicle-speed-sensing progressive power rack and pinion steering, rear-wheel drive, 4-wheel independent double-wishbone suspension, gas pressurized shock absorbers, front and rear stabilizer bars, 4-wheel power-assisted ventilated disc brakes, 4-wheel anti-lock braking system (ABS), 16" aluminum alloy wheels, 215/60R16 V-rated tires, halogen projector low beam headlamps, halogen high beam headlamps, dual power remote controlled and color coordinated outside mirrors with defoggers, variable intermittent full-area windshield wipers with mist control, monotone lower body side cladding (except white), remote entry system, electronic analog instrumentation, driver and front passenger airbag supplemental restraint system (SRS), 3-point safety belts (front and outboard rear), rear center lap belt, "easy access" front seat belts, automatic locking retractor (ALR)/emergency locking retractor (ELR), safety belts for front and rear outboard passengers, power tilt and telescoping steering column with automatic tilt-away, driver and front passenger power seat adjustments (fore/aft movement, seatback for/aft movement, cushion height, lumbar support), power windows with driver's side "auto-down" feature, retained accessory power for windows and optional moonroof, power door locks with driver's door two-turn unlock feature, R-134a CFC-free air conditioning system, walnut wood trim, automatic climate control, automatic on/off headlamps, rear window defogger with auto-off timer, vehicle and audio theft-deterrent systems, illuminated entry system, dual illuminated visor vanity mirrors, center sun visor, remote electric trunk lid and fuel-filler door releases, outside temperature indicator, Lexus Premium Audio System with AM/FM cassette (7 speakers including 10" bi-amplified subwoofer and 225-watts maximum power), automatic 3-position AM/FM power mast antenna and FM diversity antenna system, pre-wired for Lexus cellular telephone, tool kit, first-aid kit.

Accessories

Code	Description	Invoice	MSRP
DC	**Remote CD Changer**	750	1000
LA	**Leather Pkg**	1040	1300
WL	**Wheel Locks**	30	50
FT	**All-Season Tires**	NC	NC
SR	**Power Moonroof**	720	900
LM	**Trunk Mat**	38	63
CF	**Floor Mats** — carpeted	66	110
NK	**Nakamichi Radio**	825	1100
	req's leather pkg and remote CD changer		
TN	**Traction Control**	1440	1800
	incls heated front seats; req's all-season tires and leather pkg		

EDMUND'S 1995 HIGH-PERFORMANCE AUTOMOBILES

LS 400

| CODE | DESCRIPTION | INVOICE | MSRP |

1995 Lexus LS 400

LS 400

Lexus introduced an all-new LS 400 on November 15, 1994, but you wouldn't know it if not for the advertising blitz on television and in print. The car looks the same, inside and out, even though virtually every piece has been revised or redesigned. Lexus claims it is going for a corporate look to further strengthen brand identity. We think that engineers and stylists had a pretty tough time improving upon a car that really needed no improvement. Replacing the old LS 400 with a new one is akin to pouring out a gallon of milk because the expiration date is a couple of days away or buying a new set of Goodyears when the tread is still good for another 15,000 miles or trading an old LS 400 for a new one. But, what's done is done.

The new LS benefits from a roomier interior, thanks to its longer wheelbase. Trunk space has increased, and rear passengers get nearly three inches of extra leg room. The car is no bigger on the outside, and has lost a couple of hundred pounds while gaining ten horsepower and improving fuel economy from the 4.0-liter V-8. The climate and radio controls have been simplified, and the CD changer moves from the trunk to the dashboard.

Outside, the new LS is blockier, with more edges and character lines. Still, the difference is so subtle that 99 percent of the population won't be able to tell the difference between the two cars. Prices haven't increased much, so the LS is still competitively priced against such luxury sedans as the new BMW 7-Series and Jaguar's stunning new XJ6. The new LS 400 is a better car than the old one, but why spend $55,000 when two-year-old LS's can be had for the price of a new Lincoln Town Car?

LS 400

Performance and Safety

Acceleration (0-60 mph) .... 7.7 sec.	ABS .... Standard
Braking (60-0 mph) .... 121 ft.	Driver Airbag .... Standard
Cornering .... .78 g's	Passenger Airbag .... Standard
Fuel Capacity .... 22.5 gal.	Traction Control .... Optional
Fuel Economy .... City: 19 mpg	Crash Test Grade .... D: N/A P: N/A
Hwy: 25 mpg	Insurance Cost .... N/A

Edmund's Driving Impression

No doubt about it, you get a lot to like—even to love—in a Lexus. Completely civilized in its capabilities, the reworked LS 400 blends the expected luxury detailing and posh creature comforts with exhilarating road behavior.

Like a consummate, thoroughly seasoned athlete playing a gentleman's game, the supreme Lexus never flaunts its prowess. What it does is get the job done, every time, with matchless skill—a level of proficiency so masterful that it goes nearly unnoticed.

Despite a touch of body lean, the LS 400 stays stable and sure-footed through expansive curves and into difficult corners. Only a light touch is needed at the steering wheel, but it delivers welcome feedback. Except for a possible touch of road rumble, you'll ride in virtual silence.

Nothing is perfect, including a Lexus. Full-throttle downshifts can jolt a bit, and the ride isn't exactly glass-smooth. You feel most road imperfections, in fact—but more as idle curiosities than as irritants.

Braking is deceptive, as the car gives the impression that it doesn't really want to stop. You push the pedal once, with what seems an appropriate pressure—then might have to press harder to produce an actual halt.

Oh yes, lest we forget, the sticker price is rather high—far beyond the reach of most. And even with its better-than-ever performance, an LS 400 is still primarily a luxury sedan, not a sport-performance tourer. True enthusiasts probably won't fancy having this Lexus as their sole vehicle.   Still, the rewards of owning a Lexus are legion. So, if you're among today's high-earners, or just happen to win at Lotto one day soon, why not take a whirl in this Japanese dream machine?

LS 400

9100	4-Dr Sedan (auto)..	41984	51200
	Destination Charge:	480	480

Standard Equipment

LS 400: 4.0L 250 HP 4 cam 32 valve V8 engine, 4-speed electronically controlled automatic transmission with intelligence (ECT-i), vehicle-speed-sensing progressive-power rack and pinion steering, rear-wheel drive, 4-wheel independent double-wishbone suspension, gas filled shock absorbers, front and rear stabilizer bars, 4-wheel power-assisted ventilated disc brakes, 4-wheel anti-lock braking system (ABS), 16" aluminum alloy wheels, 225/60R16 V-rated tires, halogen projector low-beam headlamps, halogen high-beam headlamps, dual power remote controlled and color coordinated outside mirrors with defoggers, monotone lower body side cladding, remote entry system, electronic analog instrumentation, driver and front passenger airbag supplemental restraint system (SRS), 3-point safety belts (front and outboard rear), rear center lap belt, automatic locking retractor (ALR)/emergency locking retractor (ELR) safety belts for front and rear outboard passengers, power

LS 400 / SC 300 / SC 400   LEXUS

tilt and manual telescopic steering column with automatic tilt-away driver and front passenger power seat adjustments (fore/aft movement, seatback fore/aft movement, cushion height, lumbar support), power windows with driver's side "auto-down" feature, retained accessory power for windows and optional moonroof, power door locks with driver's two-turn unlock feature, R-134a CFC-free air conditioning system, walnut wood trim, automatic climate control system, automatic on/off headlamps, rear window defogger with auto-off timer, vehicle and audio theft-deterrent systems, dual illuminated visor vanity mirrors, center sun visor, remote electric trunk lid and fuel-filler door releases, outside temperature indicator, Lexus premium audio system with AM/FM cassette (7 speakers including 8" bi-amplified subwoofer and 225-watts maximum power), automatic three-position AM/FM power mast antenna and FM diversity antenna system, pre-wired for Lexus cellular telephone, tool kit, first-aid kit.

Accessories

CODE	DESCRIPTION	INVOICE	MSRP
DC	Remote CD Changer	750	1000
CW	Chrome Wheels	880	1100
FT	All-Season Tires	NC	NC
MO	Lexus Memory System	600	750
NK	Lexus/Nakamichi Premium Audio System	825	1100
SA	Electronic Air Suspension w/Lexus Ride Control	1360	1700
SR	Power Moonroof	800	1000
TN	Traction Control	1520	1900

incls heated front seats

1995 Lexus SC 300

SC 300 / SC 400

When Lexus decided to expand its lineup into the sport/luxury coupe class, it did things a bit differently. First, a smallish, sexy body was penned that didn't look much like the mini chrome-barges that usually populate the personal luxury segment. Next, a smooth inline six-cylinder engine was implanted in the SC 300—a creamy V-8 into the SC 400—both driving the rear wheels and

SC 300 / SC 400

giving the cars excellent acceleration. Then, a cozy interior with first-rate ergonomics and traditional Lexus opulence was created, making the cars more like 2+2s than coupes capable of carrying four in comfort. Much different from entries from Cadillac, Lincoln and even Acura, indeed.

Once the car was introduced to the public, the automotive press elevated the SC Coupe to Madonna status, proclaiming it another of a string of Lexus-engineered miracles. They were right to do so; however, the past three years have seen improvements by the competition, and the escalating yen has vaulted the SC's price to the top of the heap.

Yes, this Lexus is an outstanding example of modern carmaking art, and it offers a fantastic blend of style, luxury, performance and reliability. However, the Cadillac Eldorado Touring Coupe, with its brilliant Northstar V-8, full load of accessories, and interior room for four full-sized adults, starts to look pretty good, expecially over the SC 400 and its $47,000 base sticker.

Performance and Safety

SC 300

Acceleration (0-60 mph) .... 7.8 sec.	ABS .... Standard	
Braking (60-0 mph) .... 132 ft.	Driver Airbag .... Standard	
Cornering .... .87 g's	Passenger Airbag .... Standard	
Fuel Capacity .... 20.6 gal.	Traction Control .... Optional	
Fuel Economy .... City: 18 mpg	Crash Test Grade .... D: N/A	P: N/A
Hwy: 23 mpg	Insurance Cost .... Average	

SC 400

Acceleration (0-60 mph) .... 7.3 sec.	ABS .... Standard	
Braking (60-0 mph) .... 121 ft.	Driver Airbag .... Standard	
Cornering .... .87 g's	Passenger Airbag .... Standard	
Fuel Capacity .... 20.6 gal.	Traction Control .... Optional	
Fuel Economy .... City: 18 mpg	Crash Test Grade .... D: N/A	P: N/A
Hwy: 22 mpg	Insurance Cost .... Average	

Edmund's Driving Impression

Highway and byway expertise, not flash and dazzle, is what leads performance-luxury shoppers to a Lexus—particularly to the twin sport coupes. Simply put, we experienced nothing short of sheer bliss from the moment we slid into an SC 400's cockpit, ready to take on any form of road challenge.

Everything looks—and feels—like luxury, but with a distinctly sporting accent. Quality is obvious the moment the door shuts, like a vault closing down for the night.

The coupe's touched-up suspension dampens much of the expected nastiness when rolling through pockmarked urban stretches. On the open road, it contributes to superlative handling—accompanied by an exhilarating but smooth ride.

Driving position is superb, steering wheel magnificently positioned, visibility outstanding. Seats are firm, but oh-so-perfect, cradling you into ideal posture for a day's excitement.

Controls practically reach out to greet the driver's hand. Gauges sit in a darkened panel, lighting when the ignition is switched on—with bright red pointers and white numerals, reaching to 160 mph and 8000 rpm.

SC 300 / SC 400   LEXUS

Creature comforts include handsome leather, in a charcoal and rich maple-wood interior. Headroom isn't great, at least with a sunroof. Leg room is enormous in front, but rather snug in back, despite the coupe's ample overall dimensions.

Acceleration from the SC 400's 250-horsepower, four-cam V-8 is spirited but refined—exactly as anticipated. The SC 400's burly 16-inch tires fill the wheel well, and enable the far-from-lightweight coupe to cling persistently to the tarmac.

Even if it's not quite as fast, the six-cylinder SC 300 delivers most of the handling qualities as its potent brother, helped by this season's bigger (16-inch) rubber. Manual shift is available, too, to take full advantage of the 225-horse motor. An SC 400 comes only with "intelligent" automatic.

Oddly, taken in total an SC comes across as a little old-fashioned, despite its luscious lines, near-perfect front-seat accommodations, and undeniably up-to-date engineering. At the same time, it conveys some of the aura of 1930s classics. Either way, for those who have the bucks to ante up in this game, automotive life doesn't get much better than a two-door Lexus.

SC 300

9201	Base 2-Dr Coupe (5-spd)	32800	40000
9200	Base 2-Dr Coupe (auto)	33538	40900
Destination Charge:		470	470

Standard Equipment

SC 300: 3.0L 225HP twin-cam 24 valve in-line 6 cylinder engine, 5-speed manual transmission, vehicle speed-sensing-progressive power rack and pinion steering, rear-wheel drive, 4-wheel independent double-wishbone suspension, gas pressurized shock absorbers, front and rear stabilizer bars, 4-wheel power-assisted ventilated disc brakes, 4-wheel anti-lock braking system (ABS), 16" aluminum alloy wheels, 215/60R16 V-rated tires (choice of Goodyear Eagle GA or Bridgestone Potenza RE88), halogen projector low-beam headlamps, independent halogen high-beam headlamps, dual power remote controlled and color coordinated outside mirrors with defoggers, variable intermittent full-area windshield wipers with mist control, remote entry system, electronic analog instrumentation, driver and front passenger airbag supplemental restraint system (SRS), 3-point front safety belts for all seating positions, front passenger-slide power walk-in seat feature for easier entry/exit of rear seat passengers, automatic locking retractor (ALR)/emergency locking retractor (ELR) safety belts for front and rear passengers, front seat belt assisting arm, standard manual tilt and telescopic steering column, driver and front passenger power seat adjustments (fore/aft movement, seatback fore/aft movement, cushion height, lumbar support), power windows with driver's side "auto-down" feature, power door locks with driver's door two-turn unlock feature, R-134a CFC-free air conditioning system, maple wood trim, automatic climate control, automatic on/off headlamps, rear window defogger with auto-off timer, vehicle theft-deterrent system, illuminated entry system, dual illuminated visor vanity mirrors, center sun visor, remote electric trunk lid and fuel-filler door releases, Lexus Premium Audio System with AM/FM cassette (7 speakers including 8" bi-amplified subwoofer and 170-watts maximum power), automatic 3-position AM/FM power mast antenna and FM diversity antenna system, pre-wired for Lexus cellular telephone, toolkit, first-aid kit, passenger side cup holder, multi-adjustable power passenger seat, coat hooks, headlights on indicator, outside temperature gauge.

LEXUS   SC 300 / SC 400

CODE	DESCRIPTION	INVOICE	MSRP

Accessories

DC	Remote 12-CD Auto Changer	750	1000
HH	Heated Front Seats	320	400
	req's manual transmission		
LA	Leather Trim Pkg w/Lexus Memory System	1440	1800
NK	Lexus/Nakamichi Premium Audio System	825	1100
SR	Power Tilt & Slide Moonroof w/Sunshade	720	900
TN	Traction Control System (TRAC) w/Heated Front Seats	1440	1800
	req's automatic transmission		
CF	Carpeted Floor Mats	69	115
LM	Carpeted Trunk Mat	41	68
WL	Wheel Locks	30	50

1995 Lexus SC 400

SC 400

9220	Base 2-Dr Coupe (auto)	38000	47500
	Destination Charge:	470	470

Standard Equipment

SC 400: 4.0L 250HP 4 cam 32 valve V8 engine, 4-speed electronically controlled automatic transmission with intelligence (ECT-i), vehicle-speed-sensing progressive power rack and pinion steering, rear-wheel drive, 4-wheel independent sport-tuned double-wishbone suspension, gas-filled shock absorbers, front and rear stabilizer bars, 4-wheel power assisted ventilated disc brakes, 4-wheel anti-lock braking system (ABS), 16" aluminum alloy wheels, 225/55R16 V-rated tires (choice of Goodyear Eagle GSD or Bridgestone Potenza RE93), halogen projector low-beam headlamps, independent halogen high-beam headlamps, dual power remote-controlled and color coordinated outside mirrors with defoggers, variable intermittent full-area windshield wipers with mist control, remote entry system, electronic analog instrumentation, driver and front passenger airbag supplemental restraint system (SRS), 3-point safety belts for all seating positions, front passenger-side power

SC 300 / SC 400

walk-in seat feature for easier entry/exit of rear seat passengers, automatic locking retractor (ALR)/ emergency locking retractor (ELR) safety belts for front and rear passengers, front seatbelt assisting arms, power tilt and telescopic steering column with power automatic tilt-away, driver and front passenger power seat adjustments (fore/aft movement, seatback fore/aft movement, cushion height, lumbar support), power windows with driver's side "auto-down" feature, power door locks with driver's door two-turn unlock feature, R-134a CFC-free air conditioning system, maple wood trim, automatic climate control, automatic on/off headlamps, rear window defogger with auto-off timer, vehicle theft-deterrent systems, illuminated entry system, dual-illuminated visor-vanity mirrors, center sunvisor, remote electric trunk lid and fuel-filler door releases, Lexus premium audio system with AM/FM cassette (7-speakers including 8" bi-amplified subwoofer and 170-watts maximum power), automatic 3-position AM/FM power mast antenna and FM diversity antenna system, pre-wired for Lexus cellular telephone, toolkit, first-aid kit, passenger cup holder, headlights on indicator lamp, outside temperature gauge, coat hooks.

Accessories

CODE	DESCRIPTION	INVOICE	MSRP
DC	Remote 12-CD Auto Changer	750	1000
NK	Lexus/Nakamichi Premium Audio System	825	1100
RF	Color-Keyed Rear Spoiler	320	400
SR	Power Tilt & Slide Moonroof w/Sunshade	720	900
TN	Traction Control System (TRAC) w/Heated Front Seats	1440	1800
CF	Carpeted Floor Mats	69	115
LM	Carpeted Trunk Mat	41	68
WL	Wheel Locks	30	50

EDMUND'S NEW AUDIO TAPE!

How to Get Your Way at the Auto Dealer

You'll learn how to buy right, negotiate smart, save money, and enjoy yourself all at the same time.

see our ad on page 376 for details

LINCOLN — MARK VIII

1995 Lincoln Mark VIII

MARK VIII

Since 1984, Lincoln designers have been suffering an internal struggle about the Mark. They've been non-commital about its role in the marketplace, and have been trying to decide if creating a stunning, radical new car will alienate 'traditional' Lincoln buyers. The 1984 Mark VII had a hint of greatness, but was saddled with lots of chrome and the vestigial rear tire hump. By the end of the Mark VII's run, it had gained more supportive seats, the 5.0-liter V-8 from the Mustang GT, and an optional sport suspension. A monochrome look was available on the LSC, and the popularity of that trim level should have given the boys in Dearborn a clue. The Mark VII was a pretty good luxo-sport coupe by its demise in 1992, but the sheetmetal definitely needed an update.

The Mark VIII bowed in 1993, sporting an outstanding drivetrain and a radical new look. Unfortunately, the chrome remained, the tire hump was still affixed to the rear end, and the popular LSC model was cancelled. Hmmm...still struggling.

The Mark VIII is huge. Long front and rear overhangs contribute to the overall length, and parking this beast can be a chore. The styling is a sore point with us, but in certain dark hues, the Mark looks OK. If you're nuts over the styling, then chances are you'll like the rest of the Mark VIII.

We like Ford's modular 4.6-liter V-8. It's perfectly mated to this big coupe, and goes a long way toward selling us on the car. The interior, like the exterior, is another love/hate design study, and our staff seems evenly split on the dashboard layout. Some find it reminiscent of Honda's Prelude and wish for a version of the Mercury Cougar's outstanding wraparound cockpit, others find the Mark just fine as it is. Some controls and displays have been reworked for 1995, and fake wood has been affixed to the center console to provide some warmth to the techno-industrial interior ambiance.

Under the skin, the Mark VIII is unbeatable, and we think that buyers who like the styling of the Mark VIII will enjoy this quick, competent luxury coupe for many years to come. Those who detest the Mark's brightwork will want to wait until 1996, when a sport version is due with the sorely missed LSC's monochromatic look and more aggressive front styling.

MARK VIII   LINCOLN

| CODE | DESCRIPTION | INVOICE | MSRP |

Performance and Safety

Acceleration (0-60 mph) .... 7.1 sec.	ABS .... Standard	
Braking (60-0 mph) .... 134 ft.	Driver Airbag .... Standard	
Cornering .... .79 g's	Passenger Airbag .... Standard	
Fuel Capacity .... 18 gal.	Traction Control .... Optional	
Fuel Economy .... City: 18 mpg	Crash Test Grade .... D: N/A	P: N/A
	Hwy: 25 mpg	Insurance Cost .... Average

Edmund's Driving Impression

The real question to ask when looking at luxury or performance cars isn't how much it costs. No, the true question is this: Is it worth the price?

In the case of the Mark VIII, we think the answer is a clear yes. Or, to be prudent, a definite "almost."

Rear-drive handling is taut and tight, aided by 16-inch tires. On the expressway, this luxocoupe suffers lumps and crannies quite nicely. Urban potholes, in contrast, grow quite rough, despite the air-spring suspension. Even so, it transmits a secure sensation to passengers. All-disc braking with anti-lock brings this heavyweight to a prompt halt.

Acceleration is excellent, not only from a standstill but when stepping on the gas at 55-60 mph. As the transmission downshifts, the coupe sometimes performs a virtual leap—practically bouncing the speedometer by 10 mph or so in an instant. The four-cam 4.6-liter V-8 performs with skill and grace in this installation.

Interior design is a big selling point. Wraparound cockpit styling greets the driver and front passenger, with a sweeping appearance to the shelf-like upper dash. Fuel and heat gauges are accompanied by a 7000-rpm tach and 140-mph speedometer.

Both firm and supportive, the individual leather seats manage to combine softness and comfort with great security. The driving position is superlative; almost like the Probe GT, it can feel practically custom-made. Everything is just where the hand, or the foot, senses that it should be. This big coupe is extremely easy to drive, too, with no unpleasant surprises in handling or response.

Crawling into the rear is a bit of a battle. It's a little cramped, too, especially for the not-so-youthful folks toward whom this car is aimed. Once seated, though, it's comfortable indeed.

A "trademark" of Lincoln performance coupes for ages, the fake tire hump is nicely shaped nowadays, and doesn't seem to harm the Mark VIII body lines.

MARK VIII 8 CYL

M91	2-Dr Coupe..	33793	38800
Destination Charge:		625	625

LINCOLN — MARK VIII

Standard Equipment

MARK VIII: 4.6 liter four-cam V8 engine with aluminum block and heads, electronically controlled 4-speed automatic overdrive transmission with 3.07 rear axle ratio (includes lock-out switch), speed-sensitive variable assist rack and pinion power steering, 4-wheel disc anti-lock brake system (ABS) with self-diagnostics, power windows with driver's one-touch down feature, power door locks, P225/60R16 97V all-season BSW tires, 16" aluminum alloy lacy-spoke wheels, electronic AM/FM stereo radio with cassette player and 4-speaker premium sound system, CFC-free electronic automatic temperature control with positive shut-off registers and outside temperature, body color front/rear bumpers with bright fascia insert, bright exposed exhaust tips, decklid lock cover, flexible bright grille, body color door handles, low-profile aerodynamic halogen headlamps, cornering lamps, back-up lamps, limousine doors, body color heated remote control outside mirrors with 3-position memory, "glass-edge" type black windshield/rear window moldings, color-keyed roof-to-quarter panel moldings, body color bodyside protection moldings with bright insert, bright/black "Mark VIII" nomenclature nameplate (in rear), red illuminated rear reflex, bright-tipped taillpipe, driver and right front passenger air bag SRS, front/rear seat cigarette lighter, full length floor console includes: padded front armrest/illuminated ashtray/cigarette lighter/color-keyed leather-wrapped gearshift/rear window defrost/dual heated mirror/cup holder/storage bin; vinyl door trim panels with door map pockets/courtesy light, color-keyed door-mounted switches for: outside mirrors/illuminated window/door locks/memory seat/lockable decklid release/fuel filler door, driver's side footrest, console-mounted leather-wrapped gearshift with overdrive lockout switch, lockable illuminated glove compartment, rear seat heat registers, 4-way adjustable front head restraints, instrument panel switches for headlamp/panel dimmer, mechanical analog instrumentation includes: 140 mph speedometer/tachometer/message center/trip computer/service interval reminder; individual leather seating with shirred leather, 6-way driver and passenger power seats with Autoglide seating system, dual power recliners and dual power lumbar control, 3-position driver memory with remote recall, leather-wrapped steering wheel with center blow horn, color-keyed switches, tilt steering wheel, dual illuminated visor vanity mirrors with cloth-wrapped secondary visors, 120 amp alternator, automatic power antenna, anti-theft alarm system, 72 amp/hour maintenance-free battery, performance camshaft, trunk-mounted cargo net, child restraint tether anchorage, door-mounted decklid/fuel filler door release, rear window defroster, delayed accessory continued power for windows/moonroof/audio/windshield wipers/message center; dual exhaust, tubular exhaust headers, 18 gallon fuel tank, universal garage door opener, solar tinted glass, automatic on/off headlamps with delay, illuminated entry system, remote keyless entry system with driver door pad/two remote key fobs, underhood/luggage compartment lights, low oil pressure warning light, speed control with tap-up/tap-down feature and switch backlighting, front/rear stabilizer bars, microprocessor-controlled air spring suspension with vehicle level control and speed-sensitive height adjustment, independent air spring/rebound springs rear suspension, depressed park/semi-concealed interval wipers.

Accessories

CODE	DESCRIPTION	INVOICE	MSRP
800A	**Preferred Equipment Pkg 800A**	NC	NC
	incls front and rear floor mats		
99V	**Engine — 4.6 liter 4-cam V8**	STD	STD
44U	**Transmission — automatic electronic overdrive**	STD	STD
422	**California Emissions System**	86	100
428	**High Altitude Principal Use Emissions System**	NC	NC
—	**Tires**		
T23	P225/60VR16 BSW	STD	STD
T21	P225/60VR16 Goodyear BSW	NC	NC
—	**Wheels**		
64J	cast aluminum directional	44	50
64U	chrome directional	726	845

EDMUND'S 1995 HIGH-PERFORMANCE AUTOMOBILES

MARK VIII — LINCOLN

CODE	DESCRIPTION	INVOICE	MSRP
—	**Audio**		
916	JBL audio system	486	565
	incls cellular telephone pre-wire		
919	compact disc changer, trunk-mounted	700	815
	req's 916 JBL audio system		
41H	**Engine Block Immersion Heater**	52	60
13B	**Power Moonroof**	1302	1515
	std w/touring pkg		
153	**Front License Plate Bracket**	NC	NC
—	**Paint** — tri-coat, ivory pearlescent	258	300
Z	**Individual Leather Seats** — reclining bucket	STD	STD
553	**Electronic Traction Assist**	184	215
516	**Cellular Telephone** — integrated voice-activated	594	690
61A	**Mirror** — electrochromic auto dimming inside/outside	184	215
60E	**Touring Pkg**	1342	1560
	incls power moonroof and chrome directional wheels; avail in Southeast Region only		

FOR A SPECIAL RATE ON AN AUTO LOAN, CALL

1-800-AT-CHASE

CHASE AUTOMOTIVE FINANCE

SIMPLE ◆ FAST ◆ CONVENIENT

USE A MULTIMEDIA CD-ROM TO RESEARCH YOUR NEXT AUTOMOBILE PURCHASE

see ad on page 384 for details

EDMUND'S 1995 HIGH-PERFORMANCE AUTOMOBILES

MAZDA

626 ES

| CODE | DESCRIPTION | INVOICE | MSRP |

1995 Mazda 626 ES

626 ES

Mazda has been bleeding red ink for many years now, mostly due to home market sales woes. However, the company hasn't been igniting sales charts in the U.S. in recent years either, and we have a hard time understanding why. Mazda builds some of the most innovative, unique and fun-to-drive cars money can buy, yet they sit on showroom floors unsold.

Take the 626 ES, for example. In size and price, it competes with a wide range of cars in the U.S. market, but offers more solid engineering and sporting performance than most. It looks good but somewhat bland, with flowing organic lines, nice alloys, and an interesting dash layout. The 626, built in Flat Rock, Michigan alongside the Ford Probe (with whom the 626 shares its sweet V-6 engine) and the Mazda MX-6, was the first Japanese-branded sedan to be called a true domestic by government agencies, yet it remains as reliable as a Timex. But it sits, while Camry after Accord after Taurus roll out of neighboring dealerships.

For 1995, the 626 gets new wheels, and an optional keyless entry system. The ES comes with lots of power accessories, air conditioning, four-wheel disc brakes, alloy wheels, Mazda's 2.5-liter, 164-horsepower V6, leather seats, a moonroof, standard anti-lock brakes and an alarm. The ES is loaded, standard, and still costs thousands less than a comparably-equipped Camry.

Perhaps the tide is turning. We already recommend the 626 ES to friends who want a reliable, fun-to-drive sedan. With Accord-beating performance, Taurus-beating sophistication and Camry-beating prices, how can you go wrong with the 626?

626 MAZDA

Performance and Safety

Acceleration (0-60 mph)	7.7 sec.	ABS	Standard
Braking (60-0 mph)	122 ft.	Driver Airbag	Standard
Cornering	.79 g's	Passenger Airbag	Standard
Fuel Capacity	15.9 gal.	Traction Control	N/A
Fuel Economy	City: 20 mpg	Crash Test Grade	D: Good P: N/A
	Hwy: 26 mpg	Insurance Cost	Average

Edmund's Driving Impression

How the same platform and powertrain can produce three vehicles so different in behavior is a marvel of engineering. If the Mazda MX-6 coupe is more civilized than Ford's Probe, the closely-related Mazda sedan almost totally conceals its performance credentials. Though attractively styled, it comes across as a reliable family-carrier, not a push-it-to-the-limit highway warrior.

Softer suspended than the coupe (see page 199), the 626 sedan yields a more cushy ride, as expected by its likely owners. Oh sure, the 626 body might lean over a tad more than the coupe's in a cramped curve, but its tires stay planted to the pavement nearly as well. With a V-6 and the easy-shifting five-speed, in fact, this sedan can be almost as much fun to drive as the coupe, even if it doesn't look the part.

The sedan seems to pull just about as strongly from a standstill as the MX-6, with comparable gearshift and clutch behavior. An automatic-transmission 626 exhibits less of a sporting nature, though the essentials don't change.

Occupants feel sealed off from the hurly-burly of the road, enjoying secure and quiet-running comfort. Driving position is excellent, facing the same gauges as in the coupe. Visibility also is superior. The sedan is roomy in front and the back is comfortable for two, but a center person leans against the fold-down armrest. Seats feel nice and have side bolsters like the MX-6, but don't give the same sensation of being held in place. Doors close with a light touch, demonstrating Mazda's sterling workmanship and build quality.

We find little to complain about in a 626, which adds excellent gas mileage to its credits—though premium fuel is recommended for the V-6 engine.

626 ES

—	ES V6 4-Dr Sedan (5-spd)	19725	22395
Destination Charge:		425	425

Standard Equipment

626 ES: 2.5 liter 24-valve MFI V6 engine, alarm system, power moonroof, leather reclining front bucket seats with 8-way power driver's seat, split folding rear seat, leather-wrapped steering wheel, keyless remote entry system, dual heated power OS mirrors, dual illuminated visor vanity mirrors, fog lights, 5-speed manual transmission with overdrive, front wheel drive, power steering, rear window defroster, tachometer, bodyside moldings, remote fuel filler door release, remote trunk release, mud guards, front and rear stabilizer bars, driver and front passenger air bags, tilt steering wheel, console, trip odometer, MacPherson strut front suspension, power windows, air conditioning, power 4-wheel disc brakes w/anti-lock, power door locks, AM/FM stereo radio with cassette, power antenna, alloy wheels, speed control, variable intermittent windshield wipers, P205/55R15 high performance tires.

MAZDA — 626 / MILLENIA S

CODE	DESCRIPTION	INVOICE	MSRP
	Accessories		
—	**Transmission** — 5-speed manual w/overdrive	STD	STD
AT1	**Transmission** — 4-speed automatic w/overdrive	696	800
CE1	**California/New York Emission Equipment**	126	150
FLM	**Floor Mats** — carpeted	56	80

1995 Mazda Millenia S

MILLENIA S

By 1990, Honda, Toyota, and Nissan all had luxury divisions that offered superbly engineered cars at prices that rivaled American and European brands. Mazda was a bit slow to react, but soon had its own luxury channel planned. To be called Amati, Mazda began developing two sedans to sell through the division when it debuted in the mid-Nineties.

The rising yen and softening sales in the luxury car segment made it clear to Mazda that Amati would be nothing more than a money pit. The project was cancelled, but one of the sedans in development was nearly ready for production. Rather than consign that sedan to a future of write-ups in "Cars Japan Never Built" books, they decided to sell it as a Mazda. They named it Millenia, and priced it, in base trim, to compete with entry-level BMWs, the Nissan Maxima, and even top-of-the-line Toyota Camrys.

The Millenia is an interesting looking car, unless you're viewing it from the side or rear. The S version is powered by the only Miller-cycle engine in production, a 2.3-liter unit equipped with a supercharger and good for 210 horsepower. Millenia sports a distinctive look up front, but the rest is generic Japanese sedan, which is not a bad thing if you value quality and efficient design over individuality. In contrast to the dowdy sheetmetal, the interior is quite distinctive, in the Mazda tradition of providing excellent controls wrapped in interestingly flowing shapes.

MILLENIA S — MAZDA

Competition in the Millenia's price range is stout, but this car has what it takes to go up against the likes of the Volvo 850, Lexus ES300, and C-Class Mercedes, to name a few. If it only had something other than the Miller-cycle engine to distinguish it, like the personality most other Mazdas exhibit, we could wholeheartedly recommend it.

Performance and Safety

Acceleration (0-60 mph)	7.6 sec.	ABS	Standard
Braking (60-0 mph)	128 ft.	Driver Airbag	Standard
Cornering	.80 g's	Passenger Airbag	Standard
Fuel Capacity	18 gal.	Traction Control	Optional
Fuel Economy	City: 20 mpg	Crash Test Grade	D: N/A P: N/A
	Hwy: 28 mpg	Insurance Cost	N/A

Edmund's Driving Impression

Aside from innovative technology—specifically, that high-output Miller-cycle engine with its screw-type compressor—the Millenia fails to shine particularly brightly, either in appearance or on-the-go behavior. Countless road-testers have sung its praises, but we've not been able to get quite as excited about this distressingly ordinary sedan.

Not that it warrants jeers. Not at all. This latest sedan merely fails to match the high level of desirability exhibited by its Mazda stablemates. Apart from that smoothly purring wonder beneath the "S" edition's hood, and a pleasantly spacious interior, a Millenia simply isn't terribly inviting, in terms of ride, handling, or comfort.

Then again, the Miller V-6 almost makes up for the car's sundry shortcomings, as it accelerates with astounding swiftness. Though slightly sluggish in the first moment from a standstill, it quickly gathers steam, sending the sedan smoothly and briskly on its way. The Millenia practically blasts forward to pass or merge. There's some jerkiness in upshifts to second gear, but at highway speeds, downshifts are almost instantaneous.

Cornering with reasonable talent, a Millenia stays fairly flat on curves. Light steering is accompanied by pretty good feedback, with some understeer evident. Braking is excellent, with a soft pedal feel. Except for slight tire noise, the car runs quietly.

Smooth-riding on the highway, the car is also comfortable in urban commutes. A bit woozy and slushy, at times; but devoid of serious harshness and reasonably well-controlled.

Too-short seats head the list of interior gripes. Headroom is tight at the edge of the sunroof, in a driving position that could be better. Entry/exit and visibility aren't perfect, either.

Gauges are smallish but easy to read, including a 160-mph speedometer and 8000-rpm tachometer. Traction control is part of the package. In execution, the car's solid assembly is typical Mazda. It's in the details that this one stumbles.

MILLENIA S

—	4-Dr Sedan (auto)	27338	31400
Destination Charge:			
	Alaska	625	625
	Other States	425	425

MAZDA
MILLENIA S / MX-5 MIATA

| CODE | DESCRIPTION | INVOICE | MSRP |

Standard Equipment

MILLENIA S: 2.3L Miller Cycle V6 DOHC 24-valve engine with dual intercoolers, electronic traction control, P215/55R16 all season SBR tires, front wheel drive, power steering, anti-lock power 4-wheel disc brakes, cruise control, rear window defroster, power windows, AM/FM ETR stereo radio with cassette, power antenna, anti-theft alarm system, automatic air conditioning, tachometer, power door locks, console, trip odometer, 4-speed ECT automatic transmission with overdrive, front and rear stabilizer bars, illuminated entry system, tinted glass, aluminum alloy wheels, fog lights, dual color-keyed heated power mirrors, dual illuminated visor vanity mirrors, variable intermittent windshield wipers, remote control fuel filler door release, 8-way power driver's seat, tilt steering wheel, driver and front passenger air bags, remote control trunk release, rear seat fold-down center armrest, power moonroof, leather seats, 4-way power pass. seat, keyless remote entry system, leather door trim.

Accessories

RA4	**Radio**	960	1200
	incls Bose radio w/CD player		
RA5	**CD Player**	720	900
JCS	**Paint**	147	175
	incls deep sea metallic paint		
JCR	**Paint**	294	350
	incls white pearl metallic paint		
3C0	**4-Seasons Pkg**	252	300
	incls heated front seats, heavy-duty starter motor, heavy-duty windshield wiper motor, large capacity windshield washer tank		
PPA	**Protection Pkg**	87	125
	incls alloy wheels and carpeted floor mats		

1995 Mazda Miata

MX-5 MIATA

When Mazda announced in 1989 that it had revived the traditional roadster, enthusiasts around the world clutched their chests in horror. A Japanese company trying to capture the essence of MG, Fiat, Alfa Romeo and Lotus two-seaters of the Sixties? Blasphemy!

MX-5 MIATA — MAZDA

| CODE | DESCRIPTION | INVOICE | MSRP |

Welcome to the Nineties, when you can buy the most driving fun you've ever had for less than a Ford Taurus LX. As an added bonus, the Miata doesn't leak oil from the engine bay or water from the roof. It doesn't overheat, fry its electrical system, or scare you in the twisties. You can drive it all day without carrying tools, Go Jo, or Doan's pills. The Miata is truly a modern automotive miracle.

For 1995, this sprightly convertible gets some revised option groups. Last year, Mazda added a passenger-side airbag, side-impact protection hardware, new alloy wheels and a bigger engine good for an extra 12 horsepower. Carried over from last year is the R-Package, which turns the Miata into a race-ready street machine with drivetrain and suspension modifications. Leather seats are still available, and a new color, Montego Blue, fleshes out the color chart, joining black, red, medium blue, and white.

There is nothing like the Miata on the market today. Unless you enjoy project cars that never allow you to complete the project, the Miata is the only way to go to obtain the true roadster experience.

Performance and Safety

Acceleration (0-60 mph) .... 8.7 sec.	ABS .... Optional
Braking (60-0 mph) 128	Driver Airbag .... Standard
Cornering .... .83 g's	Passenger Airbag .... Standard
Fuel Capacity .... 12.7 gal.	Traction Control .... N/A
Fuel Economy .... City: 22 mpg	Crash Test Grade .... D: Average P: N/A
	Hwy: 28 mpg	Insurance Cost .... Average

Edmund's Driving Impression

This is not a Point A to Point B car. If you don't like driving, and view getting behind a steering wheel as a chore, then move on to the Saturn SL2 entry and don't bother reading this. The Miata is unadulterated, pure driving bliss.

Let's get the Miata's negative points out of the way first. This is not a good car for long Interstate hauls. There is no room to move around, and after a few hours you stiffen up. Plus, the sun beating on your face can get brutal, and the Miata is no good with the top up. The top merely serves as cover from rain storms, protection from chilly temperatures and as a flimsy theft deterrent device. At highway speeds with the top up, the Miata becomes the most annoying noisemaker since those goofy New Year's kazoos. If the car is not parked for the night, water droplets the size of tangerines aren't falling from the sky, or the temperature is not below forty degrees, the top should be down. Don't buy this car if you're worried about your hair. Don't buy it if you don't want to sweat a bit under the summer sun. Don't buy it if you're a traveling salesman.

Now the good stuff. The Miata carves mountain two-lanes better than a Ginsu knife does Thanksgiving turkey. It stops on a dime. Sticky Dunlop tires will loosen your butt's grip on the narrow seat before they do the car from the surface of the road. The driving position, the gauges and the steering are perfect. The simple top can be dropped or secured in less than 30 seconds from the driver's seat, and the four-speaker stereo, with headrest speakers, is audible at 80 mph in a crosswind. The ozone-safe air conditioning will cool you on warm days, and the outstanding heater will warm you on brisk ones. The exhaust note, the styling, and the handling are so gratifying you just can't stop listening, looking or driving. True, the Miata can barely out-accelerate a Toyota Corolla, but if you think driving satisfaction is about getting to 60 mph before everybody else, get back to your garage and polish the Hemi 'Cuda.

EDMUND'S 1995 HIGH-PERFORMANCE AUTOMOBILES

MAZDA  MX-5 MIATA

| CODE | DESCRIPTION | INVOICE | MSRP |

We put 3,000 miles on our test car in ten days. If you enjoy driving, are under six feet tall, and haven't driven a Miata, we'd like you to do yourself a favor. Close this book, put on your shoes, and get to the nearest Mazda dealer to take a test drive *with the top down*. If it's not summer where you are, or if today happens to be the day your city is experiencing record rainfall, save it for another time, but do it. Every American with a semblance of a heartbeat should drive this perfectly-balanced roadster at least once.

MX-5 MIATA

—	2-Dr Convertible (5-spd)	15768	17500
Destination Charge:		440	440

Standard Equipment

MIATA: 1.8 liter DOHC 16-valve I4 engine with multi-port fuel injection, sport-tuned exhaust system with stainless steel tubular header, 5-speed manual transmission with overdrive, rack and pinion steering, front and rear stabilizer bars, 4-wheel double wishbone suspension, power assist 4-wheel disc brakes, power plant frame (PPF), 14" styled steel wheels with bright center caps, P185/60R14 tires, intermittent windshield wipers, dual body color mirrors, retractable halogen headlamps with flash-to-pass feature, reclining highback bucket seats, black cloth upholstery, full carpeting, lockable glove compartment, full center console with lockable storage compartment and removable cup holder, remote trunk and fuel door release, map pockets on driver and passenger doors and passenger seatback, one-piece sun visors, two dashboard mounted courtesy lights, gauges for 8000 RPM tachometer/trip odometer/140 MPH speedometer/oil pressure/engine coolant temperature, driver/passenger-side air bag SRS, heater/defroster with 4-speed blower and side window demisters, AM/FM auto-reverse cassette stereo sound system with 2 speakers/anti-theft coding/digital clock.

Accessories

ACA	**Air Conditioning**	720	900
AT1	**Automatic Transmission** — 4-speed w/overdrive	739	850
	req's leather pkg or popular equipment pkg		
—	**Power Steering**	252	300
	incls wheel trim rings		
AB1	**Anti-Lock Brakes**	765	900
	req's leather pkg or popular equipment pkg		
RA4	**Sensory Sound System**	700	875
	req's leather pkg		
1PK	**R Pkg**	1260	1500
	incls alloy wheels, limited slip differential, front and rear air dams, rear spoiler, sport suspension		
1PE	**Popular Equipment Pkg** — models w/o auto trans	1756	2090
	models w/auto trans	1428	1700
	incls power steering, power windows, speed control, dual power OS mirrors, power antenna, limited slip differential (models w/o auto trans), headrest speakers, alloy wheels, leather-wrapped steering wheel		
1LE	**Leather Pkg** — models w/o auto trans	2507	2985
	models w/auto trans	2180	2595
	incls leather seating, vinyl top, popular equipment pkg		
FLM	**Floor Mats** — carpeted	56	80
HT1	**Removable Hard Top**	1215	1500
	incls rear window defroster; req's leather pkg or popular equipment pkg		

MX-6 LS   MAZDA

1995 Mazda MX-6 LS

MX-6 LS

Built in Flat Rock, Michigan on the same assembly line as the Mazda 626 and Ford Probe, the Mazda MX-6 is one of the sexiest shapes to grace showrooms this year. Seemingly styled after Europe's Opel Calibra, the MX-6 exudes class. With the LS option package, which includes Mazda's creamy-smooth 2.5-liter V-6, bigger tires mounted on attractive alloy wheels, four-wheel disc brakes, fog lights, power sunroof, air conditioning and an alarm system, the MX-6 is quite a performer, offering outstanding braking, handling, and acceleration. Load on the Leather Package, and the MX-6 becomes a budget Lexus SC coupe.

Unfortunately, Mazda has chosen to pack all the MX-6's go-fast goodies into the LS package, which is a $3,000 option. Added to the base car's $19,000 price tag, and with leather seating, the MX-6 is pushing $23,000, and that tally doesn't include anti-lock brakes or an automatic transmission. As a wannabe Lexus, the Mazda is a steal; as an affordable sport coupe, it's a bust. The mechanically identical Ford Probe GT, with anti-lock brakes, leather, automatic and all the amenities the Mazda offers is about three thousand dollars less expensive, and offers the utility of a hatchback with an expansive cargo area.

Depending on your needs, the Mazda MX-6 is either a good or a bad deal. One thing is constant, however. It looks exceptionally tasty.

Performance and Safety

Acceleration (0-60 mph) .... 7.6 sec.	ABS .... Optional	
Braking (60-0 mph) .... 112 ft.	Driver Airbag .... Standard	
Cornering .... .90 g's	Passenger Airbag .... Standard	
Fuel Capacity .... 15.5 gal.	Traction Control .... N/A	
Fuel Economy .... City: 20 mpg	Crash Test Grade .... D: N/A	P: N/A
	Hwy: 26 mpg	Insurance Cost .... High

EDMUND'S 1995 HIGH-PERFORMANCE AUTOMOBILES

MAZDA
MX-6 LS

Edmund's Driving Impression

Though stiffer-suspended than Mazda's 626 sedan, an MX-6 LS rides smoother, with less jiggle and jolting, than the essentially-equivalent Ford Probe GT. Not glass-placid, by any means, but in a moderately more controlled manner. All three cars share basic structure and powertrain choices, but similarities tend to cease at that point.

For one, Mazda's notchback coupe is more conservatively shaped than Probe's hatchback design, suggesting an appeal to more mature customers. If Ford's Probe feels like an eager young animal when on the move, Mazda's MX-6 has the personality of its slightly older—and more worldly—cousin. Brashness gives way to civility, though both makes convey similar action when the totals are taken.

A cool and collected 2.5-liter V-6 gives the LS its potential: namely, 164 horsepower's worth. With the easy-to-rev engine and five-speed manual shift, an MX-6 whips quickly off the line. Pickup isn't bad at moderate speeds either, even if the gearbox is in an upper ratio, but a touch of "lugging" emerges on occasion.

Despite occasional resistance, the gearbox is easy to operate. Situated in top-notch position, the gearshift most often falls from one ratio to the next, with little effort. Clutch action is generally fine, though it sometimes engages with a modest jolt.

An MX-6 delivers near-perfect control, with little need to correct the steering-wheel position, whether on the highway or city streets. Sure, the coupe sometimes bounces along urban stretches, but it corners with excellence—secure, taut, tight, adept.

Though not loud, the exhaust emits a satisfying rumble, complemented by a pleasant whine from the engine. The driver occupies a superior position, with fine visibility, but the cramped back seat is suitable only for dire emergencies.

We give both the Probe and MX-6 a hearty thumbs-up (with a stipulation or two). May as well let styling—and pocketbook contents—be your guide.

MX-6 LS

CODE	DESCRIPTION	INVOICE	MSRP
—	LS 2-Dr Coupe (5-spd)	19129	21648
	Destination Charge:	425	425

Standard Equipment

MX-6 LS: 2.5 liter V6 engine, power sunroof, alarm system, air conditioning, leather-wrapped steering wheel, power 4-wheel disc brakes, fog lights, P205/55R15 tires, aluminum alloy wheels, variable intermittent windshield wipers, 90-amp alternator, floor mats, front wheel drive, driver and front passenger air bags, 5-speed manual transmission with overdrive, rack and pinion steering with variable power assist, dual body color power mirrors, tinted glass with upper windshield sunshade band, reclining bucket seats with driver's adjustable thigh support, 60/40 split fold-down rear seatback, AM/FM stereo radio with cassette, power antenna, dual visor vanity mirrors, center console, power windows with driver's side one-touch down feature, power door locks, tilt steering wheel, cruise control, rear window defroster, remote trunk release, remote fuel filler door release, front and rear stabilizer bars, tachometer.

MX-6 LS / PROTEGE ES

Accessories

CODE	DESCRIPTION	INVOICE	MSRP
AT1	Transmission — 4-speed automatic w/overdrive	696	800
AB1	Anti-Lock Brakes	680	800
RS1	Rear Spoiler	300	375
CE1	California/New York Emissions System	126	150
1LE	Leather Pkg	880	1100

incls leather seats, power driver's seat adjuster, heated power OS mirrors, keyless remote entry system

1995 Mazda Protege ES

PROTEGE ES

The engineers and designers who were putting the finishing touches on the new Protege must have lost lots of sleep during the first half of 1994. After all, they were redesigning a compact sedan that, since its 1990 debut, had been likened to a mini Mercedes 190, and had been one of the few four-doors competing in SCCA racing events. Oh, there was that pesky upstart from Chrysler Corporation too, the Neon, but heck...it was a Chrysler; nothing to worry about.

Well, Mazda's new Protege has been on showroom floors for about six months. If the numbers of new Proteges and Neons prowling the streets of America are any indication, Mazda needs to do some quick thinking to sell at least a few Proteges.

We have some suggestions. Make the 1.8-liter engine standard on the LX model, and offer air conditioning at no extra charge. Why would Joe Consumer ante up nearly $16,600 for a five-speed Protege ES when he can get a Neon Sport with every possible option, better looks, and better performance for almost a grand less? (On the other hand, considering the Protege's cavernous interior, perhaps it makes better sense as an alternative to Ford's Contour SE.)

The new Protege, priced more competitively, would make a solid alternative to the Neon. With the 1.8-liter engine and the roomiest interior in its class, the Protege's design is competent, if not

EDMUND'S 1995 HIGH-PERFORMANCE AUTOMOBILES

MAZDA
PROTEGE ES

inspiringly styled. However, compared to many of its competitors, the Protege cannot provide the value buyers expect in a small car. Until this issue is addressed, the Protege is destined to remain invisible to consumers.

Performance and Safety

Acceleration (0-60 mph)	8.7 sec.	ABS	Standard
Braking (60-0 mph)	139 ft.	Driver Airbag	Standard
Cornering	.80 g's	Passenger Airbag	Standard
Fuel Capacity	14.5 gal.	Traction Control	N/A
Fuel Economy	City: 24 mpg	Crash Test Grade	D: N/A P: N/A
	Hwy: 31 mpg	Insurance Cost	N/A

PROTEGE ES

—	ES 4-Dr Sedan (5-spd)	14710	16145
Destination Charge:		425	425

Standard Equipment

PROTEGE ES: 1.8 liter DOHC 16-valve 4 cylinder engine, power 4-wheel disc brakes with anti-lock, air conditioning, P185/65R14 all-season SBR tires, sport seats, front wheel drive, dual air bags, 5-speed manual transmission, rack and pinion steering with power assist, tinted glass, rear window defogger, tilt steering wheel, bodyside moldings, center console with storage tray, front and rear stabilizer bars, cruise control, power windows, driver's seat with 8-way adjust, power door locks, power remote control OS mirrors, AM/FM stereo radio with cassette/clock/4 speakers, trip odometer, remote trunk release, map/reading lights, courtesy lights, passenger side visor vanity mirror.

Accessories

AT1	**Transmission** — 4-speed automatic w/overdrive	720	800
FLM	**Floor Mats**	64	80
CE1	**California/New York Emissions**	126	150
1ES	**Premium Pkg**	956	1195
	incls aluminum alloy wheels, power moonroof		
ESP	**Touring Pkg**	84	105
	incls floor mats and armrest spacer		

GET MORE MONEY FOR YOUR USED CAR BY KNOWING ITS TRUE VALUE

See our ads on pages 4 and 6

1995 Mazda RX7

RX-7

When the original RX-7 bowed in 1978, Mazda claimed it represented a return to pure sports car roots. It was rather basic, offering sparse accommodations for two, good performance and a low price. However, like most Japanese sports/GT coupes tended to, the RX-7 started getting fat with power options, advanced technology and bland styling. By 1991, the RX-7 was more of a touring coupe than a sports car. Mazda attempted to change that image in 1993.

The latest RX-7 has definitely returned to the sports car fold. It is blazingly quick, exceptionally agile, and designed with speed in mind before all else. It's still a technologically-advanced machine, and can be tailored to cater to performance purists or luxury gluttons, but at heart the RX-7 is undiluted. Buyers can order the R-2 Package or the Touring Package. They are mutually exclusive options. The R-2 Package includes lots of go-faster equipment like bone-crushing suspension calibrations and speed-rated tires. The Touring Package comes with leather seats, a power moonroof and a killer Bose sound system.

Lightweight build materials were used extensively in the RX-7 to keep weight down. Designers even drilled the brake and clutch pedals to keep extra poundage off. The result is a quick, light, but expensive car. The exterior styling is fantastic, with retro touches everywhere that make it instantly familiar. It's a beautiful piece, but the odd side glass and door handle arrangement needs to be rethought.

The RX-7 is less expensive than the Toyota Supra and Nissan 300ZX Turbo, and offers as much style and speed as either of them. Coupled with the RX-7's relative rarity, we think the Mazda is the better bet, if you can handle the stiffer suspension and tighter interior space.

MAZDA RX-7

| CODE | DESCRIPTION | INVOICE | MSRP |

Performance and Safety

Acceleration (0-60 mph) .... 5.3 sec.	ABS .... Standard
Braking (60-0 mph) .... 113 ft.	Driver Airbag .... Standard
Cornering .... .98 g's	Passenger Airbag .... Standard
Fuel Capacity .... 20 gal.	Traction Control .... N/A
Fuel Economy .... City: 17 mpg	Crash Test Grade .... D: N/A P: N/A
Hwy: 24 mpg	Insurance Cost .... Average

RX-7 (1994)

—	2-Dr Coupe (5-spd)	31493	36500
Destination Charge:		440	440

Standard Equipment

RX-7: Two-rotor inline rotary engine w/sequential twin turbochargers/air-to-air intercooler/electronic fuel injection, 5-speed manual transmission w/overdrive, engine oil cooler, power plant frame (PPF), Torsen torque-sensing limited slip differential, 4-wheel independent double-wishbone suspension, rack-and-pinion steering with engine-speed variable power assist, power assisted 4-wheel ventilated disc brakes, anti-lock braking system (ABS), 16-inch aluminum alloy wheels, 225/50VR16 radial tires, dual aerodynamic bodycolor power mirrors, tinted glass, retractable halogen headlights, light weight aluminum hood, illuminated driver's lock keyhole, intermittent windshield wipers w/variable control, driver and passenger side airbags, power windows w/driver's side one-touch down feature, power door locks, remote liftgate and fuel-door releases, seat back storage pockets, dual storage compartment behind seats, 9,000 RPM tachometer w/8,000 RPM redline, oil pressure/engine coolant temperature gauges, leather-wrapped steering wheel and shift knob, cruise control w/steering wheel mounted controls, drilled aluminum clutch and brake pedals, anti-theft alarm system, AM/FM cassette stereo w/5 speakers and automatic power antenna, air conditioning.

Accessories

AT1	**Automatic Transmission**	783	900
	NA w/Popular Equipment Group or R-2 Pkg		
1RP	**R-2 Pkg**	1640	2000
	incls Pirelli P zero Z-rated tires, twin engine oil coolers, dedicated front brake air ducts, special RZ1 suspension, rear spoiler, front airdam, front shock tower support brace, unique cloth seat upholstery, cruise control deleted; NA w/Touring Pkg		
1TR	**Touring Pkg**	3444	4200
	incls leather seating surfaces, power glass moonroof, halogen fog lights, rear window wiper/washer, Bose acoustic wave stereo music system w/compact disc player, upgraded sound insulation, rear cargo cover		
1PE	**Popular Equipment Pkg**	1476	1800
	incls leather seating surfaces, power steel sunroof and rear cargo cover; NA w/R-2 Pkg		
FLM	**Floor Mats**	58	80
CE1	**California or New York Emissions**	126	150

C-CLASS — MERCEDES-BENZ

1995 Mercedes-Benz C-Class

C-CLASS

The Baby Benz grew up last year when the C-Class replaced the 190E. The new car was substantially improved over the 190, offering better performance and more interior room. This year the C-Class lineup gets a new high-performance model and the entry-level C220 can now be equipped with traction control.

The new model is the C36, an AMG-prepared road warrior sporting fat tires, aero gimcrackery and a potent 3.6-liter engine. No pricing or performance data was available as we went to press, but expect the C36 to carry a modest BMW M3-sized price tag and deliver 60 mph in just over six seconds.

The C280 and C220 carry over unchanged from 1994. Manually rowing the automatic shifter, a C220 can get to 60 mph in less than nine seconds. The six cylinder C280 feels much quicker getting to speed, and getting there quickly doesn't mean changing your own gears. Handling is surefooted with both cars, and braking ability is quite good, although published statistics show that the C220, at 200 fewer pounds than the C280, is somewhat more agile.

These Mercedes' ooze class, substance and style, unless they're adorned with pimp-roller gold packages or other tacky add ons. The look is quite contemporary, and the car seems larger than it really is. Traditional styling cues inside and out continue the Mercedes method of evolutionary rather than revolutionary design themes.

Base prices start just over $30,000 for the C220. The stronger C280 can be had for another five grand and includes the 2.8-liter six, dual power front seats and an eight-speaker Bose stereo system. The C36 will likely render such cars as the Lexus GS300 and Cadillac Seville STS also-rans. You may want to consider BMW's 325i, the Lexus ES300, or the Mazda Millenia S before buying the Benz, but we can't help but think the C-Class is a relative bargain in this class, now that Mercedes has come down off its pedestal and is pricing its wares with some semblance of sanity.

MERCEDES-BENZ — C-CLASS

Performance and Safety

C220
Acceleration (0-60 mph) .... 8.7 sec.	ABS .... Standard
Braking (60-0 mph) .... 131 ft.	Driver Airbag .... Standard
Cornering .... .80 g's	Passenger Airbag .... Standard
Fuel Capacity .... 16.4 gal.	Traction Control .... Optional
Fuel Economy .... City: 23 mpg	Crash Test Grade .... D: Good P: Good
Hwy: 28 mpg	Insurance Cost .... N/A

C280
Acceleration (0-60 mph) .... 8.3 sec.	ABS .... Standard
Braking (60-0 mph) .... 137 ft.	Driver Airbag .... Standard
Cornering .... .78 g's	Passenger Airbag .... Standard
Fuel Capacity .... 16.4 gal.	Traction Control .... Optional
Fuel Economy .... City: 20 mpg	Crash Test Grade .... D: Good P: Good
Hwy: 26 mpg	Insurance Cost .... N/A

1995 Mercedes-Benz C-Class

C-CLASS

		Invoice	MSRP
—	C220 4-Dr Sedan (auto)	26330	30950
—	C280 4-Dr Sedan (auto)	30880	36300
Destination Charge:		475	475

EDMUND'S 1995 HIGH-PERFORMANCE AUTOMOBILES

C-CLASS — MERCEDES-BENZ

Standard Equipment

C220 SEDAN: 2.2 liter DOHC 16-valve inline 4 cylinder engine, HFM sequential multi-port fuel injection and ignition, variable intake valve timing, Control Area Network (CAN) data management system, 4-speed automatic transmission, power assisted recirculating ball steering, independent double wishbone front suspension with shock absorbers and separate coil springs, independent multi-link rear suspension with coil springs and single-tube gas-pressurized shock absorbers, anti-roll bars, power assisted 4-wheel disc brakes, anti-lock braking system (ABS), 6.5J x 15" aluminum-alloy wheels, 195/65R15 91H steel belted radial tires, sliding electric sunroof with rear pop-up feature, dual heated electrically operated outside mirrors, heated windshield washers, halogen headlamps and front fog lamps, rear fog lamp, central locking with key-operated window and sunroof closing capability and automatic starter disable, supplemental restraint system (SRS) with an air bag, knee bolster and emergency tensioning retractor (ETR) for driver and front passenger; 3-point front seat belts attached to seat frames with adjustable shoulder belts, 3-point outboard rear seat belts with automatically adjusting shoulder belts, MB-Tex upholstery, leather-trimmed steering wheel and shift knob, 10-way electrically adjustable driver's seat, 10-way manually adjustable front passenger seat, power windows with express-down control for both front windows, electrostatic dust filter and residual heat REST mode, cruise control, delayed shut-off front courtesy light, rear compartment courtesy light, front reading lamp, illuminated visor vanity mirrors, front center armrest, folding rear center armrest, beverage holder, coin tray, Zebrano wood trim, 8-speaker sound system, automatic speed-dependent volume adjustment, anti-theft coded AM/FM stereo/weatherband radio and auto-reverse cassette player, automatic electric AM/FM/cellular antenna, prewiring for optional CD changer and cellular telephone, automatic climate control with digital temperature display.

C280 SEDAN (in addition to or instead of C220 SEDAN equipment): 2.8 liter DOHC 24-valve inline 6 cylinder engine, tuned-resonance intake manifold, 10-way electrically adjustable front seats, Bose sound system.

Accessories

Code	Description	Invoice	MSRP
551	Anti-Theft Alarm System	490	590
—	Leather Upholstery — C280	1349	1625
—	Metallic Paint	481	580
116	C1 Pkg — C220 *incls heated front seats, electronic traction control, headlight washer/wipers*	1332	1605
117	C1 Pkg — C280 *incls heated front seats, automatic slip control, headlight washer/wipers*	2353	2835
118	C2 Pkg *incls split fold-down rear seat and trunk pass-through with ski sack*	274	330
119	C3 Pkg — C280 *incls power glass sunroof with pop-up feature, retractable head restraints, leather seats*	1461	1760
441	Telescopic Steering Column	129	155
414	Roof — power glass sunroof with pop-up feature	187	225
430	Head Restraints — rear seats	282	340
222	Power Passenger Seat — C220	477	575
—	Power Orthopedic Backrest Seats		
404	left front	303	365
405	right front	303	365
600	Headlight Wipers/Washers	266	320
810	Radio — high performance sound system - C220 *incls 8-speaker Bose sound system*	415	500

MERCEDES-BENZ   E-CLASS

1995 Mercedes-Benz E-Class

E-CLASS

We can hardly believe that 1995 marks the tenth year of production for the E-Class (formerly the 300 Series). The shape is still modern and attractive. The interior is still up to date, offering dual airbags and well laid-out controls. This car must have been far ahead of its time in 1986 when it was introduced.

Next year an all-new E-Class bows, sporting round headlamps and retro hood contours much like those found on the 1995 Jaguar XJ6. In light of the current car's impending demise, changes for 1995 are minimal. New alloy wheels bow this year, and an early-release E300 Diesel debuted last spring, the only model in the E-Class lineup to miss our performance requirements. The thundering E500 is gone this year, replaced by the smaller and less expensive C36.

As solid as a bank vault and much better looking, the E-Class has style, panache and performance. The model range runs the gamut from fuel-sipping and slow E300 Diesel to the slick E320 convertible. Coupes, wagons and sedans available with a 3.2-liter inline six are on the roster, but the only V-8 powered model for 1995 is the E420 sedan. All, with the exception of the E320 coupe and convertible, are priced within reach of your average Lexus or Infiniti buyer.

That three-pointed star on the hood means different things to different people. For some, it is a sign of undeniable quality; for others it is a symbol of success. Still others think it's their next belt buckle, but they don't really get it. The sedans available in this class are outstanding examples of engineering and design. Just remember that the Benz, despite its age, competes on the same level as the others, and often at a lower price.

E-CLASS MERCEDES-BENZ

Performance and Safety

E320

Acceleration (0-60 mph) .... 8.1 sec.	ABS .... Standard		
Braking (60-0 mph) .... 131 ft.	Driver Airbag .... Standard		
Cornering .... .78 g's	Passenger Airbag .... Standard		
Fuel Capacity .... 18.5 gal.(19 wagon)	Traction Control .... Optional		
Fuel Economy .... City: 20 mpg	Crash Test Grade .... D: N/A	P: N/A	
	Hwy: 26 mpg	Insurance Cost .... Low	

E420

Acceleration (0-60 mph) .... 7.2 sec.	ABS .... Standard		
Braking (60-0 mph) .... 124 ft.	Driver Airbag .... Standard		
Cornering .... .78 g's	Passenger Airbag .... Standard		
Fuel Capacity 18.5	Traction Control .... Optional		
Fuel Economy .... City: 18 mpg	Crash Test Grade .... D: N/A	P: N/A	
	Hwy: 24 mpg	Insurance Cost .... Low	

E320

CODE	DESCRIPTION	INVOICE	MSRP
—	E320 4-Dr Sedan (auto)	37010	43500
—	E320 2-Dr Cabriolet (auto)	65570	79000
—	E320 2-Dr Coupe (auto)	52290	63000
Destination Charge:		475	475

Standard Equipment

E320 SEDAN: 3.2 liter DOHC 24-valve inline 6 cylinder engine, HFM sequential multi-port fuel injection and ignition, variable intake valve timing, tuned-resonance intake manifold, Control Area Network (CAN) data management system, 4-speed automatic transmission, power assisted recirculating ball steering, independent gas-pressurized damper strut front suspension with separate coil springs, independent multi-link rear suspension with coil springs and single-tube gas-pressurized shock absorbers, anti-roll bars, power assisted 4-wheel disc brakes, anti-lock braking system (ABS), 6.5J x 15" aluminum-alloy wheels, 195/65R15 91H steel belted radial tires, sliding electric sunroof with rear pop-up feature, dual heated electrically operated outside mirrors, halogen headlamps and front fog lamps, rear fog lamp, heated windshield washer system, electrically heated rear window, central locking with key-operated window and sunroof closing capability, anti-theft alarm system with starter interlock, supplemental restraint system (SRS) with an air bag, knee bolster and emergency tensioning retractor (ETR) for driver and front passenger; 3-point outboard seat belts with adjustable front shoulder belts and automatically adjusting dual rear shoulder belts, leather upholstery, leather-trimmed steering wheel and shift knob, 10-way electrically adjustable front seats, remote-retractable dual rear headrests, power windows with express-down control for both front windows, automatic climate control, cruise control, delayed shut-off courtesy light, entrance lamps, front reading lamp,

MERCEDES-BENZ
E-CLASS

CODE	DESCRIPTION	INVOICE	MSRP

illuminated visor vanity mirrors, Zebrano wood trim, active bass sound system with 6 speakers, automatic speed-dependent volume adjustment, anti-theft coded AM/FM stereo/weatherband radio and auto-reverse cassette player, automatic electric AM/FM/cellular antenna, prewiring for optional CD changer and cellular telephone.

E320 CABRIOLET & COUPE (in addition to or instead of E320 SEDAN equipment): Electrically operated soft top (Cabriolet), pop-up roll bar with integrated head restraints (Cabriolet), wind deflector (Cabriolet), heated front seats (Cabriolet), electrically telescoping steering column, 2-position memory for driver's seat and steering column, individual rear seats, one-button automatic raising and lowering of all side windows (Cabriolet), Burl walnut trim, high performance sound system with 10 speakers (Coupe).

Accessories

Code	Description	Invoice	MSRP
471	**Automatic Traction Control** — Cabriolet	1785	2150
—	**Metallic Paint** — Sedan	552	665
	Coupe, Cabriolet	NC	NC
600	**Headlight Wipers/Washers** — Sedan	266	320
540	**Power Rear Window Sunshade**	340	410
	NA on Cabriolet		
877	**Rear Reading Lights** — Sedan	75	90
—	**Power Orthopedic Backrest Seats**		
404	left front	303	365
405	right front	303	365
441	**Power Telescoping Steering Column** — Sedan	303	365
952	**Sportline Pkg** — Coupe	905	1090
	Sedan	1581	1905
	incls sport steering, sport suspension, 4-place sport seats (Sedan)		
112	**Option Pkg E1** — Sedan	2353	2835
	incls auto traction control, heated front seats, headlight washer/wipers		
113	**Option Pkg E1** — Coupe	2137	2575
	incls auto traction control, heated front seats		
114	**Option Pkg E2** — Sedan	896	1080
	incls high performance sound system, power telescoping steering column, driver's seat memory		

E420

Code	Description	Invoice	MSRP
—	E420 4-Dr Sedan (auto)	43580	52500
	Destination Charge:	475	475

See the Automobile Dealer Directory on page 388 for a Dealer near you!

E-CLASS — MERCEDES-BENZ

Standard Equipment

E420 SEDAN: 4.2 liter twin-DOHC 32-valve V8 engine, aluminum-alloy block and head, LH sequential multi-port fuel injection, electronic ignition, anti-knock control, variable intake valve timing, Control Area Network (CAN) data management system, 4-speed automatic transmission, power assisted recirculating ball steering, independent gas-pressurized damper strut front suspension with separate coil springs, independent multi-link rear suspension with coil springs and single-tube gas-pressurized shock absorbers, anti-roll bars, power assisted 4-wheel disc brakes, anti-lock braking system (ABS), 6.5J x 15" aluminum-alloy wheels, 195/65R15 91H steel belted radial tires, sliding electric sunroof with rear pop-up feature, dual heated electrically operated outside mirrors, halogen headlamps including heated washing system with wipers, front fog lamps, rear fog lamp, heated windshield washer system, electrically heated rear window, central locking with key-operated window and sunroof closing capability, anti-theft alarm system with starter interlock, automatic electric AM/FM/cellular antenna, supplemental restraint system (SRS) with an air bag, knee bolster and emergency tensioning retractor (ETR) for driver and front passenger; 3-point outboard seat belts with adjustable front shoulder belts and automatically adjusting rear shoulder belts, leather upholstery, leather-trimmed steering wheel and shift knob, 10-way electrically adjustable front seats, 2-position memory for driver's seat (including steering column), remote-retractable dual rear head restraints, electrically telescoping steering column, power windows with one-touch down control for both front windows, automatic climate control, cruise control, delayed shut-off courtesy light, entrance lamps, front reading lamp, illuminated visor vanity mirrors, Burl walnut trim, high performance sound system with 10 speakers, automatic speed-dependent volume adjustment, anti-theft coded AM/FM stereo/weatherband radio and auto-reverse cassette player, automatic electric AM/FM/cellular antenna, pre-wiring for optional CD changer and cellular telephone

Accessories

CODE	DESCRIPTION	INVOICE	MSRP
877	**Rear Reading Lights**	75	90
540	**Power Rear Window Sunshade**	340	410
—	**Metallic Paint**	NC	NC
—	**Power Orthopedic Backrest Seats**		
404	left front	303	365
405	right front	303	365
113	**Option Pkg E1**	2137	2575
	incls auto traction control and heated front seats		

For a guaranteed low price on a new vehicle in your area, call

1-800-CAR-CLUB

MERCEDES-BENZ S600

CODE DESCRIPTION INVOICE MSRP

1995 Mercedes-Benz S-Class

S600

The massive, ostentatious Mercedes S600 sedan has a 10'4" wheelbase, is just over seventeen feet long, weighs nearly 2.5 tons, and costs as much as a three-bedroom house. A nice one. The S600 coupe, while a bit smaller externally, weighs and costs even more. And, motivating these ponderous masses of well-engineered metal are thumping V-12 engines that produce 389 horsepower and belt out 421 pounds feet of torque.

As if these statistics weren't enough to boggle the mind, each of these pudgy cars accelerates quicker than a Nissan 300ZX Turbo, stops faster than a Porsche 928 GTS, and corners better than a Cadillac Seville STS. Uh...excuse me? Isn't all this against some obscure law of physics?

Mercedes has created the ultimate automotive enigma in the S600. Everything about the car defies logic. Which might explain why S-Class sales have fallen dramatically since these behemoths were introduced a few years ago.

For 1995, Mercedes has decided to spruce the S-Class up a bit. To make the car appear less large, a character line has been stamped into the sheetmetal from bumper to bumper, just above the lower body side cladding. A new grille, taillight alterations and a more rounded trunk lid conclude Mercedes' efforts to visually lengthen and lower the car. Prices remain the same, but the cars are a bit lighter—not that you'd notice.

Mercedes has moved nearly 13,000 1994 S-Class sedans and coupes into American driveways, through October. We'll wager that fewer than 1,000 of them were of the S600 variety. Who would buy this car? We don't know, but the few who do so take possession of perhaps the most amazing automobile for sale today.

S600 — MERCEDES-BENZ

CODE	DESCRIPTION	INVOICE	MSRP

Performance and Safety

Acceleration (0-60 mph) .... 5.7 sec.		ABS .... Standard	
Braking (60-0 mph) .... 126 ft.		Driver Airbag .... Standard	
Cornering .... .79 g's		Passenger Airbag .... Standard	
Fuel Capacity .... 26.4 gal.		Traction Control .... Standard	
Fuel Economy .... City: 13 mpg		Crash Test Grade .... D: N/A	P: N/A
	Hwy: 16 mpg	Insurance Cost .... N/A	

S600

		INVOICE	MSRP
—	S600 2-Dr Coupe (auto)	110640	133300
—	S600 4-Dr Sedan (auto)	108150	130300
Destination Charge:		475	475
Gas Guzzler Tax:		3000	3000

Standard Equipment

S600 COUPE: 6.0 liter twin-DOHC 48-valve V12 engine, aluminum-alloy block and head, LH sequential multi-port fuel injection, electronic ignition, anti-knock control, variable intake valve timing, Control Area Network (CAN) data management system, 4-speed automatic transmission, automatic slip control (ASR), speed-dependent power assisted recirculating ball steering, independent double wishbone front suspension with hydropneumatic shock absorbers and separate coil springs, independent multi-link rear suspension with coil springs and hydropneumatic shock absorbers, anti-roll bars, adaptive damping system (ADS) with automatic level control, power assisted 4-wheel disc brakes, anti-lock braking system (ABS), front/rear brake force proportioning, aluminum-alloy wheels, 235/60ZR16 performance steel belted radial tires, sliding electric sunroof with rear pop-up feature, dual heated electrically operated outside mirrors, halogen headlamps including heated washing system with wipers, front fog lamps, rear fog lamp, heated windshield washer system, infrared-remote central locking of doors, trunk and fuel filler with window and sunroof closing capability, anti-theft alarm system with starter interlock, pneumatic door and trunk closing assist, automatic retracting trunk handle, pop-up reversing guides, supplemental restraint system (SRS) with an air bag, knee bolster and emergency tensioning retractor (ETR) for driver and front passenger; 3-point seat belts, premium leather upholstery, 12-way electrically adjustable front seats with multi-contour seatbacks, electrically operated tilt/telescoping steering column, electrically adjustable dual rear head restraints, heated front seats, electrically operated inside rearview mirror with automatic dimming, 3-position memory for driver's seat (including all rearview mirrors and steering column) and front passenger seat, power dual-pane side windows with front express up/down control, automatic climate control with activated charcoal filter, separate left and right controls and adjustable rear air vents; electric rear window sunshade, cruise control, delayed shut-off courtesy light, entrance lamps, front reading lamps, dual illuminated vanity mirrors, dual front cup holders, remote trunk release, Burl walnut trim, walnut-trimmed gearshift and shift gate, Bose beta sound system with 11 speakers and 245-watt output, automatic speed-dependent volume adjustment, anti-theft coded AM/FM stereo/weatherband radio and auto-reverse cassette player, integrated AM/FM antenna system, automatic electric cellular telephone antenna, trunk-mounted CD changer, integrated cellular mobile telephone.

S600 SEDAN (in addition to or instead of S600 COUPE equipment): Rear air conditioning, electrically adjustable rear seat, rear reading lamps, rear illuminated vanity mirrors, rear cup holders.

EDMUND'S 1995 HIGH-PERFORMANCE AUTOMOBILES

MERCEDES-BENZ   *S600 / SL-CLASS*

CODE	DESCRIPTION	INVOICE	MSRP

Accessories

—	Metallic Paint	NC	NC
—	Portable Telephone — cellular	747	900
414	Power Sliding Glass Sunroof	328	395
224	Power Seats — 4-place seating - Sedan	3403	4100

1995 Mercedes-Benz 320SL

SL-CLASS

The SL600 is the two-door roadster version of the conspicuous consumers that Mercedes labels the S600 sedan and coupe. The SL isn't merely a S600 coupe with no roof. It is lighter, more nimble, and based on the SL-Class of roadsters. The bloodline it shares with the gargantuan S-Class is the 6.0-liter V-12 that makes 389 horsepower and moves the car with authority. Stuffed into the SL, the V-12 is a better performer and costs less, but at a stupendous $120,000, that's kind of a moot point.

Mercedes has left the SL600 alone for model year 1995, instead concentrating on the...ahem, lowly SL320 and SL500. Prices for the SL320 and SL500 have fallen this year...dramatically. The SL320, which was base priced at $95,000 in 1994, is starting at about $80,000 this year. Likewise, the SL500 has fallen nearly ten grand to $90,000. So, do you get less car for your smaller payment? No. The SL320 gets standard traction control for 1995, and the SL500 and SL600 get a new voice-activated cellular phone that can be removed from the car and used as a portable phone.

Image-conscious buyers love the SL600, and very often, in places like Bel Air and South Beach and Scottsdale, the only SL convertibles with any visible nomenclature are of the SL600 variety. Why? Seems that buyers of the SL320 and SL500, which are visually identical to the SL600, remove the nameplates from the decklid so that other 'socially aware' folks don't know they couldn't afford the top-of-the-line Benz roadster. Pretty ridiculous, huh?

SL-CLASS MERCEDES-BENZ

We don't think you should go for the SL600. The SL500 is just as good, and better in some respects, than its more muscular brother. And with your savings you could get a Jeep Grand Cherokee for the kids to take to Keg-A-Beer University in the fall. If straight-line acceleration and social status are even less important to you, the SL320 serves nicely, and leaves almost 40 thou' in your pocket over the V-12 version.

Performance and Safety

SL320

Acceleration (0-60 mph)	7.6 sec.	ABS	Standard
Braking (60-0 mph)	104 ft.	Driver Airbag	Standard
Cornering	N/A	Passenger Airbag	Standard
Fuel Capacity	21.3 gal.	Traction Control	Standard
Fuel Economy	City: 17 mpg	Crash Test Grade	D: N/A P: N/A
	Hwy: 24 mpg	Insurance Cost	Average

SL500

Acceleration (0-60 mph)	6.3 sec.	ABS	Standard
Braking (60-0 mph)	N/A	Driver Airbag	Standard
Cornering	.82 g's	Passenger Airbag	Standard
Fuel Capacity	21.3 gal.	Traction Control	Standard
Fuel Economy	City: 16 mpg	Crash Test Grade	D: N/A P: N/A
	Hwy: 21 mpg	Insurance Cost	N/A

SL600

Acceleration (0-60 mph)	5.5	ABS	Standard
Braking (60-0 mph)	124 ft.	Driver Airbag	Standard
Cornering	.83 g's	Passenger Airbag	Standard
Fuel Capacity	21.3 gal.	Traction Control	Standard
Fuel Economy	City: 13 mpg	Crash Test Grade	D: N/A P: N/A
	Hwy: 18 mpg	Insurance Cost	N/A

USE A MULTIMEDIA CD-ROM TO RESEARCH YOUR NEXT AUTOMOBILE PURCHASE

see ad on page 384 for details

MERCEDES-BENZ

SL-CLASS

CODE	DESCRIPTION	INVOICE	MSRP
SL320			
—	2-Dr Coupe/Roadster (auto)	64990	78300
	Destination Charge:	475	475

Standard Equipment

SL320 COUPE/ROADSTER: 3.2 liter DOHC 24-valve inline 6 cylinder engine, HFM sequential multiport fuel injection and ignition, variable intake valve timing, tuned-resonance intake manifold, Control Area Network (CAN) data management system, 5-speed automatic transmission, electronic traction system (ETS), power assisted recirculating ball steering, independent damper strut front suspension with separate coil springs, independent multi-link rear suspension with coil springs and single-tube gas-pressurized shock absorbers, anti-roll bars, power assisted 4-wheel disc brakes, anti-lock braking system (ABS), 8J x 16 aluminum alloy wheels, 225/55ZR16 steel belted radial tires, automatic electric/hydraulic convertible top, removable hardtop with heated rear window, automatic pop-up roll bar, wind deflector, dual heated electrically operated outside mirrors, halogen headlamps including heated washing system with wipers, ellipsoidal front fog lamps, rear fog lamp, eccentric-sweep windshield wiper with heated washer system, infrared remote central locking of doors, trunk, interior compartments and fuel filler; key or remote operated window closing capability, anti-theft alarm system with starter interlock, supplemental restraint system (SRS) with an air bag, knee bolster and Emergency Tensioning Retractor (ETR) for driver and passenger; 3-point seat belts with automatically adjusting shoulder belts, leather upholstery, 10-way electrically adjustable seats, electrically operated tilt/telescoping steering column, electrically operated inside rearview mirror with automatic dimming, 3-position memory for driver's seat (including all rearview mirrors and steering column) and passenger seat, power windows with express-down control, automatic climate control, cruise control, delayed shut-off courtesy light, entrance lamps, dual reading lamps, dual illuminated vanity mirrors, adjustable center armrest, 6 lockable storage compartments, burl walnut trim, Bose sound system with 6 speakers, Acoustimass bass module and 200 watts output, automatic speed-dependent volume adjustment, anti-theft coded AM/FM stereo/weatherband radio and auto-reverse cassette player, automatic electric AM/FM/cellular antenna, pre-wiring for optional CD changer and mobile or portable cellular phone.

Accessories

216	**Adaptive Damping Suspension**	3432	4135
—	**Metallic Paint**	NC	NC
873	**Heated Front Seats**	469	565
—	**Power Orthopedic Back Rest**		
404	left front	303	365
405	right front	303	365
471	**Automatic Slip Control**	1370	1650

GET MORE MONEY FOR YOUR USED CAR BY KNOWING ITS TRUE VALUE

See our ads on pages 4 and 6

SL-CLASS — MERCEDES-BENZ

CODE	DESCRIPTION	INVOICE	MSRP

SL500
— 2-Dr Coupe/Roadster (auto) 74620 89900
Destination Charge: 475 475
Gas Guzzler Tax: 1300 1300

Standard Equipment

SL500 COUPE/ROADSTER: 5.0 liter twin-DOHC 32-valve V8 engine, aluminum alloy block and head, LH sequential multiport fuel injection, electronic ignition, anti-knock control, variable intake valve timing, Control Area Network (CAN) data management system, 4-speed automatic transmission, automatic slip control (ASR), power assisted recirculating ball steering, independent damper strut front suspension with separate coil springs, independent multi-link rear suspension with coil springs and single-tube gas-pressurized shock absorbers, anti-roll bars, power assisted 4-wheel disc brakes, anti-lock braking system (ABS), 8J x 16 aluminum alloy wheels, 225/55ZR16 steel belted radial tires, automatic electric/hydraulic convertible top, removable hardtop with heated rear window, automatic pop-up roll bar, wind deflector, dual heated electrically operated outside mirrors, halogen headlamps including heated washing system with wipers, ellipsoidal front fog lamps, rear fog lamp, eccentric-sweep windshield wiper with heated washer system, infrared remote central locking of doors, trunk, interior compartments and fuel filler; key or remote operated window closing capability, anti-theft alarm system with starter interlock, supplemental restraint system (SRS) with an air bag, knee bolster and Emergency Tensioning Retractor (ETR) for driver and passenger; 3-point seat belts with automatically adjusting shoulder belts, leather upholstery, 10-way electrically adjustable seats, electrically operated tilt/telescoping steering column, electrically operated inside rearview mirror with automatic dimming, 3-position memory for driver's seat (including all rearview mirrors and steering column) and passenger seat, power windows with express-down control, automatic climate control, cruise control, delayed shut-off courtesy light, entrance lamps, dual reading lamps, dual illuminated vanity mirrors, adjustable center armrest, 6 lockable storage compartments, burl walnut trim, Bose sound system with 6 speakers, Acoustimass bass module and 200 watts output, automatic speed-dependent volume adjustment, anti-theft coded AM/FM stereo/weatherband radio and auto-reverse cassette player, automatic electric AM/FM/cellular antenna, pre-wiring for optional CD changer and mobile or portable cellular phone.

Accessories

216	Adaptive Damping Suspension	3432	4135
—	Metallic Paint	NC	NC
873	Heated Front Seats	469	565
—	Power Orthopedic Back Rest		
404	left front	303	365
405	right front	303	365

See the Automobile Dealer Directory on page 388 for a Dealer near you!

MERCEDES-BENZ

SL-CLASS

CODE	DESCRIPTION	INVOICE	MSRP

SL600
—	SL600 2-Dr Coupe/Roadster (auto)	99680	120100
Destination Charge:		475	475
Gas Guzzler Tax:		2600	2600

Standard Equipment

SL600 COUPE/ROADSTER: 6.0 liter twin-DOHC 48-valve V12 engine, aluminum-alloy block and head, LH sequential multi-port fuel injection, electronic ignition, anti-knock control, variable intake valve timing, Control Area Network (CAN) data management system, 4-speed automatic transmission, automatic slip control (ASR), power assisted recirculating ball steering, independent damper strut front suspension with hydropneumatic shock absorbers and separate coil springs, independent multi-link rear suspension with coil springs and hydropneumatic shock absorbers, anti-roll bars, adaptive damping system (ADS) with automatic level control, power assisted 4-wheel disc brakes, anti-lock braking system (ABS), front/rear brake force proportioning, 8J x 16" aluminum-alloy wheels, 225/55ZR16 steel belted radial tires, automatic electric/hydraulic convertible top, removable hardtop with heated rear window, automatic pop-up roll bar, wind deflector, dual heated electrically operated outside mirrors, halogen headlamps including heated washing system with wipers, ellipsoidal front fog lamps, rear fog lamp, eccentric-sweep windshield wiper with heated washer system, infrared-remote central locking of doors, trunk interior compartments and fuel filler; key or remote operated window closing capability, anti-theft alarm system with starter interlock, supplemental restraint system (SRS) with an air bag, knee bolster and emergency tensioning retractor (ETR) for driver and passenger; 3-point seat belts with automatically adjusting shoulder belts, exclusive leather upholstery, 10-way electrically adjustable seats, heated seats, electrically operated tilt/telescoping steering column, electrically operated inside rearview mirror with automatic dimming, 3-position memory for driver's seat (including all rearview mirrors and steering column) and passenger seat, power windows with express-down control, automatic climate control, cruise control, delayed shut-off courtesy light, entrance lamps, dual reading lamps, dual illuminated vanity mirrors, adjustable center armrest, 6 lockable storage compartments, Burl walnut trim, walnut-trimmed gearshift and shift gate, Bose sound system with 6 speakers, Acoustimass bass module and 200-watt output, automatic speed-dependent volume adjustment, anti-theft coded AM/FM stereo/weatherband radio and auto-reverse cassette player, automatic electric AM/FM/cellular antenna, trunk-mounted CD changer, mobile cellular phone.

Accessories

—	**Metallic Paint**	NC	NC
141	**Portable Telephone** — cellular	747	900
—	**Power Orthopedic Backrest Seats**		
404	left front	303	365
405	right front	303	365

For a guaranteed low price on a new vehicle in your area, call

1-800-CAR-CLUB

COUGAR XR7 — MERCURY

CODE	DESCRIPTION	INVOICE	MSRP

1995 Mercury Cougar XR7

COUGAR XR7 (V8)

Mercury sells half as many Cougars as Ford does the mechanically identical Thunderbird. Not bad, considering Mercury's more limited dealer network and the Cougar's more conservative styling. The Cougar is a traditional luxo-coupe boulevardier, but when infused with Ford's potent modular 4.6-liter V-8, the Cougar's purr becomes a snarl.

Amazingly, the hefty Cougar turns in some pretty impressive performance figures. The exterior features traditional cues such as a chrome grille and formal roofline. Unfortunately, these looks make the Cougar a prime candidate for aftermarket or dealer-installed 'luxury packages' that include such gimcrackery as tacky opera lamps, fake convertible roof applications, and yucky gold trim add-ons. Not even the factory can resist cluttering Cougar's lines; a non-functional luggage rack is available on the options list. Inside, the Cougar offers first-class accommodations for five, with a sweeping dashboard that provides a cocooned cockpit feel to front passengers.

This iteration of the Cougar has been on the market since 1989, albeit with dramatic improvements over the years. If a healthy dose of luxury and traditional styling is your cup of tea, the Cougar is likely one car you'll want to consider.

Performance and Safety

Acceleration (0-60 mph)	8.5 sec.	ABS	Optional
Braking (60-0 mph)	139 ft.	Driver Airbag	Standard
Cornering	.78 g's	Passenger Airbag	Standard
Fuel Capacity	18 gal.	Traction Control	Optional
Fuel Economy	City: 17 mpg	Crash Test Grade	D: Excellent P: Excellent
	Hwy: 25 mpg	Insurance Cost	Average

EDMUND'S 1995 HIGH-PERFORMANCE AUTOMOBILES

MERCURY
COUGAR XR7

CODE   DESCRIPTION   INVOICE   MSRP

Edmund's Driving Impression

Blend richness and comfort with a strong rear-drive powertrain, and the result could be Cougar. Mercury's personal-luxury coupe borrows some of its interior plushness from the Lincoln Mark VIII, basic shape and personality from Ford Thunderbird—with a dash of Mustang thrown in.

Just sporty enough to make road trips interesting, the XR7 accelerates and handles well above the average—if not quite in the full-bore performance-car class. Rather than a muscle-flexing ride, the V-8 Cougar delivers an invigorating but well-behaved romp.

Swifter than expected when you first hit the gas, the V-8 Cougar starts to run out of steam part way up the speed scale. Merging into freeways is no chore, but don't expect to be slammed back in your seat when pulling out to pass. A 7,000-rpm tachometer on the full-gauge dash leads the driver to expect more from the engine, but it's redlined closer to a modest 5,300 revs.

Electronic controls make the transmission shift with little fanfare, quickly selecting the proper ratio for each occasion. Because the XR7 rolls along so effortlessly, an actual jolt from a pavement hump or pothole comes as a rude intrusion. Power steering has a fairly light touch, but fine responsiveness, and you never feel detached from the highway. Tires grip the road with some tenacity, but again, don't expect miracles.

If economy takes precedence over potential, the XR7 can be ordered with a 140-horsepower V-6 instead. Unlike the T-Bird, there's no supercharged engine option. Pushbutton-controlled traction assist is a sensible option for drivers in the snowbelt.

1995 Mercury Cougar XR7

COUGAR XR7 8 CYL
M62 2-Dr Sedan 15587   17305
Destination Charge: 495   495

Standard Equipment

COUGAR XR7: 4.6 liter EFI V8 engine, electronic automatic overdrive transmission with brake shift interlock feature, power rack and pinion steering, power front disc/rear drum brakes, power side windows with illuminated switches, P205/70R15 BSW all-season tires, luxury wheel covers, electronic

COUGAR XR7 — MERCURY

AM/FM stereo cassette radio with 4 speakers, manual CFC-free air conditioning with rotary controls, front and rear color-keyed soft fascia bumpers, black door handles/lock bezels, flush side/windshield/rear window glass, bright grille with bright surround and cat head, low-profile aero halogen headlamps (integrated into parking lamp/turn signal/side marker assembly), dual power remote control body color mirrors, concealed drip moldings, black windshield/rear window moldings, bright door window/quarter window moldings, color-keyed bodyside moldings, bright antenna/black bezel (RH fender), black B-pillar moldings, black decklid lock bezel, "Mercury" nomenclature (driver side front bumper), wrap-around design taillamps, driver and right front passenger air bag SRS, luxury 24 oz. color-keyed cut-pile carpeting, chimes for: headlamps on/fasten safety belts/key in ignition reminder, full length floor console with leather-wrapped floor shift/front and rear ashtrays/armrest storage/coin holder/cup holders; color-keyed soft door trim panel with lower carpeting/cloth inserts/map pockets/courtesy lamps; quarter trim panels with courtesy lights/padded armrests/cloth inserts, locking glove box, molded color-keyed cloth headliner, rear compartment heat ducts, backlighted analog performance cluster includes: tachometer/fuel gauge/coolant temperature/120-mph speedometer/oil pressure/voltmeter gauges; stalk-mounted controls for turn signals/headlamp hi-beams/flash-to-pass/interval wiper/washer; flow-through design instrument panel with passenger air bag supplemental restraint system, side window demisters, dual beam dome/map light, carpeted lighted luggage compartment with flat load floor, day/night rearview mirror, concealed driver/unconcealed passenger visor mirrors, color-keyed 3-point active safety restraints (front/rear outboard positions), lap belt (rear center), reclining individual front bucket seats with luxury cloth and leather/inertia front seat back releases/power lumbar/2-way adjustable head restraints; rear seat center fold-down armrest, 4-spoke luxury steering wheel with tilt feature/driver air bag SRS/center blow horn; 130 amp alternator, 58 amp/hour maintenance-free battery, 3-point manual safety belt system, electric drive fan, EEC-IV electronic engine controls, 18 gallon fuel tank, tinted glass, 4-speed heater/defroster system, counter-balanced hood, high-mounted rear brake light, plastic headed ignition key, theft-resistant decklid lock, push-push parking brake release, nitrogen gas-pressurized hydraulic shock absorbers, long spindle short/long arm front suspension with variable rate coil springs and stabilizer bar, independent rear suspension with variable rate coil springs and stabilizer bar, 2-speed electric windshield wipers with fluidic washers and interval feature.

Accessories

Code	Description	Invoice	MSRP
—	**Preferred Equipment Pkgs** — prices include pkg discounts		
260A	Pkg 260A	882	990
	incls group 1 (incls electric rear window defroster, illuminated entry, front floor mats), group 2 (incls fingertip speed control, leather-wrapped steering wheel, cast aluminum wheels, P215/70R15 BSW tires), group 3 (incls power lock group and 6-way power driver's seat)		
—	**Groups**		
—	Group 1	241	270
	incls electric rear window defroster, illuminated entry, front floor mats		
—	Group 2	458	515
	incls fingertip speed control, leather-wrapped steering wheel, cast aluminum wheels, P215/70R15 BSW tires		
—	Group 3	521	585
	incls power lock group (incls power door locks, power decklid release and remote fuel filler door), 6-way power driver's seat		
422	**California Emissions System**	85	95
428	**High Altitude Emissions System**	NC	NC
44L	**Transmission** — automatic w/overdrive	STD	STD
573	**Automatic Air Conditioning**	138	155
	req's autolamp system		

EDMUND'S 1995 HIGH-PERFORMANCE AUTOMOBILES

MERCURY
COUGAR XR7

CODE	DESCRIPTION	INVOICE	MSRP
45A	**Traction-Lok Axle**	85	95
	incls 3.27 axle ratio		
13B	**Power Moonroof**	658	740
	incls dual reading lights, air deflector		
474	**Autolamp System**	62	70
	incls auto headlamp on/off delay; req's air conditioning		
943	**Luxury Light Group**	124	140
	incls engine compartment light, RH instrument panel courtesy lights, dual illuminated visor mirrors		
41H	**Engine Block Immersion Heater**	18	20
153	**Front License Plate Bracket**	NC	NC
631	**Heavy Duty Battery**	23	25
144	**Keyless Remote Entry System**	191	215
	incls automatic power door locks		
553	**Electronic Traction Assist**	187	210
	req's anti-lock brakes		
552	**Anti-Lock Brakes**	503	565
—	**Paint — tri-coat**	201	225
53C	**Sport Appearance Group**	102	115
	incls BBS-style wheels, non-functional luggage rack		
—	**Audio**		
586	premium electronic AM/FM stereo w/cassette tape player	258	290
585	high-level audio w/electronic AM/FM stereo and CD player	383	430
91H	power antenna	71	80
	req's air conditioning		
—	**Seats**		
5	cloth and leather reclining bucket	NC	NC
6	leather reclining bucket	436	490
	req's seat adjuster		
21J	**seat adjuster, 6-way dual power**	258	290
—	**Tires**		
T33	P205/70R15 BSW (4)	STD	STD
T37	P215/70R15 BSW (4)	NC	NC

See Edmund's

Automobile Dealer Directory (page 388)

and the back cover of this book to enter our

$10,000 Wheel N'Deal Give-Away.

MYSTIQUE LS — MERCURY

1995 Mercury Mystique LS

MYSTIQUE LS (V6)

Ford has gambled six billion dollars on the world car project that has produced the European-market Ford Mondeo and American-market twins, Ford Contour and Mercury Mystique. These cars have to be hugely successful to make any money, and early indications are that Ford has a winning hand here.

The Mystique, in our opinion, is the most attractive of the three cars. Unlike the somewhat radical-looking Contour, the Mystique is more conservatively styled, with a traditional chrome grille and full-width taillights. Inside, the Mystique is German in flavor, sporting a tidy interior and firm seating for five adults, although the rear seat really is more suitable for two rather than three occupants. Also Germanic in feel is the chassis tuning and all-around performance of the 170-horsepower Duratec V-6. Equipped with this engine, the Mystique LS has been called one of the most fun-to-drive compacts on the road.

Dual airbags, as you would expect on an all-new car, are standard. Anti-lock brakes and traction control are optional. The well-equipped LS includes alloy wheels, fog lights, a power driver's seat and a cassette stereo. Add the equipment group that includes the V-6 engine, power convenience items, and air conditioning and the Mystique LS V-6 is rolling off the showroom floor for around $18,000.

Compared to its predecessor, the pathetic Topaz, the Mystique is much more expensive. But, considering that the average price of a car purchased in the United States has climbed to 19 grand, the Mystique LS is a bargain, and the addition of anti-lock brakes and traction control don't push the sticker far over that threshold. Well-equipped, good looking, and possessed with the road manners of a European sport sedan, the Mystique delivers value. Unfortunately for Ford, though, Chrysler has a set of trump cards, and their names are Cirrus and Stratus.

MERCURY — MYSTIQUE LS

| CODE | DESCRIPTION | INVOICE | MSRP |

Performance and Safety

Acceleration (0-60 mph) .... 7.4 sec.
Braking (60-0 mph) .... 122 ft.
Cornering .... .79 g's
Fuel Capacity .... 14.5 gal.
Fuel Economy .... City: 22 mpg
                                   Hwy: 30 mpg

ABS .... Optional
Driver Airbag .... Standard
Passenger Airbag .... Standard
Traction Control .... Optional
Crash Test Grade .... D: N/A   P: N/A
Insurance Cost .... N/A

MYSTIQUE LS V6

M66	LS 4-Dr Sedan	14611	16220
	Destination Charge:	495	495

Standard Equipment

MYSTIQUE LS V6: 2.5 liter Duratec V6 engine, 5-speed manual transaxle with overdrive, power rack and pinion steering, power 4-wheel disc brakes, decklid applique with lower bright finisher, color-keyed front/rear polycarbonate 5-mph bumpers, flush color-keyed door handles/bezels, dripless water management door construction, solar tinted glass, semi-flush side glass, bright chrome grille perimeter with center black-out and chrome "Flying M", flush aerodynamic halogen headlamps, wrap-around front/rear side marker lights, body color dual remote power mirrors, body color bodyside moldings, bright front bumper sight shield, "Mystique" nomenclature (LH lower decklid shield), "Mercury" nomenclature (RH lower decklid shield), "Flying M" nomenclature (front grille center), lower bodyside and rocker panel PVC coating, rear decklid low liftover access with decklid gas-assist struts, horizontal taillamps with full-width reflex and lower bright molding, windshield water management system, driver and right front passenger air bag SRS, center console cloth covered/padded armrests, rear seat armrest, illuminated ashtray with lighter, instrument panel clock, full length console includes: armrest/CD/cassette stowage/rear ashtray/parking brake/cup holders; molded full coverage soft door trim with armrest/cloth insert/front and rear speaker provision; door trim panels include: front stowage map pockets/carpeted lower trim/door reflectors/lighted door courtesy lights/curb illumination; driver's footrest, illuminated locking glove box with dampened door and integrated purse/litter hook, grab handles, offset hand brake (center console), 4-way adjustable front contoured head restraints, illuminated headlamp switch, color-keyed cloth-covered headliner, rear floor heat ducts, backlighted analog gauges include: 130-mph speedometer/8,000-rpm tachometer/temperature and fuel gauges/ trip odometer/flash-to-pass/oil pressure/high beam warning lights; driver-oriented functional design instrument panel includes: side window demisters/driver's knee bolsters/positive shut-off registers; lights include: front footwell/courtesy switches on all doors with delay/rear dome; child-proof rear door locks, side wall trim luggage compartment with floor carpet and spare wheel cover, Micronair pollen filtration system, day/night rearview mirror, color-keyed manual lap/shoulder belts (front and rear outboard positions), lap belt (rear center position), seatback map storage, driver seat manual lumbar adjustment, driver seat manual tilt adjustment, 60/40 split folding rear seat with carpet backing (release knobs in trunk), illuminated headlamp on/climate control switches, driver/passenger molded seat stowage bins, cloth-covered visor vanity driver and passenger mirrors, 130-amp alternator, heavy duty maintenance-free battery, brake shift interlock (automatic only), warning chimes for: key in ignition/driver's door open/lights on/seat belt reminder, remote decklid release, diagnostic plug, front wheel drive, remote fuel filler door release, electronic sequential multi-port fuel injection, 14.5 gallon fuel tank with tethered cap, solar tinted glass, 4-speed blower heater/defroster, dual note horn, 2-key system (1 for door/ignition, 1 for trunk/glove box), mini spare wheel/tire, platinum-tipped spark plugs, front/rear stabilizer bars, tilt steering column, variable intermittent windshield wipers with fluidic washer jets and flip-away wiper arm blades, P205/60RX15 BSW performance radial tires, 15" aluminum wheels, electronic AM/FM stereo radio with cassette and 4 speakers, rear quarter panel power

MYSTIQUE LS — MERCURY

CODE	DESCRIPTION	INVOICE	MSRP

antenna, fog lamps (integral in front air dam), heated driver/passenger side mirrors, color-keyed 16 oz. carpeting, front/rear floor mats, pull-out fog lamp switch, Columbo trim individual cloth front bucket seats, driver seat 10-way power adjustment includes: fore/aft/recline/tilt/height/lumbar; leather rim steering wheel with center horn and air bag SRS, electric rear defroster, performance tuned suspension.

Accessories

Code	Description	Invoice	MSRP
380A	**Pkg 380A**	1228	1380
	incls group 2 (air conditioning), group 3 (power door locks, power windows, light group, remote power locking), and speed control		
—	**Groups**		
462	**Group 2**	694	780
	incls air conditioning		
603	**Group 3**	743	835
	incls power door locks, power windows, light group, remote power locking		
445	**Transaxle — 5-speed manual**	STD	STD
44T	**Transmission — automatic overdrive**	725	815
422	**California Emission System**	85	95
428	**High Altitude Principal Use Emission System**	NC	NC
T35	**Tires — P205/60R15 BSW - LS**	STD	STD
641	**Wheels — 15" cast aluminum**	STD	STD
572	**Air Conditioning**	694	780
—	**Seats**		
21A	10-way power driver's	STD	STD
P	cloth individual bucket	STD	STD
Q	leather reclining surfaces	530	595
553	**All-Speed Traction Control**	712	800
	incls anti-lock braking system		
552	**Anti-Lock Braking System**	503	565
153	**Front License Plate Bracket**	NC	NC
13B	**Power Moonroof**	530	595
143	**Remote Locking**	143	160
41H	**Engine Block Immersion Heater**	18	20
525	**Speed Control**	191	215
—	**Audio**		
913	premium sound w/electronic AM/FM stereo/cassette	116	130
585	compact disc radio & premium sound w/electronic AM/FM stereo	240	270

EDMUND'S 1995 HIGH-PERFORMANCE AUTOMOBILES

MITSUBISHI 3000GT

1995 Mitsubishi 3000GT SL

3000GT

There are many competent sports cars on the market today. They combine blazing speed with deft handling prowess and often luxurious interiors. While they all compete within the same segment, most have a distinct flavor all their own. So it is with Mitsubishi's 3000GT.

The 3000GT SL is powered by a twin-cam 3.0-liter V-6 that pumps 222 horsepower through the front wheels. With the 3000GT's mass, the SL gets to 60 mph in a somewhat dawdley 8.5 seconds, but it shines brightly in the braking and cornering arenas—all at a $10,000 price advantage over its more muscular brother, the VR-4. Additionally, the SL comes with leather seating, standard.

All-wheel drive, a twin-turbo V-6, and gobs of torque characterize the 3000GT VR-4. The VR-4 offers blistering acceleration, but due to its hefty curb weight, suffers slight reductions in braking and cornering ability over the more subdued SL. However, most snow belt enthusiasts will likely prefer the 3000GT VR-4, or its twin the Dodge Stealth R/T Turbo, over other cars in this class for their all-wheel drive capabilities.

Inside, drivers are protected by dual airbags that reside in a scooped and binnacled dashboard that could double as the interior of the Batmobile. Generally, ergonomics are good, but we prefer a more restrained driving environment.

Due early in 1995 is a convertible version of the 3000GT that features a fully-retractable hardtop, the first in a production car since Ford installed one in the Sunliner back when cruising wasn't likely to get you popped by a gangbanger and a drive-in had more to do with watching Hitchcock than using an ATM machine.

3000GT   MITSUBISHI

Performance and Safety

3000GT SL

Acceleration (0-60 mph) .... 8.5 sec.	ABS .... Standard
Braking (60-0 mph) .... 117 ft.	Driver Airbag .... Standard
Cornering .... .89 g's	Passenger Airbag .... Standard
Fuel Capacity .... 19.8 gal.	Traction Control .... N/A
Fuel Economy .... City: 18 mpg	Crash Test Grade .... D: Excellent P: N/A
Hwy: 24 mpg	Insurance Cost .... High

3000GT VR-4

Acceleration (0-60 mph) .... 5.3 sec.	ABS .... Standard
Braking (60-0 mph) .... 122 ft.	Driver Airbag .... Standard
Cornering .... .88 g's	Passenger Airbag .... Standard
Fuel Capacity .... 19.8 gal.	Traction Control .... N/A
Fuel Economy .... City: 18 mpg	Crash Test Grade .... D: Excellent P: N/A
Hwy: 24 mpg	Insurance Cost .... High

Edmund's Driving Impression

Slither into the snug-but-comfortable cockpit of Mitsubishi's hottest number, and chances are, you'll feel right at home. Take a spin through a few countryside curves and long highway stretches, and you might *never* want to leave that driver's seat. All the more so if you've been at the wheel of the stunning and swift twin-turbo VR-4.

If the 3000GT SL is a performance dream, the VR-4 is an all-out fantasy come true. All-wheel-drive, four-wheel steering and an electronically-controlled suspension combine to deliver a sports car that takes the most demanding curves without a whimper, grasping the asphalt like it had claws. Road behavior doesn't get much better than this, inspiring a melding of driver and machine that many promise, but few deliver.

Hit the gas hard, whether from a standstill or when passing, and you're practically slammed back in your seat. To get the most out of the 320-horse engine, you have to pay close attention to the six-speed gearbox (no automatic for the VR-4). Don't expect raucous sounds to match the action, though; the VR-4 is surprisingly quiet on the highway, emitting only a modest exhaust gurgle. Gauges are great, though the supplementary ones are a little hard to see, off to the side. Operation of the Active Aero system, which raises the huge rear wing at 50 mph, is impressive but won't make much difference in handling unless you drive to work by way of a race course.

Aggressively styled, loaded with fury, the VR-4 is a prime candidate for serious enthusiasts with plenty of bucks to spend. Sure, the ride gets harsh now and then—especially in the city. In truth, it's pretty mild for such a fiery traveler. Even Sport mode won't shake your fillings out.

Anyway, if that's a worry, try a base-model or SL instead. You'll save thousands of dollars, and all three *look* sharp.

EDMUND'S 1995 HIGH-PERFORMANCE AUTOMOBILES

MITSUBISHI 3000GT

CODE	DESCRIPTION	INVOICE	MSRP

3000GT

GT24-P SL 2-Dr Coupe (5-spd)	27664	33750
GT24-P SL 2-Dr Coupe (auto)	28390	34625
GT24-T VR4 Turbo 2-Dr Coupe (6-spd)	35302	43050
Destination Charge:	470	470

Standard Equipment

3000GT SL: 4-passenger seating capacity, leather-wrapped steering wheel/manual transmission shift knob/parking brake lever, passenger area cut pile carpeting, cargo area carpeting, cloth insert door trim with carpeted lower section, carpeted floor mats, dual bi-level heater/defroster with rear seat heater ducts and variable speed fan, CFC-free refrigerant air conditioning with manual controls, power windows with one-touch driver's auto-down, power door locks with one-touch keyless locking, electric rear window defroster with timer, tilt steering column, full-function cruise control, courtesy lamps (incls dome, trunk, map, glove compartment), rear cargo cover, center console with storage areas/cup holders/coin holder/armrest, remote hood-latch/fuel door/trunk lid release, driver and front passenger air bags, 3-point seatbelts for all passengers, side-impact door beams, 4-wheel disc brakes, full instrumentation (incls 160 MPH speedometer/7000 RPM redline tachometer/fuel level gauge/oil pressure gauge/coolant temperature gauge/tripmeter/voltmeter), warning lights (include engine check, brake system, low oil pressure, low fuel door/trunk ajar, charging system, low coolant, ignition key warning chime), 4-spoke sport steering wheel, steering column mounted controls (incls headlamps, high/low beam, flash-to-pass, turn signals, windshield wipers, cruise control), rear window wiper/washer, instrument panel controls (include panel lamps dimmer, tripmeter reset, hazard flasher, heater ventilation, fog lamps, rear window defroster), digital quartz clock, ETACS-IV (incls variable speed intermittent wipers, flash-to-pass, anti-theft system, fade-out dome lamp, ignition key lockout, belt warning timer, rear window defogger timer, 30-second delay power window, exterior lights auto-off), color-keyed 5-mph bumpers, color-keyed rear spoiler with high-mounted stop lamp, bright sport dual exhaust outlets, tinted glass, halogen headlamps with auto-off and flash-to-pass, projector fog lamps, power remote sideview mirrors (dual aero-type), convex right sideview mirror, upper windshield shade band, 16 x 8 aluminum alloy wheels with locks, 225/55R16 V-rated SBR performance tires, 3.0 liter DOHC V6 engine with MVIC, electronic multi-point fuel injection, automatic valve-lash adjusters, roller-type cam followers, stainless steel dual exhaust system, 5-speed manual transmission with overdrive, strut-type independent front suspension, multi-link independent rear suspension, power assisted rack and pinion steering, on-board diagnostic system, color-coded under hood service item identification, 7-way adjustable driver seat with 5-way power adjustments, leather front seating surfaces, auxiliary 12-volt power outlet, steering wheel mounted audio controls, anti-theft system with remote keyless entry, dual sun visors with vanity mirrors deleted, anti-lock braking system (ABS), Mitsubishi/Infinity audio system (incls AM/FM cassette with graphic equalizer, 8 speakers, separate amplifier, steering wheel remote audio controls), power and diversity antenna, electric sideview mirror defroster, ECS electronically controlled suspension, security system.

3000 GT VR-4 (in addition to or instead of 3000 GT SL equipment): Cloth insert door trim with lower carpeting deleted, automatic climate control with CFC-free refrigerant air conditioning and electronic pictographic controls, dual sun visors with illuminated vanity mirrors, 180 MPH speedometer, turbocharger boost gauge replaces voltmeter, Active Aero system front air dam extension and rear spoiler, 18 x 8.5 chrome plated aluminum alloy wheels with locks, 245/40R18 Z-rated SBR performance tires, 3.0 liter DOHC V6 engine with twin turbochargers and intercoolers, engine oil cooler, Getrag 6-speed manual transmission, double-wishbone type multi-link independent rear suspension, 4-wheel steering (4WS), limited slip rear differential, full-time AWD w/VCU and center differential.

3000GT MITSUBISHI

CODE	DESCRIPTION	INVOICE	MSRP

Accessories

SR	Manual Sunroof	300	375
PR	Power Sunroof — SL	720	900
	VR4	420	525
MG	Mud Guards	85	130
CW	Chrome Wheels — SL	480	600
Y99	Yellow Pearl Paint	250	313
EA	CD Changer	488	699

1995 Mitsubishi 3000GT VR-4

For expert advice in selecting/buying/leasing a new car, call
1-900-AUTOPRO
($2.00 per minute)

EDMUND'S 1995 HIGH-PERFORMANCE AUTOMOBILES

MITSUBISHI / ECLIPSE

1995 Mitsubishi Eclipse GSX

ECLIPSE

Since 1990, the Eclipse has been giving budget-minded enthusiasts style and performance at bargain prices. This year, an all-new Eclipse bowed, sporting a thicker, more muscular look and all the character of the old car, but in a much improved package.

The GS and GS-T have front-wheel drive, but different engines. A twin-cam Chrysler motor powers the GS, while the GS-T gets a potent turbo version of a Mitsubishi 2.0-liter engine. The top-of-the-line GSX gets the Mitsubishi powerplant, and an all-wheel drive system for less than hospitable climates.

Prices have crept up a bit and the Eclipse faces stiffer competition in the sport coupe class than it did when it was first introduced in 1990. Still, with all-wheel drive, good looks, and fantastic performance, the GSX is worth consideration at $25,000. The GS and GS-T must duel with competitors that offer the same level of refinement and power, often at lower prices.

The Eclipse is essentially the same car as the Eagle Talon, but the Mitsubishi looks much better. The tail is tidier, and the roof of the Eclipse is painted the same color as the rest of the car, unlike the Talon's all-black roof treatment. Dual airbags are standard for this sleek sportster, but anti-lock brakes are optional on all models. The interior is a nice place to spend time, with an organically-shaped dashboard that sweeps in front of the driver and between the seats.

Shop carefully for a sport coupe, but definitely consider the Eclipse, especially over its less sophisticated sibling, the Talon.

ECLIPSE — MITSUBISHI

Performance and Safety

Eclipse GS

Acceleration (0-60 mph)	8.6 sec.
Braking (60-0 mph)	N/A
Cornering	.82 g's
Fuel Capacity	15.9 gal.
Fuel Economy	City: 22 mpg
	Hwy: 31 mpg

ABS	Optional	
Driver Airbag	Standard	
Passenger Airbag	Standard	
Traction Control	N/A	
Crash Test Grade	D: Good	P: Good
Insurance Cost	N/A	

Eclipse GS-T

Acceleration (0-60 mph)	6.4 sec.
Braking (60-0 mph)	116 ft.
Cornering	.86 g's
Fuel Capacity	15.9 gal.
Fuel Economy	City: 20 mpg
	Hwy: 27 mpg

ABS	Optional	
Driver Airbag	Standard	
Passenger Airbag	Standard	
Traction Control	N/A	
Crash Test Grade	D: Good	P: Good
Insurance Cost	N/A	

Eclipse GSX

Acceleration (0-60 mph)	6.4 sec.
Braking (60-0 mph)	121 ft.
Cornering	.86 g's
Fuel Capacity	15.9 gal.
Fuel Economy	City: 19 mpg
	Hwy: 25 mpg

ABS	Optional	
Driver Airbag	Standard	
Passenger Airbag	Standard	
Traction Control	N/A	
Crash Test Grade	D: Good	P: Good
Insurance Cost	N/A	

Edmund's Driving Impression

Differences from the Talon marketed by Eagle dealers aren't vast. No surprise, since both makes are produced at the same plant in Illinois.

A five-speed manual gearbox is needed to take full advantage of the GSX Turbo's supreme acceleration potential. Under hard throttle, you can feel the turbo slip into action when easing the clutch out. Release the clutch pedal too quickly, though, and the effect is largely lost.

An automatic Turbo is no slowpoke, but the transmission—despite "fuzzy logic" controls—inevitably manages to sap some of the engine's strength away. In addition, when equipped with automatic, a Turbo Eclipse's engine has five fewer horsepower and six fewer foot-pounds of torque. Manual or automatic, the gearshift lever stands tall, with a handbrake to its right.

GSX Eclipses contain a 170-mph speedometer and 9000-rpm tachometer. Those figures imply an eagerness for the turbocharged engine to rev high, but they're somewhat optimistic. Dashboard reflections in the windshield can grow annoying—a common complaint nowadays.

Biggest plus for the all-wheel-drive GSX is handling, hands-down. Expect to feel highway imperfections in the wheel, but steering is clean and precise. AWD ride isn't too bad—actually, a touch better than in the less-aggressive, two-wheel-drive GS model.

MITSUBISHI   ECLIPSE

Seats are extremely firm and hold occupants nicely, but somewhat short bottoms might cause pain after a time. Toothpick-slim legs are needed to get into the back seat, but designers obviously made an effort to contour the roofline, to achieve great front headroom.

From a standstill, a 140-horsepower GS with automatic is a bit slow off the line, but not so bad beyond that point. The eager motor revs really high, just like the base-model Talon. Downshifts come neatly for passing, without significant jerkiness, but the GS definitely does not leap. For comfortable cruising, without bruising the pocketbook too painfully, it's a worthy choice—but no performance machine, even with manual shift.

1995 Mitsubishi Eclipse GSX

ECLIPSE

CODE	DESCRIPTION	INVOICE	MSRP
EC24H	GS DOHC 3-Dr Coupe (5-spd)	14204	16329
EC24H	GS DOHC 3-Dr Coupe (auto)	14809	17019
EC24T	GS Turbo 3-Dr Coupe (5-spd)	17397	19999
EC24T	GS Turbo 3-Dr Coupe (auto)	18121	20829
EC24U	GSX Turbo AWD 3-Dr Coupe (5-spd)	19717	22929
EC24U	GSX Turbo AWD 3-Dr Coupe (auto)	20416	23739
Destination Charge:		420	420

Standard Equipment

ECLIPSE GS DOHC: 2.0 liter DOHC 16-valve 4 cylinder engine, 5-speed manual transmission with overdrive, power assisted rack and pinion steering, on-board diagnostic system, color-keyed 5-mph bumpers, hood with power bulge, tinted glass, aero-type halogen headlamps, electric rear window defroster, full wheel covers, tilt steering column, courtesy lamps, center console, remote hood latch/fuel door/trunk lid release, driver and passenger air bags, full instrumentation, power 4-wheel disc brakes, color-keyed door handles/mirror trim, full profile color-keyed air dam, sculpted side sill cladding, color-keyed rear spoiler, dual power remote aero-type sideview mirrors, 16" x 6.0" steel wheels, 205/55HR16 tires, 7-way adjustable driver's seat with dual height and reclining with memory, carpeted lower door trim, split fold-down rear seat, rear cargo cover and cargo net, ETR AM/FM stereo radio with cassette and six speakers.

ECLIPSE — MITSUBISHI

| CODE | DESCRIPTION | INVOICE | MSRP |

GS TURBO (in addition to or instead of GS DOHC equipment): 2.0 liter DOHC 16-valve 4 cylinder turbocharged/intercooled engine, dual engine stabilizers, engine oil cooler, sport-tuned shock absorbers, power windows, power door locks, cruise control, rear window wiper/washer, integrated fog lamps, turbo boost gauges and oil pressure gauge, Mitsubishi Infinity audio system (incls AM/FM stereo radio with graphic equalizer, separate amplifier, eight speakers and CD changer controls), 16. x 6.0 aluminum alloy wheels.

GSX TURBO (in addition to or instead of GS TURBO equipment): Full-time all-wheel drive, limited slip differential, 215/55VR16 tires (size 205/55VR16 w/auto trans), leather front seating surfaces with power driver's seat, leather wrapped steering wheel and manual transmission shift knob.

Accessories

Code	Description	Invoice	MSRP
SR	Power Sunroof	599	731
AB	Anti-Lock Braking System	587	716
KE	Keyless Entry System	88	136
CC	Speed Control — GS DOHC	175	213
FM	Floor Mats	32	49
MG	Mud Guards	80	123
—	Alarm System/Keyless Entry System	272	332
TL	Wheel Locks — GS DOHC	21	32
AW	Alloy Wheels — GS DOHC	276	337
LS	Leather Pkg — GS Turbo	647	789

incls leather seat trim and power driver's seat adjuster

Code	Description	Invoice	MSRP
—	**Audio**		
ED	compact disc - GS DOHC	399	599
EA	compact disc autochanger	598	899
EI	Infinity system - GS DOHC	541	660
PH	Preferred Equipment Pkg — GS DOHC	1298	1582

incls air conditioning, power windows, power door locks, rear window wiper/washer, AM/FM stereo radio w/full logic cassette

---

See Edmund's

Automobile Dealer Directory (page 388)

and the back cover of this book to enter our

$10,000 Wheel N'Deal Give-Away.

MITSUBISHI — MIRAGE LS

1995 Mitsubishi Mirage LS Coupe

MIRAGE LS COUPE

This is one of the best kept secrets in the subcompact class. The Mirage LS is relatively cheap, fast, reliable and undeniably attractive (except for the funny bumper blisters on the tail). Think about this: the car performs as well as a Dodge Neon, costs just over $14,500 with every option on it, and is blessed with a shape that won't tire soon. It has dual airbags, split-fold rear seats, alloy wheels, a powerful little 1.8-liter engine, and a bunch of other stuff most people don't expect on a car of this caliber. A CD player is optional, as is air conditioning and an automatic transmission. But incredibly, what it doesn't have, even as an option, is anti-lock brakes.

Mitsubishi, it's 1995. General Motors has been equipping such agrarian implements as the Cavalier and Beretta with standard ABS since 1991. Get with the program.

One good program Mitsubishi has subscribed to is leasing. The Mirage LS has been advertised for less than $250 per month and no money down in our neck of the woods, and we've noticed a marked increase in the numbers of Mirage LS's on the road, with those temporary tags plastered to the rear window.

We doubt the Mirage will ever crack the best-seller lists in the United States, but frugal-minded performance buyers who want a car with some exclusivity and like the idea of leasing, might find merit in this Mitsubishi.

MIRAGE LS — MITSUBISHI

CODE	DESCRIPTION	INVOICE	MSRP

Performance and Safety

Acceleration (0-60 mph) .... 8.7 sec.	ABS .... N/A
Braking (60-0 mph) .... 133 ft.	Driver Airbag .... Standard
Cornering .... .82 g's	Passenger Airbag .... Standard
Fuel Capacity .... 13.2 gal.	Traction Control .... N/A
Fuel Economy .... City: 26 mpg	Crash Test Grade .... D: N/A P: N/A
Hwy: 33 mpg	Insurance Cost .... High

MIRAGE LS COUPE

MG21-M 2-Dr Coupe (5-spd)	11315	12569
MG21-M 2-Dr Coupe (auto)	11903	13229
Destination Charge:	420	420

Standard Equipment

MIRAGE LS COUPE: 1.8 liter SOHC 16-valve 4 cylinder engine with MFI, power steering, 5-passenger seating capacity, soft-touch wraparound dash, passenger area carpeting, front and rear armrests, heating/ventilating system with 4-speed fan/dial-type controls/dual bi-level output, electric rear window defroster with automatic shut-off, center console with storage bin, remote hood/latch release, keyless locking, door map pockets, driver and passenger air bags, side-impact door beams, height adjustable driver and passenger shoulder belt, ELR/ALR switchable outboard 3-point shoulder belts, child restraint anchorages, analog instrumentation (incls speedometer/fuel level gauge/coolant temperature gauge/ backglow instrument illumination), warning lights for engine check/emergency brake system/low oil pressure/door ajar/SRS light, steering column mounted controls (incls headlamps/high-low beam/ flash-to-pass/turn signals/windshield washer and wipers), instrument panel controls (incls panel lamps dimmer, hazard flasher, heater/ventilation), radio accommodation package (antenna, full harness, radio bracket, 4 speakers), 5-mph bumpers, color-keyed integrated front and rear bumpers, color-keyed grille, black door sash accent, flush mount door handles, locking fuel-filler door with cap tether, semi-concealed windshield wipers, aero-quad halogen headlamps, stainless steel exhaust system, 4-wheel independent/multi-link rear suspension, 5-speed manual transmission with overdrive, power assist front disc/rear drum brakes, rack and pinion steering, luxury sport front bucket seats, height adjustable driver seat, adjustable front headrests, split fold-down rear seat, full cloth upholstery, cargo area carpeting, cloth insert door trim, 2-speed intermittent wipers, tilt steering column, day/ night rearview mirror, digital clock, remote fuel filler and hatch release, Convenience Pkg (incls digital clock, intermittent wipers, cloth door trim, split fold-down rear seat, full trunk trim and lamp), low fuel warning light, trip odometer, tachometer, ETR AM/FM cassette with 4 speakers, color-keyed bodyside molding, color-keyed door handles, rear spoiler, locking fuel filler door with cap tether and remote release, tinted glass, dual power remote color-keyed sideview mirrors, 185/65R14 all-season SBR tires, alloy wheels.

Accessories

AC	Air Conditioning	700	854
MG	Mud Guards	70	99
TL	Wheel Locks	21	33
FM	Floor Mats	41	64
CN	Cargo Net	25	37
ED	Compact Disc Player	407	615
VM	Value Pkg	853	853

incls air conditioning, compact disc player, wheel locks, floor mats and cargo net

EDMUND'S 1995 HIGH-PERFORMANCE AUTOMOBILES

NISSAN 240SX

1995 Nissan 240SX SE

240SX

In 1990, the Nissan corporate think tank was in high gear, producing some of the most fun-to-drive cars of any carmaker on the planet. In quick succession, Nissan dealers received new car after new car, all of them exhibiting a brash, in-your-face personality and suave good looks. The Nissan 240SX was no exception to the rule. The car was engineered with eager young drivers in mind. To keep the insurance companies at bay, a twin-cam four cylinder was the sole powerplant available. For tail-out good times, Nissan opted for rear wheel drive on the 240, and then designed a graceful body that could be had as a coupe or hatchback. Later, a convertible was offered. The 240SX was an instant hit, particularly in hatchback form.

For 1995, Nissan has been fiddling with the formula. Gone is the popular hatchback. Gone is the convertible. Gone are low prices. Gone is the brash personality. The 1995 Nissan 240SX has moved Uptown, baby. It retains rear wheel drive and the twin-cam four. It retains speedy performance. It retains suave good looks. But in trying to become a mini Infiniti, the Nissan 240SX has lost its magical charm.

This doesn't mean it's a bad car. The Nissan 240SX should do rather well with people who find the more refined, V-6-equipped Mazda MX-6 LS unsatisfactory. Inside, the 240SX displays excellent ergonomics, with rich leather seating surfaces an extra-cost frill. Load on the options, and the 240SX SE approaches $27,000.

Time for a wake-up call, Nissan. Mazda's MX-6 LS V-6 performs much better, costs thousands less, and is prettier to look at than the 240SX SE. And for those of us paying off school loans, the new Nissan 200SX, based on the soon-to-be-introduced Sentra, is closer to the original 240 in execution and price than this wannabe luxo-coupe.

240SX   NISSAN

Performance and Safety

Acceleration (0-60 mph) .... 8.3 sec.
Braking (60-0 mph) .... 125 ft.
Cornering .... .88 g's
Fuel Capacity .... 17.2 gal.
Fuel Economy .... City: 21 mpg
                                  Hwy: 26 mpg

ABS .... Optional
Driver Airbag .... Standard
Passenger Airbag .... Standard
Traction Control .... Optional
Crash Test Grade .... D: N/A   P: N/A
Insurance Cost .... N/A

1995 Nissan 240SX

240SX COUPE

Code	Description	Invoice	MSRP
26155	Base 2-Dr Coupe (5-spd)	15057	16999
26155	Base 2-Dr Coupe (auto)	15793	17829
26255	SE 2-Dr Coupe (5-spd)	18318	20679
26215	SE 2-Dr Coupe (auto)	19053	21509
	Destination Charge:	390	390

Standard Equipment

240SX COUPE: 2.4 liter DOHC 16-valve 4-cylinder engine, 5-speed manual overdrive transmission, power assisted rack and pinion steering, power assisted 4-wheel disc brakes (front vented), power windows with driver side one-touch auto-down control, 195/60HR15 high-performance all-season tires, 15-inch steel wheels with full aerodynamic wheel covers, electronically tuned AM/FM cassette stereo audio system (50 watt) with Dolby noise reduction and 4 speakers, sequential multi-point electronic fuel injection, front-engine/rear-wheel drive, independent strut-type front suspension, front stabilizer bar, halogen headlamps, body color bumpers, semi-concealed windshield wipers, tinted glass with dark upper windshield band, dual power remote controlled body color outside mirrors, integrated high-mount stop lamp, double chrome-tipped exhaust finishers, reclining low-back front bucket seats, fold-down rear seatback (trunk through rear seat), moquette fabric seat material, cloth door trim, large front door map pockets, cut-pile carpeting, tilt steering column, 2-speed and fixed intermittent windshield wipers/twin-stream washers, electric rear window defroster with timer, side

NISSAN 240SX

window defoggers, remote trunk/fuel-filler door/hood releases, center console with covered storage area, day/night rearview mirror, lockable glove box, covered visor vanity mirror, interior courtesy lamps, analog tachometer/trip odometer/speedometer/coolant temperature/fuel level gauges, digital quartz clock, rod antenna with diversity antenna system, driver and passenger side air bags, steel side-door guard beams, 3-point front/rear seat belts, front seat belt warning light, 5-mph energy-absorbing front and rear bumpers, energy-absorbing steering column.

240SX SE COUPE (in addition to or instead of 240SX COUPE equipment): Power door locks, 205/55VR16 high-performance all-season tires, 16-inch aluminum alloy wheels, electronically-tuned AM/FM/CD stereo audio system (160 watt) with 6 speakers, air conditioning with non-CFC refrigerant, rear stabilizer bar, sport-tuned suspension, front and rear spoilers, projector-style fog lamps, driver-adjustable lumbar support, moquette fabric seat material with sporty center insert, keyless remote entry with anti-theft security system (panic alarm, remote arming), cruise control, 2-speed and variable intermittent windshield wipers/twin-stream washers, white-meter analog gauge cluster with reverse-to-electroluminescent lighting, power antenna with diversity-type antenna system.

Accessories

CODE	DESCRIPTION	INVOICE	MSRP
A01	**Air Conditioning** — std on SE	851	995
J03	**Power Sunroof**	768	899
B10	**Anti-Lock Brakes**	1022	1195
	incls limited slip differential		
C01	**California Emissions**	129	150
T04	**Alloy Wheels**	342	400
	std on SE		
E07	**Pearl Glow Paint**	300	350
V04	**Convenience Pkg**	827	945
	incls speed control, power door locks & AM/FM ETR stereo radio w/CD player, std on SE; req's air cond		
X03	**Leather Pkg**	1025	1199
	incls leather seats, leather-wrapped steering wheel & dual map lights; req's alloy wheels & power sunroof on Base; req's anti-lock brakes on SE		

FOR A SPECIAL RATE ON AN AUTO LOAN, CALL

1-800-AT-CHASE

CHASE AUTOMOTIVE FINANCE
SIMPLE ♦ FAST ♦ CONVENIENT

300ZX NISSAN

1995 Nissan 300ZX Turbo

300ZX

Tired of industry jokes about its overweight and understyled mid-Eighties 300ZX, Nissan designers decided to quiet the jester by redesigning its sports car for the Nineties. First, they re-injected the sports into the car by installing a 24-valve 3.0-liter V-6 under the hood in both turbo and non-turbo form. Then, a timeless interior was created that put the driver in control of all the power under the hood. After that, a shape that was alluring yet menacing, sophisticated yet rough-edged, understated yet bold, was penned to surround the excellent passenger compartment and fine mechanicals. That was in 1990.

This year, the 300ZX still draws stares and instills lust. It is not the fastest car in its class anymore, nor the most technologically advanced, nor the most refined, but like George Foreman, the 300ZX is still champ. It does everything a sports car should do, does it well, and it looks even better than it did when it was introduced. The 300ZX is a no-apologies kind of car.

For 1995, Nissan has left well enough alone, making only a few color and trim modifications. A lighter, less-powerful, less-luxurious and, if artist's renderings and recent Nissan products are any indication, more conservative car will be arriving in about a year. Seems this model doesn't sell well in Japan because of the styling, and the home market evidently wants a 300ZX that looks like every other car on the road.

Fair enough. We'll buy ours this year while the 300ZX still has a personality. We advise you to do the same.

NISSAN   *300ZX*

Performance and Safety

300ZX

Acceleration (0-60 mph) .... 6.7 sec.	ABS .... Standard
Braking (60-0 mph) .... 124 ft.	Driver Airbag .... Standard
Cornering .... .88 g's	Passenger Airbag .... Standard
Fuel Capacity .... 18.7 gal.	Traction Control .... N/A
Fuel Economy .... City: 18 mpg	Crash Test Grade .... D: Average P: N/A
Hwy: 23 mpg	Insurance Cost .... High

300ZX Turbo

Acceleration (0-60 mph) .... 6.0 sec.	ABS .... Standard
Braking (60-0 mph) .... 124 ft.	Driver Airbag .... Standard
Cornering .... .88 g's	Passenger Airbag .... Standard
Fuel Capacity .... 18.7 gal.	Traction Control .... N/A
Fuel Economy .... City: 18 mpg	Crash Test Grade .... D: Average P: N/A
Hwy: 23 mpg	Insurance Cost .... High

300ZX (1994)

Code	Description	Invoice	MSRP
64054	2-Dr 2-Seater Coupe (5-spd)	29156	33699
64154	2-Dr 2-Seater Coupe w/T-Bar (5-spd)	30437	35179
64114	2-Dr 2-Seater Coupe w/T-Bar (auto)	31258	36129
64854	2-Dr 2-Seater Turbo Coupe w/T-Bar (5-spd)	34694	40099
64814	2-Dr 2-Seater Turbo Coupe w/T-Bar & Leather Pkg (auto)	36446	42124
64254	2-Dr 2+2 w/T-Bar (5-spd)	31571	36489
64214	2-Dr 2+2 w/T-Bar (auto)	32392	37439
64754	2-Dr Convertible (5-spd)	35368	40879
64714	2-Dr Convertible (auto)	36234	41879
	Destination Charge:	390	390

Standard Equipment

300ZX CONVERTIBLE: 3.0L DOHC 24-valve V6 engine, Nissan valve timing control system (NVCS), sequential multi-point electronic fuel injection with dual-plenum intake, Nissan direct ignition system (NDIS), 5-speed manual overdrive transmission, electronic speed-sensitive power rack-and-pinion steering, viscous limited slip differential, 4-wheel independent multi-link suspension, front and rear stabilizer bars, power 4-wheel vented disc brakes, anti-lock braking system (ABS), cast aluminum alloy wheels, high-performance steel-belted radial tires, body-color front/rear bumpers, body-color front air dam, projection-type low-beam halogen headlamps, integrated front halogen fog lamps, dual heated power remote-controlled outside mirrors w/passenger side convex mirror, fully-tinted glass, upper shaded windshield band, quad chrome-tipped exhaust finishers, 2-passenger seating, reclining front bucket seats, power driver/s seat w/7-way adjustment (3-position lumbar, seatback recline, side bolsters, forward and rear cushion tilt, headrest height and fore/aft adjustments), power passenger seat, leather seating surfaces, center console, full cut-pile carpeting w/carpeted cargo area, lockable glove box, air conditioning (non-CFC refrigerant), power windows w/driver-side auto-

300ZX   NISSAN

| CODE | DESCRIPTION | INVOICE | MSRP |

down, keyless remote entry system, power door locks, cruise control, automatic theft deterrent system, etched glass, leather-wrapped steering wheel and gear shift knob, remote fuel-filler door release, remote trunk and hood releases, passenger-side visor vanity mirror, two-speed variable intermittent windshield wipers/twin stream washers, dual overhead map lamps, interior courtesy lamps include cigarette lighter/ashtray/rear cargo area, illuminated entry system w/fade-out feature, digital quartz clock, analog-style instrumentation, tachometer, speedometer/coolant temperature/fuel level/oil pressure gauges, low fuel and door-ajar warning lamps, trip odometer, electronically tuned AM/FM stereo w/2 speakers, auto-reverse cassette player w/Dolby noise reduction, automatic power diversity-type antenna system, driver and passenger side airbags, steel side-door guard beams, 3-point manual front seat belts, front seatbelt warning lamp, dual braking system w/ABS, center high-mount rear stoplamp, 5 mph energy-absorbing front/rear bumpers, energy-absorbing steering column.

300ZX 2-SEATER: 3.0L DOHC 24-valve V6 engine, Nissan value timing control system (NVCS), sequential multi-point electronic fuel injection with dual-plenum intake, Nissan direct ignition system (NDIS), 5-speed manual overdrive transmission, electronic speed-sensitive power rack-and-pinion steering, viscous limited slip differential, 4-wheel independent multi-link suspension, front and rear stabilizer bars, power 4-wheel vented disc brakes, anti-lock braking system (ABS), cast aluminum alloy wheels, high-performance steel-belted radial tires, body-color front/rear bumpers, body color front air dam, projection-type low beam halogen headlamps, integrated front halogen fog lamps, dual-heated power remote-controlled outside mirrors with passenger-side convex mirror, full-tinted glass/upper shaded windshield band, electric rear window wiper/washer, quad chrome tipped exhaust finishers, reclining front bucket seats, driver's seat with 7-way adjustment (3-position lumbar, seatback recline, side bolsters, forward and rear cushion tilt, headrest height and fore/aft adjustments), cloth seat trim, center console, full cut-pile carpeting w/carpeted cargo area, lockable glove box, air conditioning (non-CFC refrigerant), automatic temperature control, retractable cargo area cover, power windows w/driver-side auto-down feature, power door locks, keyless remote entry system, etched glass, leather-wrapped steering wheel and gear shift knob, remote fuel-filler door release, remote hatch/trunk and hood releases, passenger side visor vanity mirror, 2-speed variable intermittent windshield wipers/twin stream washers, electric rear window defroster w/timer, side window defoggers, dual overhead map lamps, interior courtesy lamps include cigarette lighter/ashtray/rear cargo area, illuminated entry system w/fade-out feature, digital quartz clock, analog-style instrumentation, tachometer, speedometer/coolant temperature/fuel level/oil pressure gauges, low fuel and door ajar warning lamps, trip odometer, Bose audio system w/4 speakers, auto reverse cassette player w/Dolby noise reduction, automatic power diversity-type antenna system, driver and passenger side air bags, steel side-door guard beams, 3-point manual front seatbelts, front seatbelt warning lamp, dual braking system w/ABS, center high-mount rear stoplamp, 5 mph energy-absorbing front/rear bumpers, energy-absorbing steering column, cruise control, automatic theft deterrent system.

T-ROOF (in addition to or instead of 2-SEATER equipment): T-bar roof w/removable tinted glass panels, power driver's seat.

2+2 (in addition to or instead of T-ROOF equipment): 2+2 seating, fold-down rear seatback, passenger side walk-in device, 3-point manual rear seatbelts.

TURBO (in addition to or instead of 2+2 equipment): Twin-turbocharged 3.0L DOHC 24-valve V6 engine w/trim air-to-air intercoolers, engine oil cooler, super HICAS 4-wheel steering system, 2-way driver-adjustable shock absorbers, integrated body-color rear spoiler, front air dam with twin intercooler inlets, 2+2 seating deleted, fold-down rear seatback deleted, passenger-side walk-in device deleted, turbo boost gauge, 3-point manual rear seatbelts deleted.

NISSAN — 300ZX / ALTIMA

CODE	DESCRIPTION	INVOICE	MSRP

Accessories

X03	**Leather Pkg** — Coupe w/T-Bar	919	1075
	Turbo Coupe w/T-Bar	919	1075
	2+2	1090	1275
E07	**Pearlglow Paint** — Convertibles & models w/T-Bar	300	350
C01	**California Emissions**	129	150

1995 Nissan Altima GLE

ALTIMA

Talk about a runaway success. The Altima has become quite a popular car in this country, with hundreds of thousands of the jelly-bean-shaped sedans sold since its 1993 introduction. Its predecessor, the Nissan Stanza, was a practically invisible car to consumers, and we can't help but wonder whether the name change or Nissan's $27 million advertising campaign touting the Altima as an affordable luxury car dictated the tides of change.

What we do know is that the Altima has the right mix of good looks, sedan capability, spunky personality and affordable price that Honda and Toyota used to make the Accord and Camry best-sellers. The Altima is a fun car, and plays the roles of pedestrian family hauler and pseudo-sport sedan with equal aplomb. Heavily subsidized national lease deals on the GXE trim level haven't hurt sales either, and virtually guarantee an excellent used Altima market in about a year.

For 1995, Nissan tweaked the styling of the Altima a bit, with a new grille and revised taillights. Four trim levels are available: entry-level XE; mid-priced GXE; sporty SE; and luxury-oriented GLE. The GXE is the best selller, and when equipped with air conditioning, cassette stereo, automatic transmission, cruise and anti-lock brakes, stickers for just over $19,000.

Guess what. That's Ford Contour SE and Mercury Mystique LS territory, and is just a couple thou' shy of the Maxima GXE, which has all that stuff standard. The Fords perform better than the Altima,

ALTIMA NISSAN

have a slightly higher equipment content, and offer a refined V-6 powerplant. Still, the Altima lease deals are hard to beat, and it's a good car. The competition is getting better though, even from within Nissan itself.

Performance and Safety

Altima GXE

Acceleration (0-60 mph)	8.7 sec.	ABS	Optional	
Braking (60-0 mph)	130 ft.	Driver Airbag	Standard	
Cornering	.79 g's	Passenger Airbag	Standard	
Fuel Capacity	15.9 gal.	Traction Control	N/A	
Fuel Economy	City: 21 mpg	Crash Test Grade	D: Good	P: Average
	Hwy: 29 mpg	Insurance Cost	Average	

Altima SE

Acceleration (0-60 mph)	8.1 sec.	ABS	Optional	
Braking (60-0 mph)	116 ft.	Driver Airbag	Standard	
Cornering	.80 g's	Passenger Airbag	Standard	
Fuel Capacity	15.9 gal.	Traction Control	N/A	
Fuel Economy	City: 21 mpg	Crash Test Grade	D: Good	P: Average
	Hwy: 29 mpg	Insurance Cost	Average	

Edmund's Driving Impression

Our first trial with an Altima yielded a few nits to pick—flaws that, while minor, are hard to forget when evaluating the '95 model. The five-speed manual gearbox, for one, ranks as good, but not great: occasionally balky, and unwilling to reach into reverse. Seats are comfortable and supportive, but the protruding adjuster on that early Altima caught and tore our shoe—twice. It's like the horseplayer who goes through the rest of life complaining about a particular thoroughbred, unable to forgive that horse for "failing" him once at the winner's circle.

On the plus side, an Altima rides nicely, if a trifle rough on occasion. Acceleration is spirited, but hardly breathtaking. Highway pickup is pretty good with manual shift, even if you're not in the ideal gear for the occasion. Handling is capable, but not startling.

The five-speed's gearshift can be a little stiff, and the clutch demands moderate effort and a rather long push—but delivers good feel. Brakes feel light, but strong.

Seats in the SE are extra-firm, with tight side bolsters and short bottoms. Instruments—namely, a 120-mph speedometer and 8000-rpm tachometer, plus fuel and temperature gauges—are easily visible through the steering-wheel rim.

In the unusual interior, door upholstery reaches up over the door sills. There's headroom aplenty, and Nissan promotes the fact that leg room beats out Honda's Accord. The rear compartment is truly comfortable, and the trunk is rather sizable for a car of this size.

All told, not much stood out in our first trial, and that's still true today, beyond the shapely Altima styling and spacious interior. We have to wonder, too, why Nissan hasn't followed the lead of its competitors and plopped in a V-6. The 2.4-liter, 16-valve four is fine, but doesn't quite deliver the kind of performance that this well-built sedan should be able to convey.

NISSAN — ALTIMA

1995 Nissan Altima SE

ALTIMA

CODE	DESCRIPTION	INVOICE	MSRP
15655	XE 4-Dr Sedan (5-spd)	13185	14799
15615	XE 4-Dr Sedan (auto)	13924	15629
15755	GXE 4-Dr Sedan (5-spd)	13913	15799
15715	GXE 4-Dr Sedan (auto)	14644	16629
15955	SE 4-Dr Sedan (5-spd)	16520	18869
15915	SE 4-Dr Sedan (auto)	17246	19699
15815	GLE 4-Dr Sedan (auto)	17413	19889
Destination Charge:		390	390

Standard Equipment

ALTIMA - XE: 2.4 liter 16-valve SFI 4 cylinder engine, 5-speed manual transmission, power steering, power front disc/rear drum brakes, driver and front passenger air bags, tilt steering wheel, bodyside moldings, tachometer, trip odometer, rear window defroster, intermittent windshield wipers, console, cloth reclining bucket seats, remote trunk release, remote fuel filler door release, wheel covers, power OS mirrors, visor vanity mirror.

GXE (in addition to or instead of XE equipment): Power windows, power door locks.

SE (in addition to or instead of GXE equipment): Power moonroof, air conditioning, speed control, alloy wheels, fog lights, rear spoiler, sport suspension, cornering lights, power 4-wheel disc brakes, AM/FM stereo radio with cassette, cloth reclining sport bucket seats, variable intermittent windshield wipers, leather-wrapped steering wheel, bodyside moldings deleted.

GLE (in addition to or instead of GXE equipment): Automatic air conditioning, 4-speed automatic transmission with overdrive, AM/FM stereo radio with cassette and compact disc, power antenna, alloy wheels, power moonroof, alarm system, cornering lights, speed control, variable intermittent windshield wipers, illuminated visor vanity mirrors.

ALTIMA / MAXIMA — NISSAN

Accessories

CODE	DESCRIPTION	INVOICE	MSRP
B07	**Anti-Lock Brakes**	854	999
	req's F02 option pkg on XE; req's F09 option pkg on GXE		
X03	**Leather Pkg** — SE, GLE	897	1049
C01	**California Emissions System**	129	150
S07	**Speed Control** — XE w/auto trans	196	229
F02	**Option Pkg F02** — XE	1563	1829
	incls air conditioning, speed control, AM/FM stereo radio w/cassette		
F09	**Option Pkg F09** — GXE	1025	1199
	incls air conditioning, speed control, AM/FM stereo w/cassette, power antenna		

1995 Nissan Maxima SE

MAXIMA

Somehow, Nissan designers underwent a complete personality switch in the late Eighties and began producing cars whose styling was as fresh five years after introduction day as it was on introduction day. These cars were a far cry from the carved-from-a-cinderblock styling of previous Nissans. The 1989 Maxima was one of the new generation of cars to roll out of Japan, and it continued to look better year after year, aging more gracefully than Dick Clark. For 1995, Nissan replaced it with an all-new car, one with a stellar drivetrain and first-class cabin, but with a somewhat dowdy exterior and funky-ugly taillights.

First, the good stuff. Under the hood is a twin-cam, aluminum 3.0-liter V-6. It puts 190 horsepower to the ground through the front axle. A five-speed is standard on GXE and SE trim levels, but an automatic is optional. This engine is a jewel, providing swift acceleration without penalizing fuel economy.

NISSAN — MAXIMA

Inside, the Maxima sports an interior befitting an Infiniti. No coincidence here; the Maxima serves as the basis for the upcoming Infiniti I30. Roomier than the old Maxima, the new one should find nobody complaining about the accommodations.

The new Maxima's styling is growing on us, but the taillights and sculpted decklid are just too overwrought. Something closer to the Altima's tail would have been more tasteful. Also, on models not equipped with fog lights, tacky ribbed-plastic inserts fill the holes in the front fascia where they would have gone. The inserts jar the eye and detract from an otherwise clean frontal design.

Overall, the Maxima has lost some of its sex appeal, but the new engine, interior, and price structure of the car more than make up for the slight styling shortcomings.

Performance and Safety

Acceleration (0-60 mph) .... 6.6 sec.	ABS .... Optional
Braking (60-0 mph) .... 131 ft.	Driver Airbag .... Standard
Cornering .... .83 g's	Passenger Airbag .... Standard
Fuel Capacity .... 18.5 gal.	Traction Control .... N/A
Fuel Economy .... City: 21 mpg	Crash Test Grade .... D: Good P: Average
Hwy: 28 mpg	Insurance Cost .... N/A

Edmund's Driving Impression

Not only is the largest Nissan a terrific performer and a fairly nimble handler, it also delivers a stable ride (if slightly rough at times). Easy to drive, solid and strong on the move, roomy inside, the reworked Maxima feels solid and tight, fully devoid of rattles and squeaks.

Acceleration is nothing short of stunning. Despite its girth, this four-door nearly leaps ahead from a standstill, then passes and merges without a care. Automatic-transmission upshifts in the performance-oriented SE edition are smooth; often, barely noticeable. Downshifts for passing bring only a tiny delay.

Handling in the SE with its sport-tuned suspension isn't 100% precise, but close. Really close. Rock-solid and steady on the highway, the thoughtfully-engineered sedan also maneuvers easily around town. Curves and corners are consumed in a nearly-flat stance. Braking is excellent, bringing only a trace of nosedive, but quick and straight response.

Not totally silent, Maxima is pleasantly quiet, yielding only a modest roar when accelerating hard. Harsher-riding than some competitors, at least on rough urban pavement, the SE calms down on the open road. Its taut suspension responds quickly, if not always fully resiliently. Tires do a good job of trying to stay in total contact, no matter how turbulent the surface gets.

Visibility is excellent, except toward the right front. The steering wheel sits low, but feels just right. Though comfortable, seats aren't as supportive as some, producing a mild sensation of rolling forward. Front headroom is super.

Oh, one thing more: the SE gauges. You'll either adore or detest these black-on-white analog instruments, more befitting a race car than a family sedan. Like them or not, you get a 140-mph speedometer and 8000-rpm tach, plus fuel and temp readouts.

If only the sheetmetal shaping matched Maxima's muscular character—especially in SE guise—this would be a hard-to-beat performance choice.

MAXIMA

1995 Nissan Maxima SE

MAXIMA

CODE	DESCRIPTION	INVOICE	MSRP
08455	GXE 4-Dr Sedan (5-spd)	17818	19999
08415	GXE 4-Dr Sedan (auto)	18493	20999
08255	SE 4-Dr Sedan (5-spd)	18384	20999
08215	SE 4-Dr Sedan (auto)	19260	21999
08615	GLE 4-Dr Sedan (auto)	21186	24199
Destination Charge:		390	390

Standard Equipment

MAXIMA - GXE: DOHC 24-valve V6 engine, 5-speed manual transmission, power-assisted rack and pinion steering, power-assisted 4-wheel disc brakes (front vented), power windows with driver side auto-down feature, power door locks, steel wheels with full covers, electronically tuned AM/FM stereo audio system with auto-reverse cassette, Dolby noise reduction and 4 speakers, air conditioning with non-CFC refrigerant, sequential multi-point fuel injection, Nissan Direct Ignition System (NDIS), independent strut front suspension, front and rear stabilizer bars, flush-mounted halogen headlamps, flush-mounted halogen cornering lamps, semi-concealed windshield wipers, tinted glass with dark upper windshield band, dual power remote control outside mirrors with passenger side convex mirror, body color bodyside moldings, front bucket seats, multi-adjustable driver's seat with front and rear seat cushion tilt/seatback recline/2-way lumbar support and fore/aft adjustments, large front door map pockets, cut-pile carpeting, cruise control with steering wheel-mounted controls, tilt steering column, 2-speed windshield wipers with fixed intermittent feature, electric rear window defroster with timer, side window defoggers, cup holders, remote trunk/fuel filler door and hood releases, center console with large storage area and armrest, lockable glove box illuminated entry, overhead map lamp, interior courtesy lamps, ashtray and trunk courtesy lamps, tachometer/coolant temperature/fuel level gauges, low fuel warning light, trip odometer, digital clock, automatic power diversity antenna system, driver and passenger side air bags (SRS), 3-point manual seatbelts in outboard positions/rear center lap belts, child-safety rear door locks, energy-absorbing steering column/front and rear bumpers, side impact protection.

EDMUND'S 1995 HIGH-PERFORMANCE AUTOMOBILES

NISSAN MAXIMA

GLE (in addition to or instead of GXE equipment): Electronically controlled 4-speed automatic overdrive transmission, aluminum alloy wheels with bright finish, Bose electronically-tuned AM/FM cassette/CD stereo audio system with 4 amplifiers and 6 speakers, single chrome-tipped exhaust finisher, 8-way power-adjustable front driver's seat, fold-down rear seat center armrest with trunk pass-through, leather seating surfaces, leather-wrapped steering wheel and shift knob, simulated wood trim, automatic temperature control, dual illuminated visor vanity mirrors, 2-speed windshield wipers with variable intermittent feature, remote keyless entry system, theft deterrent system, driver and passenger side illuminated visor vanity mirror, automatic transmission park/lock feature.

SE (in addition to or instead of GLE equipment): 5-speed manual transmission, electronically-tuned AM/FM stereo audio system with auto-reverse cassette/Dolby noise reduction and 4 speakers, electronically controlled liquid filled front engine mount, sport-tuned suspension, halogen fog lamps, body color rear spoiler and black-out exterior trim, 8-way power adjustable front driver's seat deleted, leather seating surfaces deleted, simulated wood trim deleted, automatic temperature control deleted, dual illuminated visor vanity mirrors deleted, 2-speed windshield wipers with fixed intermittent feature, remote keyless entry system and theft deterrent feature deleted, white-faced analog-style gauges with reverse-to-electroluminescent lighting, automatic transmission park/lock feature deleted.

Accessories

Code	Description	Invoice	MSRP
B07	**Anti-Lock Brakes**	851	995
	NA GXE 5-spd		
J01	**Power Sunroof**	768	899
	NA GXE 5-spd		
C01	**California Emissions**	129	150
W08	**Cold Weather Pkg**	174	199
	incls heated front seats, heated OS mirrors, low windshield washer fluid warning light, heavy duty battery; req's anti-lock brakes and security convenience pkg; NA GXE 5-spd		
H07	**Bose Audio System w/CD Player** — SE, GXE auto	700	799
	incls AM/FM ETR stereo radio; req's power sunroof and security convenience pkg		
X03	**SE Leather Trim Pkg** — SE	939	1099
	incls leather seating surfaces, door panels with leatherette trim, automatic air conditioning controls; req's Bose audio system and security convenience pkg		
V01	**Security Convenience Pkg** — SE, GXE auto	613	700
	incls 8-way power driver's seat, keyless entry system, security system, power decklid release, variable intermittent wipers, illuminated visor vanity mirrors (GXE also incls chrome-tipped exhaust outlet and P205/60HR15 SBR all-season tires; SE req's power sunroof		

GET MORE MONEY FOR YOUR USED CAR BY KNOWING ITS TRUE VALUE

See our ads on pages 4 and 6

SENTRA SE-R

1994.5 Nissan Sentra SE-R

SENTRA SE-R

Enthusiasts have always lamented the loss of the econo-sport sedan that paved the way for cars like the Volkswagen GTI, the Dodge Omni GLH and the current Ford Escort GT. That sedan was called the BMW 2002, and it blended performance with function, offering within its sedate three-box shape the ability to speed undetected by police who were looking for brightly-colored, finned and spoilered muscle cars to yank over to the side of the road.

The BMW was affordable fun, and most of the souped-up hatchbacks that followed it never adhered to the basic formula that the Bimmer embraced—simplicity in style, with an emphasis on performance and the driving experience. Most 'pocket-rockets' were painted in bright hues, with spoilers and ground effects and hood vents to give them the boy-racer look, which only attracted attention from speed enforcers.

Then along came Nissan, in the midst of a corporate change in philosophy that dictated that cars should be good looking and fun-to-drive. In 1991, Nissan gave us the 140-horsepower Nissan Sentra SE-R, a version of the Sentra coupe stuffed with a big four cylinder, fat tires, and a tweaked suspension. Discreet fog lights, a small rear spoiler and attractive alloy wheels were the only external clues that indicated this was more than a regular Sentra. The press labeled it the modern-day BMW 2002, and Nissan hasn't goofed with the formula yet.

Unfortunately, the 1994.5 Sentra SE-R is the last of the breed. This January, it will be phased out in favor of a new coupe called the 200SX, which looks more swoopy, more speedy and more expensive. It certainly won't be the stealth-machine the SE-R is, if early-release press photos are accurate.

That all good things come to an end is an unavoidable corollary of life. The SE-R has reached the end of the line, and serious enthusiasts on a budget would do well to hurry to the nearest Nissan dealer and try to locate one of the few remaining examples of the quintessential 'pocket-rocket.'

NISSAN SENTRA SE-R

Performance and Safety

Acceleration (0-60 mph) .... 7.6 sec.	ABS .... Optional		
Braking (60-0 mph) .... 128 ft.	Driver Airbag .... Optional		
Cornering .... .82 g's	Passenger Airbag .... N/A		
Fuel Capacity .... 13.2 gal.	Traction Control .... N/A		
Fuel Economy .... City: 24 mpg	Crash Test Grade .... D: Good	P: Good	
	Hwy: 31 mpg	Insurance Cost .... Very High	

SENTRA SE-R *(1994.5)*

Code	Description	Invoice	MSRP
22454	2-Dr Sedan (5-spd)	12909	14489
22414	2-Dr Sedan (auto)	13622	15289
	Destination Charge:	390	390

Standard Equipment

SENTRA SE-R: 2.0 liter DOHC 16-valve 4 cylinder engine, sequential multi-point electronic fuel injection, 5-speed manual transmission, power rack and pinion steering, power assisted 4-wheel disc brakes, 4-wheel independent suspension, front/rear stabilizer bars, limited slip differential, front air dam, aluminum alloy wheels, halogen headlamps, fog lamps, tinted glass, dual power remote control outside mirrors with passenger side convex mirror, body color bodyside moldings, body color bumpers, bright exhaust outlet, rear spoiler, reclining front sport bucket seats, sporty velour cloth seat trim, deluxe door trim with cloth insert, front door map pockets, carpeting, dual cup holders, tilt steering column, leather-wrapped steering wheel and shift knob (manual trans), 2-speed intermittent windshield wipers/washers, rear window defroster/side window defoggers, remote trunk release, remote hood release, remote fuel filler door release, center console, lockable glove box, front and rear assist grips, tachometer, trip odometer, coolant temperature gauge, digital quartz clock.

Accessories

Code	Description	Invoice	MSRP
A01	**Air Conditioning**	851	995
S05	**Cruise Control**	197	230
B07	**Anti-Lock Braking System**	599	700
	req's value option pkg and driver's side air bag; models w/manual trans also req power sunroof		
C01	**California Emissions**	129	150
J01	**Power Sunroof**	706	825
	req's value option pkg		
H01	**Radio**	513	600
	incls AM/FM ETR stereo w/cassette		
F09	**Value Option Pkg**	1112	1300
	incls air conditioning, cruise control, AM/FM ETR stereo radio w/cassette, diversity antenna system, 4 speakers		

AURORA   OLDSMOBILE

1995 Oldsmobile Aurora

AURORA

We really want to like the Aurora. On paper, it seems to have everything in place to whip the competition. Strong performance, a Northstar-derived V-8 engine, standard anti-lock brakes and traction control, svelte sheetmetal, and prices that top out well under $34,000 fully loaded. Sounds tasty, doesn't it?

While slick overall, it looks like a Saturn SL that underwent reconstructive surgery. It weighs two tons. The wheels look like Aunt Polly's holiday condiment dishes. It barely avoids the dreaded gas-guzzler tax. The kicker is the lack of an Oldsmobile badge anywhere on the the car save for the radio. There is a reason for this omission, something having to do with reputation perhaps, and we feel that 1) it is a statement regarding GM products, Oldsmobiles in particular, and 2) it indicates a level of dishonesty on the part of General Motors.

Do they really believe that consumers stopped buying Oldsmobiles because of the name? Do they really believe that omitting the brand from the exterior of the Aurora will bring buyers into showrooms, or are they afraid that potential customers who might like the car would be embarrassed to drive it if an Oldsmobile tag was grafted onto its flanks? Whatever the reason, we think it stinks, mainly because this is the image car Oldsmobile needs as GM attempts to transform public perception of the brand.

Doesn't really matter, because there are more than a few cars at or below the Aurora's price level that look better, feel better, and perform better.

OLDSMOBILE — AURORA

| CODE | DESCRIPTION | INVOICE | MSRP |

Performance and Safety

Acceleration (0-60 mph) .... 7.4 sec.
Braking (60-0 mph) .... 127 ft.
Cornering .... .81 g's
Fuel Capacity .... 20 gal.
Fuel Economy .... City: 17 mpg
                                              Hwy: 24 mpg

ABS .... Standard
Driver Airbag .... Standard
Passenger Airbag .... Standard
Traction Control .... Standard
Crash Test Grade .... D: N/A   P: N/A
Insurance Cost .... N/A

Edmund's Driving Impression

Conventional wisdom calls Oldsmobile's latest hope a revelation, if not a revolution—the car that can keep the company afloat into the next century. Even before the first Auroras rolled off the line, critics were praising its shape, its acceleration, its ride and handling—simply everything.

It's never easy to be different, but we just haven't been able to warm up to this Olds. And when you don't care for a car as a whole, you tend to magnify its lesser flaws. We've grumbled about the distorted view out the rear window, grimaced at the rougher-than-expected ride (on harsh pavement), picked apart the odd door-window design and the overabundance of controls.

An early-production Aurora bucked once or twice when tromping the gas. Seat bottoms seemed short and low. Brakes produced a little jerk, an instant before the car eased to a halt.

Another Aurora delivered an occasional slight jolt when cruising, as though trying to slow itself down for no apparent reason. A driveline drone added to the annoyance. So did a mild misalignment in the trunklid, and rattles in the window.

Even if true, those imperfections cannot obscure the car's numerous virtues: mainly, its impressive new V-8 engine, evolved from Cadillac's Northstar System. Stomp the pedal in either Power or Normal shift mode, and the sizable sedan nearly leaps ahead. Tires clutch the pavement tightly through curves, aided by a taut suspension. Wallowing and slushiness are absent. An Aurora feels strong, solid, stable, quiet. It rides pleasantly on the expressways, if a trifle jittery over rough spots in town.

For thirty grand, you get a lot of car. What it failed to give us is joy—an urge to make an Aurora our own. You may disagree, but compare it to the far-cheaper Eighty Eight before taking delivery.

AURORA 8 CYL

R29GS 4-Dr Sedan 29017 31370
Destination Charge: 625   625

Standard Equipment

AURORA: 4.0 liter 32-valve DOHC V8 engine, front wheel drive, 4-speed electro-shift automatic overdrive transmission, rack and pinion steering with magnetic speed variable assist, front suspension (independent strut-type with lower control arms, coil springs and stabilizer bar), rear suspension (independent semi-trailing arm with lateral links, coil springs, stabilizer bar and automatic leveling), 16" x 7" 6-spoke aluminum wheels, Goodyear Eagle GA P235/60R16 radial ply BW touring tires, Freedom battery, composite halogen headlamps with flash-to-pass feature, integrated front fascia foglamps, 5-mph bumpers, bodycolor bodyside moldings, black rocker panel moldings, cornering lamps, front seats (contour bucket with 6-way power adjustment, power recliners, power lumbar supports, manually adjustable headrests, leather seating areas and driver side memory control), rear seat (bench with integrated headrests, center folding armrest with storage and dual cupholders,

AURORA — OLDSMOBILE

center pass-through to trunk and leather seating areas), front center console including floor-mounted leather-wrapped shifter and storage compartment, E-Z Kool solar control windows, courtesy lamps, illumination package activated by remote lock control, deluxe acoustical insulation, genuine walnut burl wood trim on console and door armrests, deluxe trunk trim, front and rear floor mats, ashtrays, driver and front passenger side air bags, power 4-wheel disc anti-lock brakes, all-speed traction control system, automatic programmable door locks with remote controls, Pass-Key vehicle security system, pulse wiper system, leather-wrapped tilt steering wheel with touch controls, side window defoggers, electric rear window defogger, dual horns, chime-tone warning system, automatic dual-zone air conditioner with rear seat duct and outside temperature display, power windows with driver side auto down feature and driver-controlled lockout switch, remote lock control package, cruise control, twilight sentinel automatic headlamp control, front seatback pockets, door pockets, overhead console, retained accessory power, sunvisors with auxiliary shades, extensions and map straps, power fuel filler door release, inside hood release, gas strut hood supports, inside day/night electrochromic mirror, driver and passenger lighted visor vanity mirrors, two rear assist handles, trunk cargo net, electronic clock, power trunk lid lock release, analog instrument panel including tachometer, audio system (AM/FM stereo radio with automatic tone control, cassette, CD player, 6-speaker Dimensional Sound System, power antenna).

Accessories

Code	Description	Invoice	MSRP
FE9	Federal Emission Equipment	NC	NC
NG1	Massachusetts Emission Equipment	NC	NC
YF5	California Emission Equipment	NC	NC
CF5	Sunroof — electric sliding, glass	856	995
KA1	Seats — driver/passenger heated	254	295
K05	Engine Block Heater	15	18
QQX	Autobahn Pkg	340	395
	incls Michelin P235/60VR16 SBR BW tires, 3.71 axle ratio		
UU8	Bose Acoustimass System	577	671
	incls AM/FM ETR stereo radio with seek/scan, auto reverse cassette, speaker system with rear shelf module including woofer and 6 additional speakers		
—	Cloth Seat Trim	NC	NC

1995 Oldsmobile Aurora

OLDSMOBILE — CUTLASS SUPREME

1995 Oldsmobile Cutlass Supreme Convertible

CUTLASS SUPREME 3.4L CONVERTIBLE (V6)

Sam Moses, a contributor to Auto Week magazine, said this about the Oldsmobile Cutlass Supreme Convertible: "Good-looking, strong engine, nice leather interior, but basically they've taken the world's worst-handling rental car and tried to turn it into a sports car." We don't completely agree with Moses, but he did nail down the Cutlass relatively succinctly.

It is a good looking car, and since the convertible appeared in 1990, it has gotten better every year. For 1995, it gets a much needed interior redo, and now sports a very attractive instrument panel that houses dual airbags and does away with the myriad buttons and angular edges of the old one. The twin-cam 3.4-liter engine develops 210 horsepower and moves the heavy Cutlass out reasonably quickly.

Benefiting from Oldsmobile's value pricing policy, the convertible comes loaded, standard. Among the few options are an upgraded stereo, automatic climate controls, and the engine package that provides the 3.4-liter motor. All told, the Cutlass comes in just under $28,000. Seems pricey? Consider this: the new Cavalier convertible is expected to start at 20 grand, and work its way up.

As for the wannabe sports car impression, we disagree with Moses. The Cutlass is a boulevardier, more at home cruising Main Street or covering Interstate miles. Consumers looking for real performance, good looks, and a lower price tag would do well to shop Ford or Chevy. Both the Mustang GT and Camaro Z28 convertibles can be had with the Oldsmobile's equipment for about the same price as the Cutlass, but creative fiddling with the options sheet could save thousands.

CUTLASS SUPREME — OLDSMOBILE

Performance and Safety

Acceleration (0-60 mph) .... 8.5 sec.	ABS .... Standard
Braking (60-0 mph) .... 129 ft.	Driver Airbag .... Standard
Cornering .... .79 g's	Passenger Airbag .... Standard
Fuel Capacity .... 16.5 gal.	Traction Control .... N/A
Fuel Economy .... City: 17 mpg	Crash Test Grade .... D: N/A P: N/A
Hwy: 26 mpg	Insurance Cost .... Low

CUTLASS SUPREME 3.4L CONVERTIBLE V6

Code	Description	Invoice	MSRP
T67WS	2-Dr 3.4L V6 Convertible	24120	26715
	pricing is for model when ordered w/o option pkg 1SB or 1SC		
T67WS	2-Dr 3.4L V6 Convertible	24060	26645
	pricing is for model when ordered w/ option pkg 1SB or 1SC		
Destination Charge:	....	535	535

Standard Equipment

CUTLASS SUPREME 3.4L CONVERTIBLE: 3.4 liter DOHC V6 engine, oil level monitor, special suspension, rear aero wing, dual exhaust, speed sensitive steering, driver and passenger air bags, four-season air conditioning, maintenance-free Freedom battery, 4-wheel disc anti-lock brakes, brake/transmission shift interlock, body color front/rear bumper fascias, warning chimes for: safety belts/headlamps on/key in ignition/turn signal on; full length shifting console with armrest storage and cup holder, electronic cruise control with resume and acceleration features, side window/electric rear window defoggers, pillar-mounted door handles with illuminated driver side lock, power programmable automatic door locks, interior door-pull handles, front wheel drive, dual engine cooling fans, deluxe cut-pile wall-to-wall floor carpeting, lower door panel carpeting, auxiliary front/rear carpeted floor mats, fog lamps, mini-quad headlamps with flash-to-pass provision on turn signal, interior operated hood release, gas-charged hood struts, illuminated entry package, analog gauge cluster instrument panel includes: speedometer/tachometer/gauges for fuel level/engine temperature/indicators for oil pressure/low fuel/fasten seat belts/low coolant/"service engine soon"/anti-lock brakes/engine oil level monitor/backlit illumination; keyless remote lock control package includes: illumination package/key chain transmitter; center high-mounted stop lamp, leather trimmed seating areas, light package includes: lamps for instrument panel/glove box/roof rail/courtesy/under hood/trunk; inside day/night mirror with dual reading lamps, black outside dual power mirrors, driver and passenger covered visor vanity mirrors, color-coordinated body color wheel opening moldings, Delco ETR AM/FM stereo radio with seek/scan/auto reverse cassette/digital display clock/4-speaker extended-range sound system/rear quarter power antenna; color-keyed 3-point deluxe safety belts (front/rear outboard positions), color-keyed rear center lap belt, reclining front bucket seats (6-way driver side power seat adjuster, 4-way passenger side manual seat adjuster), deluxe leather-wrapped tilt-wheel steering wheel, power folding vinyl top, electronic-shift automatic overdrive transmission with floor shifter, power trunk lid lock release, deluxe trunk trim Pass Key vehicle security system, Flo-Thru ventilation, power side windows, Soft-Ray tinted windows, wet-arm pulse wiper system, P225/60R16 SBR BW performance tires, wheels w/bolt-on discs.

OLDSMOBILE CUTLASS SUPREME / EIGHTY-EIGHT LSS

CODE	DESCRIPTION	INVOICE	MSRP

Accessories

FE9	Federal Emission Equipment	NC	NC
NG1	Massachusetts Emission Equipment	NC	NC
YF5	California Emission Equipment	NC	NC
1SB	Option Pkg 1SB	186	216
	incls driver/passenger illuminated visor mirrors, variable effort steering, 6-speaker dimensional sound system		
1SC	Option Pkg 1SC	461	536
	incls Pkg 1SB contents plus automatic climate control with driver and passenger controls, steering wheel controls for audio system and air conditioner		
AP9	Trunk Cargo Net	26	30
B84	Bodyside Moldings	52	60
K05	Engine Block Heater	15	18
UN0	Radio	86	100
	incls AM/FM audio system with compact disc		
UP0	Radio	172	200
	incls AM/FM audio system with cassette and compact disc		

1995 Oldsmobile Eighty-Eight LSS

EIGHTY-EIGHT LSS

Since 1992, the Oldsmobile LSS has been one of our favorites. It features Euro-chic styling, a stout suspension, loads of equipment, some of the nicest-looking alloy wheels we've seen from GM, and enough room to take the family to Disney World or on your own little version of Mr. Toad's Wild Ride along mountain two-lanes. The only shortcoming was somewhat uninspired acceleration out of the 3.8-liter V-6.

EIGHTY-EIGHT LSS — OLDSMOBILE

| CODE | DESCRIPTION | INVOICE | MSRP |

For 1995, Oldsmobile infuses the LSS with supercharged power from the larger Ninety-Eight model. The additional horsepower makes the competent LSS a true sports sedan that will have you hunting down and annihilating Probe GT owners, leaving them with gape-mouthed stares as they read the quickly-fading Oldsmobile badge on the rear fascia. If that's not fun, what is?

Better yet is the interior of the LSS, an ergonomic delight and aesthetic triumph. Add ample room for four (five if need be), dual airbags, anti-lock brakes and traction control, and the LSS provides everything closet enthusiasts will require for safe, speedy driving.

Compare the LSS to the Aurora. It's better looking, weighs a whopping 600 pounds less, has more interior room, gets better gas mileage, goes and handles faster, and is a year's tuition cheaper. What were they thinking?

Performance and Safety

Eighty Eight LSS

Acceleration (0-60 mph)	8.0 sec.	ABS	Standard	
Braking (60-0 mph)	137 ft.	Driver Airbag	Standard	
Cornering	.83 g's	Passenger Airbag	Standard	
Fuel Capacity	18 gal.	Traction Control	Standard	
Fuel Economy	City: 19 mpg	Crash Test Grade	D: N/A	P: N/A
	Hwy: 29 mpg	Insurance Cost	Low	

Eighty Eight LSS Supercharged

Acceleration (0-60 mph)	7.0 sec.	ABS	Standard	
Braking (60-0 mph)	137 ft.	Driver Airbag	Standard	
Cornering	.83 g's	Passenger Airbag	Standard	
Fuel Capacity	18 gal.	Traction Control	Standard	
Fuel Economy	City: 17 mpg	Crash Test Grade	D: N/A	P: N/A
	Hwy: 27 mpg	Insurance Cost	N/A	

Edmund's Driving Impression

Last season's Olds Luxury Sport Sedan was polite, well-behaved, reasonably capable—possessing just a hint of brashness beneath the skin. Now, with 35 more horsepower emanating from its base engine, the ardent lamb turns into a roaring lion. Add the new option of a supercharged V-6, cranking up 225 horses, and the lion's bellow gains several decibels.

Even the former 170-hp V-6 produced a strong pull when commanded, delivering fairly impressive acceleration for a heavy car. The Series II engine, able to stretch its strength to 6000 rpm, is sufficiently vigorous on its own to diminish the importance of the supercharger option.

Transmission shifts are barely perceptible. Downshifts for passing arrive smoothly and crisply, with virtually no delay and no "hunting" for the right gear ratio.

Feedback to the steering wheel is fine, but don't expect unfettered sports-sedan handling. This is a sophisticated, well-behaved driving experience, not a tawdry highway affair. Roll up the windows and you're riding in near-total silence, marred by no more than a mild engine growl when pounding the gas pedal.

OLDSMOBILE
EIGHTY-EIGHT LSS

If all-around comfort is one of your goals, sorry. While an LSS with its touring suspension and 16-inch rubber rides beautifully over the road, it can grow nasty in the city. Though resilient, able to deflect some roughness, that suspension simply doesn't soak up the truly awful pavement breakups.

Beautifully constructed, the Olds features such masterful touches as rounded door edges. Sport-oriented performance aside, though, it still lacks overall sparkle. While strong and capable throughout, an LSS offers few surprises—not quite as much sensation of delight as we've expected. Sure, the supercharged version conveys a bit more sass; but except for shaving the acceleration numbers, even a blown LSS isn't 100% guaranteed to set anyone's pulse pounding.

EIGHTY-EIGHT LSS 6 CYL

Code	Description	Invoice	MSRP
Y69HS	LSS 4-Dr Sedan	22930	24010
	Destination Charge:	585	585

Standard Equipment

EIGHTY-EIGHT LSS SEDAN: Driver and passenger air bags, air conditioning with rear seat duct, maintenance-free Freedom battery, power front disc/rear drum anti-lock brakes, brake/transmission shift interlock, convenience group includes: trunk lamp/covered visor vanity mirrors/chime tones for: seat belts/headlamps on/key in ignition/turn signal on; high capacity engine cooling equipment, electronic cruise control with resume and acceleration feature, side window/electric rear window defoggers, deluxe trim luggage compartment with "jack-in-the-box" tool kit, power door locks, child security rear door locks, 3800 Series II V6 sequential fuel injection engine, transverse-mounted engine with front wheel drive, cut-pile wall-to-wall floor carpeting, carpeted lower door panels, auxiliary front/rear carpeted floor mats, composite halogen headlamps with flash-to-pass feature, interior operated hood release, instrument panel analog gauge cluster includes: fuel/coolant temperature/low engine oil level indicator, center high-mounted stop lamp, light package includes: dome/instrument panel ashtray/glove box door/under hood/courtesy/warning/front and rear reading lamps; lighter, auxiliary 12-volt outlet (keyed through ignition), front license plate bracket, front door/seat back map pockets, inside day/night mirror, body color outside dual power mirrors, bright belt reveal/drip moldings, body color wheel opening moldings, body color wide lower bodyside moldings, Delco ETR AM/FM stereo radio with seek/scan/automatic tone control/auto reverse cassette/digital display clock/6-speaker Dimensional Sound system/power rear quarter antenna; color-keyed 3-point front safety belts (with height adjustment for outboard positions), color-keyed front center lap belt, color-keyed 3-point rear safety belts (with child comfort guides for outboard positions), color-keyed center rear lap belt, 55/45 divided front reclining seats with individual controls/storage armrest/dual cup holders, power rack and pinion steering, deluxe tilt-wheel vinyl rim steering wheel, four-wheel fully independent MacPherson front strut/rear coil spring suspension system, front and rear stabilizer bars, P205/70R15 SBR BW all-season tires, electronic-shift automatic overdrive transmission with column shift, trip odometer, power trunk lid lock release, Pass Key vehicle security system, Flo-Thru ventilation, covered visor vanity mirrors with auxiliary sunshades, deluxe wheel discs, 15" x 6" wheels, power side windows, Soft-Ray tinted windows (EZ Kool solar control windshield and rear window glass), pulse wiper system, Pkg 1SB (dual zone heat/ventilation/air conditioning system, 16" aluminum wheels, BW tires, overhead console with storage compartment and dual reading lamps, steering wheel touch controls, luxury/convenience package includes: keyless remote accessory control package/dual lighted visor vanity mirrors/front and rear reading lamps/power reclining 6-way adjustable driver's seat; reminder package includes: indicators for low fuel/low coolant/low oil pressure/high engine temperature/low washer fluid level; trunk cargo net, rear seat storage armrest with cup holders), Pkg R7C (LSS Package, leather trim seating areas, Comfort Package includes: electrochromic inside mirror with compass/6-way passenger side power seat adjuster with power recliner/cornering lamps, traction control system).

EDMUND'S 1995 HIGH-PERFORMANCE AUTOMOBILES

EIGHTY-EIGHT LSS / SILHOUETTE — OLDSMOBILE

Accessories

CODE	DESCRIPTION	INVOICE	MSRP
FE9	Federal Emission Equipment	NC	NC
NG1	Massachusetts Emission Equipment	NC	NC
YF5	California Emission Equipment	NC	NC
K05	Engine Block Heater	15	18
L67	Engine — supercharged 3800 V6	879	1022
UP0	Radio	172	200

incls AM/FM audio system with cassette and compact disc

1995 Oldsmobile Silhouette

SILHOUETTE (3.8L V6)

As we drew up performance parameters for this buyer's guide, we decided to relax them a bit to include a few vehicles that weren't necessarily performance-oriented, but performed well nonetheless. We expected a few pickup trucks to make the cut, and the Jeep Grand Cherokee V-8, but this minivan was a surprise.

Through careful research, we found data that put the Silhouette on the list, although information on the Silhouette's corporate twins, the Lumina Minivan and Pontiac Trans Sport, was such that those two did not qualify. We suspect that they perform much the way the Silhouette does, even if the numbers don't corroborate the theory.

The Silhouette is GM's luxury-oriented minivan. It retained the Dustbuster front styling last year while its Chevy and Pontiac siblings underwent cosmetic surgery on the vans' prominent schnozz. We think the original styling, intact on the Silhouette, is better looking. The rest of the plastic-skinned van is modern in appearance, and even borders on attractive with the Silhouette's blacked-out pillars, tinted glass, and beltline tape stripe.

A 3.8-liter V-6 propels the front wheels, and anti-lock brakes help rein the van in safely. Inside, a driver's side airbag and seating for seven is standard. The modular seats are easy to configure

OLDSMOBILE — SILHOUETTE

and remove, but interior space is limited compared to other minivans. Leather seats are optional, as are such niceties as integrated child safety seats, a CD player, a power sliding door and traction control.

Topping out with every option at just under $24,000 and offering the best performance of any minivan on the market, the Silhouette competes nicely with some of the more refined family-haulers available today.

Performance and Safety

Acceleration (0-60 mph)	9.7 sec.
Braking (60-0 mph)	146 ft.
Cornering	.75 g's
Fuel Capacity	20 gal.
Fuel Economy	City: 17 mpg
	Hwy: 25 mpg

ABS	Standard
Driver Airbag	Standard
Passenger Airbag	N/A
Traction Control	Optional
Crash Test Grade	D: N/A P: Good
Insurance Cost	Low

Edmund's Driving Impression

When GM introduced its trio of minivans—Lumina APV, Pontiac Trans Sport, and Olds Silhouette—for the 1990 model year, they were examples of futuristic styling, versatile interiors, and family-focused comfort. Performance? That seemed almost an afterthought. The first Silhouette we drove, in fact, practically sat like a slug when stomping the gas in the expressway merging lane.

After Oldsmobile and its GM mates introduced a 3.8-liter V-6 engine for the minivans, the game changed. Now, the three were able to accelerate in a manner more appropriate to their eye-catching profiles. Chevrolet and Pontiac still make the big engine an option, but it's now the only choice in a Silhouette—and the only one worth having, for anyone who insists on performance as an adjunct to practicality.

Whether from a standing start or in the pass/merge lanes, the current minivan takes off with surprising swiftness—far quicker than expected for this brand of hauler. Upshifts and downshifts from the electronically controlled four-speed automatic transmission are smooth and competent.

GM minivans even rank fairly high on the handling scale: reasonably precise in steering, able to earn a passing grade in maneuverability and nimbleness. They also absorb bumps capably, but the ride can still get a little floaty, even boatlike, on occasion. The suspension reacts quickly, though, and the body doesn't keep on bouncing after the imperfections have disappeared.

Except for a little engine noise when it's commanded to furnish peak action, quiet running is the rule. Climbing in and out is a snap. Seats are easy to remove and rearrange to other configurations.

None of the GM minivans makes our "best of them all" list. Chrysler's twins and the new Ford Windstar are simply too hard to beat. Nevertheless, the Silhouette offers a tempting assortment of virtues, with few minuses to cloud the picture.

SILHOUETTE 3.8L V6 MINIVAN

CODE	DESCRIPTION	INVOICE	MSRP
M06US	Series I Minivan	19344	20255
M06US	Series II Minivan	20776	21755
	Destination Charge:	540	540

EDMUND'S 1995 HIGH-PERFORMANCE AUTOMOBILES

SILHOUETTE — OLDSMOBILE

Standard Equipment

SILHOUETTE SERIES I: 3.8 liter V6 EFI engine, automatic transmission, driver side air bag, four-season air conditioning, front and rear air distribution system, maintenance-free Freedom battery, power front disc/rear drum anti-lock brakes, brake/transmission shift interlock, warning chimes for: seat belts/headlamps on/key in ignition/turn signal on; lower center lockable storage console with HVAC and radio controls, console dual cup holders, front and rear side window defoggers, electric rear window defogger, sliding door child security lock, door pull handles, front wheel drive, deluxe cut-pile wall-to-wall floor carpeting, carpeted lower door panels, auxiliary front and rear carpeted floor mats, fog lamps, composite halogen headlamps, interior operated hood release, instrument panel gauge cluster includes: electrically driven speedometer/tachometer/trip odometer/voltmeter/temperature and oil pressure gauges; center high-mounted stop lamp, interior liftgate assist handle, light package includes: dome reading lamps/dome lamp override switch/instrument panel/glove box courtesy/under hood lamp; front door map pockets, inside day/night mirror, black outside foldaway dual power mirrors, bodyside body color moldings, 12-volt concealed auxiliary power outlet (in rear cargo area), black roof, color-keyed 3-point front/rear safety belts (outboard positions), color-keyed center lap belt, 7-passenger seating (front - reclining buckets with folding armrests, center - 3 modular seats, rear - 2 modular seats), driver side 4-way manual seat adjuster, power rack and pinion steering, deluxe steering wheel with tilt-wheel adjustable column, MacPherson front strut/rear variable rate coil spring suspension system, P205/70R15 SBR BW all-season tires, Flo-Thru ventilation, driver and passenger covered visor vanity mirrors, 15" x 6" aluminum wheels, Soft-Ray tinted windows, solar-treated windshield, wet-arm pulse wiper system, rear window washer/wiper, power windows, power door locks, cruise control, convenience net, overhead console, rooftop luggage carrier, remote lock control package, AM/FM stereo cassette radio.

SERIES II (in addition to or instead of SERIES I equipment): Power sliding door, driver side 6-way power seat adjuster, steering wheel touch controls, leather trimmed seating areas.

Accessories

CODE	DESCRIPTION	INVOICE	MSRP
FE9	Federal Emission Equipment	NC	NC
NG1	Massachusetts Emission Equipment	NC	NC
YF5	California Emission Equipment	NC	NC
AD8	Integrated Child Seat	108	125
AD9	Integrated Dual Child Seats	194	225
AG9	Power Driver Seat Adjuster — Series I	232	270
B4A	Black Roof Paint Delete	NC	NC
C34	Auxiliary Rear Air Conditioner	387	450
K05	Engine Block Heater	15	18
NW9	Traction Control System - Series II *incls touring suspension*	477	555
U1C	Radio — Series I	220	256
	Series II *incls AM/FM audio system with compact disc*	194	226

PLYMOUTH NEON

1995 Plymouth Neon Sport

NEON

Unless you live in an igloo in the northernmost reaches of Alaska, you've heard about or seen the Neon. Hi, say the ads. Hi, say the jaunty ovoid headlights as they approach in the rearview mirror. Bye, says the raspy exhaust note as the 132-hp sedanlet blows the doors off your jalopy in the stoplight drag race.

The Neon has the compact carmakers trembling. The Escort LX is flat outdated next to this Plymouth. The new Tercel is forty horsepower and a personality off the mark. Nissan's new Sentra is expected to be much pricier and not nearly as attractive when it hits showrooms in January. This car's closest competitor in performance, price and features is the stodgy-looking Mercury Tracer LTS, a car sold in such small quantities that you probably don't even know what it is.

The Neon is a solid little sedan, and is joined by a coupe variant for 1995. Also new this year is an optional twin-cam four-cylinder motor good for 150 horsepower, which promises to make other compacts even less competitive. When the new motor comes on line, there really won't be any point in shopping around. Just drop in to any Plymouth dealer and drive off in one of the best cars in the small car class.

Performance and Safety

Acceleration (0-60 mph)	8.4 sec.
Braking (60-0 mph)	135 ft.
Cornering	.82 g's
Fuel Capacity	11.2 gal.
Fuel Economy	City: 27 mpg
	Hwy: 33 mpg

ABS	Optional
Driver Airbag	Standard
Passenger Airbag	Standard
Traction Control	N/A
Crash Test Grade	D: Average P: Average
Insurance Cost	N/A

NEON — PLYMOUTH

Driving Impression

Maybe the hype gave us some lofty expectations. Maybe the media has been brainwashed. We weren't thrilled with Chrysler's latest star. On paper, the Neon looks unbeatable. In reality, it feels cheap, like it will break if pushed too hard, and that doesn't do much for instilling pride of ownership. True, the powertrain does a marvelous job of getting the Neon down the road in a hurry and the steering is communicative, sharp and direct, but the execution of the rest of the car underwhelms. Chrysler needs to tear down a Toyota Corolla and learn about *feel*.

Moreover, the back seat is very hard to squeeze into. Despite cab-forward styling, the swoopy roofline and rear wheelwell are far too instrusive. Once in, the back seat is relatively comfortable, but head, leg, and foot room are rather tight.

Up front, the seats are mushy, and covered in a low-rent fabric. And what's with the jutting dash? It's huge, putting alot of acreage between the driver and the base of the windshield. It also encroaches on passenger space, and is constructed of hard, grained plastic. I guess Chrysler figures that with dual airbags, a soft dash isn't necessary. It sure would look nice though.

Perhaps our largest gripe was with throttle response. It's abrupt and makes smooth clutch modulation difficult. Evidently, Chrysler feels that a touchy accelerator imparts the illusion to that the car is more powerful than it actually is. Hey, the Neon is powerful. No need to fake it.

Still, very few manufacturers can touch the Neon in the affordability, performance, or styling departments. Japanese competitors are combating the negative effects of an appreciating yen, and most domestic models are far underpowered compared to the sprightly Neon. There are two models which compete with the Neon dollar-for-dollar and boast smoother, more zingy drivetrains: the Mercury Tracer LTS and the Ford Escort GT. While their styling may not be quite as daring, and the performance may not be quite as strong, they both come across as more refined, substantial and therefore fun-to-drive cars than the Neon.

NEON 4 CYL

CODE	DESCRIPTION	INVOICE	MSRP
PL42	Base 4-Dr Sedan	8815	9500
PH22	Highline 2-Dr Coupe	10416	11240
PH42	Highline 4-Dr Sedan	10416	11240
PS22	Sport 2-Dr Coupe	12285	13567
PS42	Sport 4-Dr Sedan	12015	13267
Destination Charge:		500	500

Standard Equipment

NEON - BASE: 85 amp alternator, 450 amp maintenance-free battery, 13" power front disc/rear drum brakes, 5-mph front and rear bumpers, child protection rear door locks, warning chimes (for key in ignition, headlights on, seat belts), console, 2.0 liter SOHC 16V SMPI 4 cylinder engine, stainless steel exhaust system, single halogen aero-style headlights, cloth covered headliner, mirrors (left exterior manual remote, black), rearview mirror with day/night feature, passenger side visor vanity mirror, driver and front passenger air bags, seats (cloth with vinyl trim, front high back buckets, rear fixed bench), manual steering, sun visors with driver side sunshade extension panel, ride tuned suspension, P165/80R13 all-season BSW SBR tires, T115/70D14 compact spare tire, 5-speed manual transaxle, carpet floor mat trunk dress-up, 13" steel painted bright silver wheels with black center cap, 2-speed windshield wipers.

PLYMOUTH NEON

| CODE | DESCRIPTION | INVOICE | MSRP |

HIGHLINE (in addition to or instead of BASE equipment): Front and rear body color fascias, tinted glass, mirrors (dual exterior manual remote, black), dual visor vanity mirrors (driver side covered), body color bodyside moldings, AM/FM stereo radio with clock and 4 speakers, seats (cloth with vinyl trim, front low back buckets, rear 60/40 split folding bench), premium sound insulation, 18:1 ratio power assisted steering, touring tuned suspension, P185/70R13 all-season BSW SBR tires, trunk dress-up (incls molded carpet for wheel houses, spare tire well, carpet covered spare), 13" steel wheels painted black with bright silver wheel covers, 2-speed windshield wipers with variable intermittent feature.

SPORT (in addition to or instead of HIGHLINE equipment): 14" power 4-wheel disc brakes with anti-lock, remote decklid release, rear window defroster, power door locks, 2.0 liter DOHC 16V SMPI 4 cylinder engine (Coupe), front and rear body color fascias with accent color rub strip, fog lights, "power bulge" hood design (Coupe), mirrors (dual exterior power remote, black), accent color bodyside moldings, passenger assist handles, rear decklid spoiler (Coupe), 16:1 ratio power assisted steering (Coupe), tilt steering column, performance tuned suspension (Coupe), P185/65R14 all-season touring BSW SBR tires (Sedan), P185/65R14 all-season performance BSW SBR tires (Coupe), T115/70R14 compact spare tire, 14" cast aluminum painted sparkle silver wheels (painted white with white exterior).

Accessories

—	**Quick Order Pkgs** — prices include pkg discounts		
A	**Pkg A — Base Sedan**	NC	NC
	incls model with standard equipment		
B	**Pkg B — Base Sedan**	1712	1861
	incls air conditioning, rear window defroster, manual remote dual exterior mirrors, bodyside moldings, radio (AM/FM stereo with clock and 4 speakers), power steering, tinted glass, touring tuned suspension, intermittent windshield wipers		
C	**Pkg C — Highline**	NC	NC
	incls model with standard equipment		
D	**Pkg D — Highline Coupe/Sedan**	626	703
	incls air conditioning, floor-mounted console with armrest and storage bin, remote decklid release, rear window defroster		
F	**Pkg F — Highline Coupe**	1184	1330
	Highline Sedan	1220	1371
	incls pkg D contents plus 14" front disc/rear drum brakes, power door locks, front and rear floor mats, light group, power remote dual exterior mirrors, tilt steering wheel, tachometer and low fuel light, P185/65R14 all-season touring BSW SBR tires, 14" wheel covers		
J	**Pkg J — Sport**	NC	NC
	incls model with standard equipment		
K	**Pkg K — Sport Coupe/Sedan**	557	626
	incls air conditioning, front and rear floor mats, light group, radio (AM/FM stereo with cassette, clock and 6 speakers)		
23C	**Pkg 23C "Competition" — Highline Coupe**	911	990
	incls 14" power assisted 4-wheel disc brakes, unlimited speed engine controller, front and rear body color fascias with metallic accent, bodyside moldings, heavy duty radiator, radio delete, 16:1 ratio power steering, competition suspension, tachometer with low fuel light, P185/60HR14 all-season touring BSW SBR tires, 14" bright silver cast aluminum wheels (white when ordered with white exterior)		

NEON / PLYMOUTH

CODE	DESCRIPTION	INVOICE	MSRP
23D	**Pkg 23D** — Highline Coupe	1536	1693
	incls pkg 23C "Competition" contents plus air conditioning, floor-mounted console with armrest and storage bin, rear window defroster, remote decklid release		
25A	**Pkg 25A "Competition"** — Base Sedan	1449	1575
	incls 14" power assisted 4-wheel disc brakes, unlimited speed engine controller, front and rear body color fascias with metallic accent, painted body color grille bar, tinted glass, dual exterior manual remote mirrors, heavy duty radiator, 16:1 ratio power steering, competition suspension, tachometer with low fuel light, T115/70R14 compact spare tire, P175/65HR14 all-season performance BSW SBR tires, 14" bright silver cast aluminum wheels (white when ordered with white exterior)		
25B	**Pkg 25B** — Base Sedan	2687	2981
	incls pkg 25A "Competition" contents plus air conditioning, rear window defroster, dual exterior manual remote mirrors, intermittent wipers		
ECB	**Engine** — 2.0 liter SOHC 16V SMPI		
	Base Sedan	STD	STD
	Highline	STD	STD
	Sport Coupe	STD	STD
	Sport Sedan	(89)	(100)
ECC	**Engine** — 2.0 liter DOHC 16V SMPI		
	Sport Sedan	STD	STD
	Highline Coupe w/pkg 23C or 23D	138	150
DD4/5	**Transmission** — 5-speed manual	STD	STD
DGA	**Transmission** — 3-speed automatic	496	557
4XA	**Air Conditioning Bypass** — Base w/pkg A or 25A	NC	NC
BRH	**Anti-Lock Brakes** — 13" - Base w/pkg A or B	503	565
	Highline w/pkg C or D	503	565
	NA w/AY7 on Highline models		
BRJ	**Anti-Lock Brakes** — 14" - Highline w/pkg D or F	503	565
	req's AY7		
CFK	**Child Seat** — integrated	89	100
AJP	**Power Convenience Group** — Highline Coupe w/pkg D	228	256
	Highline Sedan w/pkg D	264	297
	incls dual exterior power remote mirrors, power door locks; incld in pkg F		
GFA	**Rear Window Defroster** — req'd in New York State		
	Base Sedan w/pkg A or 25A	154	173
	incld in pkg B or 25B		
	Highline w/pkg C or 23C	154	173
	incld in pkg D, F or 23D		
NAE	**California Emissions**	91	102
NBY	**Massachusetts Emissions**	91	102
CLE	**Floor Mats** — front and rear - Base Sedan, Highline, Sport	41	46
	incld in pkg F and K		
MWG	**Luggage Rack** — roof-mounted	89	100
GTE	**Mirrors** — dual exterior, manual remote — Base Sedan w/pkg A	62	70
	incld in pkg B and 25B		
K37	**Bodyside Moldings** — Base Sedan w/pkg A	27	30
	incld in pkg B		

EDMUND'S 1995 HIGH-PERFORMANCE AUTOMOBILES

PLYMOUTH NEON

CODE	DESCRIPTION	INVOICE	MSRP
RAL	**Radio** — AM/FM stereo w/clock and 4 speakers - Base Sedan	297	334
	incld in pkg B		
RAS	**Radio** — AM/FM stereo w/cassette, clock and 6 premium speakers -		
	Base Sedan w/pkg B	223	250
	Highline	223	250
	Sport w/pkg J	223	250
	incld in pkg K		
RBG	**Radio** — AM/FM stereo w/CD player, clock and 6 premium speakers -		
	Base Sedan w/pkg B	434	488
	Highline	434	488
	Sport w/pkg J	434	488
	Sport w/pkg K	212	238
SUA	**Tilt Steering Column** — Base Sedan w/pkg B	132	148
	Sport w/pkg C or D	132	148
	incld in pkg F		
NHM	**Speed Control** — Highline w/pkg D or F	199	224
	Sport w/pkg K	199	224
JHA	**Intermittent Windshield Wipers** — Base Sedan w/pkg A	59	66
	incld in pkg B and 25B		
JFH	**Tachometer & Low Fuel Warning Light** — Highline w/pkg D	83	93
	incld in pkg F		
AY7	**14" Wheel Dress-Up** — Highline w/pkg D	71	80
	incls 14" front disc/rear drum brakes, P185/65R14 all-season touring BSW SBR tires, 14" black wheels, 14" silver wheel covers (white w/quartz center when ordered w/white exterior); incld in pkg F		
—	**Paint** — extra cost	86	97

1995 Plymouth Neon Coupe

EDMUND'S 1995 HIGH-PERFORMANCE AUTOMOBILES

BONNEVILLE   PONTIAC

| CODE | DESCRIPTION | INVOICE | MSRP |

1995 Pontiac Bonneville SSEi

BONNEVILLE

If ever there was an American sedan that combined traditional full-size sedan accoutrements with European style and class, it is this version of the Bonneville. Introduced in 1992, the Bonny competes with near-luxury offerings such as the Lexus ES300 and BMW 3-Series, but kills the competition with seating for six, dramatic styling and amazing performance capabilities for a big, front-drive four-door.

This year, the Bonneville benefits from a much more powerful base engine. The 3.8-liter V-6 pumps out 35 more horsepower than last year, which is sure to cut into sales of the supercharged SSEi model. And, if you must have the supercharged engine but don't want all the goofy aero add-ons and tacky gold trim that come standard on the SSEi, you can get the blown motor in the base model. One stipulation exists, though; you've got to order the SLE package, which gives you some of the goodies that were previously available only on the SSE. Confused? Let's clarify the Bonneville roster.

Base model is the SE, and this is the only trim level to consider. Next up is the SSE, which is basically a sporty version of the SE. The SSEi is a package available on the SSE that includes the supercharged engine and gross exterior trim. Since everything you need to build a competent sport sedan is optional on the SE, we recommend you start there.

For example, an SE with the SLE package, performance suspension, CD player with premium sound, power moonroof, traction control and 16-inch alloy wheels runs just under $27,000 and includes stuff like leather seats, anti-lock brakes, power everything and an anti-theft system. The Bonneville makes good economic sense, and doesn't punish you for spending less.

PONTIAC — BONNEVILLE

Performance and Safety

Bonneville SE and SSE (w/ 3.8-liter V-6)

Acceleration (0-60 mph) .... 8.1 sec.	ABS .... Standard
Braking (60-0 mph) .... 136 ft.	Driver Airbag .... Standard
Cornering .... .81 g's	Passenger Airbag .... Standard
Fuel Capacity .... 18 gal.	Traction Control .... Optional
Fuel Economy .... City: 19 mpg	Crash Test Grade .... D: Excellent P: Average
Hwy: 29 mpg	Insurance Cost .... Low

Bonneville SE, SSE and SSEi (w/ 3.8-liter supercharged V-6)

Acceleration (0-60 mph) .... 7.0 sec.	ABS .... Standard
Braking (60-0 mph) .... 132 ft.	Driver Airbag .... Standard
Cornering .... .81 g's	Passenger Airbag .... Standard
Fuel Capacity .... 18 gal.	Traction Control .... Optional
Fuel Economy .... City: 17 mpg	Crash Test Grade .... D: Excellent P: Average
Hwy: 25 mpg	Insurance Cost .... Low

Edmund's Driving Impression

Supercharged or not, this is one hearty highway cruiser. Accelerating a base-engine Bonneville from a standstill, you'll hardly notice—or regret—the lack of a blower. There's a definite zoom from the Series II V-6 when hitting the gas, but the car takes off with smooth, steadfast, nearly-startling haste.

Stepping on it at 55 mph doesn't produce as phenomenal a response, so the blower might be welcome part of the time. Hitting it hard at 30, the transmission takes just a moment to downshift, but comes on like a catapult—a catapult that's passed its prime, perhaps, but still capable of swift motion.

Touring mode is never wallowy or slushy: just mild firmness that imparts a secure, yet comfortable ride. Switch the suspension to Performance mode, and everything tightens crisply. Coupled with power steering that transmits excellent feedback from the road, it makes for a rigorously-controlled experience—but without much jarring or jolting.

Actually, in either mode, the Bonneville responds well to bumps, with quick and supple snubbing and no hint of clanks and jangles—even when rolling across a pothole, crack, or tar strip.

A Bonneville's body can lean a little through hard turns, but big tires hug the pathway like a panther on a hunt. The car corners quite well, but doesn't exactly rank as nimble. It's like the experienced, cautious fellow who *catches* the trapeze artist, not the brash, lightweight youngster whose acrobatic antics grab the audience's attention. This car also demonstrates Pontiac's increasingly superior assembly quality.

Easy to read by day, full gauges glow orange at night, led by the 7000-rpm tach and 120-mph speedometer. Seats are shaped so you fall into virtual craters. Seat bottoms could be longer, and we had doubts about comfort over the long haul. Leg/head space is plentiful all around.

Boosting the potential of the basic engine this year actually negates the need to opt for the supercharged edition. Not only does that save a bundle of bucks, it gives you almost the kind of performance that the blown Bonneville has delivered all along.

BONNEVILLE

CODE	DESCRIPTION		INVOICE

1995 Pontiac Bonneville SSE

BONNEVILLE 6 CYL

X69S	4-Dr SE Sedan	18828	20804
Z69S	4-Dr SSE Sedan	23353	25804
Destination Charge:		585	585

Standard Equipment

BONNEVILLE SE: 3800 Series II SFI V6 engine, electronically-controlled 4-speed automatic transmission, power rack and pinion steering, power disc/drum brakes, 4-wheel anti-lock brake system (ABS), power windows with driver's express-down feature, power door locks, P215/65R15 SBR blackwall touring tires, 15" bolt-on wheel covers, Delco ETR AM/FM stereo radio with clock and 4-speaker sound system, manual air conditioning, soft fascia type bumpers with integral rub strips, composite polymer front fenders, fog lamps, Soft-Ray tinted glass, composite halogen headlamps, sport mirrors (LH remote/RH manual), wide bodyside molding, compact spare tire, extensive acoustical insulation, driver and passenger side air bag/safety belts, 3-point active height adjustable front safety belts, cruise control, instrumentation includes: backlit/analog speedometer/fuel and coolant temperature/oil pressure/voltage/tachometer; systems monitor includes: coolant temperature light/oil pressure indicator/battery voltage light/parking brake light; lamp group includes: engine compartment light/front overhead console/ashtray/glove box/headlamp-on warning/rear assist handles/rear rail courtesy lights/trunk light; cluster warning lights include: oil pressure/check engine/brake system/security system/inflatable restraint (air bag); front and rear floor mats, covered RH/LH visor vanity mirrors, rear seat pass-through, 45/55 split bench seats with manual recliners, 4-spoke urethane steering wheel, tilt-wheel adjustable steering column, Pass-Key II theft deterrent system, extensive anti-corrosion protection with two-side galvanized steel doors/quarters/hood/decklid/rockers; Delco Freedom II battery, brake/transmission shift interlock safety feature, stainless steel single exhaust, composite polymer front fenders, front wheel drive.

BONNEVILLE SSE (in addition to or instead of SE equipment): P225/60R16 BW Eagle GA SBR touring tires, 16" cast aluminum Torque Star wheels (white wheels with white exterior, silver wheels with all other exterior colors), Delco 2001 Series ETR AM/FM stereo radio with auto reverse cassette, 6 speakers, 7-band graphic equalizer, clock, touch control, seek up/down, search and replay, leather-

BONNEVILLE

INVOICE MSRP

...with radio controls and power antenna; heated power mirrors with blue tint, ...one bodyside applique, monotone ground effects package, rear decklid ...kit, front floor console with storage and rear HVAC vents, 45/45 Doral cloth ...ted visor vanity mirrors, console with rear AC vents, overhead console with ...enience net, deluxe floor mats, decklid release, electric rear window defogger, ...system and retained accessory power, Electronic Compass/Driver Information ...: check oil level/low washer fluid/low coolant/check gauges (oil pressure, battery ..., coolant temperature)/hood ajar/door ajar/trunk ajar/lamp monitor; Twilight Sentinel, luggage compartment cargo net, deluxe front and rear floor mats, RH/LH covered illuminated visor vanity mirrors, 45/45 bucket seats with center console storage and Doral cloth trim, 6-way power bucket driver seat, 4-spoke leather-wrapped steering wheel with radio controls, rear center armrest with dual cup holders, Computer Command Ride/Handling Package (requires bucket seats), electronic load leveling, stainless steel split dual rectangular exhaust.

Accessories

Code	Description	Invoice	MSRP
1SA	**SE Group 1SA**	NC	NC
	incls vehicle with standard equipment		
1SB	**SE Group 1SB**	240	270
	incls retained accessory power illuminated entry system, Delco ETR AM/FM stereo radio with auto reverse cassette, seek/scan and clock		
1SC	**SE Group 1SC**	821	923
	incls SE 1SB contents plus deck lid release, sport LH/RH power remote mirrors, 6-way power driver seat, electric rear window defogger, variable effort steering		
1SD	**SE Group 1SD**	1410	1584
	incls SE Group 1SC contents plus power antenna, RH/LH covered illuminated visor vanity mirrors, leather-wrapped steering wheel, twilight sentinel, custom trim, remote keyless entry		
1SC/H4U	**SE Value Equipment Group 1SC/H4U**	2360	2635
	incls SE Group 1SC and H4U Sport Luxury Edition (incls. P225/60R16 BW touring tires, machine faced crosslace aluminum wheels, leather bucket seats, leather wrapped steering wheel, monotone appearance pkg, rear spoiler, power antenna)		
1SD/H4U	**SE Value Equipment Group 1SD/H4U**	2534	2830
	incls SE Group 1SD contents and H4U Sport Luxury Edition (incls. P225/60R16 BW touring tires, machine faced crosslace aluminum wheels, leather bucket seats, leather wrapped steering wheel, monotone appearance pkg, rear spoiler, power antenna)		
1SA	**SSE Group 1SA**	NC	NC
	incls vehicle with standard equipment		
1SB	**SSE Group 1SB**	1282	1440
	incls remote keyless entry, head-up display, electrochromic inside rearview mirror, automatic air conditioning, 8-speaker performance sound system, 6-way power passenger seat, theft deterrent system, traction control		
—	**Engines**		
L36	3.8 liter 3800 Series II SFI V6	STD	STD
L67	3.8 liter 3800 SFI V6 supercharged - SE	1056	1187
	incls P225/60HR16 SBR BW performance tires, 2.97 axle ratio		
	SSE	NC	NC
	req's WA6		
FE9	**Federal Emissions**	NC	NC

BONNEVILLE — PONTIAC

CODE	DESCRIPTION	INVOICE	MSRP
YF5	**California Emissions**	NC	NC
NG1	**Massachusetts Emissions**	NC	NC
—	**Tires**		
QPH	P215/65R15 BSW STL touring - SE	STD	STD
QNX	P225/60R16 BSW STL touring - SE w/o H4U & Y52	75	84
	w/H4U and/or Y52	NC	NC
QVG	P225/60HR16 BSW performance	NC	NC
	incld with L67 supercharged engine (SE)		
	req's WA6 (SSE)		
—	**Interiors**		
—	45/55 split bench w/Metrix cloth - SE	STD	STD
—	45/55 buckets w/Doral cloth - SSE	STD	STD
B20	custom interior with 45/55 split bench w/Doral cloth		
	w/o 1SD	209	235
	w/1SD	NC	NC
B20	custom interior w/bucket seats w/Doral cloth		
	w/o 1SD	449	505
	w/1SD	155	174
B20	custom interior w/bucket seats w/leather seating areas		
	w/o 1SD or H4U	1254	1409
	w/1SD and w/o H4U	915	1028
	w/H4U	NC	NC
AS7	45/55 buckets w/leather seating areas - SSE	760	854
AL7	45/55 articulating buckets w/leather seating areas - SSE		
	w/1SA	1250	1404
	w/1SB	978	1099
B57	**Monotone Appearance Pkg** — w/o H4U	178	200
	w/H4U	NC	NC
Y52	**Performance & Handling Pkg** — w/o H4U	1053	1183
	w/H4U	690	775
	incls. traction control, electronic level control, computer command ride 5-blade aluminum wheels, P225/60R16 touring BW tires		
C68	**Air Conditioning** — electronic automatic	134	150
C49	**Defogger, Electric Rear Window**	151	170
WA6	**SSEi Supercharger Pkg - SSE**	1039	1167
	incls 3.8 liter supercharged V6 engine, 2.97 axle ratio, SSEi floor mats, SSEi badging, P225/60HR16 BW performance tires		
FW1	**Computer Command Ride - SSE**	338	380
K05	**Engine Block Heater**	16	18
T2Z	**Enhancement Group** — w/o AS7, H4U or 1SD	183	206
	w/AS7 (cloth) and w/o 1SD or H4U	98	110
	w/AS7 (leather) or H4U and w/o 1SD	53	60
	w/1SD	NC	NC
US7	**Power Antenna** — w/o H4U, UT6, UP3 or 1SD	76	85
	w/H4U, UT6, UP3 or 1SD	NC	NC
AG1	**Power Seat** — 6-way driver - w/o 1SC or 1SD	271	305
	w/1SC or 1SD	NC	NC

EDMUND'S 1995 HIGH-PERFORMANCE AUTOMOBILES

PONTIAC BONNEVILLE

CODE	DESCRIPTION	INVOICE	MSRP
AG2	**Power Seat — 6-way passenger**	271	305
	w/1SB - SSE	NC	NC
UK3	**Steering Wheel Radio Controls — w/U1C or UN6**	111	125
	w/UP3 or UT6	NC	NC
UN6	**Radio — w/o 1SB, 1SC or 1SD**	174	195
	w/1SB, 1SC or 1SD	NC	NC
	incls ETR AM/FM stereo cassette with auto reverse		
U1C	**Radio — w/o 1SB, 1SC or 1SD**	263	295
	w/1SB, 1SC or 1SD	89	100
	incls ETR AM/FM stereo with compact disc player		
UW6	**6-Speaker Performance Sound System**		
	w/UN6 or U1C	89	100
	w/UT6 or UP3	NC	NC
UT6	**Radio — w/o H4U, AS7 (leather), T2Z or 1SD**	343	385
	w/AS7 (leather) or T2Z and w/o H4U or 1SD	298	335
	w/H4U or 1SD	223	250
	incls ETR AM/FM stereo cassette with auto reverse and 7-band graphic equalizer		
UP3	**Radio — SE - w/o H4U, AS7 (leather), T2Z or 1SD**	432	485
	w/AS7 (leather) or T2Z and w/o H4U or 1SD	387	435
	w/H4U or 1SD	312	350
	SSE	89	100
	incls ETR AM/FM stereo with compact disc and 7-band graphic equalizer		
AU0	**Remote Keyless Entry — SE - w/o 1SD, SSE - w/o 1SB**	120	135
	SE - w/1SD, SSE - w/1SB	NC	NC
D58	**Spoiler, Rear Deck Delete**	(98)	(110)
T43	**Spoiler, Rear Deck — w/o H4U**	98	110
	w/H4U	NC	NC
CF5	**Sunroof, Power Glass — SE - w/o B20 custom interior**	886	995
	SE - w/B20 custom interior	873	981
	SSE	873	981
NW9	**Traction Control — SE - w/o Y52**	156	175
	SE - w/Y52	NC	NC
	SSE - w/o 1SB	156	175
	SSE - w/1SB	NC	NC
PF5	**Wheels — 16" 5-blade aluminum - w/wheel locks, w/o Y52**	303	340
	w/o wheel locks, w/o Y52	288	324
	w/Y52	NC	NC
N73	**Wheels — 16" aluminum gold crosslace - SE w/wheel locks**	303	340
	SE - w/o wheel locks	288	324
	SSE	NC	NC
PA2	**Wheels — 16" aluminum machine faced - SE w/wheel locks**	303	340
	SE w/o wheel locks	288	324
	SSE	NC	NC
PA6	**Wheels — 16" aluminum sparkle silver torque star - SSE**	NC	NC

FIREBIRD / PONTIAC

1995 Pontiac Firebird Formula Convertible

FIREBIRD FORMULA/TRANS AM

Aside from a small period of history during the early '80s, Firebird has been synonymous with performance since 1967. The blue-striped Trans Am from 1969 comes to mind, along with the 1974 SD-455, the 1978 black and gold 455 T/A abused by Burt Reynolds in "Smokey and the Bandit," the orange 1978 Firebird Esprit driven to fame by James Garner in "The Rockford Files," the 1987 Turbo V-6 Indianapolis 500 pace car, and this, the current 275-horsepower Corvette-killer Formula and Trans Am for 1995.

The Firebird, in base form, is a beautiful car. The blend of angular greenhouse lines and softly bulging sheetmetal creates the automotive equivalent of Kim Basinger in a silk nightgown. Unfortunately, the bespoiled Trans Am, with its aero skirting, decklid Batwing, and peek-a-boo driving lights ruins the effect. However, the Formula provides all of the T/A's hardware goodies in a more restrained, lighter, less costly package.

The Firebird's cockpit is a nice blend of style and function, and is much better than, say, that found in a Dodge Stealth. Dual airbags and anti-lock brakes are standard, and Firebird now has an optional traction control system for the Formula and Trans Am. Additionally, convertible versions of each model were introduced in 1994, so if top-down motoring is preferable, for a boost in price it is yours.

Performance from the Corvette-derived 5.7-liter V-8 is astounding, providing enough power to get the Formula to 60 mph faster than your ten-year-old can get to 40 yards. Stay away from the well-optioned Trans Am. The Formula provides all the performance and image you need, and keeps your budget well in the black.

EDMUND'S 1995 HIGH-PERFORMANCE AUTOMOBILES

PONTIAC — FIREBIRD

CODE	DESCRIPTION	INVOICE	MSRP

Performance and Safety

Firebird Formula

Acceleration (0-60 mph)	5.8 sec.	ABS	Standard
Braking (60-0 mph)	115 ft.	Driver Airbag	Standard
Cornering	.85 g's	Passenger Airbag	Standard
Fuel Capacity	15.5 gal.	Traction Control	Optional
Fuel Economy	City: 17 mpg	Crash Test Grade	D: Excellent P: Excellent
	Hwy: 25 mpg	Insurance Cost	Very High

Firebird Trans Am

Acceleration (0-60 mph)	6.3 sec.	ABS	Standard
Braking (60-0 mph)	116 ft.	Driver Airbag	Standard
Cornering	.86 g's	Passenger Airbag	Standard
Fuel Capacity	15.5 gal.	Traction Control	Optional
Fuel Economy	City: 17 mpg	Crash Test Grade	D: Excellent P: Excellent
	Hwy: 25 mpg	Insurance Cost	Very High

Edmund's Driving Impression

Picture this: Thunderous hooves of rubber, prowling rural lanes and little-used freeway ramps. The roar of a V-8 exhaust, the manic titillation of wheelspinning takeoffs, a low-slung coupe fading into the horizon.

Either you're fantasizing about a time-machine return to the muscle-car era of the Sixties—or a test drive in a Firebird Trans Am. Camaro Z28 fanatics would disagree, but the Trans Am, a wild animal of the road, may be the prime example of modern-day muscle that can be found in a dealer's showroom.

Under Firebird Formula hoods—and that of the legendary Trans Am—throbs a 275-horsepower variant of the 5.7-liter Corvette V-8, sending its energy to a masterful six-speed manual gearbox. A four-speed automatic also handles the job, but this brawny powerplant clamors for a stick-shift.

Even if a Trans Am isn't quite the fastest car on the prairie, acceleration *feels* near-breathtaking—if the gearbox and clutch are manipulated adroitly. Clutch behavior is superb, skillfully grabbing hold of the engine's vigor. The gearbox slips between cogs with a neat "snick."

Noisy? Definitely! Trans Ammers aren't timid. Gloriously throaty exhausts try hard to awaken any dormant teenager impulses. Expect a random clunk or groan at low speeds, too.

A V-8 Firebird is far from the roughest-riding of the high-performance machines. All models maneuver handily through traffic or ambling country curves. Each can tackle a hard corner without fuss, but Trans Ams grip the asphalt with a tenacious claw. Full gauges include a 7000-rpm tach and 155-mph speedometer, and the tall wing does not obstruct visibility.

Seats are ecstasy, despite a legs-forward driving position. Firebirds aren't so easy to climb into, but a little squirming isn't too much to ask, for the pleasures that await.

Muscle-car purists may snicker, but in the snowbelt, we'd opt for the new traction control option. Nothing wrong with the less-flamboyant Formula, or even the V6-powered basic 'bird.

FIREBIRD | *PONTIAC*

| CODE | DESCRIPTION | INVOICE | MSRP |

1995 Pontiac Firebird Trans Am

FIREBIRD FORMULA/TRANS AM 8 CYL

V87S	Formula 2-Dr Coupe	17476	19099
V87S	Trans Am 2-Dr Coupe	19278	21069
V67S	Formula 2-Dr Convertible	22993	25129
V67S	Trans Am 2-Dr Convertible	24832	27139
Destination Charge:		500	500

Standard Equipment

FIREBIRD FORMULA COUPE: 5.7 liter V8 engine, 6-speed manual transmission, power 4-wheel disc brakes w/anti-lock braking system, P235/55R16 SBR touring tires, 16" x 8" bright silver sport cast aluminum wheels, air conditioning, 125 amp alternator, 3.42 axle ratio, performance suspension, power rack and pinion steering, Delco ETR AM/FM stereo radio with auto reverse cassette, clock and Delco theft lock; right rear fixed mast black antenna, soft fascia type bumpers, composite doors/fenders/fascias/roof/rear decklid/spoiler; Solar-Ray tinted glass, electrically operated concealed quartz halogen headlamps, rear license plate bracket with lamp, sport mirrors (LH remote/RH manual), waterborne base coat/two-component clearcoat finish paint, rear decklid spoiler with integrated center high-mounted stop lamp, compact spare tire, controlled-cycle windshield wipers, extensive acoustical insulation, driver and front passenger air bags, full cut-pile floor carpeting, fully carpeted cargo area, full length front console with cup holder and storage box, side window defogger, Metrix cloth seat fabric, locking glove box, hatch release, instrumentation includes: analog speedometer/tachometer/odometer/coolant temperature/oil pressure/voltmeter/trip odometer; lights include: ashtray/dome/glove box; carpeted front mats, day/night rearview mirror with reading lamps, RH/LH covered visor vanity mirrors, rear decklid release, passive driver and front passenger seat and shoulder safety belts, 3-point active safety belts (all outboard rear positions), driver and passenger 2-way manual front seats, reclining front bucket seats, folding rear seat, 4-spoke steering wheel, tilt-wheel adjustable steering column, Pass Key II theft deterrent system, extensive anti-corrosion protection, Delco Freedom II battery, brake/transmission shift interlock (with auto trans), Federal emissions system, stainless steel single converter exhaust system (dual converter California V8 with auto trans), GM Computer Command Control, low oil level monitor and warning, rear wheel drive, gas-charged monotube de carbon shock absorbers, short and long arm front suspension, front and rear stabilizer bars.

EDMUND'S 1995 HIGH-PERFORMANCE AUTOMOBILES

PONTIAC — FIREBIRD

CODE	DESCRIPTION	INVOICE	MSRP

FORMULA CONVERTIBLE (in addition to or instead of FIREBIRD FORMULA COUPE equipment): Power windows with driver side express-down feature, power automatic door locks, LH/RH remote power sport mirrors with blue glass, bodyside body color moldings, waterborne base coat/two-component clearcoat finish paint, cruise control, electric rear window defogger, lights include: rear seat courtesy light, trunk lamp; carpeted front mats, carpeted rear mats, remote keyless entry, 4-way manual front driver/2-way manual front passenger seats.

TRANS AM COUPE (in addition to or instead of FORMULA COUPE equipment): Power windows with driver side express-down feature, power automatic door locks, P245/50ZR16 speed-rated all-weather tires, Delco 2001 Series ETR AM/FM stereo radio with auto reverse cassette and 7-band graphic equalizer (includes clock/touch control/seek/search/replay/steering wheel radio controls/leather appointment group/power antenna/Delco theft lock), Hi-Performance 10-speaker system, fog lamps, LH/RH power remote sport mirrors with blue glass, bodyside body color moldings, cruise control, electric rear window defogger, rear seat courtesy lights deleted, trunk lamp deleted, rear floor mats, 4-way manual front driver/2-way manual front passenger seats, leather-wrapped steering wheel with sound system controls (includes leather-wrapped shift knob and parking brake handle).

TRANS AM CONVERTIBLE (in addition to or instead of FORMULA CONVERTIBLE equipment): Power windows with driver side express-down feature, power automatic door locks, P245/50ZR16 speed-rated all-weather tires, Delco 2001 Series ETR AM/FM stereo radio with auto reverse cassette and 7-band graphic equalizer (includes clock/touch control/seek/search/replay/steering wheel radio controls/leather appointment group/power antenna/Delco theft lock), fog lamps, LH/RH power remote sport mirrors with blue glass, bodyside body color moldings, cruise control, electric rear window defogger, rear seat courtesy lights deleted, trunk lamp deleted, 4-way manual front driver/2-way manual front passenger seats, leather-wrapped steering wheel with sound system controls (includes leather-wrapped shift knob and parking brake handle).

Accessories

Code	Description	Invoice	MSRP
1SA	**Formula Group 1SA** — incls vehicle with standard equipment	NC	NC
1SB	**Formula Group 1SB - Convertibles** — incls rear mats, bodyside moldings, power windows, power door locks, cruise control, power mirrors, electric rear window defogger	925	1076
	Coupes — incls remote keyless entry, graphic equalizer, 6-speaker sound system, steering wheel controls, power antenna and leather appointment group	437	508
1SC	**Formula Group 1SC - Coupes** — incls Group 1SB plus remote keyless entry, graphic equalizer, 10 speakers, leather steering wheel and power antenna	1448	1684
1SA	**Trans Am Group 1SA** — incls vehicle with standard equipment	NC	NC
UN6	**Radio — Formula** — incls ETR AM/FM stereo with auto reverse cassette	STD	STD
U1C	**Radio — Formula** — incls ETR AM/FM stereo radio with compact disc player	86	100
UT6	**Radio — Formula Coupes**	407	473
	Trans Am Coupe — incls ETR AM/FM stereo radio with auto reverse cassette, graphic equalizer and power antenna	342	398

FIREBIRD — PONTIAC

CODE	DESCRIPTION	INVOICE	MSRP
	Formula Convertibles (std Trans Am Conv)	321	373
	incls ETR AM/FM stereo radio with auto reverse cassette, graphic equalizer, power antenna, steering wheel controls, leather appointment group		
UP3	**Radio — Formula Coupes w/o 1SC**	493	573
	Formula Coupes w/1SC	86	100
	Trans Am Coupe	428	498
	incls ETR AM/FM stereo radio with compact disc player and graphic equalizer		
	Formula Convertibles w/o 1SB	407	473
	Formula Convertibles w/1SB	86	100
	Trans Am Convertible	86	100
	incls ETR AM/FM stereo with compact disc player and graphic equalizer, power antenna, steering wheel and leather appointment group		
LT1	**Engine — 5.7 liter SFI V8 - Formula, Trans Am**	STD	STD
FE9	**Federal Emissions**	NC	NC
YF5	**California Emissions**	86	100
NG1	**Massachusetts Emissions**	86	100
—	**Tires**		
QMT	P235/55R16 BSW touring - Formula	STD	STD
QFZ	P245/50ZR16 BSW STL (std Trans Am) - Formula	124	144
QLC	P245/50ZR16 BSW STL - Formula	194	225
	Trans Am	78	91
—	**Interiors**		
AR9	articulating bucket seats w/leather - Formula coupe	692	804
AQ9	articulating bucket seats w/leather - Formula	713	829
AR9	bucket seats w/Metrix cloth - Trans Am	STD	STD
AQ9	articulating bucket seats w/Metrix cloth - Trans Am	284	330
AQ9	articulating bucket seats w/leather - Trans Am	713	829
VK3	**License Plate Bracket, Front**	NC	NC
GU5	**Rear Performance Axle**	151	175
AU0	**Remote Keyless Entry** — std Trans Am	116	135
AG1	**Seat** — driver power 6-way	232	270
NW9	**Traction Control**	387	450
MN6	**Transmission** — 6-speed manual	STD	STD
MX0	**Transmission** — 4-speed automatic	667	775
C41	**Non Air Conditioning**	(770)	(895)
B84	**Body Color Side Moldings** — Coupe - std Trans Am	52	60
K34	**Cruise Control, Resume Speed** — Coupe - std Trans Am	194	225
C49	**Defogger, Rear Window** — Coupe - std Trans Am	146	170
CC1	**Hatch Roof, Removable** — Coupe w/locks, stowage & sunshades	856	995
B35	**Mats, Rear Floor** — Coupe - std Trans Am	13	15
DG7	**Mirrors** — Coupe - LH/RH power, blue glass (std Trans Am)	83	96
AU3	**Power Door Locks** — Coupe - std Trans Am	189	220
A31	**Power Windows** — Coupe - std Trans Am	249	290
NW9	**Traction Control**	387	450
T43	**Uplevel Spoiler** — Trans Am	301	350

EDMUND'S 1995 HIGH-PERFORMANCE AUTOMOBILES

PONTIAC — GRAND PRIX

| CODE | DESCRIPTION | INVOICE | MSRP |

1995 Pontiac Grand Prix GTP

GRAND PRIX GTP COUPE / GT SEDAN (3.4L V6)

It took General Motors ten years to bring the platform on which the Grand Prix is based to market, and since the 1988 debut of the Grand Prix and its corporate siblings, the Buick Regal and Oldsmobile Cutlass Supreme, the cars have been major money losers for the company. Originally available only as coupes, sedans joined the lineup in 1990, but were too late and too lame to capitalize on a market dominated by the Ford Taurus and Honda Accord. To remain competitive, prices for these under-engineered vehicles have remained quite low, and GM loses money on every single one it sells.

The current Grand Prix may not look much different from the car we first saw in 1988, but under the skin it's very different. A new interior was added last year, new engines power both the coupe and sedan, and low prices undercut the competition. Equipped with the optional DOHC 3.4-liter V-6, the Grand Prix is transformed into a reasonably good performer with accommodations for five adults. Each year, the Grand Prix receives improvement.

However, we do not recommend actually buying one of these cars. Style is their forte, not substance. They feel heavy, look dated, and are generally underwhelming. Granted, the GTP coupe looks like a bad boy compared to Ford's Thunderbird and the new Monte Carlo, but those cars are far more sophisticated, better looking, and are better engineered. Ditto the GT sedan, which goes up against the likes of the Ford Taurus SHO and Nissan Maxima SE. With the availablity of far better cars for slightly more money, the Grand Prix just doesn't make sense.

GRAND PRIX   PONTIAC

Performance and Safety

GTP Coupe (w/3.4-liter V-6)

Acceleration (0-60 mph) .... 7.5 sec.	ABS .... Optional		
Braking (60-0 mph) .... 137 ft.	Driver Airbag .... Standard		
Cornering .... .79 g's	Passenger Airbag .... Standard		
Fuel Capacity .... 17.1 gal.	Traction Control .... N/A		
Fuel Economy .... City: 17 mpg	Crash Test Grade .... D: Good	P: Average	
Hwy: 26 mpg	Insurance Cost .... Average		

GT Sedan (w/3.4-liter V-6)

Acceleration (0-60 mph) .... 8.7 sec. ABS .... Optional
Braking (60-0 mph) .... 135 ft. Driver Airbag .... Standard
Cornering .... .82 g's Passenger Airbag .... Standard
Fuel Capacity .... 17.1 gal. Traction Control .... N/A
Fuel Economy .... City: 17 mpg Crash Test Grade .... D: Good   P: Average
                             Hwy: 26 mpg Insurance Cost .... Average

1995 Pontiac Grand Prix GTP

GRAND PRIX GTP 3.4L COUPE V6

— 2-Dr Coupe		17914	19640
Destination Charge:		535	535

Standard Equipment

GRAND PRIX GTP 3.4L COUPE: 3.4 liter DOHC V6 engine, variable-effort power steering, power 4-wheel disc brakes w/anti-lock braking system, hood louvers, GTP nameplates, Special Edition Coupe Pkg (incls specific front/rear fascias w/round fog lamps, lower aero skirting, wheel flares, 16" Crosslace aluminum wheels or 16" 5-spoke aluminum wheels, P225/60R16 performance tires, split dual exhaust with cast aluminum tips and sport suspension), electronically-controlled 4-speed

EDMUND'S 1995 HIGH-PERFORMANCE AUTOMOBILES

PONTIAC — GRAND PRIX

automatic transmission and second gear start feature, power windows with lighted switch and LH express-down feature, automatic power door locks with unlock and relock feature, Delco 2001 Series ETR AM/FM stereo radio with seek/up-down/auto reverse cassette/clock; steering wheel radio controls (includes leather-wrapped steering wheel), electronic push button air conditioning, fixed mast black antenna, soft fascia type bumpers with integral rub strip, Soft-Ray tinted glass (flush fitting/safety laminated), mini-quad halogen headlamps, fog lamps, body color LH/RH power remote sport mirrors, compact spare tire, "wet-arm" controlled-cycle windshield wipers, extensive acoustical insulation package, driver and passenger side air bags, front floor storage console, cruise control, decklid release, electric rear window defogger, flush door handles, Cordae cloth interior, instrumentation includes: mechanical analog speedometer/tachometer/coolant temperature/fuel odometer/trip odometer; entry lighting, fully carpeted luggage compartment, day/night rearview mirror, RH/LH covered visor vanity mirrors, passive driver and front passenger seat and shoulder door safety belts, rear seat shoulder and lap belts (all outboard positions), reclining sport bucket seats, 3-passenger rear seating with integrated headrests, tilt-wheel adjustable steering column, 4-spoke leather sport steering wheel with controls and air bag (NA with base radio), lockable instrument panel compartment, front door map pockets, pocketed visors, turn signal reminder, Delco Freedom II battery, brake/transmission shift interlock, extensive anti-corrosion protection, front wheel drive, GM Computer Command Control, Pass Key II theft deterrent system.

Accessories

CODE	DESCRIPTION	INVOICE	MSRP
1SA	Group 1SA	NC	NC
	incls cruise control, covered dual visor vanity mirrors, sport mirrors (LH power/RH power convex), Delco 2001 Series AM/FM stereo radio with cassette, remote deck lid release, electric rear window defogger, front and rear floor mats, steering wheel radio controls (incls leather-wrapped steering wheel)		
FE9	Federal Emissions	NC	NC
YF5	California Emissions	89	100
NG1	Massachusetts Emissions	89	100
AR9	Interior — buckets w/Cordae cloth	STD	STD
—	Custom Interior Groups		
B20	sport buckets w/Doral cloth	348	391
B20	sport buckets w/Prado leather seating areas	771	866
UV8	Cellular Phone Provisions	31	35
K05	Engine Block Heater	16	18
UV6	Head-Up Display	223	250
U40	Trip Computer	177	199
VK3	License Plate Bracket, Front	NC	NC
US7	Power Antenna	76	85
AG1	Power Seat — driver 6-way	271	305
U1C	Radio	111	125
	incls AM/FM stereo with compact disc player		
UT6	Radio	156	175
	incls ETR AM/FM stereo with auto reverse cassette, 7-band equalizer and 8-speaker performance sound system		
UP3	Radio	245	275
	incls ETR AM/FM stereo with compact disc player, 7-band equalizer and 8-speaker performance sound system		
AU0	Remote Keyless Entry	120	135
D81	Spoiler, Rear Deck	156	175
CF5	Sunroof, Power Glass — w/B20	575	646

GRAND PRIX — PONTIAC

| CODE | DESCRIPTION | INVOICE | MSRP |

1995 Pontiac Grand Prix GT Sedan

GRAND PRIX 3.4L GT SEDAN 6 CYL

		Invoice	MSRP
—	GT 4-Dr Sedan (incls pkg 1SB)	17905	19651
—	GT 4-Dr Sedan (incls pkg 1SC)	18568	20396
Destination Charge:		535	535

Standard Equipment

GRAND PRIX 3.4L GT SEDAN: 3.4 liter DOHC V6 SFI engine, P225/60R16 performance tires, 16" 5-blade aluminum wheels, speed-sensitive power steering, power 4-wheel disc brakes with anti-lock brake system, sport suspension, split dual exhaust system, sport bucket seats, hood louvers, electronically controlled 4-speed automatic transmission, power windows with express-down feature, power automatic door locks with unlock and relock feature, electronic push button air conditioning, soft fascia type bumpers with integral rub strips, Soft-Ray tinted glass, halogen fog lamps, compact spare tire, "wet-arm" controlled-cycle windshield wipers, acoustical insulation package, driver and front passenger side air bags, front floor console with storage, tachometer, coolant temp/fuel gauges, trip odometer, entry lighting, fully carpeted luggage compartment, day/night rearview mirror, tilt-wheel adjustable steering column, front center armrest storage, lockable instrument panel compartment, front door map pockets, turn signal reminder, Delco Freedom II battery, anti-corrosion protection, front wheel drive, GM Computer Command Control Pass Key II theft deterrent system.

3.4L GT SEDAN w/PKG 1SB (in addition to or instead of 3.4L GT SEDAN equipment): Cruise control, covered dual visor vanity mirrors, sport mirrors, (LH power/RH power convex), Delco 2001 Series AM/FM stereo radio with cassette, remote decklid release, electric rear window defogger.

3.4L GT SEDAN w/PKG 1SC (in addition to or instead of 3.4L GT SEDAN w/PKG 1SB equipment): Front and rear floor mats, steering wheel radio controls, leather-wrapped steering wheel, power 6-way driver's seat, remote keyless entry, power antenna.

EDMUND'S 1995 HIGH-PERFORMANCE AUTOMOBILES

PONTIAC   GRAND PRIX

CODE	DESCRIPTION	INVOICE	MSRP

Accessories

Code	Description	Invoice	MSRP
FE9	Federal Emissions	NC	NC
YF5	California Emissions	89	100
NG1	Massachusetts Emissions	89	100
—	**Custom Interior Groups**		
B20	sport buckets w/Doral cloth — GT w/pkg 1SB	461	518
	GT w/pkg 1SC	376	423
B20	sport buckets w/Prado leather — GT w/pkg 1SB	884	993
	GT w/pkg 1SC	799	898
UV8	Cellular Phone Provisions	31	35
K05	Engine Block Heater	16	18
UV6	Head-Up Display — digital	223	250
U40	Trip Computer	177	199
VK3	Front License Plate Bracket	NC	NC
US7	Power Antenna — GT w/pkg 1SB	76	85
AG1	Power Seat — driver 6-way	271	305
UK3	Steering Wheel Radio Controls — GT w/pkg 1SB	111	125
	GT w/pkg 1SC	NC	NC
	incls leather-wrapped steering wheel		
U1C	Radio	89	100
	incls ETR AM stereo/FM stereo w/CD player		
UT6	Radio — GT w/pkg 1SB	245	275
	GT w/pkg 1SC	134	150
	incls ETR AM stereo/FM stereo w/auto-reverse cassette, 7-band equalizer, 8-speaker performance sound system and steering wheel controls		
UP3	Radio — GT w/pkg 1SB	334	375
	GT w/pkg 1SC	223	250
	incls ETR AM stereo/FM stereo w/compact disc player, 7-band equalizer, 8-speaker performance sound system and steering wheel controls		
AU0	Remote Keyless Entry — GT w/pkg 1SB	120	135
CF5	Power Glass Sunroof	575	646
NW0	Wheels — aluminum sport bright faced	NC	NC

For expert advice in selecting/buying/leasing a new car, call

1-900-AUTOPRO

($2.00 per minute)

911 CARRERA

1995 Porsche 911 Carrera

911 CARRERA

Over thirty years ago, Porsche introduced what would become one of the most recognizable vehicles on the planet—the 911. It received modifications over the next three decades, but the shape was never changed, aside from subtle tweaks. For 1995, Porsche has introduced a new 911, and much of the old one has carried over. The interior, doors, roof and floorpan are the same as last year's model. The rest is new, or substantially upgraded, including an all-new, and more forgiving, rear suspension.

You can see that the overall visual effect is a familiar one. Same can be said of the interior, which has a new airbag-equipped steering wheel and revised seats. These are not bad things, as Porsche research indicates that 911 buyers are a loyal and reliable lot. What is not the same about this much improved version of the legendary Porsche is the price.

The 1995 911 is $5,000 to $12,000 less-expensive than the 1994 model, depending on which one you buy. There is a 911 Carrera 2, the base model and most popular 911. At mid-level is a convertible version of the 911 Carrera 2. The top-of-the-line 911 is the all-wheel drive Carrera 4, which benefits from a completely new drive system that, Porsche says, makes the car more fun on sunny days without giving up wet weather traction or prowess.

Porsche is counting on the 911 to give sales a badly needed boost. We think many current 911 owners will want the latest version of Germany's premier sports car.

PORSCHE
911 CARRERA

| CODE | DESCRIPTION | INVOICE | MSRP |

Performance and Safety

911 Carrera 2
Acceleration (0-60 mph) .... 5.3 sec.	ABS .... Standard			
Braking (60-0 mph) .... 117 ft.	Driver Airbag .... Standard			
Cornering .... .92 g's	Passenger Airbag .... Standard			
Fuel Capacity .... 19.4 gal.	Traction Control .... Optional			
Fuel Economy .... City: 17 mpg	Crash Test Grade .... D: N/A	P: N/A		
Hwy: 24 mpg	Insurance Cost .... N/A			

911 Carrera 2 Cabriolet
Acceleration (0-60 mph) .... 6.1 sec.
Braking (60-0 mph) .... 113 ft.
Cornering .... .92 g's
Fuel Capacity .... 19.4 gal.
Fuel Economy .... City: 17 mpg
Hwy: 24 mpg

ABS .... Standard
Driver Airbag .... Standard
Passenger Airbag .... Standard
Traction Control .... Optional
Crash Test Grade .... D: N/A   P: N/A
Insurance Cost .... N/A

911 Carrera 4
Acceleration (0-60 mph) .... 5.4 sec.
Braking (60-0 mph) .... N/A
Cornering .... N/A
Fuel Capacity .... 19.4 gal.
Fuel Economy .... City: 16 mpg
Hwy: 23 mpg

ABS .... Standard
Driver Airbag .... Standard
Passenger Airbag .... Standard
Traction Control .... Standard
Crash Test Grade .... D: N/A   P: N/A
Insurance Cost .... N/A

Edmund's Driving Impression

Anyone accustomed to driving in ho-hum fashion, steering with a lazy finger, should steer clear of Porsches completely. To operate a 911 at all, much less seize the maximum from its potential, demands effort. You have to pay attention. Manipulate the clutch and gears with skill and caution, and you're rewarded with an unrivaled motoring experience.

Acceleration is simply phenomenal—provided that you stay in each gear for a suitable span of time, and avoid letting the rear-mounted engine over-rev. No one could ask for a sweeter gearshift lever—one that traverses through six speeds by way of long, visceral flicks of the wrist. The stiff clutch demands a strong foot, but engages gracefully.

Everybody knows that handling is Porsche's prime talent, but you must experience it to believe. Steering doesn't require a lot of effort, but you feel every last imperfection from the pavement in the steering wheel, never losing intimate kinship with the road. Sixteen-inch tires grasp the road like pincers, and 17-inchers are available for the hard-to-please. Brake response is astounding.

In the city or on rough roads, the ride gets harsh—even shaky. Yet on the highway, a 911 is surprisingly comfortable. The car practically tries to ride right over the top of bumps, to maintain the best possible grip.

911 CARRERA — PORSCHE

Back support couldn't be better, in a superlative driving position. Seats feel molded to your body—the point of perfection between stiffness and softness. The driver faces a big 8000-rpm tach head-on. To the side sits a 180-mph speedometer—a realistic figure, since the car can reach 168 mph.

As for criticisms, the gearbox doesn't like to shift into reverse—an obstacle that could be avoided by selecting a Porsche with Tiptronic transmission. Engine and tire noise can get downright screechy—though Porsche fanatics revere such commotion. Grievances pale, however, in comparison with the car's striving toward perfection. Expert at handling, created to enhance the joy of driving, this precision machine stands near the pinnacle of sports-car excellence.

1995 Porsche 911 Carrera Cabriolet

911 CARRERA

CODE	DESCRIPTION	INVOICE	MSRP
993630	Carrera 2-Dr Cabriolet (6-spd)	57045	68200
993630	Carrera 2-Dr Cabriolet (Tiptronic)	59680	71350
993330	Carrera 2-Dr Coupe (6-spd)	50145	59900
993330	Carrera 2-Dr Coupe (Tiptronic)	52780	63050
993530	Carrera 4 2-Dr Cabriolet (6-spd)	62070	74200
993130	Carrera 4 2-Dr Coupe (6-spd)	55165	65900
Destination Charge:		725	725
Gas Guzzler Tax: Carrera 4		1000	1000

Standard Equipment

911 CARRERA COUPE & CABRIOLET: 3.6 liter 270 HP aluminum alloy twin spark plug air-cooled horizontally opposed 6 cylinder engine with partial engine encapsulation, fully integrated electronic ignition and fuel injection system Digital Motor Electronics (DME) with dual knock sensor and hot film air flow sensor systems, dual-mass flywheel, 6-speed manual transmission, hydraulically activated single disc dry clutch, rack and pinion steering with force-sensitive power assist, MacPherson front strut fully independent suspension (aluminum alloy lower control arms with stabilizer bar), rear aluminum alloy fully independent multi-link LSA axle suspension (with toe correction characteristics and stabilizer bar), power assisted 4-wheel cross-drilled disc brakes with revised anti-lock braking system (ABS 5) and asbestos-free pads (aluminum alloy 4-piston caliper, internally ventilated), redesigned 5-spoke

PORSCHE
911 CARRERA

pressure-cast light alloy wheels with locks, 7J x 16 wheels with 205/55ZR16 SBR front tires, 9J x 16 wheels with 245/45ZR16 SBR rear tires, 19.4 gallon fuel tank, two door Coupe or Cabriolet with 2+2 seating, electric sliding sunroof (Coupe), full power top with automatic latching and unlatching (Cabriolet), digital electronic fog lights (integrated into front apron), modular ellipsoid headlights with variable focus and washer system, redesigned third brake light, welded unitized body construction (double-sided, zinc galvanized steel), redesigned front and rear bumpers and fenders, second generation side-impact protection, speed-dependent extendable rear spoiler, heated windshield washer nozzles, electrically adjustable and heatable outside rearview mirrors, windshield antenna with signal amplifier, two-stage rear window defroster (Coupe), tinted glass, graduated-tint windshield, redesigned outside door handles (painted to match exterior color), driver and front seat passenger air bags, front and rear 3-point inertia-reel seatbelts, redesigned interior panels, individually folding rear seat backs (Coupe), increased luggage compartment volume, redesigned partial leather reclining bucket seats with electric height adjustment, air conditioning with automatic temperature control, new particle filters for ventilation system, redesigned leather-covered steering wheel, backlit analog instrumentation (incls tachometer, oil pressure/oil temperature/oil level/fuel level gauges, corresponding warning lights), trip odometer, power windows, analog quartz clock, brake pad wear indicator, mirrors in sun visors, interior lighting with delayed shut off, cruise control, one-key central locking and alarm system with fixed light-emitting diodes, AM/FM digital display stereo cassette radio with 6 speakers and amplifier, cassette holder.

911 CARRERA 4 COUPE & CABRIOLET: 3.6 liter 270 HP aluminum alloy twin spark plug air-cooled horizontally opposed 6 cylinder engine with partial engine encapsulation, fully integrated electronic ignition and fuel injection system Digital Motor Electronics (DME) with dual knock sensor and hot film air flow sensor systems, dual mass flywheel, 6-speed manual transmission (Porsche-designed full-time all-wheel-drive system with viscous center clutch), hydraulically activated single disc dry clutch, rack and pinion steering with force-sensitive power assist, MacPherson front strut fully independent suspension (aluminum alloy lower control arms with stabilizer bar), rear aluminum alloy fully independent suspension (multi-link LSA axle with toe correction characteristics and stabilizer bar), limited slip differential with automatic brake differential (ABD) traction system and lockup, power assisted aluminum alloy 4-piston fixed caliper internally ventilated 4-wheel cross-drilled disc brakes with revised anti-lock braking system (ABS 5) and asbestos-free pads, redesigned 5-spoke pressure-cast light alloy wheels with locks, 7J x 17 front wheels with 205/50ZR17 SBR tires, 9J x 17 rear wheels with 255/40ZR17 SBR tires, 19.4 gallon fuel tank, two door Coupe or Cabriolet with 2+2 seating, electric sliding sunroof (Coupe), full power top with automatic latching and unlatching (Cabriolet), digital electronic fog lights integrated into front apron, newly developed modular ellipsoid headlights with variable focus and washer system, redesigned third brake light, welded unitized body construction (double-sided, zinc galvanized steel), redesigned front/rear bumpers and fenders, second generation side-impact protection, larger speed-dependent extendable rear spoiler, heated windshield washer nozzles, electrically adjustable and heatable outside rearview mirrors, windshield antenna with signal amplifier, two-stage rear window defroster (Coupe), tinted glass, windshield with graduated tint, redesigned outside door handles (painted to match exterior color), driver and front seat passenger air bags, 3-point inertia-reel front/rear seatbelts, redesigned interior panels, individually folding rear seat backs (Coupe), increased luggage compartment volume, redesigned partial leather reclining bucket seats with electric height adjustment, air conditioning with automatic temperature control, new particle filters for ventilation system, redesigned leather-covered steering wheel, backlit analog instrumentation (incls tachometer, oil pressure/oil temperature/oil level/fuel level gauges, corresponding warning lights), trip odometer, power windows, analog quartz clock, brake pad wear indicator, mirrors in sun visors, interior lighting with delayed shut off, cruise control, one-key central locking and alarm system with fixed light-emitting diodes, AM/FM digital display stereo cassette radio with 6 speakers and amplifier, cassette holder.

Accessories

Code	Description	Invoice	MSRP
659	Computer — on-board	338	422
—	Engine — 6 cylinder EFI 3.6 liter	STD	STD

911 CARRERA — PORSCHE

CODE	DESCRIPTION	INVOICE	MSRP
—	**Seat Adjuster**		
437	power driver's	431	538
P15	dual power	766	956
—	**Tires**		
—	P205/55ZR16 front tires, P245/45ZR16 rear tires - Carrera	STD	STD
—	P205/50ZR17 front tires, P255/40ZR17 rear tires - Carrera 4	STD	STD
—	P205/50ZR17 front tires, P255/40ZR17 rear tires - Carrera	NC	NC
	req's wheels 398		
X65	**Steering Wheel Pkg**	971	1212
	incls leather-covered ventilating cover, leather fresh air side and center dash vents, leather fresh air side vents		
X66	**Door Panel Pkg**	1515	1891
	incls leather inside door openers, leather outside mirror adjuster frame, leather radio speaker covers, leather power window switches, leather covered caps, leather door lock pin rosettes		
X67	**Seat Pkg**	1403	1751
	incls leather front backrest lock controls, leather ring plates for switch/seat adjuster, leather seat hinges, leather heat adjust switches, leather seat adjust switches		
551	**Windstop Deflector** — Cabriolets	275	344
SPP	**Power Pack Plus**	39	45
—	**Dashboard**		
X18	dark rootwood	3490	4356
X17	light rootwood	3490	4356
X19	leather - in color to sample	716	893
—	**Radio Equipment**		
X81	CD storage - left door panel	193	241
X53	CD storage - behind hand brake lever	370	461
490	hi-fi sound	745	930
	incls amplifier system; std w/radio equipment P49		
P48	CD player - Cabriolets	239	299
P53	CD player - Coupes	239	299
692	remote control CD changer	998	1245
P49	digital sound	1663	2075
	incls hi-fi amplifier system and sound		
XR7	**Wiper/Washer** — rear window - Coupes	654	817
425	**Wiper** — rear window - Coupes	273	340
Z07	**Carpeting** — cargo compartment	551	687
Z69	**Carpeting** — interior deviating standard colors	60	75
Z35	**Kneebar** — leather - in deviating current Porsche colors	40	50
	req's all leather interior		
Z31	**Kneebar** — leather	452	564
SAC	**Air Conditioning** — rapid charger	153	177
—	**Trim**		
Z44	leather armrests	209	260
XM5	leather control knobs (4)	323	403
XN3	leather fresh air side dash vents (2)	531	662
XZ4	leather glove box lock frame	67	83

PORSCHE — 911 CARRERA

CODE	DESCRIPTION	INVOICE	MSRP
XW4	leather light switch	72	90
XW3	leather rear window wiper switch	136	169
XV9	leather B-pillar seat belt covers	93	116
XM7	leather-covered glove box	74	93
XJ5	leather ignition/door key	125	156
XF7	leather-covered tray - behind parking brake	154	193
XP6	leather seat belt lock and housing	374	466
XR3	leather seat hinges (4)	269	335
XW5	leather wiper/instrument light knob	92	115
XN8	leather sun visors	464	579
XK7	leather shift knob and cover	182	227
XW1	leather seat belt rosettes (2)	122	153
Z65	leatherette beltline in deviating standard color	84	105
XX6	leather shift lever knob in deviating colors - models w/manual trans	55	68
XM9	leather turn signal/wiper switch	225	281
XW9	leather entrance panel cover	205	256
XV3	leather air conditioner/heat adjust covers	241	300
XF5	leather-covered instrument rings	354	442
XN7	leather parking brake lever	200	249
XV5	leather seat adjuster switches (6)	485	606
XJ8	leather tiptronic selector lever - models w/Tiptronic trans	197	246
XW8	leather-covered caps (2)	20	25
Z11	leather carpet welting - in current Porsche colors	857	1069
Z09	leather carpet welting - in deviating interior colors	1490	1860
XW6	leather door lock pin rosettes	67	83
XR6	leather front backrest lock controls	379	473
XF6	leather gear box tunnel	158	198
XJ4	leather ignition lock rosette	47	58
XP9	leather radio speaker covers (6)	383	478
XV1	leather-covered ventilating cover	346	432
XN4	leather fresh air center vent	278	347
XV7	leather fuel tank pull knob	53	66
XZ7	leather outside mirror adjuster frame	88	110
XN1	leather power window switches	274	342
XV2	leather fresh air side vents (2)	17	22
XV4	leather heat adjust switches (2)	149	188
XN2	leather inside door openers (2)	136	170
XW2	leather rear seat belt lock and housing	459	573
XV6	leather ring plates for switch/seat adjuster	287	359
398	**Wheels** — 5-spoke - Carrera models	1104	1378
	incls P205/50ZR17 front tires and P255/40ZR17 rear tires; std Carrera 4 models; std w/chassis P31		
—	**Battery**		
SUL	ultra-light - small	101	118
SLB	standard - large	43	50
SBE	battery eliminator	77	90

911 CARRERA — PORSCHE

CODE	DESCRIPTION	INVOICE	MSRP
—	**Paint**		
98/99	color to sample	2002	2498
Z41	pearl white metallic	9814	12249
—	metallic	830	1036
—	**Rim Caps**		
XD4	w/Porsche Crest	172	214
X89	w/Porsche Crest on painted rims	172	214
XD9	**Rims** — painted in vehicle color	865	1079
—	**Seats**		
P14	dual heated w/adjustable heating range	460	578
513	passenger's lumbar support	442	551
586	driver's lumbar support	442	551
374	sport passenger w/power height adjuster	293	365
373	sport driver w/power height adjuster	293	365
—	**Seat Trim**		
—	leather	1181	1474
982	supple leather	306	382
Z45	inlays in deviating current Porsche colors	82	103
Z51	leather front and rear in deviating current Porsche colors	559	697
Z21	**Seat Stitching** — in alternate current Porsche colors	72	90
—	**Interior Trim**		
—	special leather - Coupes	3392	4233
	Cabriolets	2657	3317
—	leather - Coupes	3046	3800
	Cabriolets	2311	2885
98	leather in deviating colors - Coupes	3225	4025
	Cabriolets	2491	3109
99	leather in color to sample - Coupes	4682	5843
	Cabriolets	3947	4927
—	**Floor Mats**		
M6	**Porsche**	81	125
XX1	front	286	357
	req's special leather interior trim		
—	**Parking Brake Lever**		
X31	light rootwood	428	535
X32	dark rootwood	428	535
498	**Model Designation Delete** — rear	NC	NC
—	**Telephone**		
S6	cellular	2195	2395
	incls exclusive console		
S88	cellular	1275	1425
	incls mounting bracket and installation kit		
—	**Headliner**		
Z27	leather in current Porsche color - Coupe	1530	1808
	incls sun visors and A & B pillars		
Z05	leather in color to sample - Coupe	2048	2556
	incls sun visors and A & B pillars		

EDMUND'S 1995 HIGH-PERFORMANCE AUTOMOBILES

PORSCHE 911 CARRERA

CODE	DESCRIPTION	INVOICE	MSRP
Z28	leatherette in deviating current Porsche colors - Coupe	56	70
—	**Chassis**		
P31	sport - Carrera Coupe	1616	2017
	incls 5-spoke wheels		
030	sport - Carrera 4 Coupe	512	639
Z53	**Head Restraints** - w/stamped Porsche crest	82	103
	req's leather seat trim		
—	**Door Trim Panels**		
X86	light rootwood	1158	1445
X87	dark rootwood	1158	1445
Z43	leather	209	260
419	**Storage** — rear compartment - Coupes	525	656
	Cabriolets	NC	NC
	deletes standard rear seat		
—	**Gear Shift Knob**		
XC8	light rootwood - models w/manual trans	289	360
XC9	dark rootwood - models w/manual trans	289	360
XP3	**Boot Cover** — leather top - Cabriolets	2069	2583
—	**Shift Lever**		
X25	light rootwood - models w/Tiptronic trans	339	423
X24	dark rootwood - models w/Tiptronic trans	339	423
—	**Axle**		
224	active brake differential - Carrera w/Tiptronic trans	732	913
	std Carrera 4		
P08	active limited slip differential - Carrera	958	1195
	std Carrera 4		

1995 Porsche 911 Carrera Cabriolet

928 GTS

| CODE | DESCRIPTION | INVOICE | MSRP |

1995 Porsche 928 GTS

928 GTS

Porsche is able to do one thing no other automaker is able to do in the United States: Sell cars long after their expiration date. The 911 was introduced just months after the Kennedy assassination. The 968 is based on an ill-fated budget-priced Porsche that first bowed in late 1976. And this car, the 928, was introduced a year later, in 1977, which makes it the freshest shape in Porsche showrooms this year. Sure, the cars are updated and improved regularly, but the shapes have remained pretty much intact since day one. And they can't figure out why sales continue to decline year after year.

928s are as rare as a good-natured political campaign ad. Sales of this grand tourer peaked in the go-go Eighties, not long after Tom Cruise dumped one into Lake Michigan in Risky Business. Today, barely 100 are sold per year—that's right, 100. In the 18 years since its introduction, Porsche has paid off the tooling and now makes a fat profit on each 928 it sells. The company claims that the 928 will continue to be sold as long as there are people who want to buy it, but at 100 sales per year we doubt the 928 will last much longer.

Powered by an aluminum 5.4-liter V-8 that produces 345 horsepower and 369 pounds feet of torque, the 928's 3600 pounds of metal, rubber, glass and leather gets down the road in a hurry. Huge brakes stop the heavy GT quickly, and the 928 grips the road better than nearly anything you can buy.

Your 85 grand buys a great car in the 928, and miniscule sales totals guarantee exclusivity. The 928 is a classic Porsche in every sense of the word, and time to obtain one fresh out of the box is running out.

PORSCHE 928 GTS

Performance and Safety

Acceleration (0-60 mph) .... 5.5 sec.	ABS .... Standard	
Braking (60-0 mph) .... 128 ft.	Driver Airbag .... Standard	
Cornering .... .91 g's	Passenger Airbag .... Standard	
Fuel Capacity .... 19.6 gal.	Traction Control .... N/A	
Fuel Economy .... City: 15 mpg	Crash Test Grade .... D: N/A	P: N/A
	Hwy: 19 mpg	Insurance Cost .... Average

928 GTS

	INVOICE	MSRP
928940 2-Dr Coupe (5-spd)	68030	82260
928920 2-Dr Coupe (auto)	68030	82260
Destination Charge:	725	725
Gas Guzzler Tax: w/5-spd trans	3000	3000
w/auto trans	2100	2100

Standard Equipment

928 GTS: 5.4 liter 345 HP aluminum alloy double overhead cam V8 engine, four valves per cylinder, EZK ignition with knock sensor system, LH Jetronic fuel injection with 2-stage resonance induction system, 5-speed manual or 4-speed automatic transmission with shift lock and key lock features, "PSD" electronically-variable limited slip differential, rack and pinion steering with force-sensitive power assist, sport shock absorbers, fully independent front suspension (aluminum alloy double A-arms with coil springs negative steering roll radius and stabilizer bar), fully independent rear suspension (aluminum alloy multi-link "Weissach" rear axle with self-stabilizing toe characteristics and stabilizer bar), race-developed aluminum alloy 4-piston fixed caliper power assisted internally ventilated 4-wheel disc brakes with anti-lock braking system (ABS) and asbestos-free pads, 5-spoke pressure-cast light alloy wheels with locks, 7.5J x 17 front wheels with 225/45ZR17 SBR tires, 9J x 17 rear wheels with 255/40ZR17 SBR tires, 22.7 gallon fuel tank, two-door Coupe with 2+2 seating and rear hatch, electric sunroof (closes automatically when vehicle is locked with key), fog and driving lights integrated in front bumper, retractable halogen headlights, welded unitized body construction (double-sided zinc galvanized steel with lightweight aluminum front fenders/hood/doors), rear spoiler (painted to match exterior color), environmentally-compatible water-based metallic paint, heated windshield washer nozzles, rear window wiper and defroster with two heat settings, electrically adjustable and heatable outside rearview mirrors, roof-mounted antenna, tinted glass, windshield with graduated tint, headlight washers, driver and front seat passenger air bags, 3-point inertia-reel front and rear seatbelts, full power front seats, front and rear leather seats, fold-out front armrests, individual folding rear seatbacks, 3-position Positrol memory for driver's seat and outside mirrors, adjustable-tilt steering column and instrument cluster, automatic climate control system with separate rear air conditioning, new particle filters for ventilation system, electric rear hatch release on driver and passenger sides, leather-covered steering wheel/gearshift lever boot, backlit analog instrumentation (incls tachometer, oil pressure/coolant temperature/fuel level/battery charge gauges), driver-information and diagnostic system monitoring 10 information functions and 22 separate warning functions, power windows, illuminated mirrors in front sun visors, rear sun visors, interior lighting with delayed shut-off, red warning lights and white courtesy lights in doors, cruise control, one-key central locking and alarm system with light-emitting diodes in door lock buttons (to show the alarm is engaged), AM/FM digital display stereo cassette radio with remote CD changer and 10 speakers (hi-fi sound system with 160-watt, 6-channel amplifier), cassette holder.

928 GTS

CODE	DESCRIPTION	INVOICE	MSRP

Accessories

- **Interior**
- — leather w/leather seat trim ... 2480 | 3096
- — special leather ... 3066 | 3826
- — leather w/cloth seat inlays ... 2480 | 3096
- **Tires**
- — P225/45ZR17 front tires and P225/40ZR17 rear tires ... STD | STD
- **Trim**

Code	Description	Invoice	MSRP
XN4	leather center instrument panel air vent	354	442
XV3	leather air conditioner/heater adjuster covers	241	300
XV1	leather defroster panel	253	315
XY1	leather console area for switch/dials	126	158
XZ9	leather safety belt tongue frame	106	133
XZ1	leather parking brake rosette	170	212
XK7	leather shift lever - models w/manual trans	182	227
XJ8	leather shift lever - models w/auto trans	221	276
XZ5	leather interior sensor cover	35	43
Z10	leatherette welting in current colors	37	46
XY3	leather seat adjuster w/covered memory switch	93	116
XY2	leather seat adjuster w/o covered memory switch	57	71
XY5	leather auto selector lever cover	198	247
XM9	leather turn signal and wiper switch	225	281
XZ2	leather rear seat belt rosettes	153	191
XZ4	leather glove box lock frame	173	216
XP7	leather rear seat belt housing cover	164	204
Z08	leather welting in current colors	911	1137
XW6	leather door lock pin rosettes (2)	113	141
XY4	leather center console frame	225	281
XP9	leather speaker covers in doors (10)	605	755
XN7	leather parking brake lever	293	365
XY8	leather frame for switches	57	71
XJ3	leather door locking knobs and rosettes (2)	233	291
XZ6	leather RH fresh air vent	44	55
XJ5	leather-covered ignition/door key	125	156
XY6	leather ashtray cover	72	90
XP6	leather front seat belt locks and housing	374	466
XV5	leather seat adjuster switches (6)	485	606
XR5	leather backrest lock controls	555	692
XZ3	leather central locking system dial area frame	122	153
XN3	leather side instrument panel air vents (2)	516	644
XY7	leather rear window wiper/windows/sunroof switches	200	249
XM6	leather door opener handle recess plates	327	408
XV4	leather heater adjuster switches (2)	149	186
XW2	leather rear seat belt lock/housing cover	459	573
XV6	leather seat adjuster switch covers (2)	287	359
XR3	leather front seat hinges (4)	269	335

EDMUND'S 1995 HIGH-PERFORMANCE AUTOMOBILES

PORSCHE 928 GTS

CODE	DESCRIPTION	INVOICE	MSRP
XZ7	leather outside mirror frame/knob/rocker	88	110
XZ8	leather luggage compartment cover rosette	237	295
—	**Engine** — V8 32-valve EFI 5.4 liter	STD	STD
XR7	**Wiper/Washer** — rear window	1011	1262
—	**Air Conditioning**		
570	increased output	NC	NC
SAC	rapid charger	153	177
XX5	**Radio Equipment** — cassette holder in left door	1232	1537
—	**Seats**		
586	driver's lumbar support	442	551
513	passenger's lumbar support	442	551
387	sport passenger's w/power height adjustment	NC	NC
383	sport driver's w/power height adjustment	NC	NC
340	heated passenger's	231	289
139	heated driver's	231	289
—	**Seat Trim**		
980	supple leather	450	561
95	leather in color to sample w/leatherette beltline	4855	6059
—	cloth	NC	NC
94	leather in deviating colors w/leatherette beltline	2893	3610
538	passenger's memory	831	1038
Z18	stitching in current colors	76	95
X73	**Leather Seat Pkg**	1583	1975
	incls leather heater adjuster switches, leather front seat hinges, leather seat adjuster switches/switch covers, leather seat backrest lock controls		
X74	**Leather Door Pkg**	1902	2374
	incls pkg 1 plus leather side instrument panel air vents, leather outside mirror frame, leather seat adjuster (with or without covered memory switch), leather RH fresh air vent, leather outside knob/rocker, leather door lock pin rosettes		
X13	**Pkg 1**	1048	1308
	incls leather speaker covers in doors, leather door locking knobs and rosettes, leather door handle recess plates/door openers; std w/leather door pkg X74		
X14	**Pkg 2**	855	1067
	incls leather front seat belt locks and housing, leather parking brake rosette, leather parking brake lever, leather rear seat belt lock/housing cover		
X15	**Pkg 3**	1570	1960
	incls leather heater adjuster switches, leather front seat hinges, leather seat adjuster switch covers, leather seat backrest lock controls, leather seat adjuster switches		
X16	**Pkg 4**	875	1092
	incls leather auto selector lever cover, leather rear window wiper switches, leather window and sunroof switches, leather shift lever, leather frame for switches, leather ashtray cover		
—	**Telephone**		
S88	cellular w/mounting bracket and installation kit	1275	1425
S8	cellular - installed	2095	2295
	incls exclusive console		
—	**Battery**		
SLB	standard - large	43	50

928 GTS — PORSCHE

CODE	DESCRIPTION	INVOICE	MSRP
SUL	ultra-light - small	101	118
—	**Shift Lever Knob**		
XC8	light rootwood - models w/manual trans	289	360
XC9	dark rootwood - models w/manual trans	289	360
XX6	leather - models w/manual trans	55	68
—	**Floor Mats**		
M8	Porsche	81	125
XX1	front	286	357
	req's special leather interior trim		
—	**Parking Brake Handle**		
X31	light rootwood	428	535
X32	dark rootwood	428	535
474	**Sport Shock Absorbers**	274	342
—	**Console**		
XL4	light rootwood	3927	4902
	incls door trim		
XL5	dark rootwood	3927	4902
	incls door trim		
418	**Bodyside Moldings**	NC	NC
XN9	**Sun Visors** — leather w/illuminated RH visor vanity mirror	537	671
SPP	**Power Pack Plus**	39	45
SBE	**Battery Eliminator**	77	90
498	**Model Designation Delete** — rear	NC	NC
—	**Paint**		
98/99	color to sample	2135	2664
Z16	**Head Restraints** — w/stamped Porsche Crest	85	106
—	**Selector Lever**		
X23	light rootwood - models w/auto trans	366	457
X22	dark rootwood - models w/auto trans	366	457
—	**Rim Caps**		
X89	ornamental	172	214
	req's rims XD9		
XD4	w/Porsche crest	172	214
XD9	**Rims** — painted in vehicle color	865	1079
Z34	**Carpet** — in deviating current color	52	65

USE A MULTIMEDIA CD-ROM TO RESEARCH YOUR NEXT AUTOMOBILE PURCHASE

see ad on page 384 for details

PORSCHE 968

| CODE | DESCRIPTION | INVOICE | MSRP |

1995 Porsche 968 Coupe

968

Back in the mid-Seventies, Porsche replaced its mid-engined, Volkswagen-powered 912 with the 924. It was sleek and sexy, with a snug-fitting interior. However, its performance left much to be desired, and the Porsche name on the tail couldn't overcome the simple fact that the 924 was not an heir to the Porsche legend. A turbocharger gave the 924 a much needed boost in acceleration, but reliability problems and the tarnished 924 image effectively killed sales.

The Eighties brought a revamped 924S and more powerful 944. The 924S had a proper Porsche engine, and was priced under $20,000. Still, not many takers. The car lasted only a few years. The 944 was much more satisfying than the 924, and came with attractively flared fenders and lots of other goodies. The 944 was quite successful, but it didn't last beyond the early Nineties, when the 968 bowed.

The 968 is still the entry-level Porsche. Base prices start at about $40,000 for the coupe, and another ten grand for the Cabrio. The 968 is a slick piece, but is the singular Porsche model that really looks its age. Next year, the 968 will be replaced by the new Boxster roadster, so get to your local Porsche dealer soon if you've been saving your pennies for a 968. The 1995 is the best iteration of the original 924 yet, and should prove rather collectible in the future.

Sports car buyers would do well to note that the 968 costs a bit less than a Nissan 300ZX Turbo, a Mitsubishi 3000GT VR-4, or a Toyota Supra Turbo. Not bad for a genuine Porsche, and one that could be considered a collector's edition. But for another three grand, the Corvette Convertible sure would be fun, wouldn't it?

968 PORSCHE

Performance and Safety

Acceleration (0-60 mph) .... 5.9 sec.	ABS .... Standard	
Braking (60-0 mph) .... 138 ft.	Driver Airbag .... Standard	
Cornering .... .90 g's	Passenger Airbag .... Standard	
Fuel Capacity .... 19.6 gal.	Traction Control .... N/A	
Fuel Economy .... City: 17 mpg	Crash Test Grade .... D: N/A	P: N/A
	Hwy: 25 mpg	Insurance Cost .... High

968

CODE	DESCRIPTION	INVOICE	MSRP
968310	2-Dr Cabriolet (6-spd)	42555	51900
968310	2-Dr Cabriolet (Tiptronic)	45135	55050
968110	2-Dr Coupe (6-spd)	32760	39950
968110	2-Dr Coupe (Tiptronic)	35340	43100
Destination Charge:		725	725

Standard Equipment

968 COUPE & CABRIOLET: 3.0 liter 236 HP aluminum alloy double overhead cam 4 cylinder engine with twin balance shafts, four valves per cylinder with Vario Cam control, fully integrated electronic ignition and fuel injection system Digital Motor Electronics (DME), dual knock sensor system, front engine and rear transaxle, twin pipe high flow exhaust system coupled with reduced flow loss metal-monolith catalytic converter, lightweight forced pistons (lightened, forged crankshaft and connecting rods), 911 Turbo-type dual-mass flywheel, six-speed manual transmission, hydraulically activated single-plate clutch, rack and pinion steering with force-sensitive power assist, front fully independent suspension (MacPherson struts, aluminum alloy lower control arms with stabilizer bar), rear fully independent suspension (coil springs, aluminum alloy semi-trailing arms and torsion bars with stabilizer bar), race-developed aluminum alloy 4-piston fixed caliper power assisted dual-circuit internally ventilated 4-wheel disc brakes with anti-lock braking system (ABS) and asbestos-free pads, 5-spoke pressure-cast light alloy wheels with locks, 7J x 16 front wheels with 205/55ZR16 SBR tires, 8J x 16 rear wheels with 225/50ZR16 SBR tires, 19.6 gallon fuel tank, 2-door Coupe with 2+2 seating and rear hatch or two-seat Cabriolet with trunk, electric tilt/removable sunroof (Coupe), power top (Cabriolet), projector-type fog lights integrated into front spoiler, pop-up variable focal point halogen headlights, welded unitized body construction (double-sided, zinc galvanized steel), new integrated design energy-absorbing front/rear bumper covers, rear spoiler (Coupe), heated windshield washer nozzles, rear window wiper (Coupe), electrically adjustable and heatable outside rearview mirrors, roof-mounted antenna (Coupe), windshield antenna with signal amplifier (Cabriolet), rear window defroster (Coupe), tinted glass, windshield with graduated tint, driver and front passenger air bags, front/rear 3-point inertia-reel seatbelts (Cabriolet - front only), reclining bucket seats with electric height adjustment, individual folding rear seatbacks (Coupe), leatherette interior with cloth seat inlays, air conditioning with automatic temperature control and outside temperature display, new particle filters for ventilation system, electric release for rear/hatch (Coupe), electric trunk release (Cabriolet), leather-covered steering wheel and gear shift lever boot, backlit instrumentation (incls tachometer, oil pressure/coolant temperature/fuel level/battery charge gauges, corresponding warning lights), trip odometer, power windows, analog quartz clock, brake pad wear indicator, mirrors in sun visors, interior lighting with delayed shut-off, cruise control, one-key central locking and alarm system with light-emitting diodes in door lock buttons (to show alarm is engaged), AM/FM digital display stereo cassette radio with 6 speakers and anti-theft coding, cassette holder, storage compartments (instead of rear seats on Cabriolet).

PORSCHE 968

CODE	DESCRIPTION	INVOICE	MSRP

Accessories

Code	Description	Invoice	MSRP
—	**Seat Adjuster**		
438	power passenger's	431	538
437	power driver's	431	538
P15	dual power	766	956
—	**Engine** — 4 cyl 16 valve EFI 3.0 liter	STD	STD
—	**Trim**		
Z20	leather hand brake lever in current Porsche colors	19	23
XV6	leather ring plates for seat adjust switch	287	359
XM9	leather turn signal/wiper switch	225	281
XV9	leather B-pillar seat belt covers	93	116
XR6	leather front backrest lock controls	379	473
XW6	leather door lock pin rosettes	113	141
XK7	leather shift knob and cover	182	227
XV5	leather seat adjuster switches (6)	485	606
XN7	leather parking brake lever	293	365
XP6	leather seat belt locks/housing	374	466
XJ5	leather-covered ignition/door key	125	156
XW2	leather rear seat belt locks/housing	459	573
XP9	leather speaker covers	140	174
XM6	leather door openers and handle recess plates (2)	293	365
XJ8	leather selector lever - models w/Tiptronic	197	246
XR3	leather front seat hinges (4)	269	335
XV4	leather heat adjuster switches (2)	149	186
XN1	leather power window/mirror switches	160	199
X48	**Light Rootwood Pkg**	1929	2407
	incls light rootwood parking brake lever, light rootwood gear shift knob/lever, light rootwood instrument carrier		
X50	**Dark Rootwood Pkg**	1929	2407
	incls dark rootwood parking brake lever, dark rootwood gear shift knob/lever, dark rootwood instrument carrier		
X45	**Leather Door Pkg**	452	564
	incls leather speaker covers, leather door openers and handle recess plates, leather door locking pin rosettes		
X46	**Leather Seat Pkg**	1410	1760
	incls leather heat adjuster switches, leather seat adjuster switches, leather front seat hinges, leather ring plates for seat adjust switches, leather front backrest lock controls		
398	**Wheels** — 5-spoke 17"	1104	1378
—	**Telephone**		
S88	cellular w/mounting bracket and installation kit	1275	1425
S	cellular - installed	1795	1995
	incls exclusive console		
—	**Battery**		
SUL	ultra-light - small	101	118
SLB	standard - large	43	50

968 PORSCHE

CODE	DESCRIPTION	INVOICE	MSRP
SBE	battery eliminator	77	90
—	**Console**		
X95	light rootwood	712	888
X96	dark rootwood	712	888
—	**Paint**		
—	metallic	660	823
98/99	color to sample	2002	2498
Z41	pearl white metallic	9814	12249
SAC	**Air Conditioning** — rapid charger	153	177
288	**Headlamp Washers**	210	262
—	**Floor Mats**		
XX1	front	286	357
	req's special leather interior		
M4	**Porsche**	81	125
220	**Limited Slip Differential Axle** — models w/manual trans	732	913
Z77	**Leather-Wrapped Steering Wheel** — in deviating current colors	20	25
—	**Interior Trim**		
98	leather w/leatherette beltline in deviating standard colors - Coupe	3810	4755
	Cabriolet	3523	4397
99	leather in color to sample w/black leatherette beltline	5240	6540
—	leather w/leatherette beltline - Coupe	3631	4532
	Cabriolet	3344	4173
—	special leather - Coupe	3977	4963
	Cabriolet	3688	4603
XX6	**Shift Lever Knob** — leather in deviating standard colors - models w/manual trans	55	68
—	**Shift Lever**		
X25	light rootwood - models w/Tiptronic	339	423
X24	dark rootwood - models w/Tiptronic	339	423
—	**Sun Visors**		
XN8	leather	464	579
XN9	leather w/illuminated RH visor vanity mirror	537	671
—	**Radio Equipment**		
490	hi-fi sound system	450	561
	incls amplifier system		
P45	**CD player** - Coupe	239	299
P46	**CD player** - Cabriolet	239	299
692	remote control CD changer	998	1245
XD9	**Rims** — painted in vehicle color	865	1079
595	**Spoiler** — color-keyed rear - Coupe	170	213
—	**Seats**		
P14	dual heated	460	578
513	passenger's lumbar support	442	551
586	driver's lumbar support	442	551
387	sport passenger w/power height adjuster	251	314
383	sport driver's w/power height adjuster	251	314

EDMUND'S 1995 HIGH-PERFORMANCE AUTOMOBILES

PORSCHE 968

CODE	DESCRIPTION	INVOICE	MSRP
	Seat Trim		
Z55	supple leather front	355	443
—	leather - Coupe	1807	2256
	Cabriolet	1561	1949
—	partial leather w/leatherette	547	682
418	**Bodyside Moldings**	280	350
	Boot Cover		
Z57	deviating current colors - Cabriolet	78	98
XP3	leather - Cabriolet	2076	2591
Z53	**Head Restraints** — stamped w/Porsche Crest	82	103
	req's leather seat trim		
498	**Model Designation Delete** — rear	NC	NC
SPP	**Power Pack Plus**	39	45
	Tires		
—	P205/55ZR16 front tires and P225/50ZR16 rear tires	STD	STD
—	P225/45ZR17 front tires and P255/40ZR17 rear tires	NA	NA
	std w/chassis P31		
Z36	**Cargo Cover** — leather in current Porsche colors - Coupe	770	963
	Door Trim Panels		
Z81	leather in deviating current color	41	51
Z80	leather	214	267
Z82	leather in full leather interior	43	53
	Kneebar		
Z31	leather	539	672
Z35	leather in deviating current colors	65	81
	Rim Caps		
X89	painted w/Porsche Crest	172	214
XD4	w/Porsche Crest	172	214
	Parking Brake Lever		
X31	light rootwood or leather in color to sample	428	535
X32	dark rootwood or leather in color to sample	428	535
	Carpet		
Z69	deviating in std color - Coupe	60	75
Z70	deviating in std color - Cabriolet	94	118
	Instrument Carrier		
XL2	light rootwood	1397	1743
XL3	dark rootwood	1397	1743
	Gear Shift Knob		
XC8	light rootwood - models w/manual trans	289	360
XC9	dark rootwood - models w/manual trans	289	360
P31	**Sport Chassis** — Coupe	1616	2017
	incls 5-spoke wheels, larger front/rear stabilizer bars, P225/45ZR17 front tires, P225/40ZR17 rear tires		

900SE

1995 Saab 900SE

900SE / SE TURBO

When General Motors bought Saab several years ago, many thought that the unique and quirky characteristics that endeared Saabs to thousands of loyal owners would vanish as GM began redesigning and introducing new models to the public. When the new 900 arrived for 1994, those fears vanished. The 900 retained its Saabish styling and handling, and the fun-loving turbo reappeared with more power just months ago.

For 1995, the changes to the Saab 900 are non-existent. A convertible version of the coupe is now for sale, and the automotive press has raved about it. The base coupe and sedan, both of which are actually cavernous hatchbacks, come with a twin-cam, 2.3-liter four cylinder good for 150 horsepower. A 170-horsepower GM V-6 is standard on the SE 5-door hatch, and boosts the base 900 into performance car territory. The SE Turbo 3-door hatchback continues the trend, with 185-horsepower wrung from a 2.0-liter unit that gets the 900 to 60 mph just one-tenth of a second slower than a Ford Mustang GT.

Inside, a traditionally high seating position in orthopedically-correct seats gives a commanding view over the short hood. The windshield is fairly upright, contributing to the excellent forward visibility. The dash is logically laid out, with clearly marked analog gauges. With the seats folded, the Saab rivals many sport utilities and minivans with its cargo volume.

Yes, the Saab has retained its Saabishness. The ignition is still floor-mounted, and the shifter still must be in reverse to remove the key. These are the reasons a small contingent of consumers pays upwards of $21,000 for the 900 each year. From a practical standpoint, there are other cars that do what the Saab does, but none with such offbeat panache.

SAAB 900SE

Performance and Safety

900 SE V-6

Acceleration (0-60 mph) .... 7.9 sec.	ABS .... Standard
Braking (60-0 mph) .... 126 ft.	Driver Airbag .... Standard
Cornering .... .80 g's	Passenger Airbag .... Standard
Fuel Capacity .... 18 gal.	Traction Control .... Optional
Fuel Economy .... City: 19 mpg	Crash Test Grade .... D: N/A P: N/A
Hwy: 27 mpg	Insurance Cost .... High

900 SE Turbo

Acceleration (0-60 mph) .... 6.8 sec.	ABS .... Standard
Braking (60-0 mph) .... 116 ft.	Driver Airbag .... Standard
Cornering .... .83 g's	Passenger Airbag .... Standard
Fuel Capacity .... 18 gal.	Traction Control .... Optional
Fuel Economy .... City: 21 mpg	Crash Test Grade .... D: N/A P: N/A
Hwy: 28 mpg	Insurance Cost .... N/A

Edmund's Driving Impression

Redesigning for '94 failed to alter Saab's European-oriented disposition, or to extinguish its idiosyncrasies. In ride, in handling, in seating and basic theme, this Swedish compact declines to follow American or Asian trends.

As a result, its fans love their Saabs, while other folks wonder what the fuss is all about—just as it's been for the nearly four decades since Saab entered the American market.

Performance is fine with manual shift. Better yet, the gearshift is a joy to operate: slightly loose in action, but precise and nearly effortless. The smooth-action clutch has a light feel and requires slight effort. Optional 4-speed automatic is electro-hydraulically controlled, with three shift modes (normal, sporty, or winter).

Standard in the 900 SE (optional in 900 S), the 170-horsepower V-6 responds well to the driver's foot, as the car escalates competently to highway speeds. That does not mean startling acceleration, but few cars feel this solid and substantial.

Where the Saab excels is in hard corners and tight curves. Even though the body can lean almost precariously, the sedan's tires don't release their hold on the pavement. Expect a little understeer in such maneuvers, which require turning the steering wheel a little more than anticipated. Except for a bit of bouncing along uneven pavement, the ride is calm and orderly.

The driver sits high, close to the steering wheel and not so far from the windshield, in a slightly off-kilter position. Some knees could bump the dashboard bottom while shifting. Interior space is snug, but occupants have ample leg/head room. Dashboards hold a 155-mph speedometer and 7000-rpm tach, and the ignition switch is mounted on the floor—one of those quaint Saab quirks.

Saab's new SE coupe uses a turbo four; the 900 S has a conventional four-cylinder engine. Even though Saab's turbos have a better reputation than most, we like the strong and sweet V-6, which comes complete with traction control.

900SE — SAAB

CODE	DESCRIPTION	INVOICE	MSRP

900SE

975MSR SE 5-Dr Hatchback (5-spd)	25381	28680
953MSR SE Turbo 3-Dr Coupe (5-spd)	25656	28990
952MT SE Turbo 2-Dr Convertible (5-spd)	34383	39520
Destination Charge:	470	470

Standard Equipment

900SE - HATCHBACK: 2.5 liter V6 170 HP engine, 4-wheel power assisted disc brakes with ABS, ventilated front discs, power assisted rack and pinion steering, independent front suspension with MacPherson struts, front and rear stabilizer bars, high speed SBR tires, 5-speed manual transmission, Saab Supplemental Restraint System (SRS) (incls driver and passenger side air bags, automatic belt tensioner system for front seat occupants), 3-point safety belts for all occupants, welded unit body construction and side-impact protection system designed in front and rear crumple zones, well-isolated fuel tank location, collapsible steering column, manually activated "child-proof" rear door locks, lock-out switch for rear power window switches, mechanically-activated rear-wheel hand brake, headlamp wiper and washer, daytime running lights, rear window wiper and washer system, color-keyed "self-restoring" bumpers and black window trim, protective bodyside moldings, aerodynamic headlamps with flush lenses and replaceable halogen bulbs, side guidance reversing lights and side-mounted direction indicator lights, front/rear fog lights, front spoiler, undercoating and anti-corrosion treatment, remote central locking and anti-theft alarm, deadlock security system, telescopic steering wheel, power windows with one-touch feature on front windows, electronic speed control with "cruise on" indicator light, electrically adjustable and heated rearview mirrors, windshield wiper/washer with interval and clean sweep feature, head restraints at front and rear outboard seating positions, 2-position fold-down back seat and fold-down rear center armrest, pass-through opening from trunk to back seat (behind center armrest), automatic headlamp shut-off and courtesy headlamp delay feature, illuminated visor vanity mirrors, interior courtesy light delay feature, luggage compartment light and built-in tool kit, heat absorbent tinted glass, electric rear window demister, two-tone luxury velour upholstery, adjustable front safety belt guide loops, rear side window demisters, front/rear plush carpet floor mats, AM/FM stereo cassette with CD changer controls (incls anti-theft lock-out code, front/rear fader control, electronic tuning with programmable AM/FM pre-sets, seek up and down tuning, auto-reverse cassette with Dolby noise reduction, full-logic cassette transport with head and roller release), automatic electric antenna, 8 acoustically engineered speakers (in six locations), analog speedometer, analog tachometer, digital odometer and trip meter, fuel and temperature gauges, dashboard "black panel" feature with integrated warning system, quartz analog clock, warning lights (incls traction control system [TCS], supplemental restraint system [SRS], anti-lock braking system [ABS], low fuel, oil pressure, battery, brake fluid), indicator lamps (incls rear demister, hand brake, high beam, open door, rear fog light),Saab Traction Control System (TCS), light alloy wheels, electric tilt/slide tinted glass sunroof with interior ventilated sunshade, CFC-free automatic climate control with interior air filtration system, power 8-way adjustable front seats with driver's side memory, leather seating surfaces, leather-wrapped steering wheel, Saab Car Computer (SCC).

SE COUPE (in addition to or instead of SE HATCHBACK equipment): 2.0 liter turbocharged 185 HP 4 cylinder engine, Saab Traction Control System (TCS) deleted, lowered sport chassis, manually activated "child-proof" rear door locks deleted, lock-out switch for rear power window switches deleted, rear spoiler.

SE CONVERTIBLE: 2.0 liter turbocharged 185 HP 4 cylinder engine, 4-wheel power assisted disc brakes with ABS, ventilated front discs, power assisted rack and pinion steering, independent front suspension with MacPherson struts, front and rear stabilizer bars, high speed SBR tires, light alloy wheels, 5-speed manual transmission, Saab Supplemental Restraint System (SRS) (incls driver and passenger air bags, automatic belt tensioner system for front seat occupants), 3-point safety belts for all occupants, welded unit-body construction and side-impact protection system designed in front and rear crumple zones, well-isolated fuel tank location, collapsible steering column, lock-out switch for rear power window switches, mechanically activated rear-wheel hand brake, headlamp

SAAB 900SE / 9000 AERO

wiper and washer, daytime running lights, electrically operated top with automatic retraction under molded boot cover, color-keyed "self-restoring" bumpers and black window trim, protective bodyside moldings, aerodynamic headlamps with flush lenses and replaceable halogen bulbs, side guidance reversing lights and side mounted direction indicator lights, front/rear fog lights, front spoiler, undercoating and anti-corrosion treatment, remote central locking and anti-theft alarm, deadlock security system, telescopic steering wheel, power windows with one-touch opening for front windows (separate switch for simultaneous operation of all side windows), electronic speed control with "cruise on" indicator light, electrically adjustable and heated rearview mirrors, windshield wiper/washer with interval and clean sweep feature, head restraints at front and rear outboard seating positions, fold-down lockable rear seat back, automatic headlamp shut-off and courtesy headlamp delay feature, illuminated visor vanity mirrors, interior courtesy light delay feature, luggage compartment light and built-in tool kit, electric rear window demister, leather seating surfaces, leather-wrapped steering wheel, front and rear plush carpet floor mats, AM/FM stereo/cassette with CD changer controls (incls anti-theft lock-out code, front/rear fader control, electronic tuning with programmable AM/FM presets, seek up and down tuning, auto-reverse cassette with Dolby noise reduction, full-logic cassette transport with head and roller release), automatic electric antenna, 8 acoustically engineered speakers (in six locations), analog speedometer, analog tachometer, digital odometer and trip meter, fuel and temperature gauges, dashboard "black panel" feature with integrated warning system, quartz analog clock, warning lights (incls Traction Control system [TCS, V6 only], Supplemental Restraint System [SRS], anti-lock braking system [ABS], low fuel, oil pressure, battery, brake fluid), indicator lamps (incls rear demister, hand brake, high beam, open door, rear fog light), CFC-free automatic climate control with interior air filtration system, power 8-way adjustable front seats with driver's side memory, CD changer, Saab Car Computer (SCC).

Accessories

972	**V6 2.5L Engine** — 900SE Convertible	467	550
—	**Automatic Transmission** — 4-spd - 900SE Hatchback & Convertible	843	995
	900SE Coupe	NA	NA

req's 2.5 liter engine on 900SE Convertible

1995 Saab 9000 Aero

9000 AERO

In the mid-Eighties, Saab advertising boasted about brisk sales, saying they sold every 900 imported to the United States, even the yellow ones. The time was right to capitalize on the company's

9000 AERO — SAAB

newfound success, and the five-door 9000 was launched as the new Saab flagship in 1986. It was available in turbo and non-turbo form, and found many buyers.

The 9000 Aero is basically the same car, but with a multitude of upgrades and gobs more turbo power. The Aero wrings 225 horsepower out of a tiny 2.3-liter four cylinder engine. To go along with this go-power, the Aero is distinguished from lesser 9000 models by its integrated fog lights, body-color side cladding, decklid spoiler and meaty tires on gray-painted three-spoke rims. It definitely looks the part.

The Aero acts the part, too. It's a fast front-driver. Braking and handling are top-notch, too. Inside, occupants are coddled by heated leather chairs in a cabin that measures in the large car category, according to the EPA. The Aero comes with everything standard. There are no options, aside from an automatic transmission and traction control. While modern-day 9000s can be had in either hatchback or sedan form, the Aero is only offered with the hatch.

For 1995, the 9000 Aero adds daytime running lights, which means everybody will see you coming, including radar gun-toting traffic cops. Overall, the 9000 Aero is an impressive car. It's packaged well, is quick, and seats passengers in extreme comfort. It's also a rare car that assures buyers of exclusivity. And, at just over $40,000, it offers consumers in the luxo-sport sedan class a dash of spice in what can be a bland group of automobiles. We don't particularly care for Saab's meld of boxy yet rounded styling, but it certainly is a different sort of car for a different sort of driver.

Performance and Safety

Acceleration (0-60 mph)	7.4 sec.	ABS	Standard
Braking (60-0 mph)	124 ft.	Driver Airbag	Standard
Cornering	.85 g's	Passenger Airbag	Standard
Fuel Capacity	17.4 gal.	Traction Control	Optional
Fuel Economy	City: 17 mpg	Crash Test Grade	D: Good P: N/A
	Hwy: 25 mpg	Insurance Cost	Low

9000 AERO

Code	Description	Invoice	MSRP
065ASR	Turbo 5-Dr Hatchback (auto)	35105	41300
065MSR	High Output Turbo 5-Dr Hatchback (5-spd)	35488	41750
	Destination Charge:	470	470

Standard Equipment

9000 AERO: 2.3 liter turbocharged 225 HP engine, water-cooled turbocharger/air-to-air charge air intercooler/engine oil cooler, Saab Trionic engine management system (incls electronc fuel injection, knock detection, charge-pressure control, Saab Direct Ignition), 5-speed overdrive manual transmission, 4-wheel power assisted disc brakes with ABS (ventilated front discs), power assisted rack and pinion steering, gas-hydraulic shock absorbers, independent front suspension with MacPherson struts, front and rear stabilizer bars, light alloy wheels, high speed SBR tires, Saab Supplemental Restraint System (SRS) (incls driver and passenger air bags, automatic belt tensioner system for front seat occupants, padded knee bolsters for front seat occupants), 3-point safety belts at all outboard seating positions, rear center lap belt, welded unit body construction (designed in front

SAAB
9000 AERO

and rear crumple zones), side-impact protection system, well-isolated fuel tank location, collapsible steering column, manually activated "child-proof" rear door locks, lock-out switch for rear door power window switches, mechanically activated rear-wheel hand brake, headlamp wiper and washer system, daytime running lights, electric tilt/slide tinted glass sunroof with interior sunshade, aerodynamic headlamps with flush lenses and replaceable halogen headlamp bulbs, color-keyed "self-restoring" bumpers and black window trim, protective bodyside moldings, side-guidance reversing lights and side-mounted direction indicator lights, front and rear fog lights, front spoiler, neutral-density dark-tinted taillight lenses, undercoating and anti-corrosion treatment, CFC-free automatic climate control with manual override and interior air filtration system, electrically heated full leather sport seats with temperature controls for both seat heaters, power 8-way adjustable front seats with driver's seat memory, electronic speed control with "cruise on" indicator light, remote central locking with anti-theft alarm, lockable center storage console, power windows with "one-touch" opening for front windows, electrically adjustable and heated rearview mirrors, rear side window demisters and electric rear window demister, windshield wiper/washer system with interval wipe feature, illuminated visor vanity mirrors, interior courtesy light delay feature, overhead console with swiveling map light/dual rear seat reading lamps, adjustable front safety belt guide loops, head restraints at front and rear outboard seating positions, leather-wrapped steering wheel, leather shift boot cover (manual trans), telescopic steering wheel, walnut instrument panel, front and rear plush carpet floor mats, fold-down rear center armrest, remote trunk/hatch release button on driver's door, luggage compartment light and built-in/removable tool kit, tinted/heat-absorbent glass, "Prestige" AM/FM stereo/cassette with removable keypad controls (incls anti-theft lock-out code and warning light, 150 watt amplifier, front/rear fader control, electronic tuning with 18 programmable AM/FM pre-sets, seek and scan up and down tuning, auto-reverse cassette with Dolby noise reduction, full-logic cassette transport with key-off eject), 10 acoustically engineered speakers, automatic electric antenna, compact disc player (pre-wired for CD changer), analog speedometer with odometer and trip meter, analog tachometer/fuel and temperature gauges, Saab Car Computer (incls digital clock), electronic display (incls voltage, outside temperature, average/inst. fuel economy, miles to empty, message prompts to check coolant and oil levels), pictogram (incls bulb failure, door/trunk open, low oil pressure), warning lights (incls Supplemental Restraint System [SRS], anti-lock braking system [ABS], low fuel, battery brake fluid, washer fluid), indicator lamps (incls rear demister, hand brake, high beam), rear window wiper/washer system, rear spoiler, three-position fold-down back seat, turbo boost pressure gauge, "shift up" indicator.

1995 Saab 9000 Aero

SC2   SATURN

1995 Saturn SC2

SATURN SC2

Since its debut for the 1991 model year, we've had mixed feelings about the Saturn SC. We wanted to like it, because General Motors was trying to revolutionize the way small cars were built in the United States. All the secrecy over the car before its introduction just added to our already high expectations. When we finally saw the car, in a dull metallic gray with darker gray body cladding and bumpers, with ultra-shiny alloy wheels of uninspired design that didn't even fill out the substantial wheel wells, massive and bulbous, rectangular taillights, we were let down. The Geo Storm was better looking, a serious detriment if ever there was one.

Inside, a massive hard plastic dash housed tiny gauges and Fisher Price switchgear. The motorized mouse seatbelt anchors were unfinished and flimsy looking. In short, we didn't see any evidence that GM had learned anything with the Saturn project, aside from pioneering the no-haggle pricing philosophy and understanding how to properly market a car.

Fortunately, the buying public turned the Saturn franchise into one of GM's bright spots, and money to improve the breed flowed easily. New wheels and the cancellation of two-tone paint greatly improved the SC's look. An entry-level model with the sedan's front clip arrived for 1993, and brighter colors lightened the exterior look a bit.

1995 brings more substantial changes. The SC2 gets an all-new interior with dual airbags and three-point seatbelts. Gauges are large and easily legible, and the new dash design visually opens up the interior a bit. New alloy wheels fill the wheel wells without a problem, and the front and rear fascias have received styling tweaks to take some of the awkwardness out of the design.

Now the Saturn SC2 is much better looking than the Storm, and many other sport coupes on the road. With good performance, low prices, and unbeatable dealer service, the Saturn SC2 is a good buy indeed.

SATURN SC2

Performance and Safety

Acceleration (0-60 mph) .... 8.4 sec.	ABS .... Optional
Braking (60-0 mph) .... 132 ft.	Driver Airbag .... Standard
Cornering .... .88 g's	Passenger Airbag .... Standard
Fuel Capacity .... 12.8 gal.	Traction Control .... Optional
Fuel Economy .... City: 24 mpg	Crash Test Grade .... D: N/A P: N/A
Hwy: 34 mpg	Insurance Cost .... High

Edmund's Driving Impression

What a prospective customer might notice first inside a Saturn coupe is its surprisingly sporty aura. You sit in an almost "arms-out" driving position, not unlike an all-out sports car. The steering wheel is beautifully positioned, with a thick rim to grasp.

Saturns have quieted down some since their 1990 debut, but the twin-cam engine (standard in SC2/SL2/SW2) still emits a surprisingly loud growl when accelerating—even a little bit.

With automatic shift, the engine revs easily to just past 6000 rpm, before slipping neatly into the next gear. Standing-start acceleration is more than adequate, but hardly performance-packed. Tromp the pedal at 55 mph, in fact, and response is kind of puny. Do it at 20 mph and the engine revs vigorously to that 6000-rpm cutoff, but liberates a lot more noise than action.

Controls are excellent, and gauges huge: a 130-mph speedometer and 8000-rpm tachometer (with 6500-rpm redline), plus fuel and temperature readouts.

Moderate bounciness on ordinary pavement demonstrates that the suspension is rather taut, even in its softer-of-two settings. The ride smooths out on the highway, but slight vibration often is evident, noticeable in the steering wheel and the floor.

Stable on the highway, with good road-grip generally, the twin-cam Saturn can grow twitchy on curves. A slight bump in the road while completing a quick turn can cause the back end to almost leap laterally for an instant, before settling down again. On the other hand, in slalom-like low-speed maneuvers, the coupe hung tight, with only mild body lean and almost no tire squeal. Precise steering sends this car just where it's pointed, with only a hint of understeer.

All-around visibility is outstanding—virtually unbeatable. Brakes inspire supreme confidence—especially with optional anti-locking. Seat bottoms are fairly short, but otherwise inviting. Coupes have virtually no backseat leg room, and sedans aren't exactly spacious back there either.

Essentially, an SL2 is an SC2 with two extra doors and a greater likelihood of fitting a couple of people into the rear. Although the coupe looks sharp, the sedan—to many eyes—suggests dowdiness. Even if a Saturn with the top engine can't quite outperform the competition, why not get one that *looks* like it could?

See the Automobile Dealer Directory on page 388 for a Dealer near you!

SC2 — SATURN

| CODE | DESCRIPTION | INVOICE | MSRP |

1995 Saturn SC2

SATURN SC2

ZZG27	SC2 2-Dr Coupe (5-spd)	11696	12995
ZZH27	SC2 2-Dr Coupe (auto)	12434	13815
Destination Charge:		360	360

Standard Equipment

SATURN SC2: Front wheel drive, 5-speed manual transmission, 5-mph front and rear bumpers, dent-resistant exterior panels on fenders, doors, quarters and fascias, integral bodyside moldings, high gloss polyurethane clearcoat paint finish, flush tinted glass, adjustable driver and front passenger head restraints, cloth door trim panels, 60/40 fold-down rear seatbacks, fabric seats, rear seat heater ducts, reclining front seatbacks, fully trimmed trunk/cargo area, AM/FM stereo radio with seek/scan tuning and four 6" speakers, digital quartz clock, rear window defogger, 3-speed intermittent windshield wipers, headlamps-on chime, high mounted audio controls, interior storage features, passenger vanity mirror, adjustable steering column, remote fuel filler door release, independent 4-wheel suspension, power front disc/rear drum brakes, rack and pinion steering, driver-side air bag, automatic shoulder/manual lap belt system for driver and front passenger, manual lap/shoulder safety belts for rear seats, flash to pass headlamps, halogen headlamps, child security rear door locks, combined low engine oil pressure and coolant level telltale, tachometer, coolant temperature gauge, centralized electrical fuse centers, long-life engine coolant, maintenance-free suspension, maintenance-free battery, scissors jack, self-adjusting accessory drive belt, stainless steel exhaust system, steel spaceframe construction, 1.9 liter DOHC 4 cylinder PFI engine, P195/60R15 radial tires.

Accessories

—	**Pkg 2**	1697	1885
	incls air conditioning, power windows, power locks, power passenger side mirrors, "sawtooth" alloy wheels, speed control		
—	**California Emissions**	63	70
—	**Massachusetts Emissions**	63	70
C60	**Air Conditioning**	815	905

EDMUND'S 1995 HIGH-PERFORMANCE AUTOMOBILES

SATURN
SC2 / SL2

CODE	DESCRIPTION	INVOICE	MSRP
K34	Speed Control	225	250
—	Anti-Lock Brakes — w/5-spd trans	653	725
	w/auto trans (incls traction control)	702	780
CF5	Power Sunroof	608	675
D80	Rear Spoiler	162	180
PG5	Alloy Wheels — "teardrop"	185	205
—	Leather Trim	608	675
UM6	Radio — AM/FM stereo w/cassette	180	200
UU6	Radio — AM/FM stereo w/cassette & equalizer	329	365
U79	Coaxial Speakers — extended range	68	75

1995 Saturn SL2

SATURN SL2

The Saturn SL2 is a good car, but we aren't particularly fond of it. We've always found the styling to be an odd mix of curves and angles, with an overall effect that fairly screams Oldsmobile Cutlass Supreme. The interior, until this year, has received sharp criticism from our staff for its slab-sided dashboard, cheesy knobs and switches, virtually vertical rear seatback, and low, uncomfortable rear seat which was more often than not covered in a material strangely reminiscent of those velour-like shirts that were popular in the late Seventies.

Performance with the SL2's twin-cam 1.9-liter engine has always been good, but somewhat raucous. We like the idea of dent and rust resistant plastic body panels, and find that the SL2 is a solid sporty sedan that pleases most drivers most of the time. The Saturn dealer network is top-notch, worrying more about customer satisfaction than lining their pockets with profits. Overall though, the Saturn Corporation has put in an immense amount of effort to produce a pretty dull transportation device that happens to handle reasonably well.

For 1995, one of our largest complaints about the SL2, the interior, has been addressed. A new dashboard debuts this year, and dual airbags replace the infuriating motorized seatbelts. Controls

SL2 SATURN

and gauges are light-years ahead of where they used to be. The back seat still needs improvement, but we expect that quibble to be resolved next year when a new SL debuts for 1996.

Oh yes, Consumer Reports claims that the Saturn line of cars is darn near bulletproof in the reliability department. Another point that proves the SL2 will satisfy most drivers most of the time, but now that the Neon is all the rage, we suspect that Saturn will have to sell the 1995 SL2 largely on the strength of a well-deserved sterling reputation.

Performance and Safety

Acceleration (0-60 mph) .... 8.7 sec.	ABS .... Optional	
Braking (60-0 mph) .... 130 ft.	Driver Airbag .... Standard	
Cornering .... .79 g's	Passenger Airbag .... Standard	
Fuel Capacity .... 12.8 gal.	Traction Control .... Optional	
Fuel Economy .... City: 24 mpg	Crash Test Grade .... D: N/A	P: N/A
	Hwy: 34 mpg	Insurance Cost .... Average

1995 Saturn SL2

SATURN SL2
ZZJ69	SL2 4-Dr Sedan(5-spd)	10796	11995
ZZK69	SL2 4-Dr Sedan (auto)	11534	12815
Destination Charge:		360	360

Standard Equipment

SATURN SL2: Front wheel drive, 5-speed manual transmission, 5-mph front and rear bumpers, dent-resistant exterior panels on fenders, doors, quarters and fascias, integral bodyside moldings, high gloss polyurethane clearcoat paint finish, flush tinted glass, adjustable driver and front passenger head restraints, cloth door trim panels, 60/40 fold-down rear seatbacks, fabric seats, rear seat heater ducts, reclining front seatbacks, fully trimmed trunk/cargo area, AM/FM stereo radio with seek/scan tuning and four 6" speakers, digital quartz clock, rear window defogger, 3-speed intermittent windshield

SATURN SL2

wipers, headlamps-on chime, high mounted audio controls, interior storage features, passenger vanity mirror, adjustable steering column, remote fuel filler door release, independent 4-wheel suspension, power front disc/rear drum brakes, rack and pinion steering, driver-side air bag, automatic shoulder/manual lap belt system for driver and front passenger, manual lap/shoulder safety belts for rear seats, flash to pass headlamps, halogen headlamps, child security rear door locks, combined low engine oil pressure and coolant level telltale, tachometer, coolant temperature gauge, centralized electrical fuse centers, long-life engine coolant, maintenance-free suspension, maintenance-free battery, scissors jack, self-adjusting accessory drive belt, stainless steel exhaust system, steel spaceframe construction, 1.9 liter DOHC 4 cylinder PFI engine, P195/60R15 radial tires.

Accessories

Code	Description	Invoice	MSRP
—	**Pkg 2**	1899	2110
	incls air conditioning, power windows, power locks, power passenger side mirrors, "sawtooth" alloy wheels, speed control		
—	**California Emissions**	63	70
—	**Massachusetts Emissions**	63	70
C60	**Air Conditioning**	815	905
K34	**Speed Control**	225	250
—	**Anti-Lock Brakes** — w/5-spd trans	653	725
	w/auto trans (incls traction control)	702	780
CF5	**Power Sunroof**	608	675
D80	**Rear Spoiler**	162	180
T96	**Fog Lights**	140	155
PH6	**Alloy Wheels** — "sawtooth"	275	305
—	**Leather Trim**	608	675
UM6	**Radio** — AM/FM stereo w/cassette	180	200
UU6	**Radio** — AM/FM stereo w/cassette & equalizer	329	365
U79	**Coaxial Speakers** — extended range	68	75

EDMUND'S NEW AUDIO TAPE!

How to Get Your Way at the Auto Dealer

You'll learn how to buy right,
negotiate smart, save money, and
enjoy yourself all at the same time.

see our ad on page 376 for details

1995 Saturn SW2

SATURN SW2

Saturn has weathered some tough criticism since its debut. Complaints about the car have ranged from stodgy styling and ineffective ergonomics to buzzy engines and a distinct lack of refinement. Because of the hype when Saturn was launched, the critics peered into the car's every nook and cranny to decide whether the car was a successful engineering coup or just more hot air from General Motors.. Now that the car has been on the market for awhile, it's easy to see through the fog of accolades and shortcomings and realize that the Saturn is becoming quite a nice little car.

The SW2, equipped with Saturn's 124-horsepower, twin-cam four cylinder and the sharp 'sawtooth' alloy wheels, is a very attractive package. The styling is getting a tad stale, and the rear end looks kind of dumpy, but for a wagon, it's not bad. Making it nicer is an all-new interior that includes dual airbags, cupholders, big gauges and rounded contours; very modern and light-years ahead of the old Saturn's slab-sided, hard plastic dashboard.

Normally, one would not associate the concept of performance with a station wagon. The SW2 is an exception, providing more than enough power and handling ability for most families. Compared to the best-seller in the class, the Ford Escort wagon, the Saturn is a rocket.

Saturn must make the SW2 remain competitive for just one more year. A redesigned wagon is due in 1996, and is expected to feature more rounded sheetmetal everywhere but in front, where a more traditional nose will replace the current car's sloping schnozz. It's a good bet that the new interior will carry over to the new car, and Saturn will likely hold the line on pricing. Whatever the case, the SW2 is a competent compact wagon.

SATURN   SW2

Performance and Safety

Acceleration (0-60 mph) .... 8.7 sec.	ABS .... Optional	
Braking (60-0 mph) .... 130 ft.	Driver Airbag .... Standard	
Cornering .... .79 g's	Passenger Airbag .... Standard	
Fuel Capacity .... 12.8 gal.	Traction Control .... Optional	
Fuel Economy .... City: 24 mpg	Crash Test Grade .... D: N/A	P: N/A
Hwy: 34 mpg	Insurance Cost .... Average	

Edmund's Driving Impression

Competent is precisely the word that comes to mind behind the wheel of Saturn's wagon. It delivers almost precisely the same quantity of competence that's conveyed by the sleek sport coupe, and also the practical-minded sedan. These are three birds of a nearly-identical feather, equally capable on the road when carrying the 124-horsepower twin-cam engine. (Saturn's 1-series vehicles use a less hearty, single-cam four-cylinder motor.)

Wagon drivers enjoy the same "arms-out" driving position and thick-grip steering wheel as their SC2/SL2 brethren. Front seats are low, steering wheel high, helping to produce a surprisingly sporty sensation—an intimacy with the road that's not so common in small wagons.

Thigh support could be better, but back support is superb, prompting a belief that one could sit here forever. Loaded with head and leg room in front, the wagon isn't nearly as spacious for three in back—especially for the unfortunate person in the center. Head room is great, but there isn't as much space for feet.

On the road, virtually all the high points of the SC2 coupe—as well its demerits—are present in the wagon. The twin-cam engine, though quieter than before, is certainly no silent runner. Instead, it's a growler. Acceleration, while spirited, tends to produce more sound than fury.

Even in Normal mode of the two-way suspension, road bumps don't go unnoticed. That makes a person reluctant even to try the Performance setting, except in short sprints.

Since the beginning, Saturn has offered one of the slickest, easiest-shifting manual gearboxes around. Still does, but the optional four-speed automatic isn't quite so alluring. Though solid in action, reasonably smooth-shifting, it's unable to extract the most from the motor.

Saturn's wagon makes a fine choice for a suburban family—satisfying each member who insists on functionality, but wouldn't mind a touch of performance pizzazz during those daily treks to the mall.

SATURN SW2
ZZJ35	SW2 4-Dr Wagon (5-spd)		11426	12695
ZZK35	SW2 4-Dr Wagon (auto)		12164	13515
Destination Charge:	....		360	360

EDMUND'S 1995 HIGH-PERFORMANCE AUTOMOBILES

SW2 — SATURN

| CODE | DESCRIPTION | INVOICE | MSRP |

Standard Equipment

SATURN SW2: Front wheel drive, 5-speed manual transmission, 5-mph front and rear bumpers, dent-resistant exterior panels on fenders, doors, quarters and fascias, integral bodyside moldings, high gloss polyurethane clearcoat paint finish, flush tinted glass, adjustable driver and front passenger head restraints, cloth door trim panels, 60/40 fold-down rear seatbacks, fabric seats, rear seat heater ducts, reclining front seatbacks, fully trimmed trunk/cargo area, AM/FM stereo radio with seek/scan tuning and four 6" speakers, digital quartz clock, rear window defogger, 3-speed intermittent windshield wipers, headlamps-on chime, high mounted audio controls, interior storage features, passenger vanity mirror, adjustable steering column, remote fuel filler door release, independent 4-wheel suspension, power front disc/rear drum brakes, rack and pinion steering, driver-side air bag, automatic shoulder/manual lap belt system for driver and front passenger, manual lap/shoulder safety belts for rear seats, flash to pass headlamps, halogen headlamps, child security rear door locks, combined low engine oil pressure and coolant level telltale, tachometer, coolant temperature gauge, centralized electrical fuse centers, long-life engine coolant, maintenance-free suspension, maintenance-free battery, scissors jack, self-adjusting accessory drive belt, stainless steel exhaust system, steel spaceframe construction, 1.9 liter DOHC 4 cylinder PFI engine, P195/60R15 radial tires.

Accessories

Code	Description	Invoice	MSRP
—	**Pkg 1**	1625	1805
	incls air conditioning, power windows, power locks, power passenger side mirror, speed control		
—	**California Emissions**	63	70
—	**Massachusetts Emissions**	63	70
C60	**Air Conditioning**	815	905
K34	**Speed Control**	225	250
—	**Anti-Lock Brakes** — w/5-spd trans	653	725
	w/auto trans (incls traction control)	702	780
T96	**Fog Lights**	140	155
PH6	**Alloy Wheels** — "sawtooth"	275	305
—	**Leather Trim**	608	675
UM6	**Radio** — AM/FM stereo w/cassette	180	200
UU6	**Radio** — AM/FM stereo w/cassette & equalizer	329	365
U79	**Coaxial Speakers** — extended range	68	75

See Edmund's

Automobile Dealer Directory (page 388)

and the back cover of this book to enter our

$10,000 Wheel N'Deal Give-Away.

SUBARU

SVX

1995 Subaru SVX

SVX

Subaru has never been what you'd call a conventional car company. When 18-foot-long V-8-powered behemoth station wagons roamed America, Subaru was busy marketing tiny, ugly, four-wheel-drive wagons primarily to consumers in the Northeast and Northwest. While the inline four cylinder engine became the compact class standard, Subaru installed horizontally-opposed 'flat' fours in its models. All the while, Subaru retained character in the styling of its wares, bucking the jelly-bean look for a more squared-off wedge thing. The Subaru XT Coupe, about which nothing was common, became Subaru's first attempt at marketing a sports coupe. The SVX replaced that oddity in 1992.

The first thing you notice about the SVX is the out-there styling. Much more attractive than the XT Coupe, the SVX is an interesting blend of curves, bulges and angles which result in a busy, overstyled car that looks too thick in the rear. Captain Kirk likely would have found the styling pleasing, but we don't. The split side glass is a neat concept that allows you to drive with the window down in a rainstorm without worrying about getting a wet arm or mussing your hair, but we suspect that in the real world of varying-height drive-thru service windows, it doesn't work well.

Inside, the SVX looks more like a luxury coupe than a sports car. Velour covers the seats in all but the top-of-the-line LSi. The swept dash is full of oddities, such as the trick stereo cover. Comfortable chairs provide surprisingly good outward visibility, but the rear view is somewhat compromised by the big decklid spoiler.

So why should you buy this Subaru? It's speedy, comfortable and with available all-wheel drive, is one of the few sports cars made for all-weather driving. Fully loaded at just over $36,000, the SVX gives good bang for the buck, and makes a strong statement about its owner. If your wacky personality matches the offbeat SVX, you've just found the car of your dreams.

SVX — **SUBARU**

| CODE | DESCRIPTION | INVOICE | MSRP |

Performance and Safety

SVX L and LS (fwd)
Acceleration (0-60 mph) .... 7.6 sec.	ABS .... Optional		
Braking (60-0 mph) .... 122 ft.	Driver Airbag .... Standard		
Cornering .... .83 g's	Passenger Airbag .... Standard		
Fuel Capacity .... 18.5 gal.	Traction Control .... N/A		
Fuel Economy .... City: 17 mpg	Crash Test Grade .... D: N/A	P: N/A	
	Hwy: 25 mpg	Insurance Cost .... Average	

SVX L and LSi (awd)
Acceleration (0-60 mph) .... 7.6 sec.	ABS .... Standard		
Braking (60-0 mph) .... 112 ft.	Driver Airbag .... Standard		
Cornering .... .92 g's	Passenger Airbag .... Standard		
Fuel Capacity .... 18.5 gal.	Traction Control .... N/A		
Fuel Economy .... City: 17 mpg	Crash Test Grade .... D: N/A	P: N/A	
	Hwy: 25 mpg	Insurance Cost .... Average	

SVX (1994)
Code	Description	Invoice	MSRP
RKA	L 2-Dr Coupe (auto)	21405	23900
RKC	LS 2-Dr Coupe (auto)	25243	28550
RKD	LSi AWD 2-Dr Coupe (auto)	29563	33850
Destination Charge:			
	New England	475	475
	New York	499	499
	Other States	445	445

Standard Equipment

SVX L: 3.3L 6 cylinder EFI 24-valve engine, 4-speed automatic transmission, front wheel drive, automatic air conditioning, speed-sensitive power steering, power 4-wheel disc brakes, cruise control, front and rear stabilizer bars, electric rear window defroster, driver's side air bag, P225/50VR16 all-season SBR tires, aluminum alloy wheels, fog lights, digital clock, AM/FM ETR stereo radio with cassette, power antenna, power windows, center console, cloth upholstery, reclining front bucket seats with folding rear, tilt steering wheel, power door locks with central locking system, variable intermittent windshield wipers, intermittent rear window wiper/washer, dual power mirrors, dual illuminated visor vanity mirrors, remote control fuel filler door release, remote control trunk release.

LS (in addition to or instead of L equipment): Power sunroof with tilt/slide feature, tinted glass, anti-lock braking system, bodycolor rear spoiler, passenger side air bag, upgraded cloth upholstery.

LSi (in addition to or instead of LS equipment): All-wheel drive, alarm system, limited slip differential, leather upholstery, leather-wrapped steering wheel, 8-way power driver's seat, split fold-down rear seat, premium AM/FM ETR stereo radio with cassette, CD player and equalizer, carpeted floor mats, dual heated power mirrors.

EDMUND'S NEW HIGH-PERFORMANCE AUTOMOBILES

SUBARU — SVX

CODE	DESCRIPTION	INVOICE	MSRP

Accessories

The following SVX accessories are dealer-installed.

Code	Description	Invoice	MSRP
R	Alarm System — L, LS	238	365
B	Floor Mats — L, LS	48	74
LPB	Air Deflector	42	65
LV1	Engine Block Heater	39	56
ENB	CD Player — L, LS	487	649

FOR A SPECIAL RATE ON AN AUTO LOAN, CALL

1-800-AT-CHASE

CHASE AUTOMOTIVE FINANCE

SIMPLE ♦ FAST ♦ CONVENIENT

EDMUND'S NEW AUDIO TAPE!

How to Get Your Way at the Auto Dealer

You'll learn how to buy right, negotiate smart, save money, and enjoy yourself all at the same time.

see our ad on page 376 for details

CAMRY   TOYOTA

1995 Toyota Camry SE

CAMRY (V6)

When Toyota revamped the Camry sedan for 1992, the automotive press called it the best sedan available for less than $20,000, likening it to a Lexus. Partially true, since Toyota dressed up a Camry and began marketing it as the Lexus ES300 that same year. Also true, the fact that the Camry was a good car for a decent price, performing its duties so flawlessly that many auto writers found it to be distinctly lacking in character after spending more than a few minutes behind the wheel.

Well, maybe it does lack a bit of panache, but the Camry wasn't designed to entertain; it is a family sedan first and foremost, a sport sedan (in V-6 trim) second. With the optional V-6, the Camry is indeed sporty. And by opting for the full-zoot XLE trim level and optional leather interior, you get nearly all the goodies from the Lexus ES300 except the more distinctive styling and brand prestige. Still, you can't even step into a Camry V-6 without shelling out $22,000, and that's for the LE model. The XLE or SE sedan and SE coupe cost another grand or two. By the time you option one out with leather, a moonroof, anti-lock brakes, and premium stereo equipment, you're looking at 26 to 28 thou' for a mid-sized sedan.

True, you do get flawless engineering and assembly quality, outstanding reliability, and the yuppie prestige currently afforded to top-rung sedans from Japan, but for almost $30,000 we can think of several other cars we'd rather have. A BMW 318i is better equipped, sports a distinct personality, and offers an unparalleled driving experience. Ditto the Volkswagen GLX and Passat GLX. A Nissan Maxima undercuts a fully-loaded Camry as well, and for the same money, General Motors serves up supercharged versions of the much bigger Pontiac Bonneville and Oldsmobile Eighty Eight LSS.

No doubt, the Camry is a great car, but the upper-echelon V-6 models compete in a class populated by other great cars, most of which are sold in numbers low enough that you won't see yourself coming or going in every suburban neighborhood you enter. Choose carefully.

TOYOTA CAMRY

Performance and Safety

Acceleration (0-60 mph) .... 7.3 sec.	ABS .... Optional
Braking (60-0 mph) .... 126 ft.	Driver Airbag .... Standard
Cornering .... .78 g's	Passenger Airbag .... Standard
Fuel Capacity .... 18.5 gal.	Traction Control .... N/A
Fuel Economy .... City: 20 mpg	Crash Test Grade .... D: Good P: Average
Hwy: 28 mpg	Insurance Cost .... Low

1995 Toyota Camry XLE

CAMRY V6

Code	Description	Invoice	MSRP
2508	LE 2-Dr Coupe (auto)	18717	21588
2506	SE 2-Dr Coupe (auto)	20121	23208
2534	LE 4-Dr Sedan (auto)	18967	21878
2544	XLE 4-Dr Sedan (auto)	21152	24398
2546	SE 4-Dr Sedan (auto)	20372	23498
	Destination Charge (approx):	400	400

Standard Equipment

CAMRY V6: 3.0 liter V6 four-cam 24-valve EFI engine, 4-speed electronically controlled automatic overdrive transmission, power 4-wheel disc brakes, anti-lock brake system (XLE), front wheel drive, variable assist power rack and pinion steering, tinted glass, halogen headlamps with "auto-off" feature, dual color-keyed power outside mirrors (black on SE), full wheel covers (LE), aluminum alloy wheels (SE, XLE), intermittent front windshield wipers (variable intermittent on XLE), air conditioning, digital quartz clock, cruise control, dual cup holders, power door locks, gauges (speedometer, tachometer, coolant temp, fuel level, odometer, tripmeter), illuminated entry/exit system (XLE), remote hood release, remote trunk release, remote fuel filler door release, 6-way adjustable driver's seat (LE Sedan, SE Coupe), 7-way adjustable driver's seat (LE Coupe, SE Sedan), 7-way adjustable power driver's seat (XLE), fabric seat trim, dual map pockets, driver's side footrest, 60/40 split fold-down rear seat with center armrest and security lock, 4-spoke tilt steering wheel, leather-wrapped

CAMRY — TOYOTA

CODE	DESCRIPTION	INVOICE	MSRP

steering wheel, power windows, deluxe ETR AM/FM stereo radio with cassette and 4 speakers, power antenna, color-keyed rear spoiler (SE), driver and front passenger air bags, 205/65HR15 SBR BW tires (V-rated on SE).

Accessories

Code	Description	Invoice	MSRP
MG	**Black Mud Guards**	40	50
AW	**Aluminum Wheels — LE**	336	420
LS	**Leather Trim Pkg — SE Sedan**	780	975
	incls adjustable leather headrests, leather seats, leather door trim		
LP	**Leather Trim Pkg — LE Coupe**	1008	1260
	incls leather door trim, adjustable leather headrests, power driver seat, leather seats, leather-wrapped steering wheel		
LA	**Leather Trim Pkg — XLE**	1000	1250
	incls leather door trim, adjustable leather headrests, leather seats, leather-wrapped steering wheel, 4-way power passenger seat		
LA	**Leather Trim Pkg — SE Coupe**	780	975
	incls leather door trim, adjustable leather headrests, leather seats, perforated steering wheel and parking brake lever		
PE	**Power Seat Pkg — LE Coupe**	184	230
CA	**California Emissions**	NC	NC
SR	**Power Glass Moonroof — tilt/slide**	776	970
	incls map light, sunshade		
CE	**Premium AM/FM ETR Radio w/Cassette**	180	240
	incls 6 speakers, diversity reception, programmable equalization		
DC	**Premium 3-In-1 Combo Radio — LE Coupe, SE, XLE**	866	1155
	incls 6 speakers, diversity reception, programmable equalization, AM/FM ETR stereo radio w/compact disc and cassette		
AB	**Anti-Lock Brakes**	779	950
	incls rear disc brakes; std on XLE		

For expert advice in selecting/buying/leasing a new car, call
1-900-AUTOPRO
($2.00 per minute)

TOYOTA — CELICA GT

1995 Toyota Celica GT

CELICA GT

The Celica has long been ahead of its time as far as styling is concerned. Seems like you just get used to the funky looks of the latest Celica and Toyota unveils a new one to challenge your retinas. This version of the Celica, while toned down somewhat from its predecessor, is still difficult to swallow at first glance. If not for the odd headlights and oversized rear spoiler, it would be a very pretty car. But it's not.

Reminding our staffers of several species of brutal underwater fish, the front styling is just too radical. However, the interior of the Celica is quite nice, with a subdued driving environment that places all the controls in all the right places. The effect is somewhat Teutonic in nature, and is nicely complimented by snug, supportive seats.

Under the hood of the GT is a 135-horsepower 2.2-liter four cylinder that moves the Celica briskly but without fanfare. Compared to most of the competition in the sport coupe class, the Celica is woefully underpowered. But boy, it's as reliable as Grandma's pumpkin pie at Thanksgiving dinner.

A new convertible version appears for 1995, and is the most attractive Celica drop-top since 1985, despite the bulging headlights and gaping air dam. Powered by the same 2.2-liter engine as the GT but hauling around some extra weight, don't expect the Celica convertible to force you back in your seat during the on-ramp dance. And at a starting cost of $24,000, we have three words for potential drop-top buyers: Mustang GT Convertible.

The Celica is solid, reasonably sporty, and has an outstanding reliability record. We can't recommend it, though, when less-expensive and speedier cars like the Probe GT, Neon Sport Coupe and Acura Integra are available for the taking.

CELICA GT — TOYOTA

Performance and Safety

Acceleration (0-60 mph) .... 8.4 sec.	ABS .... Optional
Braking (60-0 mph) .... 127 ft.	Driver Airbag .... Standard
Cornering .... .87 g's	Passenger Airbag .... Standard
Fuel Capacity .... 15.9 gal.	Traction Control .... N/A
Fuel Economy .... City: 23 mpg	Crash Test Grade .... D: N/A P: N/A
Hwy: 30 mpg	Insurance Cost .... High

1995 Toyota Celica GT Convertible

CELICA GT

Code	Description	Invoice	MSRP
2175	GT 2-Dr Coupe (5-spd)	16722	19288
2172	GT 2-Dr Coupe (auto)	17416	20088
2183	GT 2-Dr Convertible (5-spd)	21046	23998
2184	GT 2-Dr Convertible (auto)	21740	24798
2195	GT 3-Dr Liftback (5-spd)	17147	19778
2192	GT 3-Dr Liftback (auto)	17840	20578
Destination Charge (approx):		400	400

Standard Equipment

CELICA GT: 2.2 liter 4 cylinder twin-cam 16-valve EFI engine, front wheel drive, power 4-wheel disc brakes, engine oil cooler, front and rear stabilizer bars, variable assist power rack and pinion steering, suspension (independent MacPherson strut front and dual-link independent MacPherson strut rear), 5-speed manual overdrive transmission, color-keyed bumpers and door handles, Cambria cloth power convertible top (Convertible), tinted glass, halogen headlamps with "auto-off" feature, dual color-keyed power outside mirrors, full wheel covers, intermittent rear window wiper (Liftback), variable intermittent front windshield wipers, rear cargo area cover (Liftback), full carpeting with driver side footrest, digital quartz clock, center console with cover, dual cup holder, rear window defogger with timer, power door locks, gauges (speedometer, tachometer, coolant temp and fuel level, odometer, tripmeter), overhead map lights (NA on Convertible), dual visor vanity mirrors, remote hood release,

TOYOTA — CELICA GT

remote hatch/trunk release, remote fuel filler door release, 50/50 fold-down rear seat with security lock (NA on Convertible), 4-way adjustable driver's seat, tilt steering wheel, power rear quarter windows (Convertible), power windows with driver side "auto-down" feature, power door locks, driver and front passenger air bags, 205/55R15 all-season tires.

Accessories

Code	Description	Invoice	MSRP
AB	Anti-Lock Brake System	676	825
AC	Air Conditioning	780	975
AW	Aluminum Wheels	336	420
	incls 205/55R15 all-season tires		
CA	California Emissions	130	153
CL	Cruise Control	212	265
LA	Leather Pkg — Coupe & Convertible	836	1045
	incls leather trimmed seats/door trim, leather-wrapped steering wheel, 5M shift knob		
SL	Leather Sport Pkg — Liftback	1252	1565
	incls leather sport seats, leather steering wheel/shift knob, front sport suspension, aluminum wheels, 205/55R15 summer tires		
SX	Fabric Sport Pkg — Liftback	724	905
	incls fabric sport seats, leather steering wheel/shift knob, front sport suspension, aluminum wheels, 205/55R15 summer tires		
RF	Rear Spoiler — Liftback	300	375
SR	Power Moonroof — Coupe & Liftback	592	740
CE	Radio — Coupe & Liftback	149	200
	Convertible	112	150
	incls premium AM/FM radio with cassette, 6 speakers, programmable equalization, power antenna and diversity antenna		
DC	Radio — Coupe & Liftback	941	1255
	Convertible	904	1205
	incls premium 3-in-1 combo (ETR/cassette/CD player), programmable equalization, power antenna, diversity reception and 8 speakers		

See Edmund's

Automobile Dealer Directory (page 388)

and the back cover of this book to enter our

$10,000 Wheel N'Deal Give-Away.

MR2 — TOYOTA

1995 Toyota MR2 Turbo

MR2

What a dilemma. Consumer Reports gives the Toyota MR2 a recommended rating and predicts that reliability of the mid-engined sports car will be excellent. Our local Toyota technicians have told us on more than one occasion that the MR2 sure looks good, but isn't worth the money underneath the skin, citing chronic oil leak problems with the car. Who's right? Hard to call, but it illustrates that any car-buying advice you receive should be tempered with common sense and a solid understanding of what you need and want in a car.

We like the MR2, despite what the guys at the Toyota dealer tell us. We like it because it's unique, and is committed to the idea of traveling as quickly as possible with few extra people and little baggage. In short, it's a driver's car. Its svelte, sexy looks don't hurt either.

Toyota is going to cancel the MR2 soon. The car barely made it into the 1994 model year, and surprised us when our Toyota press kit revealed that it would be available in 1995. Fewer than 1500 MR2s are expected to find owners in 1994, and the number will likely be lower during the coming year.

Available in turbo and non-turbo form, the MR2 is an entertaining drive. Roadholding grip is outstanding, and straight-line acceleration with the turbo is quite brisk. Prices for the base MR2 start near the $23,000 mark—not bad for a reliable sports car with the styling of a Ferrari and the exclusivity of an exotic. If a new MR2 is what you've been waiting to buy, don't wait much longer.

TOYOTA MR2

Performance and Safety

MR2
Acceleration (0-60 mph)	8.5 sec.	ABS	Optional	
Braking (60-0 mph)	136 ft.	Driver Airbag	Standard	
Cornering	.93 g's	Passenger Airbag	Standard	
Fuel Capacity	14.3 gal.	Traction Control	N/A	
Fuel Economy	City: 21 mpg	Crash Test Grade	D: N/A	P: N/A
	Hwy: 30 mpg	Insurance Cost	Very High	

MR2 Turbo
Acceleration (0-60 mph)	6.2 sec.	ABS	Optional	
Braking (60-0 mph)	107 ft.	Driver Airbag	Standard	
Cornering	.94 g's	Passenger Airbag	Standard	
Fuel Capacity	14.3 gal.	Traction Control	N/A	
Fuel Economy	City: 20 mpg	Crash Test Grade	D: N/A	P: N/A
	Hwy: 27 mpg	Insurance Cost	Very High	

1995 Toyota MR2 Turbo

MR2

CODE	DESCRIPTION	INVOICE	MSRP
3088	Base 2-Dr Coupe (5-spd)	20313	23568
3087	Base 2-Dr Coupe (auto)	21002	24368
3098	Base 2-Dr Coupe w/T-Bar Roof (5-spd)	21821	25318
3085	Turbo 2-Dr Coupe w/T-Bar Roof (5-spd)	24708	28668
	Destination Charge:	397	397

MR2 — TOYOTA

Standard Equipment

MR2 - BASE: 2.2 liter 4 cylinder EFI 16-valve engine, front and rear color-keyed bumpers, 5-speed manual transmission, color-keyed front and rear spoilers, power 4-wheel disc brakes, black cloth interior, four-way adjustable sport seats, front and rear stabilizer bars, tinted glass, manual steering, door map pockets, tilt steering column, SBR BW tires (front - 195/55R15, rear - 225/50R15), locking glove box, assist grip, dome/map light, digital clock, driver and passenger side air bags, 6 x 15 inch aluminum alloy wheels (front), 7 x 15 inch aluminum alloy wheels (rear), 140-mph speedometer, tachometer, odometer, resettable tripmeter, fuel level gauge, coolant temperature gauge, voltmeter, bodyside and rocker panel moldings, dual color-keyed power mirrors, full carpeting, lockable right rear storage, electric rear window defroster, AM/FM ETR stereo radio with cassette and 6 speakers, manually operated antenna, air conditioning, remote decklid release, remote fuel filler door release, intermittent wipers, T-Bar roof with dual removable tinted glass panels (T-Bar), power windows (T-Bar), power door locks (T-Bar), illuminated entry/exit fade-out system (T-Bar), leather-wrapped steering wheel (T-Bar).

TURBO (in addition to or instead of BASE equipment): Turbocharged 2.0 liter 16-valve EFI 4 cylinder engine with intercooler, front air dam, retractable halogen headlamps, fog lights, 7-way adjustable driver's seat, passenger side seatback map pocket, cruise control, variable intermittent wipers, 3-compartment center console storage box, door courtesy lights, premium AM/FM ETR stereo radio with cassette, programmable equalization, 8 speakers, power antenna and diversity reception; leather-wrapped steering wheel, manual shift knob and parking brake handle; turbo boost gauge (replaces voltmeter), power windows, power door locks, illuminated entry/exit.

Accessories

Code	Description	Invoice	MSRP
AB	**Anti-Lock Brakes**	779	950
PS	**Power Steering**	590	690
CA	**California Emissions** — Base	130	153
CL	**Cruise Control** — Base	228	285
	incls intermittent windshield wipers		
SR	**Sunroof** — NA on models w/T-Bar roof	320	400
PN	**Anti-Theft System**	160	200
LD	**Limited Slip Differential** — Turbo	368	460
PO	**Power Pkg** — Base	444	555
	incls power door locks and power windows; std on T-Bar models		
CE	**Radio** — Base w/o T-Bar roof	330	440
	Base w/T-Bar roof	255	330
	incls premium AM/FM ETR radio w/cassette, 8 speakers and power antenna w/diversity reception		
DC	**Radio** — Base w/o T-Bar roof	1016	1355
	Base w/T-Bar roof	941	1255
	Turbo	686	915
	incls premium AM/FM ETR radio w/cassette, CD player, 8 speakers and power antenna w/diversity reception		
LA	**Leather Pkg** — Base w/T-Bar roof	964	1205
	Turbo	648	810

EDMUND'S 1995 HIGH-PERFORMANCE AUTOMOBILES

TOYOTA *SUPRA*

1995 Toyota Supra

SUPRA

Looking like some kind of hybrid between an F-16, a Honda Prelude and a Ferrari F40, the wide-eyed Supra arrived late in 1993 to do battle with everything from Nissan 300ZXs to Lexus SC coupes. The wild exterior cloaks an austere but inviting cabin where the first order of business is driving. Under the hood, your choice of two inline six cylinder engines: a twin-cammer good for 220 horsepower or a twin-turbo version of the same that ups output by 100 horsepower.

The automotive press has absolutely gushed about the Supra driving experience. No doubt, this is a serious driving machine. However, we've noticed that Toyota has been having trouble lately creating attractive sporting cars. The Celica is quite a good looking sportster, until the bulging 'eyes' up front seemingly follow your every move as you round the hood. The image is one of a shark ready to strike, and you find yourself wishing you had a spear to jab into one of the headlights. The Supra is also a beautiful work of art, but the hyena-like front styling is disconcerting. The Supra has a wild-eyed look, and the huge air intake below the bumper needs only a row of white teeth to guarantee that small children will never pass within twenty feet of the front end. The rear, with its rows of science-project taillights, massive rear fascia, and obnoxious wing, is just too much. Why Toyota tacked these front and rear aberrations onto an otherwise restrained and wonderfully styled body is a mystery.

As usual, though, we have a theory. In the United States, the Supra's main market, there really aren't any public roads (save for some desolate desert highway) to use the Supra to its full potential. The stylists wanted the Supra to be noticed. They wanted it to sell. So they gave it 'Look at me!' styling to generate as much of a commotion at a supermarket parking lot as it would at 120 on Interstate 10. It works.

SUPRA — TOYOTA

Performance and Safety

Supra

Acceleration (0-60 mph) .... 6.2 sec.	ABS .... Standard
Braking (60-0 mph) .... 112 ft.	Driver Airbag .... Standard
Cornering .... .88 g's	Passenger Airbag .... Standard
Fuel Capacity .... 18.5 gal.	Traction Control .... N/A
Fuel Economy .... City: 19 mpg	Crash Test Grade .... D: N/A P: N/A
Hwy: 24 mpg	Insurance Cost .... Average

Supra Turbo

Acceleration (0-60 mph) .... 5.1 sec.	ABS .... Standard
Braking (60-0 mph) .... 112 ft.	Driver Airbag .... Standard
Cornering .... .97 g's	Passenger Airbag .... Standard
Fuel Capacity .... 18.5 gal.	Traction Control .... N/A
Fuel Economy .... City: 18 mpg	Crash Test Grade .... D: N/A P: N/A
Hwy: 24 mpg	Insurance Cost .... Average

Edmund's Driving Impression

Slipping inside a Supra, it's hard to escape the sensation that you're entering an aircraft cockpit, about to face a demanding racetrack trial—and wondering if you've really prepared. Dead ahead await an 8000-rpm tach and 180-mph speedometer, joined by an abundant congregation of pushbuttons. (Full gauges aren't included: just fuel and temperature.)

Fire up the inline six-cylinder engine and the first satisfying sounds arrive. Snick the stubby but easy-to-move gearshift lever into notch Number One, ease out the heavy clutch, and the sensations escalate.

Easing through the first curve, you become suddenly aware of this Toyota's superlative handling expertise. Few cars can whip around corners nearly as adeptly.

No, the 220-horsepower normally-aspirated engine doesn't deliver the kind of acceleration that brings rocket-launchers and projectiles to mind. It's fast, but not blistering. If you absolutely must possess the max, look into the turbocharged Supra instead, with its full hundred extra horses. But you'll pay plenty more to knock a second off the 0-60 acceleration time. And a "basic" Supra is hardly a low-budget machine, either.

Instead of the slick-action five-speed installed on the regular Supra, the Turbo gets a six-speed. But no one need feel deprived for lack of a Turbo beneath his or her Supra's bonnet. Oh yes, you can request automatic instead, but it's likely to disappoint in comparison.

Controls and instruments are angled toward the driver—even the stubby gearshift lever, which moves with a positive motion between ratios. Front-seat occupants have lots of space, but forget the rear, where legroom approaches zero. Seats are stiff, their bottoms far from soft. You have to peer through a tall rear wing, through a low back window, to see what's in back of a Supra, but good mirrors help.

If your wallet is thick enough, in either form you get a 2+2 true sports car that's a joy to handle, a pleasure to drive, a delight to occupy.

TOYOTA SUPRA

CODE	DESCRIPTION	INVOICE	MSRP

SUPRA
2398	Base 2-Dr Liftback (5-spd)	30863	36900
2396	Base 2-Dr Liftback (auto)	31615	37800
2393	Base 2-Dr Liftback w/Sport Roof (5-spd)	31783	38000
2394	Base 2-Dr Liftback w/Sport Roof (auto)	32535	38900
2381	Turbo 2-Dr Liftback (6-spd)	38976	46600
2383	Turbo 2-Dr Liftback w/Sport Roof (6-spd)	39979	47800
2387	Turbo 2-Dr Liftback w/Sport Roof (auto)	38976	46600
	Destination Charge (approx):	400	400

Standard Equipment

SUPRA - BASE: Tachometer, front and rear stabilizer bars, aluminum alloy wheels, tinted glass, power door locks, power windows, driver and front passenger airbags, cargo area cover, front spoiler, cold kit, digital clock, front fog lights, digital trip odometer, diagnostic master warning lights, premium AM/FM ETR stereo w/cassette/6 speakers/theft deterrent system, power antenna w/diversity reception, front and rear color-keyed bumpers, leather-wrapped steering wheel, cruise control, tilt steering column, illuminated entry system w/automatic fade-out, halogen retractable headlights w/automatic-off system, dual color-keyed heated power mirrors, right visor vanity mirror, 3-way adjustable sport seats w/power slide and recline, driver's seat height adjustment, 2-way manual adjustable passenger seat, fold-down rear seat, automatic air conditioning, speed-sensitive power steering, anti-lock power 4-wheel disc brakes, heavy-duty electric rear window defroster w/timer, remote hatch release, variable intermittent wipers, 3.0L 6 cylinder EFI DOHC 24-valve engine, 5-speed manual transmission, rear window intermittent wipers, remote fuel-filler door release, 225/50ZR16 SBR high-performance front tires, 245/50ZR16 SBR high-performance rear tires, full cut-pile carpeting (including cargo area), lights include door/luggage area/glove box/ignition, cloth upholstery.

TURBO (in addition to or instead of BASE equipment): Engine oil cooler, sport-tuned suspension, Torsen limited slip differential, 235/45ZR17 SBR high-performance front tires, 255/40ZR17 SBR high-performance rear tires, 3.0L 6 cylinder EFI 24-valve twin turbocharged engine w/intercooler, traction control system w/indicator light, 6-speed manual transmission.

Accessories

LD	**Limited Slip Differential — Base**	368	460
LA	**Leather Trim Pkg**	880	1100
	incls leather trimmed armrests and seats		
DC	**Premium Radio — 3-in-1 combo**	739	985
	incls AM/FM ETR stereo radio w/cassette, programmable equalization and logic control, compact disc, power antenna w/diversity system, 7 speakers (includes subwoofer)		
P3	**CD Player**	455	650
	NA w/DC premium radio		
P5	**CD Player**	325	464
	NA w/DC premium radio		
CF	**Floor Mats — front and rear**	31	78
MG	**Mud Guards**	59	99
RK	**Alarm Enhancement System**	310	695
WL	**Alloy Wheel Locks**	30	50
FE	**50-State Emissions — Turbo**	NC	NC
CA	**California Emissions — Base**	130	153
RF	**Rear Spoiler**	336	420

GTI — VOLKSWAGEN

1995 Volkswagen GTI VR6

GTI VR6

In 1983, the Volkswagen GTI, a hopped-up version of the Rabbit, really brought focus on the 'pocket-rocket' class. Also known as 'nickel-missiles' for their inexpensive prices, these were generally sporty versions of pedestrian hatchbacks like the Ford Escort, Mercury Lynx and Chevrolet Citation, consisting primarily of appearance groups that included suspension revisions that made them go around corners better. The GTI was different. It wasn't so much blacked-out trim and alloy wheels but serious mechanical hardware and German road feel that made it such a hit and redefined the genre, inspiring such cars as the Dodge Omni GLH and Honda Civic Si.

The 'pocket-rocket' class has been replaced by more expensive sport coupes like the Ford Probe, Honda Prelude, and Toyota Celica—cars that have been designed specifically for the market. A few models remain faithful to the original formula of the hot-rodded econocar, such as the Ford Escort GT and Honda Civic Si, but most have retired or gone on to bigger and better things. The GTI straddles the line here, remaining a souped-up version of the workaday Golf III, but costing enough that the term 'nickel-missile' no longer applies.

At $20,000 or so, the GTI admittedly provides a lot of car for the money. It comes with just about every feature you want, and some you don't, like multi-colored upholstery and daytime running lights. It performs well, carries four people with ease, or two and enough luggage to lap America without stopping at a laundromat. Unfortunately, the Golf's basic styling remains intact on the GTI. While the GTI looks better than the Golf, it is faint praise indeed. Fortunately, however, the Golf's basic interior styling remains intact in the GTI, as do its fine road manners. This is a car that will get you speeding tickets.

Overall, the GTI is a mixed bag. It feels good, performs well, and offers more utility than most cars in this class can. We really like the GTI, but its price tag makes us want to shop around. Or try the Golf Sport, which offers much of the GTI's feel and amenities for thousands less but with a distinct drop in acceleration times.

VOLKSWAGEN *GTI*

| CODE | DESCRIPTION | INVOICE | MSRP |

Performance and Safety

Acceleration (0-60 mph) .... 6.7 sec.		ABS .... Standard	
Braking (60-0 mph) .... 120 ft.		Driver Airbag .... Standard	
Cornering .... .78 g's		Passenger Airbag .... Standard	
Fuel Capacity .... 14.5 gal.		Traction Control .... Standard	
Fuel Economy .... City: 18 mpg		Crash Test Grade .... D: N/A P: N/A	
	Hwy: 25 mpg	Insurance Cost .... N/A	

GTI VR6
1H16T4 2-Dr Coupe (5-spd)	17458	18875
Destination Charge:	390	390

Standard Equipment

GTI VR6: 2.8 liter V6 engine, 5-speed manual transmission, power 4-wheel disc brakes with anti-lock braking system, power windows with express-down feature, air conditioning, driver and front passenger air bags, alarm system, front wheel drive, traction control system, power steering, leather-wrapped tilt steering wheel, center console with storage, cruise control, tinted glass, tachometer, trip computer, trip odometer, P205/50HR15 SBR high performance all-season tires, fog lights, front and rear spoilers, front and rear stabilizer bars, sport suspension, digital clock, rear window defroster, premium AM/FM stereo radio with cassette, cloth heated reclining sport bucket sets, 60/40 split fold-down rear seat, 60 amp battery, 120 amp alternator, alloy wheels, power door locks with central locking system, power trunk release, dual horns, power tilt/slide glass sunroof, variable intermittent windshield wipers, rear window wiper/washer, cloth and leatherette door trim, color-keyed bodyside moldings, black rocker panels, dual power heated mirrors, illuminated RH visor vanity mirror, courtesy lights, map pockets.

Accessories

B0W	California Emissions System		NC	NC
B55	Massachusetts Emissions System		NC	NC
—	Clearcoat Metallic Paint		153	175
CDC	Compact Disc Changer		412	495

For a guaranteed low price on a new vehicle in your area, call

1-800-CAR-CLUB

340   **EDMUND'S 1995 HIGH-PERFORMANCE AUTOMOBILES**

JETTA GLX   VOLKSWAGEN

1995 Volkswagen Jetta III GLX

JETTA III GLX

Volkswagen's sedan version of the Golf, the Jetta, has always been one of our favorite sedans. Like most cars conceived in Germany, the Jetta has an uncanny ability to keep the driver in touch with every undulation and irregularity in the road without sacrificing comfort. It has a cavernous interior, logically laid-out controls and displays, and zippy performance. For 1995, Volkswagen has taken the driving experience up a few notches with the introduction of the Jetta GLX.

The GLX is powered by the same 2.8-liter narrow-angle V-6 that worked magic in the now defunct Corrado, the Passat, and now the brand new GTI. Soon, the entire Volkswagen lineup will have this engine under the hood of one or more models: the wimpy Eurovan gets the much-needed power infusion for 1996. But we digress.

The GLX is one of the most fun cars you can buy with four doors. Everything feels good, from the seats to the steering to the modulation of the clutch. One caveat; the shifter is rubbery and somewhat vague. Otherwise, the Jetta GLX is driving bliss.

Wouldn't know this car was so fun by looking at it. The only signs that the GLX is more than your average family sedan are the large front airdam, BBS-style wheels, and small decklid spoiler. Taurus drivers will get the message, though, when reading the GLX badge as you zoom by on the way to pick up Junior from soccer practice.

Reliability has been a problem with Volkswagens in the past. However, a new 10 year/100,000 mile warranty backs up the powertrain, and free roadside assistance is provided for the first two years of ownership.

Not that you couldn't afford to fix it once in a while. The GLX, loaded up with leather, sunroof, CD player, a fun-robbing automatic transmission and standard anti-lock brakes and traction control, doesn't crack the $23,000 barrier. Prices like these make this speedy Jetta competitive with the Dodge Intrepid ES, Toyota Camry, and Honda Accord. Sign us up.

EDMUND'S 1995 HIGH-PERFORMANCE AUTOMOBILES

VOLKSWAGEN — JETTA GLX

CODE	DESCRIPTION	INVOICE	MSRP

Performance and Safety

Acceleration (0-60 mph)	6.9 sec.	ABS	Standard
Braking (60-0 mph)	134 ft.	Driver Airbag	Standard
Cornering	.78 g's	Passenger Airbag	Standard
Fuel Capacity	14.5 gal.	Traction Control	Standard
Fuel Economy	City: 18 mpg	Crash Test Grade	D: N/A P: N/A
	Hwy: 25 mpg	Insurance Cost	N/A

1995 Volkswagen Jetta III GLX

JETTA III GLX

1H27T4 4-Dr Sedan (5-spd)	18441	19975
Destination Charge:	390	390

Standard Equipment

JETTA III GLX: 2.8 liter V6 SMFI engine, 5-speed close-ratio manual transmission, power rack and pinion steering, sport tuned suspension (including rear gas shocks), high performance power assisted 4-wheel disc brakes (front vented) with anti-lock braking system, traction control system, cruise control, CFC-free air conditioning, anti-theft vehicle alarm system with warning LED, front illuminated ashtray, electric rear window defroster, molded door trim with cloth/leatherette inserts, assist handles, coat hooks, instrumentation (incls speedometer, odometer, trip odometer, tachometer, fuel and temp gauges, digital clock), trip information computer, brake wear indicator, courtesy lights, rear reading lights, luggage compartment light, child safety rear door locks, power locking system, power trunk/fuel filler release, driver and passenger illuminated vanity mirrors, premium AM/FM cassette stereo radio with theft deterrent warning light and coding system, driver and passenger air bags, fully reclining heatable front sport seats with adjustable headrests, front seat storage trays, 60/40 split/fold rear seat, rear seat headrests (2), folding rear center armrest, leather-covered steering wheel with height adjustable steering column, front door storage pockets with rubber liners, rear door storage pockets, front seatback magazine/storage pockets, center console (incls 2 front and 1 rear beverage holders), illuminated front ashtray, leather manual trans shift knob/boot and hand brake

JETTA GLX / PASSAT GLX — VOLKSWAGEN

cover, fully lined trunk/cargo area, "Future" woven cloth seat fabric, power windows with one-touch feature, black roof-mounted antenna, 5-mph body color bumpers with black lower section, tinted glass, dual horns, front and rear daytime running lights, rectangular Eurostyle halogen headlamps, front fog lamps, defoggable power remote OS mirrors, body color side molding, black rocker panel covering, power glass tilt and slide sunroof with sunshade, black front chin spoiler, body color rear wing spoiler, space saver spare tire, 15" "BBS" lattice design without center cap alloy wheels, 205/50R15H all-season tires, 2-speed intermittent windshield wipers.

Accessories

Code	Description	Invoice	MSRP
—	Automatic Transmission — 4-speed	856	875
—	Leather Seat Trim	698	800
—	Clearcoat Metallic Paint	153	175
CDC	Compact Disc Changer	412	495
B0W	California Emissions	NC	NC
B55	Massachusetts Emissions	NC	NC

1995 Volkswagen Passat GLX Sedan

PASSAT GLX

The Passat has never sold well in the United States. Weak engines plagued the early editions, ineffective marketing has played a role, and a muddled brand identity that has defeated sales across the board have all contributed to this car's seemingly invisible presence on the sedan market. Of course, its plain-vanilla styling didn't let the Passat stand out for much recognition other than the lack of a grille on the nose.

Volkswagen has been trying to change things lately, and the Passat has received a good bit of attention. The 2.8-liter V-6 that has literally transformed Volkswagen's lineup from staid German sedans to road cars brimming with vitality is now standard on the Passat. Also new is a revised exterior design that gives this Volkswagen a much more modern, mainstream look. Passats now

VOLKSWAGEN
PASSAT GLX

come fully loaded in one trim level—the only options are an automatic transmission, a sunroof and a CD player. The warranty has been stretched to 10 years or 100,000 miles, and safety equipment like traction control and anti-lock brakes come as part of the package.

So what do you think a fully-loaded German sport sedan (or wagon) might cost? The base price of a new Passat is roughly equivalent to the price of a well-equipped Taurus GL. Surprise, surprise. We think you ought to try the Passat whether or not performance is important to you. It's a good car at a fire-sale price, with the ability to put a grin on your face every time you drive it.

Performance and Safety

Acceleration (0-60 mph) .... 8.5 sec.	ABS .... Standard
Braking (60-0 mph) .... 127 ft.	Driver Airbag .... Standard
Cornering .... .82 g's	Passenger Airbag .... Standard
Fuel Capacity .... 18.5 gal.	Traction Control .... Standard
Fuel Economy .... City: 18 mpg	Crash Test Grade .... D: N/A P: N/A
Hwy: 25 mpg	Insurance Cost .... N/A

PASSAT GLX

Code	Description	Invoice	MSRP
3A26Q5	4-Dr Sedan (5-spd)	18801	20890
3A56Q5	4-Dr Wagon (5-spd)	19185	21320
	Destination Charge:	390	390

Standard Equipment

PASSAT GLX: 2.8 liter V6 engine, 5-speed manual transmission, power 4-wheel disc brakes with ABS, power steering, air-conditioning, cruise control, front wheel drive, power windows with express-down feature, electric rear window defroster, dual air bags, power windows, central locking system, alloy wheels, P215/50HR15 performance all-season tires, tachometer, front and rear stabilizer bars, anti-theft alarm system, traction control, trip odometer, fog lights, bodyside moldings, luggage rack (Wagon), rear spoiler (Sedan), dual heated power OS mirrors, dual illuminated visor vanity mirrors, cloth reclining bucket seats, 60/40 split fold-down rear seat, leather-wrapped tilt steering wheel, intermittent rear window, wiper/washer (Wagon), premium AM/FM stereo radio w/ cassette and 8 speakers, map pockets, center console, rear seat center armrest, power trunk release (Sedan), cargo area cover (Wagon).

Accessories

—	**Automatic Transmission — 4-speed**		777	800
—	**Leather Trim**		742	850
CDC	**CD Changer — Sedan**		412	495
—	**Clearcoat Metallic Paint**		NC	NC
PW1	**All-Weather Pkg**		262	300
	incls heated front seats and windshield washer nozzles			
—	**California/Massachusetts Emissions System**		NC	NC

850 TURBO

1995 Volvo 850 Turbo

850 TURBO

Volvos can be counted upon to provide several things to drivers. A safety-engineered cabin comfortable for four large adults. Excellent heating systems that often include the front occupants' comfortable seats. A solidly-constructed vehicle that is designed to operate for longer than the the term of the purchaser's loan. Boxy styling. At times, performance is also associated with Volvo, but not since the 240 Turbos of the early-eighties has Volvo emphasized the performance capabilities of one of its vehicles as much as the 850.

Both sedan and station wagon are screamers. Powered by a turbocharged 2.3-liter four that pumps out 222 horsepower, the 850 Turbo Wagon is the most fun you'll have playing taxi for Junior and his pals. The sedan will whisk you and three clients to dinner in class and style, not to mention safety. The 1995 850 is the first production car to employ side airbags to protect occupants in the event that they are T-boned on their way to eat a T-bone.

The exterior design is traditionally Volvo, but with slightly rounded edges, like the corners in a Southwestern-style tract home. Inside, the Volvo resembles those that came before it, with high chair-like seating and a chunky but well laid-out dashboard. The one styling element of the 850 that disturbs us is the taillight design on the 850 Wagon. Long, thin, multi-colored lens assemblies are affixed to the tailgate pillars like those on GM's questionably-styled APV vans. They look too gimmicky for this otherwise attractively restrained exterior shape.

All this good stuff comes at a price. The 850 is smaller that the Volvo 940/960 range of cars. It's also pricier. While the 940 Turbo sedan and wagon may not perform as well as the 850 Turbo, and they don't offer such things as side airbags or the availability of traction control, they may be the better buy. The price difference between a base 940 Turbo Wagon and a base 850 Turbo Wagon leaves about $6,500 in change in the pocket of the 940 owner. Plus he gets more room. Decide carefully.

VOLVO 850 TURBO

Performance and Safety

Acceleration (0-60 mph) .... 7.0 sec.	ABS .... Standard
Braking (60-0 mph) .... 128 ft.	Driver Airbag .... Standard
Cornering .... .80 g's	Passenger Airbag .... Standard
Fuel Capacity .... 19.3 gal.	Traction Control .... Optional
Fuel Economy .... City: 19 mpg	Crash Test Grade .... D: Excellent P: Good
Hwy: 26 mpg	Insurance Cost .... Average

1995 Volvo 850 Turbo Wagon

850 TURBO SEDAN / WAGON

854T	4-Dr Sedan (auto)	28095	30045
855T	5-Dr Wagon (auto)	29395	32345
Destination Charge:		460	460

Standard Equipment

850 TURBO SEDAN/WAGON: Inline 2.3 liter 5 cylinder 20-valve turbocharged engine with intercooler, 4-speed automatic transmission, power-assisted rack and pinion steering, power 4-wheel disc brakes with anti-lock, drover and front passenger side air bags, side impact air bag protection sytem, 3-point seat belts and head restraints, child-proof rear door locks, CFC-free air conditioning system, electronic climate control, daytime running light system, rear fog light, integral child booster cushion (Wagon), cruise control, remote keyless entry/security system, power glass sunroof w/tilt and slide, power windows with driver's auto-down feature, central locking system, heated power outside mirrors, radio (AM/FM stereo full logic cassette, 4x25 watt amp. w/CD compatibility and anti-theft, 8 speakers), power antenna (Sedan), integrated side window antenna (Wagon), leather steering wheel w/tilt telescope steering column, front reclining bucket seats, tilt and fold front passenger seat, 8-way power adjustable driver's seat w/3-position memory, split leather upholstery, trip computer, sold or metallic paint, front suspension (MacPherson hydraulic struts w/asymmetrically mounted coil springs

850 TURBO — VOLVO

and 20mm stabilizer bar), rear suspension (Volvo patented Delta-link, semi-independent suspension with coil springs, gas charged shock absorbers and 19.5mm stabilizer bar (Sedan)), 6.5" x 16" 5-spoke swept design alloy wheels, 205/50 16" ZR MXM Michelin tires.

Accessories

Code	Description	Invoice	MSRP
—	**Rear Spoiler - Sedan**	260	325
—	**Traction Control System**	305	385
—	**Sport Suspension**	120	150
	incls extra firm shock absorbers and stabilizer bar		
—	**Burled Walnut Instrument Panel Trim**	480	600
—	**Power Seat**	395	495
	8-way adjustable w/3-position memory		
—	**Cold Weather Pkg**	360	450
	incls traction control system, heated seats, ambient temp. gauge, headlamp wiper/washer		
—	**Alloy Wheels — alloy**	NC	NC
—	**Traction Control/Cold Weather Pkg**	600	750

FOR A SPECIAL RATE ON AN AUTO LOAN, CALL

1-800-AT-CHASE

CHASE AUTOMOTIVE FINANCE

SIMPLE ♦ FAST ♦ CONVENIENT

GET MORE MONEY FOR YOUR USED CAR BY KNOWING ITS TRUE VALUE

See our ads on pages 4 and 6

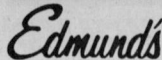# STEP-BY-STEP COSTING FORM

MAKE: EXTERIOR COLOR:
MODEL: INTERIOR COLOR:
BODY STYLE: ENGINE SIZE/TYPE:

ITEMS	MSRP	INVOICE	BEST DEAL
Basic Model Price Only			
Optional Equipment/Accessories			
1.			
2.			
3.			
4.			
5.			
6.			
7.			
8.			
9.			
10.			
11.			
12.			
13.			
14.			
TOTAL			
ADD Destination Charge			
ADD Preparation Charge			
ADD Dealer Charges ("Extras")			
ADD Advertising Fee			
ADD Dealer Profit			
SUBTRACT Rebate Amount			
SUBTRACT "Trade-In" Amount or ADD "Trade-In" Deficit			
FINAL PRICE			
ADD Sales Taxes and Fees			
TOTAL COST			

EDMUND'S 1995 HIGH-PERFORMANCE AUTOMOBILES

Specifications and EPA Mileage Ratings
1995 High-Performance Automobiles

Contents

350	Acura	361	Mazda
351	Alfa Romeo	361	Mercedes-Benz
351	Audi	363	Mercury
352	BMW	363	Mitsubishi
353	Buick	364	Nissan
353	Cadillac	365	Oldsmobile
354	Chevrolet	366	Plymouth
355	Chrysler	366	Pontiac
355	Dodge	367	Porsche
356	Eagle	368	Saab
356	Ford	369	Saturn
358	Honda	369	Subaru
358	Infiniti	370	Toyota
359	Jaguar	371	Volkswagen
360	Lexus	372	Volvo
360	Lincoln		

Specifications EPA Mileage Ratings

ACURA

	Integra GS-R Sdn	Integra GS-R Cpe	Integra LS Cpe	Integra LS Sdn	Integra RS Cpe	Integra RS Sdn	Integra Spec Edit Cpe	Integra Spec Edit Sdn	Legend GS Sdn
Length (in.)	178	172	172	178	172	178	172	178	195
Width (in.)	67.3	67.3	67.3	67.3	67.3	67.3	67.3	67.3	71.3
Height (in.)	53.9	52.6	52.6	53.9	52.6	53.9	52.6	53.9	55.1
Curb Weight (lbs.)	2765	2667	2643	2703	2529	2628	2529	2628	3571
Wheelbase (in.)	103	101	101	103	101	103	101	103	115
Front Track (in.)	58.1	58.1	58.1	58.1	58.1	58.1	58.1	58.1	61
Rear Track (in.)	57.8	57.8	57.8	57.8	57.8	57.8	57.8	57.8	60.6
Front Head Room (in.)	38.9	38.6	38.6	38.9	38.6	38.9	38.6	38.9	38.5
Rear Head Room (in.)	36	35	35	36	35	36	35	36	36.5
Front Shoulder Room (in.)	52	51.7	51.7	52	51.7	52	51.7	52	56.3
Rear Shoulder Room (in.)	50.3	48.8	48.8	50.3	48.8	50.3	48.8	50.3	56.4
Front Hip Room (in.)	50.7	50.3	50.3	50.7	50.3	50.7	50.3	50.7	53.6
Rear Hip Room (in.)	49.9	44.1	41	49.9	44.1	49.9	44.1	49.9	56
Front Leg Room (in.)	42.2	42.7	42.7	42.2	42.7	42.2	42.7	42.2	42.7
Rear Leg Room (in.)	32.7	28.1	28.1	32.7	28.1	32.7	28.1	32.7	33.5
Luggage Capacity (cu ft.)	11	13.3	13.3	11	13.3	11	13.3	11	14.8
Number of Cylinders	4	4	4	4	4	4	4	4	6
Displacement (liters)	1.8	1.8	1.8	1.8	1.8	1.8	1.8	1.8	3.2
Fuel System	PGMFI	PGMFI	PGMFI	PGMFI	PGMFI	PGMFI	PGMFI	PGMFI	PGMFI
Compression Ratio	10:1	10:1	9.2:1	9.2:1	9.2:1	9.2:1	9.2:1	9.2:1	9.6:1
Horsepower @ RPM	170@7600	170@7600	142@6300	142@6300	142@6300	142@6300	142@6300	142@6300	230@6200
Torque @ RPM	128@6200	128@6200	127@5200	127@5200	127@5200	127@5200	127@5200	127@5200	206@5000
Fuel Capacity	13.2	13.2	13.2	13.2	13.2	13.2	13.2	13.2	18
EPA City (mpg) - manual	25	25	25	25	25	25	25	25	18
EPA Hwy (mpg) - manual	31	31	31	31	31	31	31	31	26
EPA City (mpg) - auto	N/A	N/A	24	24	24	24	24	24	18
EPA Hwy (mpg) - auto	N/A	N/A	31	31	31	31	31	31	23

Specifications EPA Mileage Ratings

	ACURA Legend L Cpe	ACURA Legend LS Cpe	ACURA NSX Cpe	ALFA ROMEO 164 LS Sport Sdn	ALFA ROMEO 164 Q Sport Sdn	AUDI 90 Sdn	AUDI 90 Quattro Sdn
Length (in.)	193	193	174	184	180	180	180
Width (in.)	71.3	71.3	71.3	69.3	69.3	66.7	66.7
Height (in.)	53.7	53.7	46.1	54.7	54.7	54.3	54.7
Curb Weight (lbs.)	3516	3516	3020	3413	3406	3197	3296
Wheelbase (in.)	111	111	99.6	105	105	103	102
Front Track (in.)	61	61	59.4	59.6	59.6	57.2	57
Rear Track (in.)	60.6	60.6	60.2	58.6	58.6	57.9	58.1
Front Head Room (in.)	37.3	37.3	36.3	38.2	38.2	37.8	37.8
Rear Head Room (in.)	35.9	35.9	N/A	36.6	36.6	37.2	37.2
Front Shoulder Room (in.)	56.3	56.3	52.5	56.4	56.4	53.3	53.3
Rear Shoulder Room (in.)	54.9	54.9	N/A	56.6	56.6	52.6	52.6
Front Hip Room (in.)	53.5	53.5	53.8	57.5	57.5	N/A	N/A
Rear Hip Room (in.)	50.1	50.1	N/A	57.5	57.5	N/A	N/A
Front Leg Room (in.)	42.9	42.9	44.3	39.3	39.3	42.2	42.2
Rear Leg Room (in.)	28.7	28.7	N/A	33.9	33.9	32.5	32.5
Luggage Capacity (cu ft.)	14.1	14.1	5	17.8	17.8	14	14
Number of Cylinders	6	6	6	6	6	6	6
Displacement (liters)	3.2	3.2	3.0	3.0	3.0	2.8	2.8
Fuel System	PGMFI	PGMFI	FI	MPFI	MPFI	SMPFI	SMPFI
Compression Ratio	9.6:1	9.6:1	10.2:1	10:1	10:1	10:1	10:1
Horsepower @ RPM	230@6200	230@6200	270@7100	210@6300	230@6300	172@5500	172@5500
Torque @ RPM	206@5000	206@5000	210@5300	198@5000	202@5000	184@3000	184@3000
Fuel Capacity	18	18	18.5	17.2	17.2	17.4	16.9
EPA City (mpg) - manual	18	18	19	17	17	20	19
EPA Hwy (mpg) - manual	26	26	24	24	24	26	26
EPA City (mpg) - auto	18	18	18	15	N/A	18	18
EPA Hwy (mpg) - auto	23	23	23	22	N/A	26	26

Specifications EPA Mileage Ratings

	AUDI S6 Sdn	AUDI Sport 90 Sdn	AUDI Sport Quattro 90 Sdn	BMW 325i Sdn	BMW 325iC Conv	BMW 325is Cpe	BMW 530i Sdn	BMW 540i Sdn
Length (in.)	193	180	180	175	175	175	186	186
Width (in.)	71	66.7	66.7	66.8	67.3	67.3	68.9	68.9
Height (in.)	56.5	54.3	54.7	54.8	53.1	53.8	55.6	55
Curb Weight (lbs.)	3825	3197	3296	3087	3352	3087	3627	3693
Wheelbase (in.)	106	103	102	106	106	106	109	109
Front Track (in.)	61.5	57.2	57	55.4	55.4	55.4	57.9	57.9
Rear Track (in.)	60.1	57.9	58.1	55.9	55.9	55.9	58.9	58.9
Front Head Room (in.)	38.3	37.8	37.8	37.1	38.1	36.7	36.9	36.9
Rear Head Room (in.)	37.6	37.2	37.2	36.7	36.3	35.9	36.4	36.4
Front Shoulder Room (in.)	56.5	53.3	53.3	53.5	53.2	53.2	54.3	54.3
Rear Shoulder Room (in.)	56.2	52.6	52.6	53.3	43.6	52.1	55.2	55.2
Front Hip Room (in.)	N/A	N/A	N/A	N/A	N/A	N/A	N/A	N/A
Rear Hip Room (in.)	N/A	N/A	N/A	N/A	N/A	N/A	N/A	N/A
Front Leg Room (in.)	42.4	42.2	42.2	41.1	41.2	41.2	41.6	41.6
Rear Leg Room (in.)	34.8	32.5	32.5	34	28.1	32.7	37	37
Luggage Capacity (cu ft.)	16.4	14	14	10.3	8.9	9.2	13	13
Number of Cylinders	5	6	6	6	6	6	8	8
Displacement (liters)	2.2	2.8	2.8	2.5	2.5	2.5	3.0	4.0
Fuel System	SFI	SMPFI	SMPFI	EFI	EFI	EFI	EFI	EFI
Compression Ratio	9.3:1	10:1	10:1	10.5:1	10.5:1	10.5:1	10.5:1	10:1
Horsepower @ RPM	227@5900	172@5500	172@5500	189@5900	189@5900	189@5900	215@5800	282@5800
Torque @ RPM	258@1950	184@3000	184@3000	181@4200	181@4200	181@4200	214@4500	295@4500
Fuel Capacity	21.1	17.4	16.9	17.2	17.2	17.2	21.1	21.1
EPA City (mpg) - manual	18	20	19	19	19	19	16	14
EPA Hwy (mpg) - manual	23	26	24	28	28	28	24	23
EPA City (mpg) - auto	N/A	18	18	20	20	20	17	17
EPA Hwy (mpg) - auto	26	26	26	28	28	28	26	25

Specifications EPA Mileage Ratings

	BMW 840Ci Cpe	BMW 850CSi Cpe	BMW M3 Cpe	BUICK Park Avenue Ultra Sdn	BUICK Riviera Cpe	CADILLAC Eldorado Touring Cpe	CADILLAC Seville Touring Sdn
Length (in.)	188	188	175	206	207	202	204
Width (in.)	73	73	67.3	74.1	75	75.5	74.2
Height (in.)	52.8	52.8	52.6	55.1	55.2	53.6	54.5
Curb Weight (lbs.)	4167	4234	3180	3642	3748	3818	3892
Wheelbase (in.)	106	106	106	111	114	108	111
Front Track (in.)	61.2	61.2	56	60.4	62.5	60.9	60.9
Rear Track (in.)	61.5	61.5	56.9	60.6	62.6	60.9	60.9
Front Head Room (in.)	35.9	35.9	38.1	38.9	38.2	37.8	38
Rear Head Room (in.)	34.7	34.7	36.3	37.9	36.2	38.3	38.3
Front Shoulder Room (in.)	57.3	57.3	53.2	58.7	57.9	58.2	58.9
Rear Shoulder Room (in.)	55.3	55.3	52.1	58.9	57.9	57.6	57.5
Front Hip Room (in.)	N/A	N/A	N/A	55.1	53.7	57.6	55
Rear Hip Room (in.)	N/A	N/A	N/A	54.2	52.8	55.7	57.6
Front Leg Room (in.)	44	44	41.2	42.7	42.6	42.6	43
Rear Leg Room (in.)	26	26	32.7	40.7	37.3	36.1	39.1
Luggage Capacity (cu ft.)	9.5	9.5	9.2	20.3	17.4	15.3	14.4
Number of Cylinders	8	12	6	6	6	8	8
Displacement (liters)	4.0	5.6	3.0	3.8	3.8	4.6	4.6
Fuel System	EFI	EFI	EFI	SPFI	SPFI	TPI	TPI
Compression Ratio	10:1	9.8:1	10.5:1	8.5:1	9.4:1	10.3:1	10.3:1
Horsepower @ RPM	282@5800	372@5300	240@6000	225@5000	205@5200	300@6000	300@6000
Torque @ RPM	295@4500	402@4000	225@4250	275@3200	230@4000	295@4400	295@4400
Fuel Capacity	23.8	23.8	17.2	18	20	20	20
EPA City (mpg) - manual	N/A	N/A	19	N/A	N/A	N/A	N/A
EPA Hwy (mpg) - manual	N/A	N/A	27	N/A	N/A	N/A	N/A
EPA City (mpg) - auto	16	17	N/A	N/A	19	16	16
EPA Hwy (mpg) - auto	24	N/A	N/A	27	29	25	25

Specifications EPA Mileage Ratings

CHEVROLET

	Camaro Z28 Conv	Camaro Z28 Cpe	Caprice 5.7L Sdn	Corvette Conv	Corvette Cpe	Corvette ZR-1 Cpe	Impala SS Sdn	Lumina LS 3.4L Sdn	Monte Carlo Z34 Cpe
Length (in.)	193	193	214	179	179	179	214	201	201
Width (in.)	74.1	74.1	77.5	70.7	70.7	73.1	77.5	72.5	72.5
Height (in.)	52	51.3	55.7	47.3	46.3	46.3	54.7	55.2	53.8
Curb Weight (lbs.)	3480	3390	4061	3360	3203	3512	4036	3372	3436
Wheelbase (in.)	101	101	116	96.2	96.2	962	116	108	108
Front Track (in.)	60.7	60.7	61.8	57.7	57.7	57.7	62.3	59.1	59.5
Rear Track (in.)	60.6	60.6	62.3	59.1	59.1	60.6	62.7	59	59
Front Head Room (in.)	38	37.2	39.2	37	36.5	36.5	39.2	38.4	37.9
Rear Head Room (in.)	39	35.3	37.9	N/A	N/A	N/A	37.9	37.4	36.9
Front Shoulder Room (in.)	57.4	57.4	63.4	53.9	53.9	53.9	63.4	58.4	57.5
Rear Shoulder Room (in.)	43.5	55.8	63.4	N/A	N/A	N/A	63.4	57.4	57.6
Front Hip Room (in.)	52.8	52.8	57	43.9	49.3	49.3	57	55.4	53.4
Rear Hip Room (in.)	43.7	44.4	56.9	N/A	N/A	N/A	56.9	55.3	51.6
Front Leg Room (in.)	43	43	42.2	42	42	42	42.2	42.4	42.4
Rear Leg Room (in.)	26.8	26.8	39.5	N/A	N/A	N/A	39.5	36.6	34.9
Luggage Capacity (cu ft.)	7.6	12.9	20.4	6.6	12.6	12.6	204	15.7	15.7
Number of Cylinders	8	8	8	8	8	8	8	6	6
Displacement (liters)	5.7	5.7	5.7	5.7	5.7	5.7	5.7	3.4	3.4
Fuel System	SFI	SFI	SFI	SFI	SFI	SFI	SFI	SFI	SFI
Compression Ratio	10.5:1	10.5:1	10:1	10.5:1	10.5:1	11:1	10.5:1	9.3:1	9.3:1
Horsepower @ RPM	275@5000	275@5000	260@4800	300@5000	300@5000	405@5800	260@4800	210@5200	210@5200
Torque @ RPM	325@2000	325@2000	330@3200	340@4000	340@4000	385@5200	330@3200	215@4000	215@4000
Fuel Capacity	15.5	15.5	21	20	20	20	23	17.1	17.1
EPA City (mpg) - manual	17	17	N/A	17	17	17	N/A	N/A	N/A
EPA Hwy (mpg) - manual	26	26	N/A	27	27	25	N/A	N/A	N/A
EPA City (mpg) - auto	17	17	17	17	17	N/A	17	17	17
EPA Hwy (mpg) - auto	24	24	25	24	24	N/A	25	26	26

Specifications EPA Mileage Ratings

	CHRYSLER Concorde 3.5L Sdn	CHRYSLER LHS Sdn	DODGE Intrepid 3.5L ES Sdn	DODGE Neon Highline 2.0L SOHC Cpe	DODGE Neon Highline 2.0L SOHC Sdn	DODGE Neon Sport 2.0L DOHC Cpe	DODGE Neon Sport 2.0L SOHC Sdn	DODGE Stealth R/T Cpe
Length (in.)	202	207	202	172	172	172	172	180
Width (in.)	74.4	74.5	74.4	67.2	67.4	67.2	67.4	72.4
Height (in.)	56.3	55.9	56.3	52.8	54.8	52.8	54.8	49.1
Curb Weight (lbs.)	3376	3628	3372	2384	2320	2485	2320	3164
Wheelbase (in.)	113	113	113	104	104	104	104	97.2
Front Track (in.)	62	62	62	57.4	57.4	57.4	57.4	61.4
Rear Track (in.)	62	62	62	57.4	57.4	57.4	57.4	62.2
Front Head Room (in.)	38.4	36.9	38.4	39.6	39.6	39.6	39.6	37.1
Rear Head Room (in.)	37.5	36.7	37.5	36.5	36.5	36.5	36.5	34.1
Front Shoulder Room (in.)	59	58.8	59	52	52.5	52	52.5	55.9
Rear Shoulder Room (in.)	59	58.2	58.3	54.7	52.3	54.7	52.3	52
Front Hip Room (in.)	56.4	56.4	56.3	50.3	50.8	50.3	50.8	56.7
Rear Hip Room (in.)	60.9	61.1	60.9	53.9	50.6	53.9	50.6	46.9
Front Leg Room (in.)	42.4	42.4	42.4	42.5	42.5	42.5	42.5	44.2
Rear Leg Room (in.)	38.8	41.7	38.8	35.1	33.9	35.1	33.9	28.5
Luggage Capacity (cu ft.)	16.6	17.9	16.7	11.8	11.8	11.8	11.8	11.1
Number of Cylinders	6	6	6	4	4	4	4	6
Displacement (liters)	3.5	3.5	3.5	2.0	2.0	2.0	2.0	3.0
Fuel System	SMPI	SMPI	SMPI	SMPI	SMPI	SMPI	SMPI	SMPI
Compression Ratio	9.6:1	9.6:1	9.6:1	9.8:1	9.8:1	9.8:1	9.8:1	10:1
Horsepower @ RPM	214@5850	214@5850	214@5850	132@6000	132@6000	150@6800	132@6000	222@6000
Torque @ RPM	221@3100	221@3100	221@3100	129@5000	129@5000	131@5600	129@5000	205@4500
Fuel Capacity	18	18	18	11.2	11.2	11.2	11.2	19.8
EPA City (mpg) - manual	N/A	N/A	N/A	29	29	29	29	19
EPA Hwy (mpg) - manual	N/A	N/A	N/A	38	38	38	38	28
EPA City (mpg) - auto	18	18	18	27	27	27	27	18
EPA Hwy (mpg) - auto	26	26	26	33	33	33	33	24

Specifications EPA Mileage Ratings

	DODGE Stealth R/T Turbo Cpe	DODGE Viper Roadster	EAGLE Summit 1.8L ESi Cpe	EAGLE Talon TSi Hbk	EAGLE Talon TSi AWD Hbk	EAGLE Vision TSi Sdn	FORD Contour SE Sdn
Length (in.)	180	175	171	172	172	202	184
Width (in.)	72.4	75.7	66.1	68.7	68.7	74.4	69.1
Height (in.)	49.3	43.9	51.4	51.6	51.6	56.3	54.5
Curb Weight (lbs.)	3792	3487	2085	2866	3119	3507	2769
Wheelbase (in.)	97.2	96.2	96.1	98.8	98.8	113	107
Front Track (in.)	61.4	59.6	57.1	59.7	59.7	62	59.2
Rear Track (in.)	62.2	60.6	57.5	59.4	59.4	62	58.5
Front Head Room (in.)	37.1	N/A	38.6	37.9	37.9	38.4	39
Rear Head Room (in.)	34.1	N/A	36.4	34.1	34.1	37.5	36.7
Front Shoulder Room (in.)	55.9	53.8	53.9	53.1	53.1	59	53.9
Rear Shoulder Room (in.)	52	N/A	54.1	51.2	51.2	59	53.3
Front Hip Room (in.)	56.7	N/A	54.9	55.1	55.1	56.3	50.7
Rear Hip Room (in.)	46.9	N/A	53.7	47.2	47.2	60.9	45.5
Front Leg Room (in.)	44.2	42.6	42.9	43.3	43.3	42.4	42.4
Rear Leg Room (in.)	28.5	N/A	31.1	28.4	28.4	38.8	34.3
Luggage Capacity (cu ft.)	11.1	11.8	10.5	16.6	13.5	16.6	13.9
Number of Cylinders	6	10	4	4	4	6	6
Displacement (liters)	3.0	8.0	1.8	2.0	2.0	3.5	2.5
Fuel System	SMPI	MPI	SMPI	SMPI	SMPI	SMPI	SEFI
Compression Ratio	8:1	9.1:1	9.5:1	8.5:1	8.5:1	9.6:1	9.7:1
Horsepower @ RPM	320@6000	400@4600	113@6000	210@6000	210@6000	214@5850	170@6200
Torque @ RPM	315@2500	465@3600	116@4500	214@3000	214@3000	221@3100	165@4200
Fuel Capacity	19.8	22	13.2	15.8	15.8	18	14.5
EPA City (mpg) - manual	18	14	26	22	21	N/A	21
EPA Hwy (mpg) - manual	24	22	33	31	27	N/A	29
EPA City (mpg) - auto	N/A	N/A	N/A	N/A	N/A	18	22
EPA Hwy (mpg) - auto	N/A	N/A	33	N/A	N/A	26	30

Specifications EPA Mileage Ratings — FORD

	Escort GT 3Dr Hbk	Mustang GT Conv	Mustang GT Cpe	Probe GT 3Dr Hbk	Taurus SHO 5Spd Sdn	Taurus SHO Auto Sdn	Thunderbird Super Cpe	Thunderbird V8 LX Cpe
Length (in.)	170	182	182	180	192	192	200	200
Width (in.)	66.7	71.8	71.8	69.8	71.2	71.2	72.7	72.7
Height (in.)	52.5	53.3	53.4	51.6	54.1	54.1	53	52.5
Curb Weight (lbs.)	2459	3451	3280	2921	3118	3118	3536	3536
Wheelbase (in.)	98.4	101	101	103	106	106	113	113
Front Track (in.)	56.5	60.1	60.1	59.4	61.6	61.6	61.6	61.6
Rear Track (in.)	56.5	58.7	58.7	59.4	60.5	60.5	60.2	60.2
Front Head Room (in.)	37.4	38.1	38.2	37.8	38.3	38.3	38.1	38.1
Rear Head Room (in.)	38.6	35.7	35.9	34.8	37.6	37.6	37.5	37.5
Front Shoulder Room (in.)	53	53.6	53.6	52	57.5	57.5	59.1	59.1
Rear Shoulder Room (in.)	52.6	41.2	52.1	53.9	57.6	57.6	58.9	58.9
Front Hip Room (in.)	51.3	52.4	52.4	53.9	55.2	55.2	55.6	55.6
Rear Hip Room (in.)	46.7	41.1	48.8	48.6	54.8	54.8	56.6	56.6
Front Leg Room (in.)	41.7	42.5	42.5	43.1	41.7	41.7	42.5	42.5
Rear Leg Room (in.)	34.6	30.3	30.3	28.5	37.7	37.7	35.8	35.8
Luggage Capacity (cu ft.)	17.3	8.5	10.9	18	18	18	15.1	15.1
Number of Cylinders	4	8	8	6	6	6	6	8
Displacement (liters)	1.8	5.0	5.0	2.5	3.0	3.2	3.8	4.6
Fuel System	EFI	SEFI	SEFI	SEFI	SEFI	SEFI	SEFI	SEFI
Compression Ratio	9:1	9:1	9:1	9.2:1	9.8:1	9.8:1	8.5:1	9:1
Horsepower @ RPM	127@6500	215@4200	215@4200	164@5600	220@6200	220@6000	230@4400	205@4500
Torque @ RPM	114@4500	285@3400	285@3400	160@4000	200@4800	215@4800	330@2500	265@3200
Fuel Capacity	13.2	15.4	15.4	15.5	18.4	18.4	18	18
EPA City (mpg) - manual	25	17	17	21	18	N/A	18	N/A
EPA Hwy (mpg) - manual	31	25	25	26	26	N/A	24	N/A
EPA City (mpg) - auto	23	17	17	20	N/A	18	18	17
EPA Hwy (mpg) - auto	29	24	24	26	N/A	26	26	25

Specifications EPA Mileage Ratings

HONDA

	Accord EX Cpe	Accord EX Sdn	Civic EX Cpe	Civic del Sol VTEC Targa	Prelude Si VTEC Cpe	Prelude VTEC Cpe
Length (in.)	184	184	173	157	175	175
Width (in.)	70.1	70.1	66.9	66.7	69.5	69.5
Height (in.)	54.7	55.1	50.9	49.4	50.8	50.8
Curb Weight (lbs.)	2954	3009	2443	2522	2866	2932
Wheelbase (in.)	107	107	103	93.3	100	100
Front Track (in.)	59.6	59.6	58.1	58.1	60	60
Rear Track (in.)	59.1	59.1	57.7	57.7	59.6	59.6
Front Head Room (in.)	38.4	38.4	38	37.5	38	38
Rear Head Room (in.)	36.2	36.7	35.1	N/A	35.1	35.1
Front Shoulder Room (in.)	56	55.7	53.4	52.9	54	54
Rear Shoulder Room (in.)	53.5	54.3	52.1	N/A	50.6	50.6
Front Hip Room (in.)	51.6	52.6	49.8	49.3	52.2	52.2
Rear Hip Room (in.)	47.6	51.4	45.7	N/A	41.4	41.4
Front Leg Room (in.)	42.9	42.7	42.5	40.3	44.2	44.2
Rear Leg Room (in.)	31.3	34.3	29.3	N/A	28.1	28.1
Luggage Capacity (cu ft.)	13	13	11.8	10.5	7.9	7.9
Number of Cylinders	4	4	4	4	4	4
Displacement (liters)	2.2	2.2	1.5	1.6	2.3	2.2
Fuel System	PGMFI	PGMFI	PGMFI	PGMFI	PGMFI	PGMFI
Compression Ratio	8.8:1	8.8:1	9.2:1	10.2:1	9.8:1	10:1
Horsepower @ RPM	145@5500	145@5500	125@6600	160@7600	160@5800	190@6800
Torque @ RPM	147@4500	147@4500	106@5200	111@7000	156@4500	158@5500
Fuel Capacity	17	17	11.9	11.9	15.9	15.9
EPA City (mpg) - manual	25	25	29	26	22	22
EPA Hwy (mpg) - manual	31	31	35	30	26	26
EPA City (mpg) - auto	23	23	29	N/A	22	N/A
EPA Hwy (mpg) - auto	30	30	34	N/A	27	N/A

INFINITI

	G20t Sdn	J30 Sdn
Length (in.)	175	191
Width (in.)	66.7	69.7
Height (in.)	54.7	54.7
Curb Weight (lbs.)	2954	3527
Wheelbase (in.)	100	109
Front Track (in.)	57.9	59.1
Rear Track (in.)	57.5	59.1
Front Head Room (in.)	38.8	37.7
Rear Head Room (in.)	37.3	36.7
Front Shoulder Room (in.)	54.2	55.9
Rear Shoulder Room (in.)	54.2	56.5
Front Hip Room (in.)	52.1	54.1
Rear Hip Room (in.)	54.2	54.1
Front Leg Room (in.)	42	41.3
Rear Leg Room (in.)	33.2	30.5
Luggage Capacity (cu ft.)	14.2	10.1
Number of Cylinders	4	6
Displacement (liters)	2.0	3.0
Fuel System	SMPFI	SPFI
Compression Ratio	9.5:1	10.5:1
Horsepower @ RPM	140@6400	210@6400
Torque @ RPM	132@4800	193@4800
Fuel Capacity	15.9	19
EPA City (mpg) - manual	24	N/A
EPA Hwy (mpg) - manual	32	N/A
EPA City (mpg) - auto	22	18
EPA Hwy (mpg) - auto	28	23

Specifications EPA Mileage Ratings

	INFINITI Q45t Sdn	JAGUAR Vanden Plas Sdn	XJ12 Sdn	XJ6 Sdn	XJR Sdn	XJS 4.0 Conv	XJS 4.0 Cpe	XJS 6.0 Conv
Length (in.)	200	198	198	198	198	191	191	191
Width (in.)	71.9	81.7	81.7	81.7	81.7	74.1	74.1	74.1
Height (in.)	56.3	70.8	53.1	70.8	70.8	48.7	48.7	48.7
Curb Weight (lbs.)	4045	4105	4420	4080	4215	4022	3805	4306
Wheelbase (in.)	113	113	113	113	114	102	102	102
Front Track (in.)	61.8	59.1	59.1	59.1	59.1	58.6	58.6	58.6
Rear Track (in.)	62	59	59	59	59	59.2	59.2	59.2
Front Head Room (in.)	38.2	37.2	37.2	37.2	37.2	35.7	36.1	35.7
Rear Head Room (in.)	36.3	N/A	N/A	N/A	N/A	N/A	N/A	N/A
Front Shoulder Room (in.)	58.3	57.3	57.3	57.3	57.3	56.1	56.1	56.1
Rear Shoulder Room (in.)	57.5	N/A	N/A	N/A	N/A	N/A	N/A	N/A
Front Hip Room (in.)	55.2	N/A	N/A	N/A	N/A	N/A	N/A	N/A
Rear Hip Room (in.)	56.4	N/A	N/A	N/A	N/A	N/A	N/A	N/A
Front Leg Room (in.)	43.9	41.2	41.2	41.2	41.2	43	43	43
Rear Leg Room (in.)	32	N/A	N/A	N/A	N/A	N/A	N/A	N/A
Luggage Capacity (cu ft.)	14.8	12	12	11.1	11.1	9.4	9.4	10.6
Number of Cylinders	8	6	12	6	6	6	6	12
Displacement (liters)	4.5	4.0	6.0	4.0	4.0	4.0	4.0	6.0
Fuel System	SMPFI	EFI	EFI	EFI	EFI	EFI	EFI	EFI
Compression Ratio	10.2:1	10:1	11:1	10:1	8.5:1	10:1	10:1	11:1
Horsepower @ RPM	278@6000	245@4700	313@5350	245@4700	322@5000	237@4700	237@4700	301@5400
Torque @ RPM	292@4000	289@4000	353@3750	289@4000	378@3050	282@4000	282@4000	351@2800
Fuel Capacity	22.5	23.1	23.1	23.1	23.1	20.7	24	20.7
EPA City (mpg) - manual	N/A	N/A	N/A	N/A	N/A	N/A	N/A	N/A
EPA Hwy (mpg) - manual	N/A	N/A	N/A	N/A	N/A	N/A	N/A	N/A
EPA City (mpg) - auto	17	17	12	17	15	17	17	12
EPA Hwy (mpg) - auto	22	23	16	23	21	24	24	16

Specifications / EPA Mileage Ratings

	JAGUAR XJS 6.0 Cpe	LEXUS ES 300 Sdn	LEXUS GS 300 Sdn	LEXUS LS 400 Sdn	LEXUS SC 300 Cpe	LEXUS SC 400 Cpe	LINCOLN Mark VIII Cpe
Length (in.)	191	188	195	197	191	191	207
Width (in.)	74.1	70	70.7	72	70.5	70.5	74.8
Height (in.)	48.7	53.9	55.1	55.7	52.6	52.6	53.6
Curb Weight (lbs.)	4053	3374	3660	3650	3506	3625	3768
Wheelbase (in.)	102	103	109	112	106	106	113
Front Track (in.)	58.6	61	60.6	62	59.8	59.8	61.6
Rear Track (in.)	59.2	59.1	60.2	62	59.8	60	60.2
Front Head Room (in.)	36.1	37.8	38.3	38.9	38.3	38.3	38.1
Rear Head Room (in.)	N/A	36.6	36.8	36.9	36.1	36.1	37.5
Front Shoulder Room (in.)	56.1	56.1	57.3	57.9	56	56	58.9
Rear Shoulder Room (in.)	N/A	55.1	57.3	57.1	52.7	52.7	59.5
Front Hip Room (in.)	N/A	N/A	N/A	N/A	55.1	55.1	56.7
Rear Hip Room (in.)	N/A	N/A	N/A	N/A	39.2	39.2	56.7
Front Leg Room (in.)	43	43.5	44	43.7	44.1	44.1	42.6
Rear Leg Room (in.)	N/A	33.1	33.8	36.9	27.2	27.2	32.5
Luggage Capacity (cu ft.)	9.4	14.3	13	13.9	9.3	9.3	14.4
Number of Cylinders	12	6	6	8	6	8	8
Displacement (liters)	6.0	3.0	3.0	4.0	3.0	4.0	4.6
Fuel System	EFI	SMPFI	MPFI	SMPFI	MPFI	MPFI	SEFI
Compression Ratio	11:1	10.5:1	10:1	10.4:1	10:1	10:1	9.8:1
Horsepower @ RPM	301@5400	188@5200	220@5800	260@5300	225@6000	250@5600	280@5500
Torque @ RPM	351@2800	203@4400	210@4800	270@4500	210@4800	260@4400	285@4500
Fuel Capacity	24	18.5	21.1	22.5	20.6	20.6	18
EPA City (mpg) - manual	N/A	N/A	N/A	N/A	18	N/A	N/A
EPA Hwy (mpg) - manual	N/A	N/A	N/A	N/A	23	N/A	N/A
EPA City (mpg) - auto	12	20	18	19	17	18	18
EPA Hwy (mpg) - auto	17	28	23	25	23	23	25

360

Specifications EPA Mileage Ratings

MAZDA

	626 ES Sdn	Miata Conv	Millenia S Sdn	MX-6 LS Cpe	RX-7 Cpe
Length (in.)	184	155	190	182	169
Width (in.)	68.9	65.9	69.7	68.9	68.9
Height (in.)	55.1	48.2	54.9	51.6	48.4
Curb Weight (lbs.)	2906	2293	3391	2800	2826
Wheelbase (in.)	103	89.2	108	103	95.5
Front Track (in.)	59.1	55.5	59.8	59.1	57.5
Rear Track (in.)	59.1	56.2	59.8	59.1	57.5
Front Head Room (in.)	39.2	37.1	37.3	38.1	37.6
Rear Head Room (in.)	37.8	N/A	37	34.7	N/A
Front Shoulder Room (in.)	55.1	50.4	55.1	53.5	51.8
Rear Shoulder Room (in.)	54.7	N/A	54.2	50.9	N/A
Front Hip Room (in.)	N/A	51.7	N/A	N/A	N/A
Rear Hip Room (in.)	N/A	N/A	N/A	N/A	N/A
Front Leg Room (in.)	43.5	42.7	43.3	44	44.1
Rear Leg Room (in.)	35.8	N/A	34.1	27.7	N/A
Luggage Capacity (cu ft.)	13.8	3.6	13.3	12.4	17
Number of Cylinders	6	4	6	4	RTRY
Displacement (liters)	2.5	1.8	2.3	2.5	1.3
Fuel System	MPFI	MPFI	MPFI	MPFI	EFI
Compression Ratio	9.2:1	9:1	10:1	9.2:1	9:1
Horsepower @ RPM	164@5600	128@6500	210@5300	164@5600	255@6500
Torque @ RPM	160@4800	110@5000	210@3500	160@4800	217@5000
Fuel Capacity	15.5	12.7	18	15.5	20
EPA City (mpg) - manual	21	23	N/A	21	17
EPA Hwy (mpg) - manual	26	29	N/A	26	25
EPA City (mpg) - auto	20	22	20	20	18
EPA Hwy (mpg) - auto	26	28	28	26	24

MERCEDES-BENZ

	C220 Sdn	C280 Sdn	E320 Cabriolet
Length (in.)	177	177	184
Width (in.)	67.7	67.7	68.5
Height (in.)	56.1	56.1	54.8
Curb Weight (lbs.)	3150	3350	4025
Wheelbase (in.)	106	106	107
Front Track (in.)	58.8	58.8	59.1
Rear Track (in.)	57.6	57.6	58.7
Front Head Room (in.)	37.2	37.2	37.6
Rear Head Room (in.)	37	37	35.5
Front Shoulder Room (in.)	54.6	54.6	55.7
Rear Shoulder Room (in.)	53.9	53.9	48.7
Front Hip Room (in.)	52.8	52.8	56.8
Rear Hip Room (in.)	53.9	53.9	51
Front Leg Room (in.)	41.5	41.5	41.9
Rear Leg Room (in.)	32.8	32.8	24.8
Luggage Capacity (cu ft.)	11.6	11.6	8.1
Number of Cylinders	4	6	6
Displacement (liters)	2.2	2.8	3.2
Fuel System	SMPFI	SMPFI	SMPFI
Compression Ratio	9.8:1	10:1	10:1
Horsepower @ RPM	148@5500	194@5500	217@5500
Torque @ RPM	155@4000	199@3750	229@3750
Fuel Capacity	16.4	16.4	18.5
EPA City (mpg) - manual	N/A	N/A	N/A
EPA Hwy (mpg) - manual	N/A	N/A	N/A
EPA City (mpg) - auto	23	20	18
EPA Hwy (mpg) - auto	28	26	23

MERCEDES-BENZ

Specifications EPA Mileage Ratings

	E320 Cpe	E320 Sdn	E420 Sdn	S600 Cpe	S600 Sdn	SL320 Conv	SL500 Conv	SL600 Conv
Length (in.)	184	187	187	199	205	176	176	178
Width (in.)	68.5	68.5	68.5	74.6	74.3	71.3	71.3	71.3
Height (in.)	54.9	56.3	56.3	56.7	58.3	51.3	51.3	51.3
Curb Weight (lbs.)	3525	3525	3745	4960	5030	4090	4165	4455
Wheelbase (in.)	107	110	110	116	124	99	99	99
Front Track (in.)	59.1	59.1	59.1	63.2	63.2	60.4	60.4	60.4
Rear Track (in.)	58.7	58.7	58.7	62.2	62.2	60	60	60
Front Head Room (in.)	36	36.9	36.9	36.5	38	37.1	37.1	37.1
Rear Head Room (in.)	36.8	36.9	36.9	37.2	38.5	N/A	N/A	N/A
Front Shoulder Room (in.)	55.7	55.9	55.9	61.7	61.7	55.4	55.4	55.4
Rear Shoulder Room (in.)	50.5	55.7	55.7	56.5	61.4	N/A	N/A	N/A
Front Hip Room (in.)	53.4	53	53	56.7	58	53.2	53.2	53.2
Rear Hip Room (in.)	52.4	55.4	54	53.1	57.6	N/A	N/A	N/A
Front Leg Room (in.)	41.9	41.7	41.7	41.7	41.3	42.4	42.4	42.4
Rear Leg Room (in.)	29.6	33.5	33.5	31.5	39.6	N/A	N/A	N/A
Luggage Capacity (cu ft.)	14.4	14.6	14.6	14.2	15.6	7.9	7.9	7.9
Number of Cylinders	6	6	8	12	12	4	8	12
Displacement (liters)	3.2	3.2	4.2	6.0	6.0	3.2	5.0	6.0
Fuel System	SMPFI	SMPFI	SMPFI	SMPFI	SMPFI	SMPFI	SMPFI	SMPFI
Compression Ratio	10:1	10:1	11:1	10:1	10:1	10:1	10:1	10:1
Horsepower @ RPM	217@5500	217@5500	275@5700	389@5200	389@5200	229@5600	315@5600	389@5200
Torque @ RPM	229@3750	229@3750	295@3900	420@3800	420@3800	232@3750	345@3900	420@3800
Fuel Capacity	18.5	18.5	18.5	26.4	26.4	21.3	21.3	21.3
EPA City (mpg) - manual	N/A	N/A	N/A	N/A	N/A	N/A	N/A	N/A
EPA Hwy (mpg) - manual	N/A	N/A	N/A	N/A	N/A	N/A	N/A	N/A
EPA City (mpg) - auto	20	20	18	13	13	17	16	13
EPA Hwy (mpg) - auto	26	26	24	17	16	24	20	17

Specifications EPA Mileage Ratings

	MERCURY Cougar XR7 Cpe	MERCURY Mystique V6 LS Sdn	MITSUBISHI 3000GT SL Cpe	MITSUBISHI 3000GT VR-4 Cpe	MITSUBISHI Eclipse GS Cpe	MITSUBISHI Eclipse GS-T Cpe	MITSUBISHI Eclipse GSX Cpe	MITSUBISHI Mirage LS Cpe
Length (in.)	200	184	180	180	172	172	172	171
Width (in.)	72.7	69.1	72.4	72.4	68.3	68.7	68.7	66.5
Height (in.)	52.5	54.5	49	49.3	49.8	51	51.6	51.6
Curb Weight (lbs.)	3533	2824	3351	3781	2822	2877	3120	2125
Wheelbase (in.)	113	107	97.2	97.2	98.8	98.8	98.8	96.1
Front Track (in.)	61.6	59.2	61.4	61.4	59.6	59.6	59.6	57.1
Rear Track (in.)	60.2	58.5	62.2	62.2	59.4	59.4	59.4	57.5
Front Head Room (in.)	38.1	39	37.1	37.1	37.9	37.9	37.9	38.6
Rear Head Room (in.)	37.6	36.7	34.1	34.1	34.1	34.1	34.1	36.4
Front Shoulder Room (in.)	59.1	53.9	55.9	55.9	53.1	53.1	53.1	53.9
Rear Shoulder Room (in.)	58.9	53.3	52	52	51.2	51.2	51.2	54.1
Front Hip Room (in.)	55.6	50.7	56.7	56.7	51	55.1	55.1	52.7
Rear Hip Room (in.)	56.6	45.5	46.9	46.9	47.2	47.2	47.2	53.7
Front Leg Room (in.)	42.5	42.4	44.2	44.2	43.3	43.3	43.3	42.9
Rear Leg Room (in.)	36.5	34.3	28.5	28.5	28.4	28.4	28.4	31.1
Luggage Capacity (cu ft.)	15.1	13.9	11.1	11.1	16.6	16.6	13.5	10.5
Number of Cylinders	8	6	6	6	4	4	4	4
Displacement (liters)	4.6	2.5	3.0	3.0	2.0	2.0	2.0	1.8
Fuel System	SMPI	SEFI	MPFI	MPFI	SEFI	SEFI	SEFI	MPFI
Compression Ratio	9:1	9.7:1	10:1	8:1	9.6:1	8.5:1	8.5:1	9.5:1
Horsepower @ RPM	205@4500	170@6200	222@6000	320@6000	140@6000	210@6000	210@6000	113@6000
Torque @ RPM	265@3200	165@4200	205@4500	315@2500	130@4800	214@3000	214@3000	116@4500
Fuel Capacity	18	14.5	19.8	19.8	16.9	15.9	15.9	13.2
EPA City (mpg) - manual	N/A	21	19	18	22	23	21	26
EPA Hwy (mpg) - manual	N/A	29	25	24	32	31	27	33
EPA City (mpg) - auto	17	22	18	N/A	22	20	19	26
EPA Hwy (mpg) - auto	25	30	24	N/A	31	27	25	33

363

Specifications EPA Mileage Ratings

NISSAN

	240SX Cpe	240SX SE Cpe	300ZX 2+2	300ZX Cpe	300ZX Conv	300ZX Turbo Cpe	Altima GLE Sdn	Altima GXE Sdn	Altima SE Sdn
Length (in.)	177	177	178	170	170	170	181	181	181
Width (in.)	68.1	68.1	70.9	70.5	70.5	70.5	67.1	67.1	67.1
Height (in.)	50.8	50.8	48.1	48.3	49.5	48.4	55.9	55.9	55.9
Curb Weight (lbs.)	2753	2760	3413	3299	3446	3517	3032	2972	2968
Wheelbase (in.)	99.4	99.4	101	96.5	96.5	96.5	103	103	103
Front Track (in.)	58.3	58.3	58.9	58.9	58.9	58.9	57.7	57.7	57.7
Rear Track (in.)	57.9	57.9	60.4	60.4	60.4	61.2	57.3	57.3	57.3
Front Head Room (in.)	38.3	38.3	37.1	36.8	37.1	36.8	39.3	39.3	39.3
Rear Head Room (in.)	34.3	34.3	34.4	N/A	N/A	N/A	37.6	37.6	37.6
Front Shoulder Room (in.)	52	52	56.7	56.7	56.7	56.7	54.8	54.8	54.8
Rear Shoulder Room (in.)	42.2	42.2	55.2	N/A	N/A	N/A	54	54	54
Front Hip Room (in.)	50.6	50.6	53.5	53.5	53.5	53.5	52.8	52.8	52.8
Rear Hip Room (in.)	42.2	42.2	41.2	N/A	N/A	N/A	52.4	52.4	52.4
Front Leg Room (in.)	42.6	42.6	43	43	43	43	42.6	42.6	42.6
Rear Leg Room (in.)	20.8	20.8	22.7	N/A	N/A	N/A	34.7	34.7	34.7
Luggage Capacity (cu ft.)	8.6	8.6	11.5	23.7	5.8	23.7	14	14	14
Number of Cylinders	4	4	6	6	6	6	4	4	4
Displacement (liters)	2.4	2.4	3.0	3.0	3.0	3.0	2.4	2.4	2.4
Fuel System	SMPFI	SMPFI	MPFI	MPFI	MPFI	MPFI	SMPFI	SMPFI	SMPFI
Compression Ratio	9.5:1	9.5:1	10.5:1	10.5:1	10.5:1	8.5:1	9.2:1	9.2:1	9.2:1
Horsepower @ RPM	155@5600	155@5600	222@6400	222@6400	222@6400	300@6400	150@5600	150@5600	150@5600
Torque @ RPM	160@4400	160@4400	198@4800	198@4800	198@4800	283@3600	154@4400	154@4400	154@4400
Fuel Capacity	17.2	17.2	18.7	18.7	18.2	18.7	15.8	15.8	15.8
EPA City (mpg) - manual	22	22	18	18	18	N/A	24	24	24
EPA Hwy (mpg) - manual	28	28	24	24	24	N/A	30	30	30
EPA City (mpg) - auto	21	21	18	18	18	N/A	21	21	21
EPA Hwy (mpg) - auto	26	26	23	23	23	N/A	29	29	29

Specifications EPA Mileage Ratings

NISSAN

	Altima XE Sdn	Maxima GLE Sdn	Maxima GXE Sdn	Maxima SE Sdn	Sentra SE-R Cpe
Length (in.)	181	188	188	188	170
Width (in.)	67.1	69.7	69.7	69.7	65.6
Height (in.)	55.9	56	56	56	53.9
Curb Weight (lbs.)	2924	3097	3001	3010	2467
Wheelbase (in.)	103	106	106	106	95.7
Front Track (in.)	57.7	59.8	60.2	59.8	56.9
Rear Track (in.)	57.3	59.1	59.1	59.1	56.3
Front Head Room (in.)	39.3	40.1	40.1	40.1	38.5
Rear Head Room (in.)	37.6	37.4	37.4	37.4	36.6
Front Shoulder Room (in.)	54.8	56.8	56.8	56.8	52.6
Rear Shoulder Room (in.)	54	56.2	56.2	56.2	52.6
Front Hip Room (in.)	52.8	54.3	54.3	54.3	51.2
Rear Hip Room (in.)	52.4	55.9	55.9	55.9	53.4
Front Leg Room (in.)	42.6	43.9	43.9	43.9	41.9
Rear Leg Room (in.)	34.7	34.3	34.3	34.3	30.9
Luggage Capacity (cu ft.)	14	14.5	14.5	14.5	11.7
Number of Cylinders	4	6	6	6	4
Displacement (liters)	2.4	3.0	3.0	3.0	2.0
Fuel System	SMPFI	SMPFI	SMPFI	SMPFI	SMPI
Compression Ratio	9.2:1	10:1	10:1	10:1	9.5:1
Horsepower @ RPM	150@5600	190@5600	190@5600	190@5600	140@6400
Torque @ RPM	154@4400	205@4000	205@4000	205@4000	132@4800
Fuel Capacity	15.8	18.5	18.5	18.5	13.2
EPA City (mpg) - manual	24	N/A	22	22	23
EPA Hwy (mpg) - manual	30	N/A	27	27	31
EPA City (mpg) - auto	21	21	21	21	N/A
EPA Hwy (mpg) - auto	29	28	28	28	N/A

OLDSMOBILE

	88 LSS Sdn	88 LSS Supercharged 3.8L	Aurora Sdn
Length (in.)	200	200	205
Width (in.)	74.1	74.1	74.4
Height (in.)	55.7	55.7	55.4
Curb Weight (lbs.)	3429	3429	2779
Wheelbase (in.)	111	111	114
Front Track (in.)	60.4	60.4	62.5
Rear Track (in.)	60.4	60.4	62.6
Front Head Room (in.)	38.7	38.7	38.4
Rear Head Room (in.)	38.3	38.3	36.9
Front Shoulder Room (in.)	59	59	57.9
Rear Shoulder Room (in.)	58.3	58.3	57.9
Front Hip Room (in.)	55.4	55.4	55.1
Rear Hip Room (in.)	54.1	54.1	55.8
Front Leg Room (in.)	42.5	42.5	42.6
Rear Leg Room (in.)	38.7	38.7	38.4
Luggage Capacity (cu ft.)	17.5	17.5	16.1
Number of Cylinders	6	6	8
Displacement (liters)	3.8	3.8	4.0
Fuel System	SMPI	SMPI	TPI
Compression Ratio	9.4:1	8.5:1	10.3:1
Horsepower @ RPM	205@5200	225@5000	250@5600
Torque @ RPM	230@4000	275@3200	260@4400
Fuel Capacity	18	18	20
EPA City (mpg) - manual	N/A	N/A	N/A
EPA Hwy (mpg) - manual	N/A	N/A	N/A
EPA City (mpg) - auto	19	17	16
EPA Hwy (mpg) - auto	29	27	25

Specifications EPA Mileage Ratings

	OLDSMOBILE Cutlass Suprm 3.4L Conv	PLYMOUTH Neon Highline 2.0L SOHC Sdn	Neon Highline 2.0L SOHC Cpe	Neon Sport 2.0L DOHC Cpe	Neon Sport 2.0L SOHC Sdn	PONTIAC Bonneville SE Sdn	Bonneville Supercharged SE S
Length (in.)	194	172	172	172	172	200	200
Width (in.)	71	67.4	67.2	67.2	67.4	74.5	74.5
Height (in.)	54.3	54.8	52.8	52.8	54.8	55.7	55.7
Curb Weight (lbs.)	3629	2320	2384	2485	2320	3446	3446
Wheelbase (in.)	107	104	104	104	104	111	111
Front Track (in.)	59.5	57.4	57.4	57.4	57.4	60.4	60.4
Rear Track (in.)	58	57.4	57.4	57.4	57.4	60.3	60.3
Front Head Room (in.)	38.5	39.6	39.6	39.6	39.6	39.2	39.2
Rear Head Room (in.)	38.9	36.5	36.5	36.5	36.5	38.3	38.3
Front Shoulder Room (in.)	57.6	52.5	52	52	52.5	59.8	59.8
Rear Shoulder Room (in.)	57.2	52.3	54.7	54.7	52.3	59.4	59.4
Front Hip Room (in.)	51.9	50.8	50.3	50.3	50.8	57.2	57.2
Rear Hip Room (in.)	51.5	50.6	53.9	53.9	50.6	38.3	38.3
Front Leg Room (in.)	42.3	42.5	42.5	42.5	42.5	42.6	42.6
Rear Leg Room (in.)	34.8	33.9	35.1	35.1	33.9	38	38
Luggage Capacity (cu ft.)	12.1	11.8	11.8	11.8	11.8	18	18
Number of Cylinders	6	4	4	4	4	6	6
Displacement (liters)	3.4	2.0	2.0	2.0	2.0	3.8	3.8
Fuel System	SMPI	SMPI	SMPI	SMPI	SMPI	SPFI	SPFI
Compression Ratio	9.2:1	9.8:1	9.8:1	9.8:1	9.8:1	9.4:1	9:1
Horsepower @ RPM	210@5200	132@6000	132@6000	150@6800	132@6000	205@5200	225@5000
Torque @ RPM	215@4000	129@5000	129@5000	131@5600	129@5000	230@4000	275@3200
Fuel Capacity	16.5	11.2	11.2	11.2	11.2	18	18
EPA City (mpg) - manual	N/A	29	29	29	29	N/A	N/A
EPA Hwy (mpg) - manual	N/A	38	38	38	38	N/A	N/A
EPA City (mpg) - auto	17	27	27	27	27	19	17
EPA Hwy (mpg) - auto	26	33	33	33	33	28	25

Specifications EPA Mileage Ratings

	PONTIAC Bonneville Supercharged SSE	Firebird Formula Cpe	Firebird Formula Conv	Firebird Trans Am Conv	Firebird Trans Am Cpe	Grand Prix GT Sdn	Grand Prix GTP Cpe	**PORSCHE** 911 Carrera Cabriolet
Length (in.)	201	196	196	196	196	195	195	168
Width (in.)	74.5	74.5	74.5	74.5	74.5	71.9	71.9	68.3
Height (in.)	55.7	52	52	52	52	54.8	52.8	51.8
Curb Weight (lbs.)	3587	3373	3373	3610	3345	3318	3243	3064
Wheelbase (in.)	111	101	101	101	101	108	108	89.4
Front Track (in.)	60.8	60.7	60.7	60.7	60.7	59.5	59.5	55.3
Rear Track (in.)	60.6	60.6	60.6	60.6	60.6	58	58	56.9
Front Head Room (in.)	39.2	37.2	37.2	37.2	37.2	38.6	37.8	N/A
Rear Head Room (in.)	38.3	35.3	35.3	35.3	35.3	37.7	36.6	N/A
Front Shoulder Room (in.)	59.8	57.4	57.4	57.4	57.4	57.2	57.3	N/A
Rear Shoulder Room (in.)	59.4	55.8	55.8	55.8	55.8	57.4	57.3	N/A
Front Hip Room (in.)	57.2	52.8	52.8	52.8	52.8	53.1	52	N/A
Rear Hip Room (in.)	38.3	44.4	44.4	44.4	44.4	54.3	53	N/A
Front Leg Room (in.)	42.6	43	43	43	43	42.4	42.3	N/A
Rear Leg Room (in.)	38	28.9	28.9	28.9	28.9	36.2	34.8	N/A
Luggage Capacity (cu ft.)	18	12.9	12.9	12.9	12.9	15.5	14.9	N/A
Number of Cylinders	6	8	8	8	8	6	6	6
Displacement (liters)	3.8	5.7	5.7	5.7	5.7	3.4	3.4	3.6
Fuel System	SPFI	SPFI	SPFI	SPFI	SPFI	SPFI	SPFI	DMEFI
Compression Ratio	9:1	10.5:1	10.5:1	10.5:1	10.5:1	9.2:1	9.2:1	11.3:1
Horsepower @ RPM	225@5000	275@5000	275@5000	275@5000	275@5000	210@5000	210@5000	270@6100
Torque @ RPM	275@3200	325@2400	325@2400	325@2400	325@2400	215@4000	215@4000	243@5000
Fuel Capacity	18	15.5	15.5	15.5	15.5	17.1	17.1	19.4
EPA City (mpg) - manual	N/A	17	17	17	17	N/A	N/A	17
EPA Hwy (mpg) - manual	N/A	25	25	25	25	N/A	N/A	25
EPA City (mpg) - auto	17	17	17	17	17	17	17	17
EPA Hwy (mpg) - auto	25	24	24	24	24	27	27	24

Specifications EPA Mileage Ratings

	PORSCHE 911 Carrera Cpe	911 Carrera 4 Cabriolet	911 Carrera 4 Cpe	928 GTS Cpe	968 Cabriolet	968 Cpe	SAAB 900 SE Conv	900 SE Hbk
Length (in.)	168	168	168	178	171	171	183	183
Width (in.)	68.3	68.3	68.3	74.4	68.3	68.3	67.4	67.4
Height (in.)	51.8	51.8	51.8	50.5	50.2	50.2	56.5	56.5
Curb Weight (lbs.)	3064	3175	3175	3593	3240	3086	3190	3120
Wheelbase (in.)	89.4	89.4	89.4	98.4	94.5	94.5	102	102
Front Track (in.)	55.3	55.3	55.3	61.1	58.2	58.2	56.9	56.9
Rear Track (in.)	56.9	58	58	63.6	57.1	57.1	56.8	56.8
Front Head Room (in.)	N/A	N/A	N/A	N/A	N/A	N/A	39.3	39.3
Rear Head Room (in.)	N/A	N/A	N/A	N/A	N/A	N/A	37.9	37.8
Front Shoulder Room (in.)	N/A	N/A	N/A	N/A	N/A	N/A	N/A	N/A
Rear Shoulder Room (in.)	N/A	N/A	N/A	N/A	N/A	N/A	N/A	N/A
Front Hip Room (in.)	N/A	N/A	N/A	N/A	N/A	N/A	N/A	N/A
Rear Hip Room (in.)	N/A	N/A	N/A	N/A	N/A	N/A	N/A	N/A
Front Leg Room (in.)	N/A	N/A	N/A	N/A	N/A	42.3	42.3	
Rear Leg Room (in.)	N/A	N/A	N/A	N/A	N/A	N/A	36	36
Luggage Capacity (cu ft.)	N/A	N/A	N/A	N/A	N/A	N/A	12.5	24
Number of Cylinders	6	6	6	8	4	4	6	6
Displacement (liters)	3.6	3.6	3.6	5.4	3.0	3.0	2.5	2.5
Fuel System	DMEFI	DMEFI	DMEFI	LH-J FI	DMEFI	DMEFI	FI	FI
Compression Ratio	11.3:1	11.3:1	11.3:1	10.4:1	11:1	11:1	10.8:1	10.8:1
Horsepower @ RPM	270@6100	270@6100	270@6100	345@5700	236@6200	236@6200	170@5900	170@5900
Torque @ RPM	243@5000	243@5000	243@5000	369@4250	225@4100	225@4100	167@4200	167@4200
Fuel Capacity	19.4	19.4	19.4	22.7	19.6	19.6	18	18
EPA City (mpg) - manual	17	16	16	12	17	17	18	18
EPA Hwy (mpg) - manual	25	23	23	19	26	26	25	25
EPA City (mpg) - auto	17	N/A	N/A	15	16	16	19	19
EPA Hwy (mpg) - auto	24	N/A	N/A	19	25	25	27	27

Specifications EPA Mileage Ratings

	SAAB 900 SE Turbo Conv	SAAB 900 SE Turbo Cpe	SAAB 9000 Aero Hbk	SATURN Saturn SC2 Cpe	SATURN Saturn SL2 Sdn	SATURN Saturn SW2 Wgn	SUBARU SVX AWD LSi Cpe
Length (in.)	183	183	187	173	176	176	182
Width (in.)	67.4	67.4	69.4	67.6	67.6	67.6	69.7
Height (in.)	56.5	56.5	55.9	50.6	52.5	53.7	51.2
Curb Weight (lbs.)	3160	3060	3250	2750	2750	2750	3580
Wheelbase (in.)	102	102	105	99.2	102	102	103
Front Track (in.)	56.9	56.9	59.9	56.8	56.8	56.8	59.1
Rear Track (in.)	56.8	56.8	58.7	56	56	56	58.3
Front Head Room (in.)	39.3	39.3	38.6	37.5	38.5	38.8	37.4
Rear Head Room (in.)	37.9	37.8	37.4	35	36.3	37.4	35
Front Shoulder Room (in.)	N/A	N/A	N/A	53.7	54.3	54.3	56.1
Rear Shoulder Room (in.)	N/A	N/A	N/A	51.3	54.3	54.3	54.5
Front Hip Room (in.)	N/A	N/A	N/A	51.3	51.7	51.7	N/A
Rear Hip Room (in.)	N/A	N/A	N/A	49.2	50.7	50.7	N/A
Front Leg Room (in.)	42.3	42.3	41.7	42.6	42.5	42.5	43.5
Rear Leg Room (in.)	36	36	39	26.5	32.6	32.6	28.5
Luggage Capacity (cu ft.)	12.5	24	23.5	10.9	11.9	24	8.2
Number of Cylinders	4	4	4	4	4	4	6
Displacement (liters)	2.0	2.0	2.3	1.9	1.9	1.9	3.3
Fuel System	FI	FI	FI	PFI	PFI	PFI	SPFI
Compression Ratio	9.2:1	9.2:1	9.2:1	9.5:1	9.5:1	9.5:1	10:1
Horsepower @ RPM	185@5500	185@5500	225@5500	124@5600	124@5600	124@5600	230@5400
Torque @ RPM	194@2100	194@2100	252@1950	122@4800	122@4800	122@4800	228@4400
Fuel Capacity	18	18	17.4	12.8	12.8	12.8	18.5
EPA City (mpg) - manual	20	21	21	25	25	25	N/A
EPA Hwy (mpg) - manual	27	28	29	35	35	35	N/A
EPA City (mpg) - auto	N/A	N/A	18	24	24	24	17
EPA Hwy (mpg) - auto	N/A	N/A	27	34	34	34	25

Specifications EPA Mileage Ratings

	SUBARU SVX L Cpe	SUBARU SVX LS Cpe	TOYOTA Camry V6 LE Cpe	TOYOTA Camry V6 LE Sdn	TOYOTA Camry V6 SE Cpe	TOYOTA Camry V6 SE Sdn	TOYOTA Camry V6 XLE Sdn	TOYOTA Celica GT Conv
Length (in.)	182	182	188	188	188	188	188	177
Width (in.)	69.7	69.7	69.7	69.7	69.7	69.7	69.7	68.9
Height (in.)	51.2	51.2	54.9	55.1	54.9	55.1	55.1	51.6
Curb Weight (lbs.)	3375	3430	3219	3241	3164	3186	3274	2755
Wheelbase (in.)	103	103	103	103	103	103	103	99.9
Front Track (in.)	59.1	59.1	61	61	61	61	61	59.6
Rear Track (in.)	58.3	58.3	59	59	59	59	59	58.9
Front Head Room (in.)	38	37.4	38.4	38.4	38.4	38.4	38.4	38.7
Rear Head Room (in.)	35	35	37.4	37.1	37.4	37.1	37.1	34.1
Front Shoulder Room (in.)	56.1	56.1	56.5	56.8	56.5	56.8	56.8	52.4
Rear Shoulder Room (in.)	54.5	54.5	55.2	56.1	55.2	56.1	56.1	44.8
Front Hip Room (in.)	N/A	N/A	54.2	55.9	54.2	55.9	55.9	52.8
Rear Hip Room (in.)	N/A	N/A	53	54	53	55.4	55.4	41.2
Front Leg Room (in.)	43.5	43.5	43.5	43.5	43.5	43.5	43.5	44.2
Rear Leg Room (in.)	28.5	28.5	33	35	33	35	35	18.9
Luggage Capacity (cu ft.)	8.2	8.2	14.8	14.8	14.8	14.8	14.8	6.8
Number of Cylinders	6	6	6	6	6	6	6	4
Displacement (liters)	3.3	3.3	3.0	3.0	3.0	3.0	3.0	2.2
Fuel System	SPFI	SPFI	EFI	EFI	EFI	EFI	EFI	EFI
Compression Ratio	10:1	10:1	10.5:1	10.5:1	10.5:1	10.5:1	10.5:1	9.5:1
Horsepower @ RPM	230@5400	230@5400	188@5200	188@5200	188@5200	188@5200	188@5200	130@5400
Torque @ RPM	228@4400	228@4400	203@4400	203@4400	203@4400	203@4400	203@4400	145@4400
Fuel Capacity	18.5	18.5	18.5	18.5	18.5	18.5	18.5	15.9
EPA City (mpg) - manual	N/A	N/A	N/A	N/A	N/A	N/A	N/A	22
EPA Hwy (mpg) - manual	N/A	N/A	N/A	N/A	N/A	N/A	N/A	29
EPA City (mpg) - auto	17	17	20	20	20	20	20	23
EPA Hwy (mpg) - auto	25	25	28	28	28	28	28	30

Specifications EPA Mileage Ratings

TOYOTA

	Celica GT Cpe	Celica GT Lbk	MR2 Cpe	MR2 Turbo Cpe	Supra Lbk	Supra Turbo Lbk
Length (in.)	177	177	174	164	164	178	178
Width (in.)	68.9	68.9	66.9	66.9	71.3	71.3
Height (in.)	51	50.8	48.6	48.6	49.8	49.8
Curb Weight (lbs.)	2560	2580	2657	2888	3210	3445
Wheelbase (in.)	99.9	99.9	94.5	94.5	100	100
Front Track (in.)	59.6	59.6	57.9	57.9	59.8	59.8
Rear Track (in.)	58.9	58.9	57.1	57.1	60	60
Front Head Room (in.)	34.5	34.5	37.5	36.8	37.5	37.5
Rear Head Room (in.)	30.7	30.7	N/A	N/A	32.9	32.9
Front Shoulder Room (in.)	52.4	52.4	54	54	54.2	54.2
Rear Shoulder Room (in.)	49.9	49.9	N/A	N/A	43.8	43.8
Front Hip Room (in.)	52.8	52.8	N/A	N/A	N/A	N/A
Rear Hip Room (in.)	47.8	47.8	N/A	N/A	N/A	N/A
Front Leg Room (in.)	44.2	44.2	43.4	43.4	44	44
Rear Leg Room (in.)	26.8	26.8	N/A	N/A	23.8	23.8
Luggage Capacity (cu ft.)	10.6	16.2	6.5	6.5	10.1	10.1
Number of Cylinders	4	4	4	4	6	6
Displacement (liters)	2.2	2.2	2.2	2.0	3.0	3.0
Fuel System	EFI	EFI	EFI	EFI	SEFI	SEFI
Compression Ratio	9.5:1	9.5:1	9.5:1	8.8:1	10:1	8.5:1
Horsepower @ RPM	130@5400	130@5400	135@5400	200@6000	220@5800	320@5600
Torque @ RPM	145@4400	145@4400	145@4400	200@3200	210@4800	315@4000
Fuel Capacity	15.9	15.9	14.3	14.3	18.5	18.5
EPA City (mpg) - manual	22	22	22	20	18	17
EPA Hwy (mpg) - manual	29	29	29	27	23	24
EPA City (mpg) - auto	23	23	21	N/A	18	19
EPA Hwy (mpg) - auto	30	30	30	N/A	24	24

VOLKSWAGEN

	GTI VR6 Hbk	Jetta III GLX Sdn
Length (in.)	160	173
Width (in.)	66.7	66.7
Height (in.)	56	56.2
Curb Weight (lbs.)	2818	2915
Wheelbase (in.)	97.3	97.3
Front Track (in.)	57.1	57.1
Rear Track (in.)	56.4	56
Front Head Room (in.)	37.5	39.2
Rear Head Room (in.)	37.4	37.3
Front Shoulder Room (in.)	54	53.8
Rear Shoulder Room (in.)	54.6	52.8
Front Hip Room (in.)	52.8	53.2
Rear Hip Room (in.)	51.9	52.3
Front Leg Room (in.)	42.3	42.3
Rear Leg Room (in.)	31.5	31.5
Luggage Capacity (cu ft.)	17.5	15
Number of Cylinders	6	6
Displacement (liters)	2.8	2.8
Fuel System	SFI	SMFI
Compression Ratio	10:1	10:1
Horsepower @ RPM	172@5400	172@5800
Torque @ RPM	173@4200	173@4200
Fuel Capacity	14.5	14.5
EPA City (mpg) - manual	18	18
EPA Hwy (mpg) - manual	25	25
EPA City (mpg) - auto	N/A	18
EPA Hwy (mpg) - auto	N/A	25

	Passat GLX Sdn	Passat GLX Wgn	850 Turbo Wgn	850 Turbo Sdn
Length (in.)	182	181	185	184
Width (in.)	67.5	67.5	69.3	69.3
Height (in.)	56.4	58.7	56.9	55.7
Curb Weight (lbs.)	3140	3201	3387	3278
Wheelbase (in.)	103	103	105	105
Front Track (in.)	58.4	58.4	59.8	59.8
Rear Track (in.)	56.2	56.2	57.9	57.9
Front Head Room (in.)	39.3	39.9	38.4	38
Rear Head Room (in.)	36.6	38.3	37.9	37.3
Front Shoulder Room (in.)	55	55	57.1	57.1
Rear Shoulder Room (in.)	54	54	56.3	56.3
Front Hip Room (in.)	N/A	N/A	55.2	55.2
Rear Hip Room (in.)	N/A	N/A	55.2	55.2
Front Leg Room (in.)	45.1	45.1	41.4	41.4
Rear Leg Room (in.)	37	37	35.2	32.3
Luggage Capacity (cu ft.)	14.4	34	37.1	14.7
Number of Cylinders	6	6	5	5
Displacement (liters)	2.8	2.8	2.3	2.3
Fuel System	SMPI	SFI	EFI	EFI
Compression Ratio	10:1	10:1	8.5:1	8.5:1
Horsepower @ RPM	172@5800	172@5800	222@5200	222@5200
Torque @ RPM	177@4200	177@4200	221@2100	221@2100
Fuel Capacity	18.5	18.5	19.3	19.3
EPA City (mpg) - manual	18	18	N/A	N/A
EPA Hwy (mpg) - manual	25	25	N/A	N/A
EPA City (mpg) - auto	18	18	19	19
EPA Hwy (mpg) - auto	25	25	26	26

Specifications EPA Mileage Ratings

VOLKSWAGEN — *VOLVO*

How the fuel economy estimates are obtained:

The estimates of the number of miles a vehicle can travel on a gallon of fuel are based on results of the U.S. Environmental Protection Agency (E.P.A.) "Emissions Standards Test Procedure." This procedure is used to certify that cars, vans, and light trucks comply with the Clean Air Act, as amended. Each year, manufacturers submit new vehicle codes to the E.P.A. The procedure for testing simulates every day driving conditions. Each vehicle is tested under controlled laboratory conditions by a professional driver. By using a dynamometer to simulate driving conditions, the driver can test each vehicle under identical circumstances in exactly the same way each time. Therefore, the obtained results can be compared accurately. The test vehicles are broken in, properly maintained, and driven in test conditions which simulate warm weather and dry, level roads. The quality of the fuel used is also very closely controlled. The test conditions are those the E.P.A. must use to assure emissions measurements. However, no test can cover all possible combinations of actual road conditions, climate, driving and car-care habits of individual drivers.

CRASH TEST DATA

In 1994, the National Highway and Trafic Safety Administration (NHTSA) changed the way they rate crash test performances of the cars and trucks they run into a wall at 35 mph. Instead of using the confusing numerical scale that had been in place for years, NHTSA decided to make the data more user-friendly for interested consumers by converting to a five star rating system, just like the movie reviewer in your local paper or the lucky people AAA employs to go around the world eating and sleeping in the best hotels and restaurants.

Listed below are the results for some of the vehicles listed in this book since NHTSA adopted its new system. A five-star rating is best.

Model	Airbag System	Driver	Passenger
Acura Legend	Dual	***	****
BMW 3-Series	Dual	****	***
Cadillac Seville	Dual	****	No Data
Chevrolet Camaro	Dual	*****	*****
Chevrolet Caprice	Dual	****	**
Chevrolet Impala SS	Dual	****	**
Chevrolet S-10 Pickup	Driver	No Data	***
Chrysler Concorde	Dual	***	****
Chrysler LHS	Dual	****	****
Dodge Intrepid	Dual	****	****
Dodge Neon	Dual	***	***
Dodge Ram	Driver	*****	No Data
Dodge Stealth	Dual	*****	No Data
Eagle Vision	Dual	***	****
Ford Escort	Dual	****	No Data
Ford F-150	Driver	*****	*****
Ford Mustang	Dual	****	****

EDMUND'S 1995 HIGH-PERFORMANCE AUTOMOBILES

CRASH TEST DATA

Model	Airbag System	Driver	Passenger
Ford Probe	Dual	*****	****
Ford Taurus	Dual	****	****
Ford Thunderbird	Dual	*****	*****
GMC Sonoma Pickup	Driver	No Data	***
Honda Accord	Dual	****	***
Honda Civic	Dual	***	***
Honda Prelude	Dual	****	*****
Infiniti J30	Dual	****	****
Jeep Grand Cherokee	Driver	****	***
Lexus GS300	Dual	***	***
Mazda 626	Dual	****	*****
Mazda Miata	Dual	***	No Data
Mercedes C-Class	Dual	****	****
Mercury Cougar	Dual	*****	*****
Mitsubishi 3000GT	Dual	*****	No Data
Mitsubishi Eclipse	Dual	****	****
Nissan 300ZX	Dual	***	No Data
Nissan Altima	Dual	****	***
Nissan Maxima	Dual	****	***
Nissan Sentra	None	****	****
Oldsmobile Silhouette	Driver	No Data	****
Plymouth Neon	Dual	***	***
Pontiac Bonneville	Dual	*****	***
Pontiac Firebird	Dual	*****	*****
Pontiac Grand Prix	Dual	****	***
Saab 9000	Dual	****	No Data
Toyota Camry	Dual	****	***
Volvo 850	Dual/Side	*****	****

EDMUND'S 1995 HIGH-PERFORMANCE AUTOMOBILES

Edmund's N•E•W CONSUMER AUDIO TAPE SERIES

How To Get Your Way at the Auto Dealer

- *How to be a savvy automobile buyer*
- *Know the best time to buy*
- *How to wheel and deal when purchasing a new automobile*
- *How to prepare for and negotiate the best deal*

Burke Leon, auto-buying expert and author of *"The Insider's Guide to Buying a New or Used Automobile"*, has created for Edmund's an audio tape that instructs you in the preparation and negotiation process for getting a great deal on a new automobile. With insight and humor, the tape presents the facts, techniques, and attitude you need to out-smart the auto dealer. Covered topics include vehicle and option selection, financing/leasing and insurance, trade-in appraisal, choosing a dealer, the test drive, picking the time to buy, negotiating and closing the deal, and more.

You'll learn how to buy right, negotiate smart, save money, and enjoy yourself all at the same time.

Furthermore, the auto-buying negotiation skills you develop will help you in other important aspects of your life.

"You'll want to play this informative tape over and over again for its expert advice."
Michael G. Samet, Ph. D., Chief Information Officer, Edmund Publications Corp.

Special Price for Edmund's Readers

$9.99

*plus $3.99 ship/handling
1 cassette.*

"By buying my new Taurus on the last day of the month, I saved an additional $500" —M. Wayward, Boise, Idaho
"I got $600 more for my trade-in than I expected." —D. Applebaum, Frederick, Maryland

TO ORDER, CALL TOLL FREE:
1-800-826-8766
MC / VISA ACCEPTED

EDMUND PUBLICATIONS CORP., 300 N SEPULVEDA BLVD, SUITE 2050, EL SEGUNDO, CA 90245

Edmund's Success Story!

Dear Edmund's!

I wanted to thank you for your publication, and also, your toll-free number and 900 number.

... I decided to buy a new car, and do it on my own —without a man helping me. I was interested in a Honda Civic DX 2-Door Coupe. I saw your publication recommended in auto buying articles. I called your hotline, and one of your people told me to get my new car at $200-$300 over dealer cost, and hold at $500.

I did.

Some salespeople and dealers didn't appreciate me going in with the Edmund's prices, or that I was an educated woman consumer.

And some did. I went to a Honda dealer in Georgia. We went back and forth on the numbers, and I knew I was getting a great deal. I got the car I wanted, with automatic transmission, air-conditioning, AM/FM cassette player, pin stripes, floor mats, mud guards, paint and fabric protection. I paid $14,350 and that included tax, tag, and title. That was $300 over dealer invoice.

The manager told me that when a customer comes in with Edmund's prices, and has done their homework, they are happy to work with them. (And that women are 67% of their car buyers, so they wouldn't think of treating them badly.)

I drove my new car home that day, and I am thrilled with it. Even the other dealers congratulated me, and said I did very well.

So, thanks to **Edmund's Buyer's Guide** and their information hotline, I got the information I needed, and the car I wanted at the right price.

Sincerely,

Sandra T. Davidson
Atlanta, GA

Automobile Manufacturers
Customer Assistance Numbers

Acura 1-800-382-2238
Audi 1-800-822-2834
BMW 1-800-831-1117
Buick 1-800-521-7300
Cadillac 1-800-458-8006
Chevrolet 1-800-222-1020
Chrysler 1-800-992-1997
Dodge 1-800-992-1997
Eagle 1-800-992-1997
Ford 1-800-392-3673
Geo 1-800-222-1020
Honda 1-310-783-2000
                        toll free not available
Hyundai 1-800-633-5151
Infiniti 1-800-662-6200
Jaguar 1-201-818-8500
                        toll free not available

Lexus	1-800-255-3987
Lincoln	1-800-392-3673
Mazda	1-800-222-5500
Mercedes-Benz	1-800-222-0100
Mercury	1-800-392-3673
Mitsubishi	1-800-222-0037
Nissan	1-800-647-7261
Oldsmobile	1-800-442-6537
Plymouth	1-800-992-1997
Pontiac	1-800-762-2737
Porsche	1-800-545-8039
Saab	1-800-955-9007
Saturn	1-800-553-6000
Subaru	1-800-782-2783
Suzuki	1-800-934-0934
Toyota	1-800-331-4331
Vokswagen	1-800-822-8987
Volvo	1-800-458-1552

LEASING TIPS 1

Like most consumers, you want to know how to buy or lease the car of your choice for the best possible price. Buyers are attracted to leasing by low payments and the prospect of driving a new car every two or three years. Many people figure that a car payment is an unavoidable fact of budgetary life, and they might as well drive 'new' rather than 'old'. True, leasing is an attractive alternative, but there are some things you need to understand about leasing before jumping in feet first without a paddle. Whatever. You know what I mean.

1) Low Payments. You've seen the ads: 1994 Escort LX for $199 a month. 1994 Altima GXE for $229 a month. 1994 Infiniti Q45 for $599 a month. Zowie! Visions of new golf clubs, a 32-inch television and 2 weeks in Tahiti release endorphins at twice the Surgeon General's recommended level. Hold on a sec. Read the fine print. See where it says *'Capitalized Cost Reduction'*? That's lease-speak for 'down payment'. See where it says "36,000 miles over term?" That's lease-speak for 'You're going to the supermarket and back - and that's all folks.' Want the car for zero down? That's gonna cost you. You drive someplace more than twice a month? That's gonna cost you too.

Low payments aren't a fallacy with leasing, when taken in proper context. For example, a Ford Ranger XLT V6 stickers at about $13,900, give or take. To lease for two years with no *Capitalized Cost Reduction* (down payment), the truck will cost you about $350 per month; to lease for three years; about $275 per month. Ford allows 15,000 miles per year and charges about 11 cents per mile for each mile over the term limit. To buy the Ranger, financed for 24 months at 10% APR with no money down, you will pay $690 per month including tax and tags. For three years at 10%, the payment is $485 per month. So you see, leasing is cheaper on a monthly basis when compared to financing for the same term.

There are two flaws here. First, 60-month financing is now commonplace. The Ranger will cost $320 per month for 5 years, and still be worth a good chunk of change at the end of the loan, if cared for properly. Second, ownership is far less restrictive, even if the bank holds the title until 1999. You can drive as far as you want, paint the thing glow-in-the-dark orange with magenta stripes, and spill coffee on the seats without sweating a big wear-and-tear bill down the road. Leasing for two years costs about $8,400, and you don't own the truck at lease end. Financing for two years costs about $16,560, but you own a truck worth about $8,500 when the payment book is empty,

LEASING TIPS

which makes your actual cost a tad over $8,000. Is leasing cheaper? Monthly payments, when compared to financing over the same term, are lower. But leasing is actually more expensive in the long run.

2) Restrictions. Leasing severely restricts your use of a vehicle. Mileage allowances are limited, modifications to the vehicle can result in hefty fines at the end of the lease, and if the vehicle is not in top condition when it is returned, excessive wear-and-tear charges may be levied. Many dealers will be more lenient if you buy or lease another vehicle from them at the end of your term, but if you drop off the car and walk, prepare yourself for some lease-end misery. Be sure to define these limitations at the beginning of the lease so that you know what you're getting yourself into. Find out what will be considered excessive in the wear-and-tear department and try to negotiate the mileage limit upwards.

3) How to lease. Never walk into a dealership and announce that you want to lease a car. Don't talk payment either. Concentrate on finding a car you like and know before you go into the dealership what you can afford. Most two- and three-year lease payments are calculated based on a *residual value* (the predicted value of the vehicle at the end of the lease term) of about half of the *Manufacturer's Suggested Retail Price* (MSRP). Sales tax is generally calculated using the MSRP as well, and a *money factor,* which is lease-speak for 'interest rate', is also involved in the calculation of a lease payment.

Calculating an exact lease payment is nearly impossible, but you can arrive at an approximate ball-park figure by using the following formula, which we will illustrate using a 1995 Escort GT as an example:

1995 Ford Escort GT Base MSRP	**$12,700**
Destination Charge	**$375**
Estimated Residual Value after 2 years	(50% of MSRP)
	$12,700 / 2 = **$6,350**
Sales Tax of 6%	(MSRP + Dest.) x 6%
	($12,700 + $375) x 0.06 = **$784.50**
Money Factor of 6%	(MSRP + Residual Value) x 6%
	($12,700 + $6,350) x 0.06 = **$1,143**
Total to be paid over 2-year term	(Res. Value + Sales Tax + Money Factor)
	$6,350 + $784.50 + $1,143 = **$8,277.50**
Divide by 24 months (2-year term)	**$344.89** per month with no money down.

LEASING TIPS 3

Ford Motor Company, for example, has developed special calculators for the sole purpose of computing lease payments because the actual method is not nearly as simplistic as the one above, but using the ball-park figure of $345, you can find out whether or not an Escort GT fits your budget without having a salesman breathing down your neck, asking where he needs to be to get you to buy a car today.

Actual lease payments are affected by negotiation of the sticker price of the vehicle, term of the lease, available incentives, residual values, and layers of financial wizardry that even sales managers can't interpret without the magic of modern technology. Once you find a car you can afford, negotiate the sticker price and then explore leasing based on the negotiated price. Ask what the residual value is and subtract any rebates or incentives from the *Capitalized Cost*, which is lease-speak for 'selling price'. Use the formula above to calculate a ball-park figure, and if the dealer balks at your conclusion, ask them to explain the error of your ways.

4) Lease-end. Studies show that consumers generally like leases, right up until they end. The reason for their apprehension is routed in the dark days of *open-end leasing*, when Joe Lessee was dealt a sucker punch by the lessor on the day Joe returned the car to the leasing agent. Back then, residual values were established at the end of the lease, wear-and-tear charges maxxed out credit cards and dealers laughed all the way to the S & L.

Leasing has evolved, and with today's *closed-end leases* (the only type of lease you should consider), the lease-end fees are quite minimal, unless the car has 100,000 miles on it, a busted-up grille, and melted chocolate smeared into the upholstery. Dealers want you to buy or lease another car from them, and can be rather lenient regarding excess mileage and abnormal wear. After all, if they hit you with a bunch of trumped-up charges, you're not going to remain a loyal customer, are you?

Additionally, closed-end leasing establishes the value of the car in advance, at the beginning of the lease. Also, any fees or charges you may incur at the lease-end are spelled out in detail before you sign the lease. All the worry is removed by the existence of concrete figures.

LEASING TIPS 4

Another leasing benefit is the myriad of choices you have at the end of the term. Well, maybe not a myriad, but there are four, which is more than you have after two or three years of financing. They are:

a) Return the car to the dealer and walk away from it after paying any applicable charges such as a termination fee, wear-and-tear repairs, or excessive mileage bills. Of course, if you don't plan to buy or lease another car from the dealer, you may get hit for every minor thing, but dem's da risks.

b) Buy the car from the dealer for the residual value established at the beginning of the lease. If the car is in good shape, the residual value is probably lower than the true value of the car, making it a bargain, and many leasing companies will guarantee financing at the lowest interest rate available at the time your lease ends. We recommend this option if the lease vehicle is trashed, just to avoid the lease-end charges such a vehicle would certainly incur.

c) Use any equity in the car as leverage in a new deal with the dealer. Since residual values are generally set low, the car is likely worth more than the residual value at lease end. A well-maintained, low-mileage lease car should allow the dealer to knock off up to a couple of thousand bucks off your next deal.

d) Sell the car yourself and pay off the residual value, pocketing whatever profit you make.

Closed end leasing is a win-win situation for everybody. The manufacturer sells more cars, the dealer sells more cars, and you get low payments and a new car every couple of years. However, it is important to stress that you never own the car, and leasing could be quite restrictive. If you are a low-mileage driver who maintains cars in perfect condition, don't like tying up capital in down payments and don't mind never-ending car payments, leasing is probably just right for you. However, if you're on the road all day every day, beat the stuffing out of your wheels, enjoy a customized look or drive your cars until the wheels fall off, purchase whatever it is you're considering — it's way cheaper.

MULTIMEDIA CAR SHOPPING

WITH
THE AUTO ALMANAC CD-ROM

- √ Fun and Easy to Use
- √ Includes All New Cars and Light Trucks
- √ View Future Models
- √ Compare Vehicle MSRP and Specifications
- √ Compute Your Interest and Payments
- √ Learn About Insider Buying Tricks
- √ Save Money and Get the Right Vehicle

Use this information-packed CD-ROM in your personal computer to access a full range of photos and figures on the car of your dreams. Discover which models will provide you with the most satisfaction. Save time, hassle, and money with this total infomration source. Turn car shopping into an enjoyable experience with the <u>Auto Almanac CD-ROM</u>, a multimedia shopping excursion that can't be matched by any other product!

INTRODUCTORY PRICE FOR EDMUND'S READERS $9.99 PLUS SHIPPING/HANDLING

VISA/MASTERCARD ACCEPTED

FOR IBM PC & COMPATIBLES
REQUIRES: 386 BASED PC, DOS 5.0
OR HIGHER, WINDOWS 3.1, 4MB RAM,
2 MB FREE HARD DISK SPACE, AND
CD-ROM DRIVE

TO ORDER YOUR CD-ROM, CALL:
1-800-826-8766

THE AUTO ALMANAC IS A PRODUCT OF CE3 INC., TORRANCE, CA

READER QUESTIONNAIRE

To help us improve the information content of our books, please complete this questionnaire and mail to:

Edmund Publications Corporation
300 N. Sepulveda Blvd., Suite 2050
El Segundo, CA 90245

1. **Where did you purchase this Edmund's Book?**
   ☐ BOOKSTORE ☐ NEWSSTAND ☐ OTHER

2. **How many times have you purchased editions of Edmund's books?**
   ☐ ONCE ☐ TWICE ☐ THREE TIMES ☐ FOUR TIMES OR MORE

3. **What is your vehicle preference?**
   CHECK ONE: ☐ AMERICAN ☐ IMPORT
   CHECK ONE OR MORE: ☐ CAR ☐ VAN ☐ TRUCK ☐ SPORT UTILITY

4. **What is your budget/price for buying a new vehicle?**
   ☐ UNDER $10,000 ☐ $10-$15,000 ☐ $15-20,000 ☐ $20-30,000
   ☐ $30-$40,000 ☐ $40,000 AND UP

5. **Would you like to use a computerized version of Edmund's Price Guides?**
   ☐ NO YES, FOR: ☐ DOS ☐ WINDOWS ☐ MACINTOSH ☐ CD-ROM

ANY COMMENTS: _____
_____
_____
_____
_____

To be adviseed directly of special offers from Edmund's, please complete the following. Thank you.

NAME _____
ADDRESS _____
CITY, STATE, ZIP _____
TELEPHONE _____

Edmund's ENTRY FORM

$10,000 WHEEL N'DEAL GIVE-AWAY

Edmund's is giving away $1,000 a month to lucky readers selected at random – see our announcement on the back cover of this book. To enter the drawing, complete the form below or provide the same information on a piece of paper and mail to:

Edmund Publications Corporation
300 N. Sepulveda Blvd., Suite 2050
El Segundo, CA 90245

NAME

ADDRESS

CITY, STATE, ZIP

TELEPHONE

NAME AND YEAR OF DESIRED AUTOMOBILE

NAME, ADDRESS, AND CONTACT OF A DEALER IN YOUR AREA LISTED IN EDMUND'S AUTOMOBILE DEALER DIRECTORY (page 388) OR OBTAINED BY CALLING **1-800-996-AUTO**

WHEEL N'DEAL GIVEAWAY Official Rules.

1. Using the Automobile Dealer Directory in the back of this book, select the dealer nearest you for your desired vehicle. Simply enter and send us the name, address, and contact person for this dealer. NO PURCHASE IS NECESSARY TO PARTICIPATE OR WIN.

2. $1,000 cash prize will be awarded each month to a single entrant. Prizes will be awarded through hand-drawn drawings from all eligible entry forms timely received. The drawings will be under supervision of an independent organization (Edmund Publications' promotions department) whose decisions are final, binding and conclusive on all matters. Prizes will be awarded only if prize winner complies with these official rules. Only one winner per name or household. All prizes will be awarded.

3. Drawings will be held on the 25th day of each month starting January 1995, with the last drawing on October 25, 1995. Entry forms must be received by Edmund Publications by the end of business on the (20th) day of the month to be eligible to participate in the drawing for that month and all subsequent drawings. All eligible entry forms timely received will be automatically entered into each subsequent monthly drawing. Edmund Publications is not and will not be responsible for illegible, damaged, late, lost, or misdirected entry forms.

4. Winners will be notified by First Class Mail on or before the 15th day of the month following each drawing. Prize winners will be required to sign (a) a declaration of eligibility and release form whereby winners consent to the commercial use of their name for advertising without additional compensation and (b) any forms required by tax authorities within 21 days of notification or forfeit the prize.

5. Payment of all applicable federal, state and local taxes is the sole responsibility of and must be paid by the winner.

6. Contest is open to residents of the United States who are 18 years or older. Employees and their immediate families of Edmund Publications or any dealer listed in the Automobile Dealer Directory, or any company or individual engaged in the development, production or execution of this promotion are not eligible to participate. Residents of Florida are eligible to participate and to win prizes. Void where prohibited or restricted by law.

7. For a list of prize winners, official entry forms, or a copy of these official rules, send a stamped self-addressed envelope to: Wheel N'Deal Giveaway, c/o Edmund Publications Corp., 300 N. Sepulveda Blvd., Suite 2050, El Segundo, CA 90245.

8. Odds of winning are determined by the total number of entry forms received.

Automobile Dealer Directory

BMW

CONNECTICUT
BMW SAAB OF DARIEN
140 Ledge Road
Darien
Contact: Charles or Ron 203/656-1804

NEW YORK
PACE BMW
25 E. Main
New Rochelle
Contact: Jerry or Dave 914/636-2000

BUICK

CALIFORNIA
MAGNUSSEN PONTIAC-BUICK-GMC
550 El Camino Real
Menlo Park
Contact: Steve Bridges 415/326-4100

MICHIGAN
SUPERIOR BUICK
15101 Michigan Avenue
Dearborn
Contact: Joe 313/846-0040

OREGON
WALLACE BUICK
3515 NE Sandy Blvd
Portland
Contact: Don Forni 503/234-0221

CADILLAC

FLORIDA
ED MORSE CADILLAC
101 E. Fletcher Avenue
Tampa
Contact: Phil Raskin 813/968-8222

MASSACHUSETTS
FROST CADILLAC
399 Washington Street
Newton
Contact: Mark Gablehart 617/630-3000

CHEVROLET / GEO

ARIZONA
COURTESY CHEVROLET
1233 E. Camelback Road
Phoenix
Contact: Commercial Fleet Dept 602/279-3232

CALIFORNIA
CONNELL CHEVROLET
2828 Harbour Blvd
Costa Mesa
Contact: Eddie Cuadra or Gail Dalton 714/546-1200

AMERICAN CHEVROLET & GEO
1234 McHenry Avenue
Modesto
Contact: Commercial Sales 209/575-1606

MASSACHUSETTS
MCLAUGHLIN CHEVROLET INC.
741 Temple St. RT 27
Whitman
Contact: Ed Valante 617/447-4401

LANNAN CHEVROLET OLDSMOBILE GEO, INC.
40 Winn
Woburn
Contact: Steve Alesse 617/935-2000

MINNESOTA
FRIENDLY CHEVROLET/GEO INC.
7501 N.E. Hwy 65
Fridley
Contact: John Langworthy
or Howie Lee 612/786-6100

NEW JERSEY
FISHER CHEVROLET/OLDSMOBILE
210 S. Washington Ave.
Bergenfield
Contact: Pat Sabino 201/384-5800

PINE BELT CHEVROLET/GEO
1088 State HWY 88
Lakewood
Contact: Gil Casorla **908/363-2900**

NEW YORK
AMITY CHEVROLET INC.
20 Merick Road
Amityville
Contact: Chris Sadusky 516/264-0909

SOUNDVIEW CHEVROLET/GEO INC.
291 Main Street
New Rochelle
Contact: Mitch Kronengold 914/632-6400

NORTH CAROLINA
POWERS-SWAIN CHEVROLET/GEO
4709 Bragg Boulevard
Fayetteville
Contact: Gary Brown 800/467-5135

PENNSYLVANIA
CASTRIOTA CHEVROLET/GEO INC.
1701 West Liberty Avenue
Pittsburgh
Contact: Rocco 412/343-2100 x351

DAVID PENSKE CHEVROLET/GEO
On Mall Boulevard across from King of Prussia Mall
King of Prussia
Contact: Mark Degnan 610/337-3100 x20

TEXAS
NORMAN FREDE CHEVROLET
16801 Feather Craft
Houston
Contact: Bob Ondrias **713/486-2200**

CHRYSLER/PLYMOUTH

CALIFORNIA
CHASE CHRYSLER/PLYMOUTH/SUZUKI
2979 Auto Center Circle
Stockton
Contact: Ted Yee .... 209/956-7600 or 209/956-7617

For a Dealer in your area dial 1-800-996-Auto

Automobile Dealer Directory

CONNECTICUT
CALLARI CHRYSLER/PLYMOUTH JEEP/EAGLE
840 E. Main Street
Stamford
Contact: Anthony Viola 203/326-7800

MASSACHUSETTS
DEDHAM–WEST ROXBURY CHRYSLER/PLYMOUTH INC.
17 Eastern Avenue at Dedham Square
Dedham
Contact: Marshall Satter 617/326-4040

OHIO
BOB CALDWELL CHRYSLER/PLYMOUTH
1888 Morse
Columbus
Contact: Doug Berger 614/888-2331

PENNSYLVANIA
MAINLINE CHRYSLER/PLYMOUTH
663 Lancaster Avenue
Bryn Mahr
Contact: Jim Maloney or David Rapp 610/525-6670

SOUTH HILLS CHRYSLER/PLYMOUTH
3344 Washington Road
McMurray
Contact: Larry Winter 412/941-4300

DODGE

ILLINOIS
ANDERSON DODGE
5711 E. State
Rockford
Contact: Ron Heinkle or Mark Hauger 815/229-2000

MASSACHUSETTS
MOTOR MART DODGE
800 Washington Street
S. Attleboro
Contact: Martin Lamoreaux 508/761-5400

WESTMINSTER DODGE INC.
720 Morrissey Blvd.
Boston
Contact: Bob Bickford 800/274-9922

NEW JERSEY
MOTOR WORLD DODGE HYUNDAI
315 Rt 4 West
Paramus
Contact: Phil Bell 201/488-9000

PENNSYLVANIA
DEVON HILL DODGE
20 West Lancaster Avenue
Devon
Contact: Chuck O'Keefe 610/687-9350

LANCASTER DODGE
1475 Manheim Pike
Lancaster
Contact: Jerry Cutler or Russ Osborne 717/393-0625

NORWIN DODGE
13230 Rt 30
N. Huntington
Contact: Jack Butler or Scott Gutshall 412/864-0140

WASHINGTON
TACOMA DODGE
4101 S. Tacoma Way
Tacoma
Contact: Bob Ward/John R. 206/475-7300

WISCONSIN
DODGE CITY
4640 South 27th
Milwaukee
Contact: Frank Brugger 414/281-9100

FORD

ARIZONA
BELL FORD
2401 West Bell Road
Phoenix
Contact: Larry Barnes 602/866-1776

CALIFORNIA
AIRPORT MARINA FORD
5880 Centinela Avenue
Los Angeles
Contact: Bob Garcia 310/649-3673

EL CAJON FORD
1595 E. Main Street
El Cajon
Contact: Phil Smithey 619/579-8888

HANSEL FORD
3075 Corby Avenue
Santa Rosa
Contact: Joe, Ed or Paul 707/525-3688
or 800/956-5556

S & C FORD & CITY LEASING
2001 Market Street
San Francisco
Contact: Ron Fields 415/861-6000

SUN VALLEY AUTO PLAZA
2285 Diamond Blvd.
Concord
Contact: Geoff Dettlinger
or Dan Stillman 510/686-3325

HAWAII
CUTTER FORD/ISUZU INC.
98-015 Kamehameha Highway
Aiea
Contact: Tom Nakama or Dennis Ouchi 808/487-3811

ILLINOIS
JOE COTTON FORD
175 West North Avenue
Carol Stream
Contact: Kimberly Schweppe 708/682-9200

ARLINGTON HEIGHTS FORD
801 West Dundee Road
Arlington Heights
Contact: Randy Malkiewicz
or Richard Jacobsen 708/870-1300

MASSACHUSETTS
MAIN STREET AUTO SALES
1022 Main Street
Waltham
Contact: Justin Barrett or Julius Simon 617/894-8000

For a Dealer in your area dial 1-800-996-Auto

EDMUND'S 1995 HIGH-PERFORMANCE AUTOMOBILES

Automobile Dealer Directory

MINNESOTA
FREEWAY FORD
9700 Lyndale Avenue
Minneapolis
Contact: Dick Lewis 612/888-9481

MISSOURI
CAVALIER FORD INC.
7501 Manchester Avenue
St. Louis
Contact: Jim Danner 314/645-2780

NEW JERSEY
KEATS FORD
2865 Brunswick Park
Lawrenceville
Contact: Joseph Keats or Gary Glauser 609/883-3400
LARSON FORD, INC.
1150 State HWY 88
Lakewood
Contact: Bob Taurosa or Bob Eden 908/363-8100
MULLANE FORD
241 N. Washington Avenue
Bergenfield
Contact: Pat Moran 201/385-6500

NEW YORK
ASPEN FORD INC.
855 65th Street
Brooklyn
Contact: Pat DiDomenico or Rich Willis 718/921-9100

OHIO
PEFFLEY FORD
4600 N. Main Street
Dayton
Contact: Jake Cabay 513/278-7921

OREGON
HARVEST FORD LINCOLN/MERCURY
2833 Washburn Way
Klamath Falls
Contact: Gary Creese 503/884-3121

PENNSYLVANIA
McKEAN FORD
5151 Liberty Avenue
Pittsburgh
Contact: Fred Orendi 412/622-8800
NORRISTOWN FORD
Ridge Pike & Trooper
Norristown
Contact: Joe Lutz or Andy Stratz 215/539-5400

TEXAS
LEE JARMON FORD
1635 I-35 East
Carrollton
Contact: John Prouty 214/242-0682
LONE STAR FORD INC.
8477 North Freeway
Houston
Contact: Charlie Bradt or Teddy Dikas 713/931-3300

VIRGINIA
BEACH FORD INC.
2717 Virginia Beach Blvd.
Virginia Beach
Contact: Dick Phelps or Bob Macomber 804/486-2717
or 804/766-0497

HONDA

CALIFORNIA
GOUDY HONDA
1400 W. Main Street
Alhambra
Contact: Terry McCarton or Mike Tognetti 818/576-1114
213/283-7336, 800/423-1114

GOUDY HONDA

1400 W. Main Street, Alhambra, CA
818/576-1114 • 213/283-7336
1-800-423-1114

Contact:
Terry McCarton or
Mike Tognetti

JIM DOTEN'S HONDA
2600 Shattuck Avenue
Berkeley
Contact: Stewart Petersen, Fleet Dept 510/843-3704
SAN FRANCISCO HONDA/KIA
10 South Van Ness Ave.
San Francisco
Contact: Brent Miletich or Philip Mah 415/441-2000
Beeper 415/202-6361

CONNECTICUT
SCHALLER
HONDA OLDS MITSU SUBARU
1 Veterans Drive
New Britain
Contact: Gary Turchetta 203/223-2230

FLORIDA
HOLLYWOOD HONDA
1450 N. State Road 7
Hollywood
Contact: Tom Frondczek/Alberto Verne 305/989-1600

MASSACHUSETTS
DARTMOUTH HONDA/VOLVO
26 State Rd.
North Dartmouth
Contact: Jim Dicostanzo or Hank Costa 508/996-6800
HONDA VILLAGE
371 Washington Street
Newton
Contact: Mort Shapiro 617/965-8200

NEW JERSEY
HONDA OF ESSEX
1170 Bloomfield Ave.
West Caldwell
Contact: Sales Manager 201/808-9100

For a Dealer in your area dial 1-800-996-Auto

Automobile Dealer Directory

VIP HONDA
555 Somerset Street/Corner of Rt 22 East
North Plainfield
Contact: Ron Lombardi 908/371-3752

NEW YORK
BAY RIDGE HONDA
8801 4th Avenue
Brooklyn
Contact: Phil Donati or Mark Knipstein 718/836-4600

PACE HONDA
25 E. Main
New Rochelle
Contact: Jerry or Dave 914/636-2000

OHIO
MOTORCARS–HONDA
2953 Mayfield
Cleveland Heights
Contact: Rick Gartman 216/932-2400

TEXAS
JIM ALLEE HONDA
11300 East Northwest Hwy
Dallas
Contact: Andy Kahn 214/348-7500

WISCONSIN
DAVID HOBBS HONDA
6100 North Green Bay Avenue
Milwaukee
Contact: Randy Wilson or Tim Hansen 414/352-6100

JEEP/EAGLE

MICHIGAN
MIKE MILLER JEEP/EAGLE
6540 South Cedar
Lansing
Contact: Mike Hornberger 517/394-2770

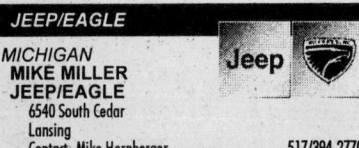

Mike Miller Jeep/Eagle
6540 SOUTH CEDAR, LANSING, MI
517-394-2770

NEW JERSEY
SALERNO DUANE JEEP/EAGLE
267 Broad Street
Summit
Contact: Steve Memolo 908/277-6700

OREGON
WALLACE JEEP/EAGLE
3515 NE Sandy Blvd
Portland
Contact: Don Forni 503/234-0221

TEXAS
JIM ALLEE OLDSMOBILE JEEP/EAGLE
12277 Shiloh Rd.
Dallas
Contact: Steve Hess 214/321-5030

LEXUS

FLORIDA
LEXUS OF KENDALL
10943 South Dixie Highway
Miami
Contact: Terry Bean 305/669-0522 x450

NEW JERSEY
PRESTIGE LEXUS
955 State Hwy 17
Ramsey
Contact: Bill Berradino 201/825-5200

LINCOLN/MERCURY

CALIFORNIA
TORRANCE LINCOLN/MERCURY VOLKS/HYUNDAI
20460 Hawthorne Blvd.
Torrance
Contact: Carol Wagner 310/370-6311

MICHIGAN
MIKE MILLER LINCOLN/MERCURY
6540 South Cedar
Lansing
Contact: Mike Hornberger **517/394-2770**

NEW JERSEY
WESTWOOD LINCOLN/MERCURY
55 Kinderkamack Road
Emerson
Contact: Charlie Featherstone 201/265-7700

NEW YORK
L & B LINCOLN/MERCURY
520 Montauk Highway
West Babylon
Contact: George Talley 516/669-2600

OREGON
HARVEST FORD LINCOLN/MERCURY
2833 Washburn Way
Klamath Falls
Contact: Gary Creese 503/884-3121

PENNSYLVANIA
NORTHEAST LINCOLN/MERCURY
7001 Roosevelt Blvd
Philadelphia
Contact: Lori Swenson 215/331-6600

For a Dealer in your area dial 1-800-996-Auto

Automobile Dealer Directory

SOUTH HILLS LINCOLN/MERCURY
2760 Washington Road
Pittsburgh
Contact: Dave Arbogast 412/941-1600

MITSUBISHI

FLORIDA
PAUL WEST MITSUBISHI
3111 N. Main Street
Gainesville
Contact: Mark Fish 904/371-3752

MASSACHUSETTS
BERNARDI MITSUBISHI
671 Worcester Rd.
Natick
Contact: Stephen Bianchi 508/655-8588

NEW JERSEY
SALERNO DUANE MITSUBISHI
267 Broad Street
Summit
Contact: Dave Walsh 908/277-6780

NISSAN

CALIFORNIA
CONCORD NISSAN INC.
1290 Concord Avenue
Concord
Contact: Jack Tarafevic, Shawn Mosley 510/676-4400

FLORIDA
PRECISION NISSAN
4600 N. Dale Mabry Hwy
Tampa
Contact: Gary Armstrong 813/870-3333

GEORGIA
TRONCALLI NISSAN
1625 Church Street
Decatur
Contact: Jeff Slocum **404/292-3853**

ILLINOIS
CONTINENTAL NISSAN
5750 South La Grange Road
Countryside
Contact: Mike Bromer/Tim Duda 708/352-9200

MASSACHUSETTS
FROST NISSAN
1180 Washington Street
West Newton
Contact: Dan Favre 617/630-3050

NEW JERSEY
CHERRY HILL NISSAN
State Hwy 39 & Cooper Landing
Cherry Hill
Contact: Marvin, Frank,
or Freeman **609/667-8300**
MOTOR WORLD NISSAN MAZDA VOLKS
340 Sylvan Avenue Rt 9W
Englewood Cliffs
Contact: Jeff Montemuro 201/568-4400
or 201/567-9000

NEW YORK
GEIS NISSAN
Rt 6 & Westbrook Drive
Peekskill
Contact: Tom Conaty
or Steve Pinto 914/528-4347x859/878

PENNSYLVANIA
CONCORDVILLE NISSAN
RT 202 South
Concordville
Contact: Gregory Brown 215/459-8900

WISCONSIN
ROSEN NISSAN INC.
5505 South 27th
Milwaukee
Contact: Scott Levy 414/282-9300

OLDSMOBILE

TEXAS
JIM ALLEE
OLDSMOBILE JEEP/EAGLE
12277 Shiloh Rd.
Dallas
Contact: Steve Hess 214/321-5030

PONTIAC

CALIFORNIA
MAGNUSSEN
PONTIAC-BUICK-GMC
550 El Camino Real
Menlo Park
Contact: Steve Bridges 415/326-4100

ILLINOIS
JOE COTTON
PONTIAC/GMC TRUCK, INC.
271 East North Avenue
Glendale Heights
Contact: Kimberly Schweppe 708/682-9200

NEW YORK
GEIS PONTIAC BUICK OLDS CADILLAC
Rt 6 & Westbrook Drive
Peekskill
Contact: Ed Rice
or Jim Lockwood 914/528-4347x811/866

OHIO
MOTORCARS–PONTIAC
2953 Mayfield
Cleveland Heights
Contact: Chris Osborne 216/932-2400

OREGON
BRESLIN PONTIAC GMC
3515 N E Sandy Boulevard
Portland
Contact: Don Forni 503/234-0221

NEW JERSEY
SALERNO DUANE PONTIAC
267 Broad Street
Summit
Contact: Steve Memolo 908/277-6700

For a Dealer in your area dial 1-800-996-Auto

Automobile Dealer Directory

TOYOTA

ARIZONA
CAMELBACK TOYOTA
1500 East Camelback Road
Phoenix
Contact: Vic Schafer 602/274-9576

CALIFORNIA
KEARNEY MESA TOYOTA
5090 Kearney Mesa Road
San Diego
Contact: Mike Hunter 619/279-8151

TOYOTA OF NORTH HOLLYWOOD
4100 Lankershim
North Hollywood
Contact: Pam Morgan or Irene Samaltanos 818/508-2900

CONNECTICUT
GIRARD TOYOTA/BMW
543 Colman Street
New London
Contact: Larry Main 203/447-3141

FLORIDA
KENDALL TOYOTA
10943 South Dixie Highway
Miami
Contact: Frank Marsala 305/665-6581 x323

PRECISION TOYOTA INC.
10909 N. Florida Avenue
Tampa
Contact: Brad Savelli or Matt Coffey 813/933-6402

MASSACHUSETTS
WOBURN FOREIGN MOTORS
394 Washington Street
Woburn
Contact: Stephan Harasim 617/933-1100

MINNESOTA
RUDY LUTHER'S TOYOTA
8801 Wayzata Blvd
Minneapolis
Contact: Larry Fenton or Curt Folstad 612/544-1313

NEW JERSEY
BOB CIASULLI MONMOUTH TOYOTA
700 State Hwy 36
Eatontown
Contact: Allison Guttman 908/544-1000

NEW YORK
GEIS TOYOTA
Rt 6 & Westbrook Drive
Peekskill
Contact: Joe Trabucco
or Pat Canavan 914/528-4347x880/894

OHIO
KINGS TOYOTA/SUZUKI
9500 Kings Automall Road
Cincinnati
Contact: Greg Plowman 513/683-5440

TEXAS
STERLING McCALL TOYOTA
9400 Southwest Freeway
Houston
Contact: Tanya Tolander 713/270-3974

VOLVO

MASSACHUSETTS
DARTMOUTH HONDA/VOLVO
26 State Rd.
North Dartmouth
Contact: Jim Dicostanzo or Hank Costa 508/996-6800

Edmund's $10,000 Wheel N'Deal Give-Away

To enter your chance to win $1,000 in a monthly drawing, see pages 386 & 387.

[Dealers, call 1-800-996-2886 to participate]

For a Dealer in your area dial 1-800-996-Auto

EDMUND'S 1995 HIGH-PERFORMANCE AUTOMOBILES

Edmund's SINGLE COPIES / ORDER FORM

Please send me:

☐ **USED CAR PRICES & RATINGS** *(includes S&H)* **$8.25**

☐ **NEW CAR PRICES**
—**American & Import** *(includes S&H)* **$8.25**

☐ **NEW PICKUPS, VANS & SPORT UTILITIES** *(includes S&H)* **$8.25**

☐ **NEW HIGH-PERFORMANCE
AUTOMOBILES** *(includes S&H)* **$8.25**

Name _____
Address _____
City, State, Zip _____
Phone _____

PAYMENT: __ MASTERCARD __ VISA __ CHECK or MONEY ORDER $ _____
Make check or money order payable to:
Edmund Publications Corporation P.O.Box 338, Shrub Oaks, NY 10588
For more information or to order by phone, call **(914) 962-6297**

Credit Card # _____ Exp. Date: _____
Cardholder Name: _____ Signature _____

Prices above are for shipping within the U.S. and Canada only. Other countries, please add $5.00 to the cover price per book (via air mail) and $2.00 to the cover price per book (surface mail). Please pay through an American Bank or with American Currency. Rates subject to change without notice.

Edmund's SUBSCRIPTIONS / ORDER FORM

BUYER'S PRICE GUIDES

Please send me a one year subscription for:

☐ **USED CAR PRICES & RATINGS**
American & Import (price includes $4 S&H) $20.00
4 issues/yr

☐ **NEW CAR PRICES**
American & Import (package price includes $3 S&H) $15.00
3 issues/yr

☐ **NEW PICKUPS, VANS & SPORT UTILITIES**
American & Import (package price includes $6 S&H) $15.00
3 issues/yr

☐ **NEW AUTOMOBILE PRICES**
American & Import (package price includes $6 S&H) $30.00
6 issues/yr:
3 NEW CAR PRICES [American & Import]
3 NEW PICKUPS, VANS & SPORT UTILITIES [American & Import]

☐ **NEW/USED AUTOMOBILE PRICES**
American & Imports (package price includes $10 S&H) $50.00
10 issues/yr:
4 USED CAR PRICES & RATINGS [American & Import]
3 NEW CAR PRICES [American & Import]
3 NEW PICKUPS, VANS & SPORT UTILITIES [American & Import]

Name _____

Address _____

City, State, Zip _____

Payment: __ MC __ Visa __ Check or Money Order —Amount $_____ Rates subject to change without notice

Make check or money order payable to:
Edmund Publications Corporation P.O.Box 338, Shrub Oaks, NY 10588
For more information or to order by phone, call **(914) 962-6297**

Credit Card # _____ Exp. Date: _____

Cardholder Name: _____ Signature _____

EDMUND'S 1995 HIGH-PERFORMANCE AUTOMOBILES

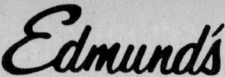

BUYER'S DECISION GUIDES
SCHEDULED RELEASE DATES FOR 1995*

VOL. 29		RELEASE DATE	COVER DATE
U2901	USED CAR PRICES & RATINGS	JAN 95	SPRING
N2901	NEW CAR PRICES [American & Import]	FEB 95	MAY 95
S2901	NEW PICKUPS, VANS & SPORT UTILITIES	FEB 95	MAY 95
U2902	USED CAR PRICES & RATINGS	APR 95	SUMMER
N2902	NEW CAR PRICES [American & Import]	MAY 95	NOV 95
S2903	NEW PICKUPS, VANS & SPORT UTILITIES	MAY 95	NOV 95
U2903	USED CAR PRICES & RATINGS	JUL 95	FALL
R2901	USED CAR RATINGS	AUG 95	1996
U2904	USED CAR PRICES & RATINGS	OCT 95	WINTER
N2903	NEW CAR PRICES [American & Import]	NOV 95	JAN 96
S2903	NEW PICKUPS, VANS & SPORT UTILITIES	NOV 95	FEB 96

VOL. 30			
U3001	USED CAR PRICES & RATINGS	JAN 96	SPRING

*Subject to Change

You can SAVE $100-$1000 or more on the purchase/lease of your next car for the cost of a single tank of gas!

With this new book, Burke and Stephanie Leon will teach you how to:

- get the best possible price for your trade-in
- calculate dealer cost to determine the price you should expect to pay
- find reasonable financing
- know if buying or leasing is best for you
- evaluate the worth of a used car
- keep the upper hand during negotiations

Packed with checklists, this book is guaranteed to save you money on your next car.

"...an excellent handbook...anyone in the market for a new car would be wise to study Leon's technique." AUTOWEEK

YES! Send me _____ copies of INSIDER'S GUIDE TO BUYING A NEW OR USED CAR.
I've enclosed $9.95 per book, plus $3.00 shipping and handling.

Charge my: ☐ Visa ☐ Mastercard

Credit Card # _____ Expiration: _____

Signature _____

Name _____

Address _____

City, State, Zip _____

EDMUND PUBLICATIONS   300 N. SEPULVEDA BLVD., SUITE. 2050, EL SEGUNDO, CA 90245

INDEX TO PERFORMANCE - A

Ranked by Overall Performance

Automobile	Accel. 0-60 (sec)	Braking 60-0 (ft)	Cornering (g's)	Page #
Toyota Supra Turbo	5.1	112	0.97	336
Toyota MR2 Turbo	6.2	107	0.94	333
Mazda RX-7	5.3	113	0.98	211
Chevrolet Corvette ZR1	5.2	117	0.92	79
BMW M3	5.6	111	0.86	45
Chevrolet Corvette LT1	5.6	115	0.92	79
Acura NSX	5.3	118	0.95	35
Dodge Viper R/T 10	4.5	129	0.97	117
Porsche 911 Carerra 2	5.3	117	0.92	291
Chevrolet Camaro Z28	5.7	112	0.88	72
Toyota Supra	6.2	112	0.88	336
Dodge Stealth R/T Turbo	5.7	120	0.90	114
Mitsubishi 3000GT VR4	5.3	122	0.88	234
BMW 850CSi	5.8	116	0.87	53
Mazda MX-6 LS	7.6	112	0.90	207
Pontiac Firebird Formula	5.8	115	0.85	281
Audi S6	6.5	115	0.87	42
Porsche 911 Carerra 4	4.9	125	0.83	291
BMW 325is	7.2	114	0.88	45
Pontiac Firebird Trans Am	6.3	116	0.86	281
Mitsubishi Eclipse GSX	6.4	116	0.86	238
Nissan 300ZX Turbo	6.0	124	0.88	247
Porsche 911 Carerra 2 Cabrio	6.0	122	0.87	291
Porsche 928 GTS	6.1	128	0.91	299
Mercedes SL600	5.5	124	0.83	222
Mitsubishi Eclipse GS-T	6.4	121	0.86	238
Eagle Talon TSi	6.4	123	0.87	121
Nissan 300ZX	6.7	124	0.88	247
Saab 900 SE Turbo	6.8	116	0.83	309
BMW 840Ci	7.4	113	0.83	53
BMW 540i	6.9	118	0.84	49
Ford Probe GT	7.5	117	0.87	140
Lexus SC 400	7.3	121	0.87	191
Ford Mustang GT	6.7	125	0.86	136
Infiniti Q45t	7.2	121	0.85	172

INDEX TO PERFORMANCE - A

Ranked by Overall Performance

Automobile	Accel. 0-60 (sec)	Braking 60-0 (ft)	Cornering (g's)	Page #
Chevrolet Impala SS	7.1	120	0.83	84
Oldsmobile 88 LSS Supercharg	7.0	134	0.78	264
Porsche 968	5.9	138	0.90	304
Dodge Stealth R/T	8.5	117	0.89	114
Mitsubishi 3000GT SL	8.5	117	0.89	234
Honda Prelude Si VTEC	7.2	131	0.89	166
Saab 9000 Aero	7.4	124	0.85	312
Honda Civic del Sol VTEC	7.4	126	0.87	164
Jaguar XJR	6.8	121	0.80	174
Ford Thunderbird SC	6.8	124	0.81	149
Subaru SVX LS	7.6	122	0.83	324
BMW 325i	7.4	126	0.85	45
Nissan 240SX	8.3	125	0.88	244
Nissan Maxima	6.6	131	0.83	253
Mercedes S600	5.7	126	0.79	220
Nissan Altima GLE, SE	8.1	116	0.80	250
Acura Integra GS-R	7.3	130	0.84	28
Honda Prelude Si	7.8	133	0.89	166
Volkswagen GTI	6.7	120	0.78	339
Alfa Romeo 164	7.2	126	0.81	37
Lexus SC 300	7.8	132	0.87	191
Toyota Celica GT	8.4	127	0.87	330
Ford Contour SE	7.4	122	0.79	128
Mercury Mystique LS V6	7.4	122	0.79	231
Acura Integra LS	7.6	127	0.82	28
Acura Integra RS	7.6	127	0.82	28
Volvo 850 Turbo	7.0	128	0.80	345
Oldsmobile Aurora	7.4	127	0.81	259
Nissan Sentra SE-R	7.6	128	0.82	257
Acura Legend LS Coupe	7.5	134	0.85	32
Pontiac Bonneville SSEi	7.0	132	0.81	275
Saturn SC2	8.4	132	0.88	315
Mazda 626 ES	7.7	122	0.79	200
Dodge Intrepid ES 3.5L	8.1	125	0.81	102
Eagle Vision TSi	8.1	125	0.81	124

EDMUND'S 1995 HIGH-PERFORMANCE AUTOMOBILES

INDEX TO PERFORMANCE - A

Ranked by Overall Performance

Automobile	Accel. 0-60 (sec)	Braking 60-0 (ft)	Cornering (g's)	Page #
Jaguar XJS	7.8	125	0.80	177
BMW 530i	7.0	132	0.80	49
Infiniti G20t	8.4	125	0.82	169
Toyota MR2	8.5	136	0.93	333
Mercedes E420	7.2	124	0.78	216
Mazda Millenia S	7.6	128	0.80	202
Acura Legend GS Sedan	8.1	129	0.82	32
Saab 900 SE	7.9	126	0.80	309
Lexus LS 400	7.7	121	0.78	189
Honda Accord EX	8.1	125	0.79	160
Toyota Camry V6	7.3	126	0.78	327
Ford Lightning	7.2	143	0.84	134
Volkswagen Passat GLX	8.5	127	0.82	343
Lexus GS 300	8.7	124	0.82	187
Lincoln Mark VIII	7.1	134	0.79	196
Cadillac Seville STS	6.5	133	0.78	65
Audi 90	8.2	129	0.80	39
Cadillac Eldorado TC	6.7	138	0.79	62
Mazda MX-5 Miata	8.7	128	0.83	204
Volkswagen Jetta GLX	6.9	134	0.78	341
Lexus ES 300	8.2	134	0.81	185
Infiniti J30	8.3	129	0.79	170
Chevrolet Monte Carlo Z34	7.8	139	0.82	90
Ford Taurus SHO	7.6	137	0.80	146
Plymouth Neon Sedan	8.4	135	0.82	270
Plymouth Neon Highline Coup	8.4	135	0.82	270
Dodge Neon Highline Coupe	8.4	135	0.82	105
Dodge Neon Sedan	8.4	135	0.82	105
Chevrolet Caprice Classic 5.7L	8.5	133	0.82	76
Pontiac Bonneville SE	8.1	136	0.81	275
Pontiac Grand Prix GTP 3.4L	7.5	137	0.79	286
Ford Escort GT	8.4	138	0.82	131
Oldsmobile Cutlass Supreme	8.5	129	0.79	252
Ford Ranger Splash 4.0L	8.3	144	0.84	143
Mitsubishi Mirage LS Coupe	8.7	133	0.82	242

INDEX TO PERFORMANCE - A

Ranked by Overall Performance

Automobile	Accel. 0-60 (sec)	Braking 60-0 (ft)	Cornering (g's)	Page #
Eagle Summit ESi Coupe	8.7	133	0.82	119
Mercedes E320	8.1	131	0.78	216
Chevrolet Lumina LS 3.4L	8.0	132	0.78	87
Buick Park Avenue Ultra	7.3	137	0.78	56
Chrysler LHS	8.7	126	0.79	99
Mercedes C220	8.7	131	0.80	213
Pontiac Grand Prix GT Sedan	8.7	135	0.82	286
Jeep Grand Cherokee V8	8.0	126	0.75	180
Nissan Altima XE, GXE	8.7	130	0.79	250
Saturn SW2	8.7	130	0.79	321
Saturn SL2	8.7	130	0.79	318
Chevrolet S-10 SS	7.9	140	0.79	94
Oldsmobile 88 LSS	8.4	134	0.78	264
Buick Riviera	7.8	139	0.78	59
Chrysler Concorde 3.5L	8.7	136	0.80	96
Mercedes C280	8.4	137	0.78	213
Mazda Protege ES	8.7	139	0.80	209
Honda Civic Coupe EX	8.4	140	0.78	162
Ford Thunderbird LX V8	8.5	139	0.78	149
Mercury Cougar XR7 V8	8.5	139	0.78	227
GMC Sonoma SLS 4.3L	7.7	146	0.77	157
Ford F-150 5.8L	8.9	144	0.75	134
Oldsmobile Silhouette	9.7	146	0.75	267

Note: Automobiles not listed in the Index to Performance-A were not ranked due to insufficient data.

INDEX TO PERFORMANCE - B

Top 25 Vehicles in Acceleration

Automobile	0-60 mph (sec)
Dodge Viper R/T 10	4.5
Porsche 911 Carerra 4	4.9
Toyota Supra Turbo	5.1
Chevrolet Corvette ZR1	5.2
Acura NSX	5.3
Mazda RX-7	5.3
Mitsubishi 3000GT VR4	5.3
Porsche 911 Carerra 2	5.3
Mercedes SL600	5.5
BMW M3	5.6
Chevrolet Corvette LT1	5.6
Chevrolet Camaro Z28	5.7
Dodge Stealth R/T Turbo	5.7
Mercedes S600	5.7
BMW 850CSi	5.8
Pontiac Firebird Formula	5.8
Porsche 968	5.9
Nissan 300ZX Turbo	6.0
Porsche 911 Carerra 2 Cabrio	6.0
Porsche 928 GTS	6.1
Toyota MR2 Turbo	6.2
Toyota Supra	6.2
Mercedes SL500	6.3
Pontiac Firebird Trans Am	6.3
Eagle Talon TSi	6.4

INDEX TO PERFORMANCE - C

Top 25 Vehicles in Braking

Automobile	60-0 mph (ft)
Mercedes SL320	104
Toyota MR2 Turbo	107
BMW M3	111
Chevrolet Camaro Z28	112
Mazda MX-6 LS	112
Toyota Supra	112
Toyota Supra Turbo	112
BMW 840Ci	113
Mazda RX-7	113
BMW 325is	114
Audi S6	115
Chevrolet Corvette LT1	115
Pontiac Firebird Formula	115
BMW 850CSi	116
Mitsubishi Eclipse GSX	116
Nissan Altima GLE, SE	116
Pontiac Firebird Trans Am	116
Saab 900 SE Turbo	116
Chevrolet Corvette ZR1	117
Dodge Stealth R/T	117
Ford Probe GT	117
Mitsubishi 3000GT SL	117
Porsche 911 Carerra 2	117
Acura NSX	118
BMW 540i	118

INDEX TO PERFORMANCE - D

Top 25 Vehicles in Cornering

Automobile	Cornering g of force
Mazda RX-7	0.98
Dodge Viper R/T 10	0.97
Toyota Supra Turbo	0.97
Acura NSX	0.95
Toyota MR2 Turbo	0.94
Toyota MR2	0.93
Chevrolet Corvette LT1	0.92
Chevrolet Corvette ZR1	0.92
Porsche 911 Carerra 2	0.92
Porsche 928 GTS	0.91
Dodge Stealth R/T Turbo	0.90
Mazda MX-6 LS	0.90
Porsche 968	0.90
Dodge Stealth R/T	0.89
Honda Prelude Si	0.89
Honda Prelude Si VTEC	0.89
Mitsubishi 3000GT SL	0.89
BMW 325is	0.88
Chevrolet Camaro Z28	0.88
Mitsubishi 3000GT VR4	0.88
Nissan 240SX	0.88
Nissan 300ZX	0.88
Nissan 300ZX Turbo	0.88
Saturn SC2	0.88
Toyota Supra	0.88

INDEX TO PERFORMANCE - E

Listed Alphabetically

Automobile	Accel. 0-60 (sec)	Braking 60-0 (ft)	Cornering (g's)	Page #
Acura Integra GS-R	7.3	130	0.84	28
Acura Integra LS	7.6	127	0.82	28
Acura Integra RS	7.6	127	0.82	28
Acura Legend GS Sedan	8.1	129	0.82	32
Acura Legend LS Coupe	7.5	134	0.85	32
Acura NSX	5.3	118	0.95	35
Alfa Romeo 164	7.2	126	0.81	37
Audi 90	8.2	129	0.80	39
Audi S6	6.5	115	0.87	42
BMW 325i	7.4	126	0.85	45
BMW 325is	7.2	114	0.88	45
BMW 530i	7.0	132	0.80	49
BMW 540i	6.9	118	0.84	49
BMW 840Ci	7.4	113	0.83	53
BMW 850CSi	5.8	116	0.87	53
BMW M3	5.6	111	0.86	45
Buick Park Avenue Ultra	7.3	137	0.78	56
Buick Riviera	7.8	139	0.78	59
Cadillac Eldorado TC	6.7	138	0.79	62
Cadillac Seville STS	6.5	133	0.78	65
Chevrolet C 1500 5.7L	9.5	143	N/A	68
Chevrolet Camaro Z28	5.7	112	0.88	72
Chevrolet Caprice Classic 5.7L	8.5	133	0.82	76
Chevrolet Corvette LT1	5.6	115	0.92	79
Chevrolet Corvette ZR1	5.2	117	0.92	79
Chevrolet Impala SS	7.1	120	0.83	84
Chevrolet Lumina LS 3.4L	8.0	132	0.78	87
Chevrolet Monte Carlo Z34	7.8	139	0.82	90
Chevrolet S-10 SS	7.9	140	0.79	94
Chrysler Concorde 3.5L	8.7	136	0.80	96
Chrysler LHS	8.7	126	0.79	99
Dodge Intrepid ES 3.5L	8.1	125	0.81	102
Dodge Neon Highline Coupe	8.4	135	0.82	105
Dodge Neon Sedan	8.4	135	0.82	105
Dodge Ram Sport 5.9L	8.5	149	N/A	110

INDEX TO PERFORMANCE - E

Listed Alphabetically

Automobile	Accel. 0-60 (sec)	Braking 60-0 (ft)	Cornering (g's)	Page #
Dodge Stealth R/T	8.5	117	0.89	114
Dodge Stealth R/T Turbo	5.7	120	0.90	114
Dodge Viper R/T 10	4.5	129	0.97	117
Eagle Summit ESi Coupe	8.7	133	0.82	119
Eagle Talon TSi	6.4	123	0.87	121
Eagle Vision TSi	8.1	125	0.81	124
Ford Contour SE	7.4	122	0.79	128
Ford Escort GT	8.4	138	0.82	131
Ford F-150 5.8L	8.9	144	0.75	134
Ford Lightning	7.2	143	0.84	134
Ford Mustang GT	6.7	125	0.86	136
Ford Probe GT	7.5	117	0.87	140
Ford Ranger Splash 4.0L	8.3	144	0.84	143
Ford Taurus SHO	7.6	137	0.80	146
Ford Thunderbird LX V8	8.5	139	0.78	149
Ford Thunderbird SC	6.8	124	0.81	149
GMC Sierra 1500 5.7L	9.5	143	N/A	154
GMC Sonoma SLS 4.3L	7.7	146	0.77	157
Honda Accord EX	8.1	125	0.79	160
Honda Civic Coupe EX	8.4	140	0.78	162
Honda Civic del Sol VTEC	7.4	126	0.87	164
Honda Prelude Si	7.8	133	0.89	166
Honda Prelude Si VTEC	7.2	131	0.89	166
Infiniti G20t	8.4	125	0.82	169
Infiniti J30	8.3	129	0.79	170
Infiniti Q45t	7.2	121	0.85	172
Jaguar XJ12	8.3	134	N/A	174
Jaguar XJ6	8.7	132	N/A	174
Jaguar XJR	6.8	121	0.80	174
Jaguar XJS	7.8	125	0.80	177
Jeep Grand Cherokee V8	8.0	126	0.75	180
Lexus ES 300	8.2	134	0.81	185
Lexus GS 300	8.7	124	0.82	187
Lexus LS 400	7.7	121	0.78	189
Lexus SC 300	7.8	132	0.87	191

INDEX TO PERFORMANCE - E

Listed Alphabetically

Automobile	Accel. 0-60 (sec)	Braking 60-0 (ft)	Cornering (g's)	Page #
Lexus SC 400	7.3	121	0.87	191
Lincoln Mark VIII	7.1	134	0.79	196
Mazda 626 ES	7.7	122	0.79	200
Mazda Millenia S	7.6	128	0.80	202
Mazda MX-5 Miata	8.7	128	0.83	204
Mazda MX-6 LS	7.6	112	0.90	207
Mazda Protege ES	8.7	139	0.80	209
Mazda RX-7	5.3	113	0.98	211
Mercedes C220	8.7	131	0.80	213
Mercedes C280	8.4	137	0.78	213
Mercedes E320	8.1	131	0.78	216
Mercedes E420	7.2	124	0.78	216
Mercedes S600	5.7	126	0.79	220
Mercedes SL320	7.6	104	N/A	222
Mercedes SL500	6.3	N/A	0.82	222
Mercedes SL600	5.5	124	0.83	222
Mercury Cougar XR7 V8	8.5	139	0.78	227
Mercury Mystique LS V6	7.4	122	0.79	231
Mitsubishi 3000GT SL	8.5	117	0.89	234
Mitsubishi 3000GT VR4	5.3	122	0.88	234
Mitsubishi Eclipse GS	8.6	N/A	0.82	238
Mitsubishi Eclipse GS-T	6.4	121	0.86	238
Mitsubishi Eclipse GSX	6.4	116	0.86	238
Mitsubishi Mirage LS Coupe	8.7	133	0.82	242
Nissan 240SX	8.3	125	0.88	244
Nissan 300ZX	6.7	124	0.88	247
Nissan 300ZX Turbo	6.0	124	0.88	247
Nissan Altima GLE, SE	8.1	116	0.80	250
Nissan Altima XE, GXE	8.7	130	0.79	250
Nissan Maxima	6.6	131	0.83	253
Nissan Sentra SE-R	7.6	128	0.82	257
Oldsmobile 88 LSS	8.4	134	0.78	264
Oldsmobile 88 LSS Supercharg	7.0	134	0.78	264
Oldsmobile Aurora	7.4	127	0.81	259
Oldsmobile Cutlass Supreme	8.5	129	0.79	252

INDEX TO PERFORMANCE - E

Listed Alphabetically

Automobile	Accel. 0-60 (sec)	Braking 60-0 (ft)	Cornering (g's)	Page #
Oldsmobile Silhouette	9.7	146	0.75	267
Plymouth Neon Highline Coup	8.4	135	0.82	270
Plymouth Neon Sedan	8.4	135	0.82	270
Pontiac Bonneville SE	8.1	136	0.81	275
Pontiac Bonneville SSEi	7.0	132	0.81	275
Pontiac Firebird Formula	5.8	115	0.85	281
Pontiac Firebird Trans Am	6.3	116	0.86	281
Pontiac Grand Prix GT Sedan	8.7	135	0.82	286
Pontiac Grand Prix GTP 3.4L	7.5	137	0.79	286
Porsche 911 Carerra 2	5.3	117	0.92	291
Porsche 911 Carerra 2 Cabrio	6.0	122	0.87	291
Porsche 911 Carerra 4	4.9	125	0.83	291
Porsche 928 GTS	6.1	128	0.91	299
Porsche 968	5.9	138	0.90	304
Saab 900 SE	7.9	126	0.80	309
Saab 900 SE Turbo	6.8	116	0.83	309
Saab 9000 Aero	7.4	124	0.85	312
Saturn SC2	8.4	132	0.88	315
Saturn SL2	8.7	130	0.79	318
Saturn SW2	8.7	130	0.79	321
Subaru SVX LS	7.6	122	0.83	324
Toyota Camry V6	7.3	126	0.78	327
Toyota Celica GT	8.4	127	0.87	330
Toyota MR2	8.5	136	0.93	333
Toyota MR2 Turbo	6.2	107	0.94	333
Toyota Supra	6.2	112	0.88	336
Toyota Supra Turbo	5.1	112	0.97	336
Volkswagen GTI	6.7	120	0.78	339
Volkswagen Jetta GLX	6.9	134	0.78	341
Volkswagen Passat GLX	8.5	127	0.82	343
Volvo 850 Turbo	7.0	128	0.80	345